S. Dorothy Rush.

Christmas '76 from Vi + Sue.

# The New Oxford Book
# of English Verse

# The New Oxford Book of English Verse

## 1250–1950

Chosen and Edited by

Helen Gardner

*Helen Gardner*

*Kettering 28 April 1977*

Clarendon Press · Oxford

*Oxford University Press, Ely House, London W.* 1

GLASGOW NEW YORK TORONTO MELBOURNE WELLINGTON
CAPE TOWN IBADAN NAIROBI DAR ES SALAAM LUSAKA ADDIS ABABA
DELHI BOMBAY CALCUTTA MADRAS KARACHI LAHORE DACCA
KUALA LUMPUR SINGAPORE HONGKONG TOKYO

ISBN 0 19 812136 9

© OXFORD UNIVERSITY PRESS 1972

FIRST PUBLISHED 1972
REPRINTED (WITH CORRECTIONS) 1972, 1973 (twice)

PRINTED IN GREAT BRITAIN
BY RICHARD CLAY (THE CHAUCER PRESS), LTD.,
BUNGAY, SUFFOLK

# PREFACE

*The Oxford Book of English Verse, 1250–1900*, chosen and edited by Arthur Quiller-Couch, appeared in 1900. It rapidly established itself as the classic anthology of English poetry, running through twenty-one impressions in the next forty years and selling nearly half a million copies. The judgement of readers confirmed, to quote the editor's preface, that he had so managed his task 'as to serve those who already love poetry and to implant that love in some young minds not yet initiated'. In 1939 Sir Arthur revised his anthology, 'having come to regret some inclusions and omissions of indolence', and extended it by nearly a hundred pages to bring it down to 1918. The revision hardly affected the first three-quarters of the original book where only some forty items were omitted and some forty added. It was after Keats, in the section that had always given least satisfaction, that Sir Arthur made most changes, dropping some seventy poems, and adding roughly the equivalent number, before extending into the first twenty years of this century. The revision did not change the nature of the anthology. It remained what it had originally been, an anthology of lyrical verse, inspired by the most famous of Victorian anthologies, Palgrave's *Golden Treasury*.

The present edition is not a revision of Q's revision but a new anthology. Like my predecessor, I have tried 'to range over the whole field of English verse' and 'to choose the best'. But any anthology that thus aims at being classic will reflect not only the personal taste of the anthologist but also the critical consensus of the age in which it is compiled. Q was of his age in holding that to choose the best meant to choose numbers 'either lyrical or epigrammatic'. This involved the virtual exclusion of Pope, the representation of poets such as Dryden, Byron, Tennyson, and Browning solely by their lyrics, and the neglect of the tradition of satiric, political, epistolary, and didactic verse in English. Since 1900 the concept of the 'best' has widened beyond the lyrical, and the reputations of poets and of individual poems have changed. Nobody today would give twenty pages to Herrick while giving only seven to Donne and five to Herbert; and it seems safe to say that nobody today would not include such famous poems as 'Ulysses', 'My Last Duchess', and 'Dover Beach' as being finely characteristic of their authors' best work.

In making this new anthology I have in many ways followed my predecessor's example. Although I have widened the range of poetry he

v

drew upon, I have followed him in excluding dramatic verse. Here context is all-important. I have also followed him in giving full representation to major poets, and have treated Hopkins, Hardy, Yeats, and Eliot, the four greatest poets of the last hundred years, as he treated Keats and Shelley. I have also not attempted to avoid the familiar, believing with him that 'the best is the best, though a hundred judges have declared it so'. I have also agreed with him in modernizing the spelling throughout (even, as far as is possible, in the medieval poems), with the exception that I have not tampered with the spelling of poems in Scots, and have left Spenser's archaic spelling as an integral part of his deliberate attempt to 'affect the ancients'. I have also, like him, resisted the temptation to gloss, except for the occasional glossing of an obsolete word; and have kept the pages free of references, hiding them away in notes at the back of the volume. On the other hand, I have not followed him in including American poets. Since I have both enlarged the range of verse he drew upon and extended my terminal date to include a particularly rich period of English verse, I reluctantly decided that I must confine myself to poets writing in these islands. It seemed impossible to do justice to American poetry without seriously restricting the selection from English. I have made one exception, and included a handful of poems by Ezra Pound, since, though he kept American nationality, he was at the centre of the modern movement in England. I hesitated whether in a book of English Verse, poems in the Scottish dialect should be included. But I decided that the Scots would be less offended at their inclusion under this title than at the omission of the Border Ballads and Burns, which are part of the cultural heritage of England as well as of Scotland.

The present volume attempts to represent the range of English non-dramatic poetry from 1250 to 1950. It includes no poet who had not established himself by 1950, although I have not felt it necessary to confine myself with absolute strictness to poems published before that date. The end of the Second World War is a genuine terminus, the impetus of the so-called modern movement having spent itself, and the last hundred pages of Q's anthology are a warning of the danger—and the unfairness—of attempting to select from poets in mid-passage. Unlike Q I have excerpted from long poems, supplying titles for the extracts. Those curious for the source of such excerpts will find references in the notes at the close. Q regarded himself as an anthologist, or 'gatherer of flowers', and did not scruple to omit verses, or to lift a couple or so of verses from a poem, give them a title, and print them as a complete poem without signalization. Such a practice runs contrary to modern feeling. Considerations of space make some shortenings inevitable; but it can be assumed that all the items here, which are not patently extracts, or noted as such in the Notes and References, are complete poems, unless an omission is signalized by dots, or, if the omission is substantial, by an asterisk. In the latter case, the extent of the omission is indicated in a note.

The poets are arranged chronologically by date of birth, with a few exceptions. For example, I have played a little with the dates at the close of the sixteenth century to place those, like Sidney or Marlowe, who died before 1600 and are strictly Elizabethans, before poets like Greville and Ralegh who survived into the Jacobean period, and I have placed Traherne before Dryden, since he died before Dryden's major works were written. I have followed Q in grouping together poems from the Song Books, though I place them at the end and not at the beginning of the Elizabethan period; and in collecting the Ballads and placing them before the Restoration poets. On the whole, and as far as it can be ascertained, the poems of individual poets are printed in order of composition, or in order of publication.

No anthologist can hope to win approval for all his inclusions and exclusions; but I hope that some who regret the absence of old favourites will discover new loves, and be stimulated to explore further some poets with whom they are not familiar. Q's bias was towards the lyrical and the poem of personal joys and sorrows. This anthology balances against poems of the private life poems that deal with public events, and historic occasions, or express convictions, religious, moral, or political. Together with what may be felt to be a too generous proportion of satire, I have also included familiar verse, and that distinctive English achievement, light verse. As well as attempting to represent the range of English poetry, I have tried to represent a poet's own range, and wherever I could have included poems of tribute to other poets. I can only hope that readers will find half the pleasure that I have found in reading and re-reading for this anthology, in the richest and most continuously lively poetic tradition in the world.

Since I was first invited to revise the Oxford Book, over ten years ago I have had cause to be grateful to many people for suggestions and discussions. My greatest debt is to the late Mr. John Hayward for many delightful hours discussing his own anthology, the *Penguin Book of English Verse*, and his *Oxford Book of Nineteenth-Century English Verse*. Among colleagues I must particularly thank Mr. John Buxton, Miss Katherine Duncan-Jones, and Professor Norman Davis, who encouraged and assisted me in modernizing medieval texts. By great good fortune, just as I was settling down to make final choices, Mrs. Bridget Bertram offered me her services as research assistant. As well as giving invaluable assistance in checking texts, tracing sources, and

# PREFACE

preparing copy for the press, she brought critical judgement and taste to our discussions of the contents. Finally I have to thank Mrs. M. A. Gordon, who, by relieving me of all domestic cares, made possible the completion of my task far sooner than without her I could have accomplished it.

HELEN GARDNER

*Oxford University*
1972

# ACKNOWLEDGEMENTS

The editor gratefully acknowledges permission to reproduce copyright poems in this book.

W. H. Auden: 'O Where are you going', Copyright 1934 and renewed 1962 by W. H. Auden; 'As I walked out one evening', 'Lullaby', 'Musée des Beaux Arts', 'In Memory of W. B. Yeats', Copyright 1940 and renewed 1968 by W. H. Auden; 'The Shield of Achilles', copyright 1952 by W. H. Auden. All from *Collected Shorter Poems 1927–1957*. Reprinted by permission of Faber & Faber Ltd., and Random House, Inc.

Hilaire Belloc: 'Matilda' and 'The Statesman' from *Cautionary Verses*. Published 1941 by Alfred A. Knopf, Inc. Reprinted by permission of Gerald Duckworth & Co. Ltd. and Alfred A. Knopf, Inc.; 'On a General Election' from *Sonnets and Verse* (Gerald Duckworth & Co. Ltd.). Reprinted by permission of A. D. Peters and Company.

John Betjeman: 'Death of King George V', 'Parliament Hill Fields', and 'The Cottage Hospital'. Reprinted by permission of John Murray (Publishers) Ltd. and Houghton Mifflin Company.

Laurence Binyon: 'For the Fallen' from *Collected Poems* and 'The Burning of the Leaves' (section i) from *The Burning of the Leaves*. Reprinted by permission of Mrs. Nicolete Gray and The Society of Authors on behalf of the Laurence Binyon Estate.

Edmund Blunden: from *Collected Poems*, 1972. Reprinted by permission of Gerald Duckworth & Co. Ltd.

Robert Bridges: from *The Poetical Works of Robert Bridges*. Reprinted by permission of The Clarendon Press, Oxford.

G. K. Chesterton: from *The Collected Poems of G. K. Chesterton*. Reprinted by permission of A. P. Watt & Son on behalf of Miss D. E. Collins and Methuen & Co. Ltd.

W. H. Davies: from *Collected Poems*. Copyright 1963 by Jonathan Cape Ltd. Reprinted by permission of Jonathan Cape Ltd. on behalf of Mrs. H. M. Davies and Wesleyan University Press, publishers.

Cecil Day-Lewis: from *Collected Poems 1954*. Copyright 1954 by C. Day-Lewis. Reprinted by permission of Jonathan Cape Ltd., The Hogarth Press and Harold Matson Company, Inc.

Keith Douglas: from *Collected Poems*. Reprinted by permission of Faber & Faber Ltd. and Chilmark Press.

T. S. Eliot: from *Collected Poems 1909–1962*. Copyright 1936, by Harcourt Brace Jovanovich, Inc.; copyright © 1943, 1963, 1964 by T. S. Eliot.

# ACKNOWLEDGEMENTS

Reprinted by permission of Faber & Faber Ltd. and Harcourt Brace Jovanovich, Inc.

William Empson: from *Collected Poems*. Copyright © 1949 by William Empson. Reprinted by permission of Chatto and Windus Ltd. and Harcourt Brace Jovanovich, Inc.

Roy Fuller: 'Translation' from *Collected Poems*. Reprinted by permission of André Deutsch Ltd. 'The Statue' from *Collected Poems*. Reprinted by permission of André Deutsch Ltd. and Curtis Brown Ltd.

Robert Graves: from *Collected Poems 1965*. Reprinted by permission of A. P. Watt and Son on behalf of Mr. Robert Graves.

Thomas Hardy: from *Collected Poems*. Copyright © 1925 by The Macmillan Company. Reprinted by permission of the Trustees of the Hardy Estate, The Macmillan Company of Canada Ltd., and Macmillan London and Basingstoke.

Ralph Hodgson: 'The Bells of Heaven' and 'The Hammers' from *Collected Poems*. Reprinted by permission of Mrs. Hodgson, St. Martin's Press, Inc., The Macmillan Company of Canada Ltd., and Macmillan London and Basingstoke.

A. E. Housman: from *The Collected Poems*. Copyright 1922 by Holt, Rinehart & Winston, Inc., Copyright 1936, 1950 by Barclays Bank Ltd. Copyright © 1964 by Robert E. Symons; 'On Wenlock Edge', 'On the Idle Hill of Summer', and 'Into My Heart an Air that Kills' from 'A Shropshire Lad'—Authorized Edition—from *Collected Poems*. Copyright 1939, 1940, © 1959 by Holt Rinehart and Winston Inc. Copyright © 1967, 1968 by Robert E. Symons. Reprinted by permission of The Society of Authors as the literary representative of the Estate of A. E. Housman, and Jonathan Cape Ltd. as publishers, and Holt, Rinehart & Winston, Inc.

James Joyce: from *Chamber Music* and in the U.S. from *Collected Poems*. Copyright © 1918 by B. W. Huebsch, renewed 1946 by Nora Joyce. Reprinted by permission of The Society of Authors as the literary representative of the Estate of James Joyce, Jonathan Cape Ltd. on behalf of the Executors of the Joyce Estate, and The Viking Press Inc.

Rudyard Kipling: 'Mandalay' from *Barrack Room Ballads*; 'Danny Deever' from *Departmental Ditties*; 'Cities and Thrones and Powers' from *Puck of Pook's Hill*; 'The Way Through the Woods' from *Rewards and Fairies*; 'Recessional' from *The Five Nations*. Reprinted by permission of A. P. Watt & Son on behalf of Mrs. George Bambridge and Macmillan & Co. Ltd. All the above poems are also reprinted by permission of Doubleday and Company, Inc. from their *Rudyard Kipling's Definitive Edition*.

D. H. Lawrence: 'Piano' (Copyright © 1920 by B. W. Huebsch, Inc., copyright renewed 1948 by Frieda Lawrence); 'Snake' (Copyright © 1923, © renewed 1951 by Frieda Lawrence); 'Bavarian Gentians' (Copyright 1933 by Frieda Lawrence); 'Giorno dei Morti' from *The Complete Poems*

x

# ACKNOWLEDGEMENTS

(William Heinemann Ltd.) edited by Vivian de Sola Pinto and Warren Roberts. Reprinted by permission of Laurence Pollinger Ltd. on behalf of the Estate of the Late Mrs. Frieda Lawrence, and The Viking Press, Inc. of New York.

Alun Lewis: from *Raider's Dawn*. Reprinted by permission of George Allen & Unwin Ltd.

Louis MacNeice: from *The Collected Poems* edited by E. R. Dodds. Copyright © The Estate of Louis MacNeice 1966. Reprinted by permission of Faber & Faber Ltd. and Oxford University Press, Inc.

John Masefield: 'Cargoes' (Copyright 1912 by The Macmillan Company, renewed 1940 by John Masefield) and 'Up on the Downs' (Copyright 1917 by John Masefield, renewed 1945 by John Masefield) from *Poems*. Reprinted by permission of The Society of Authors as the literary representative of the Estate of John Masefield, and The Macmillan Company of New York.

Alice Meynell: 'Renouncement', and 'Christ in the Universe', Reprinted by permission of Miss Sylvia Mulvey on behalf of the Literary Executors of Alice Meynell.

Edwin Muir: From *Collected Poems 1921–1958*. Copyright © 1960 by Willa Muir. Reprinted by permission of Faber & Faber Ltd. and Oxford University Press, Inc.

Wilfred Owen: from *Collected Poems*. Copyright Chatto & Windus Ltd. 1944, © 1963. Reprinted by permission of Chatto & Windus Ltd. on behalf of the Executors of the Estate of Harold Owen, and New Directions Publishing Corp., New York.

*Oxford Book of Ballads*, edited by James Kinsley. Reprinted by permission of the editor and The Clarendon Press, Oxford.

Ezra Pound: 'The River-Merchant's Wife: A Letter', 'Hugh Selwyn Mauberly III, IV, V' from *Collected Shorter Poems* (and from *Personae* in the U.S.) and 'Canto LXXXI' from *The Cantos of Ezra Pound*. *Personae* Copyright © 1926 by Ezra Pound. *The Cantos* Copyright © 1948 by Ezra Pound. Reprinted by permission of Faber & Faber Ltd. and New Directions Publishing Corporation.

Kathleen Raine: from *The Collected Poems*. Copyright © 1956 by Kathleen Raine, Hamish Hamilton, London. Reprinted by permission of the publishers.

Henry Reed: from *A Map of Verona*. Reprinted by permission of Jonathan Cape Ltd.

Anne Ridler: from *A Matter of Life and Death*. © by Anne Ridler, 1952. Reprinted by permission of Faber & Faber Ltd. and The Macmillan Company of New York.

Isaac Rosenberg: 'August 1914' and 'Break of Day in the Trenches' from

# ACKNOWLEDGEMENTS

*Collected Poems.* Copyright © 1949 by Schocken Books Inc. Reprinted by permission of Chatto and Windus Ltd. on behalf of the Author's Literary Estate, and Schocken Books Inc.

Siegfried Sassoon: from *Collected Poems 1908–1956*. Reprinted by permission of G. T. Sassoon.

Edith Sitwell: 'The Sleeping Beauty', 'Neptune-Polka', and 'Still Falls the Rain' (Macmillan). Reprinted by permission of David Higham Associates Ltd.

Stevie Smith: from *Selected Poems*. © Stevie Smith 1962, © 1964 by Stevie Smith. Reprinted by permission of the Longman Group Ltd. and New Directions Publishing Corp., New York.

Stephen Spender: 'What I expected, was', 'I think continually of those', 'Moving through the silent crowd', Copyright 1934 and renewed 1962 by Stephen Spender; 'The room above the square', Copyright 1942 by Stephen Spender. All from *Collected Poems 1928–1953*. Reprinted by permission of Faber & Faber Ltd. and Random House, Inc.

Dylan Thomas: from *Collected Poems*. Copyright 1932 by Dylan Thomas. Copyright 1939, 1946 by New Directions Publishing Corp. Reprinted by permission of J. M. Dent & Sons Ltd. and the Trustees for the copyrights of the late Dylan Thomas, and New Directions Publishing Corp., New York.

W. J. Turner: 'Romance'. Reprinted by permission of Walters Vandercom & Hart, Solicitors on behalf of Mrs. D. M. Newton Wood.

W. B. Yeats: 'Sailing to Byzantium', 'Meditations in Time of Civil War', 'The Road at my Door', 'The Stare's Nest at my Window', 'Two Songs from a Play', 'Leda and the Swan', 'Among School Children' (Copyright 1928 by The Macmillan Co., renewed 1956 by Georgie Yeats); 'The Lake Isle of Innisfree' and 'Who goes with Fergus' (Copyright 1906 by The Macmillan Company, renewed 1934 by W. B. Yeats); 'No Second Troy' (Copyright 1912 by The Macmillan Co., renewed 1940 by Bertha Georgie Yeats); 'An Irish Airman Foresees his Death' (Copyright 1919 by The Macmillan Company, renewed 1947 by Bertha Georgie Yeats); 'Easter 1916'. 'The Second Coming' (Copyright 1924 by the Macmillan Company, renewed 1952 by Bertha Georgie Yeats), 'Byzantium' (Copyright 1933 by The Macmillan Company, renewed 1961 by Bertha Georgie Yeats); and 'Lapis Lazuli', 'Long Legged Fly' and 'The Circus Animals' Desertion' (Copyright 1940 by Georgie Yeats, renewed 1968 by Bertha Georgie Yeats, Michael Butler Yeats and Anne Yeats).

Walter de la Mare: from the *Complete Poems of Walter de la Mare*, 1969. Reprinted by permission of the Literary Trustees of Walter de la Mare, and the Society of Authors as their representative.

# ANONYMOUS

## *Cuckoo Song*

SUMMER is y-comen in,
  Loudė sing, cuckoo!
Groweth seed and bloweth meed
  And spring'th the woodė now—
      Sing cuckoo!

Ewė bleateth after lamb,
  Low'th after calfė cow;
Bullock starteth, buckė farteth.
  Merry sing, cuckoo!

  Cuckoo, Cuckoo!
Well sing'st thou, cuckoo:
  Ne swike thou never now!

Sing cuckoo, now! Sing, cuckoo!
Sing cuckoo! Sing, cuckoo, now!

## *In Praise of Mary*

OF one that is so fair and bright,
   *Velut maris stella,*
Brighter than the dayės light,
   *Parens et puella,*
I cry to thee; thou see to me!
Lady, pray thy son for me,
   *Tam pia,*
That I motė come to thee,
   *Maria.*

Lady, flower of allė thing,
   *Rosa sine spina,*
Thou borė Jesu, heavenės king
   *Gratia divina.*

swike] cease

2 see to me] look on me

I

# ANONYMOUS

Of allë thou bear'st the prize,
Lady, queen of Paradise
    *Electa.*
Maidë mildë mother is
    *Effecta.*

Of carë conseil thou art best
    *Felix fecundata,*
Of allë weary thou art rest,
    *Mater honorata.*
Beseech him with mildë mood
That for us allë shed his blood
    *In cruce,*
That we moten come to him
    *In luce.*

All this worëld were forlore
    *Eva peccatrice,*
Till our Loverd was y-bore
    *De te genetrice.*
With '*Ave*' it went away
Thuster night, and com'th the day
    *Salutis.*
The wellë springeth out of thee
    *Virtutis.*

Well he wot he is thy son
    *Ventre quem portasti;*
He will not wernë thee thy boon,
    *Parvum quem lactasti.*
So hendë and so good he is,
He haveth brought us to bliss
    *Superni,*
That hath y-dit the foulë pit
    *Inferni.*

Of carë . . . best] In distress you are the best counsellor
Thuster] dark          wernë] deny          hendë] gracious
                 y-dit] shut

2

3            *The Irish Dancer*

I AM of Ireland
And of the holy land
        Of Ireland.
Good sir, pray I thee,
Of sainté charity
Come and dance with me
        In Ireland.


4        *The Maid of the Moor*

MAIDEN in the moor lay,
    In the moor lay,
Seven nighté full,
Seven nighté full,
Maiden in the moor lay,
    In the moor lay
Seven nighté full and a day.

Well was heré meat;
    What was heré meat?
The primérole and the—
The primérole and the—
Well was heré meat;
    What was heré meat?
The primérole and the violet.

Well was heré dring;
    What was heré dring?
The coldé water of the—
The coldé water of the—
Well was heré dring;
    What was heré dring?
The coldé water of the wellé-spring.

Well was heré bower
    What was heré bower?
The redé rose and the—
The redé rose and the—
Well was heré bower;
    What was heré bower?
The redé rose and the lily-flower.

# ANONYMOUS

## The Virgin's Song

5

JESU, sweetė sonė dear,
On poorful bed liest thou here,
  And that me grieveth sore;
For thy cradle is as a bere,
Ox and assė be thy fere:
  Weep I may therefóre.

Jesu, sweetė, be not wroth,
Though I n'avė clout ne cloth
  Thee on for to fold,
Thee on to foldė ne to wrap,
For I n'avė clout ne lap;
  But lay thou thy feet to my pap
  And wite thee from the cold.


# WILLIAM LANGLAND

?1330–?1400

6

## Et Incarnatus Est

LOVE is the plant of peace and most precious of virtues;
For heaven hold it ne might, so heavy it seemed,
Till it had on earth yoten himself.
Was never leaf upon linden lighter thereafter,
As when it had of the fold flesh and blood taken;
Then was it portative and piercing as the point of a needle.
May no armour it let, neither high walls.
For-thy is love leader of our Lord's folk of heaven.

---

bere] byre     fere] companions     Thee . . . fold] to fold thee in
                 lap] fold        wite] keep

6   yoten] poured out       fold] earth       portative] light to carry
                                 let] hinder

# GEOFFREY CHAUCER
## ?1343–1400

7    *The Complaint of Troilus*

'O PALACE, whilom crown of houses all,
Enluminèd with sun of allè bliss!
O ring, fro which the ruby is outfall,
O cause of woe, that cause hast been of liss!
Yet since I may no bet, fain would I kiss
Thy coldè doorès, durst I for this rout;
And farewell shrine, of which the saint is out! . . .'

From thennèsforth he rideth up and down,
And everything come him to rémembránce,
As he rode forby places of the town
In which he whilom had all his pleasánce.
'Lo, yonder saw I last my lady dance;
And in that temple, with her eyen clear,
Me caughtè first my rightè lady dear.

'And yonder have I heard full lustily
My dearè heartè laugh; and yonder play
Saw I her onès eek full blissfully.
And yonder onès to me gan she say,
"Now goodè sweetè, love me well, I pray;"
And yond so goodly gan she me behold,
That to the death mine heart is to her hold.

'And at that corner, in the yonder house
Heard I my allerliefest lady dear
So womanly, with voice melodious,
Singen so well, so goodly, and so clear,
That in my soulè yet me think'th I hear
The blissful sound; and in that yonder place
My lady first me took unto her grace.

\*

liss] joy        onès] once        allerliefest] most beloved

'O star, of which I lost have all the light,
With heartè sore well ought I to bewail,
That ever dark in torment, night by night,
Toward my death with wind in steer I sail:
For which the tenthè night, if that I fail
The guiding of thy beamès bright an hour,
My ship and me Charybdis will devour.'

\*

'Was there none other brooch you listè let
To fiefè with your newè love,' quod he,
'But thilkè brooch that I, with tearès wet,
You gave, as for a rémembránce of me?
None other cause, alas, ne haddè ye
But for despite, and eek for that ye meant
All utterly to shewen your entent.

'Through which I see that clean out of your mind
Ye have me cast; and I ne can nor may,
For all this world, within my heartè find
To unloven you a quarter of a day!
In cursèd time I born was, wellaway,
That you, that do me all this woe endure,
Yet love I best of any creatúre!'

8                    *Love Unfeigned*

O YOUNGÈ freshè folkès, he or she,
In which that love upgroweth with your age,
Repaireth home from worldly vanity,
And of your heart upcasteth the viságe
To thilkè God that after his imáge
You made, and thinketh all n'is but a fair
This world, and passeth soon as flowers fair.

And loveth him, the which that right for love
Upon a cross, our soulès for to buy,
First starf, and rose, and sit in heaven above;
For he n'ill falsen no wight, dare I say,
That will his heart all wholly on him lay.
And since he best to love is, and most meek,
What needeth feignèd lovès for to seek?

To fiefè . . . love] to endow your new love with        8 starf] died

9        *Balade*

HIDE, Absalom, thy giltė tresses clear;
    Esther, lay thou thy meekness all a-down;
Hide, Jonathan, all thy friendly mannér;
    Penelope and Marcia Catóun
    Make of your wifehood no comparisón;
        Hide ye your beauties, Isolde and Elaine:
        My lady com'th, that all this may distain.

Thy fairė body let it not appear,
    Lavine; and thou, Lucrece of Romė town,
And Polixene, that boughten love so dear,
    And Cleopatre, with all thy passión,
    Hide ye your truth of love and your renown;
        And thou, Thisbe, that hast for love such pain:
        My lady com'th, that all this may distain.

Hero, Dido, Laodámia, all y-fere,
    And Phyllis, hanging for thy Demophon,
And Cánacé, espièd by thy chere,
    Hypsípylé, betraysèd with Jasón,
    Make of your truthė neither boast ne soun;
        Nor Hypermestre or Ariadne, ye twain:
        My lady com'th, that all this may distain.


10        *Madam Eglantine*

THERE was also a nun, a Prioress,
That of her smiling was full simple and coy;
Her greatest oath was but by Saint Loy;
And she was clepèd Madam Eglantine.
Full well she sang the servicė divine,
Entunèd in her nose full seemėly,
And French she spake full fair and fetisly,
After the school of Stratford-attė-Bow,
For French of Paris was to her unknow.

distain] outshine        espièd by thy chere] found out by thy looks

    **10**   coy] demure        fetisly] elegantly

At meatė well y-taught was she withal;
She let no morsel from her lippės fall,
Ne wet her fingers in her saucė deep;
Well could she carry a morsel and well keep
That no droppė ne fell upon her breast.
In courtesy was set full much her lest.
Her over-lippė wipèd she so clean
That in her cup there was no farthing seen
Of greasė, when she drunken had her draught.
Full seemėly after her meat she raught.
And sikerly she was of great desport,
And full pleasánt, and amiable of port,
And peynèd her to counterfeitė cheer
Of court, and been estately of mannér
And to ben holden digne of reverence.
But, for to speaken of her consciénce,
She was so charitable and so pitóus
She wouldė weep, if that she saw a mouse
Caught in a trap, if it were dead or bled.
Of smallė houndės had she that she fed
With roasted flesh, or milk and wastel-bread.
But sore wept she if one of them were dead,
Or if men smote it with a yardė smart;
And all was consciénce and tender heart.
Full seemėly her wimple pinchèd was;
Her nosė tretys, her eyen grey as glass,
Her mouth full small, and thereto soft and red;
But sikerly she had a fair forehéad;
It was almost a spannė broad, I trow;
For, hardily, she was not undergrow.
Full fetis was her cloak, as I was ware.
Of small corál about her arm she bore
A pair of beadės, gauded all with green,
And thereon hung a brooch of gold full sheen,
On which there was first writ a crownèd 'A',
And after *Amor vincit omnia.*

---

deep] deeply        keep] take care        lest] mind
  peynèd her . . . ] took pains to imitate the manners of the court
digne] worthy        wastel-bread] fine white bread        yardė] stick
    smart] sharply        pinchèd] pleated        tretys] shapely
        A pair . . . green] a rosary with larger beads of green

## ANONYMOUS

11                         *Quia Amore Langueo*

IN the vale of restless mind
  I sought in mountain and in mead,
Trusting a true love for to find.
    Upon an hill then took I heed;
    A voice I heard—and near I yede—
      In great dolóur complaining tho:
    'See, dear soul, my sidès bleed,
        *Quia amore langueo.*

Upon this mount I found a tree;
  Under this tree a man sitting;
From head to foot wounded was he,
    His heartè-blood I saw bleeding;
    A seemly man to be a king
      A gracious face to look unto.
    I asked him how he had paining.
      He said: '*Quia amore langueo.*

'I am true love that false was never:
  My sister, man's soul, I lovèd her thus;
Because I would on no wise dissever,
    I left my kingdom glorious;
    I purveyed her a place full precious;
      She flit; I followed; I loved her so
    That I suffered these painès piteous,
        *Quia amore langueo.*

'My fair love and my spousè bright,
  I saved her fro beating and she hath me bet;
I clothed her in grace and heavenly light,
    This bloody surcote she hath on me set.
    For longing love I will not let;
      Sweetè strokès be these, lo!
    I have lovèd her ever as I het,
        *Quia amore langueo.*

near I yede] I went nearer          tho] then
*Quia amore langueo*] I am sick with love (Canticles 2:5)          het] promised

'I crowned her with bliss, and she me with thorn;
   I led her to chamber, and she me to die;
I brought her to worship, and she me to scorn;
   I did her reverence, and she me villainy.
To love that loveth is no maistrý;
   Her hate made never my love her foe;
Ask then no mo questions why,
   *Quia amore langueo.*

'Look unto mine handès, man!
   These gloves were given me when I her sought;
They be not white, but red and wan,
   Embroidered with blood, my spouse them bought;
They will not off, I leave them nought,
   I woo her with them wherever she go;
These hands full friendly for her fought,
   *Quia amore langueo.*

'Marvel not, man, though I sit still;
   My love hath shod me wonder strait;
She buckled my feet, as was her will,
   With sharpè nails—well thou mayst wait!
In my love was never deceit,
   For all my members I have opened her to;
My body I made her heartès bait,
   *Quia amore langueo.*

'In my side I have made her nest;
   Look in me how wide a wound is here!
This is her chamber, here shall she rest,
   That she and I may sleep in fere.
Here may she wash, if any filth were,
   Here is succour for all her woe;
Come if she will, she shall have cheer,
   *Quia amore langueo.*

To love . . . maistrý] To love one that loves is no hard task
  wan] discoloured      wonder strait] wonderfully tight
        wait] see     in fere] together

'I will abide till she be ready,
  I will her sue if she say nay;
If she be reckèless, I will be ready,
  If she be dangerous, I will her pray.
  If she do weep, then bid I nay;
    Mine arms be spread to clip her me to;
  Cry onès: I come. Now, soul, assay!
    *Quia amore langueo.*

'I sit on an hill for to see far,
  I look to the vale; my spouse I see:
Now runs she awayward, now comes she nearer,
  Yet fro mine eye-sight she may not be.
  Some wait their prey to make her flee;
    I run tofore to chastise her foe.
  Recover, my soul, again to me,
    *Quia amore langueo.*

'My sweetè spouse, will we go play?
  Apples be ripe in my gardéne
I shall clothe thee in new array,
  Thy meat shall be milk, honey, and wine.
  Now, dear soul, let us go dine,
    Thy sustenance is in my scrippè, lo!
  Tarry not now, fair spousè mine,
    *Quia amore langueo.*

'If thou be foul, I shall make thee clean;
  If thou be sick, I shall thee heal,
If thou ought mourn, I shall bemene.
  Spouse, why wilt thou nought with me deal?
  Thou foundest never love so leal;
    What wilt thou, soul, that I shall do?
  I may of unkindness thee appeal,
    *Quia amore langueo.*

dangerous] haughty       bid I nay] I shall beg her not to
wait] lie in wait for       Recover] return       bemene] condole
            thee appeal] accuse thee

'What shall I do now with my spouse?
  Abide I will her gentleness.
Would she look onės out of her house
  Of fleshly affections and uncleanness,
  Her bed is made, her bolster is bliss,
    Her chamber is chosen, such are no mo.
  Look out at the windows of kindness,
    *Quia amore langueo.*

'Long and love thou never so high,
  Yet is my love more than thine may be;
Thou gladdest, thou weepest, I sit thee by;
  Yet might thou, spouse, look onės at me!
  Spouse, should I always feedė thee
    With childės meat? Nay, love, not so!
  I prove thy love with adversity,
    *Quia amore langueo.*

'My spouse is in chamber, hold your peace;
  Make no noise, but let her sleep.
My babe shall suffer no disease,
  I may not hear my dear child weep;
  For with my pap I shall her keep.
    No wonder though I tend her to:
  This hole in my side had never been so deep,
    But *quia amore langueo.*

'Wax not weary, mine own dear wife:
  What meed is aye to live in comfórt?
For in tribulation I run more rife
  Oftentimes than in disport;
  In wealth, in woe, ever I support,
    Then, dear soul, go never me fro!
  Thy meed is markèd, when thou art mort,
    *Quia amore langueo.*

prove] test       run more rife] run to help more quickly
    markèd] assigned      mort] dead

12            *I Sing of a Maiden*

I SING of a maiden
    That is makèless:
King of all kingès
    To her son she ches.

He came all so stillè
    There his mother was
As dew in Apríllè
    That falleth on the grass.

He came all so stillè
    To his mother's bower
As dew in Apríllè
    That falleth on the flower.

He came all so stillè
    There his mother lay
As dew in Apríllè
    That falleth on the spray.

Mother and maiden
    Was never none but she;
Well may such a lady
    Goddès mother be.


13            *Adam lay y-bounden*

ADAM lay y-bounden
    Bounden in a bond;
Four thousand winter
    Thought he not too long;
And all was for an apple
    An apple that he took,
As clerkès finden written
    In theirè book.

makèless] matchless, without a mate          ches] chose
        all so stillè] as silently

    **13**   clerkès] learned men

Ne had the apple taken been,
    The apple taken been,
Ne haddè never our Lady
    A been heaven's queen.
Blessed be the time
    That apple taken was!
Therefore we may singen
    'Deo Gratias!'

14        *I Have a Gentle Cock*

I HAVE a gentle cock
    Croweth me day;
He doth me risen early
    My matins for to say.

I have a gentle cock
    Comen he is of great;
His comb is of red corál
    His tail is of jet.

I have a gentle cock
    Comen he is of kind;
His comb is of red corál
    His tail is of inde.

His leggès been of azure
    So gentle and so small;
His spurrès are of silver white
    Into the wortèwale.

His eyen are of crystal
    Locken all in amber;
And every night he percheth him
    In my lady's chamber.

14  doth] makes        of great] of great family        of kind] of noble stock
        inde] indigo            wortèwale] root                Locken] set

15

## *Jankin*

'KYRIË', so '*Kyriĕ*',
  Jankin singeth merry,
With '*eléison*'.

As I went on Yulë day
  In our procession,
Knew I jolly Jankin
  By his merry tone—
  *Kyrie eléison.*

Jankin began the office
  On the Yulë day,
And yet me think'th it does me good
  So merry gan he say
  '*Kyrie eléison*'

Jankin read the pistle
  Full fair and full well,
And yet me think'th it does me good,
  As ever have I sel.
  *Kyrie eléison.*

Jankin at the *Sanctus*
  Crack'th a merry note,
And yet me think'th it does me good—
  I payëd for his coat.
  *Kyrie eléison.*

Jankin cracketh notës
  An hundred on a knot
And yet he hack'th them smaller
  Than wortës to the pot.
  *Kyrie eléison.*


As . . . sel] as I hope always to be happy
Crack'th . . . note] divides the note into short ones

## ANONYMOUS

Jankin at the *Agnus*
    Beareth the pax-bread;
He twinkèlèd but said nought,
    And on my foot he tread.
    *Kyrie eléison.*

*Benedicamus Domino,*
    Christ from shame me shield!
*Deo gratias* thereto—
    Alas I go with child!
    *Kyrie eléison.*


# CHARLES OF ORLEANS

## ?1394–1465

16                *A Lover's Confession*

MY ghostly father, I me confess,
    First to God and then to you,
    That at a window—wot ye how?
I stole a kiss of great sweetness,
Which done was out avisedness;
    But it is done, not undone, now.
My ghostly father, I me confess,
    First to God and then to you.
But I restore it shall doubtless
    Again, if so be that I mow;
    And that to God I make avow,
And else I ask forgivéness.
My ghostly father, I me confess,
    First to God and then to you,
    That at a window—wot ye how?
I stole a kiss of great sweetness.


**16**   out avisedness] without thought

# ANONYMOUS

**17**        *Corpus Christi Carol*

*Lully, lullay, lully, lullay,*
*The falcon hath borne my make away.*

He bore him up, he bore him down;
He bore him into an orchard brown.

In that orchard there was an hall,
That was hanged with purple and pall.

And in that hall there was a bed;
It was hanged with gold so red.

And in that bed there lieth a knight,
His woundès bleeding day and night.

By that bed's side there kneeleth a may,
And she weepeth both night and day.

And by that bed's side there standeth a stone,
*Corpus Christi* written thereon.

**18**        *The Jolly Shepherd*

CAN I not sing but 'hoy'
When the jolly shepherd made so much joy?

The shepherd upon a hill he sat;
He had on him his tabard and his hat,
His tar-box, his pipe and his flagát;
His name was called Jolly, Jolly Wat,
    For he was a good herdsboy.
        With hoy!
    For in his pipe he made so much joy.

*make*] mate        *may*] maid

**18**   flagát] flask

## ANONYMOUS

The shepherd upon a hill was laid;
His dog to his girdle was taid.
He had not slept but a little braid
But '*Gloria in excelsis*' was to him said.
    With hoy!
  For in his pipe he made so much joy.

The shepherd on a hill he stood;
Round about him his sheep they yood;
He put his hand under his hood;
He saw a star as red as blood.
    With hoy!
  For in his pipe he made so much joy.

'Now farewell Mall, and also Will;
For my love go ye all still
Until I come again you till;
And evermore, Will, ring well thy bell.'
    With hoy!
  For in his pipe he made so much joy.

'Now must I go there Christ was born;
Farewell, I come again to-morn.
Dog, keep well my sheep fro the corn,
And warn well Warrock when I blow my horn.'
    With hoy!
  For in his pipe he made so much joy.

The shepherd said anon-right:
'I will go see yon ferly sight,
Whereas the angel singeth on height,
And the star that shineth so bright.'
    With hoy!
  For in his pipe he made so much joy.

When Wat to Bethlehem come was
He sweat: he had gone faster than a pace.
He found Jesu in a simple place
Between an ox and an ass.
    With hoy!
  For in his pipe he made so much joy.

braid] moment        yood] went

'Jesu, I offer to thee here my pipe,
My skirt, my tar-box, and my scrip;
Home to my fellows now will I skip,
And also look unto my sheep.'
    With hoy!
  For in his pipe he made so much joy.

'Now farewell, mine own herdsman Wat.'
'Yea, for God, Lady, even so I hat.
Lull well Jesu in thy lap,
And farewell, Joseph, with thy round cap.'
    With hoy!
  For in his pipe he made so much joy.

'Now may I well both hop and sing
For I have been at Christès bearing.
Home to my fellows now will I fling.
Christ of heaven to his bliss us bring!'
    With hoy!
  For in his pipe he made so much joy.


19           *The Bridal Morn*

THE maidens came
    When I was in my mother's bower;
I had all that I would.
    The bailey beareth the bell away;
    The lily, the rose, the rose I lay.
The silver is white, red is the gold;
The robes they lay in fold.
    The bailey beareth the bell away;
    The lily, the rose, the rose I lay.
And through the glass window shines the sun.
How should I love, and I so young?
    The bailey beareth the bell away;
    The lily, the rose, the rose I lay.

# WILLIAM CORNISH
### d. 1524

20 *The Knight and the Lady*

THE knight knocked at the castle gate;
The lady marvelled who was thereat.

To call the porter he would not blin;
The lady said he should not come in.

The portress was a lady bright;
Strangèness that lady hight.

She askèd him what was his name;
He said, 'Desire, your man, Madame.'

She said, 'Desire, what do ye here?'
He said, 'Madame, as your prisoner.'

He was counselled to brief a bill,
And show my lady his own will.

'Kindness', said she, 'would it bear,'
'And Pity', said she, 'would be there.'

Thus how they did we cannot say;
We left them there and went our way.

## ANONYMOUS

21 *Western Wind*

WESTERN wind, when will thou blow,
The small rain down can rain?
Christ, if my love were in my arms
And I in my bed again!

20 blin] cease          brief a bill] draw up a petition

# WILLIAM DUNBAR

?1460–1520

22          *Timor Mortis Conturbat Me*

I THAT in heill wes and gladnes
Am trublit now with gret seiknes
And feblit with infirmite:
    *Timor mortis conturbat me.*

Our plesance here is all vane glory,
This fals warld is bot transitory,
The flesche is brukle, the Fend is sle:
    *Timor mortis conturbat me.*

The stait of man dois change and vary,
Now sound, now seik, now blith, now sary,
Now dansand mery, now like to dee:
    *Timor mortis conturbat me.*

No stait in erd heir standis sickir;
As with the wynd wavis the wickir
Wavis this warldis vanite:
    *Timor mortis conturbat me.*

On to the ded gois all estatis,
Princis, prelotis, and potestatis,
Baith riche and pur of all degre:
    *Timor mortis conturbat me.*

He takis the knychtis in to feild,
Anarmit under helme and scheild;
Victour he is at all mellie:
    *Timor mortis conturbat me.*

*Timor mortis conturbat me*] The fear of Death troubles me (Office of the Dead)
brukle] feeble          sle] cunning          sickir] sure          wickir] willow

# WILLIAM DUNBAR

That strang unmercifull tyrand
Takis, on the moderis breist sowkand,
The bab full of benignite:
    *Timor mortis conturbat me.*

He takis the campion in the stour,
The capitane closit in the tour,
The lady in bour full of bewte:
    *Timor mortis conturbat me.*

He sparis no lord for his piscence,
Na clerk for his intelligence,
His awfull strak may no man fle:
    *Timor mortis conturbat me. . . .*

I se that makaris amang the laif
Playis heir ther pageant, syne gois to graif;
Sparit is nocht ther faculte:
    *Timor mortis conturbat me.*

He hes done petuously devour
The noble Chaucer of makaris flour,
The Monk of Bury, and Gower, all thre:
    *Timor mortis conturbat me.*

❋

Sen he hes all my brether tane
He will nocht lat me lif alane;
On forse I man his nyxt prey be:
    *Timor mortis conturbat me.*

Sen for the deid remeid is none
Best is that we for deid dispone
Eftir our deid that live may we:
    *Timor mortis conturbat me.*

campion] champion      piscence] puissance      stour] fight
      makaris] poets      the laif] the rest

23           *The Lord is Risen*

DONE is a battell on the dragon blak,
Our campioun Chryst confountet hes his force;
The yettis of hell ar brokin with a crak,
The signe triumphall rasit is of the croce,
The divillis trymmillis with hiddous voce,
The saulis ar borrowit and to the blis can go,
Chryst with his blud our ransonis dois indoce:
*Surrexit dominus de sepulchro.*

Dungin is the deidly dragon Lucifer,
The crewall serpent with the mortall stang,
The auld kene tegir with his teith on char
Quhilk in a wait hes lyne for us so lang,
Thinking to grip us in his clowis strang:
The mercifull lord wald nocht that it wer so,
He maid him for to felye of that fang:
*Surrexit dominus de sepulchro.*

He for our saik that sufferit to be slane
And lyk a lamb in sacrifice wes dicht,
Is lyk a lyone rissin up agane,
And as a gyane raxit him on hicht:
Sprungin is Aurora radius and bricht,
On loft is gone the glorius Appollo,
The blisfull day depairtit fro the nycht:
*Surrexit dominus de sepulchro.*

The grit victour agane is rissin on hicht
That for our querrell to the deth wes woundit;
The sone that wox all paill now schynis bricht,
And, dirknes clerit, our fayth is now refoundit:
The knell of mercy fra the hevin is soundit,
The Cristin ar deliverit of thair wo,
The Jowis and thair errour ar confoundit:
*Surrexit dominus de sepulchro.*

yettis] gates        borrowit] ransomed       indoce] endorse
      Dungin] struck down       on char] ajar, open
to felye of that fang] fail of his booty       dicht] made ready
          raxit him] raised himself up

The fo is chasit, the battell is done ceis,
The presone brokin, the jevellouris fleit and flemit,
The weir is gon, confermit is the peis,
The fetteris lowsit and the dungeoun temit,
The ransoun maid, the presoneris redemit,
The feild is win, ourcummin is the fo,
Dispulit of the tresur that he yemit:
*Surrexit dominus de sepulchro.*

# JOHN SKELTON

## ?1460-1529

24                     *Philip Sparrow*

*PLA ce bo!*
Who is there, who?
*Di le xi!*
Dame Margery,
*Fa, re, my, my.*
Wherefore and why, why?
For the soul of Philip Sparrow
That was late slain at Carrow,
Among the Nunnès Black.
For that sweet soulès sake,
And for all sparrows' souls,
Set in our bead-rolls,
*Pater noster qui,*
With an *Ave Mari,*
And with the corner of a Creed,
The more shall be your meed.

When I remember again
How my Philip was slain,
Never half the pain
Was between you twain,
Pyramus and Thisbe,
As then befell to me.

24   jevellouris . . . ] gaolers terrified and put to flight
         temit] emptied              yemit] kept

I wept and I wailed,
The tearès down hailed,
But nothing it availed
To call Philip again
Whom Gib, our cat, hath slain.

Gib, I say, our cat,
Worried her on that
Which I lovèd best.
It cannot be exprest
My sorrowful heaviness,
But all without redress!
For within that stound,
Half slumbering, in a sound
I fell down to the ground.

Unneth I cast mine eyes
Toward the cloudy skies.
But when I did behold
My sparrow dead and cold,
No creature but that would
Have ruèd upon me,
To behold and see
What heaviness did me pang:
Wherewith my hands I wrang,
That my sinews cracked,
As though I had been racked,
So pained and so strained
That no life wellnigh remained.

I sighed and I sobbed,
For that I was robbed
Of my sparrow's life.
O maiden, widow, and wife,
Of what estate ye be,
Of high or low degree,
Great sorrow then ye might see,
And learn to weep at me!
Such pains did me fret
That mine heart did beat,

stound] moment          sound] swoon          Unneth] hardly

25

## JOHN SKELTON

My visage pale and dead,
Wan, and blue as lead:
The pangs of hateful death
Wellnigh had stopped my breath.

*

Like Andromach, Hector's wife,
Was weary of her life,
When she had lost her joy,
Noble Hector of Troy;
In like manner alsó
Increaseth my deadly woe,
For my sparrow is go.

It was so pretty a fool,
It would sit on a stool,
And learned after my school
For to keep his cut,
With 'Philip, keep your cut!'

It had a velvet cap,
And would sit upon my lap
And seek after small worms,
And sometime white bread-crumbs;
And many times and oft
Between my breastés soft
It would lie and rest;
It was proper and prest.

Sometime he would gasp
When he saw a wasp;
A fly or a gnat,
He would fly at that;
And prettily he would pant
When he saw an ant.
Lord, how he would pry
After the butterfly!
Lord, how he would hop
After the gressop!

go] gone          keep his cut] behave himself          prest] alert
                  gressop] grasshopper

26

And when I said, 'Phip, Phip!'
Then he would leap and skip,
And take me by the lip.
Alas, it will me slo
That Philip is gone me fro!

   *Si in i qui ta tes*
Alas, I was evil at ease!
*De pro fun dis cla ma vi,*
When I saw my sparrow die!

*

### The Requiem Mass

   *Lauda, anima mea, Dominum!*
To weep with me look that ye come
All manner of birdės in your kind;
See none be left behind
To mourning look that ye fall
With dolorous songs funeral,
Some to sing, and some to say,
Some to weep, and some to pray,
Every bird in his lay.
The goldfinch, the wagtail;
The jangling jay to rail,
The fleckèd pie to chatter
Of this dolorous matter;
And robin redbreast,
He shall be the priest
The requiem mass to sing,
Softly warbeling,
With help of the red-sparrow,
And the chattering swallow,
This hearse for to hallow;
The lark with his long toe;
The spink, and the martinet alsó;
The shoveller with his broad beak;
The dotterel, that foolish peke,
And also the mad coot,
With a bald face to toot;

slo] slay      red-sparrow] sedge-warbler
spink] chaffinch      shoveller] spoonbill

The fieldfare and the snite;
The crow and the kite;
The raven, called Rolfè,
His plain-song to sol-fa;
The partridge, the quail;
The plover with us to wail;
The woodhack, that singeth 'chur'
Hoarsely, as he had the mur;
The lusty chanting nightingale;
The popinjay to tell her tale,
That toteth oft in a glass,
Shall read the Gospel at mass;
The mavis with her whistle
Shall read there the Pistle.
But with a large and a long
To keep just plain-song,
Our chanters shall be the cuckoo,
The culver, the stockdowe,
With 'peewit' the lapwing,
The Versicles shall sing.

The bittern with his bumpè,
The crane with his trumpè,
The swan of Maeander,
The goose and the gander,
The duck and the drake,
Shall watch at this wake;
The peacock so proud,
Because his voice is loud,
And hath a glorious tail,
He shall sing the Grail;
The owl, that is so foul,
Must help us to howl;
The heron so gaunt,
And the cormorant,
With the pheasant,
And the gaggling gant,
And the churlish chough;
The knot and the ruff;

snite] snipe     woodhack] woodpecker     mur] catarrh
popinjay] parrot     toteth] peeps     Grail] Gradual

The barnacle, the buzzard,
With the wild mallard;
The divendop to sleep;
The water-hen to weep;
The puffin and the teal
Money they shall deal
To pooré folk at large,
That shall be their charge;
The seamew and the titmouse;
The woodcock with the longe nose;
The throstle with her warbling;
The starling with her brabling;
The rook, with the osprey
That putteth fishes to a fray;
And the dainty curlew,
With the turtle most true.

At this *Placebo*
We may not well forgo
The countering of the coe;
The stork alsó,
That maketh his nest
In chimneys to rest;
Within those walls
No broken galls
May there abide
Of cuckoldry side,
Or else philosophy
Maketh a great lie.

The ostrich, that will eat
An horseshoe so great,
In the stead of meat,
Such fervent heat
His stomach doth fret;
He cannot well fly,
Nor sing tunably,
Yet at a brayd
He hath well assayed
To sol-fa above E-la.
*Fa*, lorell, *fa, fa!*

countering] improvising     coe] jackdaw     at a brayd] at a push

# JOHN SKELTON

*Ne quando*
*Male cantando,*
The best that we can,
To make him our bell-man,
And let him ring the bells.
He can do nothing else.

Chanticleer, our cock,
Must tell what is of the clock
By the astrology
That he hath naturally
Conceivèd and caught,
And was never taught
By Albumazer
The astronomer,
Nor by Ptolomy
Prince of astronomy,
Nor yet by Haly;
And yet he croweth daily
And nightly the tides
That no man abides,
With Partlot his hen,
Whom now and then
He plucketh by the head
When he doth her tread.

The bird of Araby,
That potentially
May never die,
And yet there is none
But one alone;
A phoenix it is
This hearse that must bless
With aromatic gums
That cost great sums,
The way of thurification
To make a fumigation,
Sweet of reflare,
And redolent of air,
This corse for to cense
With great reverence,

reflare] perfume

30

As Patriarch or Pope
In a black cope.
While he censeth the hearse,
He shall sing the verse,
*Liber a me*,
In *de, la, sol, re,*
Softly B molle
For my sparrow's soul.
Pliny sheweth all
In his *Story Natural*
What he doth find
Of this phoenix kind;
Of whose incineration
There riseth a new creation
Of the same fashion
Without alteration,
Saving that old age
Is turned into corage
Of fresh youth again;
This matter true and plain,
Plain matter indeed,
Who so list to read.

But for the eagle doth fly
Highest in the sky,
He shall be the sub-dean,
The choir to demean,
As provost principal,
To teach them their Ordinal;
Also the noble falcon,
With the ger-falcon,
The tarsel gentil,
They shall mourn soft and still
In their amice of gray;
The saker with them shall say
*Dirige* for Philip's soul;
The goshawk shall have a roll
The choristers to control;
The lanners and the merlins
Shall stand in their mourning-gowns;

demean] conduct          saker] hawk          lanners] falcons

The hobby and the musket
The censers and the cross shall fet;
The kestrel in all this wark
Shall be holy-water clerk.

And now the dark cloudy night
Chaseth away Phoebus bright,
Taking his course toward the west,
God send my sparrow's soul good rest!
*Requiem aeternam dona eis, Domine!* . . .


## *from* A Garland of Laurel

### (i)

25      *To Mistress Margery Wentworth*

WITH marjoram gentle,
    The flower of goodlihead,
Embroderèd the mantle
    Is of your maidenhead.
Plainly, I cannot glose;
    Ye be, as I devine,
The pretty primrose,
    The goodly columbine.
With marjoram gentle,
    The flower of goodlihead,
Embroderèd the mantle
    Is of your maidenhead.
Benign, courteous, and meek,
    With wordès well devised;
In you, who list to seek,
    Be virtues well comprised.
With marjoram gentle,
    The flower of goodlihead,
Embroderèd the mantle
    Is of your maidenhead.


hobby] small falcon      musket] sparrow-hawk

25    glose] flatter

(ii)

26 *To Mistress Isabel Pennell*

BY Saint Mary, my lady,
Your mammy and your daddy
Brought forth a goodly baby!

My maiden Isabel,
Reflaring rosabel.
The fragrant camomel;
  The ruddy rosary,
The sovereign rosemary,
The pretty strawberry;
  The columbine, the nept,
The jelofer well set,
The proper violet:
  Ennewèd your colour
Is like the daisy flower
After the April shower;
  Star of the morrow gray,
The blossom on the spray,
The freshest flower of May;
  Maidenly demure,
Of womanhood the lure;
Wherefore, I make you sure,
  It were an heavenly health,
It were an endless wealth,
A life for God himself,
  To hear this nightingale
Among the birdès small
Warbling in the vale,
    'Dug, dug,
  Jug, jug,
    Good year and good luck!'
    With 'Chuck, chuck, chuck, chuck!'

Reflaring rosabel] redolent rosebud      rosary] rose-bush
nept] mint      jelofer] gillyflower      Ennewèd] freshened

33

(iii)

27      *To Mistress Margaret Hussey*

MERRY Margaret,
    As midsummer flower,
Gentle as falcon
Or hawk of the tower:
With solace and gladness,
Much mirth and no madness,
All good and no badness;
    So joyously,
    So maidenly,
    So womanly
    Her demeaning
    In everything,
    Far, far passing
    That I can indite,
    Or suffice to write
Of Merry Margaret
    As midsummer flower,
Gentle as falcon
Or hawk of the tower.
    As patient and as still
And as full of good will
As fair Isaphill,
Coriander,
Sweet pomander,
Good Cassander,
Steadfast of thought,
Well made, well wrought,
Far may be sought
Ere that ye can find
So courteous, so kind,
As Merry Margaret,
    This midsummer flower,
Gentle as falcon
Or hawk of the tower.

Isaphill] Hypsipyle       Cassander] Cassandra

# SIR THOMAS WYATT

*c.* 1503–1542

28 *Remembrance*

THEY flee from me, that sometime did me seek
 With naked foot, stalking in my chamber.
I have seen them gentle, tame, and meek,
 That now are wild, and do not remember
 That sometime they put themselves in danger
  To take bread at my hand; and now they range
  Busily seeking with a continual change.

Thanked be fortune it hath been otherwise
 Twenty times better; but once, in special,
In thin array, after a pleasant guise,
 When her loose gown from her shoulders did fall,
 And she me caught in her arms long and small,
  Therewith all sweetly did me kiss
  And softly said, 'Dear heart, how like you this?'

It was no dream; I lay broad waking:
 But all is turned, thorough my gentleness,
Into a strange fashion of forsaking;
 And I have leave to go of her goodness,
 And she also to use newfangleness.
  But since that I so kindly am served,
  I would fain know what she hath deserved.

29 *To His Lute*

MY lute, awake! perform the last
Labour that thou and I shall waste,
 And end that I have now begun;
For when this song is sung and past,
 My lute, be still, for I have done.

As to be heard where ear is none,
As lead to grave in marble stone,
  My song may pierce her heart as soon.
Should we then sigh, or sing, or moan?
  No, no, my lute, for I have done.

The rocks do not so cruelly
Repulse the waves continually,
  As she my suit and affection;
So that I am past remedy,
  Whereby my lute and I have done.

Proud of the spoil that thou hast got
Of simple hearts thorough love's shot,
  By whom, unkind, thou hast them won,
Think not he hath his bow forgot,
  Although my lute and I have done.

Vengeance shall fall on thy disdain,
That mak'st but game on earnest pain;
  Think not alone under the sun
Unquit to cause thy lovers plain,
  Although my lute and I have done.

Perchance thee lie withered and old,
The winter nights that are so cold,
  Plaining in vain unto the moon;
Thy wishes then dare not be told.
  Care then who list, for I have done.

And then may chance thee to repent
The time that thou hast lost and spent
  To cause thy lovers sigh and swoon;
Then shalt thou know beauty but lent,
  And wish and want as I have done.

Now cease, my lute! this is the last
Labour that thou and I shall waste,
  And ended is that we begun;
Now is this song both sung and past.
  My lute, be still, for I have done.

30                          *An Appeal*

AND wilt thou leave me thus?
    Say nay, say nay, for shame!
    To save thee from the blame
    Of all my grief and grame.
And wilt thou leave me thus?
    Say nay! say nay!

And wilt thou leave me thus,
    That hath loved thee so long
    In wealth and woe among?
    And is thy heart so strong
As for to leave me thus?
    Say nay! say nay!

And wilt thou leave me thus,
    That hath given thee my heart,
    Never for to depart
    Neither for pain nor smart;
And wilt thou leave me thus?
    Say nay! say nay!

And wilt thou leave me thus,
    And have no more pity
    Of him that loveth thee?
    *Hélas!* thy cruelty!
And wilt thou leave me thus?
    Say nay! say nay!


31                          *Steadfastness*

FORGET not yet the tried intent
Of such a truth as I have meant;
My great travail so gladly spent
        Forget not yet!

        **30**   grame] vexation

Forget not yet when first began
The weary life ye know, since whan
The suit, the service, none tell can;
    Forget not yet!

Forget not yet the great assays,
The cruel wrong, the scornful ways,
The painful patience in denays,
    Forget not yet!

Forget not yet, forget not this,
How long ago hath been, and is,
The mind that never meant amiss
    Forget not yet!

Forget not then thine own approved,
The which so long hath thee so loved,
Whose steadfast faith yet never moved;
    Forget not this!

32                 *Farewell*

WHAT should I say,
    Since faith is dead,
And truth away
    From you is fled?
    Should I be led
        With doubleness?
        Nay, nay, mistress!

I promised you,
    And you promised me,
To be as true,
    As I would be.
    But since I see
        Your double heart,
        Farewell my part!

31   denays] denials

Though for to take
  It is not my mind,
But to forsake
  One so unkind,
  And as I find
    So will I trust,
    Farewell, unjust!

Can ye say nay,
  But that you said
That I alway
  Should be obeyed?
  And thus betrayed,
    Or that I wist,
    Farewell, unkissed!

33                          *In Eternum*

*In eternum* I was once determed
For to have loved and my mind affirmed,
That with my heart it should be confirmed
    *In eternum.*

Forthwith I found the thing that I might like,
And sought with love to warm her heart alike,
For, as methought, I should not see the like
    *In eternum.*

To trace this dance I put myself in press;
Vain hope did lead and bade I should not cease
To serve, to suffer, and still to hold my peace
    *In eternum.*

With this first rule I furthered me apace,
That, as methought, my troth had taken place
With full assurance to stand in her grace
    *In eternum.*

It was not long ere I by proof had found
That feeble building is on feeble ground;
For in her heart this word did never sound,
    *In eternum.*

*In eternum* then from my heart I kest
That I had first determined for the best;
Now in the place another thought doth rest,
    *In eternum.*


# HENRY HOWARD, EARL OF SURREY

## ?1517–1547

34         *In Windsor Castle*

So cruel prison how could betide, alas,
As proud Windsor, where I in lust and joy
With a king's son my childish years did pass
In greater feast than Priam's sons of Troy?
Where each sweet place returns a taste full sour;
The large green courts where we were wont to hove
With eyes cast up unto the maidens' tower,
And easy sighs, such as folk draw in love;
The stately sales, the ladies bright of hue,
The dances short, long tales of great delight,
With words and looks that tigers could but rue,
Where each of us did plead the other's right;
The palm-play where, despoilèd for the game,
With dazèd eyes oft we by gleams of love
Have missed the ball and got sight of our dame,
To bait her eyes, which kept the leads above;
The gravelled ground, with sleeves tied on the helm,
On foaming horse, with swords and friendly hearts,
With cheer, as though the one should overwhelm,
Where we have fought and chasèd oft with darts;
With silver drops the meads yet spread for ruth,
In active games of nimbleness and strength,
Where we did strain, trailèd by swarms of youth,
Our tender limbs that yet shot up in length;
The secret groves which oft we made resound
Of pleasant plaint and of our ladies' praise,
Recording soft what grace each one had found,
What hope of speed, what dread of long delays;

**34**   sales] chambers

The wild forest, the clothèd holts with green,
With reins avaled, and swift ybreathèd horse,
With cry of hounds and merry blasts between,
Where we did chase the fearful hart a force;
The void walls eke that harboured us each night,
Wherewith, alas! revive within my breast
The sweet accord, such sleeps as yet delight,
The pleasant dreams, the quiet bed of rest,
The secret thoughts imparted with such trust,
The wanton talk, the divers change of play,
The friendship sworn, each promise kept so just,
Wherewith we passed the winter nights away.
And with this thought the blood forsakes my face,
The tears berain my cheeks of deadly hue,
The which as soon as sobbing sighs, alas!
Upsuppèd have, thus I my plaint renew:
'O place of bliss, renewer of my woes,
Give me account where is my noble fere,
Whom in thy walls thou didst each night enclose,
To other lief, but unto me most dear.'
Echo, alas! that doth my sorrow rue,
Returns thereto a hollow sound of plaint.
Thus I alone, where all my freedom grew,
In prison pine with bondage and restraint;
And with remembrance of the greater grief
To banish the less, I find my chief relief.

35                  *Spring*

THE sootè season, that bud and bloom forth brings,
   With green hath clad the hill and eke the vale.
The nightingale with feathers new she sings;
   The turtle to her make hath told her tale.
Summer is come, for every spray now springs.
   The hart hath hung his old head on the pale;
The buck in brake his winter coat he flings;
   The fishes float with new repairèd scale;

avaled] slackened        fere] companion       lief] beloved

35   make] mate

The adder all her slough away she slings;
  The swift swallow pursueth the flies small;
The busy bee her honey now she mings;
  Winter is worn that was the flowers' bale.
And thus I see among these pleasant things
Each care decays; and yet my sorrow springs.


36                  *Consolation*

WHEN raging love with extreme pain
  Most cruelly distrains my heart,
When that my tears, as floods of rain,
  Bear witness of my woeful smart;
    When sighs have wasted so my breath
    That I lie at the point of death,

I call to mind the navy great
  That the Greeks brought to Troyë town,
And how the boistous winds did beat
  Their ships, and rent their sails adown;
    Till Agamemnon's daughter's blood
    Appeased the gods that them withstood.

And how that in those ten years' war
  Full many a bloody deed was done,
And many a lord that came full far
  There caught his bane, alas! too soon;
    And many a good knight overrun,
    Before the Greeks had Helen won.

Then think I thus: sith such repair,
  So long time war of valiant men,
Was all to win a lady fair,
  Shall I not learn to suffer then,
    And think my life well spent to be,
    Serving a worthier wight than she?

35   mings] remembers

42

Therefore I never will repent,
    But pains contented still endure;
For like as when, rough winter spent,
    The pleasant spring straight draweth in ure,
      So, after raging storms of care,
      Joyful at length may be my fare.

37              *The Seafarer*

O HAPPY dames, that may embrace
    The fruit of your delight,
Help to bewail the woeful case
    And eke the heavy plight
Of me, that wonted to rejoice
The fortune of my pleasant choice;
Good ladies, help to fill my mourning voice.

In ship, freight with rememberance
    Of thoughts and pleasures past,
He sails that hath in governance
    My life while it will last;
With scalding sighs, for lack of gale,
Furthering his hope, that is his sail,
Toward me, the sweet port of his avail.

Alas! how oft in dreams I see
    Those eyes that were my food;
Which sometime so delighted me,
    That yet they do me good;
Wherewith I wake with his return,
Whose absent flame did make me burn:
But when I find the lack, Lord, how I mourn!

When other lovers in arms across
    Rejoice their chief delight,
Drownèd in tears, to mourn my loss
    I stand the bitter night
In my window, where I may see
Before the winds how the clouds flee.
Lo! what a mariner love hath made me!

**37**   avail] disembarking

And in green waves when the salt flood
  Doth rise by rage of wind,
A thousand fancies in that mood
  Assail my restless mind.
Alas! now drencheth my sweet foe,
That with the spoil of my heart did go,
And left me; but, alas! why did he so?

And when the seas wax calm again
  To chase fro me annoy,
My doubtful hope doth cause me plain;
  So dread cuts off my joy.
Thus is my wealth mingled with woe,
And of each thought a doubt doth grow;
'Now he comes! Will he come? Alas, no, no!'

38                 *The Happy Life*

MARTIAL, the things for to attain
The happy life be these, I find:
The riches left, not got with pain;
The fruitful ground, the quiet mind;
The equal friend; no grudge nor strife;
No charge of rule nor governance;
Without disease the healthful life;
The household of continuance;
The mean diet, no delicate fare;
Wisdom joined with simplicity;
The night dischargèd of all care
Where wine may bear no sovereignty;
The chaste wife wise, without debate;
Such sleeps as may beguile the night;
Contented with thine own estate;
Neither wish death, nor fear his might.

# ROBERT WEVER
### *c.* 1550

39       *In Youth is Pleasure*

IN a herber green, asleep where I lay,
The birds sang sweet in the mids of the day;
I dreamèd fast of mirth and play.
    In youth is pleasure, in youth is pleasure.

Methought I walked still to and fro,
And from her company could not go;
But when I waked it was not so.
    In youth is pleasure, in youth is pleasure.

Therefore my heart is surely pight
Of her alone to have a sight,
Which is my joy and heart's delight.
    In youth is pleasure, in youth is pleasure.


# THOMAS SACKVILLE, EARL OF DORSET
### 1536–1608

40       *The Shield of War*

LASTLY, stood War, in glittering arms yclad,
  With visage grim, stern looks, and blackly hued;
In his right hand a naked sword he had,
  That to the hilts was all with blood imbrued;
  And in his left, that kings and kingdoms rued,
    Famine and fire he held, and therewithal
    He razèd towns and threw down towers and all.


**39**   herber] arbour        pight] fixed

Cities he sacked and realms, that whilom flowered
   In honour, glory, and rule above the best,
He overwhelmed and all their fame devoured,
    Consumed, destroyed, wasted, and never ceased,
    Till he their wealth, their name, and all oppressed;
      His face forhewed with wounds, and by his side
      There hung his targe, with gashes deep and wide.

In midst of which, depainted there, we found
   Deadly Debate, all full of snaky hair,
That with a bloody fillet was ybound,
    Out-breathing nought but discord everywhere.
    And round about were portrayed, here and there,
      The hugy hosts, Darius and his power,
      His kings, princes, his peers, and all his flower:

Whom great Macedo vanquished there in fight
   With deep slaughter, despoiling all his pride,
Pierced through his realms and daunted all his might.
    Duke Hannibal beheld I there beside,
    In Canna's field victor how he did ride,
      And woeful Romans that in vain withstood,
      And consul Paulus covered all in blood.

Yet saw I more: the fight at Thrasimene,
   And Trebery field, and eke when Hannibal
And worthy Scipio last in arms were seen
    Before Carthago gate, to try for all
    The world's empire, to whom it should befall;
      There saw I Pompey and Caesar clad in arms,
      Their hosts allied and all their civil harms:

With conquerors' hands, forbathed in their own blood,
   And Caesar weeping over Pompey's head.
Yet saw I Sulla and Marius where they stood,
    Their great cruelty and the deep bloodshed
    Of friends; Cyrus I saw and his host dead,
      And how the queen with great despite hath flung
      His head in blood of them she overcome.

Xerxes, the Persian king, yet saw I there
  With his huge host that drank the rivers dry,
Dismounted hills, and made the vales uprear,
  His host and all yet saw I plain, perdy!
  Thebès I saw, all razed how it did lie
    In heaps of stones, and Tyrus put to spoil,
    With walls and towers flat evened with the soil.

But Troy, alas! methought, above them all,
  It made mine eyes in very tears consume,
When I beheld the woeful weird befall,
  That by the wrathful will of gods was come;
  And Jove's unmovèd sentence and foredoom
    On Priam king and on his town so bent,
    I could not lin, but I must there lament.

And that the more, sith destiny was so stern
  As, force perforce, there might no force avail,
But she must fall, and by her fall we learn
  That cities, towers, wealth, world, and all shall quail.
  No manhood, might, nor nothing mought prevail;
    All were there prest full many a prince and peer,
    And many a knight that sold his death full dear:

Not worthy Hector, worthiest of them all,
  Her hope, her joy; his force is now for nought.
O Troy, Troy, Troy, there is no boot but bale;
  The hugy horse within thy walls is brought;
  Thy turrets fall, thy knights, that whilom fought
    In arms amid the field, are slain in bed,
    Thy gods defiled and all thy honour dead.

The flames upspring and cruelly they creep
  From wall to roof till all to cinders waste;
Some fire the houses where the wretches sleep;
  Some rush in here, some run in there as fast;
  In every where or sword or fire they taste;
    The walls are torn, the towers whirled to the ground,
    There is no mischief but may there be found.

lin] cease        prest] ready

Cassandra yet there saw I how they haled
　From Pallas' house, with spercled tress undone,
Her wrists fast bound, and with Greeks' rout empaled;
　And Priam eke, in vain how did he run
　To arms, whom Pyrrhus with despite hath done
　　To cruel death, and bathed him in the baign
　　Of his son's blood, before the altar slain.

But how can I describe the doleful sight
　That in the shield so livelike fair did shine?
Sith in this world I think was never wight
　Could have set forth the half, not half so fine.
　I can no more but tell how there is seen
　　Fair Ilium fall in burning red gledes down,
　　And from the soil great Troy, Neptunus' town.


# GEORGE GASCOIGNE

## 1542–1577

41　　　　　　　　*A Farewell*

'AND if I did, what then?
　Are you aggrieved therefore?
The sea hath fish for every man,
　And what would you have more?'

Thus did my mistress once
　Amaze my mind with doubt;
And popped a question for the nonce,
　To beat my brains about.

Whereto I thus replied:
　'Each fisherman can wish,
That all the seas at every tide
　Were his alone to fish.

**40**　spercled] flowing　　　　baign] bath　　　　gledes] embers

'And so did I, in vain,
  But since it may not be,
Let such fish there as find the gain,
  And leave the loss for me.

'And with such luck and loss
  I will content myself,
Till tides of turning time may toss
  Such fishers on the shelf.

'And when they stick on sands,
  That every man may see,
Then will I laugh and clap my hands,
  As they do now at me.'


# SIR EDWARD DYER

## 1543-1607

42          *My Mind to Me a Kingdom Is*

MY mind to me a kingdom is
  Such perfect joy therein I find,
That it excels all other bliss
That world affords or grows by kind.
    Though much I want which most would have,
    Yet still my mind forbids to crave.

No princely pomp, no wealthy store,
No force to win the victory,
No wily wit to salve a sore,
No shape to feed a loving eye;
    To none of these I yield as thrall,
    For why? my mind doth serve for all.

I see how plenty suffers oft,
And hasty climbers soon do fall;
I see that those which are aloft
Mishap doth threaten most of all;
    They get with toil, they keep with fear;
    Such cares my mind could never bear.

Content I live, this is my stay,
I seek no more than may suffice,
I press to bear no haughty sway;
Look, what I lack my mind supplies.
   Lo, thus I triumph like a king,
   Content with that my mind doth bring.

Some have too much, yet still do crave,
I little have, and seek no more:
They are but poor, though much they have,
And I am rich with little store:
   They poor, I rich; they beg, I give;
   They lack, I leave; they pine, I live.

I laugh not at another's loss,
I grudge not at another's gain;
No worldly waves my mind can toss,
My state at one doth still remain.
   I fear no foe, I fawn no friend;
   I loathe not life, nor dread no end.

Some weigh their pleasure by their lust,
Their wisdom by their rage of will;
Their treasure is their only trust,
A cloaked craft their store of skill:
   But all the pleasure that I find
   Is to maintain a quiet mind.

My wealth is health and perfect ease,
My conscience clear my chief defence;
I neither seek by bribes to please,
Nor by desert to breed offence.
   Thus do I live, thus will I die;
   Would all did so, as well as I.

43
## *A Silent Love*

THE lowest trees have tops, the ant her gall,
The fly her spleen, the little spark his heat;
The slender hairs cast shadows, though but small,
And bees have stings, although they be not great;
   Seas have their source, and so have shallow springs;
   And love is love, in beggars and in kings.

Where waters smoothest run, there deepest are the fords,
The dial stirs, yet none perceives it move;
The firmest faith is found in fewest words,
The turtles do not sing, and yet they love;
   True hearts have ears and eyes, no tongues to speak;
   They hear and see, and sigh, and then they break.


# SIR PHILIP SIDNEY

## 1554–1586

44     *Ye goat-herd Gods that love the*
*grassy mountains*

*Strephon.* Ye goat-herd Gods that love the grassy mountains,
   Ye Nymphs which haunt the springs in pleasant valleys,
   Ye Satyrs joyed with free and quiet forests,
   Vouchsafe your silent ears to plaining music,
   Which to my woes gives still an early morning,
   And draws the dolour on till weary evening.

*Klaius.* O Mercury, foregoer to the evening,
   O heavenly huntress of the savage mountains,
   O lovely star, entitled of the morning,
   While that my voice doth fill these woeful valleys,
   Vouchsafe your silent ears to plaining music,
   Which oft hath Echo tired in secret forests.

*Strephon.* I that was once free burgess of the forests,
   Where shade from sun and sport I sought in evening,
   I that was once esteemed for pleasant music,
   Am banished now among the monstrous mountains
   Of huge despair, and foul affliction's valleys,
   Am grown a shriek-owl to myself each morning.

*Klaius.* I that was once delighted every morning,
   Hunting the wild inhabiters of forests,
   I that was once the music of these valleys,
   So darkened am, that all my day is evening,
   Heart-broken so, that molehills seem high mountains,
   And fill the vales with cries instead of music.

*Strephon.* Long since, alas, my deadly swannish music
  Hath made itself a crier of the morning,
  And hath with wailing strength climbed highest mountains;
  Long since my thoughts more desert be than forests;
  Long since I see my joys come to their evening,
  And state thrown down to over-trodden valleys.

*Klaius.* Long since the happy dwellers of these valleys
  Have prayed me leave my strange exclaiming music,
  Which troubles their day's work and joys of evening;
  Long since I hate the night, more hate the morning;
  Long since my thoughts chase me like beasts in forests,
  And make me wish myself laid under mountains.

*Strephon.* Meseems I see the high and stately mountains
  Transform themselves to low dejected valleys;
  Meseems I hear in these ill-changèd forests
  The nightingales do learn of owls their music;
  Meseems I feel the comfort of the morning
  Turned to the mortal serene of an evening.

*Klaius.* Meseems I see a filthy cloudy evening
  As soon as sun begins to climb the mountains;
  Meseems I feel a noisome scent, the morning
  When I do smell the flowers of these valleys;
  Meseems I hear, when I do hear sweet music,
  The dreadful cries of murdered men in forests.

*Strephon.* I wish to fire the trees of all these forests;
  I give the sun a last farewell each evening;
  I curse the fiddling finders out of music;
  With envy I do hate the lofty mountains,
  And with despite despise the humble valleys;
  I do detest night, evening, day, and morning.

*Klaius.* Curse to myself my prayer is, the morning;
  My fire is more, than can be made with forests;
  My state more base, than are the basest valleys;
  I wish no evenings more to see, each evening;
  Shamèd I hate myself in sight of mountains,
  And stop mine ears, lest I grow mad with music.

*Strephon.* For she, whose parts maintained a perfect music,
    Whose beauties shined more than the blushing morning,
    Who much did pass in state the stately mountains,
    In straightness passed the cedars of the forests,
    Hath cast me, wretch, into eternal evening,
    By taking her two suns from these dark valleys.

*Klaius.* For she, with whom compared, the Alps are valleys,
    She, whose least word brings from the spheres their music,
    At whose approach the sun rose in the evening,
    Who, where she went, bore in her forehead morning,
    Is gone, is gone from these our spoilèd forests,
    Turning to deserts our best pastured mountains.

*Strephon.* These mountains witness shall, so shall these valleys,
*Klaius.* These forests eke, made wretched by our music,
    Our morning hymn this is, and song at evening.


45               *The Bargain*

    MY true love hath my heart, and I have his,
      By just exchange, one for the other given.
    I hold his dear, and mine he cannot miss,
      There never was a better bargain driven.
    His heart in me keeps me and him in one,
      My heart in him his thoughts and senses guides;
    He loves my heart, for once it was his own,
      I cherish his, because in me it bides.
    His heart his wound receivèd from my sight,
      My heart was wounded with his wounded heart;
    For as from me on him his hurt did light,
      So still methought in me his hurt did smart.
      Both equal hurt, in this change sought our bliss:
      My true love hath my heart and I have his.

46 *Philomela*

THE Nightingale, as soon as April bringeth
Unto her rested sense a perfect waking,
While late-bare Earth, proud of new clothing, springeth,
Sings out her woes, a thorn her song-book making;
And mournfully bewailing,
Her throat in tunes expresseth
What grief her breast oppresseth,
For Tereus' force on her chaste will prevailing.

*O Philomela fair, O take some gladness
That here is juster cause of plaintful sadness!
Thine earth now springs, mine fadeth;
Thy thorn without, my thorn my heart invadeth.*

Alas! she hath no other cause of anguish
But Tereus' love, on her by strong hand wroken;
Wherein she suffering, all her spirits languish,
Full womanlike complains her will was broken.
But I, who, daily craving,
Cannot have to content me,
Have more cause to lament me,
Since wanting is more woe than too much having.

*O Philomela fair, O take some gladness
That here is juster cause of plaintful sadness!
Thine earth now springs, mine fadeth;
Thy thorn without, my thorn my heart invadeth.*

47 *Sleep, baby mine, Desire*

SLEEP, baby mine, Desire, nurse Beauty singeth,
Thy cries, O baby, set mine head on aching;
The babe cries, 'Way, thy love doth keep me waking'.

Lully, lully, my babe, hope cradle bringeth
Unto my children always good rest taking;
The babe cries, 'Way, thy love doth keep me waking'.

Since, baby mine, from me thy watching springeth,
Sleep then a little, pap content is making;
The babe cries, 'Nay, for that abide I waking'.


48                          *A Farewell*

OFT have I mused, but now at length I find,
    Why those that die, men say they do depart.
'Depart!'—a word so gentle, to my mind,
    Weakly did seem to paint death's ugly dart.
But now the stars, with their strange course, do bind
    Me one to leave, with whom I leave my heart;
I hear a cry of spirits faint and blind,
    That, parting thus, my chiefest part I part.
Part of my life, the loathèd part to me,
    Lives to impart my weary clay some breath;
But that good part, wherein all comforts be,
    Now dead, doth show departure is a death—
        Yea, worse than death; death parts both woe and joy.
        From joy I part, still living in annoy.


49                          *To Sleep*

COME, Sleep, O Sleep, the certain knot of peace,
    The baiting-place of wit, the balm of woe,
The poor man's wealth, the prisoner's release,
    The indifferent judge between the high and low;
With shield of proof shield me from out the press
    Of those fierce darts Despair at me doth throw:
O make in me those civil wars to cease;
    I will good tribute pay, if thou do so.
Take thou of me smooth pillows, sweetest bed,
    A chamber deaf to noise and blind to light,
A rosy garland and a weary head;
    And if these things, as being thine by right,
        Move not thy heavy grace, thou shalt in me,
        Livelier than elsewhere, Stella's image see.

50                        *To the Sad Moon*

WITH how sad steps, O Moon, thou climb'st the skies!
    How silently, and with how wan a face!
    What! may it be that even in heavenly place
That busy archer his sharp arrows tries?
Sure, if that long-with-love-acquainted eyes
    Can judge of love, thou feel'st a lover's case:
    I read it in thy looks; thy languished grace
To me, that feel the like, thy state descries.
Then, even of fellowship, O Moon, tell me,
    Is constant love deemed there but want of wit?
Are beauties there as proud as here they be?
    Do they above love to be loved, and yet
        Those lovers scorn whom that love doth possess?
        Do they call 'virtue' there—ungratefulness?


51                      *Voices at the Window*

'WHO is it that this dark night
    Underneath my window plaineth?'
It is one who from thy sight
    Being, ah! exiled, disdaineth
Every other vulgar light.

'Why, alas! and are you he?
    Be not yet those fancies changèd?'
Dear, when you find change in me,
    Though from me you be estrangèd,
Let my change to ruin be.

'Well, in absence this will die;
    Leave to see and leave to wonder.'
Absence sure will help, if I
    Can learn how myself to sunder
From what in my heart doth lie.

'But time will these thoughts remove;
    Time doth work what no man knoweth.'
Time doth as the subject prove;
    With time still the affection groweth
In the faithful turtle dove.

'What if you new beauties see,
    Will not they stir new affection?'
I will think they pictures be,
    Image-like, of saints' perfection,
Poorly counterfeiting thee.

'But your reason's purest light
    Bids you leave such minds to nourish.'
Dear, do reason no such spite;
    Never doth thy beauty flourish
More than in my reason's sight.

'But the wrongs love bears will make
    Love at length leave undertaking.'
No, the more fools it do shake,
    In a ground of so firm making
Deeper still they drive the stake.

'Peace, I think that some give ear;
    Come no more lest I get anger.'
Bliss, I will my bliss forbear,
    Fearing, sweet, you to endanger;
But my soul shall harbour there.

'Well, begone, begone, I say,
    Lest that Argus' eyes perceive you.'
Oh, unjustest Fortune's sway,
    Which can make me thus to leave you,
And from louts to run away.

52 *Desire*

THOU blind man's mark, thou fool's self-chosen snare,
　　Fond fancy's scum, and dregs of scattered thought,
Band of all evils, cradle of causeless care,
　　Thou web of will, whose end is never wrought;
　　Desire, desire! I have too dearly bought,
With price of mangled mind, thy worthless ware;
　　Too long, too long, asleep thou hast me brought,
Who should my mind to higher things prepare.
　　But yet in vain thou hast my ruin sought,
In vain thou mad'st me to vain things aspire,
In vain thou kindlest all thy smoky fire;
　　For virtue hath this better lesson taught,
Within myself to seek my only hire,
Desiring nought but how to kill desire.


53 *Splendidis Longum Valedico Nugis*

LEAVE me, O Love, which reachest but to dust,
　　And thou, my mind, aspire to higher things!
Grow rich in that which never taketh rust:
　　Whatever fades, but fading pleasure brings.
Draw in thy beams, and humble all thy might
　　To that sweet yoke where lasting freedoms be;
Which breaks the clouds and opens forth the light
　　That doth both shine and give us sight to see.
O take fast hold! let that light be thy guide
　　In this small course which birth draws out to death,
And think how evil becometh him to slide
　　Who seeketh Heaven, and comes of heavenly breath.
　　　Then farewell, world! thy uttermost I see:
　　　Eternal Love, maintain thy life in me!

# CHIDIOCK TICHBORNE

### d. 1586

54 *Elegy*

My prime of youth is but a frost of cares,
My feast of joy is but a dish of pain,
My crop of corn is but a field of tares,
And all my good is but vain hope of gain;
The day is past, and yet I saw no sun,
And now I live, and now my life is done.

My tale was heard and yet it was not told,
My fruit is fallen and yet my leaves are green,
My youth is spent and yet I am not old,
I saw the world and yet I was not seen;
My thread is cut and yet it is not spun,
And now I live, and now my life is done.

I sought my death and found it in my womb,
I looked for life and saw it was a shade,
I trod the earth and knew it was my tomb,
And now I die, and now I was but made;
My glass is full, and now my glass is run,
And now I live, and now my life is done.

# EDMUND SPENSER

### ?1552–1599

55 *The Lay to Eliza*

Ye dayntye Nymphs, that in this blessed Brooke
Doe bathe your brest,
Forsake your watry bowres, and hether looke,
At my request:
And eke you Virgins, that on Parnasse dwell,
Whence floweth Helicon the learned well,
Helpe me to blaze
Her worthy praise,
Which in her sexe doth all excell.

Of fayre Elisa be your silver song,
        That blessed wight:
The flowre of Virgins, may shee florish long,
        In princely plight.
For shee is Syrinx daughter without spotte,
Which Pan the shepheards God of her begot:
        So sprong her grace
        Of heavenly race,
No mortall blemishe may her blotte.

See, where she sits upon the grassie greene,
        (O seemely sight)
Yclad in Scarlot like a mayden Queene,
        And Ermines white.
Upon her head a Cremosin coronet,
With Damaske roses and Daffadillies set:
        Bayleaves betweene,
        And Primroses greene
Embellish the sweete Violet.

Tell me, have ye seene her angelick face,
        Like Phoebe fayre?
Her heavenly haveour, her princely grace
        Can you well compare?
The Redde rose medled with the White yfere,
In either cheeke depeincten lively chere.
        Her modest eye,
        Her Majestie,
Where have you seene the like, but there?

I sawe Phoebus thrust out his golden hedde,
        Upon her to gaze:
But when he sawe, how broade her beames did spredde,
        It did him amaze.
He blusht to see another Sunne belowe,
Ne durst againe his fyrye face out showe:
        Let him, if he dare,
        His brightnesse compare
With hers, to have the overthrowe.

        medled] mingled        yfere] together

Shewe thy selfe, Cynthia, with thy silver rayes,
      And be not abasht:
When shee the beames of her beauty displayes,
      O how art thou dasht?
But I will not match her with Latonaes seede,
Such follie great sorow to Niobe did breede.
      Now she is a stone,
      And makes dayly mone,
Warning all other to take heede.

Pan may be proud, that ever he begot
      Such a Bellibone,
And Syrinx rejoyse, that ever was her lot
      To bear such an one.
Soone as my younglings cryen for the dam,
To her will I offer a milkwhite Lamb:
      Shee is my goddesse plaine,
      And I her shepherds swayne,
Albee forswonck and forswatt I am.

I see Calliope speede her to the place,
      Where my Goddesse shines:
And after her the other Muses trace,
      With their Violines.
Bene they not Bay braunches, which they doe beare,
All for Elisa in her hand to weare?
      So sweetely they play,
      And sing all the way,
That it a heaven is to heare.

Lo how finely the graces can it foote
      To the Instrument:
They dauncen deffly, and singen soote,
      In their meriment.
Wants not a fourth grace, to make the daunce even?
Let that rowme to my Lady be yeven:
      She shalbe a grace,
      To fyll the fourth place,
And reigne with the rest in heaven.

Bellibone] goodly one        forswonck and forswatt] tired and sweaty

# EDMUND SPENSER

And whither rennes this bevie of Ladies bright,
    Raunged in a rowe?
They bene all Ladyes of the lake behight,
    That unto her goe.
Chloris, that is the chiefest Nymph of al,
Of Olive braunches beares a Coronall:
    Olives bene for peace,
    When wars doe surcease:
Such for a Princesse bene principall.

Ye shepheards daughters, that dwell on the greene,
    Hye you there apace:
Let none come there, but that Virgins bene,
    To adorne her grace.
And when you come, whereas shee is in place,
See, that your rudenesse doe not you disgrace:
    Binde your fillets faste,
    And gird in your waste,
For more finesse, with a tawdrie lace.

Bring hether the Pincke and purple Cullambine,
    With Gelliflowres:
Bring Coronations, and Sops in wine,
    Worne of Paramoures.
Strowe me the ground with Daffadowndillies,
And Cowslips, and Kingcups, and loved Lillies:
    The pretie Pawnce,
    And the Chevisaunce,
Shall match with the fayre flowre Delice.

Now ryse up, Elisa, decked as thou art,
    In royall aray:
And now ye daintie Damsells may depart
    Echeone her way,
I feare, I have troubled your troupes to longe:
Let dame Elisa thanke you for her song.
    And if you come hether,
    When Damsines I gether,
I will part them all you among.

Sops in wine] pinks        Pawnce] pansy        Chevisaunce] ?

56                              *Easter*

MOST glorious Lord of lyfe, that on this day,
    Didst make thy triumph over death and sin:
And having harrowd hell, didst bring away
    Captivity thence captive us to win:
    This joyous day, deare Lord, with joy begin,
And grant that we, for whom thou diddest dye,
    Being with thy deare blood clene washt from sin,
May live for ever in felicity.
And that thy love we weighing worthily,
    May likewise love thee for the same againe:
And for thy sake that all lyke deare didst buy,
    With love may one another entertayne.
        So let us love, deare love, lyke as we ought,
        Love is the lesson which the Lord us taught.


57                         *Epithalamion*

YE learned sisters which have oftentimes
Beene to me ayding, others to adorne:
Whom ye thought worthy of your gracefull rymes,
That even the greatest did not greatly scorne
To heare theyr names sung in your simple layes,
But joyed in theyr prayse.
And when ye list your owne mishaps to mourne,
Which death, or love, or fortunes wreck did rayse,
Your string could soone to sadder tenor turne,
And teach the woods and waters to lament
Your dolefull dreriment.
Now lay those sorrowfull complaints aside,
And having all your heads with girland crownd,
Helpe me mine owne loves prayses to resound,
Ne let the same of any be envide
So Orpheus did for his owne bride,
So I unto my selfe alone will sing,
The woods shall to me answer and my Eccho ring.

Early before the worlds light giving lampe,
His golden beame upon the hils doth spred,
Having disperst the nights unchearefull dampe,
Doe ye awake, and with fresh lusty hed,
Go to the bowre of my beloved love,
My truest turtle dove,
Bid her awake; for Hymen is awake,
And long since ready forth his maske to move,
With his bright Tead that flames with many a flake,
And many a bachelor to waite on him,
In theyr fresh garments trim.
Bid her awake therefore and soone her dight,
For lo the wished day is come at last,
That shall for al the paynes and sorrowes past,
Pay to her usury of long delight:
And whylest she doth her dight,
Doe ye to her of joy and solace sing,
That all the woods may answer and your eccho ring.

Bring with you all the Nymphes that you can heare
Both of the rivers and the forrests greene:
And of the sea that neighbours to her neare,
Al with gay girlands goodly wel beseene.
And let them also with them bring in hand,
Another gay girland
For my fayre love of lillyes and of roses,
Bound truelove wize with a blew silke riband.
And let them make great store of bridale poses,
And let them eeke bring store of other flowers
To deck the bridale bowers.
And let the ground whereas her foot shall tread,
For feare the stones her tender foot should wrong
Be strewed with fragrant flowers all along,
And diapred lyke the discolored mead.
Which done, doe at her chamber dore awayt,
For she will waken strayt,
The whiles doe ye this song unto her sing,
The woods shall to you answer and your Eccho ring.

Tead] torch

Ye Nymphes of Mulla which with carefull heed,
The silver scaly trouts doe tend full well,
And greedy pikes which use therein to feed,
(Those trouts and pikes all others doo excell)
And ye likewise which keepe the rushy lake,
Where none doo fishes take,
Bynd up the locks the which hang scatterd light,
And in his waters which your mirror make,
Behold your faces as the christall bright,
That when you come whereas my love doth lie,
No blemish she may spie.
And eke ye lightfoot mayds which keepe the deere,
That on the hoary mountayne use to towre,
And the wylde wolves which seeke them to devoure,
With your steele darts doo chace from comming neer
Be also present heere,
To helpe to decke her and to help to sing,
That all the woods may answer and your eccho ring.

Wake now, my love, awake; for it is time.
The Rosy Morne long since left Tithones bed,
All ready to her silver coche to clyme,
And Phoebus gins to shew his glorious hed.
Hark how the cheerefull birds do chaunt theyr laies
And carroll of loves praise.
The merry Larke hir mattins sings aloft,
The thrush replyes, the Mavis descant playes,
The Ouzell shrills, the Ruddock warbles soft,
So goodly all agree with sweet consent,
To this dayes merriment.
Ah my deere love, why doe ye sleepe thus long,
When meeter were that ye should now awake,
T'awayt the comming of your joyous make,
And hearken to the birds lovelearned song,
The deawy leaves among.
For they of joy and pleasance to you sing,
That all the woods them answer and theyr eccho ring.

My love is now awake out of her dreame,
And her fayre eyes, like stars that dimmed were
With darksome cloud, now shew theyr goodly beams
More bright then Hesperus his head doth rere.
Come now, ye damzels, daughters of delight,
Helpe quickly her to dight,
But first come, ye fayre houres which were begot
In Joves sweet paradice, of Day and Night,
Which doe the seasons of the yeare allot,
And al that ever in this world is fayre
Doe make and still repayre.
And ye three handmayds of the Cyprian Queene,
The which doe still adorne her beauties pride,
Helpe to addorne my beautifullest bride:
And as ye her array, still throw betweene
Some graces to be seene,
And as ye use to Venus, to her sing,
The whiles the woods shal answer and your eccho ring.

Now is my love all ready forth to come;
Let all the virgins therefore well awayt,
And ye fresh boyes that tend upon her groome
Prepare your selves; for he is comming strayt.
Set all your things in seemely good aray
Fit for so joyfull day,
The joyfulst day that ever sunne did see.
Faire Sun, shew forth thy favourable ray,
And let thy lifull heat not fervent be
For feare of burning her sunshyny face,
Her beauty to disgrace.
O fayrest Phoebus, father of the Muse,
If ever I did honour thee aright,
Or sing the thing, that mote thy mind delight,
Doe not thy servants simple boone refuse,
But let this day, let this one day, be myne,
Let all the rest be thine.
Then I thy soverayne prayses loud wil sing,
That all the woods shal answer and theyr eccho ring.

## EDMUND SPENSER

Harke how the Minstrels gin to shrill aloud
Their merry Musick that resounds from far,
The pipe, the tabor, and the trembling Croud,
That well agree withouten breach or jar.
But most of all the Damzels doe delite,
When they their tymbrels smyte,
And thereunto doe daunce and carrol sweet,
That all the sences they doe ravish quite,
The whyles the boyes run up and downe the street,
Crying aloud with strong confused noyce,
As if it were one voyce.
Hymen, io, Hymen, Hymen, they do shout,
That even to the heavens theyr shouting shrill
Doth reach, and all the firmament doth fill,
To which the people standing all about,
As in approvance doe thereto applaud
And loud advance her laud,
And evermore they Hymen, Hymen sing,
That al the woods them answer and theyr eccho ring.

Loe where she comes along with portly pace
Lyke Phoebe from her chamber of the East,
Arysing forth to run her mighty race,
Clad all in white, that seemes a virgin best.
So well it her beseemes that ye would weene
Some angell she had beene.
Her long loose yellow locks lyke golden wyre,
Sprinckled with perle, and perling flowres a tweene,
Doe lyke a golden mantle her attyre,
And being crowned with a girland greene,
Seeme lyke some mayden Queene.
Her modest eyes abashed to behold
So many gazers, as on her do stare,
Upon the lowly ground affixed are.
Ne dare lift up her countenance too bold,
But blush to heare her prayses sung so loud,
So farre from being proud.
Nathlesse doe ye still loud her prayses sing.
That all the woods may answer and your eccho ring.

Croud] fiddle

67

Tell me, ye merchants daughters, did ye see
So fayre a creature in your towne before,
So sweet, so lovely, and so mild as she,
Adornd with beautyes grace and vertues store,
Her goodly eyes lyke Saphyres shining bright,
Her forehead yvory white,
Her cheekes lyke apples which the sun hath rudded,
Her lips lyke cherryes charming men to byte,
Her brest like to a bowle of creame uncrudded,
Her paps lyke lyllies budded,
Her snowie necke lyke to a marble towre,
And all her body like a pallace fayre,
Ascending uppe with many a stately stayre,
To honors seat and chastities sweet bowre.
Why stand ye still, ye virgins, in amaze,
Upon her so to gaze,
Whiles ye forget your former lay to sing,
To which the woods did answer and your eccho ring.

But if ye saw that which no eyes can see,
The inward beauty of her lively spright,
Garnisht with heavenly guifts of high degree,
Much more then would ye wonder at that sight,
And stand astonisht lyke to those which red
Medusaes mazeful hed.
There dwels sweet love and constant chastity,
Unspotted fayth and comely womanhood,
Regard of honour and mild modesty,
There vertue raynes as Queene in royal throne,
And giveth lawes alone.
The which the base affections doe obay,
And yeeld theyr services unto her will,
Ne thought of thing uncomely ever may
Thereto approch to tempt her mind to ill.
Had ye once seene these her celestial threasures,
And unrevealed pleasures,
Then would ye wonder and her prayses sing,
That al the woods should answer and your echo ring.

mazeful] amazing

Open the temple gates unto my love,
Open them wide that she may enter in,
And all the postes adorne as doth behove,
And all the pillours deck with girlands trim,
For to recyve this Saynt with honour dew,
That commeth in to you.
With trembling steps and humble reverence,
She commeth in, before th'almighties vew,
Of her, ye virgins, learne obedience,
When so ye come into those holy places,
To humble your proud faces:
Bring her up to th'high altar, that she may
The sacred ceremonies there partake,
The which do endlesse matrimony make,
And let the roring Organs loudly play
The praises of the Lord in lively notes,
The whiles with hollow throates
The Choristers the joyous Antheme sing,
That al the woods may answere and their eccho ring.

Behold whiles she before the altar stands
Hearing the holy priest that to her speakes
And blesseth her with his two happy hands,
How the red roses flush up in her cheekes,
And the pure snow with goodly vermill stayne,
Like crimsin dyde in grayne,
That even th'Angels which continually
About the sacred Altare doe remaine,
Forget their service and about her fly,
Ofte peeping in her face that seemes more fayre,
The more they on it stare.
But her sad eyes still fastened on the ground,
Are governed with goodly modesty,
That suffers not one looke to glaunce awry,
Which may let in a little thought unsownd.
Why blush ye, love, to give to me your hand,
The pledge of all our band?
Sing ye, sweet Angels, Alleluya sing,
That all the woods may answere and your eccho ring.

Now al is done; bring home the bride againe,
Bring home the triumph of our victory,
Bring home with you the glory of her gaine,
With joyance bring her and with jollity.
Never had man more joyfull day then this,
Whom heaven would heape with blis.
Make feast therefore now all this live long day,
This day for ever to me holy is,
Poure out the wine without restraint or stay,
Poure not by cups, but by the belly full,
Poure out to all that wull,
And sprinkle all the postes and wals with wine,
That they may sweat, and drunken be withall.
Crowne ye God Bacchus with a coronall,
And Hymen also crowne with wreathes of vine,
And let the Graces daunce unto the rest;
For they can doo it best:
The whiles the maydens doe theyr carroll sing,
To which the woods shal answer and theyr eccho ring.

Ring ye the bels, ye yong men of the towne,
And leave your wonted labors for this day:
This day is holy; doe ye write it downe,
That ye for ever it remember may.
This day the sunne is in his chiefest hight,
With Barnaby the bright,
From whence declining daily by degrees,
He somewhat loseth of his heat and light,
When once the Crab behind his back he sees.
But for this time it ill ordained was,
To chose the longest day in all the yeare,
And shortest night, when longest fitter weare:
Yet never day so long, but late would passe.
Ring ye the bels, to make it weare away,
And bonefiers make all day,
And daunce about them, and about them sing,
That all the woods may answer, and your eccho ring.

Ah when will this long weary day have end,
And lende me leave to come unto my love?
How slowly do the houres theyr numbers spend!
How slowly does sad Time his feathers move!
Hast thee, O fayrest Planet, to thy home
Within the Westerne fome:
Thy tyred steedes long since have need of rest.
Long though it be, at last I see it gloome,
And the bright evening star with golden creast
Appeare out of the East.
Fayre childe of beauty, glorious lampe of love,
That all the host of heaven in rankes doost lead,
And guydest lovers through the nightes dread,
How chearefully thou lookest from above,
And seemst to laugh atweene thy twinkling light
As joying in the sight
Of these glad many which for joy doe sing,
That all the woods them answer and their echo ring.

Now ceasse, ye damsels, your delights forepast;
Enough is it, that all the day was youres:
Now day is doen, and night is nighing fast:
Now bring the Bryde into the brydall boures.
Now night is come, now soone her disaray,
And in her bed her lay;
Lay her in lillies and in violets,
And silken courteins over her display,
And odourd sheetes, and Arras coverlets.
Behold how goodly my faire love does ly
In proud humility;
Like unto Maia, when as Jove her tooke,
In Tempe, lying on the flowry gras,
Twixt sleepe and wake, after she weary was,
With bathing in the Acidalian brooke.
Now it is night, ye damsels may be gon,
And leave my love alone,
And leave likewise your former lay to sing:
The woods no more shal answere, nor your echo ring.

Now welcome night, thou night so long expected,
That long daies labour doest at last defray,
And all my cares, which cruell love collected,
Hast sumd in one, and cancelled for aye:
Spread thy broad wing over my love and me,
That no man may us see,
And in thy sable mantle us enwrap,
From feare of perrill and foule horror free.
Let no false treason seeke us to entrap,
Nor any dread disquiet once annoy
The safety of our joy:
But let the night be calme and quietsome,
Without tempestuous storms or sad afray:
Lyke as when Jove with fayre Alcmena lay,
When he begot the great Tirynthian groome:
Or lyke as when he with thy selfe did lie,
And begot Majesty.
And let the mayds and yongmen cease to sing:
Ne let the woods them answer, nor theyr eccho ring.

Let no lamenting cryes, nor dolefull teares,
Be heard all night within nor yet without:
Ne let false whispers, breeding hidden feares,
Breake gentle sleepe with misconceived dout.
Let no deluding dreames, nor dreadful sights
Make sudden sad affrights;
Ne let housefyres, nor lightnings helpelesse harmes,
Ne let the Pouke, nor other evill sprights,
Ne let mischivous witches with theyr charmes,
Ne let hob Goblins, names whose sence we see not,
Fray us with things that be not.
Let not the shriech Oule, nor the Storke be heard,
Nor the night Raven that still deadly yels,
Nor damned ghosts cald up with mighty spels,
Nor griesly vultures make us once affeard,
Ne let th'unpleasant Quyre of Frogs still croking
Make us to wish theyr choking.
Let none of these theyr drery accents sing;
Ne let the woods them answer, nor theyr eccho ring.

But let stil Silence trew night watches keepe,
That sacred peace may in assurance rayne,
And tymely sleep, when it is tyme to sleepe,
May poure his limbs forth on your pleasant playne,
The whiles an hundred little winged loves,
Like divers fethered doves,
Shall fly and flutter round about your bed,
And in the secret darke, that none reproves,
Their prety stealthes shal worke, and snares shal spread
To filch away sweet snatches of delight,
Conceald through covert night.
Ye sonnes of Venus, play your sports at will,
For greedy pleasure, carelesse of your toyes,
Thinks more upon her paradise of joyes,
Then what ye do, albe it good or ill.
All night therefore attend your merry play,
For it will soone be day:
Now none doth hinder you, that say or sing,
Ne will the woods now answer, nor your Eccho ring.

Who is the same, which at my window peepes?
Or whose is that faire face, that shines so bright,
Is it not Cinthia, she that never sleepes,
But walkes about high heaven al the night?
O fayrest goddesse, do thou not envy
My love with me to spy:
For thou likewise didst love, though now unthought,
And for a fleece of woll, which privily
The Latmian shephard once unto thee brought,
His pleasures with thee wrought.
Therefore to us be favorable now;
And sith of wemens labours thou hast charge,
And generation goodly dost enlarge,
Encline thy will t'effect our wishfull vow,
And the chast wombe informe with timely seed,
That may our comfort breed:
Till which we cease our hopefull hap to sing,
Ne let the woods us answere, nor our Eccho ring.

And thou, great Juno, which with awful might
The lawes of wedlock still dost patronize,
And the religion of the faith first plight
With sacred rites hast taught to solemnize:
And eeke for comfort often called art
Of women in their smart,
Eternally bind thou this lovely band,
And all thy blessings unto us impart.
And thou, glad Genius, in whose gentle hand
The bridale bowre and geniall bed remaine,
Without blemish or staine,
And the sweet pleasures of theyr loves delight
With secret ayde doest succour and supply,
Till they bring forth the fruitfull progeny,
Send us the timely fruit of this same night.
And thou, fayre Hebe, and thou, Hymen free,
Grant that it may so be.
Til which we cease your further prayse to sing,
Ne any woods shal answer, nor your Eccho ring.

And ye high heavens, the temple of the gods,
In which a thousand torches flaming bright
Doe burne, that to us wretched earthly clods
In dreadful darknesse lend desired light;
And all ye powers which in the same remayne,
More then we men can fayne,
Poure out your blessing on us plentiously
And happy influence upon us raine,
That we may raise a large posterity,
Which from the earth, which they may long possesse,
With lasting happinesse,
Up to your haughty pallaces may mount,
And for the guerdon of theyr glorious merit
May heavenly tabernacles there inherit,
Of blessed Saints for to increase the count.
So let us rest, sweet love, in hope of this,
And cease till then our tymely joyes to sing,
The woods no more us answer, nor our eccho ring.

Song, made in lieu of many ornaments,
With which my love should duly have bene dect,
Which cutting off through hasty accidents,
Ye would not stay your dew time to expect,
But promist both to recompens,
Be unto her a goodly ornament,
And for short time an endlesse moniment.


*from* The Faerie Queene

(i)

58         *The Cave of Despair*

ERE long they come, where that same wicked wight
  His dwelling has, low in an hollow cave,
Farre underneath a craggie clift ypight,
  Darke, dolefull, drearie, like a greedie grave,
  That still for carrion carcases doth crave:
On top whereof aye dwelt the ghastly Owle,
  Shrieking his balefull note, which ever drave
Farre from that haunt all other chearefull fowle;
And all about it wandring ghostes did waile and howle.

And all about old stockes and stubs of trees,
  Whereon nor fruit, nor leafe was ever seene,
Did hang upon the ragged rocky knees;
  On which had many wretches hanged beene,
  Whose carcases were scattered on the greene,
And throwne about the cliffs. Arrived there,
  That bare-head knight for dread and dolefull teene,
Would faine have fled, ne durst approchen neare,
But th'other forst him stay, and comforted in feare.

That darkesome cave they enter, where they find
  That cursed man, low sitting on the ground,
Musing full sadly in his sullein mind;
  His griesie lockes, long growen, and unbound,
  Disordred hong about his shoulders round,
And hid his face; through which his hollow eyne
  Lookt deadly dull, and stared as astound;
His raw-bone cheekes through penurie and pine
Were shronke into his jawes, as he did never dine.

75

His garment nought but many ragged clouts,
  With thornes together pind and patched was,
The which his naked sides he wrapt abouts;
  And him beside there lay upon the gras
  A drearie corse, whose life away did pas,
All wallowd in his owne yet luke-warme blood,
  That from his wound yet welled fresh, alas;
In which a rustie knife fast fixed stood,
And made an open passage for the gushing flood.

Which piteous spectacle, approving trew
  The wofull tale that Trevisan had told,
When as the gentle Redcrosse knight did vew,
  With firie zeale he burnt in courage bold,
  Him to avenge, before his bloud were cold,
And to the villein said, 'Thou damned wight,
  The author of this fact we here behold,
What justice can but judge against thee right,
With thine owne bloud to price his bloud, here shed in sight?'

'What franticke fit' (quoth he) 'hath thus distraught
  Thee, foolish man, so rash a doome to give?
What justice ever other judgement taught
  But he should die who merites not to live?
  None else to death this man despayring drive
But his owne guiltie mind deserving death.
  Is then unjust to each his due to give?
Or let him die that loatheth living breath?
Or let him die at ease that liveth here uneath?

'Who travels by the wearie wandring way
  To come unto his wished home in haste,
And meetes a flood, that doth his passage stay,
  Is not great grace to helpe him over past,
  Or free his feet, that in the myre sticke fast?
Most envious man, that grieves at neighbours good,
  And fond, that joyest in the woe thou hast,
Why wilt not let him passe, that long hath stood
Upon the banke, yet wilt thy selfe not passe the flood?

'He there does now enjoy eternall rest
  And happie ease, which thou doest want and crave,
And further from it daily wanderest:
    What if some litle paine the passage have,
    That makes fraile flesh to feare the bitter wave?
Is not short paine well borne, that brings long ease,
    And layes the soule to sleepe in quiet grave?
Sleepe after toyle, port after stormie seas,
Ease after warre, death after life does greatly please.'

The knight much wondred at his suddeine wit,
  And said, 'The terme of life is limited,
Ne may a man prolong, nor shorten it;
    The souldier may not move from watchfull sted,
    Nor leave his stand, untill his Captaine bed.'
'Who life did limit by almightie doome,'
  (Quoth he) 'knowes best the termes established;
And he that points the Centonell his roome
Doth license him depart at sound of morning droome.

'Is not his deed, what ever thing is donne,
  In heaven and earth? did not he all create
To die againe? all ends that was begonne.
    Their times in his eternall booke of fate
    Are written sure, and have their certaine date.
Who then can strive with strong necessitie,
    That holds the world in his still chaunging state,
Or shunne the death ordaynd by destinie?
When houre of death is come, let none aske whence, nor why.

'The lenger life, I wote the greater sin,
  The greater sin, the greater punishment:
All those great battels, which thou boasts to win,
    Through strife and bloud-shed and avengement,
    Now praysd, hereafter deare thou shalt repent:
For life must life, and bloud must bloud repay.
    Is not enough thy evill life forespent?
For he that once hath missed the right way,
The further he doth goe, the further he doth stray.

'Then do no further goe, no further stray,
    But here lie downe, and to thy rest betake,
Th'ill to prevent, that life ensewen may.
    For what hath life, that may it loved make,
    And gives not rather cause it to forsake?
Feare, sicknesse, age, losse, labour, sorrow, strife,
    Paine, hunger, cold, that makes the hart to quake;
And ever fickle fortune rageth rife,
All which, and thousands mo do make a loathsome life.'

(ii)

59                    *The Bower of Bliss*

EFTSOONES they heard a most melodious sound,
    Of all that mote delight a daintie eare,
Such as attonce might not on living ground,
    Save in this Paradise, be heard elswhere:
    Right hard it was, for wight which did it heare,
To read what manner musicke that mote bee:
    For all that pleasing is to living eare,
Was there consorted in one harmonee,
Birdes, voyces, instruments, windes, waters, all agree.

The joyous birdes shrouded in chearefull shade,
    Their notes unto the voyce attempred sweet;
Th'Angelicall soft trembling voyces made
    To th'instruments divine respondence meet:
    The silver sounding instruments did meet
With the base murmure of the waters fall:
    The waters fall with difference discreet,
Now soft, now loud, unto the wind did call:
The gentle warbling wind low answered to all.

There, whence that Musick seemed heard to bee,
    Was the faire Witch her selfe now solacing,
With a new Lover, whom through sorceree
    And witchcraft she from farre did thither bring:
    There she had him now layd a slombering,
In secret shade, after long wanton joyes:
    Whilst round about them pleasauntly did sing
Many faire Ladies, and lascivious boyes,
That ever mixt their song with light licentious toyes.

78

And all that while, right over him she hong,
  With her false eyes fast fixed in his sight,
As seeking medicine, whence she was stong,
  Or greedily depasturing delight:
  And oft inclining downe with kisses light,
For feare of waking him, his lips bedewd,
  And through his humid eyes did sucke his spright,
Quite molten into lust and pleasure lewd;
Wherewith she sighed soft, as if his case she rewd.

The whiles some one did chaunt this lovely lay;
  'Ah see, who so faire thing doest faine to see,
In springing flowre the image of thy day;
  Ah see the Virgin Rose, how sweetly shee
  Doth first peepe forth with bashfull modestee,
That fairer seemes, the lesse ye see her may;
  Lo, see soone after, how more bold and free
Her bared bosome she doth broad display;
Loe, see soone after, how she fades, and falles away.

'So passeth, in the passing of a day,
  Of mortall life the leafe, the bud, the flowre,
Ne more doth flourish after first decay,
  That earst was sought to decke both bed and bowre,
  Of many a Ladie, and many a Paramowre:
Gather therefore the Rose, whilest yet is prime,
  For soone comes age, that will her pride deflowre:
Gather the Rose of love, whilest yet is time,
Whilest loving thou mayst loved be with equall crime.'

(iii)

### *The Garden of Adonis*

60

IN that same Gardin all the goodly flowres,
  Wherewith dame Nature doth her beautifie,
And decks the girlonds of her paramoures,
  Are fetcht: there is the first seminarie
  Of all things that are borne to live and die,
According to their kindes. Long worke it were,
  Here to account the endlesse progenie
Of all the weedes that bud and blossome there;
But so much as doth need, must needs be counted here.

It sited was in fruitfull soyle of old,
  And girt in with two walles on either side;
The one of yron, the other of bright gold,
  That none might thorough breake, nor overstride:
  And double gates it had, which opened wide,
By which both in and out men moten pas;
  Th'one faire and fresh, the other old and dride:
Old Genius the porter of them was,
Old Genius, the which a double nature has.

He letteth in, he letteth out to wend,
  All that to come into the world desire;
A thousand thousand naked babes attend
  About him day and night, which doe require,
  That he with fleshly weedes would them attire:
Such as him list, such as eternall fate
  Ordained hath, he clothes with sinfull mire,
And sendeth forth to live in mortall state,
Till they againe returne backe by the hinder gate.

After that they againe returned beene,
  They in that Gardin planted be againe;
And grow afresh, as they had never seene
  Fleshly corruption, nor mortall paine.
  Some thousand yeares so doen they there remaine;
And then of him are clad with other hew,
  Or sent into the chaungefull world againe,
Till thither they returne, where first they grew:
So like a wheele around they runne from old to new.

Ne needs there Gardiner to set, or sow,
  To plant or prune: for of their owne accord
All things, as they created were, doe grow,
  And yet remember well the mightie word,
  Which first was spoken by th'Almightie lord,
That bad them to increase and multiply:
  Ne doe they need with water of the ford,
Or of the clouds to moysten their roots dry;
For in themselves eternall moisture they imply.

Infinite shapes of creatures there are bred,
  And uncouth formes, which none yet ever knew,
And every sort is in a sundry bed
  Set by it selfe, and ranckt in comely rew:
  Some fit for reasonable soules t'indew,
Some made for beasts, some made for birds to weare,
  And all the fruitfull spawne of fishes hew
In endlesse rancks along enraunged were,
That seem'd the Ocean could not containe them there.

Daily they grow, and daily forth are sent
  Into the world, it to replenish more;
Yet is the stocke not lessened, nor spent,
  But still remaines in everlasting store,
  As it at first created was of yore.
For in the wide wombe of the world there lyes,
  In hatefull darkenesse and in deepe horrore,
An huge eternall Chaos, which supplyes
The substances of natures fruitfull progenyes.

All things from thence doe their first being fetch,
  And borrow matter, whereof they are made,
Which when as forme and feature it does ketch,
  Becomes a bodie, and doth then invade
  The state of life, out of the griesly shade.
That substance is eterne, and bideth so,
  Ne when the life decayes, and forme does fade,
Doth it consume, and into nothing go,
But chaunged is, and often altred to and fro.

The substance is not chaunged, nor altered,
  But th'only forme and outward fashion;
For every substance is conditioned
  To change her hew, and sundry formes to don,
  Meet for her temper and complexion:
For formes are variable and decay,
  By course of kind, and by occasion;
And that faire flowre of beautie fades away,
As doth the lilly fresh before the sunny ray.

Great enimy to it, and to all the rest,
    That in the Gardin of Adonis springs,
Is wicked Time, who with his scyth addrest,
    Does mow the flowring herbes and goodly things,
    And all their glory to the ground downe flings,
Where they doe wither, and are fowly mard:
    He flyes about, and with his flaggy wings
Beates downe both leaves and buds without regard,
Ne ever pittie may relent his malice hard.

Yet pittie often did the gods relent,
    To see so faire things mard, and spoyled quight:
And their great mother Venus did lament
    The losse of her deare brood, her deare delight:
    Her hart was pierst with pittie at the sight,
When walking through the Gardin, them she spyde,
    Yet no'te she find redresse for such despight.
For all that lives, is subject to that law:
All things decay in time, and to their end do draw.

But were it not, that Time their troubler is,
    All that in this delightfull Gardin growes,
Should happie be, and have immortall blis,
    For here all plentie, and all pleasure flowes
    And sweet love gentle fits emongst them throwes,
Without fell rancor, or fond gealosie;
    Franckly each paramour his leman knowes,
Each bird his mate, ne any does envie
Their goodly meriment, and gay felicitie.

There is continuall spring, and harvest there
    Continuall, both meeting at one time:
For both the boughes doe laughing blossomes beare,
    And with fresh colours decke the wanton Prime,
    And eke attonce the heavy trees they clime,
Which seeme to labour under their fruits lode:
    The whiles the joyous birdes make their pastime
Emongst the shadie leaves, their sweet abode,
And their true loves without suspition tell abrode.

no'te] could not

EDMUND SPENSER

## (iv)

61 *The Masque of Cupid*

THE first was Fancy, like a lovely boy,
　Of rare aspect, and beautie without peare;
Matchable either to that ympe of Troy,
　Whom Jove did love, and chose his cup to beare,
　Or that same daintie lad, which was so deare,
To great Alcides, that when as he dyde,
　He wailed womanlike with many a teare,
And every wood, and every valley wyde
He fild with Hylas name; the Nymphes eke Hylas cryde.

His garment neither was of silke nor say,
　But painted plumes, in goodly order dight,
Like as the sunburnt Indians do aray
　Their tawney bodies, in their proudest plight:
　As those same plumes, so seemd he vaine and light,
That by his gate might easily appeare;
　For still he far'd as dauncing in delight,
And in his hand a windy fan did beare,
That in the idle aire he mov'd still here and there.

And him beside marcht amorous Desyre,
　Who seemd of riper yeares, then th'other Swaine,
Yet was that other swayne this elders syre,
　And gave him being, commune to them twaine:
　His garment was disguised very vaine,
And his embrodered Bonet sat awry;
　Twixt both his hands few sparkes he close did straine,
Which still he blew, and kindled busily,
That soone they life conceiv'd, and forth in flames did fly.

Next after him went Doubt, who was yclad
　In a discolour'd cote, of straunge disguyse,
That at his backe a brode Capuccio had,
　And sleeves dependant Albanese-wyse:

Capuccio] hood

83

He lookt askew with his mistrustfull eyes,
And nicely trode, as thornes lay in his way,
 Or that the flore to shrinke he did avyse,
And on a broken reed he still did stay
His feeble steps, which shrunke, when hard theron he lay.

With him went Daunger, cloth'd in ragged weed,
 Made of Beares skin, that him more dreadfull made,
Yet his owne face was dreadfull, ne did need
 Straunge horrour, to deforme his griesly shade;
 A net in th'one hand, and a rustie blade
In th'other was, this Mischiefe, that Mishap;
 With th'one his foes he threatned to invade,
With th'other he his friends ment to enwrap:
For whom he could not kill, he practizd to entrap.

Next him was Feare, all arm'd from top to toe,
 Yet thought himselfe not safe enough thereby,
But feard each shadow moving to and fro,
 And his owne armes when glittering he did spy,
 Or clashing heard, he fast away did fly,
As ashes pale of hew, and wingyheeld;
 And evermore on daunger fixt his eye,
Gainst whom he alwaies bent a brasen shield,
Which his right hand unarmed fearefully did wield.

With him went Hope in rancke, a handsome Mayd,
 Of chearefull looke and lovely to behold;
In silken samite she was light arayd,
 And her faire lockes were woven up in gold;
 She alway smyld, and in her hand did hold
An holy water Sprinckle, dipt in deowe,
 With which she sprinckled favours manifold,
On whom she list, and did great liking sheowe,
Great liking unto many, but true love to feowe.

And after them Dissemblance, and Suspect
 Marcht in one rancke, yet an unequall paire:
For she was gentle, and of milde aspect,
 Courteous to all, and seeming debonaire,

Goodly adorned, and exceeding faire:
Yet was that all but painted, and purloynd,
  And her bright browes were deckt with borrowed haire:
Her deedes were forged, and her words false coynd,
And alwaies in her hand two clewes of silke she twynd.

But he was foule, ill favoured, and grim,
  Under his eyebrowes looking still askaunce;
And ever as Dissemblance laught on him,
  He lowrd on her with daungerous eyeglaunce;
  Shewing his nature in his countenance;
His rolling eyes did never rest in place,
  But walkt each where, for feare of hid mischaunce,
Holding a lattice still before his face,
Through which he still did peepe, as forward he did pace.

Next him went Griefe, and Fury matcht yfere;
  Griefe all in sable sorrowfully clad,
Downe hanging his dull head with heavy chere,
  Yet inly being more, then seeming sad:
  A paire of Pincers in his hand he had,
With which he pinched people to the hart,
  That from thenceforth a wretched life they lad,
In wilfull languor and consuming smart,
Dying each day with inward wounds of dolours dart.

But Fury was full ill appareiled
  In rags, that naked nigh she did appeare,
With ghastly lookes and dreadfull drerihed;
  For from her backe her garments she did teare,
  And from her head oft rent her snarled heare:
In her right hand a firebrand she did tosse
  About her head, still roming here and there;
As a dismayed Deare in chace embost,
Forgetfull of his safety, hath his right way lost.

After them went Displeasure and Pleasance,
  He looking lompish and full sullein sad,
And hanging downe his heavy countenance;
  She chearefull fresh and full of joyance glad,

clewes] skeins        snarled] tangled        embost] hard-pressed

85

As if no sorrow she ne felt ne drad;
That evill matched paire they seemd to bee
  An angry Waspe th'one in a viall had
Th'other in hers an hony-lady Bee;
Thus marched these sixe couples forth in faire degree.

(v)

62          *The Hill of the Graces*

UNTO this place when as the Elfin Knight
  Approcht, him seemed that the merry sound
Of a shrill pipe he playing heard on hight,
  And many feete fast thumping th'hollow ground,
  That through the woods their Eccho did rebound.
He nigher drew, to weete what mote it be;
  There he a troupe of Ladies dauncing found
Full merrily, and making gladfull glee,
And in the midst a Shepheard piping he did see.

He durst not enter into th'open greene,
  For dread of them unwares to be descryde,
For breaking of their daunce, if he were seene;
  But in the covert of the wood did byde,
  Beholding all, yet of them unespyde.
There he did see, that pleased much his sight,
  That even he him selfe his eyes envyde,
An hundred naked maidens lilly white,
All raunged in a ring, and dauncing in delight.

All they without were raunged in a ring,
  And daunced round; but in the midst of them
Three other Ladies did both daunce and sing,
  The whilest the rest them round about did hemme,
  And like a girlond did in compasse stemme:
And in the middest of those same three, was placed
  Another Damzell, as a precious gemme,
Amidst a ring most richly well enchaced,
That with her goodly presence all the rest much graced.

**62**  stemme] surround

Looke how the Crowne, which Ariadne wore
  Upon her yvory forehead that same day,
That Theseus her unto his bridale bore,
  When the bold Centaures made that bloudy fray,
  With the fierce Lapithes, which did them dismay;
Being now placed in the firmament,
  Through the bright heaven doth her beams display,
And is unto the starres an ornament,
Which round about her move in order excellent.

Such was the beauty of this goodly band,
  Whose sundry parts were here too long to tell:
But she that in the midst of them did stand,
  Seem'd all the rest in beauty to excell,
  Crownd with a rosie girlond, that right well
Did her beseeme. And ever, as the crew
  About her daunst, sweet flowres, that far did smell,
And fragrant odours they uppon her threw;
But most of all, those three did her with gifts endew.

Those were the Graces, daughters of delight,
  Handmaides of Venus, which are wont to haunt
Uppon this hill, and daunce there day and night:
  Those three to men all gifts of grace do graunt,
  And all, that Venus in her selfe doth vaunt,
Is borrowed of them. But that faire one,
  That in the midst was placed paravaunt,
Was she to whom that shepheard pypt alone,
That made him pipe so merrily, as never none.

She was to weete that jolly Shepheards lasse,
  Which piped there unto that merry rout,
That jolly shepheard, which there piped, was
  Poore Colin Clout (who knowes not Colin Clout?)
  He pypt apace, whilest they him daunst about.
Pype, jolly shepheard, pype thou now apace
  Unto thy love, that made thee low to lout:
Thy love is present there with thee in place,
Thy love is there advaunst to be another Grace.

(vi)

63         *Nature's Reply to Mutability*

So having ended, silence long ensewed,
  Ne Nature to or fro spake for a space,
But with firme eyes affixt, the ground still viewed.
  Meane while, all creatures, looking in her face,
  Expecting th'end of this so doubtfull case,
Did hang in long suspence what would ensew,
  To whether side should fall the soveraigne place:
At length, she looking up with chearefull view,
The silence brake, and gave her doome in speeches few.

'I well consider all that ye have sayd,
  And find that all things stedfastnes doe hate
And changed be: yet being rightly wayd
  They are not changed from their first estate;
  But by their change their being doe dilate:
And turning to themselves at length againe,
  Doe worke their owne perfection so by fate:
Then over them Change doth not rule and raigne:
But they raigne over change, and doe their states maintaine.

'Cease therefore, daughter, further to aspire,
  And thee content thus to be rul'd by me:
For thy decay thou seekst by thy desire;
  But time shall come that all shall changed bee,
  And from thenceforth, none no more change shall see.'
So was the Titaness put downe and whist,
  And Jove confirm'd in his imperiall see.
Then was that whole assembly quite dismist,
And Nature's selfe did vanish, whither no man wist.

\*

When I bethinke me on that speech whyleare,
  Of Mutability, and well it way:
Me seemes, that though she all unworthy were
  Of the Heav'ns Rule; yet very sooth to say,
  In all things else she beares the greatest sway.
Which makes me loath this state of life so tickle,
  And love of things so vaine to cast away;
Whose flowring pride, so fading and so fickle,
Short Time shall soon cut down with his consuming sickle.

Then gin I thinke on that which Nature sayd,
  Of that same time when no more Change shall be,
But stedfast rest of all things firmely stayd
  Upon the pillours of Eternity,
  That is contrayr to Mutabilitie:
For, all that moveth, doth in Change delight:
  But thence-forth all shall rest eternally
With Him that is the God of Sabbaoth hight:
O that great Sabbaoth God, graunt me that Sabaoths sight.

## ANTHONY MUNDAY

### 1553–1633

64                     *Beauty Bathing*

BEAUTY sat bathing by a spring
  Where fairest shades did hide her;
The winds blew calm, the birds did sing,
  The cool streams ran beside her.
My wanton thoughts enticed mine eye
  To see what was forbidden:
But better memory said, fie!
  So vain desire was chidden.
      *Hey nonny, nonny, etc.*

Into a slumber then I fell,
  When fond imagination
Seemed to see, but could not tell
  Her feature or her fashion.
But even as babes in dreams do smile,
  And sometime fall a-weeping,
So I awaked, as wise this while,
  As when I fell a-sleeping.
      *Hey nonny, nonny, etc.*

# JOHN LYLY
?1554–1606

65                          *A Serving-Men's Song*

*Granichus.*  O! for a bowl of fat Canary,
           Rich Palermo, sparkling Sherry,
           Some nectar else, from Juno's dairy;
           O! these draughts would make us merry.

*Psyllus.*  O! for a wench (I deal in faces,
           And in other daintier things);
           Tickled am I with her embraces,
           Fine dancing in such fairy rings.

*Manes.*  O! for a plump fat leg of mutton,
           Veal, lamb, capon, pig, and coney;
           None is happy but a glutton,
           None an ass but who wants money.

*Chorus.*  Wines (indeed) and girls are good,
           But brave victuals feast the blood;
           For wenches, wine, and lusty cheer,
           Jove would leap down to surfeit here.

66                          *Cards and Kisses*

CUPID and my Campaspe played
At cards for kisses, Cupid paid;
He stakes his quiver, bow, and arrows,
His mother's doves, and team of sparrows;
Loses them too; then, down he throws
The coral of his lip, the rose
Growing on's cheek (but none knows how);
With these, the crystal of his brow,
And then the dimple of his chin:
All these did my Campaspe win.
At last, he set her both his eyes;
She won, and Cupid blind did rise.
   O Love! has she done this to thee?
   What shall (alas!) become of me?

67                    *Welcome to Spring*

WHAT bird so sings, yet so does wail?
O! 'tis the ravished nightingale.
Jug, Jug, Jug, Jug, Tereu, she cries,
And still her woes at midnight rise.
Brave prick song! who is 't now we hear?
None but the lark so shrill and clear;
How at heaven's gates she claps her wings,
The morn not waking till she sings.
Hark, hark, with what a pretty throat
Poor Robin Redbreast tunes his note;
Hark how the jolly cuckoos sing
Cuckoo, to welcome in the spring,
Cuckoo, to welcome in the spring.


# NICHOLAS BRETON

?1545-1626

68                    *The Ploughman's Song*

IN the merry month of May,
In a morn by break of day,
Forth I walked by the wood side,
Whereas May was in his pride.
There I spied all alone
Phyllida and Corydon.
Much ado there was, God wot,
He would love and she would not.
She said, never man was true;
He said, none was false to you.
He said, he had loved her long;
She said, love should have no wrong.
Corydon would kiss her then;
She said, maids must kiss no men,
Till they did for good and all.
Then she made the shepherd call
All the heavens to witness truth,
Never loved a truer youth.

Thus with many a pretty oath,
Yea and nay, and faith and troth,
Such as silly shepherds use,
When they will not love abuse,
Love, which had been long deluded,
Was with kisses sweet concluded:
And Phyllida with garlands gay
Was made the Lady of the May.

69                     *A Cradle Song*

COME, little babe, come, silly soul,
Thy father's shame, thy mother's grief,
Born as I doubt to all our dole,
And to thyself unhappy chief:
 Sing lullaby and lap it warm,
 Poor soul that thinks no creature harm.

Thou little think'st and less dost know
The cause of this thy mother's moan;
Thou want'st the wit to wail her woe,
And I myself am all alone;
 Why dost thou weep? why dost thou wail,
 And knowest not yet what thou dost ail?

Come, little wretch! Ah, silly heart!
Mine only joy, what can I more?
If there be any wrong thy smart,
That may the destinies implore,
 'Twas I, I say, against my will:
 I wail the time, but be thou still.

And dost thou smile? O! thy sweet face!
Would God himself he might thee see!
No doubt thou wouldst soon purchase grace,
I know right well, for thee and me:
 But come to mother, babe, and play,
 For father false is fled away.

Sweet boy, if it by fortune chance
Thy father home again to send,
If death do strike me with his lance,
Yet mayst thou me to him commend;
    If any ask thy mother's name,
      Tell how by love she purchased blame.

Then will his gentle heart soon yield;
I know him of a noble mind;
Although a lion in the field,
A lamb in town thou shalt him find:
    Ask blessing, babe, be not afraid!
      His sugared words hath me betrayed.

Then mayst thou joy and be right glad,
Although in woe I seem to moan;
Thy father is no rascal lad,
A noble youth of blood and bone;
    His glancing looks, if he once smile,
      Right honest women may beguile.

Come, little boy, and rock asleep!
Sing lullaby, and be thou still!
I, that can do nought else but weep,
Will sit by thee and wail my fill:
    God bless my babe, and lullaby,
      From this thy father's quality.

70            *Wooing in a Dream*

    SHALL we go dance the hay, the hay?
    Never pipe could ever play
    Better shepherd's roundelay.

    Shall we go sing the song, the song?
    Never Love did ever wrong.
    Fair maids, hold hands all along.

    Shall we go learn to woo, to woo?
    Never thought came ever to,
    Better deed could better do.

Shall we go learn to kiss, to kiss?
Never heart could ever miss
Comfort, where true meaning is.

Thus at base they run, they run,
When the sport was scarce begun.
But I waked, and all was done.

# THOMAS LODGE
?1558–1625

71                     *Rosalind's Madrigal*

LOVE in my bosom like a bee
    Doth suck his sweet;
Now with his wings he plays with me,
    Now with his feet.
Within mine eyes he makes his nest,
His bed amidst my tender breast;
My kisses are his daily feast,
And yet he robs me of my rest.
    Ah, wanton, will ye?

And if I sleep, then percheth he
    With pretty flight,
And makes his pillow of my knee
    The livelong night.
Strike I my lute, he tunes the string;
He music plays if so I sing;
He lends me every lovely thing;
Yet cruel he my heart doth sting.
    Whist, wanton, still ye!

Else I with roses every day
    Will whip you hence,
And bind you, when you long to play,
    For your offence.

# THOMAS LODGE

I'll shut mine eyes to keep you in,
I'll make you fast it for your sin,
I'll count your power not worth a pin.
Alas! what hereby shall I win
    If he gainsay me?

What if I beat the wanton boy
    With many a rod?
He will repay me with annoy,
    Because a god.
Then sit thou safely on my knee,
And let thy bower my bosom be;
Lurk in mine eyes, I like of thee.
O Cupid, so thou pity me,
    Spare not, but play thee!


# GEORGE PEELE

?1558–1596

72               *Oenone and Paris*

*Oenone.*  Fair and fair, and twice so fair,
        As fair as any may be;
    The fairest shepherd on our green,
        A Love for any lady.
*Paris.*    Fair and fair, and twice so fair,
        As fair as any may be;
    Thy Love is fair for thee alone,
        And for no other lady.
*Oenone.*  My Love is fair, my Love is gay,
        As fresh as bin the flowers in May;
    And of my Love my roundelay,
    My merry, merry, merry, roundelay,
        Concludes with Cupid's curse:
    They that do change old love for new,
        Pray gods they change for worse.
*Together.*  They that do change old love for new,
        Pray gods they change for worse.

| | |
|---|---|
| *Oenone.* | Fair and fair, and twice so fair, |
| | As fair as any may be; |
| | The fairest shepherd on our green, |
| | A Love for any lady. |
| *Paris.* | Fair and fair, and twice so fair, |
| | As fair as any may be; |
| | Thy Love is fair for thee alone, |
| | And for no other lady. |
| *Oenone.* | My Love can pipe, my Love can sing, |
| | My Love can many a pretty thing, |
| | And of his lovely praises ring |
| | My merry, merry, merry roundelays. |
| | Amen to Cupid's curse: |
| | They that do change old love for new, |
| | Pray gods they change for worse. |
| *Together.* | They that do change old love for new, |
| | Pray gods they change for worse. |

73                              *What Thing is Love?*

WHAT thing is love? for sure love is a thing.
It is a prick, it is a sting,
It is a pretty, pretty thing;
It is a fire, it is a coal,
Whose flame creeps in at every hole;
And as my wit doth best devise,
Love's dwelling is in ladies' eyes,
From whence do glance love's piercing darts,
That make such holes into our hearts;
And all the world herein accord,
Love is a great and mighty lord;
And when he list to mount so high,
With Venus he in heaven doth lie,
And evermore hath been a god,
Since Mars and she played even and odd.

74 *Farewell to Arms*
   *To Queen Elizabeth*

HIS golden locks time hath to silver turned;
   O time too swift, O swiftness never ceasing!
His youth 'gainst time and age hath ever spurned,
   But spurned in vain; youth waneth by increasing:
Beauty, strength, youth, are flowers but fading seen;
Duty, faith, love, are roots, and ever green.

His helmet now shall make a hive for bees;
   And, lovers' sonnets turned to holy psalms,
A man-at-arms must now serve on his knees,
   And feed on prayers, which are age's alms:
But though from court to cottage he depart,
His saint is sure of his unspotted heart.

And when he saddest sits in homely cell,
   He'll teach his swains this carol for a song:
'Blest be the hearts that wish my sovereign well,
   Curst be the souls that think her any wrong.'
Goddess, allow this aged man his right,
To be your beadsman now, that was your knight.


75 *Bethsabe's Song*

HOT sun, cool fire, tempered with sweet air,
Black shade, fair nurse, shadow my white hair:
Shine, sun; burn, fire; breathe, air, and ease me;
Black shade, fair nurse, shroud me and please me:
Shadow, my sweet nurse, keep me from burning,
Make not my glad cause cause of mourning.
      Let not my beauty's fire
      Inflame unstaid desire,
      Nor pierce any bright eye
      That wandereth lightly.

76 *A Summer Song*

WHEN as the rye reach to the chin,
And chopcherry, chopcherry ripe within,
Strawberries swimming in the cream,
And school-boys playing in the stream;
    Then O, then O, then O my true love said,
      Till that time come again,
    She could not live a maid.

77 *The Voice from the Well*

FAIR maiden, white and red,
Comb me smooth, and stroke my head;
And thou shalt have some cockle bread.
Gently dip, but not too deep,
For fear thou make the golden beard to weep.
Fair maid, white and red,
Comb me smooth, and stroke my head;
And every hair a sheave shall be,
And every sheave a golden tree.

# ROBERT GREENE

## 1558–1592

78 *Sephestia's Lullaby*

WEEP not, my wanton, smile upon my knee;
When thou art old there's grief enough for thee.
    Mother's wag, pretty boy,
    Father's sorrow, father's joy.
    When thy father first did see
    Such a boy by him and me,
    He was glad, I was woe:
    Fortune changed made him so,
    When he left his pretty boy,
    Last his sorrow, first his joy.

Weep not, my wanton, smile upon my knee;
When thou art old there's grief enough for thee.
    Streaming tears that never stint,
    Like pearl drops from a flint,
    Fell by course from his eyes,
    That one another's place supplies:
    Thus he grieved in every part,
    Tears of blood fell from his heart,
    When he left his pretty boy,
    Father's sorrow, father's joy.

Weep not, my wanton, smile upon my knee;
When thou art old there's grief enough for thee.
    The wanton smiled, father wept;
    Mother cried, baby lept;
    More he crowed, more we cried;
    Nature could not sorrow hide.
    He must go, he must kiss
    Child and mother, baby bliss;
    For he left his pretty boy,
    Father's sorrow, father's joy.

Weep not, my wanton, smile upon my knee;
When thou art old there's grief enough for thee.

## 79 *Samela*

LIKE to Diana in her summer weed,
Girt with a crimson robe of brightest dye,
            Goes fair Samela.
Whiter than be the flocks that straggling feed,
When washed by Arethusa's fount they lie,
            Is fair Samela.
As fair Aurora in her morning gray,
Decked with the ruddy glister of her love,
            Is fair Samela.
Like lovely Thetis on a calmèd day,
When as her brightness Neptune's fancy move,
            Shines fair Samela.

Her tresses gold, her eyes like glassy streams,
Her teeth are pearl, the breasts are ivory
        Of fair Samela.
Her cheeks like rose and lily yield forth gleams,
Her brows bright arches framed of ebony:
        Thus fair Samela.
Passeth fair Venus in her bravest hue,
And Juno in the show of majesty,
        For she's Samela.
Pallas in wit, all three, if you will view,
For beauty, wit, and matchless dignity,
        Yield to Samela.


# ROBERT SOUTHWELL

## 1561–1595

80             *The Burning Babe*

As I in hoary winter's night stood shivering in the snow,
Surprised I was with sudden heat which made my heart to glow;
And lifting up a fearful eye to view what fire was near,
A pretty Babe all burning bright did in the air appear;
Who, scorchèd with excessive heat, such floods of tears did shed,
As though his floods should quench his flames which with his tears
   were fed.
'Alas!' quoth he, 'but newly born in fiery heats I fry,
Yet none approach to warm their hearts or feel my fire but I.
My faultless breast the furnace is, the fuel wounding thorns;
Love is the fire, and sighs the smoke, the ashes shame and scorns;
The fuel justice layeth on, and mercy blows the coals;
The metal in this furnace wrought are men's defilèd souls:
For which, as now on fire I am to work them to their good,
So will I melt into a bath to wash them in my blood.'
With this he vanished out of sight and swiftly shrunk away,
And straight I callèd unto mind that it was Christmas day.

81      *New Prince, New Pomp*

BEHOLD, a silly tender Babe
    In freezing winter night
In homely manger trembling lies,
    Alas, a piteous sight!

The inns are full; no man will yield
    This little pilgrim bed,
But forced he is with silly beasts
    In crib to shroud his head.

Despise him not for lying there,
    First, what he is inquire;
An orient pearl is often found
    In depth of dirty mire.

Weigh not his crib, his wooden dish,
    Nor beasts that by him feed;
Weigh not his Mother's poor attire,
    Nor Joseph's simple weed.

This stable is a Prince's court,
    This crib his chair of state;
The beasts are parcel of his pomp,
    The wooden dish his plate.

The persons in that poor attire
    His royal liveries wear;
The Prince himself is come from heaven;
    This pomp is prizèd there.

With joy approach, O Christian wight,
    Do homage to thy King;
And highly praise his humble pomp,
    Which he from heaven doth bring.

82    *New Heaven, New War*

COME to your heaven, you heavenly choirs!
Earth hath the heaven of your desires;
Remove your dwelling to your God,
A stall is now his best abode;
Sith men their homage do deny,
Come, angels, all their fault supply.

His chilling cold doth heat require,
Come, seraphins, in lieu of fire;
This little ark no cover hath,
Let cherubs' wings his body swathe;
Come, Raphael, this Babe must eat,
Provide our little Toby meat.

Let Gabriel be now his groom,
That first took up his earthly room;
Let Michael stand in his defence,
Whom love hath linked to feeble sense;
Let graces rock when he doth cry,
And angels sing his lullaby.

The same you saw in heavenly seat,
Is he that now sucks Mary's teat;
Agnize your King a mortal wight,
His borrowed weed lets not your sight;
Come, kiss the manger where he lies,
That is your bliss above the skies.

This little Babe, so few days old,
Is come to rifle Satan's fold;
All hell doth at his presence quake,
Though he himself for cold do shake;
For in this weak unarmèd wise
The gates of hell he will surprise.

With tears he fights and wins the field,
His naked breast stands for a shield;
His battering shot are babish cries,
His arrows looks of weeping eyes,
His martial ensigns cold and need,
And feeble flesh his warrior's steed.

His camp is pitchèd in a stall,
His bulwark but a broken wall;
The crib his trench, hay-stalks his stakes,
Of shepherds he his muster makes;
And thus, as sure his foe to wound,
The angels' trumps alarum sound.

My soul, with Christ join thou in fight;
Stick to the tents that he hath pight;
Within his crib is surest ward,
This little Babe will be thy guard;
If thou wilt foil thy foes with joy,
Then flit not from this heavenly boy.

## ? ROBERT SOUTHWELL

83 *Upon the Image of Death*

BEFORE my face the picture hangs,
   That daily should put me in mind
Of those cold qualms and bitter pangs,
   That shortly I am like to find:
      But yet, alas, full little I
      Do think hereon that I must die.

I often look upon a face
   Most ugly, grisly, bare, and thin;
I often view the hollow place,
   Where eyes and nose had sometimes been;
      I see the bones across that lie,
      Yet little think that I must die.

I read the label underneath,
   That telleth me whereto I must;
I see the sentence eke that saith
   'Remember, man, that thou art dust!'
      But yet, alas, but seldom I
      Do think indeed that I must die.

**82** pight] pitched

Continually at my bed's head
  A hearse doth hang, which doth me tell,
That I ere morning may be dead,
   Though now I feel myself full well:
    But yet, alas, for all this, I
    Have little mind that I must die.

The gown which I do use to wear,
  The knife wherewith I cut my meat,
And eke that old and ancient chair
  Which is my only usual seat;
   All these do tell me I must die,
   And yet my life amend not I.

My ancestors are turned to clay,
  And many of my mates are gone;
My youngers daily drop away,
  And can I think to 'scape alone?
   No, no, I know that I must die,
   And yet my life amend not I.

Not Solomon, for all his wit,
  Nor Samson, though he were so strong,
No king nor person ever yet
  Could 'scape, but death laid him along:
   Wherefore I know that I must die,
   And yet my life amend not I.

Though all the East did quake to hear
  Of Alexander's dreadful name,
And all the West did likewise fear
  To hear of Julius Caesar's fame,
   Yet both by death in dust now lie.
   Who then can 'scape, but he must die?

If none can 'scape death's dreadful dart,
  If rich and poor his beck obey,
If strong, if wise, if all do smart,
  Then I to 'scape shall have no way.
   Oh! grant me grace, O God, that I
   My life may mend, sith I must die.

# THOMAS NASHE
### 1567–1601

84                    *Spring*

SPRING, the sweet spring, is the year's pleasant king;
Then blooms each thing, then maids dance in a ring,
Cold doth not sting, the pretty birds do sing:
  Cuckoo, jug-jug, pu-we, to-witta-woo!

The palm and may make country houses gay,
Lambs frisk and play, the shepherds pipe all day,
And we hear aye birds tune this merry lay:
  Cuckoo, jug-jug, pu-we, to-witta-woo!

The fields breathe sweet, the daisies kiss our feet,
Young lovers meet, old wives a-sunning sit;
In every street these tunes our ears do greet:
  Cuckoo, jug-jug, pu-we, to-witta-woo!
    Spring, the sweet spring!

85                *In Time of Pestilence*

ADIEU, farewell earth's bliss,
This world uncertain is;
Fond are life's lustful joys,
Death proves them all but toys,
None from his darts can fly.
I am sick, I must die.
      Lord, have mercy on us!

Rich men, trust not in wealth,
Gold cannot buy you health;
Physic himself must fade,
All things to end are made.
The plague full swift goes by.
I am sick, I must die.
      Lord, have mercy on us!

## THOMAS NASHE

Beauty is but a flower
Which wrinkles will devour;
Brightness falls from the air,
Queens have died young and fair,
Dust hath closed Helen's eye.
I am sick, I must die.
  Lord, have mercy on us!

Strength stoops unto the grave,
Worms feed on Hector brave,
Swords may not fight with fate,
Earth still holds ope her gate.
Come! come! the bells do cry.
I am sick, I must die.
  Lord, have mercy on us!

Wit with his wantonness
Tasteth death's bitterness;
Hell's executioner
Hath no ears for to hear
What vain art can reply.
I am sick, I must die.
  Lord, have mercy on us!

Haste, therefore, each degree,
To welcome destiny.
Heaven is our heritage,
Earth but a player's stage;
Mount we unto the sky.
I am sick, I must die.
  Lord, have mercy on us!

# CHRISTOPHER MARLOWE
## 1564–1593

*from* Hero and Leander

(i)

86

*Love at First Sight*

ON this feast day, oh, cursèd day and hour!
Went Hero thorough Sestos, from her tower
To Venus' temple, where unhappily,
As after chanced, they did each other spy.
So fair a church as this had Venus none;
The walls were of discoloured jasper stone,
Wherein was Proteus carvèd, and o'erhead
A lively vine of green sea-agate spread,
Where by one hand light-headed Bacchus hung,
And with the other wine from grapes out-wrung.
Of crystal shining fair the pavement was;
The town of Sestos called it Venus' glass.
There might you see the gods in sundry shapes,
Committing heady riots, incest, rapes:
For know that underneath this radiant floor
Was Danae's statue in a brazen tower;
Jove slyly stealing from his sister's bed
To dally with Idalian Ganymede,
And for his love Europa bellowing loud,
And tumbling with the rainbow in a cloud;
Blood-quaffing Mars heaving the iron net
Which limping Vulcan and his Cyclops set;
Love kindling fire to burn such towns as Troy;
Silvanus weeping for the lovely boy
That now is turned into a cypress tree,
Under whose shade the wood-gods love to be.
And in the midst a silver altar stood;
There Hero sacrificing turtles' blood,
Vailed to the ground, veiling her eyelids close,
And modestly they opened as she rose:

vailed] sank

Thence flew love's arrow with the golden head,
And thus Leander was enamourèd.
Stone-still he stood, and evermore he gazed,
Till with the fire that from his countenance blazed
Relenting Hero's gentle heart was strook;
Such force and virtue hath an amorous look.

    It lies not in our power to love or hate,
For will in us is over-ruled by fate.
When two are stripped, long ere the course begin,
We wish that one should lose, the other win;
And one especially do we affect
Of two gold ingots, like in each respect.
The reason no man knows; let it suffice,
What we behold is censured by our eyes.
Where both deliberate, the love is slight;
Who ever loved, that loved not at first sight?

(ii)

87        *Amorous Neptune*

WITH that he stripped him to the ivory skin,
And crying, 'Love, I come', leaped lively in.
Whereat the sapphire-visaged god grew proud,
And made his capering Triton sound aloud,
Imagining that Ganymede, displeased,
Had left the heavens; therefore on him he seized.
Leander strived; the waves about him wound,
And pulled him to the bottom, where the ground
Was strewed with pearl, and in low coral groves
Sweet singing mermaids sported with their loves
On heaps of heavy gold, and took great pleasure
To spurn in careless sort the shipwreck treasure:
For here the stately azure palace stood,
Where kingly Neptune and his train abode.
The lusty god embraced him, called him love,
And swore he never should return to Jove.
But when he knew it was not Ganymede,
For under water he was almost dead,
He heaved him up, and looking on his face,
Beat down the bold waves with his triple mace,

Which mounted up, intending to have kissed him,
And fell in drops like tears, because they missed him.
Leander, being up, began to swim,
And looking back, saw Neptune follow him;
Whereat aghast, the poor soul 'gan to cry:
'O! let me visit Hero ere I die!'
The god put Helle's bracelet on his arm,
And swore the sea should never do him harm.
He clapped his plump cheeks, with his tresses played,
And smiling wantonly, his love bewrayed.
He watched his arms, and as they opened wide,
At every stroke betwixt them would he slide,
And steal a kiss, and then run out and dance,
And as he turned, cast many a lustful glance,
And threw him gaudy toys to please his eye,
And dive into the water, and there pry
Upon his breast, his thighs, and every limb,
And up again, and close beside him swim,
And talk of love. Leander made reply:
'You are deceived, I am no woman, I.'
Thereat smiled Neptune, and then told a tale,
How that a shepherd, sitting in a vale,
Played with a boy so lovely fair and kind,
As for his love both earth and heaven pined;
That of the cooling river durst not drink
Lest water-nymphs should pull him from the brink;
And when he sported in the fragrant lawns,
Goat-footed satyrs and up-staring fauns
Would steal him thence. Ere half this tale was done,
'Ay me!' Leander cried, 'the enamoured sun,
That now should shine on Thetis' glassy bower,
Descends upon my radiant Hero's tower.
O! that these tardy arms of mine were wings!'
And as he spake, upon the waves he springs.

88        *The Passionate Shepherd to His Love*

COME live with me and be my love,
And we will all the pleasures prove,
That hills and valleys, dales and fields,
And all the craggy mountains yields.

There we will sit upon the rocks,
And see the shepherds feed their flocks,
By shallow rivers to whose falls
Melodious birds sing madrigals.

And I will make thee beds of roses
With a thousand fragrant posies,
A cap of flowers, and a kirtle
Embroidered all with leaves of myrtle;

A gown made of the finest wool
Which from our pretty lambs we pull;
Fair linèd slippers for the cold,
With buckles of the purest gold;

A belt of straw and ivy buds,
With coral clasps and amber studs:
And if these pleasures may thee move,
Come live with me and be my love.

The shepherds' swains shall dance and sing
For thy delight each May morning:
If these delights thy mind may move,
Then live with me and be my love.

# SIR WALTER RALEGH

## ?1552–1618

89

*The Nymph's Reply to the Shepherd*

IF all the world and love were young,
And truth in every shepherd's tongue,
These pretty pleasures might me move
To live with thee and be thy love.

Time drives the flocks from field to fold,
When rivers rage and rocks grow cold,
And Philomel becometh dumb;
The rest complains of cares to come.

The flowers do fade, and wanton fields
To wayward winter reckoning yields;
A honey tongue, a heart of gall,
Is fancy's spring, but sorrow's fall.

Thy gowns, thy shoes, thy beds of roses,
Thy cap, thy kirtle, and thy posies
Soon break, soon wither, soon forgotten,
In folly ripe, in reason rotten.

Thy belt of straw and ivy buds,
Thy coral clasps and amber studs,
All these in me no means can move
To come to thee and be thy love.

But could youth last and love still breed,
Had joys no date nor age no need,
Then these delights my mind might move
To live with thee and be thy love.

90

## Walsingham

'As you came from the holy land
    Of Walsingham,
Met you not with my true love
    By the way as you came?'

'How shall I know your true love,
    That have met many one
As I went to the holy land,
    That have come, that have gone?'

'She is neither white nor brown,
    But as the heavens fair,
There is none hath a form so divine
    In the earth or the air.'

'Such an one did I meet, good Sir,
    Such an angelic face,
Who like a queen, like a nymph did appear
    By her gait, by her grace.'

'She hath left me here all alone,
　All alone as unknown,
Who sometimes did me lead with herself,
　And me loved as her own.'

'What's the cause that she leaves you alone
　And a new way doth take,
Who loved you once as her own
　And her joy did you make?'

'I have loved her all my youth,
　But now old as you see,
Love likes not the falling fruit
　From the withered tree.

'Know that Love is a careless child,
　And forgets promise past;
He is blind, he is deaf when he list
　And in faith never fast.

'His desire is a dureless content
　And a trustless joy;
He is won with a world of despair
　And is lost with a toy.

'Of womenkind such indeed is the love
　Or the word love abused,
Under which many childish desires
　And conceits are excused.

'But true Love is a durable fire
　In the mind ever burning;
Never sick, never old, never dead,
　From itself never turning.'

91    *The Passionate Man's Pilgrimage*
      *Supposed to be written by One at the Point of Death*

GIVE me my scallop-shell of quiet,
My staff of faith to walk upon,
My scrip of joy, immortal diet,
My bottle of salvation,
My gown of glory, hope's true gage,
And thus I'll take my pilgrimage.

Blood must be my body's balmer,
No other balm will there be given,
Whilst my soul like a white palmer
Travels to the land of heaven,
Over the silver mountains,
Where spring the nectar fountains;
And there I'll kiss
The bowl of bliss,
And drink my eternal fill
On every milken hill.
My soul will be a-dry before,
But after it will ne'er thirst more.

And by the happy blissful way
More peaceful pilgrims I shall see,
That have shook off their gowns of clay
And go apparelled fresh like me.
I'll bring them first
To slake their thirst,
And then to taste those nectar suckets,
At the clear wells
Where sweetness dwells,
Drawn up by saints in crystal buckets.

And when our bottles and all we
Are filled with immortality,
Then the holy paths we'll travel,
Strewed with rubies thick as gravel,
Ceilings of diamonds, sapphire floors,
High walls of coral and pearl bowers.

From thence to heaven's bribeless hall
Where no corrupted voices brawl,
No conscience molten into gold,
Nor forged accusers bought and sold,
No cause deferred, nor vain-spent journey,
For there Christ is the King's Attorney,
Who pleads for all without degrees,
And he hath angels, but no fees.

When the grand twelve million jury
Of our sins with sinful fury
'Gainst our souls black verdicts give,
Christ pleads his death, and then we live.
Be thou my speaker, taintless pleader,
Unblotted lawyer, true proceeder;
Thou movest salvation even for alms,
Not with a bribed lawyer's palms.

And this is my eternal plea
To him that made heaven, earth and sea:
Seeing my flesh must die so soon,
And want a head to dine next noon,
Just at the stroke when my veins start and spread,
Set on my soul an everlasting head.
Then am I ready, like a palmer fit,
To tread those blest paths which before I writ.

## 92    *The Lie*

Go, soul, the body's guest,
  Upon a thankless arrant;
Fear not to touch the best;
  The truth shall be thy warrant.
    Go, since I needs must die,
    And give the world the lie.

**92**    arrant] errand

Say to the court, it glows
  And shines like rotten wood;
Say to the church, it shows
  What's good, and doth no good:
    If church and court reply,
    Then give them both the lie.

Tell potentates, they live
  Acting by others' action,
Not loved unless they give,
  Not strong but by affection:
    If potentates reply,
    Give potentates the lie.

Tell men of high condition
  That manage the estate,
Their purpose is ambition,
  Their practice only hate:
    And if they once reply,
    Then give them all the lie.

Tell them that brave it most,
  They beg for more by spending,
Who, in their greatest cost,
  Seek nothing but commending:
    And if they make reply,
    Then give them all the lie.

Tell zeal it wants devotion;
  Tell love it is but lust;
Tell time it metes but motion;
  Tell flesh it is but dust:
    And wish them not reply,
    For thou must give the lie.

Tell age it daily wasteth;
  Tell honour how it alters;
Tell beauty how she blasteth;
  Tell favour how it falters:
    And as they shall reply,
    Give every one the lie.

Tell wit how much it wrangles
  In tickle points of niceness;
Tell wisdom she entangles
  Herself in over-wiseness:
    And when they do reply,
    Straight give them both the lie.

Tell physic of her boldness;
  Tell skill it is prevention;
Tell charity of coldness;
  Tell law it is contention:
    And as they do reply,
    So give them still the lie.

Tell fortune of her blindness;
  Tell nature of decay;
Tell friendship of unkindness;
  Tell justice of delay:
    And if they will reply,
    Then give them all the lie.

Tell arts they have no soundness,
  But vary by esteeming;
Tell schools they want profoundness,
  And stand too much on seeming:
    If arts and schools reply,
    Give arts and schools the lie.

Tell faith it's fled the city;
  Tell how the country erreth;
Tell, manhood shakes off pity;
  Tell, virtue least preferreth:
    And if they do reply,
    Spare not to give the lie.

So when thou hast, as I
  Commanded thee, done blabbing,
Although to give the lie
  Deserves no less than stabbing,
    Stab at thee he that will,
    No stab thy soul can kill.

93 *All the World's a Stage*

WHAT is our life? A play of passion,
Our mirth the music of division.
Our mothers' wombs the tiring-houses be,
Where we are dressed for this short comedy.
Heaven the judicious sharp spectator is,
That sits and marks still who doth act amiss.
Our graves that hide us from the searching sun
Are like drawn curtains when the play is done.
Thus march we, playing, to our latest rest.
Only we die in earnest, that 's no jest.

94 *Epitaph*

EVEN such is Time, which takes in trust
Our youth, our joys, and all we have,
And pays us but with age and dust;
Who in the dark and silent grave,
When we have wandered all our ways,
Shuts up the story of our days:
And from which earth, and grave, and dust,
The Lord shall raise me up, I trust.

# FULKE GREVILLE, LORD BROOKE
## 1554–1628

95 *Myra*

I, WITH whose colours Myra dressed her head,
  I, that ware posies of her own hand-making,
I, that mine own name in the chimneys read
  By Myra finely wrought ere I was waking;
    Must I look on, in hope time coming may
    With change bring back my turn again to play?

I, that on Sunday at the church-stile found
  A garland sweet, with true-love knots in flowers,
Which I to wear about mine arm was bound,
    That each of us might know that all was ours;
      Must I now lead an idle life in wishes,
      And follow Cupid for his loaves and fishes?

I, that did wear the ring her mother left,
  I, for whose love she gloried to be blamed,
I, with whose eyes her eyes committed theft,
    I, who did make her blush when I was named;
      Must I lose ring, flowers, blush, theft, and go naked,
      Watching with sighs, till dead love be awakèd?

I, that, when drowsy Argus fell asleep,
  Like jealousy o'erwatchèd with desire,
Was ever warnèd modesty to keep,
    While her breath, speaking, kindled Nature's fire;
      Must I look on a-cold, while others warm them?
      Do Vulcan's brothers in such fine nets arm them?

Was it for this that I might Myra see
  Washing the water, with her beauties, white?
Yet would she never write her love to me.
    Thinks wit of change, while thoughts are in delight?
      Mad girls must safely love, as they may leave;
      No man can print a kiss; lines may deceive.

96              *Chorus Sacerdotum*

    OH wearisome condition of Humanity!
    Born under one law, to another bound:
    Vainly begot, and yet forbidden vanity;
    Created sick, commanded to be sound:
    What meaneth Nature by these diverse laws?
    Passion and Reason self-division cause:
    Is it the mark or majesty of Power
    To make offences that it may forgive?
    Nature herself doth her own self deflower,
    To hate those errors she herself doth give.

For how should man think that he may not do,
If Nature did not fail, and punish too?
Tyrant to others, to herself unjust,
Only commands things difficult and hard,
Forbids us all things which it knows is lust,
Makes easy pains, impossible reward.
If Nature did not take delight in blood,
She would have made more easy ways to good.
We that are bound by vows and by promotion,
With pomp of holy sacrifice and rites,
To teach belief in good and still devotion,
To preach of Heaven's wonders and delights:
Yet when each of us in his own heart looks,
He finds the God there, far unlike his books.


# GEORGE CHAPMAN

## 1559–1634

97 *Bridal Song*

O! COME, soft rest of cares, come Night,
  Come, naked Virtue's only tire,
The reapèd harvest of the light,
  Bound up in sheaves of sacred fire.
     Love calls to war;
      Sighs his alarms,
     Lips his swords are
      The field his arms.

Come, Night, and lay thy velvet hand
  On glorious Day's outfacing face;
And all thy crownèd flames command,
  For torches to our nuptial grace.
     Love calls to war;
      Sighs his alarms,
     Lips his swords are
      The field his arms.

# MARK ALEXANDER BOYD
## 1563–1601

98                          *Sonnet*

FRA bank to bank, fra wod to wod, I rin
    Ourhailit with my feble fantasie,
Like til a leif that fallis from a tree
    Or til a reid ourblawin with the wind.
Twa gods guides me: the ane of them is blind,
    Yea, and a bairn brocht up in vanitie;
    The nixt a wyf ingenrit of the sea,
And lichter nor a dauphin with hir fin.
    Unhappie is the man for evirmair
    That teils the sand and sawis in the air;
But twyse unhappier is he, I lairn,
    That feidis in his hairt a mad desyre,
    And follows on a woman throw the fyre,
Led by a blind and teichit by a bairn.


# SAMUEL DANIEL
## 1562–1619

*Sonnets to Delia*

99                          (i)

FAIR is my Love, and cruel as she's fair
    Her brow shades frowns, although her eyes are sunny;
Her smiles are lightning, though her pride despair;
    And her disdains are gall, her favours honey.
A modest maid, decked with a blush of honour,
    Whose feet do tread green paths of youth and love,
The wonder of all eyes that look upon her,
    Sacred on earth, designed a saint above!

98   teils] tills

Chastity and Beauty, which were deadly foes,
  Live reconcilèd friends within her brow;
And had she Pity to conjoin with those,
    Then who had heard the plaints I utter now?
      For had she not been fair, and thus unkind,
      My Muse had slept, and none had known my mind.

100
## (ii)

WHEN men shall find thy flower, thy glory, pass,
  And thou with careful brow sitting alone
Received hast this message from thy glass,
  That tells thee truth and says that all is gone,
Fresh shalt thou see in me the wounds thou madest,
  Though spent thy flame, in me the heat remaining;
I that have loved thee thus before thou fadest,
  My faith shall wax, when thou art in thy waning.
The world shall find this miracle in me,
  That fire can burn when all the matter's spent;
Then what my faith hath been thyself shalt see,
  And that thou wast unkind thou mayst repent.
    Thou mayst repent that thou hast scorned my tears,
    When winter snows upon thy sable hairs.

101
## (iii)

BEAUTY, sweet Love, is like the morning dew,
  Whose short refresh upon the tender green
Cheers for a time, but till the sun doth shew,
  And straight 'tis gone as it had never been.
Soon doth it fade that makes the fairest flourish
  Short is the glory of the blushing rose,
The hue which thou so carefully dost nourish,
  Yet which at length thou must be forced to lose.
When thou, surcharged with burden of thy years,
  Shalt bend thy wrinkles homeward to the earth,
And that in beauty's lease expired appears
  The date of age, the calends of our death—
    But ah! no more; this must not be foretold,
    For women grieve to think they must be old.

102

### (iv)

CARE-CHARMER Sleep, son of the sable Night,
　　Brother to Death, in silent darkness born,
Relieve my languish, and restore the light,
　　With dark forgetting of my cares return.
And let the day be time enough to mourn
　　The shipwreck of my ill-adventured youth;
Let waking eyes suffice to wail their scorn,
　　Without the torment of the night's untruth.
Cease, dreams, the images of day-desires,
　　To model forth the passions of the morrow;
Never let rising sun approve you liars,
　　To add more grief to aggravate my sorrow.
　　　　Still let me sleep, embracing clouds in vain;
　　　　And never wake to feel the day's disdain.

103

### (v)

LET others sing of knights and paladins
　　In agèd accents and untimely words;
Paint shadows in imaginary lines,
　　Which well the reach of their high wits records:
But I must sing of thee, and those fair eyes
　　Authentic shall my verse in time to come;
When yet the unborn shall say, 'Lo where she lies,
　　Whose beauty made him speak that else was dumb.'
These are the arks, the trophies I erect,
　　That fortify thy name against old age;
And these thy sacred virtues must protect
　　Against the dark, and Time's consuming rage.
　　　　Though the error of my youth in them appear,
　　　　Suffice they shew I lived and loved thee dear.

104

### *Heavenly Eloquence*

POWER above powers, O heavenly Eloquence,
　　That with the strong rein of commanding words
Dost manage, guide, and master the eminence
　　Of men's affections, more than all their swords,
Shall we not offer to thy excellence
　　The richest treasure that our wit affords?

Thou that canst do much more with one poor pen,
　　Than all the powers of princes can effect;
And draw, divert, dispose and fashion men,
　　Better than force or rigour can direct!
Should we this ornament of glory then,
　　As the unmaterial fruits of shades, neglect?

Or should we careless come behind the rest
　　In power of words, that go before in worth;
When as our accent's equal to the best,
　　Is able greater wonders to bring forth?
When all that ever hotter spirits expressed
　　Comes bettered by the patience of the north.

And who, in time, knows whither we may vent
　　The treasure of our tongue, to what strange shores
This gain of our best glory shall be sent,
　　To enrich unknowing nations with our stores?
What worlds in the yet unformèd Occident
　　May come refined with the accents that are ours?

Or who can tell for what great work in hand
　　The greatness of our style is now ordained?
What powers it shall bring in, what spirits command?
　　What thoughts let out, what humours keep restrained?
What mischief it may powerfully withstand;
　　And what fair ends may thereby be attained?

And as for Poesy, mother of this force,
　　That breeds, brings forth, and nourishes this might,
Teaching it in a loose, yet measured course,
　　With comely motions how to go upright;
And fostering it with bountiful discourse,
　　Adorns it thus in fashions of delight:

What should I say? since it is well approved
　　The speech of Heaven, with whom they have commerce,
That only seem out of themselves removed,
　　And do with more than human skills converse:
Those numbers, wherewith Heaven and Earth are moved,
　　Show weakness speaks in prose, but power in verse.

105 *Ulysses and the Siren*

*Siren.* Come, worthy Greek! Ulysses, come;
    Possess these shores with me!
The winds and seas are troublesome
    And here we may be free.
Here may we sit and view their toil
    That travail in the deep,
And joy the day in mirth the while
    And spend the night in sleep.

*Ulysses.* Fair nymph, if fame or honour were
    To be attained with ease,
Then would I come and rest me there,
    And leave such toils as these.
But here it dwells, and here must I
    With danger seek it forth:
To spend the time luxuriously
    Becomes not men of worth.

*Siren.* Ulysses, O! be not deceived
    With that unreal name;
This honour is a thing conceived
    And rests on others' fame;
Begotten only to molest
    Our peace, and to beguile
The best thing of our life, our rest,
    And give us up to toil.

*Ulysses.* Delicious nymph, suppose there were
    Nor honour nor report,
Yet manliness would scorn to wear
    The time in idle sport;
For toil doth give a better touch
    To make us feel our joy,
And ease finds tediousness as much
    As labour yields annoy.

*Siren.* Then pleasure likewise seems the shore,
    Whereto tends all your toil,
Which you forgo to make it more,
    And perish oft the while.
Who may disport them diversely
    Find never tedious day,
And ease may have variety,
    As well as action may.

*Ulysses.* But natures of the noblest frame
    These toils and dangers please;
And they take comfort in the same
    As much as you in ease;
And with the thought of actions past
    Are recreated still;
When pleasure leaves a touch at last,
    To shew that it was ill.

*Siren.* That doth opinion only cause,
    That's out of custom bred,
Which makes us many other laws,
    Than ever nature did.
No widows wail for our delights,
    Our sports are without blood;
The world we see by warlike wights
    Receives more hurt than good.

*Ulysses.* But yet the state of things require
    These motions of unrest;
And these great spirits of high desire
    Seem born to turn them best;
To purge the mischiefs that increase
    And all good order mar,
For oft we see a wicked peace
    To be well changed for war.

*Siren.* Well, well, Ulysses, then I see
    I shall not have thee here;
And therefore I will come to thee
    And take my fortunes there.
I must be won that cannot win,
    Yet lost were I not won,
For beauty hath created been
    T'undo, or be undone.

106 *Shadows*

ARE they shadows that we see?
  And can shadows pleasure give?
Pleasures only shadows be,
  Cast by bodies we conceive,
    And are made the things we deem
    In those figures which they seem.

But these pleasures vanish fast,
  Which by shadows are expressed;
Pleasures are not, if they last;
  In their passing is their best.
    Glory is most bright and gay
    In a flash and so away.

Feed apace, then, greedy eyes
  On the wonder you behold;
Take it sudden as it flies,
  Though you take it not to hold.
    When your eyes have done their part,
    Thought must length it in the heart.

107 *Love is a Sickness*

LOVE is a sickness full of woes,
  All remedies refusing;
A plant that with most cutting grows,
  Most barren with best using.
      Why so?
More we enjoy it, more it dies;
If not enjoyed, it sighing cries,
      Hey ho.
Love is a torment of the mind,
  A tempest everlasting;
And Jove hath made it of a kind,
  Not well, nor full nor fasting.
      Why so?
More we enjoy it, more it dies;
If not enjoyed, it sighing cries,
      Hey ho.

# MICHAEL DRAYTON
## 1563–1631

### *Sonnets to Idea*

108 (i)

AN evil spirit, your beauty, haunts me still,
  Wherewith, alas! I have been long possessed,
Which ceaseth not to tempt me to each ill,
  Nor gives me once but one poor minute's rest;
In me it speaks, whether I sleep or wake,
  And when by means to drive it out I try,
With greater torments then it me doth take,
  And tortures me in most extremity;
Before my face it lays down my despairs,
  And hastes me on unto a sudden death,
Now tempting me to drown myself in tears,
  And then in sighing to give up my breath.
    Thus am I still provoked to every evil
    By this good wicked spirit, sweet angel devil.

109 (ii)

DEAR, why should you command me to my rest,
  When now the night doth summon all to sleep?
Methinks this time becometh lovers best;
  Night was ordained together friends to keep.
How happy are all other living things,
  Which though the day disjoin by several flight,
The quiet evening yet together brings,
  And each returns unto his love at night.
O thou that art so courteous else to all,
  Why shouldst thou, Night, abuse me only thus,
That every creature to his kind dost call,
  And yet 'tis thou dost only sever us?
    Well could I wish it would be ever day,
    If, when night comes, you bid me go away.

110

### (iii)

CALLING to mind since first my love begun,
   The uncertain times oft varying in their course,
How things still unexpectedly have run,
   As't please the Fates, by their resistless force,
Lastly, mine eyes amazedly have seen
   Essex great fall, Tyrone his peace to gain,
The quiet end of that long-living Queen,
   This King's fair entrance, and our peace with Spain,
We and the Dutch at length ourselves to sever.
   Thus the world doth, and evermore shall reel,
Yet to my Goddess am I constant ever,
   Howe'er blind Fortune turn her giddy wheel.
     Though heaven and earth prove both to me untrue,
     Yet am I still inviolate to you.

111

### (iv)

SINCE there's no help, come let us kiss and part.
   Nay, I have done; you get no more of me,
And I am glad, yea, glad with all my heart,
   That thus so cleanly I myself can free;
Shake hands for ever, cancel all our vows,
   And when we meet at any time again,
Be it not seen in either of our brows
   That we one jot of former love retain.
Now at the last gasp of Love's latest breath,
   When, his pulse failing, Passion speechless lies,
When Faith is kneeling by his bed of death,
   And Innocence is closing up his eyes,
     Now if thou wouldst, when all have given him over,
     From death to life thou mightst him yet recover.

## To the Virginian Voyage

YOU brave heroic minds
   Worthy your country's name,
     That honour still pursue;
     Go and subdue!
Whilst loitering hinds
   Lurk here at home with shame.

Britons, you stay too long:
   Quickly aboard bestow you,
     And with a merry gale
     Swell your stretched sail
With vows as strong
   As the winds that blow you.

Your course securely steer,
   West and by south forth keep
     Rocks, lee-shores, nor shoals
     When Eolus scowls
You need not fear;
   So absolute the deep.

And cheerfully at sea
   Success you still entice
     To get the pearl and gold,
     And ours to hold
VIRGINIA,
   Earth's only paradise.

Where nature hath in store
   Fowl, venison, and fish,
     And the fruitfullest soil
     Without your toil
Three harvests more,
   All greater than your wish.

And the ambitious vine
   Crowns with his purple mass
     The cedar reaching high
     To kiss the sky,
The cypress, pine,
   And useful sassafras.

## MICHAEL DRAYTON

To whom the Golden Age
   Still nature's laws doth give,
      No other cares attend,
      But them to defend
From winter's rage,
   That long there doth not live.

When as the luscious smell
   Of that delicious land
      Above the seas that flows
      The clear wind throws,
Your hearts to swell
   Approaching the dear strand;

In kenning of the shore
   (Thanks to God first given)
      O you the happiest men,
      Be frolic then!
Let cannons roar,
   Frighting the wide heaven.

And in regions far,
   Such heroes bring ye forth
      As those from whom we came;
      And plant our name
Under that star
   Not known unto our North.

And as there plenty grows
   Of laurel everywhere—
      Apollo's sacred tree—
      You it may see
A poet's brows
   To crown, that may sing there.

Thy *Voyages* attend,
   Industrious Hakluyt,
      Whose reading shall inflame
      Men to seek fame,
And much commend
   To after times thy wit.

113 *First Steps up Parnassus*

MY dearly lovèd friend, how oft have we
In winter evenings (meaning to be free)
To some well-chosen place used to retire,
And there with moderate meat, and wine, and fire,
Have passed the hours contentedly with chat;
Now talked of this, and then discoursed of that,
Spoke our own verses 'twixt ourselves, if not
Other men's lines which we by chance had got,
Or some stage pieces famous long before,
Of which your happy memory had store;
And I remember you much pleasèd were
Of those who livèd long ago to hear,
As well as of those of these latter times
Who have enriched our language with their rhymes,
And in succession, how still up they grew,
Which is the subject that I now pursue.
For from my cradle you must know that I
Was still inclined to noble Poesie,
And when that once *Pueriles* I had read,
And newly had my *Cato* construèd,
In my small self I greatly marvelled then,
Amongst all other, what strange kind of men
These poets were; and, pleasèd with the name,
To my mild tutor merrily I came
(For I was then a proper goodly page,
Much like a pigmy, scarce ten years of age),
Clasping my slender arms about his thigh,
'O my dear master, cannot you' (quoth I)
'Make me a poet? Do it, if you can,
And you shall see I'll quickly be a man.'
Who me thus answered smiling, 'Boy,' (quoth he)
'If you'll not play the wag, but I may see
You ply your learning, I will shortly read
Some poets to you.' Phoebus be my speed!
To't hard went I, when shortly he began,
And first read to me honest Mantuan,
Then Virgil's *Eglogues*; being entered thus,
Methought I straight had mounted Pegasus,
And in his full career could make him stop,
And bound upon Parnassus' bi-cleft top.

114     *Verses Made the Night before he Died*

So well I love thee as without thee I
Love nothing; if I might choose, I'd rather die
Than be one day debarred thy company.

Since beasts and plants do grow and live and move,
Beasts are those men that such a life approve:
He only lives that deadly is in love.

The corn, that in the ground is sown, first dies,
And of one seed do many ears arise;
Love, this world's corn, by dying multiplies.

The seeds of love first by thy eyes were thrown
Into a ground untilled, a heart unknown
To bear such fruit, till by thy hands 'twas sown.

Look as your looking-glass by chance may fall,
Divide, and break in many pieces small,
And yet shows forth the selfsame face in all,

Proportions, features, graces, just the same,
And in the smallest piece as well the name
Of fairest one deserves as in the richest frame;

So all my thoughts are pieces but of you,
Which put together makes a glass so true
As I therein no other's face but yours can view.

# WILLIAM SHAKESPEARE
## 1564–1616

*Courser and Jennet*

BUT, lo! from forth a copse that neighbours by,
  A breeding jennet, lusty, young, and proud,
Adonis' trampling courser doth espy,
  And forth she rushes, snorts and neighs aloud:
    The strong-necked steed, being tied unto a tree,
    Breaketh his rein, and to her straight goes he.

Imperiously he leaps, he neighs, he bounds,
  And now his woven girths he breaks asunder;
The bearing earth with his hard hoof he wounds,
  Whose hollow womb resounds like heaven's thunder;
    The iron bit he crusheth 'tween his teeth,
    Controlling what he was controllèd with.

His ears up-pricked, his braided hanging mane,
  Upon his compassed crest now stand on end;
His nostrils drink the air, and forth again,
  As from a furnace, vapours doth he send:
    His eye, which scornfully glisters like fire,
    Shows his hot courage and his high desire.

Sometime he trots, as if he told the steps,
  With gentle majesty and modest pride;
Anon he rears upright, curvets and leaps,
  As who should say, 'Lo! thus my strength is tried;
    And this I do to captivate the eye
    Of the fair breeder that is standing by.'

What recketh he his rider's angry stir,
  His flattering 'Holla', or his 'Stand, I say'?
What cares he now for curb or pricking spur,
  For rich caparisons or trappings gay?
    He sees his love, and nothing else he sees,
    For nothing else with his proud sight agrees.

jennet] Spanish mare

Look, when a painter would surpass the life,
  In limning out a well-proportioned steed,
His art with nature's workmanship at strife,
  As if the dead the living should exceed;
    So did this horse excel a common one,
    In shape, in courage, colour, pace and bone.

Round-hoofed, short-jointed, fetlocks shag and long,
  Broad breast, full eye, small head, and nostril wide,
High crest, short ears, straight legs and passing strong,
  Thin mane, thick tail, broad buttock, tender hide:
    Look, what a horse should have he did not lack,
    Save a proud rider on so proud a back.

Sometime he scuds far off, and there he stares;
  Anon he starts at stirring of a feather;
To bid the wind a base he now prepares,
  And whether he run or fly they know not whether;
    For through his mane and tail the high wind sings,
    Fanning the hairs, who wave like feathered wings.

He looks upon his love, and neighs unto her;
  She answers him as if she knew his mind;
Being proud, as females are, to see him woo her,
  She puts on outward strangeness, seems unkind,
    Spurns at his love and scorns the heat he feels,
    Beating his kind embracements with her heels.

Then, like a melancholy malcontent,
  He vails his tail that, like a falling plume,
Cool shadow to his melting buttock lent:
  He stamps, and bites the poor flies in his fume.
    His love, perceiving how he was enraged,
    Grew kinder, and his fury was assuaged.

His testy master goeth about to take him;
  When lo! the unbacked breeder, full of fear,
Jealous of catching, swiftly doth forsake him,
  With her the horse, and left Adonis there.
    As they were mad, unto the wood they hie them,
    Out-stripping crows that strive to over-fly them.

116          *An Outcry upon Opportunity*

'O OPPORTUNITY! thy guilt is great,
  'Tis thou that execut'st the traitor's treason;
Thou set'st the wolf where he the lamb may get;
  Whoever plots the sin, thou point'st the season;
  'Tis thou that spurn'st at right, at law, at reason;
    And in thy shady cell, where none may spy him,
    Sits Sin to seize the souls that wander by him.

'Thou mak'st the vestal violate her oath;
  Thou blow'st the fire when temperance is thawed;
Thou smother'st honesty, thou murder'st troth;
  Thou foul abettor! thou notorious bawd!
  Thou plantest scandal and displacest laud:
    Thou ravisher, thou traitor, thou false thief,
    Thy honey turns to gall, thy joy to grief!

'Thy secret pleasure turns to open shame,
  Thy private feasting to a public fast,
Thy smoothing titles to a ragged name,
  Thy sugared tongue to bitter wormwood taste:
  Thy violent vanities can never last.
    How comes it, then, vile Opportunity,
    Being so bad, such numbers seek for thee?

'When wilt thou be the humble suppliant's friend,
  And bring him where his suit may be obtained?
When wilt thou sort an hour great strifes to end?
  Or free that soul which wretchedness hath chained?
  Give physic to the sick, ease to the pained?
    The poor, lame, blind, halt, creep, cry out for thee;
    But they ne'er meet with Opportunity.

'The patient dies while the physician sleeps;
  The orphan pines while the oppressor feeds;
Justice is feasting while the widow weeps;
  Advice is sporting while infection breeds:
  Thou grant'st no time for charitable deeds:
    Wrath, envy, treason, rape, and murder's rages,
    Thy heinous hours wait on them as their pages.

sort] choose

135

### Spring and Winter

#### (i)

WHEN daisies pied and violets blue
   And lady-smocks all silver-white
And cuckoo-buds of yellow hue
   Do paint the meadows with delight,
The cuckoo then, on every tree,
Mocks married men; for thus sings he,
       Cuckoo!
Cuckoo, cuckoo! O, word of fear,
Unpleasing to a married ear!

When shepherds pipe on oaten straws,
   And merry larks are ploughmen's clocks,
When turtles tread, and rooks, and daws,
   And maidens bleach their summer smocks,
The cuckoo then, on every tree,
Mocks married men; for thus sings he,
       Cuckoo!
Cuckoo, cuckoo! O, word of fear,
Unpleasing to a married ear!

#### (ii)

WHEN icicles hang by the wall,
   And Dick the shepherd blows his nail,
And Tom bears logs into the hall,
   And milk comes frozen home in pail;
When blood is nipped, and ways be foul,
Then nightly sings the staring owl.
Tu-whit, to-who! a merry note,
While greasy Joan doth keel the pot.

When all aloud the wind doth blow,
   And coughing drowns the parson's saw,
And birds sit brooding in the snow,
   And Marian's nose looks red and raw,

118   keel] cool

When roasted crabs hiss in the bowl,
Then nightly sings the staring owl,
Tu-whit, tu-who! a merry note,
While greasy Joan doth keel the pot.

### *Fairy Songs*

119
### (i)

 OVER hill, over dale,
  Thorough bush, thorough brier,
Over park, over pale,
  Thorough flood, thorough fire,
  I do wander everywhere,
  Swifter than the moonë's sphere;
  And I serve the fairy queen,
  To dew her orbs upon the green:
  The cowslips tall her pensioners be;
  In their gold coats spots you see;
  Those be rubies, fairy favours,
  In those freckles live their savours:
I must go seek some dew-drops here,
And hang a pearl in every cowslip's ear.

120
### (ii)

 YOU spotted snakes with double tongue,
  Thorny hedgehogs, be not seen;
Newts and blind-worms, do no wrong;
  Come not near our fairy queen.

  Philomel, with melody,
  Sing in our sweet lullaby;
 Lulla, lulla, lullaby; lulla, lulla, lullaby!
   Never harm,
   Nor spell nor charm,
  Come our lovely lady nigh.
  So, good night, with lullaby.

Weaving spiders, come not here;
   Hence, you long-legged spinners, hence!
Beetles black, approach not near;
   Worm nor snail, do no offence.

     Philomel, with melody,
      Sing in our sweet lullaby;
   Lulla, lulla, lullaby; lulla, lulla, lullaby!
       Never harm,
       Nor spell nor charm,
    Come our lovely lady nigh.
    So, good night, with lullaby.

### *Songs sung in Arden*

121
### (i)

   BLOW, blow, thou winter wind,
   Thou art not so unkind
     As man's ingratitude;
   Thy tooth is not so keen,
   Because thou art not seen,
     Although thy breath be rude.
Heigh-ho! sing, heigh-ho! unto the green holly:
Most friendship is feigning, most loving mere folly.
     Then heigh-ho! the holly!
     This life is most jolly.

   Freeze, freeze, thou bitter sky,
   That dost not bite so nigh
     As benefits forgot:
   Though thou the waters warp,
   Thy sting is not so sharp
     As friend remembered not.
Heigh-ho! sing, heigh-ho! unto the green holly:
Most friendship is feigning, most loving mere folly.
     Then heigh-ho! the holly!
     This life is most jolly.

**122**
## (ii)

It was a lover and his lass,
   With a hey, and a ho, and a hey nonino,
That o'er the green corn-field did pass,
   In spring time, the only pretty ring time,
When birds do sing, hey ding a ding, ding;
Sweet lovers love the spring.

Between the acres of the rye,
   With a hey, and a ho, and a hey nonino,
Those pretty country folks would lie,
   In spring time, the only pretty ring time,
When birds do sing, hey ding a ding, ding;
Sweet lovers love the spring.

This carol they began that hour,
   With a hey, and a ho, and a hey nonino,
How that a life was but a flower
   In spring time, the only pretty ring time,
When birds do sing, hey ding a ding, ding;
Sweet lovers love the spring.

And therefore take the present time,
   With a hey, and a ho, and a hey nonino;
For love is crowned with the prime
   In spring time, the only pretty ring time,
When birds do sing, hey ding a ding, ding;
Sweet lovers love the spring.

## *Feste's Songs*

**123**
## (i)

O mistress mine, where are you roaming?
O! stay and hear; your true love's coming,
   That can sing both high and low.
Trip no further, pretty sweeting;
Journeys end in lovers meeting,
   Every wise man's son doth know.

What is love? 'Tis not hereafter;
Present mirth hath present laughter;
   What's to come is still unsure.
In delay there lies no plenty;
Then come kiss me, sweet and twenty;
   Youth's a stuff will not endure.


124
              (ii)

COME away, come away, death,
   And in sad cypress let me be laid.
Fly away, fly away, breath;
   I am slain by a fair cruel maid.
My shroud of white, stuck all with yew,
      O! prepare it.
My part of death, no one so true
      Did share it.

Not a flower, not a flower sweet,
   On my black coffin let there be strown;
Not a friend, not a friend greet
   My poor corpse, where my bones shall be thrown.
A thousand thousand sighs to save,
      Lay me, O! where
Sad true lover never find my grave,
      To weep there.


125
              (iii)

WHEN that I was and a little tiny boy,
   With hey, ho, the wind and the rain;
A foolish thing was but a toy,
   For the rain it raineth every day.

But when I came to man's estate,
   With hey, ho, the wind and the rain;
'Gainst knaves and thieves men shut their gate,
   For the rain it raineth every day.

But when I came, alas! to wive,
 With hey, ho, the wind and the rain;
By swaggering could I never thrive,
 For the rain it raineth every day.

But when I came unto my beds,
 With hey, ho, the wind and the rain;
With toss-pots still had drunken heads,
 For the rain it raineth every day.

A great while ago the world begun,
 With hey, ho, the wind and the rain;
But that's all one, our play is done,
 And we'll strive to please you every day.

126 *At the Moated Grange*

TAKE, O! take those lips away,
 That so sweetly were forsworn,
And those eyes, the break of day,
 Lights that do mislead the morn;
But my kisses bring again,
 Bring again,
Seals of love, but sealed in vain,
 Sealed in vain.

127 *Dirge for Fidele*

FEAR no more the heat o' the sun,
 Nor the furious winter's rages;
Thou thy worldly task hast done,
 Home art gone, and ta'en thy wages.
Golden lads and girls all must,
As chimney-sweepers, come to dust.

Fear no more the frown o' the great,
 Thou art past the tyrant's stroke;
Care no more to clothe and eat,
 To thee the reed is as the oak.
The sceptre, learning, physic, must
All follow this, and come to dust.

Fear no more the lightning-flash,
   Nor the all-dreaded thunder-stone;
Fear not slander, censure rash;
   Thou hast finished joy and moan.
All lovers young, all lovers must
Consign to thee, and come to dust.

No exorciser harm thee!
Nor no witchcraft charm thee!
Ghost unlaid forbear thee!
Nothing ill come near thee!
Quiet consummation have,
And renownèd be thy grave!

128               *Autolycus Sings*

WHEN daffodils begin to peer,
   With heigh! the doxy, over the dale,
Why, then comes in the sweet o' the year;
   For the red blood reigns in the winter's pale.

The white sheet bleaching on the hedge,
   With heigh! the sweet birds, O, how they sing!
Doth set my pugging tooth on edge,
   For a quart of ale is a dish for a king.

The lark, that tirra-lirra chants,
   With heigh! with heigh! the thrush and the jay,
Are summer songs for me and my aunts,
   While we lie tumbling in the hay.

*Ariel's Songs*

129               (i)

COME unto these yellow sands,
   And then take hands:
Curtsied when you have, and kissed
   The wild waves whist,
Foot it featly here and there;
And, sweet sprites, the burden bear.

Hark, hark!
  Bow, wow
The watch-dogs bark,
  Bow, wow,
Hark, hark! I hear
The strain of strutting Chanticleer
Cry, Cock-a-diddle-dow.

130
## (ii)

FULL fathom five thy father lies;
  Of his bones are coral made;
Those are pearls that were his eyes:
  Nothing of him that doth fade,
But doth suffer a sea-change
Into something rich and strange:
Sea nymphs hourly ring his knell.
          Ding-dong!
Hark! now I hear them,
          Ding-dong, bell!

131
## (iii)

WHERE the bee sucks, there suck I,
In a cowslip's bell I lie,
There I couch when owls do cry,
On the bat's back I do fly
After summer merrily.
  Merrily, merrily, shall I live now
  Under the blossom that hangs on the bough.

132
## *Sweet Music's Power*

ORPHEUS with his lute made trees
And the mountain tops that freeze
  Bow themselves when he did sing:
To his music plants and flowers
Ever sprung; as sun and showers
  There had made a lasting spring.

Every thing that heard him play,
Even the billows of the sea,
   Hung their heads and then lay by.
In sweet music is such art,
   Killing care and grief of heart
   Fall asleep, or, hearing, die.


133                 *A Bridal Song*

ROSES, their sharp spines being gone,
Not royal in their smells alone,
   But in their hue;
Maiden pinks, of odour faint,
Daisies smell-less, yet most quaint,
   And sweet thyme true;

Primrose, firstborn child of Ver,
Merry springtime's harbinger,
   With her bells dim;
Oxlips in their cradles growing,
Marigolds on death-beds blowing,
   Larks'-heels trim:

All dear Nature's children sweet
Lie 'fore bride and bridegroom's feet,
   Blessing their sense.
Not an angel of the air,
Bird melodious or bird fair,
   Be absent hence.

The crow, the slanderous cuckoo, nor
The boding raven, nor chough hoar,
   Nor chattering pie,
May on our bride-house perch or sing,
Or with them any discord bring,
   But from it fly.

## *Sonnets*

### 134 (i)

SHALL I compare thee to a summer's day?
  Thou art more lovely and more temperate:
Rough winds do shake the darling buds of May,
  And summer's lease hath all too short a date:
Sometime too hot the eye of heaven shines,
  And often is his gold complexion dimmed;
And every fair from fair sometime declines,
  By chance, or nature's changing course untrimmed;
But thy eternal summer shall not fade,
  Nor lose possession of that fair thou owest,
Nor shall Death brag thou wanderest in his shade,
  When in eternal lines to time thou growest;
    So long as men can breathe, or eyes can see,
    So long lives this, and this gives life to thee.

### 135 (ii)

WHEN in disgrace with fortune and men's eyes
  I all alone beweep my outcast state,
And trouble deaf heaven with my bootless cries,
  And look upon myself, and curse my fate,
Wishing me like to one more rich in hope,
  Featured like him, like him with friends possessed,
Desiring this man's art, and that man's scope,
  With what I most enjoy contented least;
Yet in these thoughts myself almost despising,
  Haply I think on thee, and then my state,
Like to the lark at break of day arising
  From sullen earth, sings hymns at heaven's gate;
    For thy sweet love remembered such wealth brings
    That then I scorn to change my state with kings.

136                              (iii)

WHEN to the sessions of sweet silent thought
    I summon up remembrance of things past,
I sigh the lack of many a thing I sought,
    And with old woes new wail my dear time's waste:
Then can I drown an eye, unused to flow,
    For precious friends hid in death's dateless night,
And weep afresh love's long since cancelled woe,
    And moan the expense of many a vanished sight:
Then can I grieve at grievances foregone,
    And heavily from woe to woe tell o'er
The sad account of fore-bemoanèd moan,
    Which I new pay as if not paid before.
        But if the while I think on thee, dear friend,
        All losses are restored and sorrows end.

137                              (iv)

THY bosom is endearèd with all hearts,
    Which I by lacking have supposèd dead;
And there reigns love, and all love's loving parts,
    And all those friends which I thought buried.
How many a holy and obsequious tear
    Hath dear religious love stolen from mine eye,
As interest of the dead, which now appear
    But things removed that hidden in thee lie!
Thou art the grave where buried love doth live,
    Hung with the trophies of my lovers gone,
Who all their parts of me to thee did give,
    That due of many now is thine alone.
        Their images I loved I view in thee,
        And thou, all they, hast all the all of me.

138 ## (v)

NOT marble, nor the gilded monuments
  Of princes, shall outlive this powerful rhyme;
But you shall shine more bright in these contents
  Than unswept stone, besmeared with sluttish time.
When wasteful war shall statues overturn,
  And broils root out the work of masonry,
Nor Mars his sword nor war's quick fire shall burn
  The living record of your memory.
'Gainst death and all oblivious enmity
  Shall you pace forth; your praise shall still find room
Even in the eyes of all posterity
  That wear this world out to the ending doom.
    So, till the judgement that yourself arise,
    You live in this, and dwell in lovers' eyes.

139 ## (vi)

LIKE as the waves make towards the pebbled shore,
  So do our minutes hasten to their end;
Each changing place with that which goes before,
  In sequent toil all forwards do contend.
Nativity, once in the main of light,
  Crawls to maturity, wherewith being crowned,
Crooked eclipses 'gainst his glory fight,
  And Time that gave doth now his gift confound.
Time doth transfix the flourish set on youth
  And delves the parallels in beauty's brow,
Feeds on the rarities of nature's truth,
  And nothing stands but for his scythe to mow.
    And yet to times in hope my verse shall stand,
    Praising thy worth, despite his cruel hand.

140                     (vii)

WHEN I have seen by Time's fell hand defaced
   The rich proud cost of outworn buried age;
When sometime lofty towers I see down razed,
   And brass eternal slave to mortal rage;
When I have seen the hungry ocean gain
   Advantage on the kingdom of the shore,
And the firm soil win of the watery main,
   Increasing store with loss, and loss with store;
When I have seen such interchange of state,
   Or state itself confounded to decay,
Ruin hath taught me thus to ruminate,
   That Time will come and take my Love away.
     This thought is as a death, which cannot choose
     But weep to have that which it fears to lose.


141                     (viii)

SINCE brass, nor stone, nor earth, nor boundless sea,
   But sad mortality o'ersways their power,
How with this rage shall beauty hold a plea,
   Whose action is no stronger than a flower?
O, how shall summer's honey breath hold out
   Against the wrackful siege of battering days,
When rocks impregnable are not so stout,
   Nor gates of steel so strong, but Time decays?
O fearful meditation! Where, alack,
   Shall Time's best jewel from Time's chest lie hid?
Or what strong hand can hold his swift foot back?
   Or who his spoil of beauty can forbid?
     O, none, unless this miracle have might,
     That in black ink my love may still shine bright.

142

## (ix)

TIRED with all these, for restful death I cry;
  As to behold desert a beggar born,
And needy nothing trimmed in jollity,
  And purest faith unhappily forsworn,
And gilded honour shamefully misplaced,
  And maiden virtue rudely strumpeted,
And right perfection wrongfully disgraced,
  And strength by limping sway disabled,
And art made tongue-tied by authority,
  And folly, doctor-like, controlling skill,
And simple truth miscalled simplicity,
  And captive good attending captain ill.
    Tired with all these, from these would I be gone,
    Save that, to die, I leave my Love alone.

143

## (x)

THAT time of year thou mayst in me behold
  When yellow leaves, or none, or few, do hang
Upon those boughs which shake against the cold,
  Bare ruined choirs, where late the sweet birds sang.
In me thou seest the twilight of such day
  As after sunset fadeth in the west;
Which by and by black night doth take away,
  Death's second self, that seals up all in rest.
In me thou seest the glowing of such fire,
  That on the ashes of his youth doth lie,
As the death-bed whereon it must expire,
  Consumed with that which it was nourished by.
    This thou perceiv'st, which makes thy love more strong,
    To love that well which thou must leave ere long.

144                    (xi)

FAREWELL! thou art too dear for my possessing,
　　And like enough thou know'st thy estimate:
The charter of thy worth gives thee releasing;
　　My bonds in thee are all determinate.
For how do I hold thee but by thy granting?
　　And for that riches where is my deserving?
The cause of this fair gift in me is wanting,
　　And so my patent back again is swerving.
Thyself thou gav'st, thy own worth then not knowing,
　　Or me, to whom thou gav'st it, else mistaking;
So thy great gift, upon misprision growing,
　　Comes home again, on better judgement making.
　　　Thus have I had thee, as a dream doth flatter,
　　　In sleep a king, but, waking, no such matter.


145                    (xii)

THEN hate me when thou wilt; if ever, now;
　　Now, while the world is bent my deeds to cross,
Join with the spite of fortune, make me bow,
　　And do not drop in for an after-loss:
Ah! do not, when my heart hath 'scaped this sorrow,
　　Come in the rearward of a conquered woe;
Give not a windy night a rainy morrow,
　　To linger out a purposed overthrow.
If thou wilt leave me, do not leave me last,
　　When other petty griefs have done their spite,
But in the onset come; so shall I taste
　　At first the very worst of fortune's might.
　　　And other strains of woe, which now seem woe,
　　　Compared with loss of thee will not seem so.

146

## (xiii)

THEY that have power to hurt and will do none,
    That do not do the thing they most do show,
Who, moving others, are themselves as stone,
    Unmovèd, cold, and to temptation slow—
They rightly do inherit heaven's graces,
    And husband nature's riches from expense;
They are the lords and owners of their faces,
    Others, but stewards of their excellence.
The summer's flower is to the summer sweet,
    Though to itself it only live and die;
But if that flower with base infection meet,
    The basest weed outbraves his dignity:
        For sweetest things turn sourest by their deeds;
        Lilies that fester smell far worse than weeds.

147

## (xiv)

HOW like a winter hath my absence been
    From thee, the pleasure of the fleeting year!
What freezings have I felt, what dark days seen!
    What old December's bareness everywhere!
And yet this time removed was summer's time,
    The teeming autumn, big with rich increase,
Bearing the wanton burden of the prime,
    Like widowed wombs after their lords' decease:
Yet this abundant issue seemed to me
    But hope of orphans and unfathered fruit;
For summer and his pleasures wait on thee,
    And, thou away, the very birds are mute.
        Or, if they sing, 'tis with so dull a cheer,
        That leaves look pale, dreading the winter's near.

148                          (xv)

FROM you have I been absent in the spring,
   When proud pied April, dressed in all his trim,
Hath put a spirit of youth in every thing,
   That heavy Saturn laughed and leaped with him.
Yet nor the lays of birds, nor the sweet smell
   Of different flowers in odour and in hue,
Could make me any summer's story tell,
   Or from their proud lap pluck them where they grew:
Nor did I wonder at the lily's white,
   Nor praise the deep vermilion in the rose;
They were but sweet, but figures of delight,
   Drawn after you, you pattern of all those.
      Yet seemed it winter still, and, you away,
      As with your shadow I with these did play.


149                          (xvi)

WHEN in the chronicle of wasted time
   I see descriptions of the fairest wights,
And beauty making beautiful old rhyme,
   In praise of ladies dead and lovely knights,
Then, in the blazon of sweet beauty's best,
   Of hand, of foot, of lip, of eye, of brow,
I see their antique pen would have expressed
   Even such a beauty as you master now.
So all their praises are but prophecies
   Of this our time, all you prefiguring;
And, for they looked but with divining eyes,
   They had not skill enough your worth to sing:
      For we, which now behold these present days,
      Have eyes to wonder, but lack tongues to praise.

150 (xvii)

O! NEVER say that I was false of heart,
  Though absence seemed my flame to qualify.
As easy might I from myself depart
  As from my soul, which in thy breast doth lie:
That is my home of love; if I have ranged,
  Like him that travels, I return again,
Just to the time, not with the time exchanged,
  So that myself bring water for my stain.
Never believe, though in my nature reigned
  All frailties that besiege all kinds of blood,
That it could so preposterously be stained,
  To leave for nothing all thy sum of good;
    For nothing this wide universe I call,
    Save thou, my rose; in it thou art my all.

151 (xviii)

LET me not to the marriage of true minds
  Admit impediments. Love is not love
Which alters when it alteration finds,
  Or bends with the remover to remove.
O, no! it is an ever-fixèd mark,
  That looks on tempests and is never shaken;
It is the star to every wandering bark,
  Whose worth's unknown, although his height be taken.
Love's not Time's fool, though rosy lips and cheeks
  Within his bending sickle's compass come;
Love alters not with his brief hours and weeks,
  But bears it out even to the edge of doom.
    If this be error, and upon me proved,
    I never writ, nor no man ever loved.

152                           (xix)

THE expense of spirit in a waste of shame
    Is lust in action; and till action, lust
Is perjured, murderous, bloody, full of blame,
    Savage, extreme, rude, cruel, not to trust;
Enjoyed no sooner but despisèd straight;
    Past reason hunted; and no sooner had,
Past reason hated, as a swallowed bait,
    On purpose laid to make the taker mad:
Mad in pursuit, and in possession so;
    Had, having, and in quest to have, extreme;
A bliss in proof, and proved, a very woe;
    Before, a joy proposed; behind, a dream.
        All this the world well knows; yet none knows well
        To shun the heaven that leads men to this hell.


153                           (xx)

POOR soul, the centre of my sinful earth,
    My sinful earth these rebel powers array,
Why dost thou pine within and suffer dearth,
    Painting thy outward walls so costly gay?
Why so large cost, having so short a lease,
    Dost thou upon thy fading mansion spend?
Shall worms, inheritors of this excess,
    Eat up thy charge? Is this thy body's end?
Then, soul, live thou upon thy servant's loss,
    And let that pine to aggravate thy store;
Buy terms divine in selling hours of dross;
    Within be fed, without be rich no more:
        So shalt thou feed on Death, that feeds on men,
        And Death once dead, there's no more dying then.

WILLIAM SHAKESPEARE

*The Phoenix and the Turtle*

LET the bird of loudest lay,
  On the sole Arabian tree,
  Herald sad and trumpet be,
To whose sound chaste wings obey.

But thou shrieking harbinger,
  Foul precurrer of the fiend,
  Augur of the fever's end,
To this troop come thou not near.

From this session interdict
  Every fowl of tyrant wing,
  Save the eagle, feathered king;
Keep the obsequy so strict.

Let the priest in surplice white
  That defunctive music can,
  Be the death-divining swan,
Lest the requiem lack his right.

And thou treble-dated crow,
  That thy sable gender mak'st
  With the breath thou giv'st and tak'st,
'Mongst our mourners shalt thou go.

Here the anthem doth commence:
  Love and constancy is dead;
  Phoenix and the turtle fled
In a mutual flame from hence.

So they loved, as love in twain
  Had the essence but in one;
  Two distincts, division none;
Number there in love was slain.

Hearts remote, yet not asunder;
  Distance, and no space was seen
  'Twixt the turtle and his queen;
But in them it were a wonder.

can] knows

So between them love did shine,
    That the turtle saw his right
    Flaming in the phoenix' sight;
Either was the other's mine.

Property was thus appalled,
    That the self was not the same;
    Single nature's double name
Neither two nor one was called.

Reason, in itself confounded,
    Saw division grow together,
    To themselves yet either neither,
Simple were so well compounded:

That it cried, 'How true a twain
    Seemeth this concordant one!
    Love hath reason, reason none,
If what parts can so remain.'

Whereupon it made this threne
    To the phoenix and the dove,
    Co-supremes and stars of love,
As chorus to their tragic scene.

### THRENOS

Beauty, truth, and rarity,
Grace in all simplicity,
Here enclosed in cinders lie.

Death is now the phoenix' nest;
And the turtle's loyal breast
To eternity doth rest,

Leaving no posterity:
'Twas not their infirmity,
It was married chastity.

Truth may seem, but cannot be;
Beauty brag, but 'tis not she;
Truth and beauty buried be.

Property] individuality          threne] lament

To this urn let those repair
That are either true or fair;
For these dead birds sigh a prayer.


# THOMAS CAMPION
## 1567–1620

### *Integer Vitae*

THE man of life upright,
  Whose guiltless heart is free
From all dishonest deeds
  Or thought of vanity:

The man whose silent days
  In harmless joys are spent,
Whom hopes cannot delude,
  Nor sorrow discontent:

That man needs neither towers
  Nor armour for defence,
Nor secret vaults to fly
  From thunder's violence.

He only can behold
  With unaffrighted eyes
The horrors of the deep
  And terrors of the skies.

Thus scorning all the cares
  That fate or fortune brings,
He makes the heaven his book,
  His wisdom heavenly things,

Good thoughts his only friends,
  His wealth a well-spent age,
The earth his sober inn
  And quiet pilgrimage.

156                    *Among the Shades*

WHEN thou must home to shades of underground,
    And there arrived, a new admirèd guest,
The beauteous spirits do engirt thee round,
    White Iope, blithe Helen and the rest,
To hear the stories of thy finished love
From that smooth tongue, whose music hell can move:

Then wilt thou speak of banqueting delights,
    Of masks and revels which sweet youth did make,
Of tourneys and great challenges of knights,
    And all these triumphs for thy beauty's sake.
When thou hast told these honours done to thee,
Then tell, O! tell, how thou didst murder me.


157                         *Devotion*

FOLLOW your saint, follow with accents sweet;
Haste you, sad notes, fall at her flying feet.
There, wrapped in cloud of sorrow, pity move,
And tell the ravisher of my soul I perish for her love.
But if she scorns my never-ceasing pain,
Then burst with sighing in her sight, and ne'er return again.

All that I sung still to her praise did tend.
Still she was first, still she my songs did end.
Yet she my love and music both doth fly,
The music that her echo is, and beauty's sympathy.
Then let my notes pursue her scornful flight;
It shall suffice that they were breathed, and died for her delight.


158                    *Follow thy Fair Sun*

FOLLOW thy fair sun, unhappy shadow.
    Though thou be black as night,
    And she made all of light,
Yet follow thy fair sun, unhappy shadow.

Follow her whose light thy light depriveth.
   Though here thou liv'st disgraced,
   And she in heaven is placed,
Yet follow her whose light the world reviveth.

Follow those pure beams whose beauty burneth,
   That so have scorchèd thee,
   As thou still black must be,
Till her kind beams thy black to brightness turneth.

Follow her, while yet her glory shineth.
   There comes a luckless night,
   That will dim all her light;
And this the black unhappy shade divineth.

Follow still, since so thy fates ordainèd.
   The sun must have his shade,
   Till both at once do fade,
The sun still proved, the shadow still disdainèd.


159                          *Laura*

   ROSE-CHEEKED Laura, come;
  Sing thou smoothly with thy beauty's
  Silent music, either other
    Sweetly gracing.

   Lovely forms do flow
  From concent divinely framèd;
  Heaven is music, and thy beauty's
    Birth is heavenly.

   These dull notes we sing
  Discords need for helps to grace them;
  Only beauty purely loving
    Knows no discord;

   But still moves delight,
  Like clear springs renewed by flowing,
  Ever perfect, ever in them-
    selves eternal.

160                    *In Praise of Neptune*

OF Neptune's empire let us sing,
At whose command the waves obey,
To whom the rivers tribute pay,
   Down the high mountains sliding;
To whom the scaly nation yields
Homage for the crystal fields
       Wherein they dwell;
And every sea-god pays a gem,
Yearly out of his watery cell,
To deck great Neptune's diadem.

The Tritons dancing in a ring,
Before his palace gates, do make
The water with their echoes quake,
   Like the great thunder sounding:
The sea-nymphs chant their accents shrill;
   And the Sirens, taught to kill
       With their sweet voice,
Make every echoing rock reply,
Unto their gentle murmuring noise,
The praise of Neptune's empery.


161                      *Winter Nights*

NOW winter nights enlarge
   The number of their hours,
And clouds their storms discharge
   Upon the airy towers.
Let now the chimneys blaze,
   And cups o'erflow with wine;
Let well-tuned words amaze
   With harmony divine.
Now yellow waxen lights
   Shall wait on honey Love,
While youthful revels, masks, and courtly sights
   Sleep's leaden spells remove.

This time doth well dispense
   With lovers' long discourse.
Much speech hath some defence
   Though beauty no remorse.
All do not all things well:
   Some measures comely tread,
Some knotted riddles tell,
   Some poems smoothly read.
The Summer hath his joys,
   And Winter his delights.
Though Love and all his pleasures are but toys,
   They shorten tedious nights.

162         *A Lover's Plea*

SHALL I come, sweet Love, to thee,
   When the evening beams are set?
Shall I not excluded be?
   Will you find no feignèd let?
Let me not, for pity, more
Tell the long hours at your door.

Who can tell what thief or foe
   In the covert of the night
For his prey will work my woe,
   Or through wicked foul despite?
So may I die unredressed,
Ere my long love be possessed.

But to let such dangers pass,
   Which a lover's thoughts disdain,
'Tis enough in such a place
   To attend love's joys in vain.
Do not mock me in thy bed,
While these cold nights freeze me dead.

163 *Love-Charms*

THRICE toss these oaken ashes in the air;
Thrice sit thou mute in this enchanted chair;
Then thrice three times tie up this true love's knot,
And murmur soft: 'She will, or she will not.'

Go burn these poisonous weeds in yon blue fire,
These screech-owl's feathers and this prickling briar,
This cypress gathered at a dead man's grave,
That all thy fears and cares an end may have.

Then come, you fairies, dance with me a round;
Melt her hard heart with your melodious sound.
In vain are all the charms I can devise;
She hath an art to break them with her eyes.

164 *Cherry-Ripe*

THERE is a garden in her face,
    Where roses and white lilies grow;
A heavenly paradise is that place,
    Wherein all pleasant fruits do flow.
There cherries grow which none may buy,
Till 'Cherry-ripe' themselves do cry.

Those cherries fairly do enclose
    Of orient pearl a double row,
Which when her lovely laughter shows,
    They look like rosebuds filled with snow.
Yet them nor peer nor prince can buy,
Till 'Cherry-ripe' themselves do cry.

Her eyes like angels watch them still;
    Her brows like bended bows do stand,
Threatening with piercing frowns to kill
    All that attempt with eye or hand
Those sacred cherries to come nigh,
Till 'Cherry-ripe' themselves do cry.

**165**              *O Come Quickly!*

NEVER weather-beaten sail more willing bent to shore,
    Never tired pilgrim's limbs affected slumber more,
Than my weary spright now longs to fly out of my troubled breast.
    O! come quickly, sweetest Lord, and take my soul to rest.

Ever blooming are the joys of Heaven's high Paradise.
    Cold age deafs not there our ears, nor vapour dims our eyes;
Glory there the sun outshines, whose beams the blessed only see.
    O! come quickly, glorious Lord, and raise my spright to thee.


# ANONYMOUS

**166**            *Hierusalem, my Happy Home*

HIERUSALEM, my happy home,
    When shall I come to thee?
When shall my sorrows have an end
    Thy joys when shall I see?

O happy harbour of the saints,
    O sweet and pleasant soil
In thee no sorrow may be found
    No grief, no care, no toil. . . .

No dampish mist is seen in thee,
    Nor cold nor darksome night;
There every soul shines as the sun,
    There God himself gives light.

There lust and lucre cannot dwell,
    There envy bears no sway;
There is no hunger, heat nor cold,
    But pleasure every way.

Hierusalem, Hierusalem,
    God grant I once may see
Thy endless joys, and of the same
    Partaker aye to be.

Thy walls are made of precious stones,
   Thy bulwarks diamonds square;
Thy gates are of right orient pearl,
   Exceeding rich and rare.

Thy turrets and thy pinnacles
   With carbuncles do shine;
Thy very streets are paved with gold,
   Surpassing clear and fine.

Thy houses are of ivory,
   Thy windows crystal clear,
Thy tiles are made of beaten gold,
   O God, that I were there.

Within thy gates nothing doth come
   That is not passing clean;
No spider's web, no dirt, no dust,
   No filth may there be seen.

Ah, my sweet home, Hierusalem,
   Would God I were in thee!
Would God my woes were at an end,
   Thy joys that I might see! . . .

Thy gardens and thy gallant walks
   Continually are green;
There grows such sweet and pleasant flowers
   As nowhere else are seen. . . .

Quite through the streets with silver sound
   The flood of life doth flow;
Upon whose banks on every side
   The wood of life doth grow.

There trees for evermore bear fruit
   And evermore do spring;
There evermore the angels sit
   And evermore do sing.

There David stands with harp in hand
   As master of the Quire;
Ten thousand times that man were blest
   That might this music hear.

Our Lady sings *Magnificat*
   With tune surpassing sweet;
And all the virgins bear their parts
   Sitting about her feet.

*Te Deum* doth Saint Ambrose sing,
   Saint Austin doth the like;
Old Simeon and Zachary
   Have not their songs to seek.

There Magdalen hath left her moan
   And cheerfully doth sing,
With blessed saints whose harmony
   In every street doth ring.

Hierusalem, my happy home,
   Would God I were in thee!
Would God my woes were at an end,
   Thy joys that I might see!

## *from* Song-Books

### (i)

### *The Herdmen*

167

WHAT pleasure have great princes,
   More dainty to their choice,
Than herdmen wild, who careless
   In quiet life rejoice,
And Fortune's fate not fearing
Sing sweet in summer morning?

Their dealings plain and rightful
   Are void of all deceit;
They never know how spiteful
   It is to kneel and wait
On favourite presumptuous,
Whose pride is vain and sumptuous.

All day their flocks each tendeth;
  At night they take their rest,
More quiet than who sendeth
  His ship into the East,
Where gold and pearl are plenty,
But getting very dainty.


For lawyers and their pleading
  They esteem it not a straw;
They think that honest meaning
  Is of itself a law;
Where conscience judgeth plainly,
They spend no money vainly.


O happy who thus liveth,
  Not caring much for gold,
With clothing which sufficeth
  To keep him from the cold.
Though poor and plain his diet,
Yet merry it is and quiet.


(ii)

168            *Philon the Shepherd*

WHILE that the sun with his beams hot
  Scorchèd the fruits in vale and mountain,
Philon the shepherd, late forgot,
  Sitting besides a crystal fountain
In shadow of a green oak tree,
Upon his pipe this song played he:
  'Adieu love, adieu love, untrue love!
  Your mind is light, soon lost for new love.

'So long as I was in your sight,
  I was as your heart, your soul, your treasure;
And evermore you sobbed, you sighed,
  Burning in flames beyond all measure.
Three days endured your love to me,
And it was lost in other three.
  Adieu love, adieu love, untrue love!
  Your mind is light, soon lost for new love.

'Another shepherd you did see,
  To whom your heart was soon enchainèd;
Full soon your love was leapt from me;
  Full soon my place he had obtainèd.
Soon came a third your love to win,
And we were out, and he was in.
    Adieu love, adieu love, untrue love!
    Your mind is light, soon lost for new love.

'Sure you have made me passing glad,
  That you your mind so soon removèd,
Before that I the leisure had,
  To choose you for my best belovèd;
For all my love was past and done,
Two days before it was begun.
    Adieu love, adieu love, untrue love!
    Your mind is light, soon lost for new love.'

## (iii)

### *A Pedlar*

169

FINE knacks for ladies, cheap, choice, brave and new!
  Good pennyworths! but money cannot move.
I keep a fair but for the Fair to view;
  A beggar may be liberal of love.
Though all my wares be trash, the heart is true.

Great gifts are guiles and look for gifts again;
  My trifles come as treasures from my mind.
It is a precious jewel to be plain;
  Sometimes in shell the orient'st pearls we find.
Of others take a sheaf, of me a grain.

Within this pack pins, points, laces, and gloves,
  And divers toys fitting a country fair,
But in my heart, where duty serves and loves,
  Turtles and twins, court's brood, a heavenly pair.
Happy the heart that thinks of no removes!

(iv)

170 *Tears*

WEEP you no more, sad fountains;
　What need you flow so fast?
Look how the snowy mountains
　Heaven's sun doth gently waste.
　　But my sun's heavenly eyes
　　View not your weeping,
　　That now lies sleeping
Softly, now softly lies
　　Sleeping.

Sleep is a reconciling,
　A rest that peace begets.
Doth not the sun rise smiling
　When fair at even he sets?
　　Rest you then, rest, sad eyes,
　　Melt not in weeping,
　　While she lies sleeping
Softly, now softly lies
　　Sleeping.

(v)

171 *My Lady's Tears*

I SAW my lady weep,
　And Sorrow proud to be advancèd so
In those fair eyes where all perfections keep.
　Her face was full of woe;
But such a woe, believe me, as wins more hearts,
Than Mirth can do with her enticing parts.

　Sorrow was there made fair,
　And Passion wise, tears a delightful thing;
Silence beyond all speech a wisdom rare.
　She made her sighs to sing,
And all things with so sweet a sadness move,
As made my heart at once both grieve and love.

O fairer than aught else
The world can show, leave off in time to grieve.
Enough, enough your joyful looks excels;
    Tears kills the heart, believe.
    O! strive not to be excellent in woe,
Which only breeds your beauty's overthrow.

(vi)

172    *Sister, Awake!*

SISTER, awake! close not your eyes!
    The day her light discloses,
And the bright morning doth arise
    Out of her bed of roses.

See the clear sun, the world's bright eye,
    In at our window peeping:
Lo, how he blusheth to espy
    Us idle wenches sleeping!

Therefore awake! make haste, I say,
    And let us, without staying,
All in our gowns of green so gay
    Into the Park a-maying!

(vii)

173    *No Other Choice*

FAIN would I change that note
To which fond Love hath charmed me
Long, long to sing by rote,
Fancying that that harmed me:
Yet when this thought doth come,
'Love is the perfect sum
    Of all delight,'
I have no other choice
Either for pen or voice
    To sing or write.

O Love! they wrong thee much
That say thy sweet is bitter,
When thy rich fruit is such
As nothing can be sweeter.
Fair house of joy and bliss,
Where truest pleasure is,
  I do adore thee:
I know thee what thou art,
I serve thee with my heart,
  And fall before thee.

(viii)

174     *Passing By*

THERE is a Lady sweet and kind,
Was never face so pleased my mind;
I did but see her passing by,
And yet I love her till I die.

Her gesture, motion, and her smiles,
Her wit, her voice my heart beguiles,
Beguiles my heart, I know not why,
And yet I love her till I die. . . .

Cupid is wingèd and doth range,
Her country so my love doth change:
But change she earth, or change she sky,
Yet will I love her till I die.

(ix)

175     *The Awakening*

ON a time the amorous Silvy
Said to her shepherd, 'Sweet, how do ye?
Kiss me this once and then God be wi' ye,
  My sweetest dear!
Kiss me this once and then God be wi' ye.
For now the morning draweth near.'

With that, her fairest bosom showing,
Opening her lips, rich perfumes blowing,
She said, 'Now kiss me and be going,
　　　　My sweetest dear!
Kiss me this once and then be going,
For now the morning draweth near.'

With that the shepherd waked from sleeping,
And spying where the day was peeping,
He said, 'Now take my soul in keeping,
　　　　My sweetest dear!
Kiss me and take my soul in keeping,
Since I must go, now day is near.'

(x)

176　　　　*A Madrigal*

MY Love in her attire doth show her wit,
　　It doth so well become her:
For every season she hath dressings fit,
　　For winter, spring, and summer.
No beauty she doth miss,
　　When all her robes are on:
But Beauty's self she is,
　　When all her robes are gone.

177　　　　*Aubade*

STAY, O sweet, and do not rise!
　　The light that shines comes from thine eyes;
The day breaks not: it is my heart,
　　Because that you and I must part.
　　　　Stay! or else my joys will die
　　　　And perish in their infancy

## HENRY CHETTLE
### *c.* 1560–*c.* 1607

178            *Diaphenia*

DIAPHENIA, like the daffodowndilly,
  White as the sun, fair as the lily,
Heigh ho, how I do love thee!
  I do love thee as my lambs
  Are beloved of their dams;
How blest were I if thou wouldst prove me!

  Diaphenia, like the spreading roses,
  That in thy sweets all sweets encloses,
Fair sweet, how I do love thee!
  I do love thee as each flower
  Loves the sun's life-giving power,
For, dead, thy breath to life might move me.

  Diaphenia, like to all things blessèd,
  When all thy praises are expressèd,
Dear joy, how I do love thee!
  As the birds do love the spring,
  Or the bees their careful king:
Then in requite, sweet virgin, love me!


## SIR HENRY WOTTON
### 1568–1639

179          *Elizabeth of Bohemia*

YOU meaner beauties of the night,
  That poorly satisfy our eyes
More by your number than your light,
  You common people of the skies;
  What are you when the moon shall rise?

You curious chanters of the wood,
    That warble forth Dame Nature's lays,
Thinking your passions understood
    By your weak accents; what's your praise
    When Philomel her voice shall raise?

You violets that first appear,
    By your pure purple mantles known
Like the proud virgins of the year,
    As if the spring were all your own;
    What are you when the rose is blown?

So, when my mistress shall be seen
    In form and beauty of her mind,
By virtue first, then choice, a Queen,
    Tell me, if she were not designed
    The eclipse and glory of her kind.

180  *Upon the Sudden Restraint of the Earl of Somerset,*
        *then falling from favour, 1615.*

DAZZLED thus with height of place,
Whilst our hopes our wits beguile,
No man marks the narrow space
'Twixt a prison and a smile.

Then, since Fortune's favours fade,
You that in her arms do sleep,
Learn to swim, and not to wade,
For the hearts of Kings are deep.

But, if Greatness be so blind
As to trust in towers of air,
Let it be with Goodness lined,
That at least the fall be fair.

Then, though darkened, you shall say,
When friends fail, and Princes frown,
Virtue is the roughest way,
But proves at night a bed of down.

181 *The Character of a Happy Life*

How happy is he born and taught
That serveth not another's will;
Whose armour is his honest thought,
And simple truth his utmost skill!

Whose passions not his masters are;
Whose soul is still prepared for death,
Untied unto the world by care
Of public fame or private breath;

Who envies none that chance doth raise,
Nor vice; who never understood
How deepest wounds are given by praise;
Nor rules of state, but rules of good;

Who hath his life from rumours freed;
Whose conscience is his strong retreat;
Whose state can neither flatterers feed,
Nor ruin make oppressors great;

Who God doth late and early pray
More of His grace than gifts to lend;
And entertains the harmless day
With a religious book or friend;

—This man is freed from servile bands
Of hope to rise or fear to fall:
Lord of himself, though not of lands,
And having nothing, yet hath all.

# SIR JOHN DAVIES
## 1569–1626

182 *The Praise of Dancing*

'Dancing, bright lady, then began to be,
　When the first seeds whereof the world did spring,
The fire, air, earth, and water, did agree
　By Love's persuasion, nature's mighty king,
　To leave their first discorded combating,
　　And in a dance such measure to observe,
　　As all the world their motion should preserve.

'Since when they still are carried in a round,
　And changing come one in another's place;
Yet do they neither mingle nor confound,
　But every one doth keep the bounded space
　Wherein the dance doth bid it turn or trace.
　　This wondrous miracle did Love devise,
　　For dancing is love's proper exercise.

'Like this he framed the gods' eternal bower,
　And of a shapeless and confusèd mass,
By his through-piercing and digesting power,
　The turning vault of heaven formèd was,
　Whose starry wheels he hath so made to pass,
　　As that their movings do a music frame,
　　And they themselves still dance unto the same.

\*

'For that brave sun, the father of the day,
　Doth love this earth, the mother of the night;
And, like a reveller in rich array,
　Doth dance his galliard in his leman's sight,
　Both back and forth and sideways passing light.
　　His gallant grace doth so the gods amaze,
　　That all stand still and at his beauty gaze.

'But see the earth when she approacheth near,
   How she for joy doth spring and sweetly smile;
But see again her sad and heavy cheer,
   When changing places he retires a while;
   But those black clouds he shortly will exile,
     And make them all before his presence fly,
     As mists consumed before his cheerful eye.

'Who doth not see the measure of the moon?
   Which thirteen times she danceth every year,
And ends her pavan thirteen times as soon
   As doth her brother, of whose golden hair
   She borroweth part, and proudly doth it wear.
     Then doth she coyly turn her face aside,
     That half her cheek is scarce sometimes descried.

'Next her, the pure, subtle, and cleansing fire
   Is swiftly carried in a circle even,
Though Vulcan be pronounced by many a liar
   The only halting god that dwells in heaven;
   But that foul name may be more fitly given
     To your false fire, that far from heaven is fall,
     And doth consume, waste, spoil, disorder all.

'And now behold your tender nurse, the air,
   And common neighbour that aye runs around;
How many pictures and impressions fair
   Within her empty regions are there found,
   Which to your senses dancing do propound?
     For what are breath, speech, echoes, music, winds,
     But dancings of the air, in sundry kinds?

'For, when you breathe, the air in order moves,
   Now in, now out, in time and measure true,
And when you speak, so well she dancing loves,
   That doubling oft and oft redoubling new
   With thousand forms she doth herself endue;
     For all the words that from your lips repair
     Are nought but tricks and turnings of the air.

'Hence is her prattling daughter, Echo, born,
  That dances to all voices she can hear.
There is no sound so harsh that she doth scorn,
  Nor any time wherein she will forbear
  The airy pavement with her feet to wear;
    And yet her hearing sense is nothing quick,
    For after time she endeth every trick.

'And thou, sweet music, dancing's only life,
  The ear's sole happiness, the air's best speech,
Lodestone of fellowship, charming rod of strife,
  The soft mind's paradise, the sick mind's leech,
  With thine own tongue thou trees and stones canst teach,
    That when the air doth dance her finest measure,
    Then art thou born, the gods' and men's sweet pleasure.

'Lastly, where keep the winds their revelry,
  Their violent turnings and wild whirling hays,
But in the air's tralucent gallery?
  Where she herself is turned a hundred ways,
  While with those maskers wantonly she plays.
    Yet in this misrule they such rule embrace
    As two, at once, encumber not the place.

'If then fire, air, wandering and fixed lights,
  In every province of the imperial sky,
Yield perfect forms of dancing to your sights,
  In vain I teach the ear that which the eye,
  With certain view, already doth descry;
    But for your eyes perceive not all they see,
    In this I will your senses' master be.

'For lo! the sea that fleets about the land,
  And like a girdle clips her solid waist,
Music and measure both doth understand;
  For his great crystal eye is always cast
  Up to the moon, and on her fixèd fast;
    And as she danceth in her pallid sphere,
    So danceth he about the centre here.

hays] country dances

'Sometimes his proud green waves in order set,
    One after other, flow unto the shore;
Which when they have with many kisses wet,
    They ebb away in order, as before;
    And to make known his courtly love the more,
        He oft doth lay aside his three-forked mace,
        And with his arms the timorous earth embrace.

'Only the earth doth stand forever still:
    Her rocks remove not, nor her mountains meet,
Although some wits enriched with learning's skill
    Say heaven stands firm and that the earth doth fleet,
    And swiftly turneth underneath their feet;
        Yet, though the earth is ever steadfast seen,
        On her broad breast hath dancing ever been.

'For those blue veins that through her body spread,
    Those sapphire streams which from great hills do spring,
The earth's great dugs, for every wight is fed
    With sweet fresh moisture from them issuing,
    Observe a dance in their wild wandering;
        And still their dance begets a murmur sweet,
        And still the murmur with the dance doth meet.'

183                    *Affliction*

IF aught can teach us aught, Affliction's looks,
    Making us look into ourselves so near,
Teach us to know ourselves beyond all books,
    Or all the learned schools that ever were.

This mistress lately plucked me by the ear,
    And many a golden lesson hath me taught;
Hath made my senses quick, and reason clear,
    Reformed my will, and rectified my thought.

So do the winds and thunders cleanse the air;
    So working seas settle and purge the wine;
So lopped and prunèd trees do flourish fair;
    So doth the fire the drossy gold refine.

Neither Minerva nor the learned Muse,
   Nor rules of art, nor precepts of the wise,
Could in my brain those beams of skill infuse,
   As but the glance of this dame's angry eyes.

She within lists my ranging mind hath brought,
   That now beyond myself I list not go;
Myself am centre of my circling thought,
   Only myself I study, learn, and know.

I know my body's of so frail a kind
   As force without, fevers within, can kill;
I know the heavenly nature of my mind,
   But 'tis corrupted both in wit and will;

I know my soul hath power to know all things,
   Yet is she blind and ignorant in all;
I know I am one of nature's little kings,
   Yet to the least and vilest things am thrall.

I know my life's a pain and but a span,
   I know my sense is mocked with everything;
And to conclude, I know myself a man,
   Which is a proud, and yet a wretched thing.

184         *The Soul and the Body*

But how shall we this union well express?
   Nought ties the soul; her subtlety is such,
She moves the body, which she doth possess,
   Yet no part toucheth, but by virtue's touch.

Then dwells she not therein as in a tent;
   Nor as a pilot in his ship doth sit;
Nor as the spider in his web is pent;
   Nor as the wax retains the print in it;

Nor as a vessel water doth contain;
   Nor as one liquor in another shed;
Nor as the heat doth in the fire remain;
   Nor as a voice throughout the air is spread.

But as the fair and cheerful morning light
  Doth here and there her silver beams impart,
And in an instant doth herself unite
  To the transparent air, in all and part;

Still resting whole, when blows the air divide,
  Abiding pure, when the air is most corrupted,
Throughout the air her beams dispersing wide,
  And when the air is tossed, not interrupted:

So doth the piercing soul the body fill,
  Being all in all, and all in part diffused,
Indivisible, incorruptible still,
  Not forced, encountered, troubled or confused.

And as the sun above the light doth bring,
  Though we behold it in the air below,
So from the eternal Light the soul doth spring,
  Though in the body she her powers do show.

# JOHN DONNE

### 1572–1631

185                 *Seek True Religion!*

                    THOUGH Truth and Falsehood be
Near twins, yet Truth a little elder is.
Be busy to seek her; believe me this:
He's not of none, nor worst, that seeks the best.
To adore, or scorn an image, or protest,
May all be bad. Doubt wisely; in strange way
To stand inquiring right is not to stray;
To sleep or run wrong is. On a huge hill,
Craggèd and steep, Truth stands, and he that will
Reach her, about must and about must go,
And what the hill's suddenness resists, win so.
Yet strive so, that before age, death's twilight,
Thy soul rest, for none can work in that night.

To will implies delay; therefore now do.
Hard deeds the body's pains; hard knowledge too,
The mind's endeavours reach; and mysteries
Are like the sun, dazzling, yet plain to all eyes.
Keep the truth which thou hast found; men do not stand
In so ill case here that God hath with his hand
Signed kings blank charters to kill whom they hate,
Nor are they vicars, but hangmen to Fate.
Fool and wretch, wilt thou let thy soul be tied
To man's laws, by which she shall not be tried
At the last day? Will it then boot thee
To say a Philip or a Gregory,
A Harry, or a Martin taught thee this?
Is not this excuse for mere contraries
Equally strong? Cannot both sides say so?
That thou mayst rightly obey Power, her bounds know;
Those passed, her nature and name's changed; to be
Then humble to her is idolatry.
As streams are Power is; those blest flowers that dwell
At the rough stream's calm head thrive and prove well,
But having left their roots and themselves given
To the stream's tyrannous rage, alas, are driven
Through mills and rocks and woods, and at last, almost
Consumed in going, in the sea are lost.
So perish souls which more choose men's unjust
Power from God claimed than God himself to trust.

186       *To His Mistress Desiring to Travel with*
*Him as His Page*

By our first strange and fatal interview,
By all desires which thereof did ensue,
By our long starving hopes, by that remorse
Which my words' masculine persuasive force
Begot in thee, and by the memory
Of hurts which spies and rivals threatened me,
I calmly beg; but by thy parents' wrath,
By all pains which want and divorcement hath,

**185**    mere] absolute

I conjure thee; and all those oaths which I
And thou have sworn, to seal joint constancy,
Here I unswear, and overswear them thus:
Thou shalt not love by means so dangerous.
Temper, O fair Love, love's impetuous rage,
Be my true mistress still, not my feigned page.
I'll go, and, by thy kind leave, leave behind
Thee, only worthy to nurse in my mind
Thirst to come back; O, if thou die before,
From other lands my soul towards thee shall soar.
Thy else almighty beauty cannot move
Rage from the seas, nor thy love teach them love,
Nor tame wild Boreas' harshness: thou hast read
How roughly he in pieces shiverèd
Fair Orithea, whom he swore he loved.
Fall ill or good, 'tis madness to have proved
Dangers unurged; feed on this flattery,
That absent lovers one in the other be.
Dissemble nothing, not a boy, nor change
Thy body's habit, nor mind's; be not strange
To thyself only; all will spy in thy face
A blushing womanly discovering grace.
Richly clothed apes are called apes, and as soon
Eclipsed as bright, we call the moon the moon.
Men of France, changeable chameleons,
Spittles of diseases, shops of fashions,
Love's fuellers, and the rightest company
Of players, which upon the world's stage be,
Will quickly know thee, and know thee; and alas,
The indifferent Italian, as we pass
His warm land, well content to think thee page,
Will haunt thee, with such lust and hideous rage
As Lot's fair guests were vexed: but none of these,
Nor spongy hydroptic Dutch, shall thee displease,
If thou stay here. O stay here; for, for thee
England is only a worthy gallery,
To walk in expectation, till from thence
Our great King call thee into his presence.
When I am gone, dream me some happiness;
Nor let thy looks our long-hid love confess;
Nor praise, nor dispraise me, bless, nor curse
Openly love's force; nor in bed fright thy nurse

With midnight's startings, crying out, 'O, O,
Nurse, O, my love is slain; I saw him go
O'er the white Alps, alone; I saw him, I,
Assailed, fight, taken, stabbed, bleed, fall, and die.'
Augur me better chance, except dread Jove
Think it enough for me to have had thy love.

187                    *A Storm at Sea*

BUT when I waked, I saw that I saw not;
I, and the sun, which should teach me, had forgot
East, west, day, night; and I could but say,
If the world had lasted, now it had been day.
Thousands our noises were, yet we 'mongst all
Could none by his right name, but thunder, call:
Lightning was all our light, and it rained more
Than if the sun had drunk the sea before.
Some coffined in their cabins lie, equally
Grieved that they are not dead, and yet must die;
And as sin-burdened souls from graves will creep
At the last day, some forth their cabins peep,
And tremblingly ask, 'What news?' and do hear so,
Like jealous husbands, what they would not know.
Some, sitting on the hatches, would seem there
With hideous gazing to fear away fear.
There note they the ship's sicknesses, the mast
Shaked with this ague, and the hold and waist
With a salt dropsy clogged, and all our tacklings
Snapping, like too-high-stretchèd treble strings.
And from our tattered sails rags drop down so,
As from one hanged in chains a year ago.
Even our ordnance, placed for our defence,
Strive to break loose, and 'scape away from thence.
Pumping hath tired our men, and what's the gain?
Seas into seas thrown, we suck in again;
Hearing hath deafed our sailors, and if they
Knew how to hear, there's none knows what to say.
Compared to these storms, death is but a qualm,
Hell somewhat lightsome, and the Bermuda calm.
Darkness, light's elder brother, his birth-right
Claims o'er this world, and to heaven hath chased light.

All things are one, and that one none can be,
Since all forms uniform deformity
Doth cover; so that we, except God say
Another *Fiat*, shall have no more day.
So violent, yet long, these furies be,
That though thine absence starve me, I wish not thee.

188                          *Song*

Go and catch a falling star,
   Get with child a mandrake root,
Tell me where all past years are,
   Or who cleft the Devil's foot;
Teach me to hear mermaids singing,
Or to keep off envy's stinging,
       And find
       What wind
Serves to advance an honest mind.

If thou beest born to strange sights,
   Things invisible to see,
Ride ten thousand days and nights
   Till Age snow white hairs on thee;
Thou, when thou return'st, wilt tell me
All strange wonders that befell thee,
       And swear
       No where
Lives a woman true and fair.

If thou find'st one, let me know;
   Such a pilgrimage were sweet.
Yet do not; I would not go,
   Though at next door we might meet.
Though she were true when you met her,
And last till you write your letter,
       Yet she
       Will be
False, ere I come, to two or three.

189                    *The Apparition*

WHEN by thy scorn, O murderess, I am dead,
And that thou think'st thee free
From all solicitation from me,
Then shall my ghost come to thy bed,
And thee, fained vestal, in worse arms shall see;
Then thy sick taper will begin to wink,
And he, whose thou art then, being tired before,
Will, if thou stir, or pinch to wake him, think
    Thou call'st for more,
And in false sleep will from thee shrink,
And then, poor aspen wretch, neglected thou
Bathed in a cold quicksilver sweat wilt lie
    A verier ghost than I;
What I will say, I will not tell thee now,
Lest that preserve thee; and since my love is spent,
I had rather thou shouldst painfully repent,
Than by my threatenings rest still innocent.


190                        *Song*

SWEETEST love, I do not go
    For weariness of thee,
Nor in hope the world can show
    A fitter love for me;
        But since that I
    Must die at last, 'tis best
    To use myself in jest
        Thus by fained deaths to die.

Yesternight the sun went hence,
    And yet is here today,
He hath no desire nor sense,
    Nor half so short a way:
        Then fear not me,
    But believe that I shall make
    Speedier journeys, since I take
        More wings and spurs than he.

O how feeble is man's power,
   That if good fortune fall,
Cannot add another hour,
   Nor a lost hour recall!
     But come bad chance,
And we join to it our strength,
And we teach it art and length,
   Itself o'er us to advance.

When thou sigh'st, thou sigh'st not wind,
   But sigh'st my soul away,
When thou weep'st, unkindly kind,
   My life's blood doth decay.
     It cannot be
That thou lov'st me, as thou sayst,
If in thine my life thou waste,
   Thou art the best of me.

Let not thy divining heart
   Forethink me any ill,
Destiny may take thy part,
   And may thy fears fulfil.
     But think that we
Are but turned aside to sleep;
They who one another keep
   Alive, ne'er parted be.

191           *The Undertaking*

I HAVE done one braver thing
   Than all the Worthies did,
Yet a braver thence doth spring,
   Which is, to keep that hid.

It were but madness now to impart
   The skill of specular stone.
When he which can have learned the art
   To cut it can find none.

So, if I now should utter this,
   Others (because no more
Such stuff to work upon, there is)
   Would love but as before.

But he who loveliness within
    Hath found, all outward loathes;
For he who colour loves, and skin,
    Loves but their oldest clothes.

If, as I have, you also do
    Virtue attired in woman see,
And dare love that, and say so too,
    And forget the He and She;

And if this love, though placèd so,
    From profane men you hide,
Which will no faith on this bestow,
    Or, if they do, deride:

Then you've done a braver thing
    Than all the Worthies did,
And a braver thence will spring,
    Which is, to keep that hid.


192      *A Valediction: forbidding Mourning*

As virtuous men pass mildly away,
    And whisper to their souls to go,
Whilst some of their sad friends do say
    'The breath goes now,' and some say, 'No':

So let us melt, and make no noise,
    No tear-floods, nor sigh-tempests move,
'Twere profanation of our joys
    To tell the laity our love.

Moving of the earth brings harms and fears,
    Men reckon what it did and meant;
But trepidation of the spheres,
    Though greater far, is innocent.

Dull sublunary lovers' love
    (Whose soul is sense) cannot admit
Absence, because it doth remove
    Those things which elemented it.

But we by a love so much refined
   That ourselves know not what it is,
Inter-assurèd of the mind,
   Care less eyes, lips and hands to miss.

Our two souls therefore, which are one,
   Though I must go, endure not yet
A breach, but an expansion
   Like gold to airy thinness beat.

If they be two, they are two so
   As stiff twin compasses are two;
Thy soul, the fixed foot, makes no show
   To move, but doth, if the other do.

And though it in the centre sit,
   Yet when the other far doth roam,
It leans, and hearkens after it,
   And grows erect, as it comes home.

Such wilt thou be to me, who must
   Like the other foot, obliquely run;
Thy firmness makes my circle just,
   And makes me end where I begun.

193          *The Ecstasy*

WHERE, like a pillow on a bed,
   A pregnant bank swelled up, to rest
The violet's reclining head,
   Sat we two, one another's best.

Our hands were firmly cemented
   With a fast balm, which thence did spring;
Our eye-beams twisted, and did thread
   Our eyes upon one double string;

So to entergraft our hands, as yet
   Was all our means to make us one,
And pictures on our eyes to get
   Was all our propagation.

As 'twixt two equal armies Fate
  Suspends uncertain victory,
Our souls (which to advance their state
  Were gone out) hung 'twixt her and me.

And whilst our souls negotiate there,
  We like sepulchral statues lay;
All day the same our postures were,
  And we said nothing all the day.

If any, so by love refined
  That he soul's language understood,
And by good love were grown all mind,
  Within convenient distance stood,

He (though he knew not which soul spake,
  Because both meant, both spake the same)
Might thence a new concoction take,
  And part far purer than he came.

This ecstasy doth unperplex
  (We said) and tell us what we love,
We see by this, it was not sex,
  We see, we saw not what did move:

But as all several souls contain
  Mixture of things, they know not what,
Love these mixed souls doth mix again,
  And makes both one, each this and that.

A single violet transplant,
  The strength, the colour, and the size,
(All which before was poor and scant)
  Redoubles still, and multiplies.

When love with one another so
  Interinanimates two souls,
That abler soul, which thence doth flow,
  Defects of loneliness controls.

We then, who are this new soul, know
   Of what we are composed, and made,
For the atomies of which we grow
   Are souls, whom no change can invade.

But, O alas! so long, so far
   Our bodies why do we forbear?
They are ours, though they are not we; we are
   The intelligences, they the sphere.

We owe them thanks, because they thus
   Did us, to us, at first convey,
Yielded their forces, sense, to us,
   Nor are dross to us, but allay.

On man heaven's influence works not so,
   But that it first imprints the air;
So soul into the soul may flow,
   Though it to body first repair.

As our blood labours to beget
   Spirits, as like souls as it can;
Because such fingers need to knit
   That subtle knot, which makes us man;

So must pure lovers' souls descend
   To affections, and to faculties,
Which sense may reach and apprehend,
   Else a great Prince in prison lies.

To our bodies turn we then, that so
   Weak men on love revealed may look;
Love's mysteries in souls do grow,
   But yet the body is his book.

And if some lover, such as we,
   Have heard this dialogue of one,
Let him still mark us, he shall see
   Small change, when we're to bodies gone.

194 *The Sun Rising*

BUSY old fool, unruly Sun,
    Why dost thou thus,
Through windows and through curtains call on us?
Must to thy motions lovers' seasons run?
    Saucy pedantic wretch, go chide
    Late school-boys, and sour 'prentices,
Go tell court-huntsmen that the King will ride,
Call country ants to harvest offices;
Love, all alike, no season knows, nor clime,
Nor hours, days, months, which are the rags of time.

    Thy beams, so reverend and strong
    Why shouldst thou think?
I could eclipse and cloud them with a wink,
But that I would not lose her sight so long:
    If her eyes have not blinded thine,
    Look, and tomorrow late tell me,
Whether both the Indias of spice and mine
Be where thou left'st them, or lie here with me.
Ask for those kings whom thou saw'st yesterday,
And thou shalt hear, 'All here in one bed lay.'

    She's all States, and all Princes I;
    Nothing else is.
Princes do but play us; compared to this,
All honour's mimic; all wealth alchemy.
    Thou, Sun, art half as happy as we,
    In that the world's contracted thus;
Thine age asks ease, and since thy duties be
To warm the world, that's done in warming us.
Shine here to us, and thou art everywhere;
This bed thy centre is, these walls thy sphere.

195 *The Anniversary*

ALL Kings, and all their favourites,
    All glory of honours, beauties, wits,
The sun itself, which makes times, as they pass,
Is elder by a year now than it was
When thou and I first one another saw:
All other things to their destruction draw,
    Only our love hath no decay;
This no tomorrow hath, nor yesterday,
Running it never runs from us away,
But truly keeps his first, last, everlasting day.

    Two graves must hide thine and my corse;
    If one might, death were no divorce.
Alas, as well as other Princes, we
(Who Prince enough in one another be)
Must leave at last in death these eyes and ears,
Oft fed with true oaths, and with sweet salt tears;
    But souls where nothing dwells but love
(All other thoughts being inmates) then shall prove
This, or a love increasèd there above,
When bodies to their graves, souls from their graves remove.

    And then we shall be throughly blest;
    But we no more than all the rest.
Here upon earth we're Kings, and none but we
Can be such Kings, nor of such subjects be;
Who is so safe as we? where none can do
Treason to us, except one of us two.
    True and false fears let us refrain,
Let us love nobly, and live, and add again
Years and years unto years, till we attain
To write threescore: this is the second of our reign.

196 *The Canonization*

FOR God's sake hold your tongue, and let me love,
　　Or chide my palsy, or my gout,
My five gray hairs, or ruined fortune flout;
With wealth your state, your mind with arts improve;
　　Take you a course, get you a place,
　　Observe his Honour, or his Grace,
And the King's real, or his stamped face
　　Contemplate; what you will, approve,
　　　So you will let me love.

Alas, alas, who's injured by my love?
　　What merchant's ships have my sighs drowned?
Who says my tears have overflowed his ground?
When did my colds a forward spring remove?
　　When did the heats which my veins fill
　　Add one man to the plaguy Bill?
Soldiers find wars, and lawyers find out still
　　Litigious men, which quarrels move,
　　　Though she and I do love.

Call us what you will, we're made such by love;
　　Call her one, me another fly,
We're tapers too, and at our own cost die,
And we in us find the Eagle and the Dove;
　　The Phoenix riddle hath more wit
　　By us; we two, being one, are it,
So, to one neutral thing both sexes fit.
　　We die and rise the same, and prove
　　　Mysterious by this love.

We can die by it, if not live by love,
　　And if unfit for tombs or hearse
Our legend be, it will be fit for verse;
And if no piece of chronicle we prove,
　　We'll build in sonnets pretty rooms;
　　As well a well-wrought urn becomes
The greatest ashes, as half-acre tombs;
　　And by these hymns all shall approve
　　　Us canonized for love;

And thus invoke us: 'You, whom reverend Love
  Made one another's hermitage;
You, to whom love was peace, that now is rage;
Who did the whole world's soul extract, and drove
  Into the glasses of your eyes,
  So made such mirrors, and such spies,
That they did all to you epitomize,
  Countries, towns, courts: beg from above
  A pattern of your love!'


197      *A Nocturnal upon St Lucy's Day,*
*being the shortest day*

'TIS the year's midnight, and it is the day's,
Lucy's, who scarce seven hours herself unmasks;
  The sun is spent, and now his flasks
  Send forth light squibs, no constant rays;
    The world's whole sap is sunk;
The general balm the hydroptic earth hath drunk,
Whither, as to the bed's-feet, life is shrunk,
Dead and interred; yet all these seem to laugh,
Compared with me, who am their epitaph.

Study me then, you who shall lovers be
At the next world, that is, at the next spring:
  For I am every dead thing,
  In whom love wrought new alchemy.
    For his art did express
A quintessence even from nothingness,
From dull privations, and lean emptiness:
He ruined me, and I am re-begot
Of absence, darkness, death: things which are not.

All others, from all things, draw all that's good,
Life, soul, form, spirit, whence they being have;
  I, by Love's limbeck, am the grave
  Of all, that's nothing. Oft a flood
    Have we two wept, and so
Drowned the whole world, us two; oft did we grow
To be two Chaoses, when we did show
Care to ought else; and often absences
Withdrew our souls, and made us carcasses.

     **197**  limbeck] alchemical still

But I am by her death (which word wrongs her)
Of the first nothing the elixir grown;
   Were I a man, that I were one,
    I needs must know; I should prefer,
     If I were any beast,
Some ends, some means; yea plants, yea stones detest
And love; all, all some properties invest;
If I an ordinary nothing were,
As shadow, a light, and body must be here.

But I am None; nor will my sun renew.
You lovers, for whose sake the lesser sun
   At this time to the Goat is run
    To fetch new lust, and give it you,
     Enjoy your summer all;
Since she enjoys her long night's festival,
Let me prepare towards her, and let me call
This hour her vigil, and her eve, since this
Both the year's and the day's deep midnight is.

198             *The Relic*

     WHEN my grave is broke up again
     Some second guest to entertain,
     (For graves have learned that woman-head
     To be to more than one a bed)
       And he that digs it, spies
A bracelet of bright hair about the bone,
       Will he not let us alone,
And think that there a loving couple lies
Who thought that this device might be some way
To make their souls, at the last busy day,
Meet at this grave, and make a little stay?

     If this fall in a time, or land,
     Where mis-devotion doth command,
     Then he that digs us up will bring
     Us to the Bishop and the King,

**197**   elixir] essence         to the Goat] to the zodiacal sign of Capricorn

To make us relics; then
Thou shalt be a Mary Magdalen, and I
A something else thereby;
All women shall adore us, and some men;
And since at such times miracles are sought,
I would that age were by this paper taught
What miracles we harmless lovers wrought.

First, we loved well and faithfully,
Yet knew not what we loved, nor why;
Difference of sex no more we knew
Than our guardian angels do;
Coming and going we
Perchance might kiss, but not between those meals;
Our hands ne'er touched the seals,
Which nature, injured by late law, sets free:
These miracles we did; but now alas,
All measure, and all language, I should pass,
Should I tell what a miracle she was.

## Holy Sonnets

199

### (i)

THOU hast made me, and shall thy work decay?
  Repair me now, for now mine end doth haste;
  I run to death, and death meets me as fast,
And all my pleasures are like yesterday.
I dare not move my dim eyes any way;
  Despair behind, and death before doth cast
  Such terror, and my feebled flesh doth waste
By sin in it, which it towards hell doth weigh.
Only thou art above, and when towards thee
  By thy leave I can look, I rise again;
But our old subtle foe so tempteth me
  That not one hour I can myself sustain.
    Thy grace may wing me to prevent his art,
    And thou like adamant draw mine iron heart.

200

## (ii)

At the round earth's imagined corners blow
　Your trumpets, angels, and arise, arise
　From death, you numberless infinities
Of souls, and to your scattered bodies go:
All whom the flood did, and fire shall o'erthrow,
　All whom war, dearth, age, agues, tyrannies,
　Despair, law, chance hath slain, and you whose eyes
Shall behold God, and never taste death's woe.
But let them sleep, Lord, and me mourn a space,
　For if above all these my sins abound,
'Tis late to ask abundance of thy grace
　When we are there. Here on this lowly ground
　　Teach me how to repent: for that's as good
　　As if thou hadst sealed my pardon with thy blood.

201

## (iii)

Death, be not proud, though some have callèd thee
　Mighty and dreadful, for thou art not so;
　For those whom thou think'st thou dost overthrow
Die not, poor Death, nor yet canst thou kill me.
From rest and sleep, which but thy pictures be,
　Much pleasure—then, from thee much more must flow;
　And soonest our best men with thee do go,
Rest of their bones and soul's delivery.
Thou'rt slave to fate, chance, kings and desperate men,
　And dost with poison, war, and sickness dwell;
　And poppy or charms can make us sleep as well,
And better than thy stroke. Why swell'st thou then?
　　One short sleep past, we wake eternally,
　　And death shall be no more. Death, thou shalt die.

202 (iv)

BATTER my heart, three-personed God, for you
  As yet but knock, breathe, shine, and seek to mend;
  That I may rise and stand, o'erthrow me and bend
Your force to break, blow, burn, and make me new.
I, like an usurped town to another due,
  Labour to admit you, but O, to no end.
  Reason, your viceroy in me, me should defend,
But is captived and proves weak or untrue.
Yet dearly I love you and would be loved fain,
  But am betrothed unto your enemy.
Divorce me, untie, or break that knot again,
    Take me to you, imprison me, for I,
      Except you enthrall me, never shall be free,
      Nor ever chaste except you ravish me.

203 *A Hymn*

WILT thou forgive that sin where I begun,
  Which is my sin, though it were done before?
Wilt thou forgive those sins through which I run,
  And do them still, though still I do deplore?
    When thou hast done, thou hast not done,
      For I have more.

Wilt thou forgive that sin by which I won
  Others to sin? and made my sin their door?
Wilt thou forgive that sin which I did shun
  A year or two, but wallowed in a score?
    When thou hast done, thou hast not done,
      For I have more.

I have a sin of fear, that when I have spun
  My last thread, I shall perish on the shore;
Swear by thyself, that at my death thy Sun
  Shall shine as it shines now, and heretofore;
    And, having done that, thou hast done,
      I have no more.

# BEN JONSON
## ?1573–1637

204  *Hymn to Diana*

QUEEN and huntress, chaste and fair,
  Now the sun is laid to sleep,
Seated in thy silver chair,
  State in wonted manner keep:
    Hesperus entreats thy light,
    Goddess excellently bright.

Earth, let not thy envious shade
  Dare itself to interpose;
Cynthia's shining orb was made
  Heaven to clear when day did close:
    Bless us then with wishèd sight,
    Goddess excellently bright.

Lay thy bow of pearl apart,
  And thy crystal-shining quiver;
Give unto the flying hart
  Space to breathe, how short soever:
    Thou that mak'st a day of night—
    Goddess excellently bright.

205  *Simplex Munditiis*

STILL to be neat, still to be drest,
As you were going to a feast;
Still to be powdered, still perfumed,
Lady, it is to be presumed,
Though art's hid causes are not found,
All is not sweet, all is not sound.

Give me a look, give me a face
That makes simplicity a grace;
Robes loosely flowing, hair as free:
Such sweet neglect more taketh me
Than all the adulteries of art;
They strike mine eyes, but not my heart.

206 *To Celia*

DRINK to me only with thine eyes,
    And I will pledge with mine;
Or leave a kiss but in the cup
    And I'll not look for wine.
The thirst that from the soul doth rise
    Doth ask a drink divine;
But might I of Jove's nectar sup,
    I would not change for thine.

I sent thee late a rosy wreath,
    Not so much honouring thee
As giving it a hope that there
    It could not withered be;
But thou thereon didst only breathe,
    And sent'st it back to me;
Since when it grows, and smells, I swear,
    Not of itself but thee!

207 *The Shadow*

FOLLOW a shadow, it still flies you;
    Seem to fly it, it will pursue:
So court a mistress, she denies you;
    Let her alone, she will court you.
        Say, are not women truly, then,
        Styled but the shadows of us men?

At morn and even, shades are longest;
    At noon they are or short or none:
So men at weakest, they are strongest,
    But grant us perfect, they're not known.
        Say, are not women truly, then,
        Styled but the shadows of us men?

## Epitaphs

### (i)

208            ## On my First Daughter

HERE lies to each her parents' ruth
Mary, the daughter of their youth:
Yet, all Heaven's gifts being Heaven's due,
It makes the father less to rue.
At six months' end she parted hence
With safety of her innocence;
Whose soul Heaven's Queen (whose name she bears)
In comfort of her mother's tears,
Hath placed amongst her virgin-train;
Where, while that severed doth remain,
This grave partakes the fleshly birth,
Which cover lightly, gentle earth.

### (ii)

209            ## On my Son

Farewell, thou child of my right hand, and joy;
  My sin was too much hope of thee, loved boy.
Seven years thou wert lent to me, and I thee pay,
  Exacted by thy fate, on the just day.
O, could I lose all father now! For why
  Will man lament the state he should envy?
To have so soon 'scaped world's and flesh's rage,
  And, if no other misery, yet age?
Rest in soft peace, and, asked, say here doth lie
  Ben Jonson, his best piece of poetry.
For whose sake, henceforth, all his vows be such
  As what he loves may never like too much.

(iii)

210

## On Solomon Pavy
### A child of Queen Elizabeth's Chapel

WEEP with me, all you that read
    This little story;
And know, for whom a tear you shed
    Death's self is sorry.
'Twas a child that so did thrive
    In grace and feature,
As Heaven and Nature seemed to strive
    Which owned the creature.
Years he numbered scarce thirteen
    When Fates turned cruel,
Yet three filled Zodiacs had he been
    The Stage's jewel;
And did act (what now we moan)
    Old men so duly,
As sooth the Parcae thought him one,
    He played so truly.
So, by error, to his fate
    They all consented;
But, viewing him since, alas, too late!
    They have repented;
And have sought, to give new birth,
    In baths to steep him;
But, being so much too good for earth,
    Heaven vows to keep him.

211

## Inviting a Friend to Supper

TONIGHT, grave Sir, both my poor house and I
    Do equally desire your company:
Not that we think us worthy such a guest,
    But that your worth will dignify our feast
With those that come; whose grace may make that seem
    Something, which else could hope for no esteem.

It is the fair acceptance, Sir, **creates**
   The entertainment perfect: not the cates.
Yet shall you have, to rectify your palate,
   An olive, capers, or some better salad,
Ushering the mutton; with a short-legged hen,
   If we can get her, full of eggs, and then
Lemons, and wine for sauce; to these a cony
   Is not to be despaired of for our money;
And though fowl now be scarce, yet there are clerks,
   The sky not falling, think we may have larks.
I'll tell you of more, and lie, so you will come:
   Of partridge, pheasant, wood-cock, of which some
May yet be there; and godwit, if we can;
   Knot, rail and ruff too. How so ere, my man
Shall read a piece of Virgil, Tacitus,
   Livy, or of some better book to us,
Of which we'll speak our minds, amidst our meat;
   And I'll profess no verses to repeat:
To this, if ought appear which I not know of,
   That will the pastry, not my paper show of.
Digestive cheese and fruit there sure will be;
   But that which most doth take my Muse and me
Is a pure cup of rich Canary wine,
   Which is the Mermaid's now, but shall be mine;
Of which had Horace or Anacreon tasted,
   Their lives, as do their lines, till now had lasted.
Tobacco, nectar, or the Thespian spring
   Are all but Luther's beer, to this I sing.
Of this we will sup free, but moderately,
   And we will have no Pooly or Parrot by;
Nor shall our cups make any guilty men,
   But at our parting we will be as when
We innocently met. No simple word
   That shall be uttered at our mirthful board
Shall make us sad next morning, or affright
   The liberty that we'll enjoy tonight.


Pooly or Parrot] two well-known informers

212 *The Witches' Charm*

THE owl is abroad, the bat, and the toad,
　And so is the cat-a-mountain;
The ant and the mole sit both in a hole,
　And frog peeps out o'the fountain;
The dogs they do bay, and the timbrels play,
　The spindle is now a-turning;
The moon it is red, and the stars are fled,
　But all the sky is a-burning:
The ditch is made, and our nails the spade,
With pictures full, of wax and of wool;
Their livers I stick with needles quick:
There lacks but the blood to make up the flood.

213 *The Return of Astraea*

LOOK, look! rejoice and wonder!
　That you offending mortals are
　(For all your crimes) so much the care
Of him that bears the thunder!

Jove can endure no longer
　Your great ones should your less invade,
　Or that your weak, though bad, be made
A prey unto the stronger.

And therefore means to settle
　Astraea in her seat again;
　And let down in his golden chain
The age of better metal.

Which deed he doth the rather
　That even envy may behold
　Time not enjoyed his head of gold
Alone beneath his father.

But that his care conserveth,
　As time, so all time's honours too;
　Regarding still what heaven should do,
And not what earth deserveth.

214        *The Triumph of Charis*

SEE the Chariot at hand here of Love,
    Wherein my Lady rideth!
Each that draws is a swan or a dove,
    And well the car Love guideth.
As she goes, all hearts do duty
                Unto her beauty;
And enamoured do wish, so they might
                But enjoy such a sight,
That they still were to run by her side,
Thorough swords, thorough seas, whither she would ride.

Do but look on her eyes, they do light
    All that Love's world compriseth!
Do but look on her hair, it is bright
    As Love's star when it riseth!
Do but mark, her forehead's smoother
                Than words that soothe her;
And from her arched brows such a grace
                Sheds itself through the face,
As alone there triumphs to the life
All the gain, all the good, of the elements' strife.

Have you seen but a bright lily grow
    Before rude hands have touched it?
Have you marked but the fall of the snow
    Before the soil hath smutched it?
Have you felt the wool of the beaver,
                Or swan's down ever?
Or have smelt of the bud of the brier,
                Or the nard in the fire?
Or have tasted the bag of the bee?
O so white, O so soft, O so sweet is she!

## Ode to Himself

WHERE dost thou careless lie,
  Buried in ease and sloth?
Knowledge that sleeps doth die;
And this security,
  It is the common moth,
That eats on wits, and arts, and oft destroys them both.

Are all the Aonian springs
  Dried up? lies Thespia waste?
Doth Clarius' harp want strings,
That not a nymph now sings?
  Or droop they as disgraced,
To see their seats and bowers by chattering pies defaced?

If hence thy silence be,
  As 'tis too just a cause,
Let this thought quicken thee:
Minds that are great and free
  Should not on fortune pause,
'Tis crown enough to virtue still, her own applause.

What though the greedy fry
  Be taken with false baits
Of worded balladry
And think it poesy?
  They die with their conceits,
And only piteous scorn upon their folly waits.

Then take in hand thy lyre,
  Strike in thy proper strain;
With Japhet's line, aspire
Sol's chariot for new fire,
  To give the world again:
Who aided him will thee, the issue of Jove's brain.

And since our dainty age
  Cannot endure reproof,
Make not thyself a page
To that strumpet the Stage,
  But sing high and aloof,
Safe from the wolf's black jaw, and the dull ass's hoof.

216          *The Dream*

OR scorn or pity on me take,
I must the true relation make,
     I am undone tonight;
   Love, in a subtle dream disguised,
    Hath both my heart and me surprised,
Whom never yet he durst attempt awake;
Nor will he tell me for whose sake
     He did me the delight,
        Or spite,
  But leaves me to enquire
  In all my wild desire,
    Of sleep again, who was his aid;
    And sleep so guilty and afraid
As since he dares not come within my sight.


217   *To the Immortal Memory and Friendship of that*
*Noble Pair, Sir Lucius Cary and*
*Sir Henry Morison.*

### I. i

BRAVE infant of Saguntum, clear
Thy coming forth in that great year,
When the prodigious Hannibal did crown
His rage with razing your immortal town.
Thou, looking then about,
E'er thou wert half got out,
Wise child, didst hastily return
And mad'st thy mother's womb thine urn.
How summed a circle didst thou leave mankind
Of deepest lore, could we the centre find!

### I. ii

Did wiser Nature draw thee back
From out the horror of that sack?
Where shame, faith, honour, and regard of right
Lay trampled on; the deeds of death and night

Urged, hurried forth, and hurled
Upon the affrighted world;
Sword, fire, and famine, with fell fury met,
And all on utmost ruin set;
As, could they but life's miseries foresee,
No doubt all infants would return like thee.

### I. iii

For what is life, if measured by the space,
Not by the act?
Or maskèd man, if valued by his face,
Above his fact?
Here's one out-lived his peers,
And told forth fourscore years;
He vexèd time, and busied the whole State,
Troubled both foes and friends;
But ever to no ends:
What did this stirrer but die late?
How well at twenty had he fallen or stood!
For three of his fourscore he did no good.

### II. i

He entered well, by virtuous parts,
Got up and thrived with honest arts:
He purchased friends and fame and honours then,
And had his noble name advanced with men;
But, weary of that flight,
He stooped in all men's sight
To sordid flatteries, acts of strife,
And sunk in that dead sea of life
So deep as he did then death's waters sup;
But that the cork of Title buoyed him up.

### II. ii

Alas, but Morison fell young:
He never fell, thou fall'st, my tongue.
He stood, a soldier to the last right end,
A perfect patriot, and a noble friend,
But most, a virtuous son.
All offices were done

By him, so ample, full, and round,
In weight, in measure, number, sound,
As, though his age imperfect might appear,
His life was of humanity the sphere.

## II. iii

Go now, and tell out days summed up with fears,
And make them years;
Produce thy mass of miseries on the stage,
To swell thine age;
Repeat of things a throng,
To shew thou hast been long,
Not lived; for life doth her great actions spell
By what was done and wrought
In season, and so brought
To light: her measures are—how well
Each syllable answered, and was formed, how fair:
These make the lines of life, and that's her air.

## III. i

It is not growing like a tree
In bulk, doth make man better be;
Or standing long an oak, three hundred year,
To fall a log at last, dry, bald, and sere:
A lily of a day
Is fairer far in May,
Although it fall and die that night,
It was the plant and flower of light.
In small proportions we just beauty see,
And in short measures life may perfect be.

## III. ii

Call, noble Lucius, then for wine,
And let thy looks with gladness shine:
Accept this garland, plant it on thy head,
And think, nay, know, thy Morison's not dead.
He leaped the present age,
Possessed with holy rage,
To see that bright eternal Day,
Of which we priests and poets say
Such truths as we expect for happy men,
And there he lives with memory; and Ben

### III. iii

Jonson, who sung this of him e'er he went
Himself to rest,
Or taste a part of that full joy he meant
To have expressed,
In this bright Asterism:
Where it were friendship's schism
(Were not his Lucius long with us to tarry)
To separate these twi-
Lights, the Dioscuri,
And keep the one half from his Harry.
But fate doth so alternate the design,
Whilst that in heaven, this light on earth must shine.

### IV. i

And shine as you exalted are!
Two names of friendship, but one star:
Of hearts the union: and those not by chance
Made, or indentured, or leased out to advance
The profits for a time.
No pleasures vain did chime,
Of rhymes, or riots, at your feasts,
Orgies of drink or feigned protests;
But simple love of greatness and of good,
That knits brave minds and manners more than blood.

### IV. ii

This made you first to know the Why
You liked, then after, to apply
That liking; and approach so one the t'other,
Till either grew a portion of the other:
Each stylèd by his end
The copy of his friend.
You lived to be the great surnames
And titles by which all made claims
Unto the Virtue—nothing perfect done
But as a Cary or a Morison.

### IV. iii

And such a force the fair example had,
  As they that saw
The good, and durst not practise it, were glad
  That such a law
Was left yet to mankind;
  Where they might read, and find
Friendship in deed was written, not in words:
  And with the heart, not pen,
  Of two so early men,
Whose lines her rolls were, and records;
Who, e'er the first down bloomèd on the chin,
Had sowed these fruits and got the harvest in.

218                          *Death and Love*

Though I am young, and cannot tell
    Either what Death or Love is well,
Yet I have heard they both bear darts,
    And both do aim at human hearts;
And then again I have been told
    Love wounds with heat, as Death with cold;
So that I fear they do but bring
    Extremes to touch, and mean one thing.

As in a ruin, we it call
    One thing to be blown up or fall;
Or to our end like way may have,
    By a flash of lightning or a wave:
So Love's inflamèd shaft or brand
    May kill as soon as Death's cold hand;
Except Love's fires the virtue have
    To fright the frost out of the grave.

219 *To the Memory of my Beloved*
*Mr. William Shakespeare*

I, THEREFORE, will begin. Soul of the Age!
    The applause, delight, the wonder of our Stage!
My Shakespeare, rise; I will not lodge thee by
    Chaucer, or Spenser, or bid Beaumont lie
A little further, to make thee a room:
    Thou art a monument, without a tomb,
And art alive still, while thy book doth live,
    And we have wits to read and praise to give.
That I not mix thee so, my brain excuses;
    I mean with great, but disproportioned Muses:
For, if I thought my judgement were of years,
    I should commit thee surely with thy peers,
And tell how far thou didst our Lyly out-shine,
    Or sporting Kyd, or Marlowe's mighty line.
And though thou hadst small Latin and less Greek,
    From thence to honour thee, I would not seek
For names; but call forth thundering Æschylus,
    Euripides, and Sophocles to us,
Paccuvius, Accius, him of Cordova dead,
    To life again, to hear thy buskin tread,
And shake a stage; or, when thy socks were on,
    Leave thee alone, for the comparison
Of all that insolent Greece or haughty Rome
    Sent forth, or since did from their ashes come.
Triumph, my Britain, thou hast one to show
    To whom all scenes of Europe homage owe.
He was not of an age but for all time!
    And all the Muses still were in their prime
When, like Apollo, he came forth to warm
    Our ears, or, like a Mercury, to charm!
Nature herself was proud of his designs,
    And joyed to wear the dressing of his lines!
Which were so richly spun and woven so fit
    As, since, she will vouchsafe no other wit.
The merry Greek, tart Aristophanes,
    Neat Terence, witty Plautus, now not please,

But antiquated and deserted lie
  As they were not of Nature's family.
Yet must I not give Nature all: thy Art,
  My gentle Shakespeare, must enjoy a part.
For though the poet's matter Nature be,
  His Art doth give the fashion. And that he
Who casts to write a living line must sweat,
  (Such as thine are) and strike the second heat
Upon the Muses' anvil: turn the same
  (And himself with it) that he thinks to frame;
Or for the laurel he may gain a scorn,
  For a good poet's made as well as born.
And such wert thou. . . .

# RICHARD BARNFIELD

## 1574–1627

220                 *Philomel*

As it fell upon a day
In the merry month of May,
Sitting in a pleasant shade
Which a grove of myrtles made,
Beasts did leap and birds did sing,
Trees did grow and plants did spring;
Every thing did banish moan
Save the nightingale alone.
She, poor bird, as all forlorn,
Leaned her breast up-till a thorn,
And there sung the dolefullest ditty,
That to hear it was great pity.
*Fie, fie, fie*, now would she cry,
*Teru, teru*, by and by,
That to hear her so complain
Scarce I could from tears refrain;
For her griefs so lively shown
Made me think upon mine own.
Ah! thought I, thou mourn'st in vain,
None takes pity on thy pain;

Senseless trees, they cannot hear thee,
Ruthless beasts, they will not cheer thee;
King Pandion, he is dead,
All thy friends are lapped in lead;
All thy fellow birds do sing
Careless of thy sorrowing. . . .

# JOHN FLETCHER

## 1579–1625

221

## *Hymn to Pan*

SING his praises that doth keep
   Our flocks from harm,
Pan, the father of our sheep;
   And arm in arm
Tread we softly in a round,
Whilst the hollow neighbouring ground
Fills the music with her sound.

Pan, O great god Pan, to thee
   Thus do we sing!
Thou that keep'st us chaste and free
   As the young spring:
Ever be thy honour spoke
From that place the morn is broke
To that place day doth unyoke!

222

## *Aspatia's Song*

LAY a garland on my hearse of the dismal yew;
Maidens, willow branches bear; say I died true:
My love was false, but I was firm from my hour of birth;
Upon my buried body lay lightly, gentle earth.

223                    *Away, Delights*

AWAY, delights! go seek some other dwelling,
              For I must die.
Farewell, false love! thy tongue is ever telling
              Lie after lie.
For ever let me rest now from thy smarts;
              Alas, for pity go
              And fire their hearts
That have been hard to thee! Mine was not so.

Never again deluding love shall know me,
              For I will die;
And all those griefs that think to overgrow me
              Shall be as I:
For ever will I sleep, while poor maids cry—
              'Alas, for pity stay,
              And let us die
With thee! Men cannot mock us in the clay.'


224                    *Love's Emblems*

NOW the lusty spring is seen;
       Golden yellow, gaudy blue,
       Daintily invite the view:
Everywhere on every green
Roses blushing as they blow
       And enticing men to pull,
Lilies whiter than the snow,
       Woodbines of sweet honey full:
              All love's emblems, and all cry,
              'Ladies, if not plucked, we die.'

Yet the lusty spring hath stayed;
       Blushing red and purest white
       Daintily to love invite
Every woman, every maid:

Cherries kissing as they grow,
  And inviting men to taste,
Apples even ripe below,
  Winding gently to the waist:
    All love's emblems, and all cry,
    'Ladies, if not plucked, we die.'

225                    *Hear, Ye Ladies*

HEAR, ye ladies that despise
  What the mighty Love has done;
Fear examples and be wise:
  Fair Callisto was a nun;
Leda, sailing on the stream
  To deceive the hopes of man,
Love accounting but a dream,
  Doted on a silver swan;
    Danaë, in a brazen tower,
    Where no love was, loved a shower.

Hear, ye ladies that are coy,
  What the mighty Love can do;
Fear the fierceness of the boy:
  The chaste Moon he makes to woo;
Vesta, kindling holy fires,
  Circled round about with spies,
Never dreaming loose desires,
  Doting at the altar dies;
    Ilion, in a short hour, higher
    He can build, and once more fire.

# JOHN WEBSTER
?1580–?1625

226                          *A Dirge*

CALL for the robin-redbreast and the wren,
Since o'er shady groves they hover,
And with leaves and flowers do cover
The friendless bodies of unburied men.
Call unto his funeral dole
The ant, the field-mouse, and the mole,
To rear him hillocks that shall keep him warm,
And (when gay tombs are robbed) sustain no harm;
But keep the wolf far thence, that's foe to men,
For with his nails he'll dig them up again.

227      *The Shrouding of the Duchess of Malfi*

HARK! now everything is still,
The screech-owl and the whistler shrill,
Call upon our dame aloud,
And bid her quickly don her shroud!
Much you had of land and rent;
Your length in clay's now competent:
A long war disturbed your mind;
Here your perfect peace is signed.
Of what is't fools make such vain keeping?
Sin their conception, their birth weeping,
Their life a general mist of error,
Their death a hideous storm of terror.
Strew your hair with powders sweet,
Don clean linen, bathe your feet,
And—the foul fiend more to check—
A crucifix let bless your neck:
'Tis now full tide 'tween night and day;
End your groan and come away.

228 *Vanitas Vanitatum*

ALL the flowers of the spring
Meet to perfume our burying;
These have but their growing prime,
And man does flourish but his time:
Survey our progress from our birth—
We are set, we grow, we turn to earth.
Courts adieu, and all delights,
All bewitching appetites!
Sweetest breath and clearest eye
Like perfumes go out and die;
And consequently this is done
As shadows wait upon the sun.
Vain the ambition of kings
Who seek by trophies and dead things
To leave a living name behind,
And weave but nets to catch the wind.

# RICHARD CORBET
## 1582–1635

229 *The Fairies' Farewell*

FAREWELL, rewards and Fairies,
  Good housewives now may say,
For now foul sluts in dairies
  Do fare as well as they;
And though they sweep their hearths no less
  Than maids were wont to do,
Yet who of late for cleanliness
  Finds sixpence in her shoe?

Lament, lament, old Abbies,
  The fairies' lost command;
They did but change priests' babies,
  But some have changed your land;

And all your children sprung from thence
   Are now grown Puritans,
Who live as changelings ever since
   For love of your domains.

At morning and at evening both
   You merry were and glad,
So little care of sleep or sloth
   These pretty ladies had.
When Tom came home from labour,
   Or Ciss to milking rose,
Then merrily, merrily went their tabor,
   And nimbly went their toes.

Witness those rings and roundelays
   Of theirs, which yet remain,
Were footed in Queen Mary's days
   On many a grassy plain;
But since of late Elizabeth,
   And later James, came in
They never danced on any heath
   As when the time hath been.

By which we note the Fairies
   Were of the old profession;
Their songs were Ave Marys,
   Their dances were procession.
But now, alas, they all are dead,
   Or gone beyond the seas,
Or farther for Religion fled,
   Or else they take their ease.

A tell-tale in their company
   They never could endure,
And whoso kept not secretly
   Their mirth, was punished sure.
It was a just and Christian deed
   To pinch such black and blue:
O, how the Common wealth doth need
   Such Justices as you.

Now they have left our quarters
 A Register they have
Who looketh to their Charters,
 A man both wise and grave;
An hundred of their merry pranks
 By one that I could name
Are kept in store, con twenty thanks
 To William for the same.

I marvel who his cloak would turn
 When Puck had led him round,
Or where those walking fires would burn,
 Where Cureton would be found;
How Broker would appear to be
 For whom this Age doth mourn;
But that their spirits live in thee,
 In thee, old William Chourne.

To William Chourne of Staffordshire
 Give laud and praises due,
Who every meal can mend your cheer
 With tales both old and true.
To William all give audience,
 And pray ye for his noddle,
For all the Fairies' evidence
 Were lost if that were addle.


# PHINEAS FLETCHER

## 1582–1650

230    *'Drop, Drop, Slow Tears'*

DROP, drop, slow tears
 and bathe those beauteous feet,
Which brought from heaven
 the news and Prince of peace:
Cease not, wet eyes,
 his mercies to entreat;
To cry for vengeance
 sin doth never cease:

In your deep floods
    drown all my faults and fears;
Nor let his eye
    see sin, but through my tears.


# LORD HERBERT OF CHERBURY

## 1583–1648

231                    *Elegy over a Tomb*

MUST I then see, alas! eternal night
    Sitting upon those fairest eyes,
And closing all those beams, which once did rise
        So radiant and bright,
That light and heat in them to us did prove
        Knowledge and Love?

Oh, if you did delight no more to stay
    Upon this low and earthly stage,
But rather chose an endless heritage,
        Tell us at least, we pray,
Where all the beauties that those ashes owed
        Are now bestowed?

Doth the sun now his light with yours renew?
    Have waves the curling of your hair?
Did you restore unto the sky and air
        The red, and white, and blue?
Have you vouchsafed to flowers since your death
        That sweetest breath?

Had not Heaven's lights else in their houses slept,
    Or to some private life retired?
Must not the sky and air have else conspired?
        And in their regions wept?
Must not each flower else the earth could breed
        Have been a weed?

But thus enriched may we not yield some cause
   Why they themselves lament no more?
That must have changed the course they held before,
    And broke their proper laws,
Had not your beauties given this second birth
      To Heaven and Earth?

Tell us—for oracles must still ascend,
   For those that crave them at your tomb—
Tell us, where are those beauties now become,
    And what they now intend:
Tell us, alas, that cannot tell our grief,
      Or hope relief.

232                  *To his Watch*
               *When he could not sleep*

Uncessant minutes, whilst you move you tell
   The time that tells our life, which though it run
   Never so fast or far, your new begun
Short steps shall overtake; for though life well

May 'scape his own account, it shall not yours;
   You are Death's auditors, that both divide
And sum what ere that life inspired endures
   Past a beginning, and through you we bide

THE DOOM of Fate, whose unrecalled decree
   You date, bring, execute; making what's new,
   Ill and good, old, for as we die in you,
You die in Time, Time in Eternity.

233             *Ode upon a Question Moved:*
      *Whether Love Should Continue Forever?*

Having interred her Infant-birth,
   The watery ground that late did mourn
   Was strewed with flowers for the return
Of the wished Bridegroom of the earth.

The well accorded birds did sing
   Their hymns unto the pleasant time,
   And in a sweet consorted chime
Did welcome in the cheerful Spring.

To which soft whistles of the wind,
   And warbling murmurs of a brook,
   And varied notes of leaves that shook,
An harmony of parts did bind.

While doubling joy unto each other,
   All in so rare consent was shown,
   No happiness that came alone,
Nor pleasure that was not another.

When with a love none can express,
   That mutually happy pair,
   Melander and Celinda fair,
The season with their loves did bless.

Walking thus towards a pleasant grove,
   Which did, it seemed, in new delight
   The pleasures of the time unite
To give a triumph to their love,

They stayed at last, and on the grass
   Reposèd so, as o'er his breast
   She bowed her gracious head to rest,
Such a weight as no burden was.

While over either's compassed waist
   Their folded arms were so composed
   As if in straightest bonds enclosed
They suffered for joys they did taste.

Long their fixed eyes to Heaven bent
   Unchangèd, they did never move,
   As if so great and pure a love
No glass but it could represent.

When with a sweet, though troubled, look
   She first brake silence, saying, 'Dear friend,
   O that our love might take no end,
Or never had beginning took!

'I speak not this with a false heart,'
  (Wherewith his hand she gently strained)
  'Or that would change a love maintained
With so much faith on either part.

'Nay, I protest, though Death with his
  Worst counsel should divide us here,
  His terrors could not make me fear
To come where your loved presence is.

'Only if love's fire with the breath
  Of life be kindled, I doubt
  With our last air 'twill be breathed out,
And quenchèd with the cold of death.

'That if affection be a line,
  Which is closed up in our last hour;
  O how 'twould grieve me, any power
Could force so dear a love as mine!'

She scarce had done when his shut eyes
  An inward joy did represent,
  To hear Celinda thus intent
To a love he so much did prize.

Then with a look, it seemed, denied
  All earthly power but hers, yet so
  As if to her breath he did owe
This borrowed life, he thus replied:

'O you, wherein they say souls rest
  Till they descend, pure heavenly fires,
  Shall lustful and corrupt desires
With your immortal seed be blest?

'And shall our love, so far beyond
  That low and dying appetite,
  And which so chaste desires unite,
Not hold in an eternal bond?

'Is it because we should decline,
  And wholly from our thoughts exclude,
  Objects that may the sense delude,
And study only the Divine?

'No, sure; for if none can ascend
   Even to the visible degree
   Of things created, how should we
The invisible comprehend?

'Or rather since that Power expressed
   His greatness in his works alone,
   Being here best in his creatures known,
Why is he not loved in them best?

'But is't not true, which you pretend,
   That since our love and knowledge here
   Only as parts of life appear,
So they with it should take their end?

'O no, Beloved, I am most sure,
   Those virtuous habits we acquire,
   As being with the soul entire,
Must with it evermore endure.

'For if where sins and vice reside
   We find so foul a guilt remain,
   As never dying in his stain,
Still punished in the soul doth bide;

'Much more that true and real joy,
   Which in a virtuous love is found,
   Must be more solid in its ground
Than Fate or Death can e'er destroy.

'Else should our souls in vain elect,
   And vainer yet were Heaven's laws,
   When to an everlasting Cause
They gave a perishing Effect.

'Nor here on earth then, nor above,
   Our good affection can impair;
   For where God doth admit the fair,
Think you that he excludeth Love?

'These eyes again then, eyes shall see,
　And hands again these hands enfold,
　And all chaste pleasures can be told
Shall with us everlasting be.

'For if no use of sense remain
　When bodies once this life forsake,
　Or they could no delight partake,
Why should they ever rise again?

'And if every imperfect mind
　Make love the end of knowledge here,
　How perfect will our love be, where
All imperfection is refined?

'Let then no doubt, Celinda, touch,
　Much less your fairest mind invade;
　Were not our souls immortal made,
Our equal loves can make them such.

'So when one wing can make no way,
　Two joinèd can themselves dilate,
　So can two persons propagate,
When singly either would decay.

'So when from hence we shall be gone
　And be no more, nor you, nor I,
　As one another's mystery,
Each shall be both, yet both but one.'

This said, in her up-lifted face,
　Her eyes, which did that beauty crown,
　Were like two stars, that having fallen down
Look up again to find their place:

While such a moveless silent peace
　Did seize on their becalmèd sense,
　One would have thought some Influence
Their ravished spirits did possess.

# SIR JOHN BEAUMONT
## 1583–1627

234     *Of My Dear Son, Gervase Beaumont*

CAN I, who have for others oft compiled
The songs of Death, forget my sweetest child,
Which, like a flower crushed, with a blast is dead,
And ere full time hangs down his smiling head,
Expecting with clear hope to live anew
Among the angels, fed with heavenly dew?
We have this sign of joy, that many days,
While on the earth his struggling spirit stays,
The name of Jesus in his mouth contains
His only food, his sleep, his ease from pains.
O may that sound be rooted in my mind,
Of which in him such strong effect I find.
Dear Lord, receive my son, whose winning love
To me was like a friendship, far above
The course of nature or his tender age,
Whose looks could all my bitter griefs assuage;
Let his pure soul ordained seven years to be
In that frail body, which was part of me,
Remain my pledge in Heaven, as sent to show
How to this port at every step I go.


# AURELIAN TOWNSHEND
## ?1583–?1651

235     *A Dialogue betwixt Time and a Pilgrim*

*Pilgrim.* Agèd man, that mows these fields.
*Time.*     Pilgrim, speak; what is thy will?
*Pilgrim.* Whose soil is this, that such sweet pasture yields?
       Or who art thou, whose foot stands never still?
       Or where am I? *Time.* In love.
*Pilgrim.* His Lordship lies above.

*Time.*     Yes, and below, and round about
      Wherein all sorts of flowers are growing
    Which, as the early Spring puts out,
      Time falls as fast a-mowing.

*Pilgrim.* If thou art Time, these flowers have lives,
      And then I fear
    Under some lily she I love
      May now be growing there.

*Time.*     And in some thistle or some spire of grass
    My scythe thy stalk before hers come may pass.

*Pilgrim.* Wilt thou provide it may? *Time.* No.

*Pilgrim.* Allege the cause.

*Time.*     Because Time cannot alter but obey Fate's laws.

*Chorus.* Then happy those whom Fate, that is the stronger,
    Together twists their threads, and yet draws hers the longer.

# ?FRANCIS BEAUMONT

## ?1584–1616

236       *On the Tombs in Westminster Abbey*

MORTALITY, behold, and fear,
What a change of flesh is here!
Think how many royal bones
Sleep within this heap of stones,
Hence removed from beds of ease,
Dainty fare, and what might please,
Fretted roofs, and costly shows,
To a roof that flats the nose:
Which proclaims all flesh is grass;
How the world's fair glories pass;
That there is no trust in health,
In youth, in age, in greatness, wealth;
For if such could have reprieved
Those had been immortal lived.
Know from this the world's a snare,
How that greatness is but care,
How all pleasures are but pain,
And how short they do remain:

For here they lie had realms and lands,
That now want strength to stir their hands;
Where from their pulpits sealed with dust
They preach: 'In greatness is no trust'.
Here's an acre sown indeed
With the richest royalest seed,
That the earth did e'er suck in
Since the first man died for sin.
Here the bones of birth have cried,
'Though Gods they were, as men they died'.
Here are sands (ignoble things)
Dropped from the ruined sides of kings;
With whom the poor man's earth being shown
The difference is not easily known.
Here's a world of pomp and state,
Forgotten, dead, disconsolate;
Think, then, this scythe that mows down kings
Exempts no meaner mortal things.
Then bid the wanton lady tread
Amid these mazes of the dead;
And these truly understood
More shall cool and quench the blood
Than her many sports aday,
And her nightly wanton play.
Bid her paint till day of doom,
To this favour she must come.
Bid the merchant gather wealth,
The usurer exact by stealth,
The proud man beat it from his thought,
Yet to this shape all must be brought.

# WILLIAM DRUMMOND OF HAWTHORNDEN

### 1585–1649

237 *Madrigal*

LIKE the Idalian queen,
Her hair about her eyne,
With neck and breast's ripe apples to be seen,
    At first glance of the morn
In Cyprus' gardens gathering those fair flowers
    Which of her blood were born,
I saw, but fainting saw, my paramours.
The Graces naked danced about the place,
    The winds and trees amazed
    With silence on her gazed,
The flowers did smile, like those upon her face;
And as their aspen stalks those fingers band,
    That she might read my case,
A hyacinth I wished me in her hand.

238 *Inexorable*

MY thoughts hold mortal strife;
    I do detest my life,
    And with lamenting cries,
    Peace to my soul to bring,
Oft call that prince which here doth monarchise:
    —But he, grim-grinning King,
Who caitiffs scorns, and doth the blest surprise,
Late having decked with beauty's rose his tomb,
Disdains to crop a weed, and will not come.

239             *The World a Hunt*

THE World a-hunting is:
The prey poor Man, the Nimrod fierce is Death;
His speedy greyhounds are
Lust, Sickness, Envy, Care,
Strife that ne'er falls amiss,
With all those ills which haunt us while we breathe.
Now if by chance we fly
Of these the eager chase,
Old Age with stealing pace
Casts up his nets, and there we panting die.


240             *Saint John Baptist*

THE last and greatest Herald of Heaven's King,
   Girt with rough skins, hies to the deserts wild,
Among that savage brood the woods forth bring,
   Which he than man more harmless found and mild.
His food was locusts, and what young doth spring
   With honey that from virgin hives distilled;
Parched body, hollow eyes, some uncouth thing
   Made him appear, long since from earth exiled.
There burst he forth: 'All ye, whose hopes rely
   On God, with me amidst these deserts mourn;
   Repent, repent, and from old errors turn!'
Who listened to his voice, obeyed his cry?
     Only the echoes, which he made relent,
     Rung from their marble caves 'Repent! Repent!'

# GILES FLETCHER
## ?1588–1623

241                          *The Celestial City*

IN midst of this City celestial
Where the eternal Temple should have rose,
Lightened the Idea Beatifical:
End and beginning of each thing that grows,
Whose self no end, nor yet beginning knows,
  That hath no eyes to see, nor ears to hear,
  Yet sees and hears, and is all eye, all ear,
That nowhere is contained, and yet is everywhere.

Changer of all things, yet immutable,
Before, and after all, the first, and last,
That moving all, is yet immoveable,
Great without quantity, in whose forecast,
Things past are present, things to come are past,
  Swift without motion, to whose open eye
  The hearts of wicked men unbreasted lie,
At once absent and present to them, far and nigh.

It is no flaming lustre made of light,
No sweet consent or well-timed harmony,
Ambrosia for to feast the appetite,
Or flowery odour mixed with spicery,
No soft embrace or pleasure bodily;
  And yet it is a kind of inward feast,
  A harmony that sounds within the breast,
An odour, light, embrace, in which the soul doth rest,

A heavenly feast no hunger can consume,
A light unseen, yet shines in every place,
A sound no time can steal, a sweet perfume
No winds can scatter, an entire embrace
That no satiety can e'er unlace.
  Ingraced into so high a favour there,
  The saints with their beau-peers whole worlds outwear,
And things unseen do see, and things unheard do hear.

# JOHN FORD
?1586–1639

242 *Love's Martyrs*

OH no more, no more! too late
  Sighs are spent; the burning tapers
Of a life as chaste as Fate,
  Pure as are unwritten papers,
  Are burnt out; no heat, no light
  Now remains; 'tis ever night.
Love is dead; let lovers' eyes,
  Locked in endless dreams,
  The extremes of all extremes,
Ope no more, for now Love dies.
  Now Love dies, implying
Love's Martyrs must be ever, ever dying.

# SIR FRANCIS KYNASTON
1587–1642

243 *To Cynthia : On Concealment of her Beauty*

DO not conceal thy radiant eyes,
The star-light of serenest skies,
Lest wanting of their heavenly light,
They turn to Chaos' endless night.

Do not conceal those tresses fair,
The silken snares of thy curled hair,
Lest finding neither gold, nor ore,
The curious silk-worm work no more.

Do not conceal those breasts of thine,
More snow white than the Apennine,
Lest if there be like cold or frost,
The lily be forever lost.

Do not conceal that fragrant scent,
Thy breath, which to all flowers hath lent
Perfumes, lest it being suppressed,
No spices grow in all the East.

Do not conceal thy heavenly voice,
Which makes the hearts of Gods rejoice,
Lest Music hearing no such thing,
The nightingale forget to sing.

Do not conceal, nor yet eclipse
Thy pearly teeth with coral lips,
Lest that the seas cease to bring forth
Gems, which from thee have all their worth.

Do not conceal no beauty, grace,
That's either in thy mind or face,
Lest virtue overcome by vice
Make men believe no Paradise.


# GEORGE WITHER

## 1588–1667

244
### I Loved a Lass

I LOVED a lass, a fair one,
  As fair as e'er was seen;
She was indeed a rare one,
  Another Sheba queen.
But, fool as then I was,
  I thought she loved me too,
But now, alas, she's left me,
  *Falero, lero, loo.*

Her hair like gold did glister,
  Each eye was like a star;
She did surpass her sister,
  Which passed all others far.
She would me 'honey' call,
  She'd, O! she'd kiss me too;
But now, alas, she's left me,
  *Falero, lero, loo.*

# GEORGE WITHER

In summer time to Medley
  My love and I would go;
The boatmen there stood ready,
  My love and I to row.
For cream there would we call,
  For cakes, and for prunes too;
But now, alas, she's left me,
  *Falero, lero, loo.*

Many a merry meeting
  My love and I have had;
She was my only sweeting,
  She made my heart full glad,
The tears stood in her eyes,
  Like to the morning dew;
But now, alas, she's left me,
  *Falero, lero, loo.*

And as abroad we walkèd,
  As lovers' fashion is,
Oft as we sweetly talkèd
  The sun should steal a kiss,
The wind upon her lips
  Likewise most sweetly blew;
But now, alas, she's left me,
  *Falero, lero, loo.*

Her cheeks were like the cherry,
  Her skin as white as snow;
When she was blithe and merry,
  She angel-like did show.
Her waist exceeding small,
  The fives did fit her shoe;
But now, alas, she's left me,
  *Falero, lero, loo.*

In summer time or winter
  She had her heart's desire;
I still did scorn to stint her
  From sugar, sack, or fire;
The world went round about,
  No cares we ever knew;
But now, alas, she's left me,
  *Falero, lero. loo.*

As we walked home together
 At midnight through the town,
To keep away the weather
 O'er her I'd cast my gown.
No cold my love should feel,
 Whate'er the heavens could do;
But now, alas, she's left me,
 *Falero, lero, loo.*

Like doves we would be billing,
 And clip and kiss so fast,
Yet she would be unwilling
 That I should kiss the last;
They're Judas' kisses now,
 Since that they proved untrue.
For now, alas, she's left me,
 *Falero, lero, loo.*

To maidens' vows and swearing
 Henceforth no credit give,
You may give them the hearing
 But never them believe.
They are as false as fair,
 Unconstant, frail, untrue;
For mine, alas, has left me,
 *Falero, lero, loo.*

'Twas I that paid for all things,
 'Twas others drank the wine,
I cannot now recall things,
 Live but a fool to pine.
'Twas I that beat the bush,
 The bird to others flew,
For she, alas, hath left me,
 *Falero, lero, loo.*

If ever that Dame Nature,
 For this false lover's sake,
Another pleasing creature
 Like unto her would make,
Let her remember this,
 To make the other true,
For this, alas, hath left me,
 *Falero, lero, loo.*

236

## GEORGE WITHER

No riches now can raise me,
  No want make me despair,
No misery amaze me,
  Nor yet for want I care;
I have lost a world itself,
  My earthly heaven, adieu,
Since she, alas, hath left me,
  *Falero, lero, loo.*


245                    *A Lover's Resolution*

SHALL I, wasting in despair,
Die because a woman's fair?
Or make pale my cheeks with care
'Cause another's rosy are?
Be she fairer than the day,
Or the flowery meads in May,
  If she be not so to me,
  What care I how fair she be?

Should my heart be grieved or pined
'Cause I see a woman kind?
Or a well disposèd nature
Joinèd with a lovely feature?
Be she meeker, kinder, than
Turtle-dove or pelican,
  If she be not so to me,
  What care I how kind she be?

Shall a woman's virtues move
Me to perish for her love?
Or her well-deserving known
Make me quite forget mine own?
Be she with that goodness blest
Which may gain her name of Best,
  If she be not such to me,
  What care I how good she be?

'Cause her fortune seems too high,
Shall I play the fool and die?
Those that bear a noble mind,
Where they want of riches find,

Think what with them they would do
That without them dare to woo.
   And unless that mind I see,
   What care I though great she be?

Great, or good, or kind, or fair,
I will ne'er the more despair;
If she love me, this believe,
I will die ere she shall grieve.
If she slight me when I woo,
I can scorn and let her go.
   For if she be not for me,
   What care I for whom she be?

# WILLIAM BROWNE OF TAVISTOCK

## 1591–1643

246       *The Sirens' Song*

STEER, hither steer your wingèd pines,
   All beaten mariners!
Here lie Love's undiscovered mines,
   A prey to passengers;
Perfumes far sweeter than the best
Which make the Phoenix' urn and nest.
   Fear not your ships,
Nor any to oppose you save our lips;
   But come on shore,
Where no joy dies till Love hath gotten more.

For swelling waves our panting breasts,
   Where never storms arise,
Exchange, and be awhile our guests:
   For stars gaze on our eyes.
The compass Love shall hourly sing,
And as he goes about the ring,
   We will not miss
To tell each point he nameth with a kiss.
   Then come on shore,
Where no joy dies till Love hath gotten more.

### Epitaphs

(i)

247      *In Obitum M.S. x° Maij, 1614*

MAY! Be thou never graced with birds that sing,
         Nor Flora's pride!
In thee all flowers and roses spring,
         Mine only died.

(ii)

248    *Epitaph on the Countess Dowager of Pembroke*

UNDERNEATH this sable hearse
Lies the subject of all verse;
Sidney's sister, Pembroke's mother:
Death, ere thou hast slain another
Fair and learned and good as she,
Time shall throw a dart at thee.

## ROBERT HERRICK
### 1591–1674

249      *When He would Have his Verses Read*

IN sober mornings do not thou rehearse
The holy incantation of a verse;
But when that men have both well drunk and fed,
Let my enchantments then be sung or read.
When laurel spurts i'the fire, and when the hearth
Smiles to itself and gilds the roof with mirth;
When up the Thyrse is raised, and when the sound
Of sacred Orgies flies around, around,
When the rose reigns, and locks with ointments shine,
Let rigid Cato read these lines of mine.

250 *Upon Julia's Voice*

So smooth, so sweet, so silvery, is thy voice
As, could they hear, the damned would make no noise,
But listen to thee (walking in thy chamber)
Melting melodious words to lutes of amber.


251 *Delight in Disorder*

A SWEET disorder in the dress
Kindles in clothes a wantonness:
A lawn about the shoulders thrown
Into a fine distraction:
An erring lace, which here and there
Enthrals the crimson stomacher:
A cuff neglectful, and thereby
Ribbands to flow confusedly:
A winning wave, deserving note,
In the tempestuous petticoat:
A careless shoe-string, in whose tie
I see a wild civility:
Do more bewitch me than when art
Is too precise in every part.


252 *To Dianeme*

SWEET, be not proud of those two eyes
Which starlike sparkle in their skies;
Nor be you proud that you can see
All hearts your captives, yours yet free;
Be you not proud of that rich hair
Which wantons with the love-sick air;
Whenas that ruby which you wear,
Sunk from the tip of your soft ear,
Will last to be a precious stone
When all your world of beauty's gone.

253 *Corinna's Going a-Maying*

GET up, get up for shame! the blooming morn
Upon her wings presents the god unshorn.
　　See how Aurora throws her fair
　　Fresh-quilted colours through the air:
　　Get up, sweet slug-a-bed, and see
　　The dew-bespangling herb and tree.
Each flower has wept, and bowed toward the east,
Above an hour since; yet you not drest,
　　Nay! not so much as out of bed?
　　When all the birds have matins said,
　　And sung their thankful hymns; 'tis sin,
　　Nay, profanation to keep in,
Whenas a thousand virgins on this day
Spring sooner than the lark to fetch in May.

Rise and put on your foliage, and be seen
To come forth, like the spring-time, fresh and green,
　　And sweet as Flora. Take no care
　　For jewels for your gown or hair:
　　Fear not; the leaves will strew
　　Gems in abundance upon you:
Besides, the childhood of the day has kept,
Against you come, some orient pearls unwept.
　　Come, and receive them while the light
　　Hangs on the dew-locks of the night:
　　And Titan on the eastern hill
　　Retires himself, or else stands still
Till you come forth. Wash, dress, be brief in praying:
Few beads are best when once we go a-Maying.

Come, my Corinna, come; and coming, mark
How each field turns a street, each street a park
　　Made green and trimmed with trees: see how
　　Devotion gives each house a bough
　　Or branch; each porch, each door, ere this,
　　An ark, a tabernacle is,
Made up of white-thorn neatly interwove,
As if here were those cooler shades of love.

Can such delights be in the street
And open fields, and we not see't?
Come, we'll abroad: and let's obey
The proclamation made for May,
And sin no more, as we have done, by staying;
But, my Corinna, come, let's go a-Maying.

There's not a budding boy or girl this day
But is got up and gone to bring in May.
    A deal of youth ere this is come
    Back, and with white-thorn laden home.
    Some have dispatched their cakes and cream,
    Before that we have left to dream:
And some have wept and wooed, and plighted troth,
And chose their priest, ere we can cast off sloth:
    Many a green-gown has been given;
    Many a kiss, both odd and even;
    Many a glance too has been sent
    From out the eye, love's firmament:
Many a jest told of the keys betraying
This night, and locks picked: yet we're not a-Maying!

Come, let us go, while we are in our prime,
And take the harmless folly of the time!
    We shall grow old apace, and die
    Before we know our liberty.
    Our life is short, and our days run
    As fast away as does the sun.
And as a vapour or a drop of rain,
Once lost, can ne'er be found again:
    So when or you or I are made
    A fable, song, or fleeting shade,
    All love, all liking, all delight
    Lies drowned with us in endless night.
Then, while time serves, and we are but decaying,
Come, my Corinna, come, let's go a-Maying.

254   *To the Virgins, to Make Much of Time*

> GATHER ye rosebuds while ye may,
>   Old Time is still a-flying:
> And this same flower that smiles to-day
>   To-morrow will be dying.
>
> The glorious lamp of heaven, the sun,
>   The higher he's a-getting,
> The sooner will his race be run,
>   And nearer he's to setting.
>
> That age is best which is the first,
>   When youth and blood are warmer;
> But being spent, the worse, and worst
>   Times still succeed the former.
>
> Then be not coy, but use your time,
>   And while ye may, go marry:
> For having lost but once your prime,
>   You may for ever tarry.

255   *A Meditation for His Mistress*

> You are a tulip seen today,
> But, dearest, of so short a stay
> That where you grew scarce man can say.
>
> You are a lovely July-flower,
> Yet one rude wind or ruffling shower
> Will force you hence, and in an hour.
>
> You are a sparkling rose i'th'bud,
> Yet lost ere that chaste flesh and blood
> Can shew where you or grew or stood.
>
> You are a full-spread fair-set vine,
> And can with tendrils love entwine,
> Yet dried ere you distill your wine.

You are like balm enclosèd well
In amber, or some crystal shell,
Yet lost ere you transfuse your smell.

You are a dainty violet,
Yet withered ere you can be set
Within the virgins' coronet.

You are the queen all flowers among,
But die you must, fair maid, ere long,
As he, the maker of this song.


256   *To Anthea, Who May Command Him Anything*

BID me to live, and I will live
    Thy Protestant to be;
Or bid me love, and I will give
    A loving heart to thee.

A heart as soft, a heart as kind,
    A heart as sound and free
As in the whole world thou canst find,
    That heart I'll give to thee.

Bid that heart stay, and it will stay
    To honour thy decree:
Or bid it languish quite away,
    And 't shall do so for thee.

Bid me to weep, and I will weep
    While I have eyes to see:
And, having none, yet I will keep
    A heart to weep for thee.

Bid me despair, and I'll despair
    Under that cypress-tree:
Or bid me die, and I will dare
    E'en death to die for thee.

Thou art my life, my love, my heart,
    The very eyes of me:
And hast command of every part
    To live and die for thee.

257 *To Meadows*

Ye have been fresh and green,
　Ye have been filled with flowers,
And ye the walks have been
　Where maids have spent their hours.

You have beheld how they
　With wicker arks did come
To kiss and bear away
　The richer cowslips home.

You've heard them sweetly sing,
　And seen them in a round:
Each virgin like a spring,
　With honeysuckles crowned.

But now we see none here
　Whose silvery feet did tread
And with dishevelled hair
　Adorned this smoother mead.

Like unthrifts, having spent
　Your stock and needy grown,
You're left here to lament
　Your poor estates, alone.


258 *To Daffodils*

Fair daffodils, we weep to see
　You haste away so soon;
As yet the early-rising sun
　Has not attained his noon.
　　　Stay, stay
　　　Until the hasting day
　　　Has run
　　　But to the evensong;
And, having prayed together, we
　Will go with you along.

We have short time to stay as you,
   We have as short a spring;
As quick a growth to meet decay,
   As you, or anything.
     We die
    As your hours do, and dry
     Away
    Like to the summer's rain;
Or as the pearls of morning's dew,
   Ne'er to be found again.

259       *To the Most Fair and Lovely Mistress*
             *Anne Soame, now Lady Abdie*

So smell those odours that do rise
From out the wealthy spiceries;
So smells the flower of blooming clove,
Or roses smothered in the stove;
So smells the air of spicèd wine,
Or essences of jessamine;
So smells the breath about the hives,
When well the work of honey thrives,
And all the busy factors come
Laden with wax and honey home;
So smell those neat and woven bowers,
All over-arched with orange flowers,
And almond blossoms, that do mix
To make rich these aromatics;
So smell those bracelets and those bands
Of amber chafed between the hands,
When thus enkindled they transpire
A noble perfume from the fire.
The wine of cherries, and to these,
The cooling breath of raspberries,
The smell of morning's milk and cream,
Butter of cowslips mixed with them,
Of roasted warden or baked pear,
These are not to be reckoned here;
Whenas the meanest part of her
Smells like the maiden-pomander.
Thus sweet she smells, or what can be
More liked by her, or loved by me.

260        *Upon Julia's Clothes*

WHENAS in silks my Julia goes,
Then, then, methinks, how sweetly flows
That liquefaction of her clothes!

Next, when I cast mine eyes and see
That brave vibration each way free,
—O how that glittering taketh me!

261      *Comfort to a Youth that had Lost his Love*

WHAT needs complaints,
When she a place
Has with the race
    Of saints?

In endless mirth
She thinks not on
What's said or done
    In Earth.

She sees no tears,
Or any tone
Of thy deep groan
    She hears:

Nor does she mind
Or think on't now
That ever thou
    Wast kind;

But changed above,
She likes not there,
As she did here,
    Thy love.

Forbear therefore,
And lull asleep
Thy woes, and weep
    No more.

# HENRY KING
## 1592–1669

## *Exequy upon His Wife*

ACCEPT, thou shrine of my dead saint,
Instead of dirges this complaint;
And for sweet flowers to crown thy hearse,
Receive a strew of weeping verse
From thy grieved friend, whom thou mightst see
Quite melted into tears for thee.
  Dear loss! since thy untimely fate
My task hath been to meditate
On thee, on thee! Thou art the book,
The library, whereon I look
Though almost blind. For thee, loved clay,
I languish out, not live, the day,
Using no other exercise
But what I practise with mine eyes.
By which wet glasses I find out
How lazily time creeps about
To one that mourns. This, only this,
My exercise and business is:
So I compute the weary hours
With sighs dissolvèd into showers.
  Nor wonder if my time go thus
Backward and most preposterous:
Thou hast benighted me. Thy set
This eve of blackness did beget,
Who wast my day (though overcast
Before thou hadst thy noon-tide past)
And I remember must in tears
Thou scarce hadst seen so many years
As day tells hours. By thy clear sun
My love and fortune first did run;
But thou wilt never more appear
Folded within my hemisphere,
Since both thy light and motion,
Like a fled star, is fallen and gone,
And 'twixt me and my soul's dear wish
The earth now interposèd is,

Which such a strange eclipse doth make
As ne'er was read in almanac.
  I could allow thee for a time
To darken me and my sad clime;
Were it a month, a year, or ten,
I would thy exile live till then;
And all that space my mirth adjourn,
So thou wouldst promise to return
And, putting off thy ashy shroud,
At length disperse this sorrow's cloud.
  But woe is me! the longest date
Too narrow is to calculate
These empty hopes. Never shall I
Be so much blest as to descry
A glimpse of thee, till that day come
Which shall the earth to cinders doom,
And a fierce fever must calcine
The body of this world, like thine,
My little world! That fit of fire
Once off, our bodies shall aspire
To our souls' bliss: then we shall rise,
And view ourselves with clearer eyes
In that calm region where no night
Can hide us from each other's sight.
  Meantime thou hast her, Earth: much good
May my harm do thee. Since it stood
With Heaven's will I might not call
Her longer mine, I give thee all
My short-lived right and interest
In her, whom living I loved best:
With a most free and bounteous grief,
I give thee what I could not keep.
Be kind to her, and prithee look
Thou write into thy Doomsday book
Each parcel of this rarity,
Which in thy casket shrined doth lie.
See that thou make thy reckoning straight,
And yield her back again by weight;
For thou must audit on thy trust
Each grain and atom of this dust,
As thou wilt answer him that lent,
Not gave thee, my dear monument.

So close the ground, and 'bout her shade
Black curtains draw: my bride is laid.
  Sleep on, my Love, in thy cold bed
Never to be disquieted.
My last good night! Thou wilt not wake
Till I thy fate shall overtake:
Till age, or grief, or sickness must
Marry my body to that dust
It so much loves; and fill the room
My heart keeps empty in thy tomb.
Stay for me there: I will not fail
To meet thee in that hollow vale.
And think not much of my delay;
I am already on the way,
And follow thee with all the speed
Desire can make, or sorrows breed.
Each minute is a short degree
And every hour a step towards thee.
At night when I betake to rest,
Next morn I rise nearer my west
Of life, almost by eight hours sail
Than when sleep breathed his drowsy gale.
  Thus from the sun my bottom steers,
And my day's compass downward bears.
Nor labour I to stem the tide
Through which to thee I swiftly glide.
  'Tis true, with shame and grief I yield;
Thou, like the van, first took'st the field
And gotten hast the victory
In thus adventuring to die
Before me, whose more years might crave
A just precedence in the grave.
But hark! my pulse, like a soft drum,
Beats my approach, tells thee I come;
And slow howe'er my marches be
I shall at last sit down by thee.
  The thought of this bids me go on
And wait my dissolution
With hope and comfort. Dear, (forgive
The crime) I am content to live
Divided, with but half a heart,
Till we shall meet and never part.

263 *Sic Vita*

LIKE to the falling of a star,
Or as the flights of eagles are,
Or like the fresh spring's gaudy hue,
Or silver drops of morning dew,
Or like a wind that chafes the flood,
Or bubbles which on water stood:
Even such is man, whose borrowed light
Is straight called in, and paid to night.

The wind blows out, the bubble dies;
The spring entombed in autumn lies;
The dew dries up, the star is shot;
The flight is past: and man forgot.


# FRANCIS QUARLES

## 1592–1644

264 *My Beloved is Mine and I am His*

EVEN like two little bank-dividing brooks,
    That wash the pebbles with their wanton streams,
And having ranged and searched a thousand nooks,
    Meet both at length in silver-breasted Thames
        Where in a greater current they conjoin:
So I my Best-Beloved's am, so he is mine.

Even so we met; and after long pursuit
    Even so we joined; we both became entire;
No need for either to renew a suit,
    For I was flax and he was flames of fire:
        Our firm united souls did more than twine,
So I my Best-Beloved's am, so he is mine.

If all those glittering monarchs that command
  The servile quarters of this earthly ball
Should tender in exchange their shares of land,
  I would not change my fortunes for them all:
    Their wealth is but a counter to my coin;
The world's but theirs, but my Beloved's mine.

Nay, more: if the fair Thespian ladies all
  Should heap together their diviner treasure,
That treasure should be deemed a price too small
  To buy a minute's lease of half my pleasure.
    'Tis not the sacred wealth of all the Nine
Can buy my heart from him, or his from being mine.

Nor time, nor place, nor chance, nor death can bow
  My least desires unto the least remove;
He's firmly mine by oath, I his by vow;
  He's mine by faith, and I am his by love;
    He's mine by water, I am his by wine;
Thus I my Best-Beloved's am, thus he is mine.

He is my altar, I his holy place;
  I am his guest, and he my living food;
I'm his by penitence, he mine by grace;
  I'm his by purchase, he is mine by blood;
    He's my supporting elm, and I his vine:
Thus I my Best-Beloved's am, thus he is mine.

He gives me wealth, I give him all my vows;
  I give him songs, he gives me length of days;
With wreaths of grace he crowns my conquering brows;
  And I his temples with a crown of praise,
    Which he accepts as an everlasting sign,
That I my Best-Beloved's am; that he is mine.

265                      *Epigram*

My soul, sit thou a patient looker-on;
Judge not the play before the play is done:
Her plot has many changes; every day
Speaks a new scene; the last act crowns the play.

GEORGE HERBERT
1593–1633

266                         *Redemption*

HAVING been tenant long to a rich Lord,
   Not thriving, I resolvèd to be bold,
And make a suit unto him, to afford
   A new small-rented lease, and cancel the old.
In heaven at his manor I him sought:
   They told me there that he was lately gone
About some land, which he had dearly bought
   Long since on earth, to take possession.
I straight returned, and knowing his great birth,
   Sought him accordingly in great resorts:
   In cities, theatres, gardens, parks, and courts.
At length I heard a ragged noise and mirth
     Of thieves and murderers: there I him espied,
     Who straight, *Your suit is granted*, said, and died.


267                         *Bitter-Sweet*

    AH my dear angry Lord,
    Since thou dost love, yet strike;
    Cast down, yet help afford;
    Sure I will do the like.

    I will complain, yet praise;
    I will bewail, approve;
    And all my sour-sweet days
    I will lament, and love.


268                         *Affliction*

WHEN first thou didst entice to thee my heart
        I thought the service brave:
So many joys I writ down for my part,
        Besides what I might have
Out of my stock of natural delights,
Augmented with thy gracious benefits.

I lookèd on thy furniture so fine,
    And made it fine to me:
Thy glorious household-stuff did me entwine
    And 'tice me unto thee.
Such stars I counted mine: both heaven and earth
Paid me my wages in a world of mirth.

What pleasures could I want, whose King I served
    Where joys my fellows were?
Thus argued into hopes, my thoughts reserved
    No place for grief or fear.
Therefore my sudden soul caught at the place,
And made her youth and fierceness seek thy face.

At first thou gav'st me milk and sweetnesses;
    I had my wish and way:
My days were strewed with flowers and happiness;
    There was no month but May.
But with my years sorrow did twist and grow,
And made a party unawares for woe.

My flesh began unto my soul in pain,
    'Sicknesses cleave my bones;
Consuming agues dwell in every vein,
    And tune my breath to groans.'
Sorrow was all my soul; I scarce believed,
Till grief did tell me roundly, that I lived.

When I got health, thou took'st away my life,
    And more; for my friends die:
My mirth and edge was lost; a blunted knife
    Was of more use than I.
Thus thin and lean, without a fence or friend,
I was blown through with every storm and wind.

Whereas my birth and spirit rather took
    The way that takes the town;
Thou didst betray me to a lingering book,
    And wrap me in a gown.
I was entangled in a world of strife,
Before I had the power to change my life.

Yet, for I threatened oft the siege to raise,
                Not simpering all mine age,
Thou often didst with academic praise
                Melt and dissolve my rage.
I took thy sweetened pill, till I came where
I could not go away, nor persevere.

Yet lest perchance I should too happy be
                In my unhappiness,
Turning my purge to food, thou throwest me
                Into more sicknesses.
Thus doth thy power cross-bias me, not making
Thine own gift good, yet me from my ways taking.

Now I am here, what thou wilt do with me
                None of my books will show:
I read, and sigh, and wish I were a tree;
                For sure then I should grow
To fruit or shade: at least some bird would trust
Her household to me, and I should be just.

Yet, though thou troublest me, I must be meek;
                In weakness must be stout.
Well, I will change the service, and go seek
                Some other master out.
Ah, my dear God! though I am clean forgot,
Let me not love thee, if I love thee not.

269

## Prayer

PRAYER, the Church's banquet, Angels' age,
  God's breath in man returning to his birth,
The soul in paraphrase, heart in pilgrimage,
  The Christian plummet, sounding heaven and earth;
Engine against the Almighty, sinner's tower,
  Reversèd thunder, Christ-side-piercing spear,
The six-days' world transposing in an hour,
  A kind of tune, which all things hear and fear;

Softness, and peace, and joy, and love, and bliss,
    Exalted manna, gladness of the best,
    Heaven in ordinary, man well drest,
The milky way, the bird of Paradise,
        Church-bells beyond the stars heard, the soul's blood,
        The land of spices; something understood.


270                            *Denial*

            WHEN my devotions could not pierce
                        Thy silent ears;
        Then was my heart broken, as was my verse;
                    My breast was full of fears
                        And disorder.

            My bent thoughts, like a brittle bow,
                        Did fly asunder:
        Each took his way: some would to pleasure go,
                    Some to the wars and thunder
                        Of alarms.

            As good go anywhere, they say,
                        As to benumb
        Both knees and heart, in crying night and day,
                    *Come, come, my God, O come,*
                        But no hearing.

            O that thou shouldst give dust a tongue
                        To cry to thee,
        And then not hear it crying! all day long
                    My heart was in my knee,
                        But no hearing.

            Therefore my soul lay out of sight,
                        Untuned, unstrung;
        My feeble spirit, unable to look right,
                    Like a nipped blossom, hung
                        Discontented.

            O cheer and tune my heartless breast,
                        Defer no time;
        That so thy favours granting my request,
                    They and my mind may chime,
                        And mend my rhyme.

271 *Virtue*

SWEET day, so cool, so calm, so bright,
The bridal of the earth and sky:
The dew shall weep thy fall tonight,
   For thou must die.

Sweet rose, whose hue angry and brave
Bids the rash gazer wipe his eye:
Thy root is ever in its grave,
   And thou must die.

Sweet spring, full of sweet days and roses,
A box where sweets compacted lie:
My music shows ye have your closes,
   And all must die.

Only a sweet and virtuous soul,
Like seasoned timber never gives;
But though the whole world turn to coal,
   Then chiefly lives.

272 *The Collar*

I STRUCK the board, and cried, 'No more!
    I will abroad.
What? shall I ever sigh and pine?
My lines and life are free; free as the road,
 Loose as the wind, as large as store.
   Shall I be still in suit?
 Have I no harvest but a thorn
 To let me blood, and not restore
What I have lost with cordial fruit?
     Sure there was wine
Before my sighs did dry it: there was corn
  Before my tears did drown it.
 Is the year only lost to me?
  Have I no bays to crown it?

No flowers, no garlands gay? all blasted?
$\qquad$ All wasted?
$\quad$ Not so, my heart: but there is fruit,
$\qquad$ And thou hast hands.
$\quad$ Recover all thy sigh-blown age
On double pleasures: leave thy cold dispute
Of what is fit, and not. Forsake thy cage,
$\qquad$ Thy rope of sands,
Which petty thoughts have made, and made to thee
$\quad$ Good cable, to enforce and draw,
$\qquad$ And be thy law,
$\quad$ While thou didst wink and wouldst not see.
$\qquad$ Away; take heed:
$\qquad$ I will abroad.
Call in thy death's head there: tie up thy fears.
$\qquad$ He that forbears
$\quad$ To suit and serve his need,
$\qquad$ Deserves his load.'
But as I raved and grew more fierce and wild
$\qquad$ At every word,
$\quad$ Methoughts I heard one calling, 'Child!'
$\quad$ And I replied, 'My Lord'.


273 *The Pulley*

W HEN God at first made man,
Having a glass of blessings standing by,
'Let us', said he, 'pour on him all we can:
Let the world's riches, which dispersèd lie,
$\qquad$ Contract into a span.'


So strength first made a way;
Then beauty flowed, then wisdom, honour, pleasure;
When almost all was out, God made a stay,
Perceiving that, alone of all his treasure,
$\qquad$ Rest in the bottom lay.


'For if I should', said he,
'Bestow this jewel also on my creature,
He would adore my gifts instead of me,
And rest in Nature, not the God of Nature:
$\qquad$ So both should losers be.

'Yet let him keep the rest,
But keep them with repining restlessness;
Let him be rich and weary, that at least,
If goodness lead him not, yet weariness
         May toss him to my breast.'


274                 *The Flower*

How fresh, O Lord, how sweet and clean
Are thy returns! even as the flowers in spring,
    To which, besides their own demean,
The late-past frosts tributes of pleasure bring,
         Grief melts away
         Like snow in May,
As if there were no such cold thing.


Who would have thought my shrivelled heart
Could have recovered greenness? It was gone
    Quite underground; as flowers depart
To see their mother-root, when they have blown;
         Where they together
         All the hard weather,
Dead to the world, keep house unknown.


These are thy wonders, Lord of power,
Killing and quickening, bringing down to hell
    And up to heaven in an hour;
Making a chiming of a passing-bell.
         We say amiss,
         This or that is.
Thy word is all, if we could spell.


O that I once past changing were,
Fast in thy Paradise, where no flower can wither!
    Many a spring I shoot up fair,
Offering at heaven, growing and groaning thither:
         Nor doth my flower
         Want a spring shower,
My sins and I joining together.

But while I grow in a straight line,
Still upwards bent, as if heaven were mine own,
　　Thy anger comes and I decline:
What frost to that? what pole is not the zone,
　　　　　Where all things burn,
　　　　　When thou dost turn,
　　And the least frown of thine is shown?


And now in age I bud again,
After so many deaths I live and write;
　　I once more smell the dew and rain,
And relish versing: O my only light,
　　　　　It cannot be
　　　　　That I am he
　　On whom thy tempests fell all night.


These are thy wonders, Lord of love,
To make us see we are but flowers that glide;
　　Which when we once can find and prove,
Thou hast a garden for us, where to bide.
　　　　　Who would be more,
　　　　　Swelling through store,
　　Forfeit their Paradise by their pride.


275                    *Easter*

I GOT me flowers to straw thy way,
　　I got me boughs off many a tree;
But thou wast up by break of day,
　　And brought'st thy sweets along with thee.

The sun arising in the East,
　　Though he give light, and the East perfume;
If they should offer to contest
　　With thy arising they presume.

Can there be any day but this,
　　Though many suns to shine endeavour?
We count three hundred, but we miss:
　　There is but one, and that one ever.

276 *Discipline*

THROW away thy rod,
Throw away thy wrath:
      O my God,
Take the gentle path.

For my heart's desire
Unto thine is bent:
      I aspire
To a full consent.

Not a word or look
I affect to own,
      But by book,
And thy book alone.

Though I fail, I weep;
Though I halt in pace,
      Yet I creep
To the throne of grace.

Then let wrath remove;
Love will do the deed;
      For with love
Stony hearts will bleed.

Love is swift of foot,
Love's a man of war,
      And can shoot,
And can hit from far.

Who can 'scape his bow?
That which wrought on thee,
      Brought thee low,
Needs must work on me.

Throw away thy rod:
Though man frailties hath,
      Thou art God:
Throw away thy wrath.

277                           *Love*

LOVE bade me welcome; yet my soul drew back,
                    Guilty of dust and sin.
But quick-eyed Love, observing me grow slack
                    From my first entrance in,
Drew nearer to me, sweetly questioning,
                    If I lacked anything.

'A guest', I answered, 'worthy to be here.'
                    Love said, 'You shall be he.'
'I, the unkind, ungrateful? Ah, my dear,
                    I cannot look on thee.'
Love took my hand, and smiling did reply,
                    'Who made the eyes but I?'

'Truth, Lord, but I have marred them; let my shame
                    Go where it doth deserve.'
'And know you not', says Love, 'who bore the blame?'
                    'My dear, then I will serve.'
'You must sit down', says Love, 'and taste my meat.'
                    So I did sit and eat.


# ANONYMOUS

278                      *Preparations*

YET if His Majesty, our sovereign lord,
Should of his own accord
Friendly himself invite,
And say 'I'll be your guest to-morrow night,'
How should we stir ourselves, call and command
All hands to work! 'Let no man idle stand!
'Set me fine Spanish tables in the hall;
See they be fitted all;
Let there be room to eat
And order taken that there want no meat.
See every sconce and candlestick made bright,
That without tapers they may give a light.

'Look to the presence: are the carpets spread,
The dazie o'er the head,
The cushions in the chairs,
And all the candles lighted on the stairs?
Perfume the chambers, and in any case
Let each man give attendance in his place!'
Thus, if the king were coming, would we do;
And 'twere good reason too;
For 'tis a duteous thing
To show all honour to an earthly king,
And after all our travail and our cost,
So he be pleased, to think no labour lost.
But at the coming of the King of Heaven
All 's set at six and seven;
We wallow in our sin,
Christ cannot find a chamber in the inn.
We entertain him always like a stranger,
And, as at first, still lodge him in the manger.


# THOMAS CAREW

## ?1595–1640

279                    *On the Death of Donne*

THE Muses' garden, with pedantic weeds
O'erspread, was purged by thee; the lazy seeds
Of servile imitation thrown away;
And fresh invention planted. Thou didst pay
The debts of our penurious bankrupt age,
Licentious thefts, that make poetic rage
A mimic fury, when our souls must be
Possessed, or with Anacreon's ecstasy,
Or Pindar's, not their own; the subtle cheat
Of sly exchanges, and the juggling feat
Of two-edged words, or whatsoever wrong
By ours was done the Greek or Latin tongue,
Thou hast redeemed, and opened us a mine
Of rich and pregnant fancy, drawn a line
Of masculine expression, which, had good
Old Orpheus seen, or all the ancient brood

Our superstitious fools admire and hold
Their lead more precious than thy burnished gold,
Thou hadst been their Exchequer, and no more
They each in other's dust had raked for ore.
Thou shalt yield no precedence but of time,
And the blind fate of language, whose tuned chime
More charms the outward sense. Yet thou mayst claim
From so great disadvantage greater fame;
Since to the awe of thy imperious wit
Our stubborn language bends, made only fit
With her tough thick-ribbed hoops to gird about
Thy giant fancy, which had proved too stout
For their soft melting phrases. As in time
They had the start, so did they cull the prime
Buds of invention many a hundred year,
And left the rifled fields, besides the fear
To touch their harvest; yet from those bare lands
Of what is purely thine, thy only hands
(And that thy smallest work) have gleanèd more
Than all those times and tongues could reap before.
   But thou art gone, and thy strict laws will be
Too hard for libertines in Poetry.
They will repeal the goodly exiled train
Of gods and goddesses, which in thy just reign
Were banished nobler poems; now, with these,
The silenced tales of the *Metamorphoses*
Shall stuff their lines, and swell the windy page,
Till Verse, refined by thee, in this last age
Turn ballad rhyme, or those old idols be
Adored again with new apostasy.


280                              *Song*

        Ask me no more where Jove bestows,
        When June is past, the fading rose;
        For in your beauty's orient deep
        These flowers, as in their causes, sleep.

        Ask me no more whither doth stray
        The golden atoms of the day;
        For in pure love heaven did prepare
        Those powders to enrich your hair.

Ask me no more whither doth haste
The nightingale when May is past;
For in your sweet dividing throat
She winters and keeps warm her note.

Ask me no more where those stars light
That downwards fall in dead of night;
For in your eyes they sit, and there
Fixed become as in their sphere.

Ask me no more if east or west
The Phoenix builds her spicy nest;
For unto you at last she flies,
And in your fragrant bosom dies.

281                    *Persuasions to Enjoy*

If the quick spirits in your eye
Now languish and anon must die;
If every sweet and every grace
Must fly from that forsaken face;
    Then, Celia, let us reap our joys
    Ere Time such goodly fruit destroys.

Or if that golden fleece must grow
For ever free from agèd snow;
If those bright suns must know no shade,
Nor your fresh beauties ever fade;
    Then, fear not, Celia, to bestow
    What, still being gathered, still must grow.

Thus either Time his sickle brings
In vain, or else in vain his wings.

282                    *To My Inconstant Mistress*

When thou, poor Excommunicate
    From all the joys of love, shalt see
The full reward and glorious fate
    Which my strong faith shall purchase me,
    Then curse thine own inconstancy!

A fairer hand than thine shall cure
   That heart which thy false oaths did wound;
And to my soul a soul more pure
   Than thine shall by Love's hand be bound,
   And both with equal glory crowned.

Then shalt thou weep, entreat, complain
   To Love, as I did once to thee;
When all thy tears shall be as vain
   As mine were then: for thou shalt be
   Damned for thy false apostasy.

283      *On the Lady Mary Villiers*

THE Lady Mary Villiers lies
Under this stone; with weeping eyes
The parents that first gave her birth,
And their sad friends, laid her in earth.
If any of them, Reader, were
Known unto thee, shed a tear;
Or if thyself possess a gem
As dear to thee, as this to them,
Though a stranger to this place,
Bewail in theirs thine own hard case:
   For thou perhaps at thy return
   Mayst find thy Darling in an urn.

# JAMES SHIRLEY
## 1596–1666

284      *Piping Peace*

YOU virgins that did late despair
   To keep your wealth from cruel men,
Tie up in silk your careless hair:
   Soft peace is come again.

Now lovers' eyes may gently shoot
   A flame that will not kill;
The drum was angry, but the lute
   Shall whisper what you will.

Sing Io, Io! for his sake
   That hath restored your drooping heads;
With choice of sweetest flowers make
   A garden where he treads;

Whilst we whole groves of laurel bring,
   A petty triumph to his brow,
Who is the Master of our spring
   And all the bloom we owe.

285            *Death the Leveller*

THE glories of our blood and state
   Are shadows, not substantial things;
There is no armour against Fate;
   Death lays his icy hand on kings:
      Sceptre and Crown
      Must tumble down,
And in the dust be equal made
With the poor crooked scythe and spade.

Some men with swords may reap the field,
   And plant fresh laurels where they kill:
But their strong nerves at last must yield;
   They tame but one another still:
      Early or late
      They stoop to fate,
And must give up their murmuring breath
When they, pale captives, creep to death.

The garlands wither on your brow;
   Then boast no more your mighty deeds!
Upon Death's purple altar now
   See where the victor-victim bleeds.
      Your heads must come
      To the cold tomb:
Only the actions of the just
Smell sweet and blossom in their dust.

# WILLIAM STRODE

## 1602–1645

286      *Chloris in the Snow*

I SAW fair Chloris walk alone,
When feathered rain came softly down,
As Jove descending from his Tower
To court her in a silver shower:
The wanton snow flew to her breast,
Like pretty birds into their nest,
But, overcome with whiteness there,
For grief it thawed into a tear:
    Thence falling on her garments' hem,
    To deck her, froze into a gem.

# WILLIAM HABINGTON

## 1605–1654

287      *Nox nocti indicat Scientiam*

WHEN I survey the bright
      Celestial sphere;
So rich with jewels hung that Night
  Doth like an Ethiop bride appear:

My soul her wings doth spread
      And heavenward flies,
The Almighty's mysteries to read
  In the large volumes of the skies.

For the bright firmament
      Shoots forth no flame
So silent, but is eloquent
  In speaking the Creator's name.

## WILLIAM HABINGTON

No unregarded star
             Contracts its light
Into so small a character,
   Removed far from our human sight;

But if we steadfast look
             We shall discern
In it, as in some holy book,
   How man may heavenly knowledge learn.

It tells the Conqueror
             That far-stretched power,
Which his proud dangers traffic for,
   Is but the triumph of an hour;

That from the farthest North,
             Some nation may,
Yet undiscovered, issue forth,
   And o'er his new-got conquest sway;

Some nation yet shut in
             With hills of ice
May be let out to scourge his sin,
   Till they shall equal him in vice.

And then they likewise shall
             Their ruin have;
For as yourselves your Empires fall,
   And every Kingdom hath a grave.

Thus those celestial fires,
             Though seeming mute,
The fallacy of our desires
   And all the pride of life confute:—

For they have watched since first
             The world had birth:
And found sin in itself accurst,
   And nothing permanent on Earth.

*Pretty Sport*

FINE young folly, though you were
That fair beauty I did swear,
Yet you ne'er could reach my heart.
For we courtiers learn at school
Only with your sex to fool:
Y'are not worth the serious part.

When I sigh and kiss your hand,
Cross my arms and wondering stand,
Holding parley with your eye,
Then dilate on my desires;
Swear the sun ne'er shot such fires:
All is but a handsome lie.

When I eye your curl or lace,
Gentle soul, you think your face
Straight some murder doth commit,
And your virtue doth begin
To grow scrupulous of my sin,
When I talk to show my wit.

Therefore, Madam, wear no cloud
Nor to check my love grow proud,
For in sooth I much do doubt,
'Tis the powder in your hair,
Not your breath, perfumes the air,
And your clothes that set you out.

Yet though truth has this confessed
And I vow I love in jest,
When I next begin to court,
And protest an amorous flame,
You'll swear I in earnest am.
Bedlam! this is pretty sport.

THOMAS RANDOLPH

THOMAS RANDOLPH
1605–1635

289 *An Ode to Master Anthony Stafford*
  *to Hasten Him into the Country*

   COME, spur away,
I have no patience for a longer stay,
  But must go down,
And leave the chargeable noise of this great town:
  I will the country see,
  Where old simplicity,
   Though hid in gray,
   Doth look more gay
Than foppery in plush and scarlet clad.
 Farewell, you city wits, that are
  Almost at civil war—
'Tis time that I grow wise, when all the world grows mad.

   More of my days
I will not spend to gain an idiot's praise;
  Or to make sport
For some slight Puisne of the Inns of Court.
  Then, worthy Stafford, say,
  How shall we spend the day?
   With what delights
   Shorten the nights?
When from this tumult we are got secure,
 Where mirth with all her freedom goes,
  Yet shall no finger lose;
Where every word is thought, and every thought is pure?

   There from the tree
We'll cherries pluck, and pick the strawberry;
  And every day
Go see the wholesome country girls make hay,
  Whose brown hath lovelier grace
  Than any painted face
   That I do know
   Hyde Park can show:

Where I had rather gain a kiss than meet
(Though some of them in greater state
Might court my love with plate)
The beauties of the Cheap, and wives of Lombard Street.

But think upon
Some other pleasures: these to me are none.
Why do I prate
Of women, that are things against my fate!
I never mean to wed
That torture to my bed:
My Muse is she
My love shall be.
Let clowns get wealth and heirs: when I am gone
And the great bugbear, grisly Death,
Shall take this idle breath,
If I a poem leave, that poem is my son.

Of this no more!
We'll rather taste the bright Pomona's store.
No fruit shall 'scape
Our palates, from the damson to the grape.
Then, full, we'll seek a shade,
And hear what music's made;
How Philomel
Her tale doth tell,
And how the other birds do fill the quire;
The thrush and blackbird lend their throats,
Warbling melodious notes;
We will all sports enjoy which others but desire.

Ours is the sky,
Where, at what fowl we please, our hawk shall fly:
Nor will we spare
To hunt the crafty fox or timorous hare;
But let our hounds run loose
In any ground they'll choose;
The buck shall fall,
The stag, and all.
Our pleasures must from their own warrants be,
For to my Muse, if not to me,
I'm sure all game is free:
Heaven, earth, are all but parts of her great royalty.

          And when we mean
  To taste of Bacchus' blessings now and then,
        And drink by stealth
  A cup or two to noble Barkley's health,
      I'll take my pipe and try
      The Phrygian melody;
        Which he that hears,
        Lets through his ears
  A madness to distemper all the brain:
     Then I another pipe will take
      And Doric music make,
To civilize with graver notes our wits again.

## 290        *Upon his Picture*

WHEN age hath made me what I am not now;
And every wrinkle tells me where the plough
Of time hath furrowed; when an ice shall flow
Through every vein, and all my head wear snow;
When death displays his coldness in my cheek
And I myself in my own picture seek,
Not finding what I am, but what I was,
In doubt which to believe, this or my glass;
Yet though I alter, this remains the same
As it was drawn, retains the primitive frame
And first complexion; here will still be seen
Blood on the cheek, and down upon the chin.
Here the smooth brow will stay, the lively eye,
The ruddy lip, and hair of youthful dye.
Behold what frailty we in man may see
Whose shadow is less given to change than he.

# SIR WILLIAM DAVENANT
## 1606–1668

291                          *Aubade*

THE lark now leaves his watery nest,
    And climbing shakes his dewy wings.
He takes this window for the East,
    And to implore your light he sings—
Awake, awake! the morn will never rise
Till she can dress her beauty at your eyes.

The merchant bows unto the seaman's star,
    The ploughman from the sun his season takes;
But still the lover wonders what they are
    Who look for day before his mistress wakes.
Awake, awake! break through your veils of lawn!
Then draw your curtains, and begin the dawn!

292                  *Endimion Porter and Olivia*

*Olivia.*        Before we shall again behold
            In his diurnal race the world's great eye,
                We may as silent be and cold
            As are the shades where buried lovers lie.

*Endimion.*    Olivia, 'tis no fault of love
            To lose ourselves in death, but O, I fear
                When life and knowledge is above
            Restored to us, I shall not know thee there.

*Olivia.*        Call it not Heaven, my love, where we
            Ourselves shall see, and yet each other miss:
                So much of Heaven I find in thee
            As, thou unknown, all else privation is.

*Endimion.*    Why should we doubt, before we go
            To find the knowledge which shall ever last,
                That we may there each other know?
            Can future knowledge quite destroy the past?

274

*Olivia.*        When at the bowers in the Elysian shade
            I first arrive, I shall examine where
                They dwell who love the highest virtue made;
            For I am sure to find Endimion there.

*Endimion.*     From this vexed world when we shall both retire,
            Where all are lovers, and where all rejoice,
                I need not seek thee in the Heavenly quire;
            For I shall know Olivia by her voice.

## 293        *The Philosopher and the Lover*
                  *to a Mistress Dying*

*Lover.*         Your beauty, ripe and calm and fresh
                As eastern summers are,
            Must now, forsaking time and flesh,
                Add light to some small star.

*Philosopher.* Whilst she yet lives, were stars decayed,
                Their light by hers relief might find;
            But Death will lead her to a shade
                Where Love is cold and Beauty blind.

*Lover.*         Lovers, whose priests all poets are,
                Think every mistress, when she dies,
            Is changed at least into a star:
                And who dares doubt the poets wise?

*Philosopher.* But ask not bodies doomed to die
                To what abode they go;
            Since Knowledge is but Sorrow's spy,
                It is not safe to know.

## 294        *The Soldier Going to the Field*

      PRESERVE thy sighs, unthrifty girl,
        To purify the air;
      Thy tears to thread instead of pearl
        On bracelets of thy hair.

The trumpet makes the echo hoarse
 And wakes the louder drum;
Expense of grief gains no remorse
 When sorrow should be dumb.

For I must go where lazy Peace
 Will hide her drowsy head,
And, for the sport of Kings, increase
 The number of the dead.

But first I'll chide thy cruel theft:
 Can I in war delight,
Who being of my heart bereft
 Can have no heart to fight?

Thou know'st the sacred Laws of old
 Ordained a thief should pay,
To quit him of his theft, sevenfold
 What he had stolen away.

Thy payment shall but double be;
 O then with speed resign
My own seducèd heart to me,
 Accompanied with thine.


# EDMUND WALLER
## 1606–1687

295                    *Go, Lovely Rose*

 Go, lovely Rose—
Tell her that wastes her time and me,
 That now she knows,
When I resemble her to thee,
How sweet and fair she seems to be.

 Tell her that's young,
And shuns to have her graces spied,
 That hadst thou sprung
In deserts where no men abide,
Thou must have uncommended died.

Small is the worth
Of beauty from the light retired:
    Bid her come forth,
Suffer herself to be desired,
And not blush so to be admired.

    Then die—that she
The common fate of all things rare
    May read in thee;
How small a part of time they share
That are so wondrous sweet and fair!

296 *Old Age*

THE seas are quiet when the winds give o'er;
So calm are we when passions are no more.
For then we know how vain it was to boast
Of fleeting things, so certain to be lost.
Clouds of affection from our younger eyes
Conceal that emptiness which age descries.

The soul's dark cottage, battered and decayed,
Lets in new light through chinks that Time has made:
Stronger by weakness, wiser men become
As they draw near to their eternal home.
Leaving the old, both worlds at once they view
That stand upon the threshold of the new.

# SIR RICHARD FANSHAWE

## 1608–1666

297 *Ode on His Majesty's Proclamation,*
*Commanding the Gentry to Reside on their Estates:*
*1630*

    Now war is all the world about,
    And everywhere Erynnis reigns,
    Or else, the torch so late put out,
            The stench remains.

## SIR RICHARD FANSHAWE

Holland for many years hath been
Of Christian tragedies the stage,
Yet seldom hath she played a scene
    Of bloodier rage.

And France that was not long composed,
With civil drums again resounds,
And ere the old are fully closed
    Receives new wounds.

The great Gustavus in the west
Plucks the Imperial Eagle's wing,
Than whom the earth did ne'er invest
    A fiercer king;

Revenging lost Bohemia,
And the proud wrongs which Tilly did,
And tempereth the German clay
    With Spanish blood.

What should I tell of Polish bands,
And the bloods boiling in the North?
'Gainst whom the furied Russians
    Their troops bring forth:

Both confident. This in his purse,
And needy valour set on work;
He in his axe, which oft did worse
    The invading Turk.

Who now sustains a Persian storm:
There hell, that made it, suffers schism:
This war, forsooth, was to reform
    Mahometism.

Only the island which we sow,
(A world without the world) so far
From present wounds, it cannot show
    An ancient scar.

## SIR RICHARD FANSHAWE

White Peace, the beautifullest of things
Seems here her everlasting rest
To fix, and spreads her downy wings
        Over the nest.

As when great Jove, usurping reign,
From the plagued world did her exile,
And tied her with a golden chain
        To one blest isle;

Which in a sea of plenty swam,
And turtles sang on every bough;
A safe retreat to all that came,
        As ours is now.

Yet we, as if some foe were here,
Leave the despisèd fields to clowns,
And come to save ourselves as 'twere
        In wallèd towns.

Hither we bring wives, babes, rich clothes
And gems; till now my Sovereign
The growing evil doth oppose:
        Counting in vain

His care preserves us from annoy
Of enemies his realms to invade,
Unless he force us to enjoy
        The peace he made.

To roll themselves in envied leisure
He therefore sends the landed heirs,
Whilst he proclaims not his own pleasure
        So much as theirs.

The sap and blood of the land, which fled
Into the root, and choked the heart,
Are bid their quickening power to spread
        Through every part.

O, 'twas an act not for my Muse
To celebrate, nor the dull Age
Until the country air infuse
       A purer rage!

And if the fields as thankful prove
For benefits received, as seed,
They will, to quite so great a love,
       A Virgil breed.

A Tityrus, that shall not cease
The Augustus of our world to praise
In equal verse, author of peace
       And halcyon days.

Nor let the gentry grudge to go
Into those places whence they grew,
But think them blest they may do so.
       Who would pursue

The smoky glory of the town,
That may go till his native earth,
And by the shining fire sit down
       Of his own hearth,

Free from the griping scrivener's bands,
And the more biting mercer's books;
Free from the bait of oilèd hands
       And painted looks?

The country too, even chops for rain:
You that exhale it by your power
Let the fat drops fall down again
       In a full shower.

And you bright beauties of the time,
That waste yourselves here in a blaze,
Fix to your orb and proper clime
       Your wandering rays.

Let no dark corner of the land
Be unembellished with one gem,
And those which here too thick do stand
       Sprinkle on them.

Believe me, ladies, you will find
In that sweet life more solid joys,
More true contentment to the mind
        Than all town toys.

Nor Cupid there less blood doth spill,
But heads his shafts with chaster love,
Not feathered with a sparrow's quill,
        But of a dove.

There shall you hear the nightingale,
The harmless siren of the wood,
How prettily she tells a tale
        Of rape and blood.

The lyric lark, with all beside
Of nature's feathered quire, and all
The commonwealth of flowers in its pride
        Behold you shall.

The lily, queen, the royal rose,
The gillyflower, prince of the blood,
The courtier tulip, gay in clothes,
        The regal bud,

The violet, purple senator,
How they do mock the pomp of state,
And all that at the surly door
        Of great ones wait.

Plant trees you may, and see them shoot
Up with your children, to be served
To your clean boards, and the fairest fruit
        To be preserved.

And learn to use their several gums;
'Tis innocence in the sweet blood
Of cherry, apricots and plums
        To be imbrued.

# JOHN MILTON
## 1608–1674

298    *Hymn on the Morning of Christ's Nativity,*
*Composed 1629*

IT was the winter wild,
While the Heaven-born Child
  All meanly wrapped in the rude manger lies;
Nature in awe to him
Had doffed her gaudy trim,
  With her great Master so to sympathize;
It was no season then for her
To wanton with the sun, her lusty paramour.

Only with speeches fair
She woos the gentle air
  To hide her guilty front with innocent snow,
And on her naked shame,
Pollute with sinful blame,
  The saintly veil of maiden white to throw,
Confounded that her Maker's eyes
Should look so near upon her foul deformities.

But he her fears to cease
Sent down the meek-eyed Peace;
  She, crowned with olive green, came softly sliding
Down through the turning sphere,
His ready harbinger,
  With turtle wing the amorous clouds dividing,
And waving wide her myrtle wand,
She strikes a universal peace through sea and land.

No war or battle's sound
Was heard the world around:
  The idle spear and shield were high up-hung;
The hookèd chariot stood
Unstained with hostile blood;
  The trumpet spake not to the armèd throng,
And kings sat still with awful eye,
As if they surely knew their sovran Lord was by.

But peaceful was the night
Wherein the Prince of Light
 His reign of peace upon the earth began:
The winds with wonder whist
Smoothly the waters kissed,
 Whispering new joys to the mild ocean,
Who now hath quite forgot to rave,
While birds of calm sit brooding on the charmèd wave.

The stars with deep amaze
Stand fixed in steadfast gaze,
 Bending one way their precious influence,
And will not take their flight,
For all the morning light,
 Or Lucifer that often warned them thence;
But in their glimmering orbs did glow,
Until their Lord himself bespake, and bid them go.

And though the shady gloom
Had given day her room,
 The sun himself withheld his wonted speed,
And hid his head for shame,
As his inferior flame
 The new-enlightened world no more should need;
He saw a greater Sun appear
Than his bright throne or burning axle-tree could bear.

The shepherds on the lawn,
Or ere the point of dawn,
 Sat simply chatting in a rustic row;
Full little thought they than
That the mighty Pan
 Was kindly come to live with them below;
Perhaps their loves or else their sheep,
Was all that did their silly thoughts so busy keep.

When such music sweet
Their hearts and ears did greet,
 As never was by mortal finger strook,
Divinely warbled voice
Answering the stringèd noise
 As all their souls in blissful rapture took:
The air such pleasure loth to lose,
With thousand echoes still prolongs each heavenly close.

Nature that heard such sound
Beneath the hollow round
    Of Cynthia's seat, the airy region thrilling,
Now was almost won
To think her part was done,
    And that her reign had here its last fulfilling;
She knew such harmony alone
Could hold all heaven and earth in happier union.

At last surrounds their sight
A globe of circular light,
    That with long beams the shame-faced Night arrayed,
The helmèd Cherubim
And sworded Seraphim
    Are seen in glittering ranks with wings displayed,
Harping in loud and solemn quire,
With unexpressive notes to Heaven's new-born heir.

Such music (as 'tis said)
Before was never made,
    But when of old the sons of morning sung,
While the Creator great
His constellations set,
    And the well-balanced world on hinges hung,
And cast the dark foundations deep,
And bid the weltering waves their oozy channel keep.

Ring out, ye crystal spheres,
Once bless our human ears
    (If ye have power to touch our senses so),
And let your silver chime
Move in melodious time,
    And let the bass of heaven's deep organ blow;
And with your ninefold harmony
Make up full consort to the angelic symphony.

For if such holy song
Enwrap our fancy long,
    Time will run back and fetch the age of gold,
And speckled Vanity
Will sicken soon, and die,
    And leprous Sin will melt from earthly mould,
And hell itself will pass away
And leave her dolorous mansions to the peering day.

Yea, Truth and Justice then
Will down return to men,
   Orbed in a rainbow; and, like glories wearing,
Mercy will sit between,
Throned in celestial sheen,
   With radiant feet the tissued clouds down-steering,
And heaven, as at some festival,
Will open wide the gates of her high palace hall.

But wisest Fate says no,
This must not yet be so;
   The Babe lies yet in smiling infancy,
That on the bitter cross
Must redeem our loss,
   So both himself and us to glorify;
Yet first, to those ychained in sleep,
The wakeful trump of doom must thunder through the deep.

With such a horrid clang
As on Mount Sinai rang,
   While the red fire and smouldering clouds out-brake:
The aged Earth, aghast
With terror of that blast,
   Shall from the surface to the centre shake,
When at the world's last session
The dreadful Judge in middle air shall spread his throne.

And then at last our bliss
Full and perfect is,
   But now begins; for from this happy day
The old Dragon underground,
In straiter limits bound,
   Not half so far casts his usurpèd sway,
And, wroth to see his kingdom fail,
Swinges the scaly horror of his folded tail.

The oracles are dumb,
No voice or hideous hum
   Runs through the archèd roof in words deceiving.
Apollo from his shrine
Can no more divine,
   With hollow shriek the steep of Delphos leaving.
No nightly trance or breathèd spell
Inspires the pale-eyed priest from the prophetic cell.

The lonely mountains o'er,
And the resounding shore,
   A voice of weeping heard, and loud lament,
From haunted spring and dale,
Edged with poplar pale,
   The parting Genius is with sighing sent;
With flower-inwoven tresses torn
The nymphs in twilight shade of tangled thickets mourn.

In consecrated earth,
And on the holy hearth,
   The Lars and Lemures moan with midnight plaint;
In urns and altars round,
A drear and dying sound
   Affrights the flamens at their service quaint;
And the chill marble seems to sweat,
While each peculiar power forgoes his wonted seat.

Peor and Baälim
Forsake their temples dim,
   With that twice-battered god of Palestine;
And moonèd Ashtaroth,
Heaven's queen and mother both,
   Now sits not girt with tapers' holy shine;
The Libyc Hammon shrinks his horn,
In vain the Tyrian maids their wounded Thammuz mourn.

And sullen Moloch fled,
Hath left in shadows dread
   His burning idol all of blackest hue;
In vain with cymbals' ring
They call the grisly king,
   In dismal dance about the furnace blue;
The brutish gods of Nile as fast,
Isis and Orus, and the dog Anubis haste.

Nor is Osiris seen
In Memphian grove or green,
   Trampling the unshowered grass with lowings loud;
Nor can he be at rest
Within his sacred chest,
   Nought but profoundest hell can be his shroud;
In vain with timbreled anthems dark
The sable-stolèd sorcerers bear his worshipped ark.

He feels from Judah's land
The dreaded Infant's hand,
    The rays of Bethlehem blind his dusky eyn;
Nor all the gods beside,
Longer dare abide,
    Not Typhon huge ending in snaky twine:
Our Babe, to show his Godhead true,
Can in his swaddling bands control the damnèd crew.

So when the sun in bed,
Curtained with cloudy red,
    Pillows his chin upon an orient wave,
The flocking shadows pale
Troop to the infernal jail,
    Each fettered ghost slips to his several grave,
And the yellow-skirted fays
Fly after the night-steeds, leaving their moon-loved maze.

But see, the Virgin blest
Hath laid her Babe to rest:
    Time is our tedious song should here have ending;
Heaven's youngest teemèd star,
Hath fixed her polished car,
    Her sleeping Lord with handmaid lamp attending;
And all about the courtly stable,
Bright-harnessed angels sit in order serviceable.


299                *At a Solemn Music*

BLEST pair of Sirens, pledges of heaven's joy,
Sphere-born harmonious sisters, Voice and Verse,
Wed your divine sounds, and mixed power employ
Dead things with inbreathed sense able to pierce,
And to our high-raised phantasy present
That undisturbèd song of pure concent,
Ay sung before the sapphire-coloured throne
To him that sits thereon,
With saintly shout and solemn jubilee,
Where the bright Seraphim in burning row
Their loud uplifted angel-trumpets blow,
And the Cherubic host in thousand quires
Touch their immortal harps of golden wires,

With those just spirits that wear victorious palms,
Hymns devout and holy psalms
Singing everlastingly;
That we on earth with undiscording voice
May rightly answer that melodious noise:
As once we did, till disproportioned sin
Jarred against Nature's chime, and with harsh din
Broke the fair music that all creatures made
To their great Lord, whose love their motion swayed
In perfect diapason, whilst they stood
In first obedience and their state of good.
O may we soon again renew that song,
And keep in tune with heaven, till God ere long
To his celestial consort us unite,
To live with him, and sing in endless morn of light.

### *from* Comus

#### (i)

#### *Comus speaks*

300

THE star that bids the shepherd fold
Now the top of heaven doth hold,
And the gilded car of day
His glowing axle doth allay
In the steep Atlantic stream;
And the slope sun his upward beam
Shoots against the dusky pole,
Pacing toward the other goal
Of his chamber in the east.
Meanwhile welcome joy and feast,
Midnight shout and revelry,
Tipsy dance and jollity.
Braid your locks with rosy twine,
Dropping odours, dropping wine.
Rigour now is gone to bed;
And Advice with scrupulous head,
Strict Age, and sour Severity,
With their grave saws, in slumber lie.
We that are of purer fire,
Imitate the starry quire,
Who in their nightly watchful spheres,
Lead in swift round the months and years.

The sounds and seas with all their finny drove
Now to the moon in wavering morris move
And on the tawny sands and shelves
Trip the pert fairies and the dapper elves;
By dimpled brook and fountain-brim,
The wood-nymphs, decked with daisies trim,
Their merry wakes and pastimes keep:
What hath night to do with sleep?
Night hath better sweets to prove,
Venus now wakes, and wakens Love. . . .
Come, knit hands, and beat the ground,
In a light fantastic round.

(ii)

301 *The Lady Sings*

SWEET Echo, sweetest nymph, that liv'st unseen
  Within thy airy shell
 By slow Meander's margent green,
And in the violet-embroidered vale
 Where the lovelorn nightingale
Nightly to thee her sad song mourneth well:
Canst thou not tell me of a gentle pair
 That likest thy Narcissus are?
  O if thou have
 Hid them in some flowery cave,
  Tell me but where,
 Sweet queen of parley, daughter of the sphere;
So mayst thou be translated to the skies,
And give resounding grace to all heaven's harmonies.

(iii)

302 *Sabrina*

*The Spirit.* Sabrina fair,
  Listen where thou art sitting
  Under the glassy, cool, translucent wave,
  In twisted braids of lilies knitting
  The loose train of thy amber-dropping hair;
  Listen for dear honour's sake,
  Goddess of the silver lake,
  Listen and save.

Listen and appear to us
In name of great Oceanus,
By the earth-shaking Neptune's mace,
And Tethys' grave majestic pace,
By hoary Nereus' wrinkled look,
And the Carpathian wizard's hook,
By scaly Triton's winding shell,
And old soothsaying Glaucus' spell,
By Leucothea's lovely hands,
And her son that rules the strands,
By Thetis' tinsel-slippered feet,
And the songs of Sirens sweet,
By dead Parthenope's dear tomb,
And fair Ligea's golden comb,
Wherewith she sits on diamond rocks
Sleeking her soft alluring locks;
By all the nymphs that nightly dance
Upon thy streams with wily glance,
Rise, rise, and heave thy rosy head
From thy coral-paven bed,
And bridle in thy headlong wave,
Till thou our summons answered have.
                        Listen and save!

*Sabrina.*    By the rushy-fringèd bank,
Where grows the willow and the osier dank,
        My sliding chariot stays,
Thick set with agate, and the azurn sheen
    Of turkis blue, and emerald green,
            That in the channel strays.
            Whilst from off the waters fleet
            Thus I set my printless feet
            O'er the cowslip's velvet head,
                That bends not as I tread.
            Gentle swain, at thy request
                I am here!

(iv)

303

### The Spirit Epiloguizes

To the ocean now I fly,
And those happy climes that lie
Where day never shuts his eye,
Up in the broad fields of the sky.
There I suck the liquid air,
All amidst the gardens fair
Of Hesperus, and his daughters three
That sing about the golden tree.
Along the crispèd shades and bowers
Revels the spruce and jocund Spring;
The Graces and the rosy-bosomed Hours
Thither all their bounties bring,
That there eternal summer dwells;
And west winds with musky wing
About the cedarn alleys fling
Nard and cassia's balmy smells.
Iris there with humid bow
Waters the odorous banks that blow
Flowers of more mingled hue
Than her purfled scarf can shew,
And drenches with Elysian dew
(List, mortals, if your ears be true)
Beds of hyacinth and roses,
Where young Adonis oft reposes,
Waxing well of his deep wound,
In slumber soft, and on the ground
Sadly sits the Assyrian queen.
But far above in spangled sheen
Celestial Cupid, her famed son, advanced,
Holds his dear Psyche, sweet entranced
After her wandering labours long,
Till free consent the gods among
Make her his eternal bride,
And from her fair unspotted side
Two blissful twins are to be born,
Youth and Joy; so Jove hath sworn.

But now my task is smoothly done,
I can fly, or I can run
Quickly to the green earth's end,
Where the bowed welkin slow doth bend,
And from thence can soar as soon
To the corners of the moon.

 Mortals, that would follow me,
Love Virtue, she alone is free;
She can teach ye how to climb
Higher than the sphery chime;
Or, if Virtue feeble were,
Heaven itself would stoop to her.


304         *Lycidas*

*Monody on the Death of a Friend drowned in his
passage from Chester on the Irish Seas, 1637*

YET once more, O ye laurels, and once more,
Ye myrtles brown, with ivy never sere,
I come to pluck your berries harsh and crude,
And with forced fingers rude
Shatter your leaves before the mellowing year.
Bitter constraint, and sad occasion dear,
Compels me to disturb your season due;
For Lycidas is dead, dead ere his prime,
Young Lycidas, and hath not left his peer.
Who would not sing for Lycidas? He knew
Himself to sing, and build the lofty rhyme.
He must not float upon his watery bier
Unwept, and welter to the parching wind,
Without the meed of some melodious tear.
 Begin then, Sisters of the sacred well
That from beneath the seat of Jove doth spring,
Begin, and somewhat loudly sweep the string.
Hence with denial vain and coy excuse;
So may some gentle Muse
With lucky words favour my destined urn,
And as he passes turn,
And bid fair peace be to my sable shroud.
For we were nursed upon the self-same hill
Fed the same flock, by fountain, shade, and rill.

Together both, ere the high lawns appeared
Under the opening eyelids of the morn,
We drove afield, and both together heard
What time the grey-fly winds her sultry horn,
Battening our flocks with the fresh dews of night,
Oft till the star that rose, at evening, bright
Toward heaven's descent had sloped his westering wheel.
Meanwhile the rural ditties were not mute,
Tempered to the oaten flute;
Rough Satyrs danced, and Fauns with cloven heel
From the glad sound would not be absent long,
And old Damoetas loved to hear our song.

But O the heavy change, now thou art gone,
Now thou art gone, and never must return!
Thee, Shepherd, thee the woods and desert caves,
With wild thyme and the gadding vine o'ergrown,
And all their echoes mourn.
The willows and the hazel copses green,
Shall now no more be seen,
Fanning their joyous leaves to thy soft lays.
As killing as the canker to the rose,
Or taint-worm to the weanling herds that graze,
Or frost to flowers, that their gay wardrobe wear,
When first the white-thorn blows;
Such, Lycidas, thy loss to shepherd's ear.

Where were ye, Nymphs, when the remorseless deep
Closed o'er the head of your loved Lycidas?
For neither were ye playing on the steep,
Where your old bards, the famous Druids, lie,
Nor on the shaggy top of Mona high,
Nor yet where Deva spreads her wizard stream.
Ay me, I fondly dream,
Had ye been there!—for what could that have done?
What could the Muse herself that Orpheus bore,
The Muse herself, for her enchanting son
Whom universal nature did lament,
When by the rout that made the hideous roar
His gory visage down the stream was sent,
Down the swift Hebrus to the Lesbian shore?

Alas! what boots it with uncessant care
To tend the homely slighted shepherd's trade,
And strictly meditate the thankless Muse?

Were it not better done, as others use,
To sport with Amaryllis in the shade,
Or with the tangles of Neaera's hair?
Fame is the spur that the clear spirit doth raise
(That last infirmity of noble mind)
To scorn delights, and live laborious days;
But the fair guerdon when we hope to find,
And think to burst out into sudden blaze,
Comes the blind Fury with the abhorrèd shears,
And slits the thin-spun life. 'But not the praise,'
Phoebus replied, and touched my trembling ears:
'Fame is no plant that grows on mortal soil,
Nor in the glistering foil
Set off to the world, nor in broad rumour lies,
But lives and spreads aloft by those pure eyes
And perfect witness of all-judging Jove;
As he pronounces lastly on each deed,
Of so much fame in heaven expect thy meed.'
    O fountain Arethuse, and thou honoured flood,
Smooth-sliding Mincius, crowned with vocal reeds,
That strain I heard was of a higher mood.
But now my oat proceeds,
And listens to the herald of the sea,
That came in Neptune's plea.
He asked the waves, and asked the felon winds,
What hard mishap hath doomed this gentle swain?
And questioned every gust of rugged wings
That blows from off each beakèd promontory;
They knew not of his story,
And sage Hippotades their answer brings,
That not a blast was from his dungeon strayed;
The air was calm, and on the level brine
Sleek Panope with all her sisters played.
It was that fatal and perfidious bark,
Built in the eclipse, and rigged with curses dark,
That sunk so low that sacred head of thine.
    Next Camus, reverend sire, went footing slow,
His mantle hairy, and his bonnet sedge,
Inwrought with figures dim, and on the edge
Like to that sanguine flower inscribed with woe.
'Ah, who hath reft,' quoth he, 'my dearest pledge?'

Last came, and last did go,
The Pilot of the Galilean lake;
Two massy keys he bore of metals twain
(The golden opes, the iron shuts amain).
He shook his mitred locks, and stern bespake:
'How well could I have spared for thee, young swain.
Enow of such as for their bellies' sake
Creep and intrude and climb into the fold!
Of other care they little reckoning make
Than how to scramble at the shearers' feast,
And shove away the worthy bidden guest.
Blind mouths! that scarce themselves know how to hold
A sheep-hook, or have learned aught else the least
That to the faithful herdman's art belongs!
What recks it them? What need they? They are sped;
And when they list, their lean and flashy songs
Grate on their scrannel pipes of wretched straw;
The hungry sheep look up, and are not fed,
But swoln with wind, and the rank mist they draw,
Rot inwardly, and foul contagion spread;
Besides what the grim wolf with privy paw
Daily devours apace, and nothing said;
But that two-handed engine at the door
Stands ready to smite once, and smite no more.'
    Return, Alphéus, the dread voice is past
That shrunk thy streams; return, Sicilian Muse,
And call the vales, and bid them hither cast
Their bells and flowerets of a thousand hues.
Ye valleys low, where the mild whispers use
Of shades and wanton winds and gushing brooks,
On whose fresh lap the swart star sparely looks,
Throw hither all your quaint enamelled eyes,
That on the green turf suck the honied showers,
And purple all the ground with vernal flowers.
Bring the rathe primrose that forsaken dies,
The tufted crow-toe, and pale jessamine,
The white pink, and the pansy freaked with jet,
The glowing violet,
The musk rose, and the well-attired woodbine,
With cowslips wan that hang the pensive head,
And every flower that sad embroidery wears.
Bid amaranthus all his beauty shed,
And daffadillies fill their cups with tears,

To strew the laureate hearse where Lycid lies.
For so to interpose a little ease,
Let our frail thoughts dally with false surmise;
Ay me! whilst thee the shores and sounding seas
Wash far away, where'er thy bones are hurled,
Whether beyond the stormy Hebrides,
Where thou perhaps under the whelming tide
Visit'st the bottom of the monstrous world;
Or whether thou, to our moist vows denied,
Sleep'st by the fable of Bellerus old,
Where the great Vision of the guarded mount
Looks toward Namancos, and Bayona's hold.
Look homeward, Angel, now, and melt with ruth:
And, O ye dolphins, waft the hapless youth.

Weep no more, woeful shepherds, weep no more,
For Lycidas, your sorrow, is not dead,
Sunk though he be beneath the watery floor;
So sinks the day-star in the ocean bed,
And yet anon repairs his drooping head,
And tricks his beams, and with new-spangled ore
Flames in the forehead of the morning sky:
So Lycidas sunk low, but mounted high,
Through the dear might of him that walked the waves,
Where, other groves and other streams along,
With nectar pure his oozy locks he laves,
And hears the unexpressive nuptial song,
In the blest kingdoms meek of joy and love.
There entertain him all the saints above,
In solemn troops and sweet societies,
That sing, and singing in their glory move,
And wipe the tears for ever from his eyes.
Now, Lycidas, the shepherds weep no more;
Henceforth thou art the Genius of the shore,
In thy large recompense, and shalt be good
To all that wander in that perilous flood.

Thus sang the uncouth swain to the oaks and rills,
While the still morn went out with sandals grey;
He touched the tender stops of various quills,
With eager thought warbling his Doric lay.
And now the sun had stretched out all the hills,
And now was dropped into the western bay;
At last he rose, and twitched his mantle blue:
Tomorrow to fresh woods, and pastures new.

305

## *On His Blindness*

WHEN I consider how my light is spent,
 Ere half my days, in this dark world and wide,
 And that one talent which is death to hide
 Lodged with me useless, though my soul more bent
To serve therewith my Maker, and present
 My true account, lest he returning chide,
 'Doth God exact day-labour, light denied?'
 I fondly ask. But Patience, to prevent
That murmur, soon replies: 'God doth not need
 Either man's work or his own gifts; who best
 Bear his mild yoke, they serve him best. His state
Is kingly: thousands at his bidding speed,
 And post o'er land and ocean without rest;
 They also serve who only stand and wait.'

306

## *On the Late Massacre in Piedmont*

AVENGE, O Lord, thy slaughtered saints, whose bones
 Lie scattered on the Alpine mountains cold,
 Even them who kept thy truth so pure of old
 When all our fathers worshipped stocks and stones,
Forget not; in thy book record their groans
 Who were thy sheep, and in their ancient fold
 Slain by the bloody Piedmontese that rolled
 Mother with infant down the rocks. Their moans
The vales redoubled to the hills, and they
 To heaven. Their martyred blood and ashes sow
 O'er all the Italian fields, where still doth sway
The triple tyrant, that from these may grow
 A hundredfold, who, having learnt thy way,
 Early may fly the Babylonian woe.

307 *On His Dead Wife*

METHOUGHT I saw my late espousèd saint
 Brought to me like Alcestis from the grave,
 Whom Jove's great son to her glad husband gave,
 Rescued from death by force, though pale and faint.
Mine, as whom washed from spot of childbed taint
 Purification in the old Law did save,
 And such as yet once more I trust to have
 Full sight of her in heaven without restraint,
Came vested all in white, pure as her mind.
 Her face was veiled, yet to my fancied sight
 Love, sweetness, goodness, in her person shined
So clear as in no face with more delight.
 But O as to embrace me she inclined,
 I waked, she fled, and day brought back my night.


*from* Paradise Lost

(i)

308 *Immortal Hate*

THERE the companions of his fall, o'erwhelmed
With floods and whirlwinds of tempestuous fire,
He soon discerns, and weltering by his side
One next himself in power, and next in crime,
Long after known in Palestine, and named
Beelzebub. To whom the Arch-Enemy,
And thence in heaven called Satan, with bold words
Breaking the horrid silence thus began:
 'If thou beest he—but O how fallen! how changed
From him, who in the happy realms of light,
Clothed with transcendent brightness didst outshine
Myriads though bright—if he whom mutual league,
United thoughts and counsels, equal hope
And hazard in the glorious enterprise,
Joined with me once, now misery hath joined
In equal ruin: into what pit thou seest
From what highth fallen, so much the stronger proved
He with his thunder, and till then who knew
The force of those dire arms? Yet not for those,

Nor what the potent Victor in his rage
Can else inflict, do I repent or change,
Though changed in outward lustre, that fixed mind
And high disdain, from sense of injured merit,
That with the mightiest raised me to contend
And to the fierce contention brought along
Innumerable force of Spirits armed
That durst dislike his reign, and me preferring,
His utmost power with adverse power opposed
In dubious battle on the plains of heaven,
And shook his throne. What though the field be lost?
All is not lost; the unconquerable will,
And study of revenge, immortal hate,
And courage never to submit or yield:
And what is else not to be overcome?
That glory never shall his wrath or might
Extort from me. To bow and sue for grace
With suppliant knee, and deify his power
Who from the terror of this arm so late
Doubted his empire, that were low indeed,
That were an ignominy and shame beneath
This downfall; since by fate the strength of gods
And this empyreal substance cannot fail,
Since through experience of this great event,
In arms not worse, in foresight much advanced,
We may with more successful hope resolve
To wage by force or guile eternal war
Irreconcilable to our grand Foe,
Who now triumphs, and in the excess of joy
Sole reigning holds the tyranny of heaven.'

(ii)

*Holy Light*

309

HAIL, holy Light, offspring of Heaven first-born,
Or of the Eternal coeternal beam
May I express thee unblamed? since God is light,
And never but in unapproachèd light
Dwelt from eternity, dwelt then in thee,
Bright effluence of bright essence increate.
Or hear'st thou rather pure ethereal stream,
Whose fountain who shall tell? Before the sun,

Before the heavens thou wert, and at the voice
Of God, as with a mantle didst invest
The rising world of waters dark and deep,
Won from the void and formless infinite.
Thee I revisit now with bolder wing,
Escaped the Stygian pool, though long detained
In that obscure sojourn, while in my flight
Through utter and through middle darkness borne
With other notes than to the Orphean lyre
I sung of Chaos and eternal Night,
Taught by the Heavenly Muse to venture down
The dark descent, and up to reascend,
Though hard and rare. Thee I revisit safe,
And feel thy sovran vital lamp; but thou
Revisit'st not these eyes, that roll in vain
To find thy piercing ray, and find no dawn;
So thick a drop serene hath quenched their orbs,
Or dim suffusion veiled. Yet not the more
Cease I to wander where the Muses haunt
Clear spring, or shady grove, or sunny hill,
Smit with the love of sacred song; but chief
Thee, Sion, and the flowery brooks beneath
That wash thy hallowed feet, and warbling flow,
Nightly I visit; nor sometimes forget
Those other two equalled with me in fate,
So were I equalled with them in renown,
Blind Thamyris and blind Maeonides,
And Tiresias and Phineus prophets old:
Then feed on thoughts that voluntary move
Harmonious numbers, as the wakeful bird
Sings darkling, and in shadiest covert hid
Tunes her nocturnal note. Thus with the year
Seasons return; but not to me returns
Day, or the sweet approach of even or morn,
Or sight of vernal bloom, or summer's rose,
Or flocks, or herds, or human face divine;
But cloud instead, and ever-during dark
Surrounds me, from the cheerful ways of men
Cut off, and for the book of knowledge fair
Presented with a universal blank
Of Nature's works to me expunged and rased,
And wisdom at one entrance quite shut out.
So much the rather thou, celestial Light,

Shine inward, and the mind through all her powers
Irradiate, there plant eyes, all mist from thence
Purge and disperse, that I may see and tell
Of things invisible to mortal sight.

(iii)

*Evived in Paradise*

310

### *Evening in Paradise*

Now came still evening on, and twilight grey
Had in her sober livery all things clad;
Silence accompanied, for beast and bird,
They to their grassy couch, these to their nests
Were slunk, all but the wakeful nightingale;
She all night long her amorous descant sung;
Silence was pleased. Now glowed the firmament
With living sapphires; Hesperus that led
The starry host, rode brightest, till the moon
Rising in clouded majesty, at length
Apparent queen unveiled her peerless light,
And o'er the dark her silver mantle threw;
    When Adam thus to Eve: 'Fair consort, the hour
Of night, and all things now retired to rest,
Mind us of like repose; since God hath set
Labour and rest, as day and night to men
Successive, and the timely dew of sleep
Now falling with soft slumbrous weight inclines
Our eyelids; other creatures all day long
Rove idle, unemployed, and less need rest;
Man hath his daily work of body or mind
Appointed, which declares his dignity,
And the regard of Heaven on all his ways;
While other animals unactive range,
And of their doings God takes no account.
Tomorrow ere fresh morning streak the east
With first approach of light, we must be risen,
And at our pleasant labour, to reform
Yon flowery arbours, yonder alleys green,
Our walks at noon, with branches overgrown,
That mock our scant manuring and require
More hands than ours to lop their wanton growth.
Those blossoms also, and those dropping gums,
That lie bestrewn unsightly and unsmooth,

Ask riddance, if we mean to tread with ease;
Meanwhile, as nature wills, night bids us rest.'
   To whom thus Eve with perfect beauty adorned:
'My author and disposer, what thou bid'st
Unargued I obey; so God ordains.
God is thy law, thou mine; to know no more
Is woman's happiest knowledge, and her praise.
With thee conversing, I forget all time,
All seasons, and their change, all please alike.
Sweet is the breath of morn, her rising sweet,
With charm of earliest birds; pleasant the sun,
When first on this delightful land he spreads
His orient beams, on herb, tree, fruit, and flower,
Glistering with dew; fragrant the fertile earth
After soft showers; and sweet the coming on
Of grateful evening mild, then silent night
With this her solemn bird, and this fair moon
And these the gems of heaven, her starry train:
But neither breath of morn, when she ascends
With charm of earliest birds, nor rising sun
On this delightful land, nor herb, fruit, flower,
Glistering with dew, nor fragrance after showers,
Nor grateful evening mild, nor silent night
With this her solemn bird, nor walk by moon
Or glittering starlight, without thee is sweet.

### (iv)

311                *The Banishment*

So spake our mother Eve, and Adam heard
Well pleased, but answered not; for now too nigh
The Archangel stood, and from the other hill
To their fixed station, all in bright array
The Cherubim descended; on the ground
Gliding metéorous, as evening mist
Risen from a river o'er the marish glides,
And gathers ground fast at the labourer's heel
Homeward returning. High in front advanced,
The brandished sword of God before them blazed
Fierce as a comet; which with torrid heat,
And vapour as the Libyan air adust,

Began to parch that temperate clime; whereat
In either hand the hastening Angel caught
Our lingering parents, and to the eastern gate
Led them direct, and down the cliff as fast
To the subjected plain; then disappeared.
They, looking back, all the eastern side beheld
Of Paradise, so late their happy seat,
Waved over by that flaming brand, the gate
With dreadful faces thronged and fiery arms.
Some natural tears they dropped, but wiped them soon;
The world was all before them, where to choose
Their place of rest, and Providence their guide:
They hand in hand, with wandering steps and slow,
Through Eden took their solitary way.

### *from* Samson Agonistes

312

### (i)

O HOW comely it is and how reviving
To the spirits of just men long oppressed,
When God into the hands of their deliverer
Puts invincible might
To quell the mighty of the earth, the oppressor,
The brute and boisterous force of violent men,
Hardy and industrious to support
Tyrannic power, but raging to pursue
The righteous and all such as honour truth!
He all their ammunition
And feats of war defeats
With plain heroic magnitude of mind
And celestial vigour armed;
Their armouries and magazines contemns,
Renders them useless, while
With winged expedition
Swift as the lightning glance he executes
His errand on the wicked, who surprised,
Lose their defence, distracted and amazed.
  But patience is more oft the exercise
Of saints, the trial of their fortitude,
Making them each his own deliverer,

And victor over all
That tyranny or fortune can inflict;
Either of these is in thy lot,
Samson, with might endued
Above the sons of men; but sight bereaved
May chance to number thee with those
Whom patience finally must crown.

### (ii)

313

ALL is best, though we oft doubt,
What the unsearchable dispose
Of Highest Wisdom brings about,
And ever best found in the close.
Oft he seems to hide his face,
But unexpectedly returns
And to his faithful champion hath in place
Bore witness gloriously; whence Gaza mourns,
And all that band them to resist
His uncontrollable intent:
His servants he, with new acquist
Of true experience from this great event,
With peace and consolation hath dismissed,
And calm of mind, all passion spent.

# SIR JOHN SUCKLING

## 1609–1642

314

### *A Doubt of Martyrdom*

O FOR some honest lover's ghost,
    Some kind unbodied post
    Sent from the shades below!
    I strangely long to know
Whether the nobler chaplets wear
Those that their mistress' scorn did bear
    Or those that were used kindly.

For whatsoe'er they tell us here
        To make those sufferings dear,
        'Twill there, I fear, be found
        That to the being crowned
To have loved alone will not suffice,
Unless we also have been wise
        And have our loves enjoyed.

What posture can we think him in
        That, here unloved, again
        Departs, and's thither gone
        Where each sits by his own?
Or how can that Elysium be
Where I my mistress still must see
        Circled in other's arms?

For there the judges all are just,
        And Sophonisba must
        Be his whom she held dear,
        Not his who loved her here.
The sweet Philoclea, since she died,
Lies by her Pirocles his side,
        Not by Amphialus.

Some bays, perchance, or myrtle bough
        For difference crowns the brow
        Of those kind souls that were
        The noble martyrs here:
And if that be the only odds
(As who can tell?), ye kinder gods,
        Give me the woman here!

315                    *The Constant Lover*

        OUT upon it, I have loved
            Three whole days together!
        And am like to love three more,
            If it hold fair weather.

        Time shall moult away his wings
            Ere he shall discover
        In the whole wide world again
            Such a constant lover.

But a pox upon't, no praise
    There is due at all to me:
Love with me had made no stay,
    Had it any been but she.

Had it any been but she,
    And that very very face,
There had been at least ere this
    A dozen dozen in her place.

316                *Why so Pale and Wan*

WHY so pale and wan, fond lover?
      Prithee, why so pale?
Will, when looking well can't move her,
      Looking ill prevail?
      Prithee, why so pale?

Why so dull and mute, young sinner?
      Prithee, why so mute?
Will, when speaking well can't win her,
      Saying nothing do 't?
      Prithee, why so mute?

Quit, quit for shame! This will not move;
      This cannot take her.
If of herself she will not love,
      Nothing can make her:
      The devil take her!

# SIDNEY GODOLPHIN

## 1610–1643

317                *Wise Men and Shepherds*

LORD, when the wise men came from far,
Led to thy cradle by a star,
Then did the shepherds too rejoice,
Instructed by thy angel's voice.
Blest were the wise men in their skill,
And shepherds in their harmless will.

# SIDNEY GODOLPHIN

Wise men, in tracing Nature's laws,
Ascend unto the highest cause;
Shepherds with humble fearfulness
Walk safely, though their light be less.
Though wise men better know the way,
It seems no honest heart can stray.

There is no merit in the wise
But love, the shepherds' sacrifice.
Wise men, all ways of knowledge passed,
To the shepherds' wonder come at last.
To know can only wonder breed,
And not to know is wonder's seed.

A wise man at the altar bows,
And offers up his studied vows,
And is received. May not the tears,
Which spring too from a shepherd's fears,
And sighs upon his frailty spent,
Though not distinct, be eloquent?

'Tis true, the object sanctifies
All passions which within us rise,
But since no creature comprehends
The cause of causes, end of ends,
He who himself vouchsafes to know
Best pleases his creator so.

When then our sorrows we apply
To our own wants and poverty,
When we look up in all distress,
And our own misery confess,
Sending both thanks and prayers above,
Then, though we do not know, we love.

# JAMES GRAHAM,
# MARQUIS OF MONTROSE

### 1612–1650

318          *I'll Never Love Thee More*

My dear and only love, I pray
    That little world of thee
Be governed by no other sway
    Than purest monarchy;
For if confusion have a part
    (Which virtuous souls abhor),
And hold a synod in thine heart,
    I'll never love thee more.

Like Alexander I will reign,
    And I will reign alone;
My thoughts did evermore disdain
    A rival on my throne.
He either fears his fate too much,
    Or his deserts are small,
That dares not put it to the touch,
    To gain or lose it all.

And in the empire of thine heart,
    Where I should solely be,
If others do pretend a part
    Or dare to vie with me,
Or if Committees thou erect,
    And go on such a score,
I'll laugh and sing at thy neglect,
    And never love thee more.

But if thou wilt prove faithful then,
    And constant of thy word,
I'll make thee glorious by my pen
    And famous by my sword;
I'll serve thee in such noble ways
    Was never heard before;
I'll crown and deck thee all with bays,
    And love thee more and more.

319 *Epitaph on Charles I*

GREAT, good and just, could I but rate
My grief to thy too rigid fate!
I'd weep the world in such a strain
As it would once deluge again:
But since thy loud-tongued blood demands supplies
More from Briareus' hands than Argus' eyes,
I'll tune thy elegies to trumpet sounds,
And write thy epitaph in blood and wounds.


# THOMAS JORDAN

?1612–1685

320 *The Epicure*
*Sung by one in the Habit of a Town Gallant*

LET us drink and be merry, dance, joke, and rejoice,
With Claret and Sherry, Theorbo and Voice;
The changeable world to our joy is unjust,
All treasure uncertain, then down with your dust.
  In frolic dispose your pounds, shillings and pence,
  For we shall be nothing a hundred years hence.

We'll kiss and be free with Nan, Betty, and Philly,
Have oysters and lobsters, and maids by the belly;
Fish-dinners will make a lass spring like a flea,
Dame Venus (Love's goddess) was born of the sea.
  With her and with Bacchus we'll tickle the sense,
  For we shall be past it a hundred years hence.

Your most beautiful bit that hath all eyes upon her,
That her honesty sells for a hogo of honour;
Whose lightness and brightness doth shine in such splendour
That none but the stars are thought fit to attend her,
  Though now she be pleasant and sweet to the sense,
  Will be damnably mouldy a hundred years hence.

320   hogo] taint, or flavour

Then why should we turmoil in cares and in fears,
Turn all our tranquillity to sighs and to tears?
Let's eat, drink and play till the worms do corrupt us,
'Tis certain that *post mortem nulla Voluptas.*
   Let's deal with our damsels, that we may from thence
   Have broods to succeed us a hundred years hence. . . .


# RICHARD CRASHAW

## ?1612–1649

321                        *On Hope*
         *By Way of Question and Answer Between*
         *Abraham Cowley and Richard Crashaw*

Cowley.    *Hope, whose weak being ruined is*
           *Alike if it succeed and if it miss;*
           *Whom ill and good doth equally confound,*
           *And both the horns of Fate's dilemma wound;*
              *Vain shadow! that doth vanish quite*
              *Both at full noon and perfect night.*
           *The Fates have not a possibility*
                 *Of blessing thee.*
           *If things then from their ends we happy call,*
           *'Tis Hope is the most hopeless thing of all.*


Crashaw.   Dear Hope! Earth's dowry and Heaven's debt,
           The entity of things that are not yet.
           Subtlest but surest being! thou by whom
           Our nothing hath a definition.
              Fair cloud of fire, both shade and light,
              Our life in death, our day in night.
              Fates cannot find out a capacity
                 Of hurting thee;
           From thee their thin dilemma with blunt horn
           Shrinks, like the sick moon at the wholesome morn.


**320**   *post mortem . . .* ] there is no pleasure after death

# RICHARD CRASHAW

*Cowley.*　　*Hope, thou bold taster of delight,*
*Who, instead of doing so, devour'st it quite;*
*Thou bring'st us an estate, yet leav'st us poor,*
*By clogging it with legacies before.*
　　*The joys which we entire should wed*
　　*Come deflowered virgins to our bed.*
　　*Good fortunes without gain imported be,*
　　　　*So mighty custom's paid to thee.*
*For joy, like wine, kept close doth better taste:*
*If it take air before, its spirits waste.*

*Crashaw.*　　Thou art Love's legacy under lock
Of Faith, the steward of our growing stock.
Our crown-lands lie above, yet each meal brings
A seemly portion for the sons of kings.
　　Nor will the virgin joys we wed
　　Come less unbroken to our bed
　　Because that from the bridal cheek of bliss
　　　　Thou thus steal'st down a distant kiss:
Hope's chaste kiss wrongs no more joy's maidenhead,
Than spousal rites prejudge the marriage-bed.

　　Fair Hope! our earlier Heaven! by thee
Young Time is taster to Eternity.
The generous wine with age grows strong, not sour,
Nor need we kill thy fruit to smell thy flower.
Thy golden head never hangs down
　　Till in the lap of Love's full noon
　　It falls and dies: Oh no, it melts away
　　　　As doth the dawn into the day,
As lumps of sugar lose themselves, and twine
Their subtle essence with the soul of wine.

*Cowley.*　　*Hope, Fortune's cheating lottery,*
*Where for one prize an hundred blanks there be;*
*Fond archer Hope, who tak'st thine aim so far*
*That still or short or wide thine arrows are.*
　　*Thine empty cloud the eye itself deceives*
　　*With shapes that our own fancy gives:*
　　*A cloud which gilt and painted now appears*
　　　　*But must drop presently in tears.*
*When thy false beams o'er Reason's light prevail,*
*By* ignes fatui, *not North stars, we sail.*

Crashaw.    Fortune, alas, above the world's law wars;
Hope kicks the curled heads of conspiring stars.
Her keel cuts not the waves, where our winds stir,
And Fate's whole lottery is one blank to her.
    Her shafts and she fly far above,
    And forage in the fields of light and love.
    Sweet Hope! kind cheat! fair fallacy! by thee
      We are not where or what we be,
But what and where we would be: thus art thou
Our absent presence, and our future now.

Cowley.    *Brother of Fear! more gaily clad,*
*The merrier fool of the two, yet quite as mad.*
*Sire of Repentance! child of fond Desire,*
*That blows the chymic's and the lover's fire,*
    *Still leading them insensibly on*
    *With the strange witchcraft of* Anon.
    *By thee the one doth changing Nature through*
    *Her endless labyrinths pursue,*
*And the other chases woman, while she goes*
*More ways and turns than hunted Nature knows.*

Crashaw.    Faith's sister! nurse of fair Desire!
Fear's antidote! a wise and well-stayed fire,
Tempered 'twixt cold despair and torrid joy,
Queen Regent in young Love's minority.
    Though the vexed chymic vainly chases
    His fugitive gold through all her faces,
    And loves more fierce, more fruitless fires assay
    One face more fugitive than all they,
True Hope's a glorious huntress, and her chase
The God of Nature in the field of Grace.

322          *The Shepherds' Hymn*

Tityrus.    Gloomy night embraced the place
    Where the noble Infant lay.
The Babe looked up and showed his face;
    In spite of darkness, it was day.
It was thy day, Sweet, and did rise
Not from the East, but from thine eyes.

# RICHARD CRASHAW

*Thyrsis.*    Winter chid aloud, and sent
              The angry North to wage his wars;
         The North forgot his fierce intent
              And left perfumes instead of scars.
         By those sweet eyes' persuasive powers,
         Where he meant frost, he scattered flowers.

*Both.*      We saw thee in thy balmy nest,
              Bright dawn of our eternal day!
         We saw thine eyes break from their East
              And chase the trembling shades away.
         We saw thee, and we blessed the sight;
         We saw thee by thine own sweet light.

*Tityrus.*   Poor world, said I, what wilt thou do
              To entertain this starry stranger?
         Is this the best thou canst bestow,
              A cold, and not too cleanly manger?
         Contend, ye powers of heaven and earth,
         To fit a bed for this huge birth.

*Thyrsis.*   Proud world, said I, cease your contest,
              And let the mighty Babe alone,
         The phoenix builds the phoenix' nest,
              Love's architecture is his own.
         The Babe whose birth embraves this morn
         Made his own bed ere he was born.

*Tityrus.*   I saw the curled drops, soft and slow,
              Come hovering o'er the place's head,
         Offering their whitest sheets of snow,
              To furnish the fair infant's bed.
         Forbear, said I, be not too bold;
         Your fleece is white, but 'tis too cold.

*Thyrsis.*   I saw the obsequious Seraphins
              Their rosy fleece of fire bestow,
         For well they now can spare their wings,
              Since Heaven itself lies here below.
         Well done, said I, but are you sure
         Your down, so warm, will pass for pure?

*Tityrus.*    No, no, your King's not yet to seek
        Where to repose his royal head;
    See, see, how soon his new-bloomed cheek
        'Twixt mother's breasts is gone to bed!
    Sweet choice, said we; no way but so,
    Not to lie cold, yet sleep in snow.

*Both.*    We saw thee in thy balmy nest,
        Bright dawn of our eternal day!
    We saw thine eyes break from their East
        And chase the trembling shades away.
    We saw thee and we blessed the sight;
    We saw thee by thine own sweet light.

*Full Chorus.* Welcome, all wonders in one sight!
        Eternity shut in a span,
    Summer in winter, day in night,
        Heaven in earth and God in Man;
    Great little one! whose all embracing birth
    Lifts earth to heaven, stoops heaven to earth.

    Welcome! though not to gold nor silk,
        To more than Caesar's birthright is:
    Two sister-seas of virgin-milk,
        With many a rarely-tempered kiss
    That breathes at once both Maid and Mother,
    Warms in the one, cools in the other.

    She sings thy tears asleep, and dips
        Her kisses in thy weeping eye,
    She spreads the red leaves of thy lips
        That in their buds yet blushing lie,
    She 'gainst those mother-diamonds tries
    The points of her young eagle's eyes.

    Welcome! though not to those gay flies
        Gilded in the beams of earthly kings,
    Slippery souls in smiling eyes,
        But to poor shepherds, home-spun things,
    Whose wealth's their flock, whose wit to be
    Well read in their simplicity.

Yet when young April's husband showers
   Shall bless the fruitful Maia's bed,
We'll bring the first-born of her flowers
   To kiss thy feet and crown thy head.
To thee, dread Lamb! whose love must keep
The shepherds more than they their sheep.

To thee, meek Majesty, soft King
   Of simple graces and sweet loves,
Each of us his lamb will bring
   Each his pair of silver doves;
Till burnt at last in fire of thy fair eyes,
Our selves become our own best sacrifice.

323      *A Hymn to the Name and Honour of*
            *the Admirable Saint Teresa*

    *Love, thou art absolute, sole Lord*
    *Of life and death.* To prove the word,
    We'll now appeal to none of all
    Those thy old soldiers, great and tall,
    Ripe men of martyrdom, that could reach down
    With strong arms their triumphant crown:
    Such as could with lusty breath
    Speak loud into the face of death
    Their great Lord's glorious name; to none
    Of those whose spacious bosoms spread a throne
    For Love at large to fill. Spare blood and sweat,
    And see him take a private seat,
    Making his mansion in the mild
    And milky soul of a soft child.
    Scarce hath she learnt to lisp the name
    Of martyr, yet she thinks it shame
    Life should so long play with that breath
    Which spent can buy so brave a death.
    She never undertook to know
    What death with love should have to do;
    Nor hath she e'er yet understood
    Why to show love, she should shed blood.
    Yet though she cannot tell you why,
    She can love, and she can die.

RICHARD CRASHAW

Scarce hath she blood enough to make
A guilty sword blush for her sake;
Yet hath she a heart dare hope to prove
How much less strong is death than love. . . .

Since 'tis not to be had at home,
She'll travel for a martyrdom.
No home for hers confesses she,
But where she may a martyr be.
She'll to the Moors and trade with them
For this unvalued Diadem;
She'll offer them her dearest breath,
With Christ's name in't, in change for death.
She'll bargain with them, and will give
Them God, and teach them how to live
In him; or, if they this deny,
For him she'll teach them how to die.
So shall she leave amongst them sown
Her Lord's blood, or at least her own.
Farewell then, all the world, adieu!
Teresa is no more for you.
Farewell all pleasures, sports, and joys,
Never till now esteemèd toys!
Farewell whatever dear may be,
Mother's arms or father's knee!
Farewell house, and farewell home!
She's for the Moors and martyrdom.

Sweet not so fast! Lo, thy fair Spouse,
Whom thou seek'st with so swift vows,
Calls thee back, and bids thee come
To embrace a milder martyrdom. . . .

O how oft shalt thou complain
Of a sweet and subtle pain!
Of intolerable joys!
Of a death, in which who dies
Loves his death, and dies again,
And would forever so be slain;
And lives and dies, and knows not why
To live, but that he thus may never leave to die!
How kindly will thy gentle heart
Kiss the sweetly-killing dart,

And close in his embraces keep
Those delicious wounds that weep
Balsam to heal themselves with! Thus,
When these thy deaths so numerous
Shall all at last die into one,
And melt thy soul's sweet mansion;
Like a soft lump of incense, hasted
By too hot a fire, and wasted
Into perfuming clouds, so fast
Shalt thou exhale to heaven at last,
In a resolving sigh, and then,
O what? Ask not the tongues of men.

   Angels cannot tell. Suffice
Thyself shall feel thine own full joys,
And hold them fast forever. There,
So soon as thou shalt first appear,
The Moon of maiden stars, thy white
Mistress, attended by such bright
Souls as thy shining self, shall come,
And in her first ranks make thee room;
Where 'mongst her snowy family
Immortal welcomes wait for thee.
O what delight, when revealed Life shall stand
And teach thy lips heaven with his hand,
On which thou now mayst to thy wishes
Heap up thy consecrated kisses!
What joys shall seize thy soul, when she
Bending her blessed eyes on thee,
Those second smiles of heaven, shall dart
Her mild rays through thy melting heart!
Angels, thy old friends, there shall greet thee,
Glad at their own home now to meet thee.
All thy good works which went before,
And waited for thee at the door,
Shall own thee there, and all in one
Weave a constellation
Of crowns with which the King, thy Spouse,
Shall build up thy triumphant brows.

All thy old woes shall now smile on thee,
And thy pains sit bright upon thee;
All thy sorrows here shall shine,
And thy sufferings be divine.
Tears shall take comfort, and turn gems,
And wrongs repent to diadems.
Even thy deaths shall live, and new
Dress the soul that erst they slew.
Thy wounds shall blush to such bright scars
As keep account of the Lamb's wars.
Those rare works where thou shalt leave writ
Love's noble history, with wit
Taught thee by none but him, while here
They feed our souls, shall clothe thine there.
Each heavenly word, by whose hid flame
Our hard hearts shall strike fire, the same
Shall flourish on thy brows, and be
Both fire to us, and flame to thee;
Whose light shall live bright in thy face
By glory, in our hearts by grace.
Thou shalt look round about, and see
Thousands of crowned souls throng to be
Themselves thy crown; sons of thy vows,
The virgin-births, with which thy sovereign Spouse
Made fruitful thy fair soul. Go now,
And with them all about thee bow
To him. 'Put on', he'll say, 'put on,
My rosy Love, that thy rich zone,
Sparkling with the sacred flames
Of thousand souls, whose happy names
Heaven keeps upon thy score: thy bright
Life brought them first to kiss the light
That kindled them to stars; and so
Thou with the Lamb, thy Lord, shalt go;
And whereso'er he sets his white
Steps, walk with him those ways of light,
Which who in death would live to see
Must learn in life to die like thee.'

324
## The Flaming Heart
### Upon the Book and Picture of
### the Seraphical Saint Teresa

O THOU undaunted daughter of desires!
By all thy dower of lights and fires;
By all the eagle in thee, all the dove;
By all thy lives and deaths of love;
By thy large draughts of intellectual day,
And by thy thirsts of love more large than they;
By all thy brim-filled bowls of fierce desire,
By thy last morning's draught of liquid fire;
By the full kingdom of that final kiss
That seized thy parting soul, and sealed thee His,
By all the Heavens thou hast in Him
(Fair sister of the seraphim!);
By all of Him we have in thee;
Leave nothing of myself in me.
Let me so read thy life, that I
Unto all life of mine may die!


325
## An Epitaph upon Husband and Wife
### Who died and were buried together

To these whom death again did wed
This grave's the second marriage-bed.
For though the hand of Fate could force
'Twixt soul and body a divorce,
It could not sever man and wife,
Because they both lived but one life.
Peace, good reader, do not weep;
Peace, the lovers are asleep.
They, sweet turtles, folded lie
In the last knot that love could tie.
Let them sleep, let them sleep on,
Till this stormy night be gone,
And the eternal morrow dawn;
Then the curtains will be drawn,
And they wake into a light
Whose day shall never die in night.

# SAMUEL BUTLER
## 1613–1680

### *from* Hudibras

#### (i)

326      *Presbyterian Knight*

WHEN civil fury first grew high,
And men fell out they knew not why;
When hard words, jealousies and fears
Set folks together by the ears,
And made them fight like mad or drunk
For Dame Religion as for punk,
Whose honesty they all durst swear for,
Though not a man of them knew wherefore;
When Gospel-trumpeter, surrounded
With long-eared rout, to battle sounded,
And pulpit, drum ecclesiastic,
Was beat with fist instead of a stick:
Then did Sir Knight abandon dwelling
And out he rode a Colonelling.

*

For his Religion it was fit
To match his learning and his wit:
'Twas Presbyterian true blue,
For he was of that stubborn crew
Of errant Saints, whom all men grant
To be the true Church Militant:
Such as do build their Faith upon
The holy Text of pike and gun;
Decide all controversies by
Infallible artillery;
And prove their Doctrine orthodox
By Apostolic blows and knocks;
Call fire and sword and desolation
A godly-thorough-Reformation,
Which always must be carried on
And still be doing, never done,

As if Religion were intended
For nothing else but to be mended.
A sect whose chief devotion lies
In odd perverse antipathies,
In falling out with that or this,
And finding somewhat still amiss;
More peevish, cross and splenetick
Than dog distract or monkey sick;
That with more care keep holy-day
The wrong, than others the right way;
Compound for sins they are inclined to,
By damning those they have no mind to;
Still so perverse and opposite
As if they worshipped God for spite.
The selfsame thing they will abhor
One way, and long another for.
Free-will they one way disavow,
Another, nothing else allow.
All piety consists therein
In them, in other men all sin.
Rather than fail they will defy
That which they love most tenderly,
Quarrel with minced pies, and disparage
Their best and dearest friend, plum-porridge;
Fat pig and goose itself oppose,
And blaspheme custard through the nose.
The Apostles of this fierce Religion,
Like Mahomet's, were ass and widgeon,
To whom our Knight by fast instinct
Of wit and temper was so linked
As if hypocrisy and nonsense
Had got the advowson of his conscience.

### (ii)

### *Independent Squire*

327

A SQUIRE he had whose name was Ralph,
That in the adventure went his half.
(Though writers, for more stately tone,
Do call him Ralpho: 'tis all one:
And when we can with metre safe,
We'll call him so, if not plain Raph.)

\*

## SAMUEL BUTLER

His knowledge was not far behind
The Knight's, but of another kind,
And he another way came by it:
Some call it gifts, and some New Light;
A liberal art, that costs no pains
Of study, industry or brains.
His wits were sent him for a token,
But in the carriage cracked and broken.
Like commendation ninepence, crooked
With to and from my love, it looked.
He ne'er considered it, as loath
To look a gift-horse in the mouth,
And very wisely would lay forth
No more upon it than 'twas worth.
But as he got it freely, so
He spent it frank and freely too.
For Saints themselves will sometimes be
Of gifts that cost them nothing, free.
By means of this, with *hem* and *cough*,
Prolongers to enlightened snuff,
He could deep mysteries unriddle
As easily as thread a needle;
For as of vagabonds we say
That they are ne'er beside their way,
Whate'er men speak by this New Light,
Still they are sure to be i'th' right.
'Tis a dark-lantern of the Spirit,
Which none see by but those that bear it:
A Light that falls down from on high
For spiritual trades to cozen by;
An *Ignis Fatuus* that bewitches,
And leads men into pools and ditches,
To make them dip themselves, and sound
For Christendom in dirty pond;
To dive like wildfowl for Salvation,
And fish to catch Regeneration.
This Light inspires, and plays upon
The nose of Saint like bagpipe-drone,
And speaks through hollow empty soul,
As through a trunk or whispering hole,
Such language as no mortal ear
But spiritual eavesdroppers can hear.

So Phoebus or some friendly Muse
Into small poets song infuse,
Which they at secondhand rehearse
Through reed or bagpipe, verse for verse.

# JOHN CLEVELAND
## 1613–1658

328 *Epitaph on the Earl of Strafford*

HERE lies wise and valiant dust,
Huddled up 'twixt fit and just,
Strafford, who was hurried hence
'Twixt treason and convenience.
He spent his time here in a mist,
A Papist, yet a Calvinist;
His Prince's nearest joy and grief,
He had, yet wanted, all relief;
The prop and ruin of the State,
The peoples' violent love and hate;
One in extremes loved and abhorred.
Riddles lie here, or in a word,
Here lies blood, and let it lie
Speechless still, and never cry.

# ABRAHAM COWLEY
## 1618–1667

329 *The Wish*

WELL then! I now do plainly see
This busy world and I shall ne'er agree.
The very honey of all earthly joy
Does of all meats the soonest cloy;
 And they, methinks, deserve my pity
Who for it can endure the stings,
The crowd, and buzz, and murmurings,
 Of this great hive, the city.

Ah, yet, ere I descend to the grave,
May I a small house and large garden have;
And a few friends, and many books, both true,
Both wise, and both delightful too!
   And since love ne'er will from me flee,
A mistress moderately fair,
And good as guardian angels are,
   Only beloved and loving me.

O fountains! when in you shall I
Myself eased of unpeaceful thoughts espy?
O fields! O woods! when, when shall I be made
The happy tenant of your shade?
   Here's the spring-head of Pleasure's flood:
Here's wealthy Nature's treasury,
Where all the riches lie that she
   Has coined and stamped for good.

Pride and ambition here
Only in far-fetched metaphors appear;
Here nought but winds can hurtful murmurs scatter,
And nought but Echo flatter.
   The gods, when they descended, hither
From heaven did always choose their way:
And therefore we may boldly say
   That 'tis the way too thither.

How happy here should I
And one dear She live, and embracing die!
She who is all the world, and can exclude,
In deserts, solitude.
   I should have then this only fear:
Lest men, when they my pleasures see,
Should hither throng to live like me,
   And so make a city here.

330                     *Drinking*

THE thirsty earth soaks up the rain,
And drinks and gapes for drink again;
The plants suck in the earth, and are
With constant drinking fresh and fair;
The sea itself (which one would think
Should have but little need of drink)
Drinks ten thousand rivers up,
So filled that they o'erflow the cup.
The busy Sun (and one would guess
By 's drunken fiery face no less)
Drinks up the sea, and when he's done,
The Moon and Stars drink up the Sun:
They drink and dance by their own light,
They drink and revel all the night:
Nothing in Nature's sober found,
But an eternal health goes round.
Fill up the bowl, then, fill it high,
Fill all the glasses there—for why
Should every creature drink but I?
Why, man of morals, tell me why?


331      *On the Death of Mr. William Harvey*

IT was a dismal and a fearful night,
Scarce could the morn drive on the unwilling light,
When Sleep, Death's image, left my troubled breast
     By something liker Death possest.
My eyes with tears did uncommanded flow,
     And on my soul hung the dull weight
     Of some intolerable fate.
What bell was that? Ah me! too much I know.

My sweet companion, and my gentle peer,
Why hast thou left me thus unkindly here,
Thy end forever, and my life to moan?
     O thou hast left me all alone!
Thy soul and body, when death's agony
     Besieged around thy noble heart,
     Did not with more reluctance part
Than I, my dearest Friend, do part from thee.

My dearest Friend, would I had died for thee!
Life and this world henceforth will tedious be.
Nor shall I know hereafter what to do
    If once my griefs prove tedious too.
Silent and sad I walk about all day,
      As sullen ghosts stalk speechless by
      Where their hid treasures lie;
Alas, my treasure's gone, why do I stay?

He was my friend, the truest friend on earth;
A strong and mighty influence joined our birth.
Nor did we envy the most sounding name
    By Friendship given of old to Fame.
None but his brethren he, and sisters, knew
      Whom the kind youth preferred to me;
      And even in that we did agree,
For much above myself I loved them too.

Say, for you saw us, ye immortal lights,
How oft unwearied have we spent the nights,
Till the Ledaean stars, so famed for love,
    Wondered at us from above?
We spent them not in toys, in lusts, or wine,
      But search of deep Philosophy,
      Wit, Eloquence, and Poetry,
Arts which I loved, for they, my Friend, were thine.

Ye fields of Cambridge, our dear Cambridge, say,
Have ye not seen us walking every day?
Was there a tree about which did not know
    The love betwixt us two?
Henceforth, ye gentle trees, forever fade;
      Or your sad branches thicker join
      And into darksome shades combine,
Dark as the grave wherein my friend is laid. . . .

# RICHARD LOVELACE
## 1618–1657

332     *To Lucasta, Going to the Wars*

TELL me not, sweet, I am unkind,
   That from the nunnery
Of thy chaste breast and quiet mind
   To war and arms I fly.

True, a new mistress now I chase,
   The first foe in the field;
And with a stronger faith embrace
   A sword, a horse, a shield.

Yet this inconstancy is such
   As you too shall adore;
I could not love thee, dear, so much,
   Loved I not honour more.

333     *The Grasshopper:*
*To My Noble Friend, Mr. Charles Cotton*

O THOU that swing'st upon the waving hair
   Of some well-fillèd oaten-beard,
Drunk every night with a delicious tear
   Dropped thee from heaven, where now thou art reared.

The joys of earth and air are thine entire,
   That with thy feet and wings dost hop and fly;
And when thy poppy works thou dost retire
   To thy carved acorn-bed to lie.

Up with the day, the sun thou welcom'st then,
   Sport'st in the gilt-plaits of his beams,
And all these merry days mak'st merry men,
   Thyself, and melancholy streams.

But ah, the sickle! golden ears are cropped;
   Ceres and Bacchus bid good-night;
Sharp frosty fingers all your flowers have topped
   And what scythes spared, winds shave off quite.

Poor verdant fool! and now green ice! thy joys,
    Large and as lasting as thy perch of grass,
Bid us lay in 'gainst winter rain, and poise
    Their floods with an o'er flowing glass.

Thou best of men and friends! we will create
    A genuine summer in each other's breast;
And spite of this cold time and frozen fate
    Thaw us a warm seat to our rest.

Our sacred hearths shall burn eternally
    As vestal flames; the north-wind, he
Shall strike his frost-stretched wings, dissolve and fly
    This Etna in epitome.

Dropping December shall come weeping in,
    Bewail the usurping of his reign;
But when in showers of old Greek we begin
    Shall cry he hath his crown again!

Night as clear Hesper shall our tapers whip
    From the light casements where we play,
And the dark hag from her black mantle strip,
    And stick there everlasting day.

Thus richer than untempted kings are we,
    That asking nothing, nothing need:
Though Lord of all what seas embrace, yet he
    That wants himself is poor indeed.


334           *To Althea, from Prison*

    WHEN Love with unconfinèd wings
        Hovers within my gates;
    And my divine Althea brings
        To whisper at the grates;
    When I lie tangled in her hair,
        And fettered to her eye;
    The Gods that wanton in the air
        Know no such liberty.

RICHARD LOVELACE

When flowing cups run swiftly round
   With no allaying Thames,
Our careless heads with roses bound
   Our hearts with loyal flames;
When thirsty grief in wine we steep,
   When healths and draughts go free,
Fishes that tipple in the deep
   Know no such liberty.

When, like committed linnets, I
   With shriller throat shall sing
The sweetness, mercy, majesty,
   And glories of my King;
When I shall voice aloud how good
   He is, how great should be,
Enlargèd winds that curl the flood
   Know no such liberty.

Stone walls do not a prison make,
   Nor iron bars a cage;
Minds innocent and quiet take
   That for an hermitage;
If I have freedom in my love,
   And in my soul am free;
Angels alone that soar above
   Enjoy such liberty.


# ANDREW MARVELL

## 1621-1678

335
*An Horation Ode
upon Cromwell's Return from Ireland,
1650*

THE forward youth that would appear
Must now forsake his Muses dear,
   Nor in the shadows sing
   His numbers languishing.

'Tis time to leave the books in dust,
And oil the unusèd armour's rust,
    Removing from the wall
    The corslet of the hall.

So restless Cromwell could not cease
In the inglorious arts of peace,
    But through adventurous war
    Urgèd his active star:

And like the three-forked lightning, first
Breaking the clouds where it was nurst,
    Did thorough his own side
    His fiery way divide:

For 'tis all one to courage high,
The emulous, or enemy;
    And with such, to enclose
    Is more than to oppose.

Then burning through the air he went
And palaces and temples rent;
    And Caesar's head at last
    Did through his laurels blast.

'Tis madness to resist or blame
The force of angry Heaven's flame;
    And if we would speak true,
    Much to the man is due,

Who, from his private gardens, where
He lived reservèd and austere
    (As if his highest plot
    To plant the bergamot),

Could by industrious valour climb
To ruin the great work of time,
    And cast the Kingdom old
    Into another mould.

Though Justice against Fate complain,
And plead the ancient rights in vain—
    But those do hold or break
    As men are strong or weak—

ANDREW MARVELL

Nature, that hateth emptiness,
Allows of penetration less,
 And therefore must make room
 Where greater spirits come.

What field of all the civil wars
Where his were not the deepest scars?
 And Hampton shows what part
 He had of wiser art;

Where, twining subtle fears with hope,
He wove a net of such a scope
 That Charles himself might chase
 To Car'sbrook's narrow case;

That thence the Royal Actor borne
The tragic scaffold might adorn:
 While round the armèd bands
 Did clap their bloody hands.

He nothing common did or mean
Upon that memorable scene,
 But with his keener eye
 The axe's edge did try;

Nor called the Gods, with vulgar spite,
To vindicate his helpless right;
 But bowed his comely head
 Down, as upon a bed.

This was that memorable hour
Which first assured the forcèd power:
 So when they did design
 The Capitol's first line,

A bleeding head, where they begun,
Did fright the architects to run;
 And yet in that the State
 Foresaw its happy fate!

And now the Irish are ashamed
To see themselves in one year tamed:
 So much one man can do
 That does both act and know.

They can affirm his praises best,
And have, though overcome, confest
　　How good he is, how just
　　And fit for highest trust;

Nor yet grown stiffer with command,
But still in the Republic's hand—
　　How fit he is to sway
　　That can so well obey!

He to the Commons' feet presents
A Kingdom for his first year's rents,
　　And, what he may, forbears
　　His fame, to make it theirs:

And has his sword and spoils ungirt
To lay them at the public's skirt.
　　So when the falcon high
　　Falls heavy from the sky,

She, having killed, no more does search
But on the next green bough to perch,
　　Where, when he first does lure,
　　The falconer has her sure.

What may not then our Isle presume
While victory his crest does plume?
　　What may not others fear,
　　If thus he crown each year?

A Caesar he, ere long, to Gaul,
To Italy an Hannibal,
　　And to all States not free
　　Shall climacteric be.

The Pict no shelter now shall find
Within his particoloured mind,
　　But from this valour sad
　　Shrink underneath the plaid,

Happy, if in the tufted brake
The English hunter him mistake,
　　Nor lay his hounds in near
　　The Caledonian deer.

But thou, the War's and Fortune's son,
March indefatigably on;
    And for the last effect,
    Still keep thy sword erect:

Besides the force it has to fright
The spirits of the shady night,
    The same arts that did gain
    A power, must it maintain.

336          *The Definition of Love*

MY Love is of a birth as rare
As 'tis for object strange and high:
It was begotten by Despair
Upon Impossibility.

Magnanimous Despair alone
Could show me so divine a thing,
Where feeble Hope could ne'er have flown
But vainly flapped its tinsel wing.

And yet I quickly might arrive
Where my extended soul is fixt,
But Fate does iron wedges drive,
And always crowds itself betwixt.

For Fate with jealous eye does see
Two perfect Loves; nor lets them close:
Their union would her ruin be,
And her tyrannic power depose.

And therefore her decrees of steel
Us as the distant Poles have placed,
(Though Love's whole World on us doth wheel)
Not by themselves to be embraced.

Unless the giddy Heaven fall,
And Earth some new convulsion tear;
And, us to join, the World should all
Be cramped into a planisphere.

As lines so Loves oblique may well
Themselves in every angle greet:
But ours so truly parallel,
Though infinite, can never meet.

Therefore the Love which us doth bind
But Fate so enviously debars,
Is the conjunction of the Mind,
And opposition of the Stars.

337 *To His Coy Mistress*

HAD we but world enough, and time,
This coyness, Lady, were no crime.
We would sit down and think which way
To walk and pass our long love's day.
Thou by the Indian Ganges' side
Shouldst rubies find: I by the tide
Of Humber would complain. I would
Love you ten years before the Flood,
And you should, if you please, refuse
Till the conversion of the Jews.
My vegetable love should grow
Vaster than empires, and more slow;
An hundred years should go to praise
Thine eyes and on thy forehead gaze;
Two hundred to adore each breast;
But thirty thousand to the rest;
An age at least to every part,
And the last age should show your heart;
For, Lady, you deserve this state,
Nor would I love at lower rate.
    But at my back I always hear
Time's wingèd chariot hurrying near;
And yonder all before us lie
Deserts of vast eternity.
Thy beauty shall no more be found,
Nor, in thy marble vault, shall sound
My echoing song: then worms shall try
That long preserved virginity,
And your quaint honour turn to dust,
And into ashes all my lust:

The grave's a fine and private place,
But none, I think, do there embrace.
　　Now therefore, while the youthful hue
Sits on thy skin like morning dew,
And while thy willing soul transpires
At every pore with instant fires,
Now let us sport us while we may,
And now, like amorous birds of prey,
Rather at once our time devour
Than languish in his slow-chapt power.
Let us roll all our strength and all
Our sweetness up into one ball,
And tear our pleasures with rough strife
Thorough the iron gates of life:
Thus, though we cannot make our sun
Stand still, yet we will make him run.

338

## The Garden

HOW vainly men themselves amaze
To win the palm, the oak, or bays,
And their uncessant labours see
Crowned from some single herb or tree,
Whose short and narrow-vergèd shade
Does prudently their toils upbraid;
While all flowers and all trees do close
To weave the garlands of repose!

Fair Quiet, have I found thee here,
And Innocence, thy sister dear?
Mistaken long, I sought you then
In busy companies of men:
Your sacred plants, if here below,
Only among the plants will grow:
Society is all but rude
To this delicious solitude.

No white nor red was ever seen
So amorous as this lovely green.
Fond lovers, cruel as their flame,
Cut in these trees their mistress' name:

Little, alas! they know or heed
How far these beauties hers exceed!
Fair trees! wheresoe'er your barks I wound,
No name shall but your own be found.

When we have run our passions' heat,
Love hither makes his best retreat:
The gods, that mortal beauty chase,
Still in a tree did end their race;
Apollo hunted Daphne so,
Only that she might laurel grow;
And Pan did after Syrinx speed
Not as a nymph, but for a reed.

What wondrous life is this I lead!
Ripe apples drop about my head;
The luscious clusters of the vine
Upon my mouth do crush their wine;
The nectarine and curious peach
Into my hands themselves do reach;
Stumbling on melons, as I pass,
Ensnared with flowers, I fall on grass.

Meanwhile the mind from pleasure less
Withdraws into its happiness;
The mind, that Ocean where each kind
Does straight its own resemblance find;
Yet it creates, transcending these,
Far other worlds, and other seas;
Annihilating all that's made
To a green thought in a green shade.

Here at the fountain's sliding foot,
Or at some fruit-tree's mossy root,
Casting the body's vest aside,
My soul into the boughs does glide;
There, like a bird, it sits and sings,
Then whets and combs its silver wings,
And, till prepared for longer flight,
Waves in its plumes the various light.

Such was that happy Garden-state
While man there walked without a mate:
After a place so pure and sweet,
What other help could yet be meet!
But 'twas beyond a mortal's share
To wander solitary there:
Two paradises 'twere in one,
To live in Paradise alone.

How well the skilful gardener drew
Of flowers and herbs this dial new!
Where, from above, the milder sun
Does through a fragrant zodiac run:
And, as it works, the industrious bee
Computes its time as well as we.
How could such sweet and wholesome hours
Be reckoned, but with herbs and flowers.

## 339 *Bermudas*

WHERE the remote Bermudas ride
In the ocean's bosom unespied,
From a small boat, that rowed along,
The listening winds received this song.
   'What should we do but sing his praise
That led us through the watery maze,
Unto an isle so long unknown,
And yet far kinder than our own?
Where he the huge sea-monsters wracks,
That lift the deep upon their backs.
He lands us on a grassy stage,
Safe from the storms' and prelates' rage.
He gave us this eternal spring,
Which here enamels everything;
And sends the fowls to us in care,
On daily visits through the air.
He hangs in shades the orange bright,
Like golden lamps in a green night,
And does in the pomegranates close
Jewels more rich than Ormus shows.
He makes the figs our mouths to meet,
And throws the melons at our feet;

But apples plants of such a price
No tree could ever bear them twice.
With cedars, chosen by his hand,
From Lebanon, he stores the land;
And makes the hollow seas that roar
Proclaim the ambergris on shore.
He cast (of which we rather boast)
The Gospel's pearl upon our coast,
And in these rocks for us did frame
A temple, where to sound his Name.
Oh let our voice his praise exalt,
Till it arrive at heaven's vault,
Which thence, perhaps, rebounding may
Echo beyond the Mexique Bay.'
   Thus sung they, in the English boat,
An holy and a cheerful note,
And all the way, to guide their chime,
With falling oars they kept the time.

340           *The Fair Singer*

To make a final conquest of all me,
Love did compose so sweet an enemy,
In whom both beauties to my death agree,
Joining themselves in fatal harmony;
That while she with her eyes my heart does bind,
She with her voice might captivate my mind.

I could have fled from one but singly fair:
My disentangled soul itself might save,
Breaking the curlèd trammels of her hair.
But how should I avoid to be her slave,
Whose subtle art invisibly can wreath
My fetters of the very air I breath?

It had been easy fighting in some plain,
Where victory might hang in equal choice;
But all resistance against her is vain,
Who has the advantage both of eyes and voice;
And all my forces needs must be undone,
She having gainèd both the wind and sun.

341        *The Picture of Little T.C. in*
*a Prospect of Flowers*

SEE with what simplicity
This nymph begins her golden days!
In the green grass she loves to lie,
And there with her fair aspect tames
The wilder flowers, and gives them names;
But only with the roses plays,
                And them does tell
What colour best becomes them, and what smell.

Who can foretell for what high cause
This darling of the gods was born?
Yet this is she whose chaster laws
The wanton Love shall one day fear,
And, under her command severe,
See his bow broke and ensigns torn.
                Happy who can
Appease this virtuous enemy of man!

O then let me in time compound
And parley with those conquering eyes,
Ere they have tried their force to wound;
Ere with their glancing wheels they drive
In triumph over hearts that strive,
And them that yield but more despise:
                Let me be laid,
Where I may see thy glories from some shade.

Meantime, whilst every verdant thing
Itself does at thy beauty charm,
Reform the errors of the Spring;
Make that the tulips may have share
Of sweetness, seeing they are fair,
And roses of their thorns disarm;
                But most procure
That violets may a longer age endure.

But O, young beauty of the woods,
Whom Nature courts with fruits and flowers,
Gather the flowers, but spare the buds;
Lest Flora, angry at thy crime
To kill her infants in their prime,
Do quickly make the example yours;
        And ere we see,
Nip in the blossom all our hopes and thee.

342        *The Mower to the Glow-worms*

YE living lamps, by whose dear light
The nightingale does sit so late
And studying all the summer night,
Her matchless songs does meditate;

Ye country comets, that portend
No war, nor prince's funeral,
Shining unto no higher end
Than to presage the grasses' fall;

Ye glow-worms, whose officious flame
To wandering mowers shows the way,
That in the night have lost their aim,
And after foolish fires do stray;

Your courteous lights in vain you waste,
Since Juliana here is come,
For she my mind hath so displaced
That I shall never find my home.

343      *The Garden of Appleton House,*
*Laid out by Lord Fairfax in Figure of a Fort*

WHEN in the east the morning ray
Hangs out the colours of the day,
The bee through these known alleys hums
Beating the dian with its drums.
Then flowers their drowsy eyelids raise,
Their silken ensigns each displays,
And dries its pan yet dank with dew,
And fills its flask with odours new.

These, as their Governor goes by,
In fragrant volleys they let fly;
And to salute their Governess
Again as great a charge they press:
None for the Virgin Nymph, for she
Seems with the flowers a flower to be.
And think so still! though not compare
With breath so sweet, or cheek so fair.

Well shot, ye firemen! Oh how sweet
And round your equal fires do meet,
Whose shrill report no ear can tell,
But echoes to the eye and smell.
See how the flowers, as at parade,
Under their colours stand displayed:
Each regiment in order grows,
That of the tulip, pink and rose.

But when the vigilant patrol
Of stars walks round about the Pole,
Their leaves, that to the stalks are curled,
Seem to their staves the ensigns furled.
Then in some flower's beloved hut
Each bee as sentinel is shut;
And sleeps so too: but, if once stirred,
She runs you through, or asks the Word.

O thou, that dear and happy isle,
The Garden of the World erewhile,
Thou Paradise of four seas,
Which Heaven planted us to please,
But, to exclude the World, did guard
With watery, if not flaming, sword:
What luckless apple did we taste
To make us mortal, and thee waste?

Unhappy! shall we never more
That sweet militia restore,
When gardens only had their towers,
And all the garrisons were flowers,
When roses only arms might bear,
And men did rosy garlands wear?
Tulips, in several colours barred,
Were then the Switzers of our guard.

The gardener had the soldier's place,
And his more gentle forts did trace.
The nursery of all things green
Was then the only magazine.
The winter quarters were the stoves,
Where he the tender plants removes.
But war all this doth overgrow:
We ordnance plant and powder sow.

# HENRY VAUGHAN

## 1621–1695

344 *The Retreat*

HAPPY those early days, when I
Shined in my angel-infancy!
Before I understood this place
Appointed for my second race,
Or taught my soul to fancy aught
But a white celestial thought;
When yet I had not walked above
A mile or two from my first love,
And looking back, at that short space,
Could see a glimpse of his bright face;
When on some gilded cloud, or flower,
My gazing soul would dwell an hour,
And in those weaker glories spy
Some shadows of eternity;
Before I taught my tongue to wound
My conscience with a sinful sound,
Or had the black art to dispense
A several sin to every sense,
But felt through all this fleshly dress
Bright shoots of everlastingness.

O how I long to travel back,
And tread again that ancient track!
That I might once more reach that plain
Where first I left my glorious train;

From whence the enlightened spirit sees
That shady City of Palm-trees.
But ah! my soul with too much stay
Is drunk, and staggers in the way.
Some men a forward motion love,
But I by backward steps would move,
And when this dust falls to the urn
In that state I came, return.

345                            *Peace*

My soul, there is a country
    Far beyond the stars,
Where stands a wingèd sentry
    All skilful in the wars:
There above noise and danger
    Sweet Peace sits crowned with smiles,
And One born in a manger
    Commands the beauteous files.
He is thy gracious friend
    And—O my soul, awake!—
Did in pure love descend
    To die here for thy sake.
If thou canst get but thither,
    There grows the flower of Peace,
The Rose that cannot wither,
    Thy fortress, and thy ease.
Leave then thy foolish ranges
    For none can thee secure,
But one who never changes,
    Thy God, thy life, thy cure.

346

They are all gone into the world of light!
    And I alone sit lingering here;
Their very memory is fair and bright,
    And my sad thoughts doth clear.

It glows and glitters in my cloudy breast
  Like stars upon some gloomy grove,
Or those faint beams in which this hill is dressed,
  After the sun's remove.

I see them walking in an air of glory,
  Whose light doth trample on my days:
My days, which are at best but dull and hoary,
  Mere glimmering and decays.

O holy Hope! and high Humility,
  High as the heavens above!
These are your walks, and you have showed them me,
  To kindle my cold love.

Dear beauteous Death! the jewel of the Just,
  Shining nowhere but in the dark;
What mysteries do lie beyond thy dust,
  Could man outlook that mark!

He that hath found some fledged bird's nest may know,
  At first sight, if the bird be flown;
But what fair well or grove he sings in now,
  That is to him unknown.

And yet, as angels in some brighter dreams
  Call to the soul, when man doth sleep;
So some strange thoughts transcend our wonted themes,
  And into glory peep.

If a star were confined into a tomb,
  Her captive flames must needs burn there;
But when the hand that locked her up gives room,
  She'll shine through all the sphere.

O Father of eternal life, and all
  Created glories under thee!
Resume thy spirit from this world of thrall
  Into true liberty.

Either disperse these mists, which blot and fill
  My perspective still as they pass,
Or else remove me hence unto that hill,
  Where I shall need no glass.

## *The World*

I SAW Eternity the other night
Like a great Ring of pure and endless light,
    All calm as it was bright;
And round beneath it, Time, in hours, days, years,
    Driven by the spheres,
Like a vast shadow moved, in which the world
    And all her train were hurled.
The doting Lover in his quaintest strain
    Did there complain;
Near him, his lute, his fancy, and his flights,
    Wit's sour delights;
With gloves and knots, the silly snares of pleasure;
    Yet his dear treasure
All scattered lay, while he his eyes did pour
    Upon a flower.

The darksome Statesman hung with weights and woe,
Like a thick midnight fog, moved there so slow
    He did nor stay nor go;
Condemning thoughts, like sad eclipses, scowl
    Upon his soul,
And clouds of crying witnesses without
    Pursued him with one shout.
Yet digged the mole, and, lest his ways be found,
    Worked under ground,
Where he did clutch his prey; but One did see
    That policy.
Churches and altars fed him, perjuries
    Were gnats and flies;
It rained about him blood and tears, but he
    Drank them as free.

The fearful Miser on a heap of rust
Sat pining all his life there, did scarce trust
    His own hands with the dust;
Yet would not place one piece above, but lives
    In fear of thieves.
Thousands there were as frantic as himself,
    And hugged each one his pelf.

The downright Epicure placed heaven in sense
  And scorned pretence;
While others, slipped into a wide excess,
  Said little less;
The weaker sort, slight, trivial wares enslave,
  Who think them brave;
And poor despisèd Truth sat counting by
  Their victory.

Yet some, who all this while did weep and sing,
And sing and weep, soared up into the Ring;
  But most would use no wing.
'O fools', said I, 'thus to prefer dark night
  Before true light,
To live in grots, and caves, and hate the day
  Because it shows the way,
The way which from this dead and dark abode
  Leads up to God,
A way where you might tread the sun, and be
  More bright than he.'
But as I did their madness so discuss,
  One whispered thus,
*This Ring the Bridegroom did for none provide*
  *But for his Bride.*

348

## Man

WEIGHING the steadfastness and state
Of some mean things which here below reside,
Where birds like watchful clocks the noiseless date
  And intercourse of times divide,
Where bees at night get home and hive, and flowers
  Early, as well as late,
Rise with the sun, and set in the same bowers;

  I would (said I) my God would give
The staidness of these things to man! for these
To his divine appointments ever cleave,
  And no new business breaks their peace;
The birds nor sow, nor reap, yet sup and dine,
  The flowers without clothes live,
Yet Solomon was never dressed so fine.

Man hath still either toys, or care,
He hath no root, nor to one place is tied,
But ever restless and irregular
    About this earth doth run and ride,
He knows he hath a home, but scarce knows where,
      He says it is so far
That he hath quite forgot how to go there.

He knocks at all doors, strays and roams,
Nay, hath not so much wit as some stones have,
Which in the darkest nights point to their homes
    By some hid sense their Maker gave;
Man is the shuttle, to whose winding quest
      And passage through these looms
God ordered motion, but ordained no rest.

349               *The Night*

THROUGH that pure Virgin-shrine,
That sacred veil drawn o'er thy glorious noon
That men might look and live as glow-worms shine,
    And face the moon,
Wise Nicodemus saw such light
As made him know his God by night.

Most blest believer he!
Who in that land of darkness and blind eyes
Thy long-expected healing wings could see,
    When thou didst rise,
And what can never more be done
Did at midnight speak with the Sun!

O who will tell me where
He found thee at that dead and silent hour!
What hallowed solitary ground did bear
    So rare a flower,
Within whose sacred leaves did lie
The fullness of the Deity.

No mercy-seat of gold,
No dead and dusty cherub, nor carved stone,
But his own living works did my Lord hold
    And lodge alone;
  Where trees and herbs did watch and peep
  And wonder, while the Jews did sleep.

Dear night! this world's defeat;
The stop to busy fools; care's check and curb;
The day of spirits; my soul's calm retreat
    Which none disturb!
  Christ's progress, and his prayer time;
  The hours to which high Heaven doth chime.

God's silent searching flight:
When my Lord's head is filled with dew, and all
His locks are wet with the clear drops of night;
    His still soft call;
  His knocking time; the soul's dumb watch,
  When spirits their fair kindred catch.

Were all my loud, evil days
Calm and unhaunted as is thy dark tent,
Whose peace but by some angel's wing or voice
    Is seldom rent,
  Then I in Heaven all the long year
  Would keep and never wander here.

But living where the sun
Doth all things wake, and where all mix and tire
Themselves and others, I consent and run
    To every mire,
  And by this world's ill-guiding light,
  Err more than I can do by night.

There is in God, some say,
A deep, but dazzling darkness, as men here
Say it is late and dusky, because they
    See not all clear.
  O for that night! where I in him
  Might live invisible and dim.

350 *The Waterfall*

WITH what deep murmurs through time's silent stealth
Doth thy transparent, cool, and watery wealth
   Here flowing fall,
   And chide and call,
As if his liquid loose retinue stayed
Lingering, and were of this steep place afraid,
   The common pass
   Where, clear as glass,
   All must descend
   Not to an end;
But quickened by this deep and rocky grave,
Rise to a longer course more bright and brave.

  Dear stream! dear bank, where often I
  Have sat, and pleased my pensive eye,
  Why, since each drop of thy quick store
  Runs thither, whence it flowed before,
  Should poor souls fear a shade or night,
  Who came, sure, from a sea of light?
  Or since those drops are all sent back
  So sure to thee, that none doth lack,
  Why should frail flesh doubt any more
  That what God takes, he'll not restore?
  O useful Element and clear!
  My sacred wash and cleanser here,
  My first consigner unto those
  Fountains of life, where the Lamb goes,
  What sublime truths, and wholesome themes
  Lodge in thy mystical, deep streams!
  Such as dull man can never find,
  Unless that Spirit lead his mind,
  Which first upon thy face did move,
  And hatched all with his quickening love.
  As this loud brook's incessant fall
  In streaming rings restagnates all,
  Which reach by course the bank, and then
  Are no more seen, just so pass men.
  O my invisible estate,
  My glorious liberty, still late!
  Thou art the channel my soul seeks,
  Not this with cataracts and creeks.

351 *Quickness*

FALSE life! a foil and no more, when
        Wilt thou be gone?
Thou foul deception of all men
That would not have the true come on.

Thou art a moon-like toil; a blind
        Self-posing state;
A dark contest of waves and wind;
A mere tempestuous debate.

Life is a fixed, discerning light,
        A knowing joy;
No chance, or fit; but ever bright,
And calm and full, yet doth not cloy.

'Tis such a blissful thing, that still
        Doth vivify,
And shine and smile, and hath the skill
To please without Eternity.

Thou art a toilsome mole, or less,
        A moving mist;
But life is what none can express,
*A quickness which my God hath kissed.*


# THOMAS STANLEY
## 1625–1678

352 *The Magnet*

ASK the Empress of the night
  How the hand which guides her sphere,
Constant in unconstant light,
  Taught the waves her yoke to bear,
And did thus by loving force
Curb or tame the rude sea's course.

## THOMAS STANLEY

Ask the female palm how she
   First did woo her husband's love;
And the magnet, ask how he
   Doth the obsequious iron move;
Waters, plants and stones know this,
That they love, not what love is.

Be not then less kind than these,
   Or from love exempt alone;
Let us twine like amorous trees,
   And like rivers melt in one;
Or if thou more cruel prove
Learn of steel and stones to love.


## JOHN BUNYAN
### 1628–1688

353    *The Shepherd Boy Sings in
the Valley of Humiliation*

HE that is down needs fear no fall,
   He that is low, no pride;
He that is humble ever shall
   Have God to be his guide.

I am content with what I have,
   Little be it or much:
And, Lord, contentment still I crave,
   Because Thou savest such.

Fullness to such a burden is
   That go on pilgrimage:
Here little, and hereafter bliss,
   Is best from age to age.

## THOMAS TRAHERNE
### 1638–1674

354                                *News*

N EWS from a foreign country came
As if my treasure and my wealth lay there;
So much it did my heart inflame,
'Twas wont to call my Soul into mine ear;
    Which thither went to meet
      The approaching sweet,
    And on the threshold stood
To entertain the unknown Good.
      It hovered there
    As if 'twould leave mine ear,
And was so eager to embrace
    The joyful tidings as they came,
'Twould almost leave its dwelling-place
    To entertain the same.

As if the tidings were the things,
My very joys themselves, my foreign treasure—
    Or else did bear them on their wings—
With so much joy they came, with so much pleasure.
      My Soul stood at the gate
        To recreate
      Itself with bliss, and to
Be pleased with speed. A fuller view
      It fain would take,
    Yet journeys back would make
Unto my heart; as if 'twould fain
    Go out to meet, yet stay within
To fit a place to entertain
    And bring the tidings in.

What sacred instinct did inspire
My soul in childhood with a hope so strong?
What secret force moved my desire
To expect my joys beyond the seas, so young?
      Felicity I knew
        Was out of view,

And being here alone,
I saw that happiness was gone
From me! For this
I thirsted absent bliss,
And thought that sure beyond the seas,
Or else in something near at hand—
I knew not yet—since naught did please
I knew—my Bliss did stand.

But little did the infant dream
That all the treasures of the world were by:
And that himself was so the cream
And crown of all which round about did lie.
Yet thus it was: the Gem,
The Diadem,
The ring enclosing all
That stood upon this earthy ball,
The Heavenly eye,
Much wider than the sky,
Wherein they all included were,
The glorious Soul, that was the King
Made to possess them, did appear
A small and little thing!

# ANONYMOUS

## Ballads and Songs

355
### *Thomas the Rhymer*

TRUE Thomas lay on Huntlie bank,
A ferlie he spied wi' his e'e;
And there he saw a ladye bright
Come riding down by the Eildon Tree.

Her shirt was o' the grass-green silk,
Her mantle o' the velvet fine;
At ilka tett of her horse's mane
Hung fifty siller bells and nine.

355   ferlie] marvel          ilka tett] each tuft

True Thomas, he pulled aff his cap
  And louted low down to his knee:
'All hail, thou mighty Queen of Heaven!
  For thy peer on earth I never did see.'

'O no, O no, Thomas,' she said,
  'That name does not belang to me;
I am but the Queen of fair Elfland
  That am hither come to visit thee.

'Harp and carp, Thomas,' she said,
  'Harp and carp along wi' me,
And if ye dare to kiss my lips,
  Sure of your bodie I will be.'

'Betide me weal, betide me woe,
  That weird shall never daunton me.'
Syne he has kissed her rosy lips
  All underneath the Eildon Tree.

'Now ye maun go wi' me,' she said,
  'True Thomas, ye maun go wi' me;
And ye maun serve me seven years
  Through weal or woe, as may chance to be.'

She mounted on her milk-white steed,
  She's ta'en True Thomas up behind;
And aye whene'er her bridle rung
  The steed flew swifter than the wind.

O they rade on, and farther on—
  The steed gaed swifter than the wind—
Until they reached a desart wide
  And living land was left behind.

'Light down, light down now, True Thomas,
  And lean your head upon my knee;
Abide and rest a little space
  And I will shew you ferlies three.

carp] sing

354

## ANONYMOUS

'O see ye not yon narrow road
    So thick beset with thorns and briers?
That is the path of righteousness,
    Though after it but few enquires.

'And see ye not that braid, braid road
    That lies across that lily leven?
That is the path of wickedness,
    Though some call it the road to heaven.

'And see not ye that bonny road
    That winds about the fernie brae?
That is the road to fair Elfland,
    Where thou and I this night maun gae.

'But, Thomas, ye maun hold your tongue
    Whatever ye may hear or see,
For if you speak word in Elflyn land
    Ye'll ne'er get back to your ain countrie.'

O they rade on, and farther on,
    And they waded through rivers aboon the knee,
And they saw neither sun nor moon
    But they heard the roaring of the sea.

It was mirk, mirk night and there was nae stern light
    And they waded through red blude to the knee;
For a' the blude that's shed on earth
    Rins through the springs o' that countrie.

Syne they came on to a garden green
    And she pu'd an apple frae a tree:
'Take this for thy wages, True Thomas,
    It will give thee the tongue that can never lie.'

'My tongue is mine ain,' True Thomas said,
    'A gudely gift ye wad gie to me;
I neither dought to buy nor sell
    At fair or tryst where I may be;

lily leven] lovely lea       stern] star       dought] dare       tryst] market

'I dought neither speak to prince or peer
 Nor ask of grace from fair ladye.'
'Now hold thy peace,' the lady said,
 For as I say, so must it be.'

He has gotten a coat of the even cloth
 And a pair of shoes of velvet green;
And till seven years were gane and past
 True Thomas on earth was never seen.

356                    *Tam Lin*

O I FORBID you, maidens a'
 That wear gowd on your hair,
To come, or gae by Carterhaugh,
 For young Tom-lin is there.

There's nane that gaes by Carterhaugh
 But they leave him a wad;
Either their rings, or green mantles,
 Or else their maidenhead.

Janet has kilted her green kirtle,
 A little aboon her knee;
And she has broded her yellow hair
 A little aboon her bree;
And she's awa to Carterhaugh
 As fast as she can hie.

When she cam to Carterhaugh
 Tom-lin was at the well,
And there she fand his steed standing
 But away was himsel.

She had na pu'd a double rose,
 A rose but only tway,
Till up then started young Tom-lin,
 Says, 'Lady, thou's pu' nae mae.

356    wad] forfeit        at the well] under enchantment

'Why pu's thou the rose, Janet,
  And why breaks thou the wand?
Or why comes thou to Carterhaugh
  Withoutten my command?'

'Carterhaugh it is my ain,
  My daddie gave it me;
I'll come and gang by Carterhaugh
  And ask nae leave at thee.'

Janet has kilted her green kirtle
  A little aboon her knee,
And she has snooded her yellow hair
  A little aboon her bree,
And she is to her father's ha,
  As fast as she can hie.

Four and twenty ladies fair
  Were playing at the ba',
And out then cam the fair Janet,
  Ance the flower amang them a'.

Four and twenty ladies fair
  Were playing at the chess,
And out then cam the fair Janet,
  As green as onie glass.

Out then spak an auld grey knight,
  Lay o'er the castle-wa',
And says, 'Alas, fair Janet, for thee,
  But we'll be blamed a'.'

'Haud your tongue, ye auld-faced knight,
  Some ill death may ye die,
Father my bairn on whom I will,
  I'll father nane on thee.'

Out then spak her father dear,
  And he spak meek and mild,
'And ever alas, sweet Janet,' he says,
  'I think thou gaes wi' child.'

'If that I gae wi' child, father,
  Mysel maun bear the blame;
There's ne'er a laird about your ha',
  Shall get the bairn's name.

'If my Love were an earthly knight,
  As he's an elfin grey;
I wad na gie my ain true-love
  For nae lord that ye hae.

'The steed that my true-love rides on,
  Is lighter than the wind;
Wi' siller he is shod before,
  Wi' burning gowd behind.'

Janet has kilted her green kirtle
  A little aboon her knee;
And she has snooded her yellow hair
  A little aboon her bree;
And she's awa to Carterhaugh
  As fast as she can hie.

When she cam to Carterhaugh,
  Tom-lin was at the well;
And there she fand his steed standing,
  But away was himsel.

She had na pu'd a double rose,
  A rose but only tway,
Till up then started young Tom-lin,
  Says, 'Lady, thou pu's nae mae.

'Why pu's thou the rose, Janet,
  Amang the groves sae green,
And a' to kill the bonie babe
  That we gat us between.'

'O tell me, tell me, Tom-lin', she says,
  'For's sake that died on tree,
If e'er ye was in holy chapel,
  Or Christendom did see.'

'Roxbrugh he was my grandfather,
  Took me with him to bide,
And ance it fell upon a day
  That wae did me betide.

'Ance it fell upon a day,
  A cauld day and a snell,
When we were frae the hunting come
  That frae my horse I fell.

'The queen o' Fairies she caught me,
  In yon green hill to dwell,
And pleasant is the fairy-land;
  But, an eerie tale to tell!

'Ay at the end of seven years
  We pay a tiend to hell;
I am sae fair and fu' o' flesh
  I'm feared it be mysel.

'But the night is Halloween, lady,
  The morn is Hallowday;
Then win me, win me, an ye will,
  For weel I wat ye may.

'Just at the mirk and midnight hour
  The fairy folk will ride;
And they that wad their truelove win,
  At Milescross they maun bide.'

'But how shall I thee ken, Tom-lin,
  O how my true-love know,
Amang sae mony unco knights
  The like I never saw.'

'O first let pass the black, lady,
  And syne let pass the brown;
But quickly run to the milk-white steed,
  Pu ye his rider down;

    snell] bitter        tiend] tithe

'For I'll ride on the milk-white steed,
  And ay nearest the town;
Because I was an earthly knight
  They gie me that renown.

'My right hand will be gloved, lady,
  My left hand will be bare;
Cockt up shall my bonnet be,
  And kaimed down shall my hair;
And thae's the tokens I gie thee,
  Nae doubt I will be there.

'They'll turn me in your arms, lady,
  Into an ask and adder,
But hald me fast and fear me not,
  I am your bairn's father.

'They'll turn me to a bear sae grim,
  And then a lion bold;
But hold me fast and fear me not,
  As ye shall love your child.

'Again they'll turn me in your arms
  To a red het gaud of airn;
But hold me fast and fear me not,
  I'll do to you nae harm.

'And last they'll turn me, in your arms,
  Into the burning lead;
Then throw me into well-water,
  O throw me in wi' speed!

'And then I'll be your ain true-love,
  I'll turn a naked knight:
Then cover me wi' your green mantle,
  And cover me out o'sight.'

Gloomy, gloomy was the night,
  And eerie was the way,
As fair Jenny in her green mantle
  To Milescross she did gae.

ask] eft, lizard        het gaud of airn] hot iron bar

360

About the middle o' the night
   She heard the bridles ring;
This lady was as glad at that
   As any earthly thing.

First she let the black pass by,
   And syne she let the brown;
But quickly she ran to the milk-white steed
   And pu'd the rider down.

Sae weel she minded what he did say
   And young Tom-lin did win;
Syne covered him wi' her green mantle
   As blythe's a bird in spring.

Out then spak the queen o' Fairies,
   Out of a bush o' broom;
'Them that has gotten young Tom-lin,
   Has gotten a stately groom.'

Out then spak the queen o' Fairies,
   And an angry queen was she;
'Shame betide her ill-fared face,
   And an ill death may she die,
For she's ta'en awa the boniest knight
   In a' my companie.

'But had I kenned, Tom-lin,' she says,
   'What now this night I see,
I wad hae ta'en out thy twa grey e'en,
   And put in twa een o' tree.'

357         *Sir Patrick Spence*

THE king sits in Dumferling toune,
   Drinking the blude-reid wine:
'O whar will I get a guid sailor,
   To sail this schip of mine?'

tree] wood

Up and spak an eldern knicht,
    Sat at the king's richt kne:
'Sir Patrick Spence is the best sailor,
    That sails upon the se.'

The king has written a braid letter,
    And signed it wi' his hand;
And sent it to Sir Patrick Spence,
    Was walking on the sand.

The first line that Sir Patrick red,
    A loud lauch lauched he:
The next line that Sir Patrick red,
    The teir blinded his e'e.

'O wha is this has don this deid,
    This ill deid don to me;
To send me out this time o' the yeir,
    To sail upon the se?

'Mak haste, mak haste, my mirry men all,
    Our guid schip sails the morne.'
'O say na sae, my master deir,
    For I feir a deadlie storme.

'Late, late yestreen I saw the new moone
    Wi' the auld moone in hir arme;
And I feir, I feir, my deir master,
    That we will com to harme.'

O our Scots nobles wer richt laith
    To weet their cork-heiled schoone;
Bot lang owre a' the play wer played,
    Thair hats they swam aboone.

O lang, lang may thair ladies sit
    Wi' thair fans into their hand,
Or eir they se Sir Patrick Spence
    Cum sailing to the land.

O lang, lang may the ladies stand
    Wi' thair gold kems in their hair,
Waiting for thair ain deir lords,
    For they'll se thame na mair.

Haf owre, haf owre to Aberdour,
   It's fiftie fadom deip:
And thair lies guid Sir Patrick Spence,
   Wi' the Scots lords at his feit.

## 358 *Edward, Edward*

'WHY dois your brand sae drop wi' bluid,
       Edward, Edward?
Why dois your brand sae drop wi' bluid?
   And why sae sad gang yee, O?'
'O, I hae killed my hauke sae guid,
       Mither, mither:
O, I hae killed my hauke sae guid:
   And I had nae mair bot hee, O.'

'Your haukis bluid was nevir sae reid,
       Edward, Edward.
Your haukis bluid was nevir sae reid,
   My deir son I tell thee, O.'
'O, I hae killed my reid-roan steid,
       Mither, mither:
O, I hae killed my reid-roan steid,
   That erst was sae fair and free, O.'

'Your steid was auld, and ye hae gat mair,
       Edward, Edward:
Your steid was auld, and ye hae gat mair,
   Sum other dule ye drie, O.'
'O, I hae killed my fadir deir,
       Mither, mither,
O, I hae killed my fadir deir,
   Alas! and wae is me, O!'

'And whatten penance wul ye drie for that,
       Edward, Edward?
And whatten penance will ye drie for that?
   My deir son, now tell me, O.'
'Ile set my feit in yonder boat,
       Mither, mither:
Ile set my feit in yonder boat,
   And Ile fare ovir the sea, O.'

358 dule ye drie] grief you are suffering

'And what wul ye doe wi' your towirs and your ha',
        Edward, Edward?
And what wul ye doe wi' your towirs and your ha',
   That were sae fair to see, O?'
'Ile let them stand til they doun fa',
        Mither, mither:
Ile let them stand til they doun fa',
   For here nevir mair maun I bee, O.'

'And what wul ye leive to your bairns and your wife,
        Edward, Edward?
And what wul ye leive to your bairns and your wife,
   Whan ye gang ovir the sea, O?'
'The warldis room, let thame beg throw life,
        Mither, mither:
The warldis room, let thame beg throw life,
   For thame nevir mair wul I see, O.'

'And what wul ye leive to your ain mither deir,
        Edward, Edward?
And what wul ye leive to your ain mither deir?
   My deir son, now tell me, O.'
'The curse of hell frae me sall ye beir,
        Mither, mither:
The curse of hell frae me sall ye beir,
   Sic counseils ye gave to me, O.'

359              *Mary Hamilton*

O MARY HAMILTON to the kirk is gane
   Wi' ribbons in her hair;
An' the king thocht mair o' Marie
   Then onie that were there.

Mary Hamilton's to the preaching gane
   Wi' ribbons on her breast;
An' the king thocht mair o' Marie
   Than he thocht o' the priest.

Syne word is through the palace gane,
   I heard it tauld yestreen,
The king loes Mary Hamilton
   Mair than he loes his queen.

A sad tale through the town is gaen,
　　A sad tale on the morrow:
Oh Mary Hamilton has born a babe
　　And slain it in her sorrow.

And down then cam the auld queen,
　　Goud tassels tied her hair:
'What did ye wi' the wee wee bairn
　　That I heard greet sae sair?'

'There ne'er was a bairn into my room,
　　An' as little designs to be;
'T was but a stitch o' my sair side
　　Cam owre my fair bodie.'

'Rise up now, Marie,' quo' the queen,
　　'Rise up, an' come wi' me,
For we maun ride to Holyrood
　　A gay wedding to see.'

The queen was drest in scarlet fine,
　　Her maidens all in green;
An' every town that they cam through
　　Took Marie for the queen.

But little wist Marie Hamilton
　　As she rode oure the lea
That she was gaun to Edinbro' town
　　Her doom to hear and dree.

When she cam to the Netherbow Port
　　She laughed loud laughters three;
But when she reached the gallows-tree
　　The tears blinded her e'e.

'Yestreen the queen had four Maries,
　　The nicht she'll hae but three;
There's Marie Seaton, an' Marie Beaton,
　　An' Marie Carmichael, an' me.

dree] suffer

365

'Oh aften have I dressed my queen
  An' put gowd in her hair;
The gallows-tree is my reward
  An' shame maun be my share.

'Oh aften hae I dressed my queen
  An' saft, saft made her bed;
An' now I've got for my reward
  The gallows-tree to tread.

'There's a health to all gallant sailors
  That sail upon the sea:
Oh never let on to my father and mither
  The death that I maun dee.

'An' I charge ye, all ye mariners,
  When ye sail owre the main,
Let neither my father nor mither know
  But that I'm comin hame.

'Oh little did my mither ken,
  That day she cradled me,
What lands I was to tread in
  Or what death I should dee.'

360                *The Wife of Usher's Well*

THERE lived a wife at Usher's Well
  And a wealthy wife was she;
She had three stout and stalwart sons
  And sent them o'er the sea.

They hadna been a week from her,
  A week but barely ane,
Whan word came to the carline wife
  That her three sons were gane.

They hadna been a week from her,
  A week but barely three,
Whan word came to the carline wife
  That her sons she'd never see.

**360**  carline] old

**366**

# ANONYMOUS

'I wish the wind may never cease,
  Nor fishes in the flood,
Till my three sons come hame to me
  In earthly flesh and blood.'

It fell about the Martinmas
  Whan nights are lang and mirk,
The carline wife's three sons came hame
  And their hats were o' the birk.

It neither grew in syke nor ditch
  Nor yet in ony sheugh,
But at the gates o' Paradise
  That birk grew fair eneugh.

'Blow up the fire, my maidens,
  Bring water from the well;
For a' my house shall feast this night
  Since my three sons are well.'

And she has made to them a bed,
  She's made it large and wide,
And she's ta'en her mantle her about,
  Sat down at the bed-side.

Up then crew the red, red cock
  And up and crew the gray;
The eldest to the youngest said,
  ' 'Tis time we were away.'

The cock he hadna crawed but once
  And clapped his wings at a'
Whan the youngest to the eldest said,
  'Brother, we must awa.

'The cock doth craw, the day doth daw,
  The channerin' worm doth chide;
Gin we be mist out o' our place
  A sair pain we maun bide.

birk] birch         syke] small stream
sheugh] trench         channerin'] fretting

'Fare ye weel, my mother dear;
Fareweel to barn and byre;
And fare ye weel, the bonny lass
That kindles my mother's fire.'

361   *A Lyke-Wake Dirge*

THIS ae nighte, this ae nighte,
  —*Every nighte and alle,*
Fire and fleet and candle-lighte,
  *And Christe receive thy saule.*

When thou from hence away art past,
  —*Every nighte and alle,*
To Whinny-muir thou com'st at last;
  *And Christe receive thy saule.*

If ever thou gavest hosen and shoon,
  —*Every nighte and alle,*
Sit thee down and put them on;
  *And Christe receive thy saule.*

If hosen and shoon thou ne'er gav'st nane
  —*Every nighte and alle,*
The whinnes sall prick thee to the bare bane;
  *And Christe receive thy saule.*

From Whinny-muir when thou mayst pass,
  —*Every nighte and alle,*
To Brig o' Dread thou com'st at last;
  *And Christe receive thy saule.*

From Brig o' Dread when thou mayst pass,
  —*Every nighte and alle,*
To Purgatory fire thou com'st at last;
  *And Christe receive thy saule.*

If ever thou gavest meat or drink,
  —*Every nighte and alle,*
The fire sall never make thee shrink;
  *And Christe receive thy saule.*

If meat or drink thou ne'er gav'st nane,
  —*Every nighte and alle,*
The fire will burn thee to the bare bane;
  *And Christe receive thy saule.*

This ae nighte, this ae nighte,
  —*Every nighte and alle,*
Fire and fleet and candle-lighte,
  *And Christe receive thy saule.*

362                    *Loving Mad Tom*

FROM the hag and hungry goblin
That into rags would rend ye
All the spirits that stand by the naked man
In the Book of Moons defend ye!
That of your five sound senses
You never be forsaken
Nor wander from yourselves with Tom
Abroad to beg your bacon.

      While I do sing 'Any food, any feeding,
      Feeding, drink, or clothing'
      Come dame or maid, be not afraid,
      Poor Tom will injure nothing.

O thirty bare years have I
Twice twenty been enragèd,
And of forty been three times fifteen
In durance soundly cagèd
On the lordly lofts of Bedlam,
With stubble soft and dainty,
Brave bracelets strong, sweet whip's ding dong,
With wholesome hunger plenty.

      And now I sing etc.

With a thought I took for Maudlin
And a cruise of cockle pottage
With a thing thus tall, sky bless you all,
I befell into this dotage.

369

## ANONYMOUS

I slept not since the Conquest,
Till then I never wakèd,
Till the roguish boy of love where I lay
Me found and stripped me naked.

    And now I sing etc.

When I short have shorn my sour face
And swigged my horny barrel
In an oaken inn I pound my skin
As a suit of gilt apparel.
The moon's my constant Mistress
And the lonely owl my marrow,
The flaming drake and the nightcrow make
Me music to my sorrow.

    And now I sing etc.

The palsy plagues my pulses
When I prig their pigs or pullen,
Your culvers take, or matchless make
Your chanticleer, or sullen;
When I want provant, with Humphrey
I sup; and when benighted
I repose in Paul's with waking souls,
Yet never am affrighted.

    But I do sing etc.

I know more than Apollo,
For oft when he lies sleeping
I see the stars at bloody wars
In the wounded welkin weeping;
The moon embrace her shepherd
And the queen of Love her warrior,
While the first doth horn the star of morn
And the next the heavenly Farrier.

    While I do sing etc.

provant] provisions       Humphrey . . . Paul's] Persons loitering in
St Paul's were said to be 'dining with Duke Humphrey', i.e. going supperless

The Gipsy snap and Pedro
Are none of Tom's comradoes.
The punk I scorn and the cutpurse sworn
And the roaring boys' bravado.
The meek, the white, the gentle,
Me handle, touch, and spare not,
But those that cross Tom Rynosseros
Do what the panther dare not.

    Although I sing etc.

With an host of furious fancies,
Whereof I am commander,
With a burning spear, and a horse of air,
To the wilderness I wander.
By a knight of ghosts and shadows
I summoned am to tourney,
Ten leagues beyond the wide world's end.
Me thinks it is no journey.

    Yet will I sing etc.

# JOHN DRYDEN

## 1631–1700

**363**    *London After the Great Fire, 1666*

METHINKS already from this chymic flame
I see a city of more precious mould,
Rich as the town which gives the Indies name,
With silver paved and all divine with gold.

Already, labouring with a mighty fate,
She shakes the rubbish from her mounting brow,
And seems to have renewed her charter's date,
Which Heaven will to the death of time allow.

More great than human now and more August,
New deified she from her fires does rise:
Her widening streets on new foundations trust,
And, opening, into larger parts she flies.

Before, she like some shepherdess did show
Who sat to bathe her by a river's side,
Not answering to her fame, but rude and low,
Nor taught the beauteous arts of modern pride.

Now like a maiden queen she will behold
From her high turrets hourly suitors come;
The East with incense and the West with gold
Will stand like suppliants to receive her doom.

The silver Thames, her own domestic flood,
Shall bear her vessels like a sweeping train,
And often wind, as of his mistress proud,
With longing eyes to meet her face again.

The wealthy Tagus and the wealthier Rhine
The glory of their towns no more shall boast,
And Seine, that would with Belgian rivers join,
Shall find her lustre stained and traffic lost.

The venturous merchant who designed more far
And touches on our hospitable shore,
Charmed with the splendour of this northern star,
Shall here unlade him and depart no more.

364      *The Crown Prince of Dullness*

ALL human things are subject to decay,
And, when Fate summons, monarchs must obey:
This Flecknoe found, who, like Augustus, young
Was called to empire, and had governed long:
In prose and verse was owned without dispute,
Through all the realms of Nonsense, absolute.
This aged Prince now flourishing in peace,
And blest with issue of a large increase,
Worn out with business, did at length debate
To settle the succession of the State:
And pondering which of all his sons was fit
To reign, and wage immortal war with Wit,
Cried, ' 'Tis resolved; for Nature pleads that he
Should only rule who most resembles me:

Shadwell alone my perfect image bears,
Mature in dullness from his tender years.
Shadwell alone, of all my sons, is he
Who stands confirmed in full stupidity.
The rest to some faint meaning make pretence,
But Shadwell never deviates into sense.
Some beams of Wit on other souls may fall,
Strike through, and make a lucid interval;
But Shadwell's genuine night admits no ray,
His rising fogs prevail upon the day:
Besides, his goodly fabric fills the eye,
And seems designed for thoughtless majesty:
Thoughtless as monarch oaks, that shade the plain,
And, spread in solemn state, supinely reign.'


## *from* Absalom and Achitophel

### (i)

**365**     *Achitophel: the Earl of Shaftesbury*

So several factions from this first ferment
Work up to foam, and threat the government.
Some by their friends, more by themselves thought wise,
Opposed the power to which they could not rise.
Some had in courts been great and, thrown from thence,
Like fiends were hardened in impenitence.
Some by their Monarch's fatal mercy grown
From pardoned rebels kinsmen to the throne
Were raised in power and public office high:
Strong bands, if bands ungrateful men could tie.
   Of these the false Achitophel was first,
A name to all succeeding ages curst:
For close designs and crooked counsels fit,
Sagacious, bold, and turbulent of wit,
Restless, unfixed in principles and place,
In power unpleased, impatient of disgrace;
A fiery soul, which, working out its way,
Fretted the pigmy body to decay
And o'er-informed the tenement of clay.
A daring pilot in extremity,
Pleased with the danger, when the waves went high,

He sought the storms; but, for a calm unfit,
Would steer too nigh the sands to boast his wit.
Great wits are sure to madness near allied
And thin partitions do their bounds divide;
Else, why should he, with wealth and honour blest,
Refuse his age the needful hours of rest?
Punish a body which he could not please,
Bankrupt of life, yet prodigal of ease?
And all to leave what with his toil he won
To that unfeathered two-legged thing, a son,
Got, while his soul did huddled notions try,
And born a shapeless lump, like anarchy.
In friendship false, implacable in hate,
Resolved to ruin or to rule the state;
To compass this the triple bond he broke,
The pillars of the public safety shook,
And fitted Israel for a foreign yoke;
Then, seized with fear, yet still affecting fame,
Usurped a patriot's all-atoning name.
So easy still it proves in factious times
With public zeal to cancel private crimes.
How safe is treason and how sacred ill,
Where none can sin against the people's will,
Where crowds can wink and no offence be known,
Since in another's guilt they find their own!
   Yet fame deserved no enemy can grudge;
The statesman we abhor, but praise the judge.
In Israel's courts ne'er sat an Abbethdin
With more discerning eyes or hands more clean,
Unbribed, unsought, the wretched to redress,
Swift of despatch and easy of access.
Oh! had he been content to serve the crown
With virtues only proper to the gown,
Or had the rankness of the soil been freed
From cockle that oppressed the noble seed,
David for him his tuneful harp had strung
And Heaven had wanted one immortal song.
But wild Ambition loves to slide, not stand,
And Fortune's ice prefers to Virtue's land.

(ii)

366   *Zimri: the Duke of Buckingham*

A NUMEROUS host of dreaming Saints succeed,
Of the true old enthusiastic breed:
'Gainst form and order they their power employ,
Nothing to build and all things to destroy.
But far more numerous was the herd of such
Who think too little and who talk too much. . . .
Such were the tools; but a whole Hydra more
Remains of sprouting heads too long to score.
    Some of their chiefs were Princes of the land;
In the first rank of these did Zimri stand,
A man so various that he seemed to be
Not one, but all mankind's epitome:
Stiff in opinions, always in the wrong,
Was everything by starts and nothing long;
But, in the course of one revolving moon,
Was chemist, fiddler, statesman, and buffoon;
Then all for women, painting, rhyming, drinking,
Besides ten thousand freaks that died in thinking.
Blest madman, who could every hour employ
With something new to wish or to enjoy!
Railing and praising were his usual themes,
And both, to show his judgement, in extremes:
So over-violent or over-civil
That every man with him was God or Devil.
In squandering wealth was his peculiar art;
Nothing went unrewarded but desert.
Beggared by fools, whom still he found too late,
He had his jest, and they had his estate.
He laughed himself from Court; then sought relief
By forming parties, but could ne'er be chief:
For, spite of him, the weight of business fell
On Absalom and wise Achitophel;
Thus wicked but in will, of means bereft,
He left not faction, but of that was left.

367 *Vox Populi*

HE preaches to the crowd that power is lent,
But not conveyed, to kingly government;
That claims successive bear no binding force;
That Coronation Oaths are things of course;
Maintains the multitude can never err,
And sets the people in the papal chair.
The reason's obvious: interest never lies;
The most have still their interest in their eyes;
The power is always theirs, and power is ever wise.
Almighty Crowd, thou shortenest all dispute;
Power is thy essence, Wit thy attribute!
Nor faith nor reason make thee at a stay,
Thou leap'st o'er all eternal truths, in thy Pindaric way!
Athens, no doubt, did righteously decide,
When Phocion and when Socrates were tried:
As righteously they did those dooms repent;
Still they were wise, whatever way they went.
Crowds err not, though to both extremes they run;
To kill the Father, and recall the Son.
Some think the fools were most as times went then,
But now the world's o'er-stocked with prudent men.
The common cry is even religion's test;
The Turk's is, at Constantinople, best;
Idols in India, Popery at Rome;
And our own worship only true at home.
And true but for the time; 'tis hard to know
How long we please it shall continue so.
This side today, and that tomorrow burns;
So all are God-a'mighties in their turns.
A tempting doctrine, plausible and new;
What fools our fathers were, if this be true!

368    *To the Memory of Mr. Oldham*

FAREWELL, too little and too lately known,
Whom I began to think and call my own;
For sure our souls were near allied, and thine
Cast in the same poetic mould with mine.
One common note on either lyre did strike,
And knaves and fools we both abhorred alike:
To the same goal did both our studies drive,
The last set out the soonest did arrive.
Thus Nisus fell upon the slippery place,
While his young friend performed and won the race.
O early ripe! to thy abundant store
What could advancing age have added more?
It might (what Nature never gives the young)
Have taught the numbers of thy native tongue.
But Satire needs not those, and Wit will shine
Through the harsh cadence of a rugged line.
A noble error, and but seldom made,
When poets are by too much force betrayed.
Thy generous fruits, though gathered ere their prime
Still showed a quickness; and maturing time
But mellows what we write to the dull sweets of Rhyme.
Once more, hail and farewell; farewell, thou young,
But ah too short, Marcellus of our tongue;
Thy brows with ivy, and with laurels bound;
But Fate and gloomy Night encompass thee around.


369    *Confessio Fidei*

WHAT weight of ancient witness can prevail,
If private reason hold the public scale?
But, gracious God, how well dost thou provide
For erring judgements an unerring guide!
Thy throne is darkness in the abyss of light,
A blaze of glory that forbids the sight.
O teach me to believe thee thus concealed,
And search no farther than thyself revealed;
But her alone for my director take,
Whom thou hast promised never to forsake!

My thoughtless youth was winged with vain desires;
My manhood, long misled by wandering fires,
Followed false lights; and when their glimpse was gone
My pride struck out new sparkles of her own.
Such was I, such by nature still I am;
Be thine the glory and be mine the shame!
Good life be now my task; my doubts are done;
What more could fright my faith than Three in One?
Can I believe eternal God could lie
Disguised in mortal mould and infancy,
That the great Maker of the world could die?
And, after that, trust my imperfect sense
Which calls in question his omnipotence?
Can I my reason to my faith compel,
And shall my sight and touch and taste rebel?
Superior faculties are set aside;
Shall their subservient organs be my guide?
Then let the moon usurp the rule of day,
And winking tapers show the sun his way;
For what my senses can themselves perceive
I need no revelation to believe.

370 *Farewell, Ungrateful Traitor*

FAREWELL, ungrateful traitor,
Farewell, my perjured swain,
Let never injured creature
Believe a man again.
The pleasure of possessing
Surpasses all expressing,
But 'tis too short a blessing,
And love too long a pain.

'Tis easy to deceive us
In pity of your pain,
But when we love you leave us
To rail at you in vain.
Before we have descried it
There is no bliss beside it,
But she that once has tried it
Will never love again.

The passion you pretended
Was only to obtain,
But when the charm is ended
The charmer you disdain.
Your love by ours we measure
Till we have lost our treasure,
But dying is a pleasure,
When living is a pain.

371    *Alexander's Feast: or The Power of Music.*
        *An Ode in Honour of St. Cecilia's Day,*
                        *1697*

### I

'TWAS at the royal feast, for Persia won
          By Philip's warlike son:
        Aloft in awful state
        The god-like hero sate
          On his imperial throne:
        His valiant peers were placed around;
Their brows with roses and with myrtles bound.
        (So should desert in arms be crowned:)
The lovely Thaïs by his side,
Sat like a blooming Eastern bride
In flower of youth and beauty's pride.
        Happy, happy, happy pair!
        None but the Brave
        None but the Brave
        None but the Brave deserves the Fair.

#### CHORUS

*Happy, happy, happy pair!*
*None but the Brave*
*None but the Brave*
*None but the Brave deserves the Fair.*

### II

Timotheus placed on high
        Amid the tuneful choir,
        With flying fingers touched the lyre:
The trembling notes ascend the sky,
                        And heavenly joys inspire.

The song began from Jove;
Who left his blissful seats above,
(Such is the power of mighty Love.)
A dragon's fiery form belied the god:
Sublime on radiant spires he rode,
  When he to fair Olympia pressed,
  And while he sought her snowy breast:
Then, round her slender waist he curled,
And stamped an image of himself, a sovereign of the world.
The listening crowd admire the lofty sound,
'A present Deity,' they shout around:
'A present Deity,' the vaulted roofs rebound.
  With ravished ears
  The Monarch hears,
  Assumes the god,
  Affects to nod,
 And seems to shake the spheres.

CHORUS

*With ravished ears*
*The Monarch hears,*
*Assumes the god,*
*Affects to nod,*
*And seems to shake the spheres.*

III

The praise of Bacchus then the sweet musician sung,
  Of Bacchus ever fair and ever young;
  The jolly god in triumph comes;
  Sound the trumpets, beat the drums:
   Flushed with a purple grace
   He shows his honest face;
Now give the hautboys breath: he comes, he comes!
  'Bacchus, ever fair and young,
   Drinking joys did first ordain;
  Bacchus' blessings are a treasure;
  Drinking is the soldier's pleasure;
   Rich the treasure,
   Sweet the pleasure;
   Sweet is pleasure after pain.'

# JOHN DRYDEN

*Bacchus' blessings are a treasure ;*
*Drinking is the soldier's pleasure ;*
    *Rich the treasure,*
    *Sweet the pleasure ;*
*Sweet is pleasure after pain.*

## IV

Soothed with the sound the King grew vain,
    Fought all his battles o'er again;
And thrice he routed all his foes, and thrice he slew the slain.
        The master saw the madness rise,
        His glowing cheeks, his ardent eyes;
        And while he heaven and earth defied,
        Changed his hand, and checked his pride.
            He chose a mournful Muse
            Soft pity to infuse:
        He sung Darius great and good,
            By too severe a fate,
        Fallen, fallen, fallen, fallen,
            Fallen from his high estate
                    And weltering in his blood;
        Deserted at his utmost need
        By those his former bounty fed;
        On the bare earth exposed he lies,
        With not a friend to close his eyes.

With downcast looks the joyless victor sate,
        Revolving in his altered soul
        The various turns of chance below;
        And, now and then, a sigh he stole,
        And tears began to flow.

*Revolving in his altered soul*
    *The various turns of chance below;*
*And, now and then, a sigh he stole,*
    *And tears began to flow.*

## V

The mighty master smiled to see
That love was in the next degree:
'Twas but a kindred sound to move,
For pity melts the mind to love.
  Softly sweet, in Lydian measures
  Soon he soothed his soul to pleasures.
  'War', he sung, 'is toil and trouble;
  Honour but an empty bubble.
   Never ending, still beginning,
  Fighting still, and still destroying;
   If the world be worth thy winning,
  Think, O think it worth enjoying.
   Lovely Thaïs sits beside thee,
   Take the good the Gods provide thee.'

The many rend the skies with loud applause;
So Love was crowned, but Music won the cause.
  The Prince, unable to conceal his pain,
    Gazed on the Fair
    Who caused his care,
   And sighed and looked, sighed and looked,
  Sighed and looked, and sighed again:
At length, with love and wine at once oppressed,
The vanquished victor sunk upon her breast.

### CHORUS

  *The Prince, unable to conceal his pain,*
    *Gazed on the Fair*
    *Who caused his care,*
   *And sighed and looked, sighed and looked,*
  *Sighed and looked, and sighed again :*
*At length, with love and wine at once oppressed,*
*The vanquished victor sunk upon her breast.*

## VI

Now strike the golden lyre again,
A louder yet, and yet a louder strain.
Break his bands of sleep asunder,
And rouse him, like a rattling peal of thunder.

Hark, hark, the horrid sound
　　Has raised up his head,
　　As awaked from the dead,
　　And amazed he stares around.
'Revenge, revenge!' Timotheus cries,
　　'See the Furies arise!
　　See the snakes that they rear,
　　How they hiss in their hair,
　　And the sparkles that flash from their eyes!
　　Behold a ghastly band,
　　Each a torch in his hand!
Those are Grecian ghosts that in battle were slain,
　　　　　　　　And unburied remain
　　　　　　　　Inglorious on the plain.
　　　　　Give the vengeance due
　　　　　To the valiant crew.
Behold how they toss their torches on high,
　　How they point to the Persian abodes,
And glittering temples of their hostile gods!'
The Princes applaud with a furious joy,
And the King seized a flambeau, with zeal to destroy;
　　　　Thaïs led the way
　　　　To light him to his prey,
And, like another Helen, fired another Troy.

### CHORUS

*And the King seized a flambeau, with zeal to destroy;*
　　　*Thaïs led the way*
　　　*To light him to his prey,*
*And, like another Helen, fired another Troy.*

# VII

　　Thus, long ago,
Ere heaving bellows learned to blow,
　　While organs yet were mute;
Timotheus, to his breathing flute
　　And sounding lyre,
Could swell the soul to rage, or kindle soft desire.
　　At last divine Cecilia came,
　　Inventress of the vocal frame;

The sweet Enthusiast, from her sacred store,
 Enlarged the former narrow bounds,
 And added length to solemn sounds,
With Nature's mother wit, and arts unknown before.
 Let old Timotheus yield the prize,
  Or both divide the crown;
 He raised a mortal to the skies,
  She drew an angel down.

### GRAND CHORUS

*At last divine Cecilia came,*
 *Inventress of the vocal frame;*
*The sweet Enthusiast, from her sacred store,*
 *Enlarged the former narrow bounds,*
 *And added length to solemn sounds,*
*With Nature's mother wit, and arts unknown before.*
 *Let old Timotheus yield the prize,*
  *Or both divide the crown;*
 *He raised a mortal to the skies,*
  *She drew an angel down.*

372      *Songs from* The Secular Masque

*Diana.* With horns and with hounds I waken the day,
 And hie to my woodland walks away;
 I tuck up my robe, and am buskined soon,
 And tie to my forehead a waxing moon.
 I course the fleet stag, unkennel the fox,
 And chase the wild goats o'er summits of rocks;
 With shouting and hooting we pierce through the sky,
 And Echo turns hunter and doubles the cry.

*Chorus.* *Then our age was in its prime,*
  *Free from rage, and free from crime,*
  *A very merry, dancing, drinking,*
  *Laughing, quaffing, and unthinking time.*

*Mars.*   Inspire the vocal brass, inspire;
        The world is past its infant age:
            Arms and honour,
            Arms and honour,
        Set the martial mind on fire,
        And kindle manly rage.
        Mars has looked the sky to red;
        And Peace, the lazy good, is fled.
        Plenty, Peace, and Pleasure fly;
            The sprightly green
        In woodland walks no more is seen;
        The sprightly green has drunk the Tyrian dye.

*Momus.*  Thy sword within the scabbard keep,
           And let mankind agree;
        Better the world were fast asleep.
           Than kept awake by thee.
        The fools are only thinner,
           With all our cost and care;
        But neither side a winner,
           For things are as they were.

*Venus.*  Calms appear when storms are past,
        Love will have his hour at last:
        Nature is my kindly care;
        Mars destroys, and I repair;
        Take me, take me, while you may;
        Venus comes not every day.

*Chorus.*  *All, all of a piece throughout:*
        *Thy chase had a beast in view;*
        *Thy wars brought nothing about;*
        *Thy lovers were all untrue.*
        *'Tis well an old age is out,*
        *And time to begin a new.*

# CHARLES SACKVILLE, EARL OF DORSET

1638–1706

373                    *Song*

*Written at Sea in the First Dutch War (1665),*
*the night before an Engagement*

To all you ladies now at land
  We men at sea indite;
But first would have you understand
  How hard it is to write:
The Muses now, and Neptune too,
We must implore to write to you—
    With a fa, la, la, la, la.

For though the Muses should prove kind,
  And fill our empty brain,
Yet if rough Neptune rouse the wind
  To wave the azure main,
Our paper, pen, and ink, and we,
Roll up and down our ships at sea—
    With a fa, la, la, la, la.

Then if we write not by each post,
  Think not we are unkind;
Nor yet conclude our ships are lost
  By Dutchmen or by wind:
Our tears we'll send a speedier way,
The tide shall bring them twice a day—
    With a fa, la, la, la, la.

The King with wonder and surprise
  Will swear the seas grow bold,
Because the tides will higher rise
  Than e'er they did of old:
But let him know it is our tears
Bring floods of grief to Whitehall stairs—
    With a fa, la, la, la, la.

386

Should foggy Opdam chance to know
   Our sad and dismal story,
The Dutch would scorn so weak a foe,
   And quit their fort at Goree:
For what resistance can they find
From men who've left their hearts behind?—
     With a fa, la, la, la, la.

Let wind and weather do its worst,
   Be you to us but kind;
Let Dutchmen vapour, Spaniards curse,
   No sorrow we shall find:
'Tis then no matter how things go,
Or who's our friend, or who's our foe—
     With a fa, la, la, la, la.

To pass our tedious hours away
   We throw a merry main,
Or else at serious ombre play;
   But why should we in vain
Each other's ruin thus pursue?
We were undone when we left you—
     With a fa, la, la, la, la.

But now our fears tempestuous grow
   And cast our hopes away;
Whilst you, regardless of our woe,
   Sit careless at a play:
Perhaps permit some happier man
To kiss your hand, or flirt your fan—
     With a fa, la, la, la, la.

When any mournful tune you hear,
   That dies in every note
As if it sighed with each man's care
   For being so remote,
Think then how often love we've made
To you, when all those tunes were played—
     With a fa, la, la, la, la.

In justice you cannot refuse
   To think of our distress,
When we for hopes of honour lose
   Our certain happiness:
All those designs are but to prove
Ourselves more worthy of your love—
   With a fa, la, la, la, la.

And now we've told you all our loves,
   And likewise all our fears,
In hopes this declaration moves
   Some pity for our tears:
Let's hear of no inconstancy—
We have too much of that at sea—
   With a fa, la, la, la, la.

# SIR CHARLES SEDLEY
## 1639–1701

374       *To Celia*

NOT, Celia, that I juster am
   Or better than the rest!
For I would change each hour, like them,
   Were not my heart at rest.

But I am tied to very thee
   By every thought I have;
Thy face I only care to see,
   Thy heart I only crave.

All that in woman is adored
   In thy dear self I find—
For the whole sex can but afford
   The handsome and the kind.

Why then should I seek further store,
   And still make love anew?
When change itself can give no more,
   'Tis easy to be true!

375                              *Song*

LOVE still has something of the sea,
    From whence his mother rose;
No time his slaves from Doubt can free,
    Nor give their thoughts repose:

They are becalmed in clearest days,
    And in rough weather tost;
They wither under cold delays,
    Or are in tempests lost.

One while they seem to touch the port,
    Then straight into the main,
Some angry wind in cruel sport
    The vessel drives again.

At first Disdain and Pride they fear,
    Which if they chance to 'scape,
Rivals and Falsehood soon appear
    In a more dreadful shape.

By such degrees to Joy they come,
    And are so long withstood,
So slowly they receive the sum,
    It hardly does them good.

'Tis cruel to prolong a pain,
    And to defer a joy,
Believe me, gentle Celemene,
    Offends the wingèd Boy.

An hundred thousand oaths your fears
    Perhaps would not remove;
And if I gazed a thousand years
    I could no deeper love.

376 *Phyllis Knotting*

HEARS not my Phyllis how the birds
   Their feathered mates salute?
They tell their passion in their words;
   Must I alone be mute?
Phyllis, *without frown or smile,*
*Sat and knotted all the while.*

The God of Love in thy bright eyes
   Does like a tyrant reign;
But in thy heart a child he lies,
   Without his dart or flame.
Phyllis, *without frown or smile,*
*Sat and knotted all the while.*

So many months in silence past,
   And yet in raging love,
Might well deserve one word at last
   My passion should approve.
Phyllis, *without frown or smile,*
*Sat and knotted all the while.*

Must then your faithful swain expire,
   And not one look obtain,
Which he, to sooth his fond desire,
   Might pleasingly explain?
Phyllis, *without frown or smile,*
*Sat and knotted all the while.*

# APHRA BEHN

1640–1689

377 *Song*

LOVE in fantastic triumph sate
   Whilst bleeding hearts around him flowed,
For whom fresh pains he did create
   And strange tyrannic power he showed:

From thy bright eyes he took his fires,
   Which round about in sport he hurled;
But 'twas from mine he took desires
   Enough to undo the amorous world.

From me he took his sighs and tears,
   From thee his pride and cruelty;
From me his languishments and fears,
   And every killing dart from thee.
Thus thou and I the god have armed
   And set him up a deity;
But my poor heart alone is harmed,
   Whilst thine the victor is, and free!

# JOHN WILMOT,
# EARL OF ROCHESTER
## 1647–1680

### The Mistress

**378**

AN age in her embraces passed
   Would seem a winter's day,
Where life and light with envious haste
   Are torn and snatched away.

But oh, how slowly minutes roll
   When absent from her eyes,
That feed my love, which is my soul:
   It languishes and dies.

For then no more a soul, but shade,
   It mournfully does move
And haunts my breast, by absence made
   The living tomb of love.

You wiser men, despise me not
   Whose lovesick fancy raves
On shades of souls, and heaven knows what:
   Short ages live in graves.

Whene'er those wounding eyes, so full
   Of sweetness, you did see,
Had you not been profoundly dull,
   You had gone mad like me.

Nor censure us, you who perceive
   My best beloved and me
Sigh and lament, complain and grieve:
   You think we disagree.

Alas! 'tis sacred jealousy,
   Love raised to an extreme:
The only proof 'twixt her and me
   We love, and do not dream.

Fantastic fancies fondly move
   And in frail joys believe,
Taking false pleasure for true love;
   But pain can ne'er deceive.

Kind jealous doubts, tormenting fears,
   And anxious cares, when past,
Prove our hearts' treasure fixed and dear,
   And make us blest at last.

379                                  *Return*

ABSENT from thee, I languish still;
   Then ask me not, when I return?
The straying fool 'twill plainly kill
   To wish all day, all night to mourn.

Dear! from thine arms then let me fly,
   That my fantastic mind may prove
The torments it deserves to try
   That tears my fixed heart from my love.

When, wearied with a world of woe,
   To thy safe bosom I retire
Where love and peace and truth does flow,
   May I contented there expire,

Lest, once more wandering from that heaven,
    I fall on some base heart unblest,
Faithless to thee, false, unforgiven,
    And lose my everlasting rest.


380                    *Love and Life*

ALL my past life is mine no more;
    The flying hours are gone,
Like transitory dreams given o'er
Whose images are kept in store
    By memory alone.

Whatever is to come is not:
    How can it then be mine?
The present moment's all my lot,
And that, as fast as it is got,
    Phyllis, is wholly thine.

Then talk not of inconstancy,
    False hearts, and broken vows;
If I, by miracle, can be
This livelong minute true to thee,
    'Tis all that heaven allows.


381                    *Homo Sapiens*

WERE I (who to my cost already am
One of those strange, prodigious creatures, man)
A spirit free to choose, for my own share,
What case of flesh and blood I pleased to wear,
I'd be a dog, a monkey, or a bear,
Or anything but that vain animal
Who is so proud of being rational.
    The senses are too gross, and he'll contrive
A sixth, to contradict the other five,
And before certain instinct, will prefer
Reason, which fifty times for one does err;
Reason, an *ignis fatuus* in the mind,
Which, leaving light of nature, sense, behind,

393

Pathless and dangerous wandering ways it takes
Through error's fenny bogs and thorny brakes;
Whilst the misguided follower climbs with pain
Mountains of whimseys, heaped in his own brain;
Stumbling from thought to thought, falls headlong down
Into doubt's boundless sea, where, like to drown,
Books bear him up awhile, and make him try
To swim with bladders of philosophy;
In hopes still to o'ertake the escaping light,
The vapour dances in his dazzling sight
Till, spent, it leaves him to eternal night.
Then old age and experience, hand in hand,
Lead him to death, and make him understand,
After a search so painful and so long,
That all his life he has been in the wrong.
Huddled in dirt the reasoning engine lies,
Who was so proud, so witty, and so wise.


# MATTHEW PRIOR

### 1664–1721

382      *To a Child of Quality*
*Five Years Old, 1704. The Author then Forty*

LORDS, knights, and squires, the numerous band
    That wear the fair Miss Mary's fetters,
Were summoned by her high command
    To show their passion by their letters.

My pen amongst the rest I took,
    Lest those bright eyes, that cannot read,
Should dart their kindling fires, and look
    The power they have to be obeyed.

Nor quality, nor reputation,
    Forbid me yet my flame to tell;
Dear Five-years-old befriends my passion,
    And I may write till she can spell.

For, while she makes her silkworms beds
  With all the tender things I swear;
Whilst all the house my passion reads,
  In papers round her baby's hair;

She may receive and own my flame,
  For, though the strictest prudes should know it,
She'll pass for a most virtuous dame,
  And I for an unhappy poet.

Then too, alas! when she shall tear
  The lines some younger rival sends,
She'll give me leave to write, I fear,
  And we shall still continue friends.

For, as our different ages move,
  'Tis so ordained (would Fate but mend it!)
That I shall be past making love
  When she begins to comprehend it.

383
*A Letter*
*To Lady Margaret Cavendish Holles-Harley,*
*when a Child*

MY noble, lovely, little Peggy,
Let this my First Epistle beg ye,
At dawn of morn, and close of even,
To lift your heart and hands to Heaven.
In double beauty say your prayer:
*Our Father* first, then *Notre Père*.
And, dearest child, along the day,
In every thing you do and say,
Obey and please my lord and lady,
So God shall love and angels aid ye.

If to these precepts you attend,
No second letter need I send,
And so I rest your constant friend.

384 *Jinny the Just*

RELEASED from the noise of the butcher and baker
Who, my old friends be thanked, did seldom forsake her,
And from the soft duns of my landlord the Quaker,

From chiding the footmen and watching the lasses,
From Nell that burned milk too, and Tom that brake glasses
(Sad mischiefs through which a good housekeeper passes!)

From some real care but more fancied vexation,
From a life parti-coloured half reason half passion,
Here lies after all the best wench in the nation.

From the Rhine to the Po, from the Thames to the Rhone,
Joanna or Janneton, Jinny or Joan,
'Twas all one to her by what name she was known.

For the idiom of words very little she heeded,
Provided the matter she drove at succeeded,
She took and gave languages just as she needed.

So for kitchen and market, for bargain and sale,
She paid English or Dutch or French down on the nail,
But in telling a story she sometimes did fail;

Then begging excuse as she happened to stammer,
With respect to her betters but none to her grammar,
Her blush helped her out and her jargon became her.

Her habit and mien she endeavoured to frame
To the different *gout* of the place where she came,
Her outside still changed, but her inside the same:

At the Hague in her slippers and hair as the mode is,
At Paris all falbalowed fine as a goddess,
And at censuring London in smock sleeves and bodice.

She ordered affairs that few people could tell
In what part about her that mixture did dwell
Of Frau, or Mistress, or Mademoiselle.

For her surname and race let the heralds e'en answer;
Her own proper worth was enough to advance her,
And he who liked her little valued her grandsire.

But from what house soever her lineage may come
I wish my own Jinny but out of her tomb,
Though all her relations were there in her room.

Of such terrible beauty she never could boast
As with absolute sway o'er all hearts rules the roast
When J—— bawls out to the chair for a toast;

But of good household features her person was made,
Nor by faction cried up, nor of censure afraid,
And her beauty was rather for use than parade.

Her blood so well mixed and flesh so well pasted
That, though her youth faded, her comeliness lasted;
The blue was worn off but the plum was well tasted.

Less smooth than her skin, and less white than her breast,
Was this polished stone beneath which she lies pressed:
Stop, reader, and sigh while thou think'st on the rest.

With a just trim of virtue her soul was endued,
Not affectedly pious nor secretly lewd
She cut even between the coquette and the prude;

And her will with her duty so equally stood
That, seldom opposed, she was commonly good,
And did pretty well, doing just what she would.

Declining all power she found means to persuade,
Was then most regarded when most she obeyed,
The mistress in truth when she seemed but the maid.

Such care of her own proper actions she took
That on other folks lives she had no time to look,
So censure and praise were struck out of her book.

Her thought still confined to its own little sphere,
She minded not who did excel or did err
But just as the matter related to her.

Then too when her private tribunal was reared
Her mercy so mixed with her judgement appeared
That her foes were condemned and her friends always cleared.

Her religion so well with her learning did suit
That in practice sincere and in controverse mute,
She showed she knew better to live than dispute.

Some parts of the Bible by heart she recited,
And much in historical chapters delighted,
But in points about faith she was something short-sighted;

So notions and modes she referred to the schools,
And in matters of conscience adhered to two rules:
To advise with no bigots and jest with no fools.

And scrupling but little, enough she believed,
By charity ample small sins she retrieved,
And when she had new clothes she always received.

Thus still whilst her morning unseen fled away,
In ordering the linen and making the tea,
That she scarce could have time for the psalms of the day;

And while after dinner the night came so soon
That half she proposed very seldom was done;
With twenty God bless me's, how this day is gone!

While she read and accounted and paid and abated,
Ate and drank, played and worked, laughed and cried, loved
    and hated,
As answered the end of her being created:

In the midst of her age came a cruel disease,
Which neither her broths nor receipts could appease;
So down dropped her clay, may her soul be at peace.

Retire from this sepulchre all the profane,
Ye that love for debauch, or that marry for gain;
Retire lest ye trouble the Manes of J——.

But thou that know'st love above interest or lust,
Strew the myrtle and rose on this once beloved dust,
And shed one pious tear upon Jinny the Just.

Tread soft on her grave, and do right to her honour,
Let neither rude hand nor ill tongue light upon her,
Do all the small favours that now can be done her.

And when what thou liked shall return to her clay,
For so I'm persuaded she must do one day,
Whatever fantastic J—— Asgill may say,

When as I have done now, thou shalt set up a stone
For something however distinguished or known,
May some pious friend the misfortune bemoan,
And make thy concern by reflection his own.

385    *Written in the Beginning of*
       *Mezeray's History of France*

WHATE'ER thy countrymen have done
By law and wit, by sword and gun,
    In thee is faithfully recited:
And all the living world, that view
Thy work, give thee the praises due,
    At once instructed and delighted.

Yet for the fame of all these deeds
What beggar in the Invalides,
    With lameness broke, with blindness smitten,
Wished ever decently to die,
To have been either Mezeray
    Or any monarch he has written?

It strange, dear Author, yet it true is,
That down from Pharamond to Louis
    All covet life, yet call it pain;
All feel the ill, yet shun the cure:
Can sense this paradox endure?
    Resolve me, Cambray or Fontaine.

The man in graver Tragic known,
Though his best part long since was done,
    Still on the stage desires to tarry;
And he who played the Harlequin
After the jest still loads the scene,
    Unwilling to retire, though weary.

386      *Answer to Chloe Jealous*

DEAR Chloe, how blubbered is that pretty face!
Thy cheek all on fire, and thy hair all uncurled.
Prithee, quit this caprice; and (as old Falstaff says)
Let us e'en talk a little like folks of this world.

How canst thou presume thou hast leave to destroy
The beauties which Venus but lent to thy keeping?
Those looks were designed to inspire love and joy:
More ordinary eyes may serve people for weeping.

To be vexed at a trifle or two that I writ
Your judgement at once and my passion you wrong:
You take that for fact which will scarce be found wit:
'Od's life! must one swear to the truth of a song?

What I speak, my fair Chloe, and what I write, shows
The difference there is betwixt Nature and Art:
I court others in verse, but I love thee in prose;
And they have my whimsies, but thou hast my heart.

The God of us verse-men, you know, child, the sun,
How after his journeys he sets up his rest:
If at morning o'er Earth 'tis his fancy to run,
At night he reclines on his Thetis's breast.

So when I am wearied with wandering all day,
To thee, my delight, in the evening I come;
No matter what beauties I saw in my way,
They were but my visits, but thou art my home.

Then finish, dear Chloe, this pastoral war,
And let us like Horace and Lydia agree:
For thou art a girl as much brighter than her
As he was a poet sublimer than me.

# WILLIAM CONGREVE
## 1670–1729

387          *Pious Selinda*

PIOUS Selinda goes to prayers,
  If I but ask the favour;
And yet the tender fool's in tears,
  When she believes I'll leave her.

Would I were free from this restraint,
  Or else had hopes to win her;
Would she would make of me a saint,
  Or I of her a sinner.

388          *False though she be*

FALSE though she be to me and love,
  I'll ne'er pursue revenge;
For still the charmer I approve
  Though I deplore her change.

In hours of bliss we oft have met:
  They could not always last;
And though the present I regret,
  I'm grateful for the past.

# JONATHAN SWIFT
## 1667–1745

389          *A Description of the Morning*

NOW hardly here and there a hackney-coach
Appearing, showed the ruddy morn's approach.
Now Betty from her master's bed had flown,
And softly stole to discompose her own.
The slipshod 'prentice from his master's door
Had pared the dirt and sprinkled round the floor.

Now Moll had whirled her mop with dexterous airs,
Prepared to scrub the entry and the stairs.
The youth with broomy stumps began to trace
The kennel-edge, where wheels had worn the place.
The small-coal-man was heard with cadence deep,
'Till drowned in shriller notes of chimney-sweep.
Duns at his Lordship's gate began to meet,
And brickdust Moll had screamed through half a street.
The turnkey now his flock returning sees,
Duly let out a-nights to steal for fees.
The watchful bailiffs take their silent stands,
And schoolboys lag, with satchels in their hands.

390        *Verses on the Death of Doctor Swift*

THE time is not remote when I
Must by the course of nature die:
When I foresee my special friends
Will try to find their private ends:
Though it is hardly understood
Which way my death can do them good;
Yet, thus methinks I hear 'em speak:
'See how the Dean begins to break,
Poor gentleman, he droops apace,
You plainly find it in his face;
That old vertigo in his head
Will never leave him till he's dead:
Besides, his memory decays,
He recollects not what he says,
He cannot call his friends to mind,
Forgets the place where last he dined,
Plies you with stories o'er and o'er—
He told them fifty times before.
How does he fancy we can sit
To hear his out-of-fashioned wit?
But he takes up with younger folks,
Who for his wine will bear his jokes,
Faith, he must make his stories shorter,
Or change his comrades once a quarter;
In half the time he talks them round,
There must another set be found.

# JONATHAN SWIFT

For poetry, he's past his prime,
He takes an hour to find a rhyme;
His fire is out, his wit decayed,
His fancy sunk, his muse a jade.
I'd have him throw away his pen,
But there's no talking to some men.'

And then their tenderness appears,
By adding largely to my years:
'He's older than he would be reckoned,
And well remembers Charles the Second.'

'He hardly drinks a pint of wine,
And that, I doubt, is no good sign.
His stomach too begins to fail:
Last year we thought him strong and hale,
But now he's quite another thing;
I wish he may hold out till spring.'

Then hug themselves, and reason thus;
'It is not yet so bad with us.'

\*

Suppose me dead; and then suppose
A club assembled at the Rose,
Where from discourse of this and that
I grow the subject of their chat;
And, while they toss my name about,
With favour some, and some without,
One quite indifferent in the cause
My character impartial draws:

'The Dean, if we believe report,
Was never ill-received at Court;
As for his works in verse and prose,
I own myself no judge of those;
Nor can I tell what critics thought 'em,
But this I know, all people bought 'em;
As with a moral view designed
To cure the vices of mankind;
His vein, ironically grave,
Exposed the fool, and lashed the knave;
To steal a hint was never known,
But what he writ was all his own.

He never thought an honour done him
Because a Duke was proud to own him;
Would rather slip aside, and choose
To talk with wits in dirty shoes;
Despised the fools with Stars and Garters,
So often seen caressing Chartres;
He never courted men in station
Nor persons had in admiration;
Of no man's greatness was afraid,
Because he sought for no man's aid.
Though trusted long in great affairs
He gave himself no haughty airs;
Without regarding private ends
Spent all his credit for his friends;
And only chose the wise and good,
No flatterers, no allies in blood;
But succoured virtue in distress,
And seldom failed of good success,
As numbers in their hearts must own,
Who, but for him, had been unknown.

With Princes kept a due decorum,
But never stood in awe before 'em;
And to her Majesty, God bless her,
Would speak as free as to her dresser;
She thought it his peculiar whim,
Nor took it ill as come from him.
He followed David's lesson just,
"In Princes never put thy trust."
And would you make him truly sour,
Provoke him with "a slave in power";
The Irish senate, if you named,
With what impatience he declaimed!
Fair LIBERTY was all his cry;
For her he stood prepared to die;
For her he boldly stood alone;
For her he oft exposed his own.
Two kingdoms, just as faction led,
Had set a price upon his head,
But not a traitor could be found
To sell him for six hundred pound.

Had he but spared his tongue and pen
He might have rose like other men;
But power was never in his thought,
And wealth he valued not a groat;
Ingratitude he often found,
And pitied those who meant the wound;
But kept the tenor of his mind
To merit well of human kind;
Nor made a sacrifice of those
Who still were true, to please his foes.
He laboured many a fruitless hour
To reconcile his friends in power;
Saw mischief by a faction brewing,
While they pursued each other's ruin.
But, finding vain was all his care,
He left the Court in mere despair.'

\*

'Perhaps I may allow, the Dean
Had too much satire in his vein,
And seemed determined not to starve it
Because no age could more deserve it.
Yet malice never was his aim:
He lashed the vice, but spared the name.
No individual could resent
Where thousands equally were meant.
His satire points at no defect
But what all mortals may correct;
For he abhorred that senseless tribe,
Who call it humour when they jibe;
He spared a hump or crooked nose
Whose owners set not up for beaux.
True genuine dullness moved his pity,
Unless it offered to be witty.
Those who their ignorance confessed
He ne'er offended with a jest,
But laughed to hear an idiot quote
A verse from Horace, learned by rote.

He knew an hundred pleasant stories,
With all the turns of Whigs and Tories:
Was cheerful to his dying day,
And friends would let him have his way.

He gave the little wealth he had
To build a house for fools and mad:
And shewed by one satiric touch
No nation wanted it so much;
That kingdom he hath left his debtor,
I wish it soon may have a better.'

391          *The Day of Judgement*

WITH a whirl of thought oppressed
I sink from reverie to rest.
An horrid vision seized my head,
I saw the graves give up their dead.
Jove, armed with terrors, burst the skies,
And thunder roars, and lightning flies!
Amazed, confused, its fate unknown,
The world stands trembling at his throne.
While each pale sinner hangs his head,
Jove, nodding, shook the Heavens, and said,
'Offending race of human kind,
By nature, reason, learning, blind;
You who through frailty stepped aside,
And you who never fell—through pride;
You who in different sects have shammed,
And come to see each other damned;
(So some folks told you, but they knew
No more of Jove's designs than you):
The world's mad business now is o'er,
And I resent these pranks no more.
I to such blockheads set my wit!
I damn such fools!—Go, go, you're bit.'

# ISAAC WATTS

## 1674–1748

392     *The Day of Judgement*

WHEN the fierce North-wind with his airy forces
Rears up the Baltic to a foaming fury;
And the red lightning with a storm of hail comes
    Rushing amain down;

How the poor sailors stand amazed and tremble,
While the hoarse thunder, like a bloody trumpet,
Roars a loud onset to the gaping waters,
    Quick to devour them.

Such shall the noise be, and the wild disorder
(If things eternal may be like these earthly),
Such the dire terror when the great Archangel
    Shakes the creation;

Tears the strong pillars of the vault of Heaven,
Breaks up old marble, the repose of princes;
See the graves open, and the bones arising,
    Flames all around them.

Hark, the shrill outcries of the guilty wretches!
Lively bright horror and amazing anguish
Stare through their eyelids, while the living worm lies
    Gnawing within them.

Thoughts, like old vultures, prey upon their heart-strings,
And the smart twinges, when their eye beholds the
Lofty Judge frowning, and a flood of vengeance
    Rolling afore him.

Hopeless immortals! how they scream and shiver,
While devils push them to the pit wide-yawning,
Hideous and gloomy, to receive them headlong
    Down to the centre!

Stop here, my fancy: (all away, ye horrid
Doleful ideas!) come, arise to Jesus,
How he sits God-like! and the saints around him
    Throned, yet adoring!

O may I sit there when he comes triumphant,
Dooming the nations! then ascend to glory,
While our Hosannas all along the passage
                  Shout the Redeemer!

393                *Sweet Muse, Descend*

SWEET Muse, descend and bless the shade,
    And bless the evening grove;
Business, and noise, and day are fled,
    And every care but love.

But hence, ye wanton young and fair,
    Mine is a purer flame;
No Phyllis shall infect the air,
    With her unhallowed name.

Jesus has all my powers possessed,
    My hopes, my fears, my joys:
He, the dear Sovereign of my breast,
    Shall still command my voice.

Some of the fairest choirs above
    Shall flock around my song,
With joy to hear the name they love
    Sound from a mortal tongue.

His charms shall make my numbers flow,
    And hold the falling floods,
While silence sits on every bough,
    And bends the listening woods.

I'll carve our passion on the bark,
    And every wounded tree
Shall drop and bear some mystic mark
    That Jesus died for me.

The swains shall wonder when they read,
    Inscribed on all the grove,
That Heaven itself came down, and bled
    To win a mortal's love.

# JOHN GAY
## 1685-1732

394            *Over the Hills and Far Away*

*Macheath.* Were I laid on Greenland's coast,
          And in my arms embraced my lass,
          Warm amidst eternal frost,
          Too soon the half-year's night would pass.
*Polly.*      Were I sold on Indian soil,
          Soon as the burning day was closed,
          I could mock the sultry toil
          When on my charmer's breast reposed.
*Macheath.* And I would love you all the day,
*Polly.*      Every night would kiss and play,
*Macheath.* If with me you'd fondly stray
*Polly.*      Over the hills and far away.


395            *Youth and Love*

    YOUTH's the season made for joys,
      Love is then our duty,
    She alone who that employs,
      Well deserves her beauty.
        Let's be gay,
        While we may,
  Beauty's a flower despised in decay.
*Chorus.* Youth's the season, etc.

    Let us drink and sport today,
      Ours is not to-morrow.
    Love with Youth flies swift away,
      Age is nought but sorrow.
        Dance and sing,
        Time's on the wing.
  Life never knows the return of spring.
*Chorus.* Let us drink, etc.

396                *Song*

O RUDDIER than the cherry,
O sweeter than the berry,
   O Nymph more bright
   Than moonshine night,
Like kidlings blithe and merry.
Ripe as the melting cluster,
No lily has such lustre,
   Yet hard to tame,
   As raging flame,
And fierce as storms that bluster.

# ALEXANDER POPE
### 1688–1744

397            *Sylvan Delights*

SEE what delights in sylvan scenes appear!
Descending Gods have found Elysium here.
In woods bright Venus with Adonis strayed,
And chaste Diana haunts the forest-shade.
Come, lovely nymph, and bless the silent hours,
When swains from shearing seek their nightly bowers;
When weary reapers quit the sultry field,
And crowned with corn, their thanks to Ceres yield,
This harmless grove no lurking viper hides,
But in my breast the serpent Love abides.
Here bees from blossoms sip the rosy dew,
But your Alexis knows no sweets but you.
Oh deign to visit our forsaken seats,
 The mossy fountains, and the green retreats!
Where'er you walk, cool gales shall fan the glade,
Trees, where you sit, shall crowd into a shade:
Where'er you tread, the blushing flowers shall rise,
And all things flourish where you turn your eyes.

398               *A Little Learning*

A LITTLE learning is a dangerous thing;
Drink deep, or taste not the Pierian spring:
There shallow draughts intoxicate the brain,
And drinking largely sobers us again.
Fired at first sight with what the Muse imparts,
In fearless youth we tempt the heights of Arts;
While from the bounded level of our mind
Short views we take, nor see the lengths behind,
But, more advanced, behold with strange surprise
New distant scenes of endless science rise!
So pleased at first the towering Alps we try,
Mount o'er the vales, and seem to tread the sky;
The eternal snows appear already past,
And the first clouds and mountains seem the last:
But those attained, we tremble to survey
The growing labours of the lengthened way;
The increasing prospect tires our wandering eyes,
Hills peep o'er hills, and Alps on Alps arise!

*from* The Rape of the Lock

(i)

399               *The Toilet*

AND now, unveiled, the Toilet stands displayed,
Each silver vase in mystic order laid.
First, robed in white, the Nymph intent adores,
With head uncovered, the Cosmetic powers.
A heavenly Image in the glass appears,
To that she bends, to that her eyes she rears;
The inferior Priestess, at her altar's side,
Trembling, begins the sacred rites of Pride.
Unnumbered treasures ope at once, and here
The various offerings of the world appear;
From each she nicely culls with curious toil,
And decks the Goddess with the glittering spoil.
This casket India's glowing gems unlocks,
And all Arabia breathes from yonder box.

The tortoise here and elephant unite,
Transformed to combs, the speckled and the white.
Here files of pins extend their shining rows,
Puffs, powders, patches, Bibles, billet-doux.
Now awful Beauty puts on all its arms;
The fair each moment rises in her charms,
Repairs her smiles, awakens every grace,
And calls forth all the wonders of her face;
Sees by degrees a purer blush arise,
And keener lightnings quicken in her eyes.
The busy sylphs surround their darling care,
These set the head, and those divide the hair,
Some fold the sleeve, whilst others plait the gown;
And Betty's praised for labours not her own.

## (ii)

### The Voyage on the Thames

NOT with more glories, in the ethereal plain,
The Sun first rises o'er the purpled main,
Than, issuing forth, the rival of his beams
Launched on the bosom of the silver Thames.
Fair nymphs and well-dressed youths around her shone,
But every eye was fixed on her alone.
On her white breast a sparkling cross she wore,
Which Jews might kiss, and Infidels adore.
Her lively looks a sprightly mind disclose,
Quick as her eyes, and as unfixed as those:
Favours to none, to all she smiles extends;
Oft she rejects, but never once offends.
Bright as the sun, her eyes the gazers strike,
And, like the sun, they shine on all alike,
Yet graceful ease, and sweetness void of pride,
Might hide her faults, if Belles had faults to hide:
If to her share some female errors fall,
Look on her face, and you'll forget 'em all.

*

But now secure the painted vessel glides,
The sun-beams trembling on the floating tides;
While melting music steals upon the sky,
And softened sounds along the waters die;

Smooth flow the waves, the Zephyrs gently play,
Belinda smiled, and all the world was gay.
All but the Sylph—with careful thoughts oppressed,
The impending woe sat heavy on his breast.
He summons straight his denizens of air;
The lucid squadrons round the sails repair:
Soft o'er the shrouds aerial whispers breathe,
That seemed but Zephyrs to the train beneath.
Some to the sun their insect-wings unfold,
Waft on the breeze, or sink in clouds of gold;
Transparent forms, too fine for mortal sight,
Their fluid bodies half dissolved in light.
Loose to the wind their airy garments flew,
Thin glittering textures of the filmy dew,
Dipped in the richest tincture of the skies,
Where light disports in ever-mingling dyes,
While every beam new transient colours flings,
Colours that change whene'er they wave their wings.

401

## *An Epistle*
### *To Miss Blount, On her Leaving the Town after the Coronation*

As some fond virgin, whom her mother's care
Drags from the town to wholesome country air,
Just when she learns to roll a melting eye,
And hear a spark, yet think no danger nigh;
From the dear man unwilling she must sever,
Yet takes one kiss before she parts forever:
Thus from the world fair Zephalinda flew,
Saw others happy, and with sighs withdrew;
Not that their pleasures caused her discontent,
She sighed not that *They* stayed, but that *She* went.
She went, to plain-work, and to purling brooks,
Old-fashioned halls, dull aunts, and croaking rooks:
She went from opera, park, assembly, play,
To morning-walks, and prayers three hours a day,
To part her time 'twixt reading and Bohea,
To muse, and spill her solitary tea,
Or o'er cold coffee trifle with the spoon;
Count the slow clock, and dine exact at noon,

Divert her eyes with pictures in the fire,
Hum half a tune, tell stories to the squire;
Up to her godly garret after seven,
There starve and pray, for that's the way to heaven.
　Some Squire, perhaps, you take delight to rack;
Whose game is Whisk, whose treat a toast in sack;
Who visits with a gun, presents you birds,
Then gives a smacking buss, and cries, 'No words!'
Or with his hound comes hallowing from the stable,
Makes love with nods, and knees beneath a table;
Whose laughs are hearty, though his jests are coarse,
And loves you best of all things—but his horse.
　In some fair evening, on your elbow laid,
You dream of triumphs in the rural shade;
In pensive thought recall the fancied scene,
See Coronations rise on every green;
Before you pass the imaginary sights
Of Lords, and Earls, and Dukes, and gartered Knights,
While the spread fan o'ershades your closing eyes;
Then give one flirt, and all the vision flies.
Thus vanish sceptres, coronets, and balls,
And leave you in lone woods, or empty walls!
　So when your slave, at some dear idle time,
(Not plagued with head-aches, or the want of rhyme)
Stands in the streets, abstracted from the crew,
And while he seems to study, thinks of you;
Just when his fancy points your sprightly eyes,
Or sees the blush of Parthenissa rise,
Gay pats my shoulder, and you vanish quite,
Streets, chairs, and coxcombs rush upon my sight;
Vexed to be still in town, I knit my brow,
Look sour, and hum a tune, as you may now.


402　*Elegy to the Memory of an Unfortunate Lady*

　WHAT beckoning ghost, along the moonlight shade
Invites my step, and points to yonder glade?
'Tis she!—But why that bleeding bosom gored,
Why dimly gleams the visionary sword?
Oh, ever beauteous, ever friendly! tell,
Is it, in Heaven, a crime to love too well?

To bear too tender, or too firm a heart,
To act a Lover's or a Roman's part?
Is there no bright reversion in the sky
For those who greatly think, or bravely die?

Why bade ye else, ye Powers, her soul aspire
Above the vulgar flight of low desire?
Ambition first sprung from your blest abodes,
The glorious fault of angels and of gods;
Thence to their images on earth it flows,
And in the breasts of kings and heroes glows.
Most souls, 'tis true, but peep out once an age,
Dull sullen prisoners in the body's cage:
Dim lights of life, that burn a length of years
Useless, unseen, as lamps in sepulchres;
Like Eastern kings a lazy state they keep,
And close confined in their own palace sleep.

From these perhaps (ere Nature bade her die)
Fate snatched her early to the pitying sky.
As into air the purer spirits flow,
And separate from their kindred dregs below;
So flew the soul to its congenial place,
Nor left one virtue to redeem her race.

But thou, false guardian of a charge too good,
Thou, mean deserter of thy brother's blood!
See on these ruby lips the trembling breath,
These cheeks, now fading at the blast of death;
Cold is that breast which warmed the world before,
And those love-darting eyes must roll no more.
Thus, if eternal justice rules the ball,
Thus shall your wives, and thus your children fall:
On all the line a sudden vengeance waits,
And frequent hearses shall besiege your gates.
These passengers shall stand, and pointing say
(While the long funerals blacken all the way)
'Lo! these were they, whose souls the Furies steeled
And cursed with hearts unknowing how to yield.'
Thus unlamented pass the proud away,
The gaze of fools, and pageant of a day!
So perish all whose breast ne'er learned to glow
For others' good, or melt at others' woe.

What can atone (Oh ever-injured shade!)
Thy fate unpitied, and thy rites unpaid?

No friend's complaint, no kind domestic tear
Pleased thy pale ghost, or graced thy mournful bier.
By foreign hands thy dying eyes were closed,
By foreign hands thy decent limbs composed,
By foreign hands thy humble grave adorned,
By strangers honoured, and by strangers mourned!
What though no friends in sable weeds appear,
Grieve for an hour, perhaps, then mourn a year,
And bear about the mockery of woe
To midnight dances, and the public show?
What though no weeping Loves thy ashes grace,
Nor polished marble emulate thy face?
What though no sacred earth allow thee room,
Nor hallowed dirge be muttered o'er thy tomb?
Yet shall thy grave with rising flowers be dressed,
And the green turf lie lightly on thy breast:
There shall the morn her earliest tears bestow,
There the first roses of the year shall blow;
While angels with their silver wings o'ershade
The ground, now sacred by thy relics made.
    So peaceful rests, without a stone, a name,
What once had beauty, titles, wealth, and fame.
How loved, how honoured once, avails thee not,
To whom related, or by whom begot;
A heap of dust alone remains of thee:
'Tis all thou art, and all the proud shall be!
    Poets themselves must fall, like those they sung;
Deaf the praised ear, and mute the tuneful tongue.
Even he, whose soul now melts in mournful lays,
Shall shortly want the generous tear he pays;
Then from his closing eyes thy form shall part,
And the last pang shall tear thee from his heart;
Life's idle business at one gasp be o'er,
The Muse forgot, and thou beloved no more!

403                *On a Certain Lady at Court*

I KNOW the thing that's most uncommon;
    (Envy, be silent, and attend!)
I know a reasonable woman,
    Handsome and witty, yet a friend.

Not warped by passion, awed by rumour,
    Not grave through pride, or gay through folly,
An equal mixture of good humour,
    And sensible soft melancholy.

'Has she no faults then' (Envy says) 'Sir?'
    Yes, she has one, I must aver;
When all the world conspires to praise her,
    The woman's deaf, and does not hear.

404                        *Know Thyself*

KNOW then thyself, presume not God to scan;
The proper study of mankind is Man.
Placed on this isthmus of a middle state,
A being darkly wise and rudely great:
With too much knowledge for the Sceptic side,
With too much weakness for the Stoic's pride,
He hangs between; in doubt to act or rest,
In doubt to deem himself a God or Beast,
In doubt his mind or body to prefer;
Born but to die, and reasoning but to err;
Alike in ignorance, his reason such
Whether he thinks too little or too much:
Chaos of thought and passion, all confused;
Still by himself abused, or disabused;
Created half to rise and half to fall;
Great lord of all things, yet a prey to all;
Sole judge of truth, in endless error hurled:
The glory, jest, and riddle of the world!

405                  *The Duke of Buckingham*

IN the worst inn's worst room, with mat half-hung,
The floors of plaster, and the walls of dung,
On once a flock-bed, but repaired with straw,
With tape-tied curtains, never meant to draw,
The George and Garter dangling from that bed
Where tawdry yellow strove with dirty red,
Great Villiers lies—alas, how changed from him,
That life of pleasure, and that soul of whim!

Gallant and gay, in Cliveden's proud alcove,
The bower of wanton Shrewsbury and love;
Or just as gay, at Council, in a ring
Of mimicked statesmen, and their merry King.
No Wit to flatter, left of all his store!
No fool to laugh at, which he valued more.
There, victor of his health, of fortune, friends,
And fame, this lord of useless thousands ends.

## Characters

### (i)

406

### Atticus

PEACE to all such! But were there one whose fires
True Genius kindles, and fair Fame inspires;
Blest with each talent and each art to please,
And born to write, converse, and live with ease;
Should such a man, too fond to rule alone,
Bear, like the Turk, no brother near the throne,
View him with scornful, yet with jealous eyes,
And hate for arts that caused himself to rise;
Damn with faint praise, assent with civil leer,
And without sneering, teach the rest to sneer;
Willing to wound, and yet afraid to strike,
Just hint a fault, and hesitate dislike;
Alike reserved to blame, or to commend,
A timorous foe, and a suspicious friend;
Dreading even fools, by flatterers besieged,
And so obliging, that he ne'er obliged;
Like Cato give his little Senate laws,
And sit attentive to his own applause;
While Wits and Templars every sentence raise,
And wonder with a foolish face of praise—
Who but must laugh, if such a man there be?
Who would not weep, if Atticus were he!

(ii)

## *Sporus*

LET Sporus tremble—'What? That thing of silk,
Sporus, that mere white curd of ass's milk?
Satire or sense, alas, can Sporus feel,
Who breaks a butterfly upon a wheel?'
   Yet let me flap this bug with gilded wings,
This painted child of dirt, that stinks and stings;
Whose buzz the witty and the fair annoys,
Yet wit ne'er tastes, and beauty ne'er enjoys:
So well-bred spaniels civilly delight
In mumbling of the game they dare not bite.
Eternal smiles his emptiness betray,
As shallow streams run dimpling all the way.
Whether in florid impotence he speaks,
And, as the prompter breathes, the puppet squeaks;
Or at the ear of Eve, familiar Toad,
Half-froth, half-venom, spits himself abroad,
In puns, or politics, or tales, or lies,
Or spite, or smut, or rhymes, or blasphemies.
His wit all see-saw, between that and this,
Now high, now low, now Master up, now Miss,
And he himself one vile antithesis.
Amphibious thing! that acting either part,
The trifling head, or the corrupted heart,
Fop at the toilet, flatterer at the board,
Now trips a lady, and now struts a lord.
Eve's tempter thus the rabbins have exprest,
A cherub's face, a reptile all the rest;
Beauty that shocks you, parts that none will trust,
Wit that can creep, and pride that licks the dust.

(iii)

## *Chloe*

'YET Chloe sure was formed without a spot'—
Nature in her then erred not, but forgot.
'With every pleasing, every prudent part,
Say, what can Chloe want?'—She wants a heart.

She speaks, behaves, and acts just as she ought;
But never, never, reached one generous thought.
Virtue she finds too painful an endeavour,
Content to dwell in decencies forever.
So very reasonable, so unmoved,
As never yet to love, or to be loved.
She, while her lover pants upon her breast,
Can mark the figures on an Indian chest;
And when she sees her friend in deep despair,
Observes how much a chintz exceeds mohair.
Forbid it Heaven, a favour or a debt
She e'er should cancel—but she may forget.
Safe is your secret still in Chloe's ear;
But none of Chloe's shall you ever hear.
Of all her Dears she never slandered one,
But cares not if a thousand are undone.
Would Chloe know if you're alive or dead?
She bids her footman put it in her head.
Chloe is prudent—would you too be wise?
Then never break your heart when Chloe dies.

409       *Apologia pro Vita Sua*

NOT Fortune's worshipper, nor Fashion's fool,
Not Lucre's madman, nor Ambition's tool,
Not proud, nor servile: be one poet's praise
That, if he pleased, he pleased by manly ways:
That flattery, even to kings, he held a shame,
And thought a lie in verse or prose the same:
That not in Fancy's maze he wandered long,
But stooped to Truth, and moralised his song:
That not for Fame, but Virtue's better end,
He stood the furious foe, the timid friend,
The damning critic, half-approving wit,
The coxcomb hit, or fearing to be hit;
Laughed at the loss of friends he never had,
The dull, the proud, the wicked, and the mad;
The distant threats of vengeance on his head,
The blow unfelt, the tear he never shed,
The tale revived, the lie so oft o'erthrown,
The imputed trash, and dullness not his own,

The morals blackened when the writings 'scape,
The libelled person, and the pictured shape;
Abuse, on all he loved, or loved him, spread,
A friend in exile, or a father dead;
The whisper, that to greatness still too near,
Perhaps yet vibrates on his Sovereign's ear—
Welcome, for thee, fair Virtue, all the past:
For thee, fair Virtue, welcome even the last!

410        *The Triumph of Vice*

VIRTUE may choose the high or low degree,
'Tis just alike to Virtue, and to me;
Dwell in a monk, or light upon a king,
She's still the same, beloved, contented thing.
Vice is undone, if she forgets her birth,
And stoops from Angels to the dregs of Earth:
But 'tis the fall degrades her to a whore;
Let Greatness own her, and she's mean no more:
Her birth, her beauty, crowds and courts confess,
Chaste matrons praise her, and grave bishops bless;
In golden chains the willing world she draws,
And hers the Gospel is, and hers the Laws,
Mounts the tribunal, lifts her scarlet head,
And sees pale Virtue carted in her stead.
Lo! at the wheels of her triumphal car,
Old England's Genius, rough with many a scar,
Dragged in the dust! His arms hang idly round,
His flag inverted trails along the ground!
Our youth, all liveried o'er with foreign gold,
Before her dance: behind her crawl the old!
See thronging millions to the pagod run,
And offer country, parent, wife, or son!
Hear her black trumpet through the land proclaim,
That 'NOT TO BE CORRUPTED IS THE SHAME'.
In soldier, churchman, patriot, man in power,
'Tis avarice all, ambition is no more!
See, all our nobles begging to be slaves!
See, all our fools aspiring to be knaves!
The wit of cheats, the courage of a whore,
Are what ten thousand envy and adore:

421

All, all look up, with reverential awe,
At crimes that 'scape, or triumph o'er the Law:
While truth, worth, wisdom, daily they decry—
'Nothing is sacred now but villainy.'
    Yet may this verse (if such a verse remain)
Show there was one who held it in disdain.

411            *The Power of Ridicule*

ASK you what provocation I have had?
The strong antipathy of Good to Bad.
When Truth or Virtue an affront endures,
The affront is mine, my friend, and should be yours.
Mine, as a foe professed to false pretence,
Who think a coxcomb's honour like his sense;
Mine, as a friend to every worthy mind;
And mine as man, who feel for all mankind.
    F. You're strangely proud.
                    P. So proud, I am no slave:
So impudent, I own myself no knave:
So odd, my country's ruin makes me grave.
Yes, I am proud; I must be proud to see
Men not afraid of God, afraid of me:
Safe from the Bar, the Pulpit, and the Throne,
Yet touched and shamed by Ridicule alone.
    O sacred weapon! left for Truth's defence,
Sole dread of Folly, Vice, and Insolence!
To all but Heaven-directed hands denied,
The Muse may give thee, but the God must guide;
Reverent I touch thee! but with honest zeal;
To rouse the watchmen of the public weal,
To Virtue's work provoke the tardy Hall,
And goad the Prelate slumbering in his stall.
Ye tinsel Insects! whom a Court maintains,
That counts your beauties only by your stains,
Spin all your cobwebs o'er the eye of day!
The Muse's wing shall brush you all away:
All his Grace preaches, all his Lordship sings,
All that makes Saints of Queens, and Gods of Kings,
All, all but Truth, drops dead-born from the press,
Like the last Gazette, or the last Address.

*The Triumph of Dullness*

In vain, in vain,—the all-composing hour
Resistless falls: the Muse obeys the Power.
She comes! She comes! The sable throne behold
Of Night primaeval, and of Chaos old!
Before her, Fancy's gilded clouds decay,
And all its varying rainbows die away.
Wit shoots in vain its momentary fires,
The meteor drops, and in a flash expires.
As one by one, at dread Medea's strain,
The sickening stars fade off the ethereal plain;
As Argus' eyes by Hermes' wand opprest,
Closed one by one to everlasting rest;
Thus at her felt approach, and secret might,
Art after Art goes out, and all is Night.
See skulking Truth to her old cavern fled,
Mountains of Casuistry heaped o'er her head!
Philosophy, that leaned on Heaven before,
Shrinks to her second cause, and is no more.
Physic of Metaphysic begs defence,
And Metaphysic calls for aid on Sense!
See Mystery to Mathematics fly!
In vain! they gaze, turn giddy, rave and die.
Religion blushing veils her sacred fires,
And unawares Morality expires.
Nor public flame, nor private, dares to shine;
Nor human spark is left, nor glimpse divine!
Lo! thy dread Empire, Chaos, is restored;
Light dies before thy uncreating word:
Thy hand, great Anarch, lets the curtain fall;
And Universal Darkness buries All.

## HENRY CAREY

### d. 1743

413        *Sally in our Alley*

OF all the girls that are so smart
   There's none like pretty Sally;
She is the darling of my heart,
   And she lives in our alley.
There is no lady in the land
   Is half so sweet as Sally;
She is the darling of my heart,
   And she lives in our alley.

Her father he makes cabbage-nets,
   And through the streets does cry 'em;
Her mother she sells laces long
   To such as please to buy 'em:
But sure such folks could ne'er beget
   So sweet a girl as Sally!
She is the darling of my heart,
   And she lives in our alley.

When she is by, I leave my work,
   I love her so sincerely;
My master comes like any Turk,
   And bangs me most severely:
But let him bang his bellyful,
   I'll bear it all for Sally;
She is the darling of my heart,
   And she lives in our alley.

Of all the days that's in the week
   I dearly love but one day—
And that's the day that comes betwixt
   A Saturday and Monday;
For then I'm drest all in my best
   To walk abroad with Sally;
She is the darling of my heart,
   And she lives in our alley.

My master carries me to church,
  And often am I blamed
Because I leave him in the lurch
  As soon as text is named;
I leave the church in sermon-time
  And slink away to Sally;
She is the darling of my heart,
  And she lives in our alley.

When Christmas comes about again,
  O, then I shall have money;
I'll hoard it up, and box and all
  I'll give it to my honey:
And would it were ten thousand pounds,
  I'd give it all to Sally,
She is the darling of my heart,
  And she lives in our alley.

My master and the neighbours all,
  Make game of me and Sally,
And, but for her, I'd better be
  A slave and row a galley;
But when my seven long years are out,
  O, then I'll marry Sally;
O, then we'll wed, and then we'll bed—
  But not in our alley!

# ANONYMOUS

414                    *The Vicar of Bray*

IN good King Charles's golden days,
  When loyalty no harm meant;
A furious High-Church man I was,
  And so I gained preferment.
Unto my flock I daily preached,
  'Kings are by God appointed,
And damned are those who dare resist,
  Or touch the Lord's Anointed.'

And this is Law, I will maintain
Unto my dying day, Sir,
That whatsoever King shall reign,
I will be Vicar of Bray, Sir!

When royal James possessed the Crown,
And Popery grew in fashion,
The Penal Law I hooted down,
And read the Declaration:
The Church of Rome I found would fit
Full well my constitution,
And I had been a Jesuit
But for the Revolution.
And this is Law, etc.

When William our Deliverer came
To heal the Nation's grievance,
I turned the cat in pan again,
And swore to him allegiance:
Old principles I did revoke,
Set Conscience at a distance,
Passive Obedience is a joke,
A jest is Non-Resistance.
And this is Law, etc.

When glorious Anne became our Queen,
The Church of England's glory,
Another face of things was seen,
And I became a Tory:
Occasional Conformists base
I damned, and Moderation,
And thought the Church in danger was
From such prevarication.
And this is Law, etc.

When George in pudding time came o'er,
And moderate men looked big, Sir,
My principles I changed once more,
And so became a Whig, Sir:
And thus preferment I procured
From our Faith's Great Defender,
And almost every day abjured
The Pope and the Pretender.
And this is Law, etc.

The illustrious House of Hanover,
  And Protestant Succession,
To these I lustily will swear,
  Whilst they can keep possession:
For in my Faith and Loyalty
  I never once will falter,
But George my lawful King shall be,
  Except the times should alter.
    And this is Law, etc.


# JOHN BYROM

## 1692–1763

415      *My Spirit Longeth for Thee*

MY spirit longeth for thee
  Within my troubled breast,
Although I be unworthy
  Of so divine a guest.

Of so divine a guest
  Unworthy though I be,
Yet has my heart no rest
  Unless it come from thee.

Unless it come from thee,
  In vain I look around;
In all that I can see,
  No rest is to be found.

No rest is to be found
  But in thy blessed Love;
O! let my wish be crowned,
  And send it from above!

# JAMES THOMSON
## 1700–1748

416 *A Winter Night*

WITH the fierce rage of winter deep suffused,
An icy gale, oft shifting, o'er the pool
Breathes a blue film, and in its mid-career
Arrests the bickering stream. The loosened ice,
Let down the flood, and half dissolved by day,
Rustles no more; but to the sedgy bank
Fast grows, or gathers round the pointed stone,
A crystal pavement, by the breath of Heaven
Cemented firm; till, seized from shore to shore,
The whole imprisoned river growls below.
Loud rings the frozen earth, and hard reflects
A double noise; while at his evening watch
The village dog deters the nightly thief;
The heifer lows; the distant water-fall
Swells in the breeze; and, with the hasty tread
Of traveller, the hollow-sounding plain
Shakes from afar. The full ethereal round,
Infinite worlds disclosing to the view,
Shines out intensely keen; and, all one cope
Of starry glitter, glows from Pole to Pole.
From Pole to Pole the rigid influence falls
Through the still night, incessant, heavy, strong,
And seizes Nature fast. It freezes on;
Till morn, late-rising o'er the drooping world,
Lifts her pale eye unjoyous.

417 *Spring Flowers*

ALONG the blushing borders bright with dew,
And in yon mingled wilderness of flowers,
Fair-handed Spring unbosoms every grace:
Throws out the snow-drop and the crocus first;
The daisy, primrose, violet darkly blue,

And polyanthus of unnumbered dyes;
The yellow wall-flower, stained with iron brown,
And lavish stock that scents the garden round:
From the soft wing of vernal breezes shed,
Anemonies; auriculas, enriched
With shining meal o'er all their velvet leaves;
And full ranunculas, of glowing red.
Then comes the tulip-race, where Beauty plays
Her idle freaks: from family diffused
To family, as flies the father-dust,
The varied colours run; and while they break
On the charmed eye, the exulting florist marks,
With secret pride, the wonders of his hand.
No gradual bloom is wanting; from the bud,
First-born of Spring, to Summer's musky tribes:
Nor hyacinths, deep-purpled; nor jonquils,
Of potent fragrance; nor narcissus fair,
As o'er the fabled fountain hanging still;
Nor broad carnations, nor gay-spotted pinks;
Nor, showered from every bush, the damask-rose:
Infinite numbers, delicacies, smells,
With hues on hues expression cannot paint,
The breath of Nature, and her endless bloom.

418                 *The Autumnal Moon*

THE western sun withdraws the shortened day,
And humid evening, gliding o'er the sky
In her chill progress, to the ground condensed
The vapours throws. Where creeping waters ooze,
Where marshes stagnate, and where rivers wind,
Cluster the rolling fogs, and swim along
The dusky-mantled lawn. Meanwhile the moon
Full-orbed, and breaking through the scattered clouds,
Shews her broad visage in the crimsoned east.
Turned to the sun direct, her spotted disc,
(Where mountains rise, umbrageous dales descend,
And oceans roll, as optic tube descries)
A smaller earth, gives all its blaze again,
Void of its flame, and sheds a softer day.
Now through the passing cloud she seems to stoop,

Now up the pure cerulean rides sublime.
Wide the pale deluge floats, and streaming mild
O'er the skied mountain to the shadowy vale,
While rocks and floods reflect the quivering gleam,
The whole air whitens with a boundless tide
Of silver radiance, trembling round the world.

# CHARLES WESLEY

## 1707–1788

419        *Wrestling Jacob*

COME, O thou Traveller unknown,
   Whom still I hold, but cannot see,
My company before is gone,
   And I am left alone with thee,
With thee all night I mean to stay,
And wrestle till the break of day.

I need not tell thee who I am,
   My misery, or sin declare,
Thyself hast called me by my name,
   Look on thy hands, and read it there,
But who, I ask thee, who art thou?
Tell me thy name, and tell me now.

In vain thou strugglest to get free,
   I never will unloose my hold:
Art thou the Man that died for me?
   The secret of thy love unfold.
Wrestling I will not let thee go,
Till I thy name, thy nature know.

Wilt thou not yet to me reveal
   Thy new, unutterable name?
Tell me, I still beseech thee, tell;
   To know it now resolved I am.
Wrestling I will not let thee go,
Till I thy name, thy nature know.

'Tis all in vain to hold thy tongue,
   Or touch the hollow of my thigh:
Though every sinew be unstrung,
   Out of my arms thou shalt not fly.
Wrestling I will not let thee go,
Till I thy name, thy nature know.

What though my shrinking flesh complain,
   And murmur to contend so long,
I rise superior to my pain,
   When I am weak then I am strong,
And when my all of strength shall fail,
I shall with the God-Man prevail.

My strength is gone, my nature dies,
   I sink beneath thy weighty hand,
Faint to revive, and fall to rise;
   I fall, and yet by faith I stand,
I stand, and will not let thee go,
Till I thy name, thy nature know.

Yield to me now—for I am weak;
   But confident in self-despair:
Speak to my heart, in blessings speak,
   Be conquered by my instant prayer,
Speak, or thou never hence shalt move,
And tell me, if thy name is Love.

'Tis Love, 'tis Love! Thou died'st for me,
   I hear thy whisper in my heart.
The morning breaks, the shadows flee:
   Pure Universal Love thou art;
To me, to all, thy bowels move,
Thy nature and thy name is Love.

My prayer hath power with God; the Grace
   Unspeakable I now receive,
Through Faith I see thee face to face,
   I see thee face to face, and live:
In vain I have not wept, and strove,
Thy nature and thy name is Love.

I know thee, Saviour, who thou art,
   Jesus, the feeble sinner's friend;
Nor wilt thou with the night depart,
   But stay, and love me to the end;
Thy mercies never shall remove,
Thy nature and thy name is Love.

The Sun of Righteousness on me
   Hath rose with healing in his wings,
Withered my nature's strength; from thee
   My soul its life and succour brings,
My help is all laid up above;
Thy nature and thy name is Love.

Contented now upon my thigh
   I halt, till life's short journey end;
All helplessness, all weakness I,
   On thee alone for strength depend,
Nor have I power, from thee, to move;
Thy nature and thy name is Love.

Lame as I am, I take the prey,
   Hell, earth, and sin with ease o'ercome;
I leap for joy, pursue my way,
   And as a bounding hart fly home,
Through all eternity to prove
Thy nature and thy name is Love.


# SAMUEL JOHNSON

## 1709–1784

420        *The Scholar's Life*

WHEN first the college rolls receive his name,
The young enthusiast quits his ease for fame;
Through all his veins the fever of renown
Burns from the strong contagion of the gown;
O'er Bodley's dome his future labours spread,
And Bacon's mansion trembles o'er his head.

Are these thy views? Proceed, illustrious youth,
And Virtue guard thee to the throne of Truth!
Yet should thy soul indulge the generous heat,
Till captive Science yields her last retreat;
Should Reason guide thee with her brightest ray,
And pour on misty Doubt resistless day;
Should no false Kindness lure to loose delight,
Nor Praise relax, nor Difficulty fright;
Should tempting Novelty thy cell refrain,
And Sloth effuse her opiate fumes in vain;
Should Beauty blunt on fops her fatal dart,
Nor claim the triumph of a lettered heart;
Should no Disease thy torpid veins invade,
Nor Melancholy's phantoms haunt thy shade;
Yet hope not life from grief or danger free,
Nor think the doom of man reversed for thee:
Deign on the passing world to turn thine eyes,
And pause awhile from letters, to be wise;
There mark what ills the scholar's life assail,
Toil, envy, want, the patron, and the jail.
See nations slowly wise, and meanly just,
To buried merit raise the tardy bust.
If dreams yet flatter, once again attend,
Hear Lydiat's life, and Galileo's end.

421        *Charles XII of Sweden*

ON what foundation stands the warrior's pride,
How just his hopes let Swedish Charles decide;
A frame of adamant, a soul of fire,
No dangers fright him, and no labours tire;
O'er love, o'er fear, extends his wide domain,
Unconquered lord of pleasure and of pain;
No joys to him pacific sceptres yield,
War sounds the trump, he rushes to the field;
Behold surrounding kings their power combine,
And one capitulate, and one resign;
Peace courts his hand, but spreads her charms in vain;
'Think nothing gained,' he cries, 'till nought remain,
On Moscow's walls till Gothic standards fly,
And all be mine beneath the polar sky.'

The march begins in military state,
And nations on his eye suspended wait;
Stern Famine guards the solitary coast,
And Winter barricades the realms of Frost;
He comes, not want and cold his course delay;—
Hide, blushing Glory, hide Pultowa's day:
The vanquished hero leaves his broken bands,
And shows his miseries in distant lands;
Condemned a needy supplicant to wait,
While ladies interpose, and slaves debate.
But did not Chance at length her error mend?
Did no subverted empire mark his end?
Did rival monarchs give the fatal wound?
Or hostile millions press him to the ground?
His fall was destined to a barren strand,
A petty fortress, and a dubious hand;
He left the name, at which the world grew pale,
To point a moral, or adorn a tale.

422 *The Power of Prayer*

WHERE then shall Hope and Fear their objects find?
Must dull Suspence corrupt the stagnant mind?
Must helpless man, in ignorance sedate,
Roll darkling down the torrent of his fate?
Must no dislike alarm, no wishes rise,
No cries attempt the mercies of the skies?
Enquirer, cease, petitions yet remain,
Which heaven may hear, nor deem religion vain.
Still raise for good the supplicating voice,
But leave to heaven the measure and the choice,
Safe in his power, whose eyes discern afar
The secret ambush of a specious prayer.
Implore his aid, in his decisions rest,
Secure whate'er he gives, he gives the best.
Yet when the sense of sacred presence fires,
And strong devotion to the skies aspires,
Pour forth thy fervours for a healthful mind,
Obedient passions, and a will resigned;
For love, which scarce collective man can fill;
For patience, sovereign o'er transmuted ill;

SAMUEL JOHNSON

For faith, that panting for a happier seat,
Counts death kind Nature's signal of retreat:
These goods for man the laws of heaven ordain,
These goods he grants, who grants the power to gain;
With these celestial wisdom calms the mind,
And makes the happiness she does not find.

423    *A Short Song of Congratulation*

LONG-EXPECTED one-and-twenty,
Lingering year at last is flown:
Pomp and pleasure, pride and plenty,
Great Sir John, are all your own.

Loosened from the minor's tether,
Free to mortgage or to sell,
Wild as wind, and light as feather,
Bid the slaves of thrift farewell.

Call the Betties, Kates, and Jennies,
Every name that laughs at care;
Lavish of your grandsire's guineas,
Show the spirit of an heir.

All that prey on vice and folly
Joy to see their quarry fly;
Here the gamester light and jolly,
There the lender grave and sly.

Wealth, Sir John, was made to wander,
Let it wander as it will;
See the jockey, see the pander,
Bid them come and take their fill.

When the bonny blade carouses,
Pockets full, and spirits high,
What are acres? What are houses?
Only dirt, or wet or dry.

If the guardian or the mother
Tell the woes of wilful waste,
Scorn their counsel, scorn their pother:
You can hang or drown at last!

435

424    *On the Death of Mr. Robert Levet*
       *A Practiser in Physic*

CONDEMNED to Hope's delusive mine,
  As on we toil from day to day,
By sudden blasts or slow decline
  Our social comforts drop away.

Well tried through many a varying year,
  See Levet to the grave descend;
Officious, innocent, sincere,
  Of every friendless name the friend.

Yet still he fills affection's eye,
  Obscurely wise and coarsely kind;
Nor, lettered Arrogance, deny
  Thy praise to merit unrefined.

When fainting nature called for aid,
  And hovering death prepared the blow,
His vigorous remedy displayed
  The power of art without the show.

In Misery's darkest cavern known,
  His useful care was ever nigh,
Where hopeless Anguish poured his groan,
  And lonely Want retired to die.

No summons mocked by chill delay,
  No petty gain disdained by pride;
The modest wants of every day
  The toil of every day supplied.

His virtues walked their narrow round,
  Nor made a pause, nor left a void;
And sure the Eternal Master found
  The single talent well employed.

The busy day, the peaceful night,
  Unfelt, uncounted, glided by;
His frame was firm—his powers were bright,
  Though now his eightieth year was nigh.

Then with no fiery throbbing pain,
　　No cold gradations of decay,
Death broke at once the vital chain,
　　And freed his soul the nearest way.


# WILLIAM SHENSTONE

## 1714–1763

425　　　　*Written at an Inn at Henley*

To thee, fair freedom! I retire
　　From flattery, cards, and dice, and din:
Nor art thou found in mansions higher
　　Than the low cot, or humble inn.

'Tis here with boundless power I reign;
　　And every health which I begin
Converts dull port to bright champagne,
　　Such freedom crowns it, at an inn.

I fly from pomp, I fly from plate!
　　I fly from falsehood's specious grin!
Freedom I love, and form I hate,
　　And choose my lodgings at an inn.

Here, waiter! take my sordid ore,
　　Which lackeys else might hope to win;
It buys what courts have not in store,
　　It buys me freedom, at an inn.

And now once more I shape my way
　　Through rain or shine, through thick or thin,
Secure to meet, at close of day,
　　With kind reception, at an inn.

Whoe'er has travelled life's dull round,
　　Where'er his stages may have been,
May sigh to think he still has found
　　The warmest welcome at an inn.

# THOMAS GRAY
## 1716–1771

426     *Ode on a Distant Prospect of Eton College*

YE distant spires, ye antique towers,
That crown the watery glade,
Where grateful Science still adores
Her Henry's holy shade;
And ye that from the stately brow
Of Windsor's heights the expanse below
Of grove, of lawn, of mead survey,
Whose turf, whose shade, whose flowers among
Wanders the hoary Thames along
His silver-winding way.

Ah, happy hills, ah, pleasing shade,
Ah, fields beloved in vain,
Where once my careless childhood strayed,
A stranger yet to pain!
I feel the gales, that from ye blow,
A momentary bliss bestow,
As waving fresh their gladsome wing,
My weary soul they seem to soothe,
And, redolent of joy and youth,
To breathe a second spring.

Say, Father Thames, for thou hast seen
Full many a sprightly race
Disporting on thy margent green
The paths of pleasure trace,
Who foremost now delight to cleave
With pliant arm thy glassy wave?
The captive linnet which enthrall?
What idle progeny succeed
To chase the rolling circle's speed,
Or urge the flying ball?

While some on earnest business bent
Their murmuring labours ply
'Gainst graver hours, that bring constraint
To sweeten liberty:
Some bold adventurers disdain
The limits of their little reign,
And unknown regions dare descry:
Still as they run they look behind,
They hear a voice in every wind,
And snatch a fearful joy.

Gay hope is theirs by fancy fed,
Less pleasing when possessed;
The tear forgot as soon as shed,
The sunshine of the breast:
Theirs buxom health of rosy hue,
Wild wit, invention ever-new,
And lively cheer of vigour born;
The thoughtless day, the easy night,
The spirits pure, the slumbers light,
That fly the approach of morn.

Alas, regardless of their doom,
The little victims play!
No sense have they of ills to come,
Nor care beyond today:
Yet see how all around 'em wait
The ministers of human fate,
And black Misfortune's baleful train!
Ah, show them where in ambush stand
To seize their prey the murtherous band!
Ah, tell them, they are men!

These shall the fury Passions tear,
The vultures of the mind,
Disdainful Anger, pallid Fear,
And Shame that skulks behind;
Or pining Love shall waste their youth,
Or Jealousy with rankling tooth,
That inly gnaws the secret heart,
And Envy wan, and faded Care,
Grim-visaged comfortless Despair,
And Sorrow's piercing dart.

Ambition this shall tempt to rise,
Then whirl the wretch from high,
To bitter Scorn a sacrifice,
And grinning Infamy.
The stings of Falsehood those shall try,
And hard Unkindness' altered eye,
That mocks the tear it forced to flow;
And keen Remorse with blood defiled,
And moody Madness laughing wild
Amid severest woe.

Lo, in the vale of years beneath
A grisly troop are seen,
The painful family of Death,
More hideous than their Queen:
This racks the joints, this fires the veins,
That every labouring sinew strains,
Those in the deeper vitals rage:
Lo, Poverty, to fill the band,
That numbs the soul with icy hand,
And slow-consuming Age.

To each his sufferings: all are men,
Condemned alike to groan;
The tender for another's pain,
The unfeeling for his own.
Yet ah! why should they know their fate?
Since sorrow never comes too late,
And happiness too swiftly flies.
Thought would destroy their paradise.
No more; where ignorance is bliss,
'Tis folly to be wise.

427        *On the Death of Richard West*

IN vain to me the smiling mornings shine,
    And reddening Phoebus lifts his golden fire:
The birds in vain their amorous descant join,
    Or cheerful fields resume their green attire:

These ears, alas! for other notes repine,
  A different object do these eyes require.
My lonely anguish melts no heart but mine;
  And in my breast the imperfect joys expire.
Yet morning smiles the busy race to cheer,
  And new-born pleasure brings to happier men;
The fields to all their wonted tribute bear;
  To warm their little loves the birds complain.
I fruitless mourn to him that cannot hear,
  And weep the more because I weep in vain.


428        *Ode on the Death of a Favourite Cat*
           *Drowned in a Tub of Gold Fishes*

          'TWAS on a lofty vase's side,
          Where China's gayest art had dyed
            The azure flowers, that blow;
          Demurest of the tabby kind,
          The pensive Selima reclined,
            Gazed on the lake below.

          Her conscious tail her joy declared;
          The fair round face, the snowy beard,
            The velvet of her paws,
          Her coat that with the tortoise vies,
          Her ears of jet and emerald eyes,
            She saw; and purred applause.

          Still had she gazed; but 'midst the tide
          Two angel forms were seen to glide,
            The Genii of the stream:
          Their scaly armour's Tyrian hue
          Through richest purple to the view
            Betrayed a golden gleam.

          The hapless nymph with wonder saw:
          A whisker first and then a claw,
            With many an ardent wish,
          She stretched in vain to reach the prize.
          What female heart can gold despise?
            What cat's averse to fish?

Presumptuous maid! with looks intent
Again she stretched, again she bent,
   Nor knew the gulf between.
(Malignant Fate sat by and smiled)
The slippery verge her feet beguiled,
   She tumbled headlong in.

Eight times emerging from the flood
She mewed to every watery god,
   Some speedy aid to send.
No dolphin came, no Nereid stirred:
Nor cruel Tom nor Susan heard.
   A favourite has no friend!

From hence, ye beauties, undeceived,
Know, one false step is ne'er retrieved,
   And be with caution bold.
Not all that tempts your wandering eyes
And heedless hearts is lawful prize;
   Nor all that glisters gold.

429
## *Elegy*
### *Written in a Country Churchyard*

THE curfew tolls the knell of parting day,
The lowing herd wind slowly o'er the lea,
The ploughman homeward plods his weary way,
And leaves the world to darkness and to me.

Now fades the glimmering landscape on the sight,
And all the air a solemn stillness holds,
Save where the beetle wheels his droning flight,
And drowsy tinklings lull the distant folds;

Save that from yonder ivy-mantled tower
The moping owl does to the moon complain
Of such as, wandering near her secret bower,
Molest her ancient solitary reign.

Beneath those rugged elms, that yew-tree's shade,
Where heaves the turf in many a mouldering heap,
Each in his narrow cell for ever laid,
The rude forefathers of the hamlet sleep.

The breezy call of incense-breathing morn,
The swallow twittering from the straw-built shed,
The cock's shrill clarion or the echoing horn,
No more shall rouse them from their lowly bed.

For them no more the blazing hearth shall burn,
Or busy housewife ply her evening care:
No children run to lisp their sire's return,
Or climb his knees the envied kiss to share.

Oft did the harvest to their sickle yield,
Their furrow oft the stubborn glebe has broke;
How jocund did they drive their team afield!
How bowed the woods beneath their sturdy stroke!

Let not Ambition mock their useful toil,
Their homely joys and destiny obscure;
Nor Grandeur hear, with a disdainful smile,
The short and simple annals of the poor.

The boast of heraldry, the pomp of power,
And all that beauty, all that wealth e'er gave,
Awaits alike the inevitable hour.
The paths of glory lead but to the grave.

Nor you, ye Proud, impute to these the fault,
If Memory o'er their tomb no trophies raise,
Where through the long-drawn aisle and fretted vault
The pealing anthem swells the note of praise.

Can storied urn or animated bust
Back to its mansion call the fleeting breath?
Can Honour's voice provoke the silent dust,
Or Flattery soothe the dull cold ear of Death?

Perhaps in this neglected spot is laid
Some heart once pregnant with celestial fire;
Hands that the rod of empire might have swayed,
Or waked to ecstasy the living lyre.

But Knowledge to their eyes her ample page
Rich with the spoils of time did ne'er unroll;
Chill Penury repressed their noble rage,
And froze the genial current of the soul.

Full many a gem of purest ray serene
The dark unfathomed caves of ocean bear:
Full many a flower is born to blush unseen,
And waste its sweetness on the desert air.

Some village-Hampden that with dauntless breast
The little tyrant of his fields withstood;
Some mute inglorious Milton here may rest,
Some Cromwell guiltless of his country's blood.

The applause of listening senates to command,
The threats of pain and ruin to despise,
To scatter plenty o'er a smiling land,
And read their history in a nation's eyes,

Their lot forbade: nor circumscribed alone
Their growing virtues, but their crimes confined;
Forbade to wade through slaughter to a throne,
And shut the gates of mercy on mankind,

The struggling pangs of conscious truth to hide,
To quench the blushes of ingenuous shame,
Or heap the shrine of Luxury and Pride
With incense kindled at the Muse's flame.

Far from the madding crowd's ignoble strife
Their sober wishes never learned to stray;
Along the cool sequestered vale of life
They kept the noiseless tenor of their way.

Yet even these bones from insult to protect
Some frail memorial still erected nigh,
With uncouth rhymes and shapeless sculpture decked,
Implores the passing tribute of a sigh.

Their name, their years, spelt by the unlettered muse,
The place of fame and elegy supply:
And many a holy text around she strews,
That teach the rustic moralist to die.

For who to dumb Forgetfulness a prey,
This pleasing anxious being e'er resigned,
Left the warm precincts of the cheerful day,
Nor cast one longing lingering look behind?

On some fond breast the parting soul relies,
Some pious drops the closing eye requires;
Even from the tomb the voice of Nature cries,
Even in our ashes live their wonted fires.

For thee who, mindful of the unhonoured dead,
Dost in these lines their artless tale relate;
If chance, by lonely Contemplation led,
Some kindred spirit shall inquire thy fate,

Haply some hoary-headed swain may say,
'Oft have we seen him at the peep of dawn
Brushing with hasty steps the dews away
To meet the sun upon the upland lawn.

'There at the foot of yonder nodding beech
That wreathes its old fantastic roots so high,
His listless length at noontide would he stretch,
And pore upon the brook that babbles by.

'Hard by yon wood, now smiling as in scorn,
Muttering his wayward fancies he would rove,
Now drooping, woeful wan, like one forlorn,
Or crazed with care, or crossed in hopeless love.

'One morn I missed him on the customed hill,
Along the heath and near his favourite tree;
Another came; nor yet beside the rill,
Nor up the lawn, nor at the wood was he;

'The next with dirges due in sad array
Slow through the church-way path we saw him borne.
Approach and read (for thou canst read) the lay,
Graved on the stone beneath yon aged thorn.'

### The Epitaph

*Here rests his head upon the lap of earth*
*A youth to Fortune and to Fame unknown.*
*Fair Science frowned not on his humble birth,*
*And Melancholy marked him for her own.*

*Large was his bounty and his soul sincere,*
*Heaven did a recompense as largely send:*
*He gave to Misery all he had, a tear,*
*He gained from Heaven ('twas all he wished) a friend.*

*No farther seek his merits to disclose,*
*Or draw his frailties from their dread abode,*
*(There they alike in trembling hope repose)*
*The bosom of his Father and his God.*

430

## The Bard

### I. 1

'RUIN seize thee, ruthless king!
Confusion on thy banners wait,
Though fanned by Conquest's crimson wing
They mock the air with idle state.
Helm nor hauberk's twisted mail,
Nor even thy virtues, tyrant, shall avail
To save thy secret soul from nightly fears,
From Cambria's curse, from Cambria's tears!'
Such were the sounds, that o'er the crested pride
Of the first Edward scattered wild dismay,
As down the steep of Snowdon's shaggy side
He wound with toilsome march his long array.
Stout Gloucester stood aghast in speechless trance:
'To arms!' cried Mortimer, and couched his quivering lance.

### I. 2

On a rock, whose haughty brow
Frowns o'er old Conway's foaming flood,
Robed in the sable garb of woe,
With haggard eyes the Poet stood;
(Loose his beard and hoary hair
Streamed, like a meteor, to the troubled air)
And, with a master's hand and prophet's fire,
Struck the deep sorrows of his lyre.
'Hark, how each giant-oak and desert cave
Sighs to the torrent's awful voice beneath!
O'er thee, oh King! their hundred arms they wave
Revenge on thee in hoarser murmurs breathe;
Vocal no more, since Cambria's fatal day,
To high-born Hoel's harp or soft Llewellyn's lay.

## I. 3

'Cold is Cadwallo's tongue,
That hushed the stormy main:
Brave Urien sleeps upon his craggy bed:
Mountains, ye mourn in vain
Modred, whose magic song
Made huge Plinlimmon bow his cloud-topped head.
On dreary Arvon's shore they lie,
Smeared with gore and ghastly pale:
Far, far aloof the affrighted ravens sail;
The famished eagle screams and passes by.
Dear lost companions of my tuneful art,
Dear as the light that visits these sad eyes,
Dear as the ruddy drops that warm my heart,
Ye died amidst your dying country's cries—
No more I weep. They do not sleep.
On yonder cliffs, a grisly band,
I see them sit, they linger yet,
Avengers of their native land;
With me in dreadful harmony they join,
And weave with bloody hands the tissue of thy line.

## II. 1

' "Weave the warp and weave the woof,
The winding-sheet of Edward's race.
Give ample room and verge enough
The characters of hell to trace.
Mark the year and mark the night,
When Severn shall re-echo with affright
The shrieks of death, through Berkeley's roofs that ring,
Shrieks of an agonizing King!
She-wolf of France, with unrelenting fangs,
That tear'st the bowels of thy mangled mate,
From thee be born who o'er thy country hangs
The scourge of Heaven. What terrors round him wait!
Amazement in his van, with Flight combined,
And Sorrow's faded form, and Solitude behind.

## II. 2

' "Mighty Victor, mighty Lord,
Low on his funeral couch he lies!
No pitying heart, no eye, afford
A tear to grace his obsequies.
Is the sable warrior fled?
Thy son is gone. He rests among the dead.
The swarm that in thy noon-tide beam were born?
Gone to salute the rising morn.
Fair laughs the morn and soft the zephyr blows,
While proudly riding o'er the azure realm
In gallant trim the gilded vessel goes;
Youth on the prow and Pleasure at the helm;
Regardless of the sweeping whirlwind's sway,
That, hushed in grim repose, expects his evening-prey.

## II. 3

' "Fill high the sparkling bowl,
The rich repast prepare,
Reft of a crown, he yet may share the feast:
Close by the regal chair
Fell Thirst and Famine scowl
A baleful smile upon their baffled guest.
Heard ye the din of battle bray,
Lance to lance and horse to horse?
Long years of havoc urge their destined course,
And through the kindred squadrons mow their way.
Ye Towers of Julius, London's lasting shame,
With many a foul and midnight murther fed,
Revere his consort's faith, his father's fame,
And spare the meek usurper's holy head.
Above, below, the rose of snow,
Twined with her blushing foe, we spread:
The bristled Boar in infant-gore
Wallows beneath the thorny shade.
Now, brothers, bending o'er the accursed loom,
Stamp we our vengeance deep and ratify his doom.

### III. 1

' "Edward, lo! to sudden fate
(Weave we the woof. The thread is spun.)
Half of thy heart we consecrate.
(The web is wove. The work is done.)"
Stay, oh stay! nor thus forlorn
Leave me unblessed, unpitied, here to mourn:
In yon bright track, that fires the western skies,
They melt, they vanish from my eyes.
But oh! what solemn scenes on Snowdon's height
Descending slow their glittering skirts unroll?
Visions of glory, spare my aching sight,
Ye unborn ages, crowd not on my soul!
No more our long-lost Arthur we bewail.
All-hail, ye genuine kings, Britannia's issue, hail!

### III. 2

'Girt with many a baron bold
Sublime their starry fronts they rear;
And gorgeous dames, and statesmen old
In bearded majesty, appear.
In the midst a form divine!
Her eye proclaims her of the Briton-line;
Her lion-port, her awe-commanding face,
Attempered sweet to virgin-grace.
What strings symphonious tremble in the air,
What strains of vocal transport round her play!
Hear from the grave, great Taliessin, hear;
They breathe a soul to animate thy clay.
Bright Rapture calls and, soaring as she sings,
Waves in the eye of heaven her many-coloured wings.

### III. 3

'The verse adorn again
Fierce war and faithful love,
And truth severe, by fairy fiction dressed.
In buskined measures move
Pale Grief and pleasing Pain,
With Horror, tyrant of the throbbing breast.

A voice as of the cherub-choir
Gales from blooming Eden bear;
And distant warblings lessen on my ear,
That lost in long futurity expire.
Fond impious man, think'st thou yon sanguine cloud,
Raised by thy breath, has quenched the orb of day?
Tomorrow he repairs the golden flood,
And warms the nations with redoubled ray.
Enough for me: with joy I see
The different doom our fates assign.
Be thine despair and sceptred care;
To triumph, and to die, are mine.'
He spoke, and headlong from the mountain's height
Deep in the roaring tide he plunged to endless night.

# WILLIAM COLLINS

## 1721–1759

431        *Ode to Simplicity*

O THOU by Nature taught
To breathe her genuine thought,
In numbers warmly pure and sweetly strong:
    Who first on mountains wild
    In Fancy, loveliest child,
Thy babe or Pleasure's, nursed the powers of song!

    Thou, who with hermit heart
    Disdain'st the wealth of art,
And gauds and pageant weeds and trailing pall:
    But com'st a decent maid
    In Attic robe arrayed,
O chaste unboastful nymph, to thee I call!

    By all the honeyed store
    On Hybla's thymy shore,
By all her blooms and mingled murmurs dear;
    By her, whose love-lorn woe
    In evening musings slow
Soothed sweetly sad Electra's poet's ear:

By old Cephisus deep,
  Who spread his wavy sweep
In warbled wanderings round thy green retreat,
  On whose enamelled side
  When holy Freedom died
No equal haunt allured thy future feet.

  O sister meek of Truth,
  To my admiring youth
Thy sober aid and native charms infuse!
  The flowers that sweetest breathe,
  Though Beauty culled the wreath,
Still ask thy hand to range their ordered hues.

  While Rome could none esteem
  But Virtue's patriot theme,
You loved her hills and led her laureate band:
  But stayed to sing alone
  To one distinguished throne,
And turned thy face, and fled her altered land.

  No more, in hall or bower,
  The passions own thy power,
Love, only Love, her forceless numbers mean:
  For thou hast left her shrine,
  Nor olive more nor vine
Shall gain thy feet to bless the servile scene.

  Though taste, though genius bless
  To some divine excess,
Faints the cold work till thou inspire the whole;
  What each, what all supply
  May court, may charm our eye,
Thou, only thou canst raise the meeting soul!

  Of these let others ask
  To aid some mighty task:
I only seek to find thy temperate vale,
  Where oft my reed might sound
  To maids and shepherds round,
And all thy sons, O Nature, learn my tale.

432 *How Sleep the Brave*

How sleep the brave, who sink to rest
By all their country's wishes blest!
When Spring, with dewy fingers cold,
Returns to deck their hallowed mould,
She there shall dress a sweeter sod
Than Fancy's feet have ever trod.

By fairy hands their knell is rung,
By forms unseen their dirge is sung;
There Honour comes, a pilgrim grey,
To bless the turf that wraps their clay,
And Freedom shall awhile repair
To dwell a weeping hermit there!

433 *Ode to Evening*

If aught of oaten stop or pastoral song
May hope, chaste Eve, to soothe thy modest ear,
        Like thy own solemn springs,
        Thy springs and dying gales,
O nymph reserved, while now the bright-haired sun
Sits in yon western tent, whose cloudy skirts,
        With brede ethereal wove,
        O'erhang his wavy bed;
Now air is hushed, save where the weak-eyed bat
With short shrill shriek flits by on leathern wing,
        Or where the beetle winds
        His small but sullen horn,
As oft he rises midst the twilight path,
Against the pilgrim borne in heedless hum:
        Now teach me, maid composed,
        To breathe some softened strain,
Whose numbers stealing through thy darkening vale
May not unseemly with its stillness suit;
        As musing slow, I hail
        Thy genial loved return!

For when thy folding star arising shows
His paly circlet, at his warning lamp
  The fragrant Hours, and elves
  Who slept in flowers the day,
And many a nymph who wreathes her brows with sedge,
And sheds the freshening dew, and, lovelier still,
  The Pensive Pleasures sweet,
  Prepare thy shadowy car.
Then lead, calm votaress, where some sheety lake
Cheers the lone heath, or some time-hallowed pile,
  Or upland fallows grey,
  Reflect its last cool gleam.
But when chill blustering winds or driving rain
Forbid my willing feet, be mine the hut
  That from the mountain's side
  Views wilds and swelling floods,
And hamlets brown, and dim-discovered spires,
And hears their simple bell, and marks o'er all
  Thy dewy fingers draw
  The gradual dusky veil.
While Spring shall pour his showers, as oft he wont,
And bathe thy breathing tresses, meekest Eve!
  While Summer loves to sport
  Beneath thy lingering light;
While sallow Autumn fills thy lap with leaves,
Or Winter, yelling through the troublous air,
  Affrights thy shrinking train,
  And rudely rends thy robes;
So long, sure-found beneath the sylvan shed,
Shall Fancy, Friendship, Science, rose-lipped Health,
  Thy gentlest influence own,
  And hymn thy favourite name!

434      *Dirge in Cymbeline*

  To fair Fidele's grassy tomb
   Soft maids and village hinds shall bring
  Each opening sweet of earliest bloom,
   And rifle all the breathing spring.

No wailing ghost shall dare appear
　　To vex with shrieks this quiet grove;
But shepherd lads assemble here,
　　And melting virgins own their love.

No withered witch shall here be seen,
　　No goblins lead their nightly crew;
The female fays shall haunt the green,
　　And dress thy grave with pearly dew!

The red-breast oft at evening hours
　　Shall kindly lend his little aid:
With hoary moss and gathered flowers,
　　To deck the ground where thou art laid.

When howling winds and beating rain
　　In tempests shake the sylvan cell,
Or midst the chase on every plain,
　　The tender thought on thee shall dwell.

Each lonely scene shall thee restore,
　　For thee the tear be duly shed:
Beloved, till life could charm no more,
　　And mourned, till Pity's self be dead.

435                  *The Stormy Hebrides*

UNBOUNDED is thy range; with varied style
　　Thy Muse may, like those feathery tribes which spring
　　From their rude rocks, extend her skirting wing
Round the moist marge of each cold Hebrid isle,
To that hoar pile which still its ruin shows:
　　In whose small vaults a pigmy-folk is found,
Whose bones the delver with his spade upthrows,
　　And culls them, wondering, from the hallowed ground!
Or thither, where beneath the showery west
　　The mighty kings of three fair realms are laid;
Once foes, perhaps, together now they rest.
　　No slaves revere them and no wars invade:

Yet frequent now, at midnight's solemn hour,
　　The rifted mounds their yawning cells unfold,
And forth the monarchs stalk with sovereign power
　　In pageant robes, and wreathed with sheeny gold,
And on their twilight tombs aerial council hold.

But O, o'er all, forget not Kilda's race,
　　On whose bleak rocks, which brave the wasting tides,
　　Fair Nature's daughter, Virtue, yet abides!
Go, just as they, their blameless manners trace!
Then to my ear transmit some gentle song
　　Of those whose lives are yet sincere and plain,
Their bounded walks the ragged cliffs along,
　　And all their prospect but the wintry main.
With sparing temperance, at the needful time,
　　They drain the sainted spring or, hunger-pressed,
Along the Atlantic rock undreading climb,
　　And of its eggs despoil the solan's nest.
Thus blest in primal innocence they live,
　　Sufficed and happy with that frugal fare
Which tasteful toil and hourly danger give.
　　Hard is their shallow soil, and bare;
Nor ever vernal bee was heard to murmur there!


# CHRISTOPHER SMART

## 1722–1771

436　　　　*A Song to David*

O THOU, that sitst upon a throne,
With harp of high majestic tone,
　　To praise the King of kings;
And voice of heaven-ascending swell,
Which, while its deeper notes excel,
　　Clear, as a clarion, rings:

To bless each valley, grove and coast,
And charm the cherubs to the post
　　Of gratitude in throngs;
To keep the days on Zion's mount,
And send the year to his account,
　　With dances and with songs:

O Servant of God's holiest charge,
The minister of praise at large,
  Which thou mayst now receive;
From thy blest mansion hail and hear,
From topmost eminence appear
  To this the wreath I weave.

*

O DAVID, highest in the list
Of worthies, on God's ways insist,
  The genuine word repeat:
Vain are the documents of men,
And vain the flourish of the pen
  That keeps the fool's conceit.

PRAISE above all—for praise prevails;
Heap up the measure, load the scales,
  And good to goodness add:
The generous soul her Saviour aids,
But peevish obloquy degrades;
  The Lord is great and glad.

For ADORATION all the ranks
Of angels yield eternal thanks,
  And DAVID in the midst;
With God's good poor, which, last and least
In man's esteem, thou to thy feast,
  O blessed bride-groom, bidst.

For ADORATION seasons change,
And order, truth, and beauty range,
  Adjust, attract, and fill:
The grass the polyanthus cheques;
And polished porphyry reflects,
  By the descending rill.

Rich almonds colour to the prime
For ADORATION; tendrils climb,
  And fruit-trees pledge their gems;
And Ivis with her gorgeous vest
Builds for her eggs her cunning nest,
  And bell-flowers bow their stems.

Ivis] humming bird

With vinous syrup cedars spout;
From rocks pure honey gushing out,
   For ADORATION springs:
All scenes of painting crowd the map
Of nature; to the mermaid's pap
   The scalèd infant clings.

The spotted ounce and playsome cubs
Run rustling 'mongst the flowering shrubs,
   And lizards feed the moss;
For ADORATION beasts embark,
While waves upholding halcyon's ark
   No longer roar and toss.

While Israel sits beneath his fig,
With coral root and amber sprig
   The weaned adventurer sports;
Where to the palm the jasmin cleaves,
For ADORATION 'mongst the leaves
   The gale his peace reports.

Increasing days their reign exalt,
Nor in the pink and mottled vault
   The opposing spirits tilt;
And, by the coasting reader spied,
The silverlings and crusions glide
   For ADORATION gilt.

For ADORATION ripening canes
And cocoa's purest milk detains
   The western pilgrim's staff;
Where rain in clasping boughs inclosed,
And vines with oranges disposed,
   Embower the social laugh.

Now labour his reward receives,
For ADORATION counts his sheaves
   To peace, her bounteous prince;
The nectarine his strong tint imbibes,
And apples of ten thousand tribes,
   And quick peculiar quince.

The wealthy crops of whitening rice,
'Mongst thyine woods and groves of spice,
   For ADORATION grow;
And, marshalled in the fencèd land,
The peaches and pomegranates stand,
   Where wild carnations blow.

The laurels with the winter strive;
The crocus burnishes alive
   Upon the snow-clad earth;
For ADORATION myrtles stay
To keep the garden from dismay,
   And bless the sight from dearth.

The pheasant shows his pompous neck;
And ermine, jealous of a speck,
   With fear eludes offence:
The sable, with his glossy pride,
For ADORATION is descried,
   Where frosts the wave condense.

The cheerful holly, pensive yew,
And holy thorn, their trim renew;
   The squirrel hoards his nuts:
All creatures batten o'er their stores,
And careful nature all her doors
   For ADORATION shuts.

For ADORATION, DAVID's psalms
Lift up the heart to deeds of alms;
   And he, who kneels and chants,
Prevails his passions to control,
Finds meat and medicine to the soul,
   Which for translation pants.

For ADORATION, beyond match,
The scholar bullfinch aims to catch
   The soft flute's ivory touch;
And, careless on the hazel spray,
The daring redbreast keeps at bay
   The damsel's greedy clutch.

# CHRISTOPHER SMART

For ADORATION, in the skies,
The Lord's philosopher espies
   The Dog, the Ram, and Rose;
The planets ring, Orion's sword;
Nor is his greatness less adored
   In the vile worm that glows.

For ADORATION on the strings
The western breezes work their wings,
   The captive ear to sooth.—
Hark! 'tis a voice—how still, and small—
That makes the cataracts to fall,
   Or bids the sea be smooth.

For ADORATION, incense comes
From bezoar, and Arabian gums;
   And on the civet's fur.
But as for prayer, or ere it faints,
Far better is the breath of saints
   Than galbanum and myrrh.

For ADORATION from the down,
Of damsons to the anana's crown,
   God sends to tempt the taste;
And while the luscious zest invites,
The sense, that in the scene delights,
   Commands desire be chaste.

For ADORATION, all the paths
Of grace are open, all the baths
   Of purity refresh;
And all the rays of glory beam
To deck the man of God's esteem,
   Who triumphs o'er the flesh.

For ADORATION, in the dome
Of Christ the sparrows find an home;
   And on his olives perch:
The swallow also dwells with thee,
O man of God's humility,
   Within his Saviour's CHURCH.

strings] strings of the Æolian harp         anana] pineapple

Sweet is the dew that falls betimes,
And drops upon the leafy limes;
   Sweet Hermon's fragrant air:
Sweet is the lily's silver bell,
And sweet the wakeful tapers smell
   That watch for early prayer.

Sweet the young nurse with love intense,
Which smiles o'er sleeping innocence;
   Sweet when the lost arrive:
Sweet the musician's ardour beats,
While his vague mind's in quest of sweets
   The choicest flowers to hive.

Sweeter in all the strains of love,
The language of thy turtle dove,
   Paired to thy swelling chord;
Sweeter with every grace endued,
The glory of thy gratitude,
   Respired unto the Lord.

Strong is the horse upon his speed;
Strong in pursuit the rapid glede,
   Which makes at once his game:
Strong the tall ostrich on the ground;
Strong through the turbulent profound
   Shoots xiphias to his aim.

Strong is the lion—like a coal
His eye-ball—like a bastion's mole
   His chest against the foes:
Strong, the gier-eagle on his sail,
Strong against tide, the enormous whale
   Emerges as he goes.

But stronger still, in earth and air,
And in the sea, the man of prayer;
   And far beneath the tide;
And in the seat to faith assigned,
Where ask is have, where seek is find,
   Where knock is open wide.

xiphias] the sword-fish

Beauteous the fleet before the gale;
Beauteous the multitudes in mail,
   Ranked arms and crested heads:
Beauteous the garden's umbrage mild,
Walk, water, meditated wild,
   And all the bloomy beds.

Beauteous the moon full on the lawn;
And beauteous, when the veil's withdrawn,
   The virgin to her spouse:
Beauteous the temple decked and filled,
When to the heaven of heavens they build
   Their heart-directed vows.

Beauteous, yea beauteous more than these,
The shepherd king upon his knees,
   For his momentous trust;
With wish of infinite conceit,
For man, beast, mute, the small and great,
   And prostrate dust to dust.

Precious the bounteous widow's mite;
And precious, for extreme delight,
   The largess from the churl:
Precious the ruby's blushing blaze,
And alba's blest imperial rays,
   And pure cerulean pearl.

Precious the penitential tear;
And precious is the sigh sincere,
   Acceptable to God:
And precious are the winning flowers,
In gladsome Israel's feast of bowers,
   Bound on the hallowed sod.

More precious that diviner part
Of David, even the Lord's own heart,
   Great, beautiful, and new:
In all things where it was intent,
In all extremes, in each event,
   Proof—answering true to true.

Glorious the sun in mid career;
Glorious the assembled fires appear;
   Glorious the comet's train:
Glorious the trumpet and alarm;
Glorious the almighty stretched-out arm;
   Glorious the enraptured main:

Glorious the northern lights astream;
Glorious the song, when God's the theme
   Glorious the thunder's roar:
Glorious hosanna from the den;
Glorious the catholic amen;
   Glorious the martyr's gore:

Glorious—more glorious is the crown
Of him that brought salvation down
   By meekness, called thy Son;
Thou that stupendous truth believed,
And now the matchless deed's achieved,
   DETERMINED, DARED, and DONE.

437    *The Nativity of Our Lord and Saviour*

WHERE is this stupendous stranger?
   Swains of Solyma advise,
Lead me to my Master's manger,
   Shew me where my Saviour lies.

O most Mighty! O most Holy!
   Far beyond the seraph's thought,
Art thou then so mean and lowly,
   As unheeded prophets taught?

O the magnitude of meekness!
   Worth from worth immortal sprung;
O the strength of infant weakness,
   If eternal is so young!

If so young and thus eternal,
   Michael tune the shepherd's reed,
Where the scenes are ever vernal.
   And the loves be love indeed!

See the God blasphemed and doubted
    In the schools of Greece and Rome,
See the powers of darkness routed,
    Taken at their utmost gloom.

Nature's decorations glisten
    Far above their usual trim;
Birds on box and laurels listen,
    As so near the cherubs hymn.

Boreas now no longer winters
    On the desolated coast;
Oaks no more are riven in splinters
    By the whirlwind and his host.

Spinks and ouzels sing sublimely
    'We too have a Saviour born';
Whiter blossoms burst untimely
    On the blest Mosaic thorn.

God all-bounteous, all creative,
    Whom no ills from good dissuade,
Is incarnate and a native
    Of the very world he made.

# OLIVER GOLDSMITH

## 1730–1774

438        *Song*

WHEN lovely woman stoops to folly,
    And finds too late that men betray,
What charm can sooth her melancholy,
    What art can wash her guilt away?

The only art her guilt to cover,
    To hide her shame from every eye,
To give repentance to her lover,
    And wring his bosom—is to die.

*Sweet Auburn*

SWEET Auburn, loveliest village of the plain,
Where health and plenty cheered the labouring swain,
Where smiling spring its earliest visit paid,
And parting summer's lingering blooms delayed,
Dear lovely bowers of innocence and ease,
Seats of my youth, when every sport could please,
How often have I loitered o'er thy green,
Where humble happiness endeared each scene!
How often have I paused on every charm,
The sheltered cot, the cultivated farm,
The never failing brook, the busy mill,
The decent church that topped the neighbouring hill,
The hawthorn bush, with seats beneath the shade,
For talking age, and whispering lovers made!
How often have I blest the coming day,
When toil remitting lent its turn to play,
And all the village train from labour free
Led up their sports beneath the spreading tree,
While many a pastime circled in the shade,
The young contending as the old surveyed;
And many a gambol frolicked o'er the ground,
And slights of art and feats of strength went round;
And still as each repeated pleasure tired,
Succeeding sports the mirthful band inspired;
The dancing pair that simply sought renown
By holding out to tire each other down;
The swain mistrustless of his smutted face,
While secret laughter tittered round the place;
The bashful virgin's side-long looks of love,
The matron's glance that would those looks reprove!
These were thy charms, sweet village; sports like these,
With sweet succession taught even toil to please;
These round thy bowers their cheerful influence shed
These were thy charms—but all these charms are fled.
  Sweet smiling village, loveliest of the lawn,
Thy sports are fled, and all thy charms withdrawn;
Amidst thy bowers the tyrant's hand is seen
And desolation saddens all thy green:
One only master grasps the whole domain,
And half a tillage stints thy smiling plain;

No more thy glassy brook reflects the day,
But choked with sedges, works its weedy way;
Along thy glades, a solitary guest,
The hollow sounding bittern guards its nest;
Amidst thy desert walks the lapwing flies,
And tires their echoes with unvaried cries.
Sunk are thy bowers, in shapeless ruin all,
And the long grass o'ertops the mouldering wall;
And trembling, shrinking from the spoiler's hand,
Far, far away thy children leave the land.

Ill fares the land, to hastening ills a prey,
Where wealth accumulates, and men decay:
Princes and lords may flourish, or may fade;
A breath can make them, as a breath has made;
But a bold peasantry, their country's pride,
When once destroyed, can never be supplied.

# THOMAS OSBERT MORDAUNT

## 1730–1809

**440**

### *Sound, Sound the Clarion*

SOUND, sound the clarion, fill the fife!
 Throughout the sensual world proclaim,
One crowded hour of glorious life
 Is worth an age without a name.

# JOHN SCOTT OF AMWELL

## 1730–1783

**441**

### *The Drum*

I HATE that drum's discordant sound,
Parading round, and round, and round:
To thoughtless youth it pleasure yields,
And lures from cities and from fields,
To sell their liberty for charms
Of tawdry lace, and glittering arms;
And when Ambition's voice commands,
To march, and fight, and fall, in foreign lands.

I hate that drum's discordant sound,
Parading round, and round, and round:
To me it talks of ravaged plains,
And burning towns, and ruined swains,
And mangled limbs, and dying groans,
And widows' tears, and orphans' moans;
And all that Misery's hand bestows.
To fill the catalogue of human woes.


# WILLIAM COWPER

## 1731–1800

442       *Light Shining out of Darkness*

GOD moves in a mysterious way,
   His wonders to perform;
He plants his footsteps in the sea,
   And rides upon the storm.

Deep in unfathomable mines
   Of never failing skill
He treasures up his bright designs,
   And works his sovereign will.

Ye fearful saints, fresh courage take,
   The clouds ye so much dread
Are big with mercy, and shall break
   In blessings on your head.

Judge not the Lord by feeble sense,
   But trust him for his grace;
Behind a frowning providence,
   He hides a smiling face.

His purposes will ripen fast,
   Unfolding every hour;
The bud may have a bitter taste,
   But sweet will be the flower.

Blind unbelief is sure to err,
　And scan his work in vain;
God is his own interpreter,
　And he will make it plain.


443　　　　*The Shrubbery*
　　　*Written in a Time of Affliction*

OH, happy shades—to me unblest,
　Friendly to peace, but not to me,
How ill the scene that offers rest,
　And heart that cannot rest, agree!

This glassy stream, that spreading pine,
　Those alders quivering to the breeze,
Might sooth a soul less hurt than mine,
　And please, if any thing could please.

But fixed unalterable care
　Foregoes not what she feels within,
Shows the same sadness everywhere,
　And slights the season and the scene.

For all that pleased in wood or lawn,
　While peace possessed these silent bowers,
Her animating smile withdrawn,
　Has lost its beauties and its powers.

The saint or moralist should tread
　This moss-grown alley, musing, slow;
They seek, like me, the secret shade,
　But not, like me, to nourish woe.

Me fruitful scenes and prospects waste
　Alike admonish not to roam;
These tell me of enjoyments past,
　And those of sorrows yet to come.

444  *On the Loss of the Royal George*

1782

TOLL for the brave—
The brave! that are no more:
   All sunk beneath the wave,
Fast by their native shore.
   Eight hundred of the brave,
Whose courage well was tried,
   Had made the vessel heel
And laid her on her side;
   A land-breeze shook the shrouds,
And she was overset;
   Down went the Royal George,
With all her crew complete.

Toll for the brave—
Brave Kempenfelt is gone,
   His last sea-fight is fought,
His work of glory done.
   It was not in the battle,
No tempest gave the shock,
   She sprang no fatal leak,
She ran upon no rock;
   His sword was in the sheath,
His fingers held the pen,
   When Kempenfelt went down
With twice four hundred men.

Weigh the vessel up,
Once dreaded by our foes,
   And mingle with your cup
The tears that England owes;
   Her timbers yet are sound,
And she may float again,
   Full charged with England's thunder,
And plough the distant main;
   But Kempenfelt is gone,
His victories are o'er;
   And he and his eight hundred
Must plough the wave no more.

445 *The Poplar-Field*

THE poplars are felled, farewell to the shade
And the whispering sound of the cool colonnade,
The winds play no longer, and sing in the leaves,
Nor Ouse on his bosom their image receives.

Twelve years have elapsed since I last took a view
Of my favourite field and the bank where they grew,
And now in the grass behold they are laid,
And the tree is my seat that once lent me a shade.

The blackbird has fled to another retreat
Where the hazels afford him a screen from the heat,
And the scene where his melody charmed me before,
Resounds with his sweet-flowing ditty no more.

My fugitive years are all hasting away,
And I must ere long lie as lowly as they,
With a turf on my breast, and a stone at my head,
Ere another such grove shall arise in its stead.

'Tis a sight to engage me, if any thing can,
To muse on the perishing pleasures of man;
Though his life be a dream, his enjoyments, I see,
Have a being less durable even than he.

446 *The Castaway*

OBSCUREST night involved the sky,
  The Atlantic billows roared,
When such a destined wretch as I,
  Washed headlong from on board,
Of friends, of hope, of all bereft,
His floating home for ever left.

No braver chief could Albion boast
  Than he with whom he went,
Nor ever ship left Albion's coast,
  With warmer wishes sent.
He loved them both, but both in vain,
Nor him beheld, nor her again.

Not long beneath the whelming brine,
   Expert to swim, he lay;
Nor soon he felt his strength decline,
   Or courage die away;
But waged with death a lasting strife,
Supported by despair of life.

He shouted: nor his friends had failed
   To check the vessel's course,
But so the furious blast prevailed,
   That, pitiless perforce,
They left their outcast mate behind,
And scudded still before the wind.

Some succour yet they could afford;
   And, such as storms allow,
The cask, the coop, the floated cord,
   Delayed not to bestow.
But he (they knew) nor ship, nor shore,
Whate'er they gave, should visit more.

Nor, cruel as it seemed, could he
   Their haste himself condemn,
Aware that flight, in such a sea,
   Alone could rescue them;
Yet bitter felt it still to die
Deserted, and his friends so nigh.

He long survives, who lives an hour
   In ocean, self-upheld;
And so long he, with unspent power,
   His destiny repelled;
And ever, as the minutes flew,
Entreated help, or cried—Adieu!

At length, his transient respite past,
   His comrades, who before
Had heard his voice in every blast,
   Could catch the sound no more.
For then, by toil subdued, he drank
The stifling wave, and then he sank.

No poet wept him: but the page
  Of narrative sincere,
That tells his name, his worth, his age,
  Is wet with Anson's tear.
And tears by bards or heroes shed
Alike immortalize the dead.

I therefore purpose not, or dream,
  Descanting on his fate,
To give the melancholy theme
  A more enduring date:
But misery still delights to trace
Its semblance in another's case.

No voice divine the storm allayed,
  No light propitious shone;
When, snatched from all effectual aid,
  We perished, each alone:
But I beneath a rougher sea,
And whelmed in deeper gulfs than he.

# THOMAS CHATTERTON

## 1752–1770

447                    *Song from Ælla*

O! SYNGE untoe mie roundelaie,
O! droppe the brynie teare wythe mee,
Daunce ne moe atte hallie daie,
Lycke a reynynge ryver bee;
    Mie love ys dedde,
    Gon to hys death-bedde,
    Al under the wyllowe tree.

Blacke hys cryne as the wyntere nyghte,
Whyte hys rode as the sommer snowe,
Rodde hys face as the mornynge lyghte,
Cale he lyes ynne the grave belowe;
    Mie love ys dedde,
    Gon to hys deathe-bedde,
    Al under the wyllowe tree.

**447**   cryne] hair         rode] complexion         Cale] cold

Swote hys tyngue as the throstles note,
Quycke ynn daunce as thoughte canne bee,
Defte hys taboure, codgelle stote,
O! hee lyes bie the wyllowe tree;
                Mie love ys dedde,
                Gonne to hys deathe-bedde,
                Alle underre the wyllowe tree.

Harke! the ravenne flappes hys wynge,
In the briered delle belowe;
Harke! the dethe-owle loude dothe synge,
To the nyghte-mares as heie goe;
                Mie love ys dedde,
                Gonne to hys deathe-bedde,
                Al under the wyllowe tree.

See! the whyte moone sheenes onne hie;
Whyterre ys mie true loves shroude;
Whyterre yanne the mornynge skie,
Whyterre yanne the evenynge cloude;
                Mie love ys dedde,
                Gon to hys deathe-bedde,
                Al under the wyllowe tree.

Heere, uponne mie true loves grave,
Schalle the baren fleurs be layde,
Nee one hallie Seyncte to save
Al the celness of a mayde.
                Mie love ys dedde,
                Gonne to hys death-bedde,
                Alle under the wyllowe tree.

Wythe mie hondes I'lle dente the brieres
Rounde his hallie corse to gre,
Ouphante fairie, lyghte youre fyres,
Heere mie boddie stylle schalle bee.
                Mie love ys dedde,
                Gon to hys death-bedde,
                Al under the wyllowe tree.

heie] they          celness] coldness          Ouphante] Elfin

472

Comme, wythe acorne-coppe & thorne,
Drayne mie hartys blodde awaie;
Lyfe and all yttes goode I scorne,
Daunce bie nete, or feaste by daie.
    Mie love ys dedde,
    Gon to hys death-bedde,
    Al under the wyllowe tree.

Waterre wytches, crownede wythe reytes,
Bere mee to yer leathalle tyde.
I die; I comme; mie true love waytes.
Thos the damselle spake, and dyed.

# GEORGE CRABBE

## 1754-1832

448            *Rural Life*

I GRANT indeed that fields and flocks have charms
For him that grazes or for him that farms;
But when amid such pleasing scenes I trace
The poor laborious natives of the place,
And see the mid-day sun, with fervid ray,
On their bare heads and dewy temples play;
While some, with feebler heads and fainter hearts,
Deplore their fortune, yet sustain their parts:
Then shall I dare these real ills to hide
In tinsel trappings of poetic pride?
No; cast by Fortune on a frowning coast,
Which neither groves nor happy valleys boast;
Where other cares than those the Muse relates,
And other shepherds dwell with other mates;
By such examples taught, I paint the Cot,
As Truth will paint it, and as Bards will not:
Nor you, ye poor, of lettered scorn complain,
To you the smoothest song is smooth in vain;
O'ercome by labour, and bowed down by time,
Feel you the barren flattery of a rhyme?
Can poets soothe you, when you pine for bread,
By winding myrtles round your ruined shed?

Can their light tales your weighty griefs o'erpower,
Or glad with airy mirth the toilsome hour?
   Lo! where the heath, with withering brake grown o'er,
Lends the light turf that warms the neighbouring poor;
From thence a length of burning sand appears,
Where the thin harvest waves its withered ears;
Rank weeds, that every art and care defy,
Reign o'er the land, and rob the blighted rye:
There thistles stretch their prickly arms afar,
And to the ragged infant threaten war;
There poppies nodding, mock the hope of toil;
There the blue bugloss paints the sterile soil;
Hardy and high, above the slender sheaf,
The slimy mallow waves her silky leaf;
O'er the young shoot the charlock throws a shade,
And clasping tares cling round the sickly blade;
With mingled tints the rocky coasts abound,
And a sad splendour vainly shines around.
   So looks the nymph whom wretched arts adorn,
Betrayed by man, then left for man to scorn;
Whose cheek in vain assumes the mimic rose,
While her sad eyes the troubled breast disclose;
Whose outward splendour is but folly's dress,
Exposing most, when most it gilds distress.

449            *The Lady of the Manor*

     NEXT died the Lady who yon Hall possessed;
And here they brought her noble bones to rest.
In Town she dwelt;—forsaken stood the Hall:
Worms ate the floors, the tapestry fled the wall:
No fire the kitchen's cheerless grate displayed;
No cheerful light the long-closed sash conveyed;
The crawling worm, that turns a summer-fly,
Here spun his shroud and laid him up to die
The winter-death:—upon the bed of state,
The bat shrill-shrieking wooed his flickering mate;
To empty rooms the curious came no more,
From empty cellars turned the angry poor,
And surly beggars cursed the ever-bolted door.
To one small room the steward found his way,
Where tenants followed to complain and pay;

Yet no complaint before the Lady came,
The feeling servant spared the feeble dame;
Who saw her farms with his observing eyes,
And answered all requests with his replies:—
She came not down, her falling groves to view;
Why should she know, what one so faithful knew?
Why come, from many clamorous tongues to hear,
What one so just might whisper in her ear?
Her oaks or acres, why with care explore;
Why learn the wants, the sufferings of the poor;
When one so knowing all their worth could trace,
And one so piteous governed in her place?

Lo! now, what dismal sons of Darkness come,
To bear this daughter of Indulgence home;
Tragedians all, and well arranged in black!
Who nature, feeling, force, expression lack;
Who cause no tear, but gloomily pass by,
And shake their sables in the wearied eye,
That turns disgusted from the pompous scene,
Proud without grandeur, with profusion, mean!
The tear for kindness past affection owes;
For worth deceased the sigh from reason flows;
E'en well-feigned passion for our sorrows call,
And real tears for mimic miseries fall:
But this poor farce has neither truth nor art,
To please the fancy or to touch the heart;
Unlike the darkness of the sky, that pours
On the dry ground its fertilizing showers;
Unlike to that which strikes the soul with dread,
When thunders roar and forky fires are shed;
Dark but not awful, dismal but yet mean,
With anxious bustle moves the cumbrous scene;
Presents no objects tender or profound,
But spreads its cold unmeaning gloom around.

When woes are feigned, how ill such forms appear;
And oh! how needless, when the woe's sincere.

Slow to the vault they come, with heavy tread,
Bending beneath the Lady and her lead;
A case of elm surrounds that ponderous chest,
Close on that case the crimson velvet's pressed;
Ungenerous this, that to the worm denies,
With niggard caution, his appointed prize;

For now, ere yet he works his tedious way,
Through cloth and wood and metal to his prey,
That prey dissolving shall a mass remain,
That fancy loathes and worms themselves disdain.
　　　But see! the master-mourner makes his way,
To end his office for the coffined clay;
Pleased that our rustic men and maids behold
His plate like silver, and his studs like gold,
As they approach to spell the age, the name,
And all the titles of the illustrious dame.—
This as (my duty done) some scholar read,
A village-father looked disdain and said:
'Away, my friends! why take such pains to know
What some brave marble soon in church shall show?
Where not alone her gracious name shall stand,
But how she lived—the blessing of the land;
How much we all deplored the noble dead,
What groans we uttered and what tears we shed;
Tears, true as those, which in the sleepy eyes
Of weeping cherubs on the stone shall rise;
Tears, true as those, which, ere she found her grave,
The noble Lady to our sorrows gave.'

450　　　　　*Peter Grimes; the Outcast*

THUS by himself compelled to live each day,
To wait for certain hours the tide's delay;
At the same times the same dull views to see,
The bounding marsh-bank and the blighted tree;
The water only, when the tides were high,
When low, the mud half-covered and half-dry;
The sun-burnt tar that blisters on the planks,
And bank-side stakes in their uneven ranks;
Heaps of entangled weeds that slowly float,
As the tide rolls by the impeded boat.
　　When tides were neap, and, in the sultry day,
Through the tall bounding mud-banks made their way,
Which on each side rose swelling, and below
The dark warm flood ran silently and slow;
There anchoring, Peter chose from man to hide,
There hang his head, and view the lazy tide
In its hot slimy channel slowly glide;

Where the small eels that left the deeper way
For the warm shore, within the shallows play;
Where gaping mussels, left upon the mud,
Slope their slow passage to the fallen flood;—
Here dull and hopeless he'd lie down and trace
How sidelong crabs had scrawled their crooked race;
Or sadly listen to the tuneless cry
Of fishing gull or clanging golden-eye;
What time the sea-birds to the marsh would come,
And the loud bittern, from the bull-rush home,
Gave from the salt-ditch side the bellowing boom:
He nursed the feelings these dull scenes produce,
And loved to stop beside the opening sluice;
Where the small stream, confined in narrow bound,
Ran with a dull, unvaried, saddening sound;
Where all, presented to the eye or ear,
Oppressed the soul with misery, grief, and fear.

451                        *Frenzy*

THEN was I cast from out my state;
  Two fiends of darkness led my way;
They waked me early, watched me late,
  My dread by night, my plague by day!
Oh! I was made their sport, their play,
  Through many a stormy troubled year;
And how they used their passive prey
  Is sad to tell:—but you shall hear.

                    *

Those fiends upon a shaking fen
  Fixed me, in dark tempestuous night;
There never trod the foot of men,
  There flocked the fowl in wintry flight;
There danced the moor's deceitful light
  Above the pool where sedges grow;
And when the morning-sun shone bright,
  It shone upon a field of snow.

They hung me on a bough so small,
   The rook could build her nest no higher;
They fixed me on the trembling ball
That crowns the steeple's quivering spire;
They set me where the seas retire,
   But drown with their returning tide;
And made me flee the mountain's fire,
   When rolling from its burning side.

I've hung upon the ridgy steep
   Of cliffs, and held the rambling brier;
I've plunged below the billowy deep,
   Where air was sent me to respire;
I've been where hungry wolves retire;
   And (to complete my woes) I've ran
Where Bedlam's crazy crew conspire
   Against the life of reasoning man.

I've furled in storms the flapping sail,
   By hanging from the topmast-head;
I've served the vilest slaves in jail,
   And picked the dunghill's spoil for bread;
I've made the badger's hole my bed,
   I've wandered with a gipsy crew;
I've dreaded all the guilty dread,
   And done what they would fear to do.

On sand, where ebbs and flows the flood,
   Midway they placed and bade me die;
Propped on my staff, I stoutly stood
   When the swift waves came rolling by;
And high they rose, and still more high,
   Till my lips drank the bitter brine;
I sobbed convulsed, then cast mine eye,
   And saw the tide's re-flowing sign.

And then, my dreams were such as nought
   Could yield but my unhappy case;
I've been of thousand devils caught,
   And thrust into that horrid place,
Where reign dismay, despair, disgrace;
   Furies with iron fangs were there,
To torture that accursed race,
   Doomed to dismay, disgrace, despair.

## 452 *His Late Wife's Wedding-Ring*

THE ring so worn, as you behold,
So thin, so pale, is yet of gold:
The passion such it was to prove;
Worn with life's cares, love yet was love.

# WILLIAM BLAKE

## 1757–1827

## 453 *To the Muses*

WHETHER on Ida's shady brow,
    Or in the chambers of the East,
The chambers of the sun, that now
    From ancient melody have ceased;

Whether in Heaven ye wander fair,
    Or the green corners of the earth,
Or the blue regions of the air,
    Where the melodious winds have birth;

Whether on crystal rocks ye rove,
    Beneath the bosom of the sea
Wandering in many a coral grove,
    Fair Nine, forsaking Poetry!

How have you left the ancient love
    That bards of old enjoyed in you!
The languid strings do scarcely move!
    The sound is forced, the notes are few!

## 454 *The Prince of Love*

HOW sweet I roamed from field to field,
    And tasted all the summer's pride,
'Till I the prince of love beheld,
    Who in the sunny beams did glide!

He showed me lilies for my hair,
  And blushing roses for my brow;
He led me through his gardens fair,
  Where all his golden pleasures grow.

With sweet May dews my wings were wet,
  And Phoebus fired my vocal rage;
He caught me in his silken net,
  And shut me in his golden cage.

He loves to sit and hear me sing,
  Then, laughing, sports and plays with me;
Then stretches out my golden wing,
  And mocks my loss of liberty.


455          *Piping Down the Valleys Wild*

PIPING down the valleys wild,
Piping songs of pleasant glee,
On a cloud I saw a child,
And he laughing said to me:

'Pipe a song about a Lamb!'
So I piped with merry cheer.
'Piper, pipe that song again.'
So I piped: he wept to hear.

'Drop thy pipe, thy happy pipe,
Sing thy songs of happy cheer.'
So I sung the same again,
While he wept with joy to hear.

'Piper, sit thee down and write
In a book, that all may read.'
So he vanished from my sight,
And I plucked a hollow reed,

And I made a rural pen,
And I stained the water clear,
And I wrote my happy songs
Every child may joy to hear.

456 *The Divine Image*

To Mercy, Pity, Peace, and Love
All pray in their distress;
And to these virtues of delight
Return their thankfulness.

For Mercy, Pity, Peace, and Love
Is God, our father dear,
And Mercy, Pity, Peace, and Love,
Is Man, his child and care.

For Mercy has a human heart,
Pity a human face,
And Love, the human form divine,
And Peace, the human dress.

Then every man, of every clime,
That prays in his distress,
Prays to the human form divine,
Love, Mercy, Pity, Peace.

And all must love the human form,
In heathen, turk, or jew;
Where Mercy, Love, and Pity dwell
There God is dwelling too.


457 *Holy Thursday*

'Twas on a Holy Thursday, their innocent faces clean,
The children walking two and two, in red and blue and green,
Grey-headed beadles walked before, with wands as white as snow,
Till into the high dome of Paul's they like Thames' waters flow.

O what a multitude they seemed, these flowers of London town!
Seated in companies they sit, with radiance all their own.
The hum of multitudes was there, but multitudes of lambs,
Thousands of little boys and girls raising their innocent hands.

Now like a mighty wind they raise to Heaven the voice of song,
Or like harmonious thunderings the seats of Heaven among.
Beneath them sit the aged men, wise guardians of the poor;
Then cherish pity, lest you drive an angel from your door.

458                 *Hear the Voice of the Bard*

HEAR the voice of the Bard!
Who present, past, and future sees;
Whose ears have heard
The Holy Word
That walked among the ancient trees,

Calling the lapsèd soul,
And weeping in the evening dew;
That might control
The starry pole,
And fallen, fallen light renew!

'O Earth, O Earth, return!
Arise from out the dewy grass;
Night is worn,
And the morn
Rises from the slumberous mass.

Turn away no more;
Why wilt thou turn away?
The starry floor,
The watery shore,
Is given thee till the break of day.'

459                 *The Clod and the Pebble*

'LOVE seeketh not itself to please,
Nor for itself hath any care,
But for another gives its ease,
And builds a Heaven in Hell's despair.'

So sung a little Clod of Clay
Trodden with the cattle's feet,
But a Pebble of the brook
Warbled out these metres meet:

'Love seeketh only self to please,
To bind another to its delight,
Joys in another's loss of ease,
And builds a Hell in Heaven's despite.'

460                    *The Sick Rose*

O ROSE, thou art sick!
The invisible worm
That flies in the night,
In the howling storm,

Has found out thy bed
Of crimson joy,
And his dark secret love
Does thy life destroy.


461                    *The Tiger*

TIGER! Tiger! burning bright
In the forests of the night,
What immortal hand or eye
Could frame thy fearful symmetry?

In what distant deeps or skies
Burned the fire of thine eyes?
On what wings dare he aspire?
What the hand dare seize the fire?

And what shoulder, and what art,
Could twist the sinews of thy heart?
And when thy heart began to beat,
What dread hand? And what dread feet?

What the hammer? What the chain?
In what furnace was thy brain?
What the anvil? What dread grasp
Dare its deadly terrors clasp?

When the stars threw down their spears,
And watered heaven with their tears,
Did he smile his work to see?
Did he who made the Lamb make thee?

Tiger! Tiger! burning bright
In the forests of the night,
What immortal hand or eye
Dare frame thy fearful symmetry?

462 *London*

I WANDER through each chartered street,
Near where the chartered Thames does flow,
And mark in every face I meet
Marks of weakness, marks of woe.

In every cry of every man,
In every infant's cry of fear,
In every voice, in every ban,
The mind-forged manacles I hear.

How the chimney-sweeper's cry
Every blackening church appalls;
And the hapless soldier's sigh
Runs in blood down palace walls.

But most through midnight streets I hear
How the youthful harlot's curse
Blasts the newborn infant's tear,
And blights with plagues the marriage hearse.

463 *To Tirzah*

WHATE'ER is born of Mortal Birth
Must be consumèd with the Earth,
To rise from Generation free:
Then what have I to do with thee?

The Sexes sprung from Shame and Pride,
Blowed in the morn; in evening died;
But Mercy changed Death into Sleep;
The Sexes rose to work and weep.

Thou, Mother of my Mortal Part,
With cruelty didst mould my heart,
And with false self-deceiving tears
Didst bind my Nostrils, Eyes, and Ears;

Didst close my tongue in senseless clay,
And me to Mortal Life betray:
The Death of Jesus set me free:
Then what have I to do with thee?

464                    *The Secrets of the Earth*

THE eternal gates' terrific porter lifted the northern bar:
Thel entered in and saw the secrets of the land unknown.
She saw the couches of the dead, and where the fibrous roots
Of every heart on earth infixes deep its restless twists:
A land of sorrows and of tears where never smile was seen.

She wandered in the land of clouds through valleys dark, listening
Dolours and lamentations; waiting oft beside a dewy grave
She stood in silence, listening to the voices of the ground,
Till to her own grave plot she came, and there she sat down,
And heard this voice of sorrow breathed from the hollow pit.

'Why cannot the Ear be closed to its own destruction?
Or the glistening Eye to the poison of a smile?
Why are Eyelids stored with arrows ready drawn,
Where a thousand fighting men in ambush lie?
Or an Eye of gifts and graces showering fruits and coined gold?
Why a Tongue impressed with honey from every wind?
Why an Ear, a whirlpool fierce to draw creations in?
Why a Nostril wide inhaling terror, trembling, and affright?
Why a tender curb upon the youthful burning boy?
Why a little curtain of flesh on the bed of our desire?'


465                    *Never Seek to Tell thy Love*

NEVER seek to tell thy love
Love that never told can be;
For the gentle wind does move
Silently, invisibly.

I told my love, I told my love,
I told her all my heart,
Trembling, cold, in ghastly fears—
Ah, she doth depart.

Soon as she was gone from me
A traveller came by
Silently, invisibly—
O, was no deny.

466                    *Eternity*

HE who bends to himself a joy
Does the wingèd life destroy;
But he who kisses the joy as it flies
Lives in eternity's sunrise.


467                    *Jerusalem*

AND did those feet in ancient time
Walk upon England's mountains green?
And was the holy Lamb of God
On England's pleasant pastures seen?

And did the Countenance Divine
Shine forth upon our clouded hills?
And was Jerusalem builded here
Among these dark Satanic Mills?

Bring me my Bow of burning gold!
Bring me my Arrows of desire!
Bring me my Spear! O clouds, unfold!
Bring me my Chariot of fire!

I will not cease from Mental Fight,
Nor shall my Sword sleep in my hand,
Till we have built Jerusalem
In England's green and pleasant land.


468                *The Vision of Beulah*

THOU hearest the nightingale begin the Song of Spring.
The lark sitting upon his earthy bed, just as the morn
Appears, listens silent; then springing from the waving cornfield, loud
He leads the Choir of Day: trill, trill, trill, trill,
Mounting upon the wings of light into the great expanse,
Re-echoing against the lovely blue and shining heavenly shell,
His little throat labours with inspiration; every feather
On throat and breast and wings vibrates with the effluence Divine.

All nature listens silent to him, and the awful Sun
Stands still upon the mountain looking on this little bird
With eyes of soft humility and wonder, love and awe.
Then loud from their green covert all the birds begin their song:
The thrush, the linnet and the goldfinch, robin and the wren,
Awake the Sun from his sweet reverie upon the mountain.
The nightingale again assays his song, and through the day
And through the night warbles luxuriant, every bird of song
Attending his loud harmony with admiration and love.

Thou perceivest the flowers put forth their precious odours,
And none can tell how from so small a centre comes such sweets,
Forgetting that within that centre Eternity expands
Its ever-during doors that Og and Anak fiercely guard.
First, e'er the morning breaks, joy opens in the flowery bosoms,
Joy even to tears, which the Sun rising dries; first the wild thyme
And meadow-sweet, downy and soft, waving among the reeds,
Light springing on the air, lead the sweet dance: they wake
The honeysuckle sleeping on the oak; the flaunting beauty
Revels along upon the wind; the white-thorn, lovely may,
Opens her many lovely eyes listening; the rose still sleeps,
None dare to wake her; soon she bursts her crimson-curtained bed
And comes forth in the majesty of beauty; every flower,
The pink, the jessamine, the wall-flower, the carnation,
The jonquil, the mild lily, opes her heavens; every tree
And flower and herb soon fill the air with an innumerable dance,
Yet all in order sweet and lovely. Men are sick with love.

# ROBERT BURNS

1759–1796

469        *Address to the Unco Guid*

O YE wha are sae guid yoursel,
   Sae pious and sae holy,
Ye've nought to do but mark and tell
   Your neebour's fauts and folly!
Whase life is like a weel-gaun mill,
   Supplied wi' store o' water,
The heapet happer's ebbing still,
   And still the clap plays clatter.

Hear me, ye venerable Core,
  As counsel for poor mortals,
That frequent pass douce Wisdom's door
  For glaikit Folly's portals;
I, for their thoughtless, careless sakes,
  Would here propone defences,
Their donsie tricks, their black mistakes,
  Their failings and mischances.

Ye see your state wi' theirs compared,
  And shudder at the niffer;
But cast a moment's fair regard
  What maks the mighty differ?
Discount what scant occasion gave,
  That purity ye pride in,
And (what's aft mair than a' the lave)
  Your better art o' hiding.

Think, when your castigated pulse
  Gies now and then a wallop,
What ragings must his veins convulse,
  That still eternal gallop:
Wi' wind and tide fair i' your tail,
  Right on ye scud your sea-way;
But in the teeth o' baith to sail,
  It maks an unco leeway.

See Social-life and Glee sit down,
  All joyous and unthinking,
Till, quite transmugrified, they're grown
  Debauchery and Drinking:
O would they stay to calculate
  The eternal consequences;
Or your more dreaded hell to state,
  Damnation of expenses!

Ye high, exalted, virtuous Dames,
  Tied up in godly laces,
Before ye gie poor Frailty names,
  Suppose a change o' cases;

douce] sober       glaikit] giddy       donsie] unlucky
                   niffer] exchange

A dear-loved lad, convenience snug,
 A treacherous inclination—
But, let me whisper i' your lug,
 Ye're aiblins nae temptation.

Then gently scan your brother Man,
 Still gentler sister Woman;
Though they may gang a kennin wrang,
 To step aside is human:
One point must still be greatly dark,
 The moving *Why* they do it:
And just as lamely can ye mark,
 How far perhaps they rue it.

Who made the heart, 'tis *He* alone
 Decidedly can try us,
He knows each chord, its various tone,
 Each spring, its various bias:
Then at the balance let's be mute,
 We never can adjust it;
What's *done* we partly may compute,
 But know not what's *resisted*.

470      *Auld Lang Syne*

SHOULD auld acquaintance be forgot,
 And never brought to min'?
Should auld acquaintance be forgot,
 And auld lang syne?

  For auld lang syne, my dear,
   For auld lang syne,
  We'll tak a cup o' kindness yet,
   For auld lang syne.

We twa hae run about the braes,
 And pu'd the gowans fine;
But we've wandered mony a weary foot
 Sin' auld lang syne.

  aiblins] perhaps    a kennin] a little
    470 gowans] daisies

We twa hae paidled i' the burn,
  From morning sun till dine;
But seas between us braid hae roared
  Sin' auld lang syne.

And there's a hand, my trusty fiere,
  And gie's a hand o' thine:
And we'll tak a right guid-willie waught,
  For auld lang syne.

And surely ye'll be your pint-stowp,
  And surely I'll be mine;
And we'll tak a cup o' kindness yet
  For auld lang syne.

471           *John Anderson, my Jo*

JOHN ANDERSON my jo, John,
  When we were first acquent,
Your locks were like the raven,
  Your bonnie brow was brent;
But now your brow is beld, John,
  Your locks are like the snow;
But blessings on your frosty pow,
  John Anderson, my jo.

John Anderson my jo, John,
  We clamb the hill thegither;
And mony a canty day, John,
  We've had wi' ane anither:
Now we maun totter down, John,
  And hand in hand we'll go,
And sleep thegither at the foot,
  John Anderson, my jo.

472           *The Silver Tassie*

Go fetch to me a pint o' wine,
  An' fill it in a silver tassie;
That I may drink, before I go,
  A service to my bonnie lassie.

That boat rocks at the pier o' Leith,
  Fu' loud the wind blaws frae the ferry,
The ship rides by the Berwick-law,
  And I maun leave my bonnie Mary.

The trumpets sound, the banners fly,
  The glittering spears are rankèd ready;
The shouts o' war are heard afar,
  The battle closes thick and bloody;
But it's no the roar o' sea or shore
  Wad mak me langer wish to tarry;
Nor shout o' war that's heard afar,
  It's leaving thee, my bonnie Mary.

473                *The Banks o' Doon*

YE banks and braes o' bonnie Doon,
  How can ye bloom sae fresh and fair?
How can ye chant, ye little birds,
  And I sae weary fu' o' care?
Thou'lt break my heart, thou warbling bird,
  That wantons thro' the flowering thorn:
Thou minds me o' departed joys,
  Departed never to return.

Aft hae I roved by bonnie Doon,
  To see the rose and woodbine twine;
And ilka bird sang o' its love,
  And fondly sae did I o' mine.
Wi' lightsome heart I pu'd a rose,
  Fu' sweet upon its thorny tree;
And my fause lover stole my rose,
  But ah! he left the thorn wi' me.

474                *A Red, Red Rose*

MY love is like a red, red rose
  That's newly sprung in June:
My love is like the melody
  That's sweetly played in tune.

As fair art thou, my bonnie lass,
  So deep in love am I:
And I will love thee still, my dear,
  Till a' the seas gang dry.

Till a' the seas gang dry, my dear,
  And the rocks melt wi' the sun:
And I will love thee still, my dear,
  While the sands o' life shall run.

And fare thee weel, my only love,
  And fare thee weel a while!
And I will come again, my love,
  Thou' it were ten thousand mile.


475                    *Bonnie Lesley*

O SAW ye bonnie Lesley
  As she gaed o'er the Border?
She's gane, like Alexander,
  To spread her conquests farther.

To see her is to love her,
  And love but her for ever;
For Nature made her what she is,
  And never made anither!

Thou art a queen, fair Lesley,
  Thy subjects we, before thee:
Thou art divine, fair Lesley,
  The hearts o' men adore thee.

The Deil he could na skaith thee,
  Or aught that wad belang thee;
He'd look into thy bonnie face,
  And say, 'I canna wrang thee.'

The Powers aboon will tent thee;
  Misfortune sha'na steer thee;
Thou'rt like themsel' sae lovely,
  That ill they'll ne'er let near thee.

**475**   tent] take care of          steer] molest

Return again, fair Lesley,
   Return to Caledonie!
That we may brag we hae a lass
   There's nane again sae bonnie.


476      *Robert Bruce's March to Bannockburn*

SCOTS, wha hae wi' Wallace bled,
Scots, wham Bruce has aften led,
Welcome to your gory bed,
   Or to victory!

Now's the day, and now's the hour;
See the front o' battle lour,
See approach proud Edward's power—
   Chains and slavery!

Wha will be a traitor knave?
Wha can fill a coward's grave?
Wha sae base as be a slave?—
   Let him turn, and flee!

Wha for Scotland's King and Law
Freedom's sword will strongly draw,
Freeman stand or freeman fa',
   Let him follow me!

By Oppression's woes and pains,
By your sons in servile chains,
We will drain our dearest veins,
   But they shall be free!

Lay the proud usurpers low!
Tyrants fall in every foe!
Liberty's in every blow!
   Let us do, or die!

477 *O wert Thou in the Cauld Blast*

O WERT thou in the cauld blast,
　On yonder lea, on yonder lea,
My plaidie to the angry airt,
　I'd shelter thee, I'd shelter thee.
Or did misfortune's bitter storms
　Around thee blaw, around thee blaw,
Thy bield should be my bosom,
　To share it a', to share it a'.

Or were I in the wildest waste,
　Sae black and bare, sae black and bare,
The desert were a Paradise,
　If thou wert there, if thou wert there.
Or were I monarch o' the globe,
　Wi' thee to reign, wi' thee to reign,
The brightest jewel in my crown
　Wad be my queen, wad be my queen.

# SAMUEL ROGERS

## 1763–1855

478 *A Wish*

MINE be a cot beside the hill;
　A bee-hive's hum shall soothe my ear;
A willowy brook, that turns a mill,
　With many a fall shall linger near.

The swallow oft beneath my thatch
　Shall twitter from her clay-built nest;
Oft shall the pilgrim lift the latch
　And share my meal, a welcome guest.

Around my ivied porch shall spring
　Each fragrant flower that drinks the dew;
And Lucy at her wheel shall sing
　In russet gown and apron blue.

**477**　bield] shelter

SAMUEL ROGERS

The village church among the trees,
  Where first our marriage vows were given,
With merry peals shall swell the breeze
  And point with taper spire to Heaven.


# WILLIAM WORDSWORTH
## 1770–1850

### *Lucy*

479

### (i)

STRANGE fits of passion have I known:
And I will dare to tell,
But in the Lover's ear alone,
What once to me befell.

When she I loved looked every day
Fresh as a rose in June,
I to her cottage bent my way,
Beneath an evening-moon.

Upon the moon I fixed my eye,
All over the wide lea;
With quickening pace my horse drew nigh
Those paths so dear to me.

And now we reached the orchard-plot;
And, as we climbed the hill,
The sinking moon to Lucy's cot
Came near, and nearer still.

In one of those sweet dreams I slept,
Kind Nature's gentlest boon!
And all the while my eyes I kept
On the descending moon.

My horse moved on; hoof after hoof
He raised, and never stopped:
When down behind the cottage roof,
At once, the bright moon dropped.

495

What fond and wayward thoughts will slide
Into a Lover's head!
'O mercy!' to myself I cried,
'If Lucy should be dead!'

480                          (ii)

SHE dwelt among the untrodden ways
   Beside the springs of Dove,
A Maid whom there were none to praise
   And very few to love:

A violet by a mossy stone
   Half hidden from the eye!
Fair as a star, when only one
   Is shining in the sky.

She lived unknown, and few could know
   When Lucy ceased to be;
But she is in her grave, and oh,
   The difference to me!

481                          (iii)

I TRAVELLED among unknown men,
   In lands beyond the sea;
Nor, England! did I know till then
   What love I bore to thee.

'Tis past, that melancholy dream!
   Nor will I quit thy shore
A second time; for still I seem
   To love thee more and more.

Among thy mountains did I feel
   The joy of my desire;
And she I cherished turned her wheel
   Beside an English fire.

Thy mornings showed, thy nights concealed,
  The bowers where Lucy played;
And thine too is the last green field
  That Lucy's eyes surveyed.

482                          (iv)

THREE years she grew in sun and shower;
Then Nature said, 'A lovelier flower
  On earth was never sown;
This child I to myself will take;
She shall be mine, and I will make
  A lady of my own.

'Myself will to my darling be
Both law and impulse: and with me
  The girl, in rock and plain,
In earth and heaven, in glade and bower,
Shall feel an overseeing power
  To kindle or restrain.

'She shall be sportive as the fawn
That wild with glee across the lawn
  Or up the mountain springs;
And hers shall be the breathing balm,
And hers the silence and the calm
  Of mute insensate things.

'The floating clouds their state shall lend
To her; for her the willow bend;
  Nor shall she fail to see
Even in the motions of the storm
Grace that shall mould the maiden's form
  By silent sympathy.

'The stars of midnight shall be dear
To her; and she shall lean her ear
  In many a secret place
Where rivulets dance their wayward round,
And beauty born of murmuring sound
  Shall pass into her face.

'And vital feelings of delight
Shall rear her form to stately height,
  Her virgin bosom swell;
Such thoughts to Lucy I will give
While she and I together live
  Here in this happy dell.'

Thus Nature spake—The work was done—
How soon my Lucy's race was run!
  She died, and left to me
This heath, this calm and quiet scene;
The memory of what has been,
  And never more will be.

483

(v)

A SLUMBER did my spirit seal;
  I had no human fears:
She seemed a thing that could not feel
  The touch of earthly years.

No motion has she now, no force;
  She neither hears nor sees;
Rolled round in earth's diurnal course,
  With rocks, and stones, and trees.

484

## Resolution and Independence

THERE was a roaring in the wind all night;
The rain came heavily and fell in floods;
But now the sun is rising calm and bright;
The birds are singing in the distant woods;
Over his own sweet voice the stock-dove broods;
The jay makes answer as the magpie chatters;
And all the air is filled with pleasant noise of waters.

All things that love the sun are out of doors;
The sky rejoices in the morning's birth;
The grass is bright with rain-drops;—on the moors
The hare is running races in her mirth;
And with her feet she from the plashy earth
Raises a mist; that, glittering in the sun,
Runs with her all the way, wherever she doth run.

I was a Traveller then upon the moor;
I saw the hare that raced about with joy;
I heard the woods and distant waters roar;
Or heard them not, as happy as a boy:
The pleasant season did my heart employ:
My old remembrances went from me wholly;
And all the ways of men, so vain and melancholy.

But, as it sometimes chanceth, from the might
Of joy in minds that can no further go,
As high as we have mounted in delight
In our dejection do we sink as low;
To me that morning did it happen so;
And fears and fancies thick upon me came;
Dim sadness—and blind thoughts, I knew not, nor could name.

I heard the sky-lark warbling in the sky;
And I bethought me of the playful hare:
Even such a happy Child of earth am I;
Even as these blissful creatures do I fare;
Far from the world I walk, and from all care;
But there may come another day to me—
Solitude, pain of heart, distress, and poverty.

My whole life I have lived in pleasant thought,
As if life's business were a summer mood;
As if all needful things would come unsought
To genial faith, still rich in genial good;
But how can he expect that others should
Build for him, sow for him, and at his call
Love him, who for himself will take no heed at all?

I thought of Chatterton, the marvellous Boy,
The sleepless Soul that perished in his pride;
Of Him who walked in glory and in joy
Following his plough, along the mountain-side:
By our own spirits are we deified:
We Poets in our youth begin in gladness;
But thereof come in the end despondency and madness.

Now, whether it were by peculiar grace,
A leading from above, a something given,
Yet it befell that, in this lonely place,
When I with these untoward thoughts had striven,
Beside a pool bare to the eye of heaven
I saw a Man before me unawares:
The oldest man he seemed that ever wore grey hairs.

As a huge stone is sometimes seen to lie
Couched on the bald top of an eminence;
Wonder to all who do the same espy,
By what means it could thither come, and whence;
So that it seems a thing endued with sense:
Like a sea-beast crawled forth, that on a shelf
Of rock or sand reposeth, there to sun itself;

Such seemed this Man, not all alive nor dead,
Nor all asleep—in his extreme old age:
His body was bent double, feet and head
Coming together in life's pilgrimage;
As if some dire constraint of pain, or rage
Of sickness felt by him in times long past,
A more than human weight upon his frame had cast.

Himself he propped, limbs, body, and pale face,
Upon a long grey staff of shaven wood:
And, still as I drew near with gentle pace,
Upon the margin of that moorish flood
Motionless as a cloud the old Man stood,
That heareth not the loud winds when they call;
And moveth all together, if it move at all.

At length, himself unsettling, he the pond
Stirred with his staff, and fixedly did look
Upon the muddy water, which he conned,
As if he had been reading in a book:
And now a stranger's privilege I took;
And, drawing to his side, to him did say,
'This morning gives us promise of a glorious day'.

A gentle answer did the old Man make,
In courteous speech which forth he slowly drew:
And him with further words I thus bespake,
'What occupation do you there pursue?
This is a lonesome place for one like you.'
Ere he replied, a flash of mild surprise
Broke from the sable orbs of his yet-vivid eyes.

His words came feebly, from a feeble chest,
But each in solemn order followed each,
With something of a lofty utterance drest—
Choice word and measured phrase, above the reach
Of ordinary men; a stately speech;
Such as grave Livers do in Scotland use,
Religious men, who give to God and man their dues.

He told, that to these waters he had come
To gather leeches, being old and poor:
Employment hazardous and wearisome!
And he had many hardships to endure:
From pond to pond he roamed, from moor to moor;
Housing, with God's good help, by choice or chance;
And in this way he gained an honest maintenance.

The old Man still stood talking by my side;
But now his voice to me was like a stream
Scarce heard; nor word from word could I divide;
And the whole body of the Man did seem
Like one whom I had met with in a dream;
Or like a man from some far region sent,
To give me human strength, by apt admonishment.

My former thoughts returned: the fear that kills;
And hope that is unwilling to be fed;
Cold, pain, and labour, and all fleshly ills;
And mighty Poets in their misery dead.
—Perplexed, and longing to be comforted,
My question eagerly did I renew,
'How is it that you live, and what is it you do?'

He with a smile did then his words repeat;
And said that, gathering leeches, far and wide
He travelled; stirring thus about his feet
The waters of the pools where they abide.
'Once I could meet with them on every side;
But they have dwindled long by slow decay;
Yet still I persevere, and find them where I may.'

While he was talking thus, the lonely place,
The old Man's shape, and speech—all troubled me:
In my mind's eye I seemed to see him pace
About the weary moors continually,
Wandering about alone and silently.
While I these thoughts within myself pursued,
He, having made a pause, the same discourse renewed.

And soon with this he other matter blended,
Cheerfully uttered, with demeanour kind,
But stately in the main; and when he ended,
I could have laughed myself to scorn to find
In that decrepit Man so firm a mind.
'God,' said I, 'be my help and stay secure;
I'll think of the Leech-gatherer on the lonely moor!'

485

My heart leaps up when I behold
    A rainbow in the sky:
So was it when my life began;
So is it now I am a man;
So be it when I shall grow old,
    Or let me die!
The Child is father of the Man;
And I could wish my days to be
Bound each to each by natural piety.

486                  *Upon Westminster Bridge*
                        *Sept. 3, 1802*

EARTH has not anything to show more fair:
    Dull would he be of soul who could pass by
    A sight so touching in its majesty:
This City now doth, like a garment, wear
The beauty of the morning; silent, bare,
    Ships, towers, domes, theatres, and temples lie
    Open unto the fields, and to the sky;
All bright and glittering in the smokeless air.
Never did sun more beautifully steep
    In his first splendour, valley, rock, or hill;
Ne'er saw I, never felt, a calm so deep!
    The river glideth at his own sweet will:
Dear God! the very houses seem asleep;
    And all that mighty heart is lying still!


487      *On the Extinction of the Venetian Republic,*
                        *1802*

ONCE did She hold the gorgeous East in fee;
    And was the safeguard of the West: the worth
    Of Venice did not fall below her birth,
Venice, the eldest Child of Liberty.
She was a maiden City, bright and free;
    No guile seduced, no force could violate;
    And, when she took unto herself a Mate,
She must espouse the everlasting Sea.
And what if she had seen those glories fade,
    Those titles vanish, and that strength decay;
Yet shall some tribute of regret be paid
    When her long life hath reached its final day:
Men are we, and must grieve when even the Shade
    Of that which once was great, is passed away.

488       *To Toussaint L'Ouverture,*
    *Leader of the African Slaves of San Domingo,*
          *Imprisoned by Napoleon*

TOUSSAINT, the most unhappy man of men!
    Whether the whistling rustic tend his plough
    Within thy hearing, or thy head be now
Pillowed in some deep dungeon's earless den;—
O miserable Chieftain! where and when
    Wilt thou find patience! Yet die not; do thou
    Wear rather in thy bonds a cheerful brow:
Though fallen thyself, never to rise again,
Live, and take comfort. Thou hast left behind
    Powers that will work for thee; air, earth, and skies;
There's not a breathing of the common wind
    That will forget thee; thou hast great allies;
    Thy friends are exultations, agonies,
And love, and man's unconquerable mind.


489

IT is not to be thought of that the Flood
    Of British freedom, which, to the open sea
    Of the world's praise, from dark antiquity
Hath flowed, 'with pomp of waters, unwithstood',—
Roused though it be full often to a mood
    Which spurns the check of salutary bands,—
    That this most famous Stream in bogs and sands
Should perish; and to evil and to good
Be lost for ever. In our halls is hung
    Armoury of the invincible Knights of old:
We must be free or die, who speak the tongue
    That Shakespeare spake; the faith and morals hold
Which Milton held.—In every thing we are sprung
    Of Earth's first blood, have titles manifold.

490          *The Solitary Reaper*

BEHOLD her, single in the field,
   Yon solitary Highland Lass!
Reaping and singing by herself;
   Stop here, or gently pass!
Alone she cuts and binds the grain,
And sings a melancholy strain;
O listen! for the vale profound
Is overflowing with the sound.

No nightingale did ever chaunt
   More welcome notes to weary bands
Of travellers in some shady haunt,
   Among Arabian sands:
A voice so thrilling ne'er was heard
In spring-time from the cuckoo-bird,
Breaking the silence of the seas
Among the farthest Hebrides.

Will no one tell me what she sings?—
   Perhaps the plaintive numbers flow
For old, unhappy, far-off things,
   And battles long ago:
Or is it some more humble lay,
Familiar matter of to-day?
Some natural sorrow, loss, or pain,
That has been, and may be again?

Whate'er the theme, the maiden sang
   As if her song could have no ending;
I saw her singing at her work,
   And o'er the sickle bending;—
I listened, motionless and still;
And, as I mounted up the hill,
The music in my heart I bore,
Long after it was heard no more.

491 *Daffodils*

I WANDERED lonely as a cloud
　That floats on high o'er vales and hills,
When all at once I saw a crowd,
　A host, of golden daffodils;
Beside the lake, beneath the trees,
Fluttering and dancing in the breeze.

Continuous as the stars that shine
　And twinkle on the Milky Way,
They stretched in never-ending line
　Along the margin of a bay:
Ten thousand saw I at a glance,
Tossing their heads in sprightly dance.

The waves beside them danced, but they
　Out-did the sparkling waves in glee:
A poet could not but be gay,
　In such a jocund company:
I gazed—and gazed—but little thought
What wealth the show to me had brought:

For oft, when on my couch I lie
　In vacant or in pensive mood,
They flash upon that inward eye
　Which is the bliss of solitude;
And then my heart with pleasure fills,
And dances with the daffodils.

492 *A Complaint*

THERE is a change—and I am poor;
Your love hath been, nor long ago,
A fountain at my fond heart's door,
Whose only business was to flow;
And flow it did; not taking heed
Of its own bounty, or my need.

What happy moments did I count!
Blest was I then all bliss above!
Now, for that consecrated fount
Of murmuring, sparkling, living love,
What have I? shall I dare to tell?
A comfortless and hidden well.

A well of love—it may be deep—
I trust it is,—and never dry:
What matter? if the waters sleep
In silence and obscurity.
—Such change, and at the very door
Of my fond heart, hath made me poor.

493                    *Personal Talk*

I AM not one who much or oft delight
    To season my fireside with personal talk,—
    Of friends, who live within an easy walk,
Or neighbours, daily, weekly, in my sight:
And, for my chance-acquaintance, ladies bright,
    Sons, mothers, maidens withering on the stalk,
    These all wear out of me, like forms, with chalk
Painted on rich men's floors, for one feast-night.
Better than such discourse doth silence long,
    Long, barren silence, square with my desire;
To sit without emotion, hope, or aim,
    In the loved presence of my cottage-fire,
And listen to the flapping of the flame,
Or kettle whispering its faint undersong.

494

THE world is too much with us; late and soon,
    Getting and spending, we lay waste our powers:
    Little we see in Nature that is ours;
We have given our hearts away, a sordid boon!
This sea that bares her bosom to the moon;
    The winds that will be howling at all hours,
    And are up-gathered now like sleeping flowers;
For this, for everything, we are out of tune;

It moves us not.—Great God! I'd rather be
  A Pagan suckled in a creed outworn;
So might I, standing on this pleasant lea,
  Have glimpses that would make me less forlorn;
Have sight of Proteus rising from the sea;
  Or hear old Triton blow his wreathèd horn.


495                          *Ode*
       *Intimations of Immortality from Recollections*
                  *of Early Childhood*

    THERE was a time when meadow, grove, and stream,
          The earth, and every common sight,
                  To me did seem
              Apparelled in celestial light,
      The glory and the freshness of a dream.
    It is not now as it hath been of yore;—
                Turn wheresoe'er I may,
                  By night or day,
    The things which I have seen I now can see no more.

              The rainbow comes and goes,
              And lovely is the rose;
              The moon doth with delight
        Look round her when the heavens are bare;
              Waters on a starry night
              Are beautiful and fair;
        The sunshine is a glorious birth;
        But yet I know, where'er I go,
    That there hath passed away a glory from the earth.

    Now, while the birds thus sing a joyous song,
          And while the young lambs bound
              As to the tabor's sound,
    To me alone there came a thought of grief:
    A timely utterance gave that thought relief,
              And I again am strong:
    The cataracts blow their trumpets from the steep;
    No more shall grief of mine the season wrong;
    I hear the echoes through the mountains throng,
    The winds come to me from the fields of sleep,

And all the earth is gay;
Land and sea
Give themselves up to jollity,
And with the heart of May
Doth every beast keep holiday;—
Thou Child of Joy,
Shout round me, let me hear thy shouts, thou happy
Shepherd-boy!

Ye blessed creatures, I have heard the call
Ye to each other make; I see
The heavens laugh with you in your jubilee;
My heart is at your festival,
My head hath its coronal,
The fullness of your bliss, I feel—I feel it all.
O evil day! if I were sullen
While Earth herself is adorning,
This sweet May-morning,
And the children are culling
On every side,
In a thousand valleys far and wide,
Fresh flowers; while the sun shines warm,
And the babe leaps up on his mother's arm:—
I hear, I hear, with joy I hear!
—But there's a tree, of many, one,
A single field which I have looked upon,
Both of them speak of something that is gone:
The pansy at my feet
Doth the same tale repeat:
Whither is fled the visionary gleam?
Where is it now, the glory and the dream?

Our birth is but a sleep and a forgetting:
The Soul that rises with us, our life's Star,
Hath had elsewhere its setting,
And cometh from afar:
Not in entire forgetfulness,
And not in utter nakedness,
But trailing clouds of glory do we come
From God, who is our home:
Heaven lies about us in our infancy!

Shades of the prison-house begin to close
  Upon the growing Boy,
But he beholds the light, and whence it flows,
  He sees it in his joy;
The Youth, who daily farther from the east
  Must travel, still is Nature's priest,
   And by the vision splendid
   Is on his way attended;
At length the Man perceives it die away,
And fade into the light of common day.

Earth fills her lap with pleasures of her own;
  Yearnings she hath in her own natural kind;
And, even with something of a mother's mind,
   And no unworthy aim,
  The homely nurse doth all she can
To make her foster-child, her inmate Man,
  Forget the glories he hath known,
And that imperial palace whence he came.

Behold the Child among his new-born blisses,
A six years' darling of a pigmy size!
See, where 'mid work of his own hand he lies,
Fretted by sallies of his mother's kisses,
With light upon him from his father's eyes!
See, at his feet, some little plan or chart,
Some fragment from his dream of human life,
Shaped by himself with newly-learnèd art;
   A wedding or a festival,
   A mourning or a funeral;
    And this hath now his heart,
   And unto this he frames his song:
    Then will he fit his tongue
To dialogues of business, love, or strife;
    But it will not be long
    Ere this be thrown aside,
    And with new joy and pride
The little actor cons another part;
Filling from time to time his 'humorous stage'
With all the Persons, down to palsied Age,
That Life brings with her in her equipage;
   As if his whole vocation
   Were endless imitation.

Thou, whose exterior semblance doth belie
      Thy soul's immensity;
Thou best philosopher, who yet dost keep
Thy heritage, thou eye among the blind,
That, deaf and silent, read'st the eternal deep,
Haunted for ever by the eternal mind,—
      Mighty prophet! Seer blest!
      On whom those truths do rest,
Which we are toiling all our lives to find,
In darkness lost, the darkness of the grave;
Thou, over whom thy Immortality
Broods like the Day, a master o'er a slave,
A presence which is not to be put by;
Thou little Child, yet glorious in the might
Of heaven-born freedom on thy being's height,
Why with such earnest pains dost thou provoke
The years to bring the inevitable yoke,
Thus blindly with thy blessedness at strife?
Full soon thy soul shall have her earthly freight,
And custom lie upon thee with a weight,
Heavy as frost, and deep almost as life!

      O joy! that in our embers
      Is something that doth live,
      That nature yet remembers
      What was so fugitive!
The thought of our past years in me doth breed
Perpetual benediction: not indeed
For that which is most worthy to be blest—
Delight and liberty, the simple creed
Of childhood, whether busy or at rest,
With new-fledged hope still fluttering in his breast:—
      Not for these I raise
      The song of thanks and praise;
    But for those obstinate questionings
    Of sense and outward things,
    Fallings from us, vanishings;
    Blank misgivings of a Creature
Moving about in worlds not realized,
High instincts before which our mortal Nature
Did tremble like a guilty thing surprised:
      But for those first affections,
      Those shadowy recollections,

Which, be they what they may,
Are yet the fountain-light of all our day,
Are yet a master-light of all our seeing;
Uphold us, cherish, and have power to make
Our noisy years seem moments in the being
Of the eternal Silence: truths that wake,
                To perish never:
Which neither listlessness, nor mad endeavour,
                Nor Man nor Boy,
Nor all that is at enmity with joy,
Can utterly abolish or destroy!
        Hence in a season of calm weather
            Though inland far we be,
Our souls have sight of that immortal sea
            Which brought us hither,
        Can in a moment travel thither,
And see the children sport upon the shore,
And hear the mighty waters rolling evermore.

Then sing, ye birds, sing, sing a joyous song!
            And let the young lambs bound
            As to the tabor's sound!
We in thought will join your throng,
            Ye that pipe and ye that play,
            Ye that through your hearts to-day
            Feel the gladness of the May!
What though the radiance which was once so bright
Be now for ever taken from my sight,
        Though nothing can bring back the hour
Of splendour in the grass, of glory in the flower;
            We will grieve not, rather find
            Strength in what remains behind;
            In the primal sympathy
            Which having been must ever be;
            In the soothing thoughts that spring
            Out of human suffering;
            In the faith that looks through death,
In years that bring the philosophic mind.

And O ye Fountains, Meadows, Hills, and Groves,
Forbode not any severing of our loves!
Yet in my heart of hearts I feel your might;
I only have relinquished one delight
To live beneath your more habitual sway.
I love the brooks which down their channels fret,
Even more than when I tripped lightly as they;
The innocent brightness of a new-born Day
        Is lovely yet;
The clouds that gather round the setting sun
Do take a sober colouring from an eye
That hath kept watch o'er man's mortality;
Another race hath been, and other palms are won.
Thanks to the human heart by which we live,
Thanks to its tenderness, its joys, and fears,
To me the meanest flower that blows can give
Thoughts that do often lie too deep for tears.

## *from* The Prelude

### *Childhood and School-Time*

496                (i)

   FAIR seed-time had my soul, and I grew up
Fostered alike by beauty and by fear;
Much favoured in my birthplace, and no less
In that beloved Vale to which, ere long,
I was transplanted. Well I call to mind
('Twas at an early age, ere I had seen
Nine summers) when upon the mountain slope
The frost and breath of frosty wind had snapped
The last autumnal crocus, 'twas my joy
To wander half the night among the cliffs
And the smooth hollows, where the woodcocks ran
Along the open turf. In thought and wish
That time, my shoulder all with springes hung,
I was a fell destroyer. On the heights
Scudding away from snare to snare, I plied
My anxious visitation, hurrying on,
Still hurrying, hurrying onward; moon and stars
Were shining o'er my head; I was alone,

And seemed to be a trouble to the peace
That was among them. Sometimes it befell
In these night-wanderings, that a strong desire
O'erpowered my better reason, and the bird
Which was the captive of another's toils
Became my prey; and, when the deed was done
I heard among the solitary hills
Low breathings coming after me, and sounds
Of indistinguishable motion, steps
Almost as silent as the turf they trod.
Nor less in springtime when on southern banks
The shining sun had from his knot of leaves
Decoyed the primrose flower, and when the vales
And woods were warm, was I a plunderer then
In the high places, on the lonesome peaks
Where'er, among the mountains and the winds,
The mother-bird had built her lodge. Though mean
My object, and inglorious, yet the end
Was not ignoble. Oh! when I have hung
Above the raven's nest, by knots of grass
And half-inch fissures in the slippery rock
But ill sustained, and almost, as it seemed,
Suspended by the blast which blew amain,
Shouldering the naked crag; Oh! at that time,
While on the perilous ridge I hung alone,
With what strange utterance did the loud dry wind
Blow through my ears! the sky seemed not a sky
Of earth, and with what motion moved the clouds!

497                    (ii)

WISDOM and Spirit of the universe!
Thou Soul that art the Eternity of Thought!
That giv'st to forms and images a breath
And everlasting motion! not in vain,
By day or star-light thus from my first dawn
Of childhood didst thou intertwine for me
The passions that build up our human soul,
Not with the mean and vulgar works of man,
But with high objects, with enduring things,

With life and nature, purifying thus
The elements of feeling and of thought,
And sanctifying, by such discipline,
Both pain and fear, until we recognize
A grandeur in the beatings of the heart.

Nor was this fellowship vouchsafed to me
With stinted kindness. In November days,
When vapours, rolling down the valleys, made
A lonely scene more lonesome; among woods
At noon, and 'mid the calm of summer nights,
When, by the margin of the trembling lake,
Beneath the gloomy hills I homeward went
In solitude, such intercourse was mine;
'Twas mine among the fields both day and night,
And by the waters all the summer long.

And in the frosty season, when the sun
Was set, and visible for many a mile
The cottage windows through the twilight blazed,
I heeded not the summons:—happy time
It was, indeed, for all of us; to me
It was a time of rapture: clear and loud
The village clock tolled six; I wheeled about,
Proud and exulting, like an untired horse,
That cares not for his home.—All shod with steel,
We hissed along the polished ice, in games
Confederate, imitative of the chase
And woodland pleasures, the resounding horn,
The pack loud bellowing, and the hunted hare.
So through the darkness and the cold we flew,
And not a voice was idle; with the din,
Meanwhile, the precipices rang aloud,
The leafless trees, and every icy crag
Tinkled like iron, while the distant hills
Into the tumult sent an alien sound
Of melancholy, not unnoticed, while the stars,
Eastward, were sparkling clear, and in the west
The orange sky of evening died away.

Not seldom from the uproar I retired
Into a silent bay, or sportively
Glanced sideway, leaving the tumultuous throng,
To cut across the image of a star
That gleamed upon the ice: and oftentimes
When we had given our bodies to the wind,
And all the shadowy banks, on either side,
Came sweeping through the darkness, spinning still
The rapid line of motion; then at once
Have I, reclining back upon my heels,
Stopped short, yet still the solitary cliffs
Wheeled by me, even as if the earth had rolled
With visible motion her diurnal round;
Behind me did they stretch in solemn train
Feebler and feebler, and I stood and watched
Till all was tranquil as a dreamless sleep.

## 498

SURPRISED by joy—impatient as the wind
  I turned to share the transport—Oh! with whom
  But thee, deep buried in the silent tomb,
That spot which no vicissitude can find?
Love, faithful love, recalled thee to my mind—
  But how could I forget thee? Through what power,
  Even for the least division of an hour,
Have I been so beguiled as to be blind
To my most grievous loss!—That thought's return
  Was the worst pang that sorrow ever bore,
Save one, one only, when I stood forlorn,
  Knowing my heart's best treasure was no more;
That neither present time, nor years unborn
  Could to my sight that heavenly face restore.

499 *Valediction to the River Duddon*

I THOUGHT of Thee, my partner and my guide,
  As being past away.—Vain sympathies!
  For, backward, Duddon! as I cast my eyes,
I see what was, and is, and will abide;
Still glides the Stream, and shall for ever glide;
  The Form remains, the Function never dies;
  While we, the brave, the mighty, and the wise,
We Men, who in our morn of youth defied
The elements, must vanish;—be it so!
  Enough, if something from our hands have power
  To live, and act, and serve the future hour;
And if, as toward the silent tomb we go,
  Through love, through hope, and faith's transcendent
    dower,
We feel that we are greater than we know.

500 *Mutability*

FROM low to high doth dissolution climb,
  And sink from high to low, along a scale
  Of awful notes, whose concord shall not fail;
A musical but melancholy chime,
Which they can hear who meddle not with crime,
  Nor avarice, nor over-anxious care.
  Truth fails not; but her outward forms that bear
The longest date do melt like frosty rime,
That in the morning whitened hill and plain
And is no more; drop like the tower sublime
  Of yesterday, which royally did wear
His crown of weeds, but could not even sustain
  Some casual shout that broke the silent air,
Or the unimaginable touch of Time.

501 *Extempore Effusion upon the Death of James Hogg*

WHEN first, descending from the moorlands,
I saw the stream of Yarrow glide
Along a bare and open valley,
The Ettrick Shepherd was my guide.

When last along its banks I wandered,
Through groves that had begun to shed
Their golden leaves upon the pathways,
My steps the Border-minstrel led.

The mighty Minstrel breathes no longer,
'Mid mouldering ruins low he lies;
And death upon the braes of Yarrow,
Has closed the Shepherd-poet's eyes:

Nor has the rolling year twice measured,
From sign to sign, its steadfast course,
Since every mortal power of Coleridge
Was frozen at its marvellous source;

The rapt One, of the godlike forehead,
The heaven-eyed creature sleeps in earth:
And Lamb, the frolic and the gentle,
Has vanished from his lonely hearth.

Like clouds that rake the mountain-summits,
Or waves that own no curbing hand,
How fast has brother followed brother,
From sunshine to the sunless land!

Yet I, whose lids from infant slumber
Were earlier raised, remain to hear
A timid voice, that asks in whispers,
'Who next will drop and disappear?'

Our haughty life is crowned with darkness,
Like London with its own black wreath,
On which with thee, O Crabbe! forth-looking,
I gazed from Hampstead's breezy heath.

As if but yesterday departed,
Thou too art gone before; but why,
O'er ripe fruit, seasonably gathered,
Should frail survivors heave a sigh?

Mourn rather for that holy spirit,
Sweet as the spring, as ocean deep;
For her who, ere her summer faded,
Has sunk into a breathless sleep.

No more of old romantic sorrows,
For slaughtered youth or love-lorn maid!
With sharper grief is Yarrow smitten,
And Ettrick mourns with her their poet dead.

# SIR WALTER SCOTT

1771–1832

502 *Patriotism*

BREATHES there the man, with soul so dead,
Who never to himself hath said,
　This is my own, my native land!
Whose heart hath ne'er within him burned,
As home his footsteps he hath turned,
　From wandering on a foreign strand!
If such there breathe, go, mark him well;
For him no Minstrel raptures swell;
High though his titles, proud his name,
Boundless his wealth as wish can claim;
Despite those titles, power, and pelf,
The wretch, concentred all in self,
Living, shall forfeit fair renown,
And, doubly dying, shall go down
To the vile dust, from whence he sprung,
Unwept, unhonoured, and unsung.

O Caledonia! stern and wild,
Meet nurse for a poetic child!
Land of brown heath and shaggy wood,
Land of the mountain and the flood,
Land of my sires! what mortal hand
Can e'er untie the filial band,
That knits me to thy rugged strand!
Still as I view each well-known scene,
Think what is now, and what hath been,

Seems as, to me, of all bereft,
Sole friends thy woods and streams were left;
And thus I love them better still,
Even in extremity of ill.
By Yarrow's stream still let me stray,
Though none should guide my feeble way;
Still feel the breeze down Ettrick break,
Although it chill my withered cheek;
Still lay my head by Teviot Stone,
Though there, forgotten and alone,
The Bard may draw his parting groan.

503                     *Lochinvar*

O, YOUNG Lochinvar is come out of the west,
Through all the wide Border his steed was the best;
And save his good broadsword he weapons had none,
He rode all unarmed, and he rode all alone.
So faithful in love, and so dauntless in war,
There never was knight like the young Lochinvar.

He stayed not for brake, and he stopped not for stone,
He swam the Eske river where ford there was none;
But ere he alighted at Netherby gate,
The bride had consented, the gallant came late:
For a laggard in love, and a dastard in war,
Was to wed the fair Ellen of brave Lochinvar.

So boldly he entered the Netherby Hall,
Among bride's-men, and kinsmen, and brothers, and all:
Then spoke the bride's father, his hand on his sword,
(For the poor craven bridegroom said never a word)
'O come ye in peace here, or come ye in war,
Or to dance at our bridal, young Lord Lochinvar?'

'I long wooed your daughter, my suit you denied;—
Love swells like the Solway, but ebbs like its tide—
And now am I come, with this lost love of mine,
To lead but one measure, drink one cup of wine.
There are maidens in Scotland more lovely by far,
That would gladly be bride to the young Lochinvar.'

The bride kissed the goblet: the knight took it up,
He quaffed off the wine, and he threw down the cup.
She looked down to blush, and she looked up to sigh,
With a smile on her lips, and a tear in her eye.
He took her soft hand, ere her mother could bar,—
'Now tread we a measure!' said the young Lochinvar.

So stately his form and so lovely her face,
That never a hall such a galliard did grace;
While her mother did fret, and her father did fume,
And the bridegroom stood dangling his bonnet and plume;
And the bride-maidens whispered, ''Twere better by far,
To have matched our fair cousin with young Lochinvar.'

One touch to her hand, and one word in her ear,
When they reached the hall-door, and the charger stood near;
So light to the croup the fair lady he swung,
So light to the saddle before her he sprung!
'She is won! we are gone, over bank, bush, and scaur;
They'll have fleet steeds that follow,' quoth young Lochinvar.

There was mounting 'mong Graemes of the Netherby clan;
Forsters, Fenwicks, and Musgraves, they rode and they ran:
There was racing and chasing on Cannobie Lee,
But the lost bride of Netherby ne'er did they see.
So daring in love, and so dauntless in war,
Have ye e'er heard of gallant like young Lochinvar?

504                    *Soldier, Rest!*

SOLDIER, rest! thy warfare o'er,
    Sleep the sleep that knows not breaking;
Dream of battled fields no more,
    Days of danger, nights of waking.
In our isle's enchanted hall,
    Hands unseen thy couch are strewing,
Fairy strains of music fall,
    Every sense in slumber dewing.
Soldier, rest! thy warfare o'er,
Dream of fighting fields no more:
Sleep the sleep that knows not breaking,
Morn of toil, nor night of waking.

No rude sound shall reach thine ear,
   Armour's clang, or war-steed champing,
Trump nor pibroch summon here
   Mustering clan, or squadron tramping.
Yet the lark's shrill fife may come
   At the day-break from the fallow,
And the bittern sound his drum,
   Booming from the sedgy shallow.
Ruder sounds shall none be near,
Guards nor warders challenge here,
Here's no war-steed's neigh and champing,
Shouting clans, or squadrons stamping.

Huntsman, rest! thy chase is done;
   While our slumbrous spells assail ye,
Dream not, with the rising sun,
   Bugles here shall sound reveille.
Sleep! the deer is in his den;
   Sleep! thy hounds are by thee lying;
Sleep! nor dream in yonder glen,
   How thy gallant steed lay dying.
Huntsman, rest! thy chase is done,
Think not of the rising sun,
For at dawning to assail ye,
Here no bugles sound reveille.


505                 *The Rover's Farewell*

A WEARY lot is thine, fair maid,
   A weary lot is thine!
To pull the thorn thy brow to braid,
   And press the rue for wine.
A lightsome eye, a soldier's mien,
   A feather of the blue,
A doublet of the Lincoln green—
   No more of me you knew,
      My Love!
No more of me you knew.

'This morn is merry June, I trow,
　　The rose is budding fain;
But she shall bloom in winter snow
　　Ere we two meet again.'
—He turned his charger as he spake
　　Upon the river shore,
He gave his bridle-reins a shake,
　　Said 'Adieu for evermore,
　　　　My Love!
And adieu for evermore.'

506　　　　*Madge Wildfire's Song*

PROUD Maisie is in the wood,
　　Walking so early;
Sweet Robin sits on the bush,
　　Singing so rarely.

'Tell me, thou bonny bird,
　　When shall I marry me?'
—'When six braw gentlemen
　　Kirkward shall carry ye.'

'Who makes the bridal bed,
　　Birdie, say truly?'
—'The grey-headed sexton
　　That delves the grave duly.

'The glow-worm o'er grave and stone
　　Shall light thee steady;
The owl from the steeple sing
　　Welcome, proud lady!'

507　　　　*Lucy Ashton's Song*

LOOK not thou on beauty's charming;
Sit thou still when kings are arming;
Taste not when the wine-cup glistens;
Speak not when the people listens;
Stop thine ear against the singer;
From the red gold keep thy finger;
Vacant heart and hand and eye,
Easy live and quiet die.

# SAMUEL TAYLOR COLERIDGE
### 1772–1834

508                               *Frost at Midnight*

THE Frost performs its secret ministry,
Unhelped by any wind. The owlet's cry
Came loud—and hark, again! loud as before.
The inmates of my cottage, all at rest,
Have left me to that solitude, which suits
Abstruser musings: save that at my side
My cradled infant slumbers peacefully.
'Tis calm indeed! so calm, that it disturbs
And vexes meditation with its strange
And extreme silentness. Sea, hill, and wood,
This populous village! Sea, and hill, and wood,
With all the numberless goings-on of life,
Inaudible as dreams! the thin blue flame
Lies on my low-burnt fire, and quivers not;
Only that film, which fluttered on the grate,
Still flutters there, the sole unquiet thing.
Methinks, its motion in this hush of nature
Gives it dim sympathies with me who live,
Making it a companionable form,
Whose puny flaps and freaks the idling Spirit
By its own moods interprets, everywhere
Echo or mirror seeking of itself,
And makes a toy of Thought.

                               But O! how oft,
How oft, at school, with most believing mind,
Presageful, have I gazed upon the bars,
To watch that fluttering *stranger*! and as oft
With unclosed lids, already had I dreamt
Of my sweet birth-place, and the old church-tower,
Whose bells, the poor man's only music, rang
From morn to evening, all the hot Fair-day,
So sweetly, that they stirred and haunted me
With a wild pleasure, falling on mine ear
Most like articulate sounds of things to come!
So gazed I, till the soothing things I dreamt,
Lulled me to sleep, and sleep prolonged my dreams!

And so I brooded all the following morn,
Awed by the stern preceptor's face, mine eye
Fixed with mock study on my swimming book:
Save if the door half opened, and I snatched
A hasty glance, and still my heart leaped up,
For still I hoped to see the *stranger's* face,
Townsman, or aunt, or sister more beloved,
My play-mate when we both were clothed alike!

    Dear Babe, that sleepest cradled by my side,
Whose gentle breathings, heard in this deep calm,
Fill up the interspersèd vacancies
And momentary pauses of the thought!
My babe so beautiful! it thrills my heart
With tender gladness, thus to look at thee,
And think that thou shalt learn far other lore,
And in far other scenes! For I was reared
In the great city, pent 'mid cloisters dim,
And saw nought lovely but the sky and stars.
But *thou*, my babe! shalt wander like a breeze
By lakes and sandy shores, beneath the crags
Of ancient mountain, and beneath the clouds,
Which image in their bulk both lakes and shores
And mountain crags: so shalt thou see and hear
The lovely shapes and sounds intelligible
Of that eternal language, which thy God
Utters, who from eternity doth teach
Himself in all, and all things in himself.
Great universal Teacher! he shall mould
Thy spirit, and by giving make it ask.

    Therefore all seasons shall be sweet to thee,
Whether the summer clothe the general earth
With greenness, or the redbreast sit and sing
Betwixt the tufts of snow on the bare branch
Of mossy apple-tree, while the nigh thatch
Smokes in the sun-thaw; whether the eave-drops fall
Heard only in the trances of the blast,
Or if the secret ministry of frost
Shall hang them up in silent icicles,
Quietly shining to the quiet Moon.

509    *The Rime of the Ancient Mariner*

### PART I

An ancient Mariner
meeteth three
Gallants bidden to a
wedding-feast, and
detaineth one.

IT is an ancient Mariner
And he stoppeth one of three.
'By thy long grey beard and glittering eye,
Now wherefore stopp'st thou me?

The Bridegroom's doors are opened wide,
And I am next of kin;
The guests are met, the feast is set:
Mayst hear the merry din.'

He holds him with his skinny hand,
'There was a ship,' quoth he.
'Hold off! unhand me, grey-beard loon!'
Eftsoons his hand dropt he.

The Wedding-
Guest is spellbound
by the eye of the old
seafaring man, and
constrained to hear
his tale.

He holds him with his glittering eye—
The Wedding-Guest stood still,
And listens like a three years' child:
The Mariner hath his will.

The Wedding-Guest sat on a stone:
He cannot choose but hear;
And thus spake on that ancient man,
The bright-eyed Mariner.

'The ship was cheered, the harbour cleared,
Merrily did we drop

The Mariner tells
how the ship sailed
southward with a
good wind and fair
weather, till it
reached the Line.

Below the kirk, below the hill,
Below the lighthouse top.

The Sun came up upon the left,
Out of the sea came he!
And he shone bright, and on the right
Went down into the sea.

Higher and higher every day,
Till over the mast at noon—'
The Wedding-Guest here beat his breast,
For he heard the loud bassoon.

# SAMUEL TAYLOR COLERIDGE

The Wedding-
Guest heareth the
bridal music; but
the Mariner con-
tinueth his tale.

The bride hath paced into the hall,
Red as a rose is she;
Nodding their heads before her goes
The merry minstrelsy.

The Wedding-Guest he beat his breast,
Yet he cannot choose but hear;
And thus spake on that ancient man,
The bright-eyed Mariner.

The ship driven by a
storm toward the
South Pole.

'And now the STORM-BLAST came, and he
Was tyrannous and strong:
He struck with his o'ertaking wings,
And chased us south along.

With sloping masts and dipping prow,
As who pursued with yell and blow
Still treads the shadow of his foe,
And forward bends his head,
The ship drove fast, loud roared the blast,
And southward aye we fled.

And now there came both mist and snow,
And it grew wondrous cold:
And ice, mast-high, came floating by,
As green as emerald.

The land of ice, and
of fearful sounds,
where no living
thing was to be seen.

And through the drifts the snowy clifts
Did send a dismal sheen:
Nor shapes of men nor beasts we ken—
The ice was all between.

The ice was here, the ice was there,
The ice was all around:
It cracked and growled, and roared and howled,
Like noises in a swound!

Till a great sea-bird,
called the Albatross,
came through the
snow-fog, and was
received with great
joy and hospitality.

At length did cross an Albatross,
Thorough the fog it came;
As if it had been a Christian soul,
We hailed it in God's name.

527

It ate the food it ne'er had eat,
And round and round it flew.
The ice did split with a thunder-fit;
The helmsman steered us through!

And lo! the
Albatross proveth a
bird of good omen,
and followeth the
ship as it returned
northward through
fog and floating ice.

And a good south wind sprung up behind;
The Albatross did follow,
And every day, for food or play,
Came to the mariners' hollo!

In mist or cloud, on mast or shroud,
It perched for vespers nine;
Whiles all the night, through fog-smoke white,
Glimmered the white Moon-shine.'

The ancient Mariner
inhospitably killeth
the pious bird of
good omen.

'God save thee, ancient Mariner!
From the fiends, that plague thee thus!—
Why look'st thou so?'—'With my cross-bow
I shot the ALBATROSS.'

## PART II

'The Sun now rose upon the right:
Out of the sea came he,
Still hid in mist, and on the left
Went down into the sea.

And the good south wind still blew behind,
But no sweet bird did follow,
Nor any day for food or play
Came to the mariners' hollo!

His shipmates cry
out against the
ancient Mariner, for
killing the bird of
good luck.

And I had done a hellish thing,
And it would work 'em woe:
For all averred, I had killed the bird
That made the breeze to blow.
Ah wretch! said they, the bird to slay,
That made the breeze to blow!

But when the fog cleared off, they justify the same, and thus make themselves accomplices in the crime.

Nor dim nor red, like God's own head,
The glorious Sun uprist:
Then all averred, I had killed the bird
That brought the fog and mist.
'Twas right, said they, such birds to slay,
That bring the fog and mist.

The fair breeze continues; the ship enters the Pacific Ocean, and sails northward, even till it reaches the Line.

The fair breeze blew, the white foam flew,
The furrow followed free;
We were the first that ever burst
Into that silent sea.

Down dropt the breeze, the sails dropt down,
'Twas sad as sad could be;
And we did speak only to break

The ship hath been suddenly becalmed.

The silence of the sea!

All in a hot and copper sky,
The bloody Sun, at noon,
Right up above the mast did stand,
No bigger than the Moon.

Day after day, day after day,
We stuck, nor breath nor motion;
As idle as a painted ship
Upon a painted ocean.

And the Albatross begins to be avenged.

Water, water, every where,
And all the boards did shrink;
Water, water, every where,
Nor any drop to drink.

The very deep did rot: O Christ!
That ever this should be!
Yea, slimy things did crawl with legs
Upon the slimy sea.

About, about, in reel and rout
The death-fires danced at night;
The water, like a witch's oils,
Burnt green, and blue and white.

A Spirit had
followed them; one
of the invisible in-
habitants of this
planet, neither
departed souls nor
And some in dreams assurèd were
Of the Spirit that plagued us so;
Nine fathom deep he had followed us
From the land of mist and snow.

angels; concerning whom the learned Jew Josephus, and the Platonic Constanti-
nopolitan, Michael Psellus, may be consulted. They are very numerous, and there
is no climate or element without one or more.

And every tongue, through utter drought,
Was withered at the root;
We could not speak, no more than if
We had been choked with soot.

The shipmates, in
their sore distress,
would fain throw
the whole guilt on
the ancient Mariner:
in sign whereof they
hang the dead sea-
bird round his neck.
Ah! well a-day! What evil looks
Had I from old and young!
Instead of the cross, the Albatross
About my neck was hung.'

## PART III

'There passed a weary time. Each throat
Was parched, and glazed each eye.
A weary time! a weary time!
How glazed each weary eye,
The ancient Mariner
beholdeth a sign in
the element afar off.
When looking westward, I beheld
A something in the sky.

At first it seemed a little speck,
And then it seemed a mist;
It moved and moved, and took at last
A certain shape, I wist.

A speck, a mist, a shape, I wist!
And still it neared and neared:
As if it dodged a water-sprite,
It plunged and tacked and veered.

At its nearer
approach, it seemeth
him to be a ship;
and at a dear ran-
som he freeth his
speech from the
bonds of thirst.
With throats unslaked, with black lips baked,
We could nor laugh nor wail;
Through utter drought all dumb we stood!
I bit my arm, I sucked the blood,
And cried, A sail! a sail!

With throats unslaked, with black lips baked,
Agape they heard me call:
*A flash of joy;*  Gramercy! they for joy did grin,
And all at once their breath drew in,
As they were drinking all.

*And horror follows.*
*For can it be a ship*  See! see! (I cried) she tacks no more!
*that comes onward*  Hither to work us weal;
*without wind or*  Without a breeze, without a tide,
*tide?*  She steadies with upright keel!

The western wave was all a-flame.
The day was well nigh done!
Almost upon the western wave
Rested the broad bright Sun;
When that strange shape drove suddenly
Betwixt us and the Sun.

*It seemeth him but*  And straight the Sun was flecked with bars,
*the skeleton of a*  (Heaven's Mother send us grace!)
*ship.*  As if through a dungeon-grate he peered
With broad and burning face.

Alas! (thought I, and my heart beat loud)
*And its ribs are seen*  How fast she nears and nears!
*as bars on the face*  Are those *her* sails that glance in the Sun,
*of the setting Sun.*  Like restless gossameres?
*The Spectre-*
*Woman and her*
*Death-mate, and no*  Are those *her* ribs through which the Sun
*other on board the*  Did peer, as through a grate?
*skeleton ship.*  And is that Woman all her crew?
Is that a DEATH? and are there two?
Is DEATH that woman's mate?

*Like vessel, like*  *Her* lips were red, *her* looks were free,
*crew!*  Her locks were yellow as gold:
Her skin was as white as leprosy,
The Night-mare LIFE-IN-DEATH was she,
Who thicks man's blood with cold.

*Death and Life-in-*  The naked hulk alongside came,
*Death have diced for*  And the twain were casting dice;
*the ship's crew, and*  "The game is done! I've won! I've won!"
*she (the latter)*  Quoth she, and whistles thrice.
*winneth the ancient*
*Mariner.*

No twilight within
the courts of the
Sun.

The Sun's rim dips; the stars rush out:
At one stride comes the dark;
With far-heard whisper, o'er the sea,
Off shot the spectre-bark.

At the rising of
the Moon,

We listened and looked sideways up!
Fear at my heart, as at a cup,
My life-blood seemed to sip!
The stars were dim, and thick the night,
The steersman's face by his lamp gleamed white;
From the sails the dew did drip—
Till clomb above the eastern bar
The hornèd Moon, with one bright star
Within the nether tip.

One after another,

One after one, by the star-dogged Moon,
Too quick for groan or sigh,
Each turned his face with a ghastly pang,
And cursed me with his eye.

His shipmates drop
down dead.

Four times fifty living men,
(And I heard nor sigh nor groan)
With heavy thump, a lifeless lump,
They dropped down one by one.

But Life-in-Death
begins her work
on the ancient
Mariner.

The souls did from their bodies fly,—
They fled to bliss or woe!
And every soul, it passed me by,
Like the whizz of my cross-bow!'

## PART IV

The Wedding-
Guest feareth that a
Spirit is talking to
him;

'I fear thee, ancient Mariner!
I fear thy skinny hand!
And thou art long, and lank, and brown,
As is the ribbed sea-sand.

I fear thee and thy glittering eye,
And thy skinny hand, so brown.'—

*But the ancient Mariner assureth him of his bodily life, and proceedeth to relate his horrible penance.*

'Fear not, fear not, thou Wedding-Guest!
This body dropt not down.

Alone, alone, all, all alone,
Alone on a wide wide sea!
And never a saint took pity on
My soul in agony.

*He despiseth the creatures of the calm,*

The many men, so beautiful!
And they all dead did lie:
And a thousand thousand slimy things
Lived on; and so did I.

*And envieth that they should live, and so many lie dead.*

I looked upon the rotting sea,
And drew my eyes away;
I looked upon the rotting deck,
And there the dead men lay.

I looked to heaven, and tried to pray;
But or ever a prayer had gusht,
A wicked whisper came, and made
My heart as dry as dust.

I closed my lids, and kept them close,
And the balls like pulses beat;
For the sky and the sea, and the sea and the sky
Lay like a load on my weary eye,
And the dead were at my feet.

*But the curse liveth for him in the eye of the dead men.*

The cold sweat melted from their limbs,
Nor rot nor reek did they:
The look with which they looked on me
Had never passed away.

An orphan's curse would drag to hell
A spirit from on high;
But oh! more horrible than that
Is the curse in a dead man's eye!
Seven days, seven nights, I saw that curse,
And yet I could not die.

*In his loneliness and fixedness he yearneth towards the journeying Moon, and the stars that still sojourn, yet still move onward; and every-where the blue sky belongs to them, and is their appoint-ed rest, and their native country and their own natural homes, which they enter unannounced, as lords that are certainly expected and yet there is a silent joy at their arrival.*

The moving Moon went up the sky,
And no where did abide:
Softly she was going up,
And a star or two beside—

Her beams bemocked the sultry main,
Like April hoar-frost spread;
But where the ship's huge shadow lay,
The charmèd water burnt alway
A still and awful red.

*By the light of the Moon he beholdeth God's creatures of the great calm.*

Beyond the shadow of the ship,
I watched the water-snakes:
They moved in tracks of shining white,
And when they reared, the elfish light
Fell off in hoary flakes.

Within the shadow of the ship
I watched their rich attire:
Blue, glossy green, and velvet black,
They coiled and swam; and every track
Was a flash of golden fire.

*Their beauty and their happiness.*

O happy living things! no tongue
Their beauty might declare:
A spring of love gushed from my heart,

*He blesseth them in his heart.*

And I blessed them unaware:
Sure my kind Saint took pity on me,
And I blessed them unaware.

*The spell begins to break.*

The self-same moment I could pray;
And from my neck so free
The Albatross fell off, and sank
Like lead into the sea.'

### PART V

'Oh sleep! it is a gentle thing,
Beloved from pole to pole!
To Mary Queen the praise be given!
She sent the gentle sleep from Heaven,
That slid into my soul.

534

By grace of the holy
Mother, the ancient
Mariner is refreshed
with rain.

The silly buckets on the deck,
That had so long remained,
I dreamt that they were filled with dew;
And when I awoke, it rained.

My lips were wet, my throat was cold,
My garments all were dank;
Sure I had drunken in my dreams,
And still my body drank.

I moved, and could not feel my limbs:
I was so light—almost
I thought that I had died in sleep,
And was a blessed ghost.

He heareth sounds
and seeth strange
sights and
commotions in the
sky and the element.

And soon I heard a roaring wind:
It did not come anear;
But with its sound it shook the sails,
That were so thin and sere.

The upper air burst into life!
And a hundred fire-flags sheen,
To and fro they were hurried about!
And to and fro, and in and out,
The wan stars danced between.

And the coming wind did roar more loud,
And the sails did sigh like sedge;
And the rain poured down from one black cloud;
The Moon was at its edge.

The thick black cloud was cleft, and still
The Moon was at its side:
Like waters shot from some high crag,
The lightning fell with never a jag,
A river steep and wide.

The bodies of the
ship's crew are
inspired and the ship
moves on;

The loud wind never reached the ship,
Yet now the ship moved on!
Beneath the lightning and the Moon
The dead men gave a groan.

They groaned, they stirred, they all uprose,
Nor spake, nor moved their eyes;
It had been strange, even in a dream,
To have seen those dead men rise.

The helmsman steered, the ship moved on;
Yet never a breeze up-blew;
The mariners all 'gan work the ropes,
Where they were wont to do;
They raised their limbs like lifeless tools—
We were a ghastly crew.

The body of my brother's son
Stood by me, knee to knee:
The body and I pulled at one rope,
But he said nought to me.'

'I fear thee, ancient Mariner!'
'Be calm, thou Wedding-Guest!
'Twas not those souls that fled in pain,
Which to their corses came again,
But a troop of spirits blest:

But not by the souls of the men, nor by daemons of earth or middle air, but by a blessed troop of angelic spirits, sent down by the invocation of the guardian saint.

For when it dawned—they dropped their arms,
And clustered round the mast;
Sweet sounds rose slowly through their mouths,
And from their bodies passed.

Around, around, flew each sweet sound,
Then darted to the Sun;
Slowly the sounds came back again,
Now mixed, now one by one.

Sometimes a-dropping from the sky
I heard the sky-lark sing;
Sometimes all little birds that are,
How they seemed to fill the sea and air
With their sweet jargoning!

And now 'twas like all instruments,
Now like a lonely flute;
And now it is an angel's song,
That makes the heavens be mute.

It ceased; yet still the sails made on
A pleasant noise till noon,
A noise like of a hidden brook
In the leafy month of June,
That to the sleeping woods all night
Singeth a quiet tune.

Till noon we quietly sailed on,
Yet never a breeze did breathe:
Slowly and smoothly went the ship,
Moved onward from beneath.

The lonesome Spirit from the South Pole carries on the ship as far as the Line, in obedience to the angelic troop, but still requireth vengeance.

Under the keel nine fathom deep,
From the land of mist and snow,
The spirit slid: and it was he
That made the ship to go.
The sails at noon left off their tune,
And the ship stood still also.

The Sun, right up above the mast,
Had fixed her to the ocean:
But in a minute she 'gan stir,
With a short uneasy motion—
Backwards and forwards half her length
With a short uneasy motion.

Then like a pawing horse let go,
She made a sudden bound:
It flung the blood into my head,
And I fell down in a swound.

The Polar Spirit's fellow-daemons, the invisible inhabitants of the element, take part in his wrong; and two of them relate, one to the other, that penance long and heavy for the ancient Mariner hath been accorded to the Polar Spirit, who returneth southward.

How long in that same fit I lay,
I have not to declare;
But ere my living life returned,
I heard and in my soul discerned
Two voices in the air.

"Is it he?" quoth one, "Is this the man?
By him who died on cross,
With his cruel bow he laid full low
The harmless Albatross.

537

The spirit who bideth by himself
In the land of mist and snow,
He loved the bird that loved the man
Who shot him with his bow."

The other was a softer voice,
As soft as honey-dew:
Quoth he, "The man hath penance done,
And penance more will do.'"

## Part VI

### FIRST VOICE

' "But tell me, tell me! speak again,
Thy soft response renewing—
What makes that ship drive on so fast?
What is the ocean doing?"

### SECOND VOICE

"Still as a slave before his lord,
The ocean hath no blast;
His great bright eye most silently
Up to the Moon is cast—

If he may know which way to go;
For she guides him smooth or grim.
See, brother, see! how graciously
She looketh down on him."

### FIRST VOICE

"But why drives on that ship so fast,
Without or wave or wind?"

### SECOND VOICE

"The air is cut away before,
And closes from behind.

Fly, brother, fly! more high, more high!
Or we shall be belated:
For slow and slow that ship will go,
When the Mariner's trance is abated."

The Mariner hath
been cast into a
trance; for the
angelic power
causeth the vessel
to drive northward
faster than human
life could endure.

# SAMUEL TAYLOR COLERIDGE

The supernatural
motion is retarded;
the Mariner awakes,
and his penance
begins anew.

I woke, and we were sailing on
As in a gentle weather:
'Twas night, calm night, the moon was high;
The dead men stood together.

All stood together on the deck,
For a charnel-dungeon fitter:
All fixed on me their stony eyes,
That in the Moon did glitter.

The pang, the curse, with which they died,
Had never passed away:
I could not draw my eyes from theirs,
Nor turn them up to pray.

The curse is finally
expiated.

And now this spell was snapt: once more
I viewed the ocean green,
And looked far forth, yet little saw
Of what had else been seen—

Like one, that on a lonesome road
Doth walk in fear and dread,
And having once turned round walks on,
And turns no more his head;
Because he knows, a frightful fiend
Doth close behind him tread.

But soon there breathed a wind on me,
Nor sound nor motion made:
Its path was not upon the sea,
In ripple or in shade.

It raised my hair, it fanned my cheek
Like a meadow-gale of spring—
It mingled strangely with my fears,
Yet it felt like a welcoming.

Swiftly, swiftly flew the ship,
Yet she sailed softly too:
Sweetly, sweetly blew the breeze—
On me alone it blew.

<table>
<tr><td>And the ancient<br>Mariner beholdeth<br>his native country.</td><td>

Oh! dream of joy! is this indeed<br>
The light-house top I see?<br>
Is this the hill? is this the kirk?<br>
Is this mine own countree?

</td></tr>
</table>

And the ancient
Mariner beholdeth
his native country.

Oh! dream of joy! is this indeed
The light-house top I see?
Is this the hill? is this the kirk?
Is this mine own countree?

We drifted o'er the harbour-bar,
And I with sobs did pray—
O let me be awake, my God!
Or let me sleep alway.

The harbour-bay was clear as glass,
So smoothly it was strewn!
And on the bay the moonlight lay,
And the shadow of the Moon.

The rock shone bright, the kirk no less,
That stands above the rock:
The moonlight steeped in silentness
The steady weathercock.

And the bay was white with silent light,
Till rising from the same,
*The angelic spirits* Full many shapes, that shadows were,
*leave the dead* In crimson colours came.
*bodies,*

*And appear in their* A little distance from the prow
*own forms of light.* Those crimson shadows were:
I turned my eyes upon the deck—
Oh, Christ! what saw I there!

Each corse lay flat, lifeless and flat,
And, by the holy rood!
A man all light, a seraph-man,
On every corse there stood.

This seraph-band, each waved his hand:
It was a heavenly sight!
They stood as signals to the land,
Each one a lovely light;

This seraph-band, each waved his hand,
No voice did they impart—
No voice; but oh! the silence sank
Like music on my heart.

But soon I heard the dash of oars,
I heard the Pilot's cheer;
My head was turned perforce away
And I saw a boat appear.

The Pilot and the Pilot's boy,
I heard them coming fast:
Dear Lord in Heaven! it was a joy
The dead men could not blast.

I saw a third—I heard his voice:
It is the Hermit good!
He singeth loud his godly hymns
That he makes in the wood.
He'll shrieve my soul, he'll wash away
The Albatross's blood.'

## Part VII

The Hermit of the<br>Wood,

'This Hermit good lives in that wood
Which slopes down to the sea.
How loudly his sweet voice he rears!
He loves to talk with marineres
That come from a far countree.

He kneels at morn, and noon, and eve—
He hath a cushion plump:
It is the moss that wholly hides
The rotted old oak-stump.

The skiff-boat neared: I heard them talk,
"Why, this is strange, I trow!
Where are those lights so many and fair,
That signal made but now?"

Approacheth the<br>ship with wonder.

"Strange, by my faith!" the Hermit said—
"And they answered not our cheer!
The planks looked warped! and see those sails,
How thin they are and sere!
I never saw aught like to them,
Unless perchance it were

Brown skeletons of leaves that lag
My forest-brook along;
When the ivy-tod is heavy with snow,
And the owlet whoops to the wolf below,
That eats the she-wolf's young."

"Dear Lord! it hath a fiendish look—
(The Pilot made reply)
I am a-feared"—"Push on, push on!"
Said the Hermit cheerily.

The boat came closer to the ship,
But I nor spake nor stirred;
The boat came close beneath the ship,
And straight a sound was heard.

*The ship suddenly
sinketh.*

Under the water it rumbled on,
Still louder and more dread:
It reached the ship, it split the bay;
The ship went down like lead.

*The ancient
Mariner is saved in
the Pilot's boat.*

Stunned by that loud and dreadful sound,
Which sky and ocean smote,
Like one that hath been seven days drowned
My body lay afloat;
But swift as dreams, myself I found
Within the Pilot's boat.

Upon the whirl, where sank the ship,
The boat spun round and round;
And all was still, save that the hill
Was telling of the sound.

I moved my lips—the Pilot shrieked
And fell down in a fit;
The holy Hermit raised his eyes,
And prayed where he did sit.

I took the oars: the Pilot's boy,
Who now doth crazy go
Laughed loud and long, and all the while
His eyes went to and fro.
"Ha! Ha!" quoth he, "full plain I see,
The Devil knows how to row."

And now, all in my own countree,
I stood on the firm land!
The Hermit stepped forth from the boat,
And scarcely he could stand.

The ancient Mariner
earnestly entreateth
the Hermit to
shrieve him; and the
penance of life falls
on him.

"O shrieve me, shrieve me, holy man!"
The Hermit crossed his brow.
"Say quick," quoth he, "I bid thee say—
What manner of man art thou?"

Forthwith this frame of mine was wrenched
With a woful agony,
Which forced me to begin my tale;
And then it left me free.

And ever and anon
throughout his
future life an agony
constraineth him to
travel from land to
land;

Since then, at an uncertain hour,
That agony returns:
And till my ghastly tale is told,
This heart within me burns.

I pass, like night, from land to land;
I have strange power of speech;
That moment that his face I see,
I know the man that must hear me:
To him my tale I teach.

What loud uproar bursts from that door!
The wedding-guests are there:
But in the garden-bower the bride
And bride-maids singing are:
And hark the little vesper bell,
Which biddeth me to prayer!

O Wedding-Guest! this soul hath been
Alone on a wide wide sea:
So lonely 'twas, that God himself
Scarce seemèd there to be.

O sweeter than the marriage-feast,
'Tis sweeter far to me,
To walk together to the kirk
With a goodly company!—

To walk together to the kirk
And all together pray,
While each to his great Father bends,
Old men, and babes, and loving friends
And youths and maidens gay!

*And to teach, by
his own example,
love and reverence
to all things that
God made and
loveth.*

Farewell, farewell! but this I tell
To thee, thou Wedding-Guest!
He prayeth well, who loveth well
Both man and bird and beast.

He prayeth best, who loveth best
All things both great and small;
For the dear God who loveth us,
He made and loveth all.'

The Mariner, whose eye is bright,
Whose beard with age is hoar,
Is gone: and now the Wedding-Guest
Turned from the bridegroom's door.

He went like one that hath been stunned,
And is of sense forlorn:
A sadder and a wiser man,
He rose the morrow morn.

510                    *Kubla Khan*

IN Xanadu did Kubla Khan
    A stately pleasure-dome decree:
Where Alph, the sacred river, ran
Through caverns measureless to man
    Down to a sunless sea.
So twice five miles of fertile ground
    With walls and towers were girdled round:
And there were gardens bright with sinuous rills
Where blossomed many an incense-bearing tree;
And here were forests ancient as the hills,
Enfolding sunny spots of greenery.

But O, that deep romantic chasm which slanted
Down the green hill athwart a cedarn cover!
A savage place! as holy and enchanted
As e'er beneath a waning moon was haunted
By woman wailing for her demon-lover!
And from this chasm, with ceaseless turmoil seething,
As if this earth in fast thick pants were breathing,
A mighty fountain momently was forced;
Amid whose swift half-intermitted burst
Huge fragments vaulted like rebounding hail,
Or chaffy grain beneath the thresher's flail:
And 'mid these dancing rocks at once and ever
It flung up momently the sacred river.
Five miles meandering with a mazy motion
Through wood and dale the sacred river ran,
Then reached the caverns measureless to man,
And sank in tumult to a lifeless ocean:
And 'mid this tumult Kubla heard from far
Ancestral voices prophesying war!

    The shadow of the dome of pleasure
      Floated midway on the waves;
    Where was heard the mingled measure
      From the fountain and the caves.
  It was a miracle of rare device,
  A sunny pleasure-dome with caves of ice!

    A damsel with a dulcimer
      In a vision once I saw:
    It was an Abyssinian maid,
      And on her dulcimer she played,
    Singing of Mount Abora.
    Could I revive within me,
      Her symphony and song,
  To such a deep delight 'twould win me,
  That with music loud and long,
  I would build that dome in air,
  That sunny dome! those caves of ice!
  And all who heard should see them there,
  And all should cry, Beware! Beware!
  His flashing eyes, his floating hair!

Weave a circle round him thrice,
  And close your eyes with holy dread,
  For he on honey-dew hath fed,
And drunk the milk of Paradise.


511                    *Dejection: an Ode*

  Late, late yestreen I saw the new Moon,
  With the old Moon in her arms;
  And I fear, I fear, my Master dear!
  We shall have a deadly storm.
            *Ballad of Sir Patrick Spence*

WELL! If the Bard was weather-wise, who made
  The grand old ballad of Sir Patrick Spence,
  This night, so tranquil now, will not go hence
Unroused by winds, that ply a busier trade
Than those which mould yon cloud in lazy flakes,
Or the dull sobbing draft, that moans and rakes
Upon the strings of this Æolian lute,
    Which better far were mute.
  For lo! the New-moon winter-bright!
  And overspread with phantom light,
  (With swimming phantom light o'erspread
  But rimmed and circled by a silver thread)
I see the old Moon in her lap, foretelling
  The coming-on of rain and squally blast.
And oh! that even now the gust were swelling,
  And the slant night-shower driving loud and fast!
Those sounds which oft have raised me, whilst they awed,
    And sent my soul abroad,
Might now perhaps their wonted impulse give,
Might startle this dull pain, and make it move and live!

A grief without a pang, void, dark, and drear,
  A stifled, drowsy, unimpassioned grief,
  Which finds no natural outlet, no relief,
    In word, or sigh, or tear—
O Lady! in this wan and heartless mood,
To other thoughts by yonder throstle wooed,

All this long eve, so balmy and serene,
Have I been gazing on the western sky,
  And its peculiar tint of yellow green:
And still I gaze—and with how blank an eye!
And those thin clouds above, in flakes and bars,
That give away their motion to the stars;
Those stars, that glide behind them or between,
Now sparkling, now bedimmed, but always seen:
Yon crescent Moon, as fixed as if it grew
In its own cloudless, starless lake of blue;
I see them all so excellently fair,
I see, not feel, how beautiful they are!

     My genial spirits fail;
     And what can these avail
To lift the smothering weight from off my breast?
     It were a vain endeavour,
     Though I should gaze for ever
On that green light that lingers in the west:
I may not hope from outward forms to win
The passion and the life, whose fountains are within.

O Lady! we receive but what we give,
And in our life alone does Nature live:
Ours is her wedding garment, ours her shroud!
  And would we aught behold, of higher worth,
Than that inanimate cold world allowed
To the poor loveless ever-anxious crowd,
  Ah! from the soul itself must issue forth
A light, a glory, a fair luminous cloud
     Enveloping the Earth—
And from the soul itself must there be sent
  A sweet and potent voice, of its own birth,
Of all sweet sounds the life and element!

O pure of heart! thou need'st not ask of me
What this strong music in the soul may be!
What, and wherein it doth exist,
This light, this glory, this fair luminous mist,
This beautiful and beauty-making power.
  Joy, virtuous Lady! Joy that ne'er was given,
Save to the pure, and in their purest hour,
Life, and Life's effluence, cloud at once and shower,

Joy, Lady! is the spirit and the power,
Which wedding Nature to us gives in dower
   A new Earth and new Heaven,
Undreamt of by the sensual and the proud—
Joy is the sweet voice, Joy the luminous cloud—
     We in ourselves rejoice!
And thence flows all that charms or ear or sight,
   All melodies the echoes of that voice,
All colours a suffusion from that light.

There was a time when, though my path was rough,
   This joy within me dallied with distress,
And all misfortunes were but as the stuff
   Whence Fancy made me dreams of happiness:
For hope grew round me, like the twining vine,
And fruits, and foliage, not my own, seemed mine.
But now afflictions bow me down to earth:
Nor care I that they rob me of my mirth;
    But oh! each visitation
Suspends what nature gave me at my birth,
   My shaping spirit of Imagination.
For not to think of what I needs must feel,
   But to be still and patient, all I can;
And haply by abstruse research to steal
   From my own nature all the natural man—
   This was my sole resource, my only plan:
Till that which suits a part infects the whole,
And now is almost grown the habit of my soul.

Hence, viper thoughts, that coil around my mind,
    Reality's dark dream!
I turn from you, and listen to the wind,
   Which long has raved unnoticed. What a scream
Of agony by torture lengthened out
That lute sent forth! Thou Wind, that rav'st without,
   Bare crag, or mountain-tairn, or blasted tree,
Or pine-grove whither woodman never clomb,
Or lonely house, long held the witches' home,
   Methinks were fitter instruments for thee,
Mad Lutanist! who in this month of showers,
Of dark-brown gardens, and of peeping flowers,

Mak'st Devils' yule, with worse than wintry song,
The blossoms, buds, and timorous leaves among.
  Thou Actor, perfect in all tragic sounds!
Thou mighty Poet, e'en to frenzy bold!
    What tell'st thou now about?
    'Tis of the rushing of an host in rout,
  With groans, of trampled men, with smarting wounds—
At once they groan with pain, and shudder with the cold!
But hush! there is a pause of deepest silence!
  And all that noise, as of a rushing crowd,
With groans, and tremulous shudderings—all is over—
It tells another tale, with sounds less deep and loud!
    A tale of less affright,
    And tempered with delight,
As Otway's self had framed the tender lay,—
    'Tis of a little child
    Upon a lonesome wild,
Not far from home, but she hath lost her way:
And now moans low in bitter grief and fear,
And now screams loud, and hopes to make her mother hear.

'Tis midnight, but small thoughts have I of sleep:
Full seldom may my friend such vigils keep!
Visit her, gentle Sleep! with wings of healing,
  And may this storm be but a mountain-birth,
May all the stars hang bright above her dwelling,
  Silent as though they watched the sleeping Earth!
    With light heart may she rise,
    Gay fancy, cheerful eyes,
  Joy lift her spirit, joy attune her voice;
To her may all things live, from pole to pole,
Their life the eddying of her living soul!
  O simple spirit, guided from above,
Dear Lady! friend devoutest of my choice,
Thus may'st thou ever, evermore rejoice.


512    *Time Real and Imaginary: an Allegory*

    ON the wide level of a mountain's head
    (I knew not where, but 'twas some faery place),
    Their pinions, ostrich-like, for sails outspread,
    Two lovely children run an endless race,

A sister and a brother!
This far outstripped the other;
Yet ever runs she with reverted face,
And looks and listens for the boy behind:
For he, alas! is blind!
O'er rough and smooth with even step he passed,
And knows not whether he be first or last.

513            *Work without Hope*

ALL Nature seems at work. Slugs leave their lair—
The bees are stirring—birds are on the wing—
And Winter, slumbering in the open air,
Wears on his smiling face a dream of Spring!
And I, the while, the sole unbusy thing,
Nor honey make, nor pair, nor build, nor sing.

Yet well I ken the banks where amaranths blow,
Have traced the fount whence streams of nectar flow.
Bloom, O ye amaranths! bloom for whom ye may,
For me ye bloom not! Glide, rich streams, away!
With lips unbrightened, wreathless brow, I stroll:
And would you learn the spells that drowse my soul?
Work without Hope draws nectar in a sieve,
And Hope without an object cannot live.


# WALTER SAVAGE LANDOR

## 1775–1864

514        *Corinna, to Tanagra, from Athens*

TANAGRA! think not I forget
   Thy beautifully storeyed streets;
Be sure my memory bathes yet
   In clear Thermodon, and yet greets
The blythe and liberal shepherd-boy
Whose sunny bosom swells with joy
When we accept his matted rushes
Upheaved with sylvan fruit; away he bounds, and blushes.

I promise to bring back with me
 What thou with transport wilt receive,
The only proper gift for thee,
 Of which no mortal shall bereave
In later times thy mouldering walls,
Until the last old turret falls;
A crown, a crown from Athens won,
A crown no God can wear, beside Latona's son.

There may be cities who refuse
 To their own child the honours due,
And look ungently on the Muse;
 But ever shall those cities rue
The dry, unyielding, niggard breast,
Offering no nourishment, no rest,
To that young head which soon shall rise
Disdainfully, in might and glory, to the skies.

Sweetly where caverned Dirce flows
 Do white-armed maidens chaunt my lay,
Flapping the while with laurel-rose
 The honey-gathering tribes away;
And sweetly, sweetly Attick tongues
Lisp your Corinna's early songs;
To her with feet more graceful come
The verses that have dwelt in kindred breasts at home.

O let thy children lean aslant
 Against the tender mother's knee,
And gaze into her face, and want
 To know what magic there can be
In words that urge some eyes to dance,
While others as in holy trance
Look up to heaven: be such my praise!
Why linger? I must haste, or lose the Delphic bays.

515

MOTHER, I cannot mind my wheel;
 My fingers ache, my lips are dry:
O, if you felt the pain I feel!
 But O, who ever felt as I?

No longer could I doubt him true—
    All other men may use deceit;
He always said my eyes were blue,
    And often swore my lips were sweet.


## *To Ianthe*

516                  (i)

PAST ruined Ilion Helen lives,
    Alcestis rises from the shades;
Verse calls them forth; 'tis verse that gives
    Immortal youth to mortal maids.

Soon shall Oblivion's deepening veil
    Hide all the peopled hills you see,
The gay, the proud, while lovers hail
    These many summers you and me.


517                  (ii)

FROM you, Ianthe, little troubles pass
    Like little ripples down a sunny river;
Your pleasures spring like daisies in the grass,
    Cut down, and up again as blithe as ever.


518               *Dirce*

STAND close around, ye Stygian set,
    With Dirce in one boat conveyed!
Or Charon, seeing, may forget
    That he is old and she a shade.

519 *Rose Aylmer*

AH, what avails the sceptred race!
  Ah, what the form divine!
What every virtue, every grace!
  Rose Aylmer, all were thine.

Rose Aylmer, whom these wakeful eyes
  May weep, but never see,
A night of memories and of sighs
  I consecrate to thee.

520 *Ternissa*

TERNISSA! you are fled!
I say not to the dead,
But to the happy ones who rest below:
  For, surely, surely, where
  Your voice and graces are,
Nothing of death can any feel or know.
  Girls who delight to dwell
  Where grows most asphodel,
Gather to their calm breasts each word you speak:
  The mild Persephone
  Places you on her knee,
And your cool palm smoothes down stern Pluto's cheek.

521

I STROVE with none, for none was worth my strife.
Nature I loved and, next to Nature, Art:
I warmed both hands before the fire of Life;
It sinks, and I am ready to depart.

522

DEATH stands above me, whispering low
  I know not what into my ear:
Of his strange language all I know
  Is, there is not a word of fear.

# CHARLES LAMB
## 1775–1834

523     *The Old Familiar Faces*

I HAVE had playmates, I have had companions,
In my days of childhood, in my joyful school-days,
All, all are gone, the old familiar faces.

I have been laughing, I have been carousing,
Drinking late, sitting late, with my bosom cronies,
All, all are gone, the old familiar faces.

I loved a love once, fairest among women:
Closed are her doors on me, I must not see her—
All, all are gone, the old familiar faces.

I have a friend, a kinder friend has no man;
Like an ingrate, I left my friend abruptly;
Left him, to muse on the old familiar faces.

Ghost-like I paced round the haunts of my childhood,
Earth seemed a desert I was bound to traverse,
Seeking to find the old familiar faces.

Friend of my bosom, thou more than a brother,
Why wert not thou born in my father's dwelling?
So might we talk of the old familiar faces—

How some they have died, and some they have left me,
And some are taken from me; all are departed;
All, all are gone, the old familiar faces.

# THOMAS CAMPBELL
## 1777–1844

524        *Ye Mariners of England*

YE Mariners of England
  That guard our native seas!
Whose flag has braved a thousand years
  The battle and the breeze!
Your glorious standard launch again
  To match another foe;
And sweep through the deep,
  While the stormy winds do blow!
While the battle rages loud and long
  And the stormy winds do blow.

The spirits of your fathers
  Shall start from every wave—
For the deck it was their field of fame,
  And Ocean was their grave:
Where Blake and mighty Nelson fell
  Your manly hearts shall glow,
As ye sweep through the deep,
  While the stormy winds do blow!
While the battle rages loud and long
  And the stormy winds do blow.

Britannia needs no bulwarks,
  No towers along the steep;
Her march is o'er the mountain-waves,
  Her home is on the deep.
With thunders from her native oak
  She quells the floods below,
As they roar on the shore,
  When the stormy winds do blow!
When the battle rages loud and long,
  And the stormy winds do blow.

The meteor flag of England
  Shall yet terrific burn;
Till danger's troubled night depart
  And the star of peace return.

Then, then, ye ocean-warriors!
　　Our song and feast shall flow
To the fame of your name,
　　When the storm has ceased to blow!
When the fiery fight is heard no more,
　　And the storm has ceased to blow.

525　　　　　　　*Hohenlinden*

ON Linden, when the sun was low,
All bloodless lay the untrodden snow,
And dark as winter was the flow
　　Of Iser, rolling rapidly.

But Linden saw another sight,
When the drum beat, at dead of night,
Commanding fires of death to light
　　The darkness of her scenery.

By torch and trumpet fast arrayed,
Each horseman drew his battle blade,
And furious every charger neighed
　　To join the dreadful revelry.

Then shook the hills, with thunder riven;
Then rushed the steed, to battle driven;
And, louder than the bolts of heaven,
　　Far flashed the red artillery.

But redder yet that light shall glow,
On Linden's hills of stainèd snow;
And bloodier yet, the torrent flow
　　Of Iser, rolling rapidly.

'Tis morn; but scarce yon level sun
Can pierce the war-clouds, rolling dun,
Where furious Frank, and fiery Hun,
　　Shout in their sulphurous canopy.

The combat deepens. On, ye brave,
Who rush to glory, or the grave!
Wave, Munich, all thy banners wave,
　　And charge with all thy chivalry!

THOMAS CAMPBELL

Few, few shall part, where many meet!
The snow shall be their winding sheet,
And every turf, beneath their feet,
   Shall be a soldier's sepulchre.


# THOMAS MOORE
1779–1852

      *The Light of Other Days*

OFT, in the stilly night,
  Ere slumber's chain has bound me,
Fond Memory brings the light
  Of other days around me:
  The smiles, the tears
  Of boyhood's years,
  The words of love then spoken;
    The eyes that shone,
    Now dimmed and gone,
  The cheerful hearts now broken!
Thus, in the stilly night,
  Ere slumber's chain has bound me,
Sad Memory brings the light
  Of other days around me.

When I remember all
  The friends, so linked together.
I've seen around me fall
  Like leaves in wintry weather,
    I feel like one
    Who treads alone
  Some banquet-hall deserted,
    Whose lights are fled,
    Whose garlands dead,
  And all but he departed!
Thus, in the stilly night,
  Ere slumber's chain has bound me.
Sad Memory brings the light
  Of other days around me.

527　　　　　　　*At the Mid Hour of Night*

AT the mid hour of night, when stars are weeping, I fly
To the lone vale we loved, when life shone warm in thine eye;
　　And I think that, if spirits can steal from the regions of air
　　To revisit past scenes of delight, thou wilt come to me there,
And tell me our love is remembered even in the sky.

Then I sing the wild song it once was such rapture to hear,
When our voices commingling breathed like one on the ear;
　　And as Echo far off through the vale my sad orison rolls,
　　I think, O my love! 'tis thy voice from the Kingdom of Souls
Faintly answering still the notes that once were so dear.


# JAMES LEIGH HUNT
## 1784–1859

528　　　　　　　*The Nile*

IT flows through old hushed Egypt and its sands,
　　Like some grave mighty thought threading a dream,
　　And times and things, as in that vision, seem
Keeping along it their eternal stands,—
Caves, pillars, pyramids, the shepherd bands
　　That roamed through the young world, the glory extreme
　　Of high Sesostris, and that southern beam,
The laughing queen that caught the world's great hands.
Then comes a mightier silence, stern and strong,
As of a world left empty of its throng,
　　And the void weighs on us; and then we wake,
And hear the fruitful stream lapsing along
　　Twixt villages, and think how we shall take
　　Our own calm journey on for human sake.

529 *Abou Ben Adhem*

ABOU BEN ADHEM (may his tribe increase!)
Awoke one night from a deep dream of peace,
And saw, within the moonlight in his room,
Making it rich, and like a lily in bloom,
An angel writing in a book of gold:—
Exceeding peace had made Ben Adhem bold,
And to the presence in the room he said,
   'What writest thou?'—The vision raised its head,
And with a look made of all sweet accord,
Answered, 'The names of those who love the Lord.'
'And is mine one?' said Abou. 'Nay, not so,'
Replied the angel. Abou spoke more low,
But cheerly still; and said, 'I pray thee, then,
Write me as one that loves his fellow men.'
   The angel wrote, and vanished. The next night
It came again with a great wakening light,
And showed the names whom love of God had blest,
And lo! Ben Adhem's name led all the rest.

530 *Rondeau*

JENNY kissed me when we met,
   Jumping from the chair she sat in;
Time, you thief, who love to get
   Sweets into your list, put that in!
Say I'm weary, say I'm sad,
   Say that health and wealth have missed me,
Say I'm growing old, but add,
   Jenny kissed me.

# THOMAS LOVE PEACOCK
## 1785–1866

531      *The War Song of Dinas Vawr*

THE mountain sheep are sweeter,
But the valley sheep are fatter;
We therefore deemed it meeter
To carry off the latter.
We made an expedition;
We met a host, and quelled it;
We forced a strong position,
And killed the men who held it.

On Dyfed's richest valley,
Where herds of kine were brousing,
We made a mighty sally,
To furnish our carousing.
Fierce warriors rushed to meet us;
We met them, and o'erthrew them:
They struggled hard to beat us;
But we conquered them, and slew them.

As we drove our prize at leisure,
The king marched forth to catch us:
His rage surpassed all measure,
But his people could not match us.
He fled to his hall-pillars;
And, ere our force we led off,
Some sacked his house and cellars,
While others cut his head off.

We there, in strife bewildering,
Spilt blood enough to swim in:
We orphaned many children,
And widowed many women.
The eagles and the ravens
We glutted with our foemen;
The heroes and the cravens,
The spearmen and the bowmen.

We brought away from battle,
And much their land bemoaned them,
Two thousand head of cattle,
And the head of him who owned them:
Ednyfed, king of Dyfed,
His head was borne before us;
His wine and beasts supplied our feasts,
And his overthrow, our chorus.

## 532 *Newark Abbey*
### *August, 1842, with a reminiscence of August, 1807*

I GAZE where August's sunbeam falls
Along these gray and lonely walls,
Till in its light absorbed appears
The lapse of five-and thirty years.
　　If change there be, I trace it not
In all this consecrated spot:
No new imprint of Ruin's march
On roofless wall and frameless arch:
The woods, the hills, the fields, the stream,
Are basking in the selfsame beam:
The fall, that turns the unseen mill,
As then it murmured, murmurs still.
It seems as if in one were cast
The present and the imaged past;
Spanning, as with a bridge sublime,
That fearful lapse of human time;
That gulf, unfathomably spread
Between the living and the dead.
　　For all too well my spirit feels
The only change this scene reveals.
The sunbeams play, the breezes stir,
Unseen, unfelt, unheard by her,
Who, on that long-past August day,
Beheld with me these ruins gray.
　　Whatever span the fates allow,
Ere I shall be as she is now,
Still, in my bosom's inmost cell,
Shall that deep-treasured memory dwell;
That, more than language can express,
Pure miracle of loveliness,

Whose voice so sweet, whose eyes so bright,
Were my soul's music, and its light,
In those blest days when life was new,
And hope was false, but love was true.

533                    *Rich and Poor*

THE poor man's sins are glaring;
In the face of ghostly warning
    He is caught in the fact
    Of an overt act—
Buying greens on Sunday morning.

The rich man's sins are hidden
In the pomp of wealth and station;
    And escape the sight
    Of the children of light,
Who are wise in their generation.

The rich man has a kitchen,
And cooks to dress his dinner;
    The poor who would roast
    To the baker's must post,
And thus becomes a sinner.

The rich man has a cellar,
And a ready butler by him;
    The poor must steer
    For his pint of beer
Where the saint can't choose but spy him.

The rich man's painted windows
Hide the concerts of the quality;
    The poor can but share
    A cracked fiddle in the air,
Which offends all sound morality.

The rich man is invisible
In the crowd of his gay society;
    But the poor man's delight
    Is a sore in the sight,
And a stench in the nose of piety.

## THOMAS LOVE PEACOCK

The rich man has a carriage
Where no rude eye can flout him;
The poor man's bane
Is a third class train,
With the day-light all about him.

The rich man goes out yachting,
Where sanctity can't pursue him;
The poor goes afloat
In a fourpenny boat,
Where the bishop groans to view him.

# GEORGE GORDON NOEL, LORD BYRON

### 1788-1824

534

SHE walks in beauty, like the night
Of cloudless climes and starry skies;
And all that's best of dark and bright
Meet in her aspect and her eyes:
Thus mellowed to that tender light
Which heaven to gaudy day denies.

One shade the more, one ray the less,
Had half impaired the nameless grace
Which waves in every raven tress,
Or softly lightens o'er her face;
Where thoughts serenely sweet express
How pure, how dear their dwelling-place.

And on that cheek, and o'er that brow,
So soft, so calm, yet eloquent,
The smiles that win, the tints that glow,
But tell of days in goodness spent,
A mind at peace with all below,
A heart whose love is innocent.

535

WHEN we two parted
   In silence and tears,
Half broken-hearted
   To sever for years,
Pale grew thy cheek and cold,
   Colder thy kiss;
Truly that hour foretold
   Sorrow to this.

The dew of the morning
   Sunk chill on my brow—
It felt like the warning
   Of what I feel now.
Thy vows are all broken,
   And light is thy fame;
I hear thy name spoken,
   And share in its shame.

They name thee before me,
   A knell to mine ear;
A shudder comes o'er me—
   Why wert thou so dear?
They know not I knew thee,
   Who knew thee too well:—
Long, long shall I rue thee,
   Too deeply to tell.

In secret we met—
   In silence I grieve,
That thy heart could forget,
   Thy spirit deceive.
If I should meet thee
   After long years,
How should I greet thee?
   With silence and tears.

536 *The Eve of Waterloo*

THERE was a sound of revelry by night,
   And Belgium's Capital had gathered then
   Her Beauty and her Chivalry, and bright
   The lamps shone o'er fair women and brave men;
   A thousand hearts beat happily; and when
   Music arose with its voluptuous swell,
   Soft eyes looked love to eyes which spake again,
   And all went merry as a marriage bell;
But hush! hark! a deep sound strikes like a rising knell!

Did ye not hear it?—No; 'twas but the wind,
   Or the car rattling o'er the stony street;
   On with the dance! let joy be unconfined;
   No sleep till morn, when Youth and Pleasure meet
   To chase the glowing Hours with flying feet—
   But hark!—that heavy sound breaks in once more,
   As if the clouds its echo would repeat;
   And nearer, clearer, deadlier than before!
Arm! Arm! it is—it is—the cannon's opening roar!

Within a windowed niche of that high hall
   Sate Brunswick's fated chieftain; he did hear
   That sound the first amidst the festival,
   And caught its tone with Death's prophetic ear;
   And when they smiled because he deemed it near,
   His heart more truly knew that peal too well
   Which stretched his father on a bloody bier,
   And roused the vengeance blood alone could quell;
He rushed into the field, and, foremost fighting, fell.

Ah! then and there was hurrying to and fro,
   And gathering tears, and tremblings of distress,
   And cheeks all pale, which but an hour ago
   Blushed at the praise of their own loveliness;
   And there were sudden partings, such as press
   The life from out young hearts, and choking sighs
   Which ne'er might be repeated; who could guess
   If ever more should meet those mutual eyes,
Since upon night so sweet such awful morn could rise!

# GEORGE GORDON NOEL, LORD BYRON

And there was mounting in hot haste: the steed,
  The mustering squadron, and the clattering car,
  Went pouring forward with impetuous speed,
  And swiftly forming in the ranks of war;
  And the deep thunder peal on peal afar;
  And near, the beat of the alarming drum
  Roused up the soldier ere the morning star;
  While thronged the citizens with terror dumb,
Or whispering, with white lips—'The foe! They come!
    they come!'

And wild and high the 'Cameron's Gathering' rose!
  The war-note of Lochiel, which Albyn's hills
  Have heard, and heard, too, have her Saxon foes:—
  How in the noon of night that pibroch thrills,
  Savage and shrill! But with the breath which fills
  Their mountain-pipe, so fill the mountaineers
  With the fierce native daring which instils
  The stirring memory of a thousand years,
And Evan's, Donald's fame rings in each clansman's ears!

And Ardennes waves above them her green leaves,
  Dewy with nature's tear-drops, as they pass,
  Grieving, if aught inanimate e'er grieves,
  Over the unreturning brave,—alas!
  Ere evening to be trodden like the grass
  Which now beneath them, but above shall grow
  In its next verdure, when this fiery mass
  Of living valour, rolling on the foe
And burning with high hope, shall moulder cold and low.

Last noon beheld them full of lusty life,
  Last eve in Beauty's circle proudly gay,
  The midnight brought the signal-sound of strife,
  The morn the marshalling in arms,—the day
  Battle's magnificently-stern array!
  The thunder-clouds close o'er it, which when rent
  The earth is covered thick with other clay
  Which her own clay shall cover, heaped and pent,
Rider and horse,—friend, foe,—in one red burial blent!

537 *The Dying Gladiator*

I SEE before me the Gladiator lie:
   He leans upon his hand—his manly brow
   Consents to death, but conquers agony,
   And his drooped head sinks gradually low—
   And through his side the last drops, ebbing slow
From the red gash, fall heavy, one by one,
Like the first of a thunder-shower; and now
The arena swims around him—he is gone,
Ere ceased the inhuman shout which hailed the wretch
    who won.

He heard it, but he heeded not—his eyes
   Were with his heart and that was far away;
   He recked not of the life he lost nor prize,
   But where his rude hut by the Danube lay,
   *There* were his young barbarians all at play,
   *There* was their Dacian mother—he, their sire,
Butchered to make a Roman holiday—
All this rushed with his blood—Shall he expire
And unavenged?—Arise! ye Goths, and glut your ire!

538 *from* The Prisoner of Chillon

A KIND of change came in my fate,
My keepers grew compassionate;
I know not what had made them so,
They were inured to sights of woe,
But so it was:—my broken chain
With links unfastened did remain,
And it was liberty to stride,
Along my cell from side to side,
And up and down, and then athwart,
And tread it over every part;
And round the pillars one by one,
Returning where my walk begun,
Avoiding only, as I trod,
My brothers' graves without a sod;

For if I thought with heedless tread
My step profaned their lowly bed,
My breath came gaspingly and thick,
And my crushed heart felt blind and sick.

I made a footing in the wall,
  It was not therefrom to escape,
For I had buried one and all,
  Who loved me in a human shape;
And the whole earth would henceforth be
A wider prison unto me:
No child, no sire, no kin had I,
No partner in my misery;
I thought of this, and I was glad,
For thought of them had made me mad;
But I was curious to ascend
To my barred windows, and to bend
Once more, upon the mountains high,
The quiet of a loving eye.

I saw them, and they were the same,
They were not changed like me in frame;
I saw their thousand years of snow
On high—their wide long lake below,
And the blue Rhone in fullest flow;
I heard the torrents leap and gush
O'er channelled rock and broken bush;
I saw the white-walled distant town,
And whiter sails go skimming down;
And then there was a little isle,
Which in my very face did smile,
  The only one in view;
A small green isle, it seemed no more,
Scarce broader than my dungeon floor,
But in it there were three tall trees,
And o'er it blew the mountain breeze,
And by it there were waters flowing,
And on it there were young flowers growing,
  Of gentle breath and hue.
The fish swam by the castle wall,
And they seemed joyous each and all;
The eagle rode the rising blast,
Methought he never flew so fast

As then to me he seemed to fly;
And then new tears came in my eye,
And I felt troubled—and would fain
I had not left my recent chain;
And when I did descend again,
The darkness of my dim abode
Fell on me as a heavy load;
It was as is a new-dug grave,
Closing o'er one we sought to save,—
And yet my glance, too much opprest,
Had almost need of such a rest.

It might be months, or years, or days,
   I kept no count, I took no note,
I had no hope my eyes to raise,
   And clear them of their dreary mote;
At last men came to set me free;
   I asked not why, and recked not where;
It was at length the same to me,
Fettered or fetterless to be,
   I learned to love despair.
And thus when they appeared at last,
And all my bonds aside were cast,
These heavy walls to me had grown
A hermitage—and all my own!
And half I felt as they were come
To tear me from a second home:
With spiders I had friendship made,
And watched them in their sullen trade,
Had seen the mice by moonlight play,
And why should I feel less than they?
We were all inmates of one place,
And I, the monarch of each race,
Had power to kill—yet, strange to tell!
In quiet we had learned to dwell;
My very chains and I grew friends,
So much a long communion tends
To make us what we are:—even I
Regained my freedom with a sigh.

539  *Prometheus*

TITAN! to whose immortal eyes
　The sufferings of mortality,
　Seen in their sad reality,
Were not as things that gods despise;
What was thy pity's recompense?
A silent suffering, and intense;
The rock, the vulture, and the chain,
All that the proud can feel of pain,
The agony they do not show,
The suffocating sense of woe,
　Which speaks but in its loneliness,
And then is jealous lest the sky
Should have a listener, nor will sigh
　Until its voice is echoless.

Titan! to thee the strife was given
　Between the suffering and the will,
　Which torture where they cannot kill;
And the inexorable Heaven,
And the deaf tyranny of Fate,
The ruling principle of Hate,
Which for its pleasure doth create
The things it may annihilate,
Refused thee even the boon to die:
The wretched gift Eternity
Was thine—and thou hast borne it well.
All that the Thunderer wrung from thee
Was but the menace which flung back
On him the torments of thy rack;
The fate thou didst so well foresee,
But would not to appease him tell;
And in thy Silence was his Sentence,
And in his Soul a vain repentance,
And evil dread so ill dissembled,
That in his hand the lightnings trembled.

Thy Godlike crime was to be kind,
　To render with thy precepts less
　The sum of human wretchedness,
And strengthen Man with his own mind;

But baffled as thou wert from high,
Still in thy patient energy,
In the endurance, and repulse
    Of thine impenetrable Spirit,
Which Earth and Heaven could not convulse,
    A mighty lesson we inherit:
Thou art a symbol and a sign
    To Mortals of their fate and force;
Like thee, Man is in part divine,
    A troubled stream from a pure source;
And Man in portions can foresee
His own funereal destiny;
His wretchedness, and his resistance,
And his sad unallied existence:
To which his Spirit may oppose
Itself—an equal to all woes,
    And a firm will, and a deep sense,
Which even in torture can descry
    Its own concentered recompense,
Triumphant where it dares defy,
And making Death a Victory.

540                  *Italy versus England*

WITH all its sinful doings, I must say,
    That Italy's a pleasant place to me,
Who love to see the sun shine every day,
    And vines (not nailed to walls) from tree to tree
Festooned, much like the back scene of a play,
    Or melodrame, which people flock to see,
When the first act is ended by a dance
In vineyards copied from the South of France.

I like on autumn evenings to ride out,
    Without being forced to bid my groom be sure
My cloak is round his middle strapped about,
    Because the skies are not the most secure;
I know too that, if stopped upon my route,
    Where the green alleys windingly allure,
Reeling with grapes red wagons choke the way.—
In England 'twould be dung, dust, or a dray.

I also like to dine on becaficas,
   To see the sun set, sure he'll rise to-morrow,
Not through a misty morning twinkling weak as
   A drunken man's dead eye in maudlin sorrow,
But with all Heaven to himself; the day will break as
   Beauteous as cloudless, nor be forced to borrow
That sort of farthing candlelight which glimmers
Where reeking London's smoky cauldron simmers.

I love the language, that soft bastard Latin,
   Which melts like kisses from a female mouth,
And sounds as if it should be writ on satin,
   With syllables which breathe of the sweet South,
And gentle liquids gliding all so pat in,
   That not a single accent seems uncouth,
Like our harsh northern whistling, grunting guttural,
Which we're obliged to hiss, and spit, and sputter all.

I like the women too (forgive my folly!),
   From the rich peasant cheek of ruddy bronze,
And large black eyes that flash on you a volley
   Of rays that say a thousand things at once,
To the high Dama's brow, more melancholy,
   But clear, and with a wild and liquid glance,
Heart on her lips, and soul within her eyes,
Soft as her clime, and sunny as her skies.

Eve of the land which still is Paradise!
   Italian Beauty! didst thou not inspire
Raphael, who died in thy embrace, and vies
   With all we know of Heaven, or can desire,
In what he hath bequeathed us?—in what guise,
   Though flashing from the fervour of the lyre,
Would *words* describe thy past and present glow,
While yet Canova can create below?

'England! with all thy faults I love thee still',
   I said at Calais, and have not forgot it;
I like to speak and lucubrate my fill;
   I like the government (but that is not it);
I like the freedom of the press and quill;
   I like the Habeas Corpus (when we've got it);
I like a Parliamentary debate,
Particularly when 'tis not too late;

I like the taxes, when they're not too many;
　　I like a seacoal fire, when not too dear;
I like a beef-steak, too, as well as any;
　　Have no objection to a pot of beer;
I like the weather,—when it is not rainy,
　　That is, I like two months of every year.
And so God save the Regent, Church, and King!
Which means that I like all and every thing.

Our standing army, and disbanded seamen,
　　Poor's rate, Reform, my own, the nation's debt,
Our little riots just to show we're free men,
　　Our trifling bankruptcies in the Gazette,
Our cloudy climate, and our chilly women,
　　All these I can forgive, and those forget,
And greatly venerate our recent glories,
And wish they were not owing to the Tories.

541　　　　　*So, we'll go no more a-roving*

So, we'll go no more a-roving
　　So late into the night,
Though the heart be still as loving,
　　And the moon be still as bright.

For the sword outwears its sheath,
　　And the soul wears out the breast,
And the heart must pause to breathe,
　　And love itself have rest.

Though the night was made for loving,
　　And the day returns too soon,
Yet we'll go no more a-roving
　　By the light of the moon.

542 *Growing Old*

BUT now at thirty years my hair is grey—
   (I wonder what it will be like at forty?
I thought of a peruke the other day—)
   My heart is not much greener; and, in short, I
Have squandered my whole summer while 'twas May,
   And feel no more the spirit to retort; I
Have spent my life, both interest and principal,
And deem not, what I deemed, my soul invincible.

No more—no more—Oh! never more on me
   The freshness of the heart can fall like dew,
Which out of all the lovely things we see
   Extracts emotions beautiful and new;
Hived in our bosoms like the bag o' the bee.
   Think'st thou the honey with those objects grew?
Alas! 'twas not in them, but in thy power
To double even the sweetness of a flower.

No more—no more—Oh! never more, my heart,
   Canst thou be my sole world, my universe!
Once all in all, but now a thing apart,
   Thou canst not be my blessing or my curse:
The illusion's gone for ever, and thou art
   Insensible, I trust, but none the worse,
And in thy stead I've got a deal of judgement,
Though Heaven knows how it ever found a lodgement.

My days of love are over; me no more
   The charms of maid, wife, and still less of widow,
Can make the fool of which they made before,—
   In short, I must not lead the life I did do;
The credulous hope of mutual minds is o'er,
   The copious use of claret is forbid too,
So for a good old-gentlemanly vice,
I think I must take up with avarice.

Ambition was my idol, which was broken
   Before the shrines of Sorrow, and of Pleasure;
And the two last have left me many a token
   O'er which reflection may be made at leisure:

Now, like Friar Bacon's Brazen Head, I've spoken,
   'Time is, Time was, Time's past': a chymic treasure
Is glittering Youth, which I have spent betimes—
My heart in passion, and my head on rhymes.

What is the end of Fame? 'tis but to fill
   A certain portion of uncertain paper:
Some liken it to climbing up a hill,
   Whose summit, like all hills, is lost in vapour;
For this men write, speak, preach, and heroes kill,
   And bards burn what they call their 'midnight taper',
To have, when the original is dust,
A name, a wretched picture and worse bust.

What are the hopes of man? Old Egypt's King
   Cheops erected the first Pyramid
And largest, thinking it was just the thing
   To keep his memory whole, and mummy hid;
But somebody or other rummaging,
   Burglariously broke his coffin's lid:
Let not a monument give you or me hopes,
Since not a pinch of dust remains of Cheops.

But I, being fond of true philosophy,
   Say very often to myself, 'Alas!
All things that have been born were born to die,
   And flesh (which Death mows down to hay) is grass;
You've passed your youth not so unpleasantly,
   And if you had it o'er again—'twould pass—
So thank your stars that matters are no worse,
And read your Bible, sir, and mind your purse.'

543               *The Isles of Greece*

    THE isles of Greece! the isles of Greece
       Where burning Sappho loved and sung,
    Where grew the arts of war and peace,
       Where Delos rose, and Phœbus sprung!
    Eternal summer gilds them yet,
    But all, except their sun, is set.

The Scian and the Teian muse,
  The hero's harp, the lover's lute,
Have found the fame your shores refuse:
  Their place of birth alone is mute
To sounds which echo further west
Than your sires' 'Islands of the Blest.'

The mountains look on Marathon—
  And Marathon looks on the sea;
And musing there an hour alone,
  I dreamed that Greece might still be free;
For standing on the Persians' grave,
I could not deem myself a slave.

A king sate on the rocky brow
  Which looks o'er sea-born Salamis;
And ships, by thousands, lay below,
  And men in nations;—all were his!
He counted them at break of day—
And when the sun set, where were they?

And where are they? and where art thou,
  My country? On thy voiceless shore
The heroic lay is tuneless now—
  The heroic bosom beats no more!
And must thy lyre, so long divine,
Degenerate into hands like mine?

'Tis something in the dearth of fame,
  Though linked among a fettered race,
To feel at least a patriot's shame,
  Even as I sing, suffuse my face;
For what is left the poet here?
For Greeks a blush—for Greece a tear.

Must *we* but weep o'er days more blest?
  Must *we* but blush?—Our fathers bled.
Earth! render back from out thy breast
  A remnant of our Spartan dead!
Of the three hundred grant but three,
To make a new Thermopylæ!

What, silent still? and silent all?
   Ah! no;—the voices of the dead
Sound like a distant torrent's fall,
   And answer, 'Let one living head,
But one, arise,—we come, we come!'
'Tis but the living who are dumb.

In vain—in vain: strike other chords;
   Fill high the cup with Samian wine!
Leave battles to the Turkish hordes,
   And shed the blood of Scio's vine!
Hark! rising to the ignoble call—
How answers each bold Bacchanal!

You have the Pyrrhic dance as yet;
   Where is the Pyrrhic phalanx gone?
Of two such lessons, why forget
   The nobler and the manlier one?
You have the letters Cadmus gave—
Think ye he meant them for a slave?

Fill high the bowl with Samian wine!
   We will not think of themes like these!
It made Anacreon's song divine:
   He served—but served Polycrates—
A tyrant; but our masters then
Were still, at least, our countrymen.

The tyrant of the Chersonese
   Was freedom's best and bravest friend;
*That* tyrant was Miltiades!
   O that the present hour would lend
Another despot of the kind!
Such chains as his were sure to bind.

Fill high the bowl with Samian wine!
   On Suli's rock, and Parga's shore,
Exists the remnant of a line
   Such as the Doric mothers bore;
And there, perhaps, some seed is sown,
The Heracleidan blood might own.

Trust not for freedom to the Franks—
　They have a king who buys and sells;
In native swords and native ranks
　The only hope of courage dwells:
But Turkish force and Latin fraud
Would break your shield, however broad.

Fill high the bowl with Samian wine!
　Our virgins dance beneath the shade—
I see their glorious black eyes shine;
　But gazing on each glowing maid,
My own the burning tear-drop laves,
To think such breasts must suckle slaves.

Place me on Sunium's marbled steep,
　Where nothing, save the waves and I,
May hear our mutual murmurs sweep;
　There, swan-like, let me sing and die:
A land of slaves shall ne'er be mine—
Dash down yon cup of Samian wine!

544　　　　　*Love and Death:*
　　　　　　*Last Lines*

I WATCHED thee when the foe was at our side,
　Ready to strike at him—or thee and me,
Were safety hopeless—rather than divide
　Aught with one loved save love and liberty.

I watched thee on the breakers, when the rock
　Received our prow and all was storm and fear,
And bade thee cling to me through every shock;
　This arm would be thy bark, or breast thy bier.

I watched thee when the fever glazed thine eyes,
　Yielding my couch and stretched me on the ground,
When overworn with watching, ne'er to rise
　From thence if thou an early grave hadst found.

The earthquake came, and rocked the quivering wall,
　And men and nature reeled as if with wine.
Whom did I seek around the tottering hall?
　For thee. Whose safety first provide for? Thine.

And when convulsive throes denied my breath
  The faintest utterance to my fading thought,
To thee—to thee—e'en in the gasp of death
  My spirit turned, oh! oftener than it ought.

Thus much and more; and yet thou lov'st me not,
  And never wilt! Love dwells not in our will.
Nor can I blame thee, though it be my lot
  To strongly, wrongly, vainly love thee still.


# CHARLES WOLFE

## 1791–1823

545                *The Burial of Sir John Moore*
                    *after Corunna*

NOT a drum was heard, not a funeral note,
  As his corse to the rampart we hurried;
Not a soldier discharged his farewell shot
  O'er the grave where our hero we buried.

We buried him darkly at dead of night,
  The sods with our bayonets turning,
By the struggling moonbeam's misty light
  And the lanthorn dimly burning.

No useless coffin enclosed his breast,
  Not in sheet or in shroud we wound him;
But he lay like a warrior taking his rest
  With his martial cloak around him.

Few and short were the prayers we said,
  And we spoke not a word of sorrow;
But we steadfastly gazed on the face that was dead,
  And we bitterly thought of the morrow.

We thought, as we hollowed his narrow bed
  And smoothed down his lonely pillow,
That the foe and the stranger would tread o'er his head,
  And we far away on the billow!

Lightly they'll talk of the spirit that's gone,
　　And o'er his cold ashes upbraid him—
But little he'll reck, if they let him sleep on
　　In the grave where a Briton has laid him.

But half of our heavy task was done
　　When the clock struck the hour for retiring;
And we heard the distant and random gun
　　That the foe was sullenly firing.

Slowly and sadly we laid him down,
　　From the field of his fame fresh and gory;
We carved not a line, and we raised not a stone,
　　But we left him alone with his glory.

# PERCY BYSSHE SHELLEY

## 1792–1822

546　　*Ozymandias*

I MET a traveller from an antique land
Who said: Two vast and trunkless legs of stone
Stand in the desert . . . Near them, on the sand,
Half sunk, a shattered visage lies, whose frown,
And wrinkled lip, and sneer of cold command,
Tell that its sculptor well those passions read
Which yet survive, stamped on these lifeless things,
The hand that mocked them, and the heart that fed:
And on the pedestal these words appear:
'My name is Ozymandias, king of kings:
Look on my works, ye Mighty, and despair!'
Nothing beside remains. Round the decay
Of that colossal wreck, boundless and bare
The lone and level sands stretch far away.

547            *England in 1819*

AN old, mad, blind, despised, and dying king,—
Princes, the dregs of their dull race, who flow
Through public scorn,—mud from a muddy spring,—
Rulers who neither see, nor feel, nor know,
But leech-like to their fainting country cling,
Till they drop, blind in blood, without a blow,—
A people starved and stabbed in the untilled field,—
An army, which liberticide and prey
Makes as a two-edged sword to all who wield,—
Golden and sanguine laws which tempt and slay;
Religion Christless, Godless—a book sealed;
A Senate,—Time's worst statute unrepealed,—
Are graves, from which a glorious Phantom may
Burst, to illumine our tempestuous day.

548            *from* Prometheus Unbound

*A Voice in the Air sings*

LIFE of Life! thy lips enkindle
    With their love the breath between them;
And thy smiles before they dwindle
    Make the cold air fire; then screen them
In those looks, where whoso gazes
Faints, entangled in their mazes.

Child of Light! thy limbs are burning
    Through the vest which seems to hide them;
As the radiant lines of morning
    Through the clouds ere they divide them;
And this atmosphere divinest
Shrouds thee wheresoe'er thou shinest.

Fair are others; none beholds thee,
    But thy voice sounds low and tender
Like the fairest, for it folds thee
    From the sight, that liquid splendour,
And all feel, yet see thee never,
As I feel now, lost for ever!

Lamp of Earth! where'er thou movest
  Its dim shapes are clad with brightness,
And the souls of whom thou lovest
  Walk upon the winds with lightness,
Till they fail, as I am failing,
Dizzy, lost, yet unbewailing!


### Asia Replies

My soul is an enchanted boat,
  Which, like a sleeping swan, doth float
Upon the silver waves of thy sweet singing;
  And thine doth like an angel sit
  Beside the helm conducting it,
Whilst all the winds with melody are ringing.
  It seems to float ever, for ever,
  Upon that many-winding river,
  Between mountains, woods, abysses,
  A paradise of wildernesses!
Till, like one in slumber bound,
Borne to the ocean, I float down, around,
Into a sea profound, of ever-spreading sound:

  Meanwhile thy spirit lifts its pinions
  In music's most serene dominions;
Catching the winds that fan that happy heaven.
  And we sail on, away, afar,
  Without a course, without a star,
But, by the instinct of sweet music driven;
  Till through Elysian garden islets
  By thee, most beautiful of pilots,
  Where never mortal pinnace glided,
  The boat of my desire is guided:
Realms where the air we breathe is love,
Which in the winds and on the waves doth move,
Harmonizing this earth with what we feel above.

  We have passed Age's icy caves,
  And Manhood's dark and tossing waves,
And Youth's smooth ocean, smiling to betray:
  Beyond the glassy gulfs we flee
  Of shadow-peopled Infancy,
Through Death and Birth, to a diviner day;

A paradise of vaulted bowers,
Lit by downward-gazing flowers,
And watery paths that wind between
Wildernesses calm and green,
Peopled by shapes too bright to see,
And rest, having beheld; somewhat like thee;
Which walk upon the sea, and chant melodiously!

549 *Ode to the West Wind*

I

O WILD West Wind, thou breath of Autumn's being,
 Thou from whose unseen presence the leaves dead
Are driven like ghosts from an enchanter fleeing,

 Yellow, and black, and pale, and hectic red,
Pestilence-stricken multitudes! O thou
 Who chariotest to their dark wintry bed

The wingèd seeds, where they lie cold and low,
 Each like a corpse within its grave, until
Thine azure sister of the Spring shall blow

 Her clarion o'er the dreaming earth, and fill
(Driving sweet buds like flocks to feed in air)
 With living hues and odours plain and hill;

Wild Spirit, which art moving everywhere;
Destroyer and preserver; hear, O hear!

II

Thou on whose stream, 'mid the steep sky's commotion,
 Loose clouds like earth's decaying leaves are shed,
Shook from the tangled boughs of heaven and ocean,

 Angels of rain and lightning! there are spread
On the blue surface of thine airy surge,
 Like the bright hair uplifted from the head

Of some fierce Maenad, even from the dim verge
 Of the horizon to the zenith's height,
The locks of the approaching storm. Thou dirge

Of the dying year, to which this closing night
Will be the dome of a vast sepulchre,
   Vaulted with all thy congregated might

Of vapours, from whose solid atmosphere
Black rain, and fire, and hail will burst: O hear!

### III

Thou who didst waken from his summer dreams
   The blue Mediterranean, where he lay,
Lulled by the coil of his crystalline streams,

   Beside a pumice isle in Baiae's bay,
And saw in sleep old palaces and towers
   Quivering within the wave's intenser day,

All overgrown with azure moss, and flowers
   So sweet, the sense faints picturing them! Thou
For whose path the Atlantic's level powers

   Cleave themselves into chasms, while far below
The sea-blooms and the oozy woods which wear
   The sapless foliage of the ocean, know

Thy voice, and suddenly grow gray with fear,
And tremble and despoil themselves: O hear!

### IV

If I were a dead leaf thou mightest bear;
   If I were a swift cloud to fly with thee;
A wave to pant beneath thy power, and share

   The impulse of thy strength, only less free
Than thou, O uncontrollable! if even
   I were as in my boyhood, and could be

The comrade of thy wanderings over heaven,
   As then, when to outstrip thy skiey speed
Scarce seemed a vision—I would ne'er have striven

   As thus with thee in prayer in my sore need.
O! lift me as a wave, a leaf, a cloud!
   I fall upon the thorns of life! I bleed!

A heavy weight of hours has chained and bowed
One too like thee—tameless, and swift, and proud.

### V

Make me thy lyre, even as the forest is:
   What if my leaves are falling like its own?
The tumult of thy mighty harmonies

   Will take from both a deep autumnal tone,
Sweet though in sadness. Be thou, Spirit fierce,
   My spirit! Be thou me, impetuous one!

Drive my dead thoughts over the universe,
   Like withered leaves, to quicken a new birth;
And, by the incantation of this verse,

   Scatter, as from an unextinguished hearth
Ashes and sparks, my words among mankind!
   Be through my lips to unawakened earth

The trumpet of a prophecy! O Wind,
If Winter comes, can Spring be far behind?

550          *Ode to a Skylark*

HAIL to thee, blithe spirit!
   Bird thou never wert—
That from heaven or near it
   Pourest thy full heart
In profuse strains of unpremeditated art.

Higher still and higher
   From the earth thou springest,
Like a cloud of fire;
   The blue deep thou wingest,
And singing still dost soar, and soaring ever singest.

In the golden lightning
   Of the sunken sun,
O'er which clouds are brightening,
   Thou dost float and run,
Like an unbodied joy whose race is just begun.

The pale purple even
    Melts around thy flight;
Like a star of heaven,
    In the broad daylight
Thou art unseen, but yet I hear thy shrill delight—

Keen as are the arrows
    Of that silver sphere
Whose intense lamp narrows
    In the white dawn clear,
Until we hardly see, we feel that it is there.

All the earth and air
    With thy voice is loud,
As, when night is bare,
    From one lonely cloud
The moon rains out her beams, and heaven is overflowed.

What thou art we know not;
    What is most like thee?
From rainbow clouds there flow not
    Drops so bright to see,
As from thy presence showers a rain of melody:—

Like a poet hidden
    In the light of thought,
Singing hymns unbidden,
    Till the world is wrought
To sympathy with hopes and fears it heeded not:

Like a high-born maiden
    In a palace tower,
Soothing her love-laden
    Soul in secret hour
With music sweet as love, which overflows her bower:

Like a glow-worm golden
    In a dell of dew,
Scattering unbeholden
    Its aërial hue
Among the flowers and grass which screen it from the view:

# PERCY BYSSHE SHELLEY

Like a rose embowered
    In its own green leaves,
By warm winds deflowered,
    Till the scent it gives
Makes faint with too much sweet these heavy-winged thieves:

Sound of vernal showers
    On the twinkling grass,
Rain-awakened flowers—
    All that ever was
Joyous and clear and fresh—thy music doth surpass.

Teach us, sprite or bird,
    What sweet thoughts are thine:
I have never heard
    Praise of love or wine
That panted forth a flood of rapture so divine.

Chorus hymeneal,
    Or triumphal chant,
Matched with thine would be all
    But an empty vaunt—
A thing wherein we feel there is some hidden want.

What objects are the fountains
    Of thy happy strain?
What fields, or waves, or mountains?
    What shapes of sky or plain?
What love of thine own kind? what ignorance of pain?

With thy clear keen joyance
    Languor cannot be:
Shadow of annoyance
    Never came near thee:
Thou lovest, but ne'er knew love's sad satiety.

Waking or asleep,
    Thou of death must deem
Things more true and deep
    Than we mortals dream,
Or how could thy notes flow in such a crystal stream?

We look before and after,
 And pine for what is not:
Our sincerest laughter
 With some pain is fraught;
Our sweetest songs are those that tell of saddest thought.

Yet, if we could scorn
 Hate and pride and fear,
If we were things born
 Not to shed a tear,
I know not how thy joy we ever should come near.

Better than all measures
 Of delightful sound,
Better than all treasures
 That in books are found,
Thy skill to poet were, thou scorner of the ground!

Teach me half the gladness
 That thy brain must know;
Such harmonious madness
 From my lips would flow,
The world should listen then, as I am listening now.

551    *To Maria Gisborne in England, from Italy*

 You are not here! the quaint witch Memory sees,
In vacant chairs, your absent images,
And points where once you sat, and now should be
But are not.—I demand if ever we
Shall meet as then we met;—and she replies,
Veiling in awe her second-sighted eyes;
'I know the past alone—but summon home
My sister Hope,—she speaks of all to come.'
But I, an old diviner, who knew well
Every false verse of that sweet oracle,
Turned to the sad enchantress once again,
And sought a respite from my gentle pain,
In citing every passage o'er and o'er
Of our communion—how on the sea-shore
We watched the ocean and the sky together,
Under the roof of blue Italian weather;

How I ran home through last year's thunder-storm,
And felt the transverse lightning linger warm
Upon my cheek—and how we often made
Feasts for each other, where good will outweighed
The frugal luxury of our country cheer,
As well it might, were it less firm and clear
Than ours must ever be;—and how we spun
A shroud of talk to hide us from the sun
Of this familiar life, which seems to be
But is not:—or is but quaint mockery
Of all we would believe, and sadly blame
The jarring and inexplicable frame
Of this wrong world:—and then anatomize
The purposes and thoughts of men whose eyes
Were closed in distant years;—or widely guess
The issue of the earth's great business,
When we shall be as we no longer are—
Like babbling gossips safe, who hear the war
Of winds, and sigh, but tremble not;—or how
You listened to some interrupted flow
Of visionary rhyme,—in joy and pain
Struck from the inmost fountains of my brain,
With little skill perhaps;—or how we sought
Those deepest wells of passion or of thought
Wrought by wise poets in the waste of years,
Staining their sacred waters with our tears;
Quenching a thirst ever to be renewed! . . .
                              You are now
In London, that great sea, whose ebb and flow
At once is deaf and loud, and on the shore
Vomits its wrecks, and still howls on for more.
Yet in its depth what treasures! You will see
That which was Godwin,—greater none than he
Though fallen—and fallen on evil times—to stand
Among the spirits of our age and land,
Before the dread tribunal of *to come*
The foremost,—while Rebuke cowers pale and dumb.
You will see Coleridge—he who sits obscure
In the exceeding lustre and the pure
Intense irradiation of a mind,
Which, with its own internal lightning blind,
Flags wearily through darkness and despair—
A cloud-encircled meteor of the air,

A hooded eagle among blinking owls.—
You will see Hunt—one of those happy souls
Which are the salt of the earth, and without whom
This world would smell like what it is—a tomb;
Who is, what others seem; his room no doubt
Is still adorned with many a cast from Shout,
With graceful flowers tastefully placed about;
And coronals of bay from ribbons hung,
And brighter wreaths in neat disorder flung;
The gifts of the most learned among some dozens
Of female friends, sisters-in-law, and cousins.
And there is he with his eternal puns,
Which beat the dullest brain for smiles, like duns
Thundering for money at a poet's door;
Alas! it is no use to say, 'I'm poor!'
Or oft in graver mood, when he will look
Things wiser than were ever read in book,
Except in Shakespeare's wisest tenderness.—
You will see Hogg,—and I cannot express
His virtues,—though I know that they are great,
Because he locks, then barricades the gate
Within which they inhabit;—of his wit
And wisdom, you'll cry out when you are bit.
He is a pearl within an oyster shell,
One of the richest of the deep;—and there
Is English Peacock, with his mountain Fair,
Turned into a Flamingo;—that shy bird
That gleams i' the Indian air—have you not heard
When a man marries, dies, or turns Hindoo,
His best friends hear no more of him?—but you
Will see him, and will like him too, I hope,
With the milk-white Snowdonian Antelope
Matched with this cameleopard—his fine wit
Makes such a wound, the knife is lost in it;
A strain too learned for a shallow age,
Too wise for selfish bigots; let his page,
Which charms the chosen spirits of the time,
Fold itself up for the serener clime
Of years to come, and find its recompense
In that just expectation.—Wit and sense,
Virtue and human knowledge; all that might
Make this dull world a business of delight,

Are all combined in Horace Smith.—And these,
With some exceptions, which I need not tease
Your patience by descanting on,—are all
You and I know in London.

                    I recall
My thoughts, and bid you look upon the night.
As water does a sponge, so the moonlight
Fills the void, hollow, universal air—
What see you?—unpavilioned Heaven is fair,
Whether the moon, into her chamber gone,
Leaves midnight to the golden stars, or wan
Climbs with diminished beams the azure steep;
Or whether clouds sail o'er the inverse deep,
Piloted by the many-wandering blast,
And the rare stars rush through them dim and fast:—
All this is beautiful in every land.—
But what see you beside?—a shabby stand
Of Hackney coaches—a brick house or wall
Fencing some lonely court, white with the scrawl
Of our unhappy politics;—or worse—
A wretched woman reeling by, whose curse
Mixed with the watchman's, partner of her trade,
You must accept in place of serenade—
Or yellow-haired Pollonia murmuring
To Henry, some unutterable thing.
I see a chaos of green leaves and fruit
Built round dark caverns, even to the root
Of the living stems that feed them—in whose bowers
There sleep in their dark dew the folded flowers;
Beyond, the surface of the unsickled corn
Trembles not in the slumbering air, and borne
In circles quaint, and ever-changing dance,
Like wingèd stars the fire-flies flash and glance,
Pale in the open moonshine, but each one
Under the dark trees seems a little sun,
A meteor tamed; a fixed star gone astray
From the silver regions of the milky way;—
Afar the Contadino's song is heard,
Rude, but made sweet by distance—and a bird
Which cannot be the Nightingale, and yet
I know none else that sings so sweet as it
At this late hour;—and then all is still—
Now—Italy or London, which you will!

552 *Mourn not for Adonais*

PEACE, peace! he is not dead, he doth not sleep—
He hath awakened from the dream of life—
'Tis we, who lost in stormy visions, keep
With phantoms an unprofitable strife,
And in mad trance, strike with our spirit's knife
Invulnerable nothings.—*We* decay
Like corpses in a charnel; fear and grief
Convulse us and consume us day by day,
And cold hopes swarm like worms within our living clay.

He has outsoared the shadow of our night;
Envy and calumny and hate and pain,
And that unrest which men miscall delight,
Can touch him not and torture not again;
From the contagion of the world's slow stain
He is secure, and now can never mourn
A heart grown cold, a head grown gray in vain;
Nor, when the spirit's self has ceased to burn,
With sparkless ashes load an unlamented urn.

He lives, he wakes—'tis Death is dead, not he;
Mourn not for Adonais.—Thou young Dawn,
Turn all thy dew to splendour, for from thee
The spirit thou lamentest is not gone;
Ye caverns and ye forests, cease to moan!
Cease, ye faint flowers and fountains, and thou Air,
Which like a mourning veil thy scarf hadst thrown
O'er the abandoned Earth, now leave it bare
Even to the joyous stars which smile on its despair!

He is made one with Nature: there is heard
His voice in all her music, from the moan
Of thunder, to the song of night's sweet bird;
He is a presence to be felt and known
In darkness and in light, from herb and stone,
Spreading itself where'er that Power may move
Which has withdrawn his being to its own;
Which wields the world with never-wearied love,
Sustains it from beneath, and kindles it above.

He is a portion of the loveliness
Which once he made more lovely: he doth bear
His part, while the one Spirit's plastic stress
Sweeps through the dull dense world, compelling there,
All new successions to the forms they wear;
Torturing the unwilling dross that checks its flight
To its own likeness, as each mass may bear;
And bursting in its beauty and its might
From trees and beasts and men into the Heaven's light.

The splendours of the firmament of time
May be eclipsed, but are extinguished not;
Like stars to their appointed height they climb,
And death is a low mist which cannot blot
The brightness it may veil. When lofty thought
Lifts a young heart above its mortal lair,
And love and life contend in it, for what
Shall be its earthly doom, the dead live there
And move like winds of light on dark and stormy air.

\*

The One remains, the many change and pass;
Heaven's light forever shines, Earth's shadows fly;
Life, like a dome of many-coloured glass,
Stains the white radiance of Eternity,
Until Death tramples it to fragments.—Die,
If thou wouldst be with that which thou dost seek!
Follow where all is fled!—Rome's azure sky,
Flowers, ruins, statues, music, words, are weak
The glory they transfuse with fitting truth to speak.

Why linger, why turn back, why shrink, my Heart?
Thy hopes are gone before: from all things here
They have departed; thou shouldst now depart!
A light is passed from the revolving year,
And man, and woman; and what still is dear
Attracts to crush, repels to make thee wither.
The soft sky smiles,—the low wind whispers near:
'Tis Adonais calls! oh, hasten thither,
No more let Life divide what Death can join together.

That Light whose smile kindles the Universe,
That Beauty in which all things work and move,
That Benediction which the eclipsing Curse
Of birth can quench not, that sustaining Love
Which through the web of being blindly wove
By man and beast and earth and air and sea,
Burns bright or dim, as each are mirrors of
The fire for which all thirst; now beams on me,
Consuming the last clouds of cold mortality.

The breath whose might I have invoked in song
Descends on me; my spirit's bark is driven,
Far from the shore, far from the trembling throng
Whose sails were never to the tempest given;
The massy earth and spherèd skies are riven!
I am borne darkly, fearfully, afar;
Whilst, burning through the inmost veil of Heaven,
The soul of Adonais, like a star,
Beacons from the abode where the Eternal are.

553                    *Hellas*

THE world's great age begins anew,
    The golden years return,
The earth doth like a snake renew
    Her winter weeds outworn:
Heaven smiles, and faiths and empires gleam
Like wrecks of a dissolving dream.

A brighter Hellas rears its mountains
    From waves serener far;
A new Peneus rolls his fountains
    Against the morning star;
Where fairer Tempes bloom, there sleep
Young Cyclads on a sunnier deep.

A loftier Argo cleaves the main,
    Fraught with a later prize;
Another Orpheus sings again,
    And loves, and weeps, and dies;
A new Ulysses leaves once more
Calypso for his native shore.

O write no more the tale of Troy,
   If earth Death's scroll must be—
Nor mix with Laian rage the joy
   Which dawns upon the free,
Although a subtler Sphinx renew
Riddles of death Thebes never knew.

Another Athens shall arise,
   And to remoter time
Bequeath, like sunset to the skies,
   The splendour of its prime;
And leave, if naught so bright may live,
All earth can take or Heaven can give.

Saturn and Love their long repose
   Shall burst, more bright and good
Than all who fell, than One who rose,
   Than many unsubdued:
Not gold, not blood, their altar dowers,
But votive tears and symbol flowers.

O cease! must hate and death return?
   Cease! must men kill and die?
Cease! drain not to its dregs the urn
   Of bitter prophecy!
The world is weary of the past—
O might it die or rest at last!

554        *To* ......................

ONE word is too often profaned
   For me to profane it;
One feeling too falsely disdained
   For thee to disdain it;
One hope is too like despair
   For prudence to smother;
And pity from thee more dear
   Than that from another.

I can give not what men call love:
　　But wilt thou accept not
The worship the heart lifts above
　　And the heavens reject not,
The desire of the moth for the star,
　　Of the night for the morrow,
The devotion to something afar
　　From the sphere of our sorrow?

555

MUSIC, when soft voices die,
Vibrates in the memory;
Odours, when sweet violets sicken,
Live within the sense they quicken.

Rose leaves, when the rose is dead,
Are heaped for the beloved's bed;
And so thy thoughts, when thou art gone,
Love itself shall slumber on.

556　　　　　　*Song*

A WIDOW bird sate mourning for her love
　　Upon a wintry bough;
The frozen wind crept on above,
　　The freezing stream below.

There was no leaf upon the forest bare,
　　No flower upon the ground,
And little motion in the air
　　Except the mill-wheel's sound.

557　　　　*A Lament*

O WORLD! O life! O time!
On whose last steps I climb,
　　Trembling at that where I had stood before;
When will return the glory of your prime?
　　　　No more—Oh, never more!

Out of the day and night
A joy has taken flight;
　Fresh spring, and summer, and winter hoar,
Move my faint heart with grief, but with delight
　　No more—Oh, never more!

558　　　　　*A Dirge*

　　Rough wind, that moanest loud
　　　Grief too sad for song;
　　Wild wind, when sullen cloud
　　　Knells all the night long;
　　Sad storm, whose tears are vain,
　　Bare woods, whose branches strain,
　　Deep caves and dreary main,—
　　　Wail, for the world's wrong!

# JOHN CLARE

## 1793–1864

559　　　　　*February*

　　The snow has left the cottage top;
　　　The thatch moss grows in brighter green;
　　And eaves in quick succession drop,
　　　Where grinning icicles have been,
　　Pit-patting with a pleasant noise
　　　In tubs set by the cottage-door;
　　While ducks and geese, with happy joys,
　　　Plunge in the yard-pond brimming o'er.

　　The sun peeps through the window-pane;
　　　Which children mark with laughing eye,
　　And in the wet street steal again
　　　To tell each other spring is nigh:
　　Then, as young hope the past recalls,
　　　In playing groups they often draw,
　　To build beside the sunny walls
　　　Their spring-time huts of sticks or straw.

And oft in pleasure's dreams they hie
  Round homesteads by the village side,
Scratching the hedgerow mosses by,
  Where painted pooty shells abide,
Mistaking oft the ivy spray
  For leaves that come with budding spring,
And wondering, in their search for play,
  Why birds delay to build and sing.

The milkmaid singing leaves her bed,
  As glad as happy thoughts can be,
While magpies chatter o'er her head
  As jocund in the change as she:
Her cows around the closes stray,
  Nor lingering wait the foddering-boy,
Tossing the molehills in their play,
  And staring round with frolic joy.

The shepherd now is often seen
  Near warm banks o'er his hook to bend,
Or o'er a gate or stile to lean,
  Chattering to a passing friend:
Ploughmen go whistling to their toils,
  And yoke again the rested plough;
And, mingling o'er the mellow soils,
  Boys shout, and whips are noising now.

The barking dogs, by lane and wood,
  Drive sheep afield from foddering ground;
And Echo, in her summer mood,
  Briskly mocks the cheering sound.
The flocks, as from a prison broke,
  Shake their wet fleeces in the sun,
While, following fast, a misty smoke
  Reeks from the moist grass as they run.

No more behind his master's heels
  The dog creeps on his winter-pace;
But cocks his tail, and o'er the fields
  Runs many a wild and random chase,
Following, in spite of chiding calls,
  The startled cat with harmless glee,
Scaring her up the weed-green walls,
  Or mossy mottled apple-tree.

As crows from morning perches fly,
 He barks and follows them in vain;
E'en larks will catch his nimble eye,
 And off he starts and barks again,
With breathless haste and blinded guess,
 Oft following where the hare hath gone,
Forgetting, in his joy's excess,
 His frolic puppy-days are done.

The hedgehog, from his hollow root,
 Sees the wood-moss clear of snow,
And hunts the hedge for fallen fruit—
 Crab, hip, and winter-bitten sloe;
But often checked by sudden fears,
 As shepherd-dog his haunt espies,
He rolls up in a ball of spears,
 And all his barking rage defies.

The gladdened swine bolt from the sty,
 And round the yard in freedom run,
Or stretching in their slumbers lie
 Beside the cottage in the sun.
The young horse whinnies to his mate
 And, sickening from the thresher's door,
Rubs at the straw-yard's banded gate,
 Longing for freedom on the moor.

The small birds think their wants are o'er,
 To see the snow-hills fret again,
And, from the barn's chaff-littered door,
 Betake them to the greening plain.
The woodman's robin startles coy,
 Nor longer to his elbow comes,
To peck, with hunger's eager joy,
 'Mong mossy stulps the littered crumbs.

'Neath hedge and walls that screen the wind,
 The gnats for play will flock together;
And e'en poor flies some hope will find
 To venture in the mocking weather;
From out their hiding-holes again,
 With feeble pace, they often creep
Along the sun-warmed window-pane,
 Like dreaming things that walk in sleep.

# JOHN CLARE

The mavis thrush with wild delight,
  Upon the orchard's dripping tree,
Mutters, to see the day so bright,
  Fragments of young Hope's poesy:
And oft Dame stops her buzzing wheel
  To hear the robin's note once more,
Who tootles while he pecks his meal
  From sweetbrier hips beside the door.

The sunbeams on the hedges lie,
  The south wind murmurs summer-soft;
The maids hang out white clothes to dry
  Around the elder-skirted croft:
A calm of pleasure listens round,
  And almost whispers winter by;
While Fancy dreams of summer's sound,
  And quiet rapture fills the eye.

Thus Nature of the spring will dream
  While south winds thaw; but soon again
Frost breathes upon the stiffening stream,
  And numbs it into ice: the plain
Soon wears its mourning garb of white;
  And icicles, that fret at noon,
Will eke their icy tails at night
  Beneath the chilly stars and moon.

Nature soon sickens of her joys,
  And all is sad and dumb again.
Save merry shouts of sliding boys
  About the frozen furrowed plain.
The foddering-boy forgets his song,
  And silent goes with folded arms;
And croodling shepherds bend along,
  Crouching to the whizzing storms.

560            *I am*

I AM: yet what I am none cares or knows,
    My friends forsake me like a memory lost;
I am the self-consumer of my woes,
    They rise and vanish in oblivious host,
Like shades in love and death's oblivion lost;
And yet I am, and live with shadows tost

Into the nothingness of scorn and noise,
    Into the living sea of waking dreams,
Where there is neither sense of life nor joys,
    But the vast shipwreck of my life's esteems;
And e'en the dearest—that I loved the best—
Are strange—nay, rather stranger than the rest.

I long for scenes where man has never trod,
    A place where woman never smiled or wept;
There to abide with my Creator, God,
    And sleep as I in childhood sweetly slept:
Untroubling and untroubled where I lie,
The grass below—above the vaulted sky.


561

            LOVE lives beyond
        The tomb, the earth, which fades like dew!
            I love the fond,
        The faithful, and the true.

            Love lives in sleep,
        The happiness of healthy dreams:
            Eve's dews may weep,
        But love delightful seems.

            'Tis seen in flowers,
        And in the morning's pearly dew;
            In earth's green hours,
        And in the heaven's eternal blue.

            'Tis heard in spring
        When light and sunbeams, warm and kind,
            On angel's wing
        Bring love and music to the mind.

And where is voice,
So young, so beautiful, and sweet
    As nature's choice,
Where spring and lovers meet?

    Love lives beyond
The tomb, the earth, the flowers, and dew.
    I love the fond,
The faithful, young, and true.

# JOHN KEATS

## 1795–1821

562         *On First Looking into Chapman's Homer*

MUCH have I travelled in the realms of gold,
    And many goodly states and kingdoms seen;
    Round many western islands have I been
Which bards in fealty to Apollo hold.
Oft of one wide expanse had I been told
    That deep-browed Homer ruled as his demesne:
    Yet did I never breathe its pure serene
Till I heard Chapman speak out loud and bold:
Then felt I like some watcher of the skies
    When a new planet swims into his ken;
Or like stout Cortez, when with eagle eyes
    He stared at the Pacific—and all his men
Looked at each other with a wild surmise—
    Silent, upon a peak in Darien.

563         *The Song of the Indian Maid*

BENEATH my palm-trees, by the river side,
I sat a-weeping: in the whole world wide
There was no one to ask me why I wept,—
        And so I kept
Brimming the water-lily cups with tears
        Cold as my fears.

Beneath my palm-trees, by the river side,
I sat a-weeping: what enamoured bride,
Cheated by shadowy wooer from the clouds,
    But hides and shrouds
Beneath dark palm-trees by a river side?

And as I sat, over the light blue hills
There came a noise of revellers: the rills
Into the wide stream came of purple hue—
    'Twas Bacchus and his crew!
The earnest trumpet spake, and silver thrills
From kissing cymbals made a merry din—
    'Twas Bacchus and his kin!
Like to a moving vintage down they came,
Crowned with green leaves, and faces all on flame;
All madly dancing through the pleasant valley,
    To scare thee, Melancholy!
O then, O then, thou wast a simple name!
And I forgot thee, as the berried holly
By shepherds is forgotten, when in June
Tall chestnuts keep away the sun and moon:—
    I rushed into the folly!

Within his car, aloft, young Bacchus stood,
Trifling his ivy-dart, in dancing mood,
    With sidelong laughing;
And little rills of crimson wine imbrued
His plump white arms and shoulders, enough white
    For Venus' pearly bite;
And near him rode Silenus on his ass,
Pelted with flowers as he on did pass
    Tipsily quaffing.

'Whence came ye, merry Damsels! whence came ye,
So many, and so many, and such glee?
Why have ye left your bowers desolate,
    Your lutes, and gentler fate?'—
'We follow Bacchus! Bacchus on the wing,
    A-conquering!
Bacchus, young Bacchus! good or ill betide,
We dance before him thorough kingdoms wide:—
Come hither, lady fair, and joinèd be
    To our wild minstrelsy!'

'Whence came ye, jolly Satyrs! whence came ye,
So many, and so many, and such glee?
Why have ye left your forest haunts, why left
      Your nuts in oak-tree cleft?'—
'For wine, for wine we left our kernel tree;
For wine we left our heath, and yellow brooms,
      And cold mushrooms;
For wine we follow Bacchus through the earth;
Great god of breathless cups and chirping mirth!
Come hither, lady fair, and joinèd be
      To our mad minstrelsy!'

Over wide streams and mountains great we went,
And, save when Bacchus kept his ivy tent,
Onward the tiger and the leopard pants,
      With Asian elephants:
Onward these myriads—with song and dance,
With zebras striped, and sleek Arabians' prance,
Web-footed alligators, crocodiles,
Bearing upon their scaly backs, in files,
Plump infant laughers mimicking the coil
Of seamen, and stout galley-rowers' toil:
With toying oars and silken sails they glide,
      Nor care for wind and tide.

Mounted on panthers' furs and lions' manes,
From rear to van they scour about the plains;
A three days' journey in a moment done;
And always, at the rising of the sun,
About the wilds they hunt with spear and horn,
      On spleenful unicorn.

I saw Osirian Egypt kneel adown
      Before the vine-wreath crown!
I saw parched Abyssinia rouse and sing
      To the silver cymbals' ring!
I saw the whelming vintage hotly pierce
      Old Tartary the fierce!
The kings of Ind their jewel-sceptres vail,
And from their treasures scatter pearlèd hail;
Great Brahma from his mystic heaven groans,
      And all his priesthood moans,
Before young Bacchus' eye-wink turning pale.

Into these regions came I, following him,
Sick-hearted, weary—so I took a whim
To stray away into these forests drear,
    Alone, without a peer:
And I have told thee all thou mayest hear.

564           *Ode to a Nightingale*

My heart aches, and a drowsy numbness pains
  My sense, as though of hemlock I had drunk,
Or emptied some dull opiate to the drains
  One minute past, and Lethe-wards had sunk:
'Tis not through envy of thy happy lot,
  But being too happy in thy happiness,
    That thou, light-wingèd Dryad of the trees,
      In some melodious plot
Of beechen green, and shadows numberless,
  Singest of summer in full-throated ease.

O for a draught of vintage! that hath been
  Cooled a long age in the deep-delvèd earth,
Tasting of Flora and the country-green,
  Dance, and Provençal song, and sunburnt mirth!
O for a beaker full of the warm South!
  Full of the true, the blushful Hippocrene,
    With beaded bubbles winking at the brim,
      And purple-stainèd mouth;
That I might drink, and leave the world unseen,
  And with thee fade away into the forest dim:

Fade far away, dissolve, and quite forget
  What thou among the leaves hast never known,
The weariness, the fever, and the fret
  Here, where men sit and hear each other groan;
Where palsy shakes a few, sad, last grey hairs,
  Where youth grows pale, and spectre-thin, and dies;
    Where but to think is to be full of sorrow
      And leaden-eyed despairs;
Where Beauty cannot keep her lustrous eyes,
  Or new Love pine at them beyond to-morrow.

Away! away! for I will fly to thee,
  Not charioted by Bacchus and his pards,
But on the viewless wings of Poesy,
  Though the dull brain perplexes and retards:
Already with thee! tender is the night,
  And haply the Queen-Moon is on her throne,
    Clustered around by all her starry Fays;
      But here there is no light,
Save what from heaven is with the breezes blown
  Through verdurous glooms and winding mossy ways.

I cannot see what flowers are at my feet,
  Nor what soft incense hangs upon the boughs,
But, in embalmèd darkness, guess each sweet
  Wherewith the seasonable month endows
The grass, the thicket, and the fruit-tree wild;
  White hawthorn, and the pastoral eglantine;
    Fast fading violets covered up in leaves;
      And mid-May's eldest child,
The coming musk-rose, full of dewy wine,
  The murmurous haunt of flies on summer eves.

Darkling I listen; and for many a time
  I have been half in love with easeful Death,
Called him soft names in many a musèd rhyme,
  To take into the air my quiet breath;
Now more than ever seems it rich to die,
  To cease upon the midnight with no pain,
    While thou art pouring forth thy soul abroad
      In such an ecstasy!
Still wouldst thou sing, and I have ears in vain—
  To thy high requiem become a sod.

Thou wast not born for death, immortal Bird!
  No hungry generations tread thee down;
The voice I hear this passing night was heard
  In ancient days by emperor and clown:
Perhaps the self-same song that found a path
  Through the sad heart of Ruth, when, sick for home,
    She stood in tears amid the alien corn;
      The same that oft times hath
Charmed magic casements, opening on the foam
  Of perilous seas, in faery lands forlorn.

Forlorn! the very word is like a bell
  To toll me back from thee to my sole self!
Adieu! the fancy cannot cheat so well
  As she is famed to do, deceiving elf.
Adieu! adieu! thy plaintive anthem fades
    Past the near meadows, over the still stream,
      Up the hill-side; and now 'tis buried deep
        In the next valley-glades:
  Was it a vision, or a waking dream?
  Fled is that music:—do I wake or sleep?

565          *Ode on a Grecian Urn*

Thou still unravished bride of quietness,
  Thou foster-child of Silence and slow Time,
Sylvan historian, who canst thus express
  A flowery tale more sweetly than our rhyme:
What leaf-fringed legend haunts about thy shape
    Of deities or mortals, or of both,
      In Tempe or the dales of Arcady?
  What men or gods are these? What maidens loth?
What mad pursuit? What struggle to escape?
    What pipes and timbrels? What wild ecstasy?

Heard melodies are sweet, but those unheard
  Are sweeter; therefore, ye soft pipes, play on;
Not to the sensual ear, but, more endeared,
  Pipe to the spirit ditties of no tone:
Fair youth, beneath the trees, thou canst not leave
    Thy song, nor ever can those trees be bare;
      Bold Lover, never, never canst thou kiss,
Though winning near the goal—yet, do not grieve;
    She cannot fade, though thou hast not thy bliss,
  For ever wilt thou love, and she be fair!

Ah, happy, happy boughs! that cannot shed
  Your leaves, nor ever bid the Spring adieu;
And, happy melodist, unwearièd,
  For ever piping songs for ever new;

More happy love! more happy, happy love!
  For ever warm and still to be enjoyed,
    For ever panting and for ever young;
All breathing human passion far above,
    That leaves a heart high-sorrowful and cloyed,
      A burning forehead, and a parching tongue.

Who are these coming to the sacrifice?
  To what green altar, O mysterious priest,
Lead'st thou that heifer lowing at the skies,
    And all her silken flanks with garlands drest?
What little town by river or sea-shore,
    Or mountain-built with peaceful citadel,
      Is emptied of this folk, this pious morn?
And, little town, thy streets for evermore
    Will silent be; and not a soul, to tell
      Why thou art desolate, can e'er return.

O Attic shape! fair attitude! with brede
  Of marble men and maidens overwrought,
With forest branches and the trodden weed;
    Thou, silent form! dost tease us out of thought
As doth eternity. Cold Pastoral!
    When old age shall this generation waste,
      Thou shalt remain, in midst of other woe
Than ours, a friend to man, to whom thou sayst,
'Beauty is truth, truth beauty,—that is all
      Ye know on earth, and all ye need to know.'

566                    *Ode to Psyche*

O GODDESS! hear these tuneless numbers, wrung
  By sweet enforcement and remembrance dear,
And pardon that thy secrets should be sung
    Even into thine own soft-conchèd ear:
Surely I dreamed today, or did I see
    The wingèd Psyche with awakened eyes?
I wandered in a forest thoughtlessly,
    And, on the sudden, fainting with surprise,

Saw two fair creatures, couchèd side by side
  In deepest grass, beneath the whispering roof
  Of leaves and trembled blossoms, where there ran
          A brooklet, scarce espied:
'Mid hushed, cool-rooted flowers fragrant-eyed,
  Blue, silver-white, and budded Tyrian.
They lay calm-breathing on the bedded grass;
  Their arms embracèd, and their pinions too;
  Their lips touched not, but had not bade adieu,
As if disjoinèd by soft-handed slumber,
And ready still past kisses to outnumber
  At tender eye-dawn of aurorean love:
          The wingèd boy I knew
  But who wast thou, O happy, happy dove?
          His Psyche true!

O latest-born and loveliest vision far
  Of all Olympus' faded hierarchy!
Fairer than Phoebe's sapphire-regioned star,
  Or Vesper, amorous glow-worm of the sky;
Fairer than these, though temple thou hast none,
          Nor altar heaped with flowers;
Nor Virgin choir to make delicious moan
          Upon the midnight hours;
No voice, no lute, no pipe, no incense sweet
  From chain-swung censer teeming;
No shrine, no grove, no oracle, no heat
  Of pale-mouthed prophet dreaming.

O brightest! though too late for antique vows,
  Too, too late for the fond believing lyre,
When holy were the haunted forest boughs,
  Holy the air, the water, and the fire;
Yet even in these days so far retired
  From happy pieties, thy lucent fans,
  Fluttering among the faint Olympians,
I see, and sing, by my own eyes inspired.
So let me be thy choir, and make a moan
          Upon the midnight hours;
Thy voice, thy lute, thy pipe, thy incense sweet
  From swingèd censer teeming:
Thy shrine, thy grove, thy oracle, thy heat
  Of pale-mouthed prophet dreaming.

Yes, I will be thy priest, and build a fane
  In some untrodden region of my mind,
Where branchèd thoughts, new grown with pleasant pain,
  Instead of pines shall murmur in the wind:
Far, far around shall those dark-clustered trees
  Fledge the wild-ridgèd mountains steep by steep;
And there by zephyrs, streams, and birds, and bees,
  The moss-lain Dryads shall be lulled to sleep;
And in the midst of this wide quietness
A rosy sanctuary will I dress
With the wreathed trellis of a working brain,
  With buds, and bells, and stars without a name,
With all the gardener Fancy e'er could feign,
  Who, breeding flowers, will never breed the same;
And there shall be for thee all soft delight
      That shadowy thought can win,
A bright torch, and a casement ope at night,
      To let the warm Love in!

567         *Ode on Melancholy*

No, no! go not to Lethe, neither twist
  Wolf's-bane, tight-rooted, for its poisonous wine;
Nor suffer thy pale forehead to be kist
  By nightshade, ruby grape of Proserpine;
Make not your rosary of yew-berries,
  Nor let the beetle, nor the death-moth be
    Your mournful Psyche, nor the downy owl
A partner in your sorrow's mysteries;
  For shade to shade will come too drowsily,
    And drown the wakeful anguish of the soul.

But when the melancholy fit shall fall
  Sudden from heaven like a weeping cloud,
That fosters the droop-headed flowers all,
  And hides the green hill in an April shroud;
Then glut thy sorrow on a morning rose,
  Or on the rainbow of the salt sand-wave,
    Or on the wealth of globèd peonies;
Or if thy mistress some rich anger shows,
  Emprison her soft hand, and let her rave,
    And feed deep, deep upon her peerless eyes.

She dwells with Beauty—Beauty that must die;
  And Joy, whose hand is ever at his lips
Bidding adieu; and aching Pleasure nigh,
  Turning to poison while the bee-mouth sips:
Ay, in the very temple of Delight
  Veiled Melancholy has her sovran shrine,
    Though seen of none save him whose strenuous tongue
Can burst Joy's grape against his palate fine;
  His soul shall taste the sadness of her might,
    And be among her cloudy trophies hung.

568               *To Autumn*

SEASON of mists and mellow fruitfulness!
  Close bosom-friend of the maturing sun;
Conspiring with him how to load and bless
  With fruit the vines that round the thatch-eaves run;
To bend with apples the mossed cottage-trees,
  And fill all fruit with ripeness to the core;
    To swell the gourd, and plump the hazel shells
With a sweet kernel; to set budding more,
  And still more, later flowers for the bees,
  Until they think warm days will never cease,
    For Summer has o'erbrimmed their clammy cells.

Who hath not seen thee oft amid thy store?
  Sometimes whoever seeks abroad may find
Thee sitting careless on a granary floor,
  Thy hair soft-lifted by the winnowing wind,
Or on a half-reaped furrow sound asleep,
  Drowsed with the fume of poppies, while thy hook
    Spares the next swath and all its twinèd flowers;
And sometimes like a gleaner thou dost keep
  Steady thy laden head across a brook;
  Or by a cider-press, with patient look,
    Thou watchest the last oozings hours by hours.

Where are the songs of Spring? Ay, where are they?
  Think not of them, thou hast thy music too,—
While barred clouds bloom the soft-dying day,
  And touch the stubble-plains with rosy hue;

Then in a wailful choir the small gnats mourn
  Among the river sallows, borne aloft
    Or sinking as the light wind lives or dies;
And full-grown lambs loud bleat from hilly bourn;
  Hedge-crickets sing; and now with treble soft
  The redbreast whistles from a garden-croft;
    And gathering swallows twitter in the skies.

569                 *Stanzas*

In a drear-nighted December,
  Too happy, happy tree,
Thy branches ne'er remember
  Their green felicity:
The north cannot undo them,
With a sleety whistle through them;
Nor frozen thawings glue them
  From budding at the prime.

In a drear-nighted December,
  Too happy, happy brook,
Thy bubblings ne'er remember
  Apollo's summer look;
But with a sweet forgetting,
They stay their crystal fretting,
Never, never petting
  About the frozen time.

Ah! would 'twere so with many
  A gentle girl and boy!
But were there ever any
  Writhed not at passèd joy?
To know the change and feel it,
When there is none to heal it,
Nor numbèd sense to steel it,
  Was never said in rhyme.

570 *La Belle Dame Sans Merci*

'O WHAT can ail thee, knight-at-arms,
    Alone and palely loitering?
The sedge has withered from the lake,
    And no birds sing.

'O what can ail thee, knight-at-arms,
    So haggard and so woe-begone?
The squirrel's granary is full,
    And the harvest's done.

'I see a lily on thy brow
    With anguish moist and fever dew;
And on thy cheek a fading rose
    Fast withereth too.'

'I met a lady in the meads,
    Full beautiful—a faery's child,
Her hair was long, her foot was light,
    And her eyes were wild.

'I made a garland for her head,
    And bracelets too, and fragrant zone;
She looked at me as she did love,
    And made sweet moan.

'I set her on my pacing steed
    And nothing else saw all day long,
For sideways would she lean, and sing
    A faery's song.

'She found me roots of relish sweet,
    And honey wild and manna dew,
And sure in language strange she said,
    "I love thee true!"

'She took me to her elfin grot,
    And there she wept and sighed full sore;
And there I shut her wild, wild eyes
    With kisses four.

'And there she lullèd me asleep,
　And there I dreamed—Ah! woe betide!
The latest dream I ever dreamed
　On the cold hill's side.

'I saw pale kings and princes too,
　Pale warriors, death-pale were they all;
Who cried—"La belle Dame sans Merci
　Hath thee in thrall!"

'I saw their starved lips in the gloam
　With horrid warning gapèd wide,
And I awoke and found me here
　On the cold hill's side.

'And this is why I sojourn here
　Alone and palely loitering,
Though the sedge is withered from the lake,
　And no birds sing.'

## 571 *Last Sonnet*

BRIGHT star, would I were steadfast as thou art—
　Not in lone splendour hung aloft the night,
And watching, with eternal lids apart,
　Like Nature's patient sleepless Eremite,
The moving waters at their priest-like task
　Of pure ablution round earth's human shores,
Or gazing on the new soft-fallen mask
　Of snow upon the mountains and the moors—
No—yet still steadfast, still unchangeable,
　Pillowed upon my fair love's ripening breast,
To feel for ever its soft fall and swell,
　Awake for ever in a sweet unrest,
　　Still, still to hear her tender-taken breath,
　　And so live ever—or else swoon to death.

572          *To Fanny Brawne*

THIS living hand, now warm and capable
Of earnest grasping, would, if it were cold
And in the icy silence of the tomb,
So haunt thy days and chill thy dreaming nights
That thou wouldst wish thine own heart dry of blood
So in my veins red life might stream again,
And thou be conscience-calmed—see here it is—
I hold it towards you.

# GEORGE DARLEY
## 1795–1846

573

WHEREFORE, unlaurelled Boy,
    Whom the contemptuous Muse will not inspire,
With a sad kind of joy,
    Still sing'st thou to thy solitary lyre?

The melancholy winds
    Pour through unnumbered reeds their idle woes:
And every Naiad finds
    A stream to weep her sorrow as it flows.

Her sighs unto the air
    The wood-maid's native oak doth broadly tell:
And Echo's fond despair
    Intelligible rocks re-syllable.

Wherefore then should not I,
    Albeit no haughty Muse my breast inspire,
Fated of grief to die,
    Impart it to a solitary lyre?

# GEORGE DARLEY

574            *Serenade of a Loyal Martyr*

SWEET in her green cell the Flower of Beauty slumbers,
    Lulled by the faint breezes sighing through her hair;
Sleeps she, and hears not the melancholy numbers
    Breathed to my sad lute amid the lonely air?

Down from the high cliffs the rivulet is teeming
    To wind round the willow banks that lure him from above:
O that in tears from my rocky prison streaming,
    I too could glide to the bower of my love!

Ah! where the woodbines with sleepy arms have wound her
    Opes she her eyelids at the dream of my lay,
Listening like the dove, while the fountains echo round her,
    To her lost mate's call in the forests far away?

Come then, my Bird!—for the peace thou ever bearest,
    Still heaven's messenger of comfort to me,
Come!—this fond bosom, my faithfullest! my fairest!
    Bleeds with its death-wound, but deeper yet for thee.


*from* Nepenthe

575              *The Phoenix*

O BLEST unfabled Incense Tree,
That burns in glorious Araby,
With red scent chalicing the air,
Till earth-life grow Elysian there!

Half buried to her flaming breast
In this bright tree, she makes her nest,
Hundred-sunned Phoenix! when she must
Crumble at length to hoary dust!

Her gorgeous death-bed! her rich pyre
Burnt up with aromatic fire!
Her urn, sight high from spoiler men!
Her birth-place when self-born again!

The mountainless green wilds among,
Here ends she her unechoing song!
With amber tears and odorous sighs
Mourned by the desert where she dies!

Laid like the young fawn mossily
In sun-green vales of Araby,
I woke, hard by the Phoenix tree
That with shadeless boughs flamed over me,
And upward called by a dumb cry
With moonbroad orbs of wonder, I
Beheld the immortal Bird on high
Glassing the great sun in her eye.
Steadfast she gazed upon his fire,
Still her destroyer and her sire!
As if to his her soul of flame
Had flown already, whence it came;
Like those that sit and glare so still,
Intense with their death struggle, till
We touch, and curdle at their chill!—
But breathing yet while she doth burn
The deathless Daughter of the sun!
Slowly to crimson embers turn
The beauties of the brightsome one.
O'er the broad nest her silver wings
Shook down their wasteful glitterings;
Her brinded neck high-arched in air
Like a small rainbow faded there;
But brighter glowed her plumy crown
Mouldering to golden ashes down;
With fume of sweet woods, to the skies,
Pure as a Saint's adoring sighs,
Warm as a prayer in Paradise,
Her life-breath rose in sacrifice!
The while with shrill triumphant tone
Sounding aloud, aloft, alone,
Ceaseless her joyful deathwail she
Sang to departing Araby!
Deep melancholy wonder drew
Tears from my heartspring at that view.
Like cresset shedding its last flare
Upon some wistful mariner,

The Bird, fast blending with the sky,
Turned on me her dead-gazing eye
Once—and as surge to shallow spray
Sank down to vapoury dust away!

O, fast her amber blood doth flow
    From the heart-wounded Incense Tree,
Fast as earth's deep-embosomed woe
    In silent rivulets to the sea!

Beauty may weep her fair first-born,
    Perchance in as resplendent tears,
Such golden dewdrops bow the corn
    When the stern sickleman appears.

But oh! such perfume to a bower
    Never allured sweet-seeking bee,
As to sip fast that nectarous shower
    A thirstier minstrel drew in me!

576              *Hundred-Gated Thebes*

HUNDRED-GATED City! thou
With gryphoned arch and avenue
For denizen giants, serve they now
But to let one poor mortal through?
Wide those streaming gates of war
Ran once with many a conqueror,
Horseman and chariot, to the sound
Of the dry serpent blazoning round
Theban Sesostris' dreaded name.
Where is now the loud acclaim?
Where the trample and the roll,
Shaking staid Earth like a mole?
Sunk to a rush's sigh!—Farewell,
Thou bleached wilderness o'erblown
By treeless winds, unscythable
Sandbanks, with peeping rocks bestrown,
That for thy barrenness seem'st to be
The bed of some retreated sea!
City of Apis, shrine and throne,

GEORGE DARLEY

Fare thee well! dispeopled sheer
Of thy mighty millions, here
Giant thing inhabits none,
But vast Desolation!

# THOMAS HOOD

1799–1845

*I Remember, I Remember*

I REMEMBER, I remember,
The house where I was born,
The little window where the sun
Came peeping in at morn;
He never came a wink too soon,
Nor brought too long a day,
But now, I often wish the night
Had borne my breath away!

I remember, I remember,
The roses, red and white,
The violets, and the lily-cups,
Those flowers made of light!
The lilacs where the robin built,
And where my brother set
The laburnum on his birthday,—
The tree is living yet!

I remember, I remember,
Where I was used to swing,
And thought the air must rush as fresh
To swallows on the wing;
My spirit flew in feathers then,
That is so heavy now,
And summer pools could hardly cool
The fever on my brow!

I remember, I remember,
The fir trees dark and high;
I used to think their slender tops
Were close against the sky:
It was a childish ignorance,
But now 'tis little joy
To know I'm farther off from heaven
Than when I was a boy.

578                     *Silence*

THERE is a silence where hath been no sound,
   There is a silence where no sound may be,
   In the cold grave—under the deep, deep sea,
Or in wide desert where no life is found,
Which hath been mute, and still must sleep profound;
   No voice is hushed—no life treads silently,
   But clouds and cloudy shadows wander free,
That never spoke, over the idle ground:
But in green ruins, in the desolate walls,
   Of antique palaces, where Man hath been,
Though the dun fox, or wild hyena, calls,
   And owls, that flit continually between,
Shriek to the echo, and the low winds moan,
There the true Silence is, self-conscious and alone.

579                     *Ruth*

SHE stood breast high amid the corn,
Clasped by the golden light of morn,
Like the sweetheart of the sun,
Who many a glowing kiss had won.

On her cheek an autumn flush,
Deeply ripened;—such a blush
In the midst of brown was born,
Like red poppies grown with corn.

Round her eyes her tresses fell,
Which were blackest none could tell,
But long lashes veiled a light,
That had else been all too bright.

And her hat, with shady brim,
Made her tressy forehead dim;—
Thus she stood amid the stooks,
Praising God with sweetest looks:—

Sure, I said, heaven did not mean,
Where I reap thou shouldst but glean,
Lay thy sheaf adown and come,
Share my harvest and my home.

580                *The Death-Bed*

WE watched her breathing through the night,
Her breathing soft and low,
As in her breast the wave of life
Kept heaving to and fro!

So silently we seemed to speak—
So slowly moved about!
As we had lent her half our powers
To eke her living out!

Our very hopes belied our fears
Our fears our hopes belied—
We thought her dying when she slept,
And sleeping when she died!

For when the morn came dim and sad—
And chill with early showers,
Her quiet eyelids closed—she had
Another morn than ours!

# THOMAS BABINGTON MACAULAY, LORD MACAULAY

### 1800–1859

581      *A Jacobite's Epitaph*

To my true king I offered free from stain
Courage and faith; vain faith, and courage vain.
For him I threw lands, honours, wealth, away,
And one dear hope, that was more prized than they.
For him I languished in a foreign clime,
Gray-haired with sorrow in my manhood's prime;
Heard on Lavernia Scargill's whispering trees,
And pined by Arno for my lovelier Tees;
Beheld each night my home in fevered sleep,
Each morning started from the dream to weep;
Till God, who saw me tried too sorely, gave
The resting-place I asked, an early grave.
O thou, whom chance leads to this nameless stone,
From that proud country which was once mine own,
By those white cliffs I never more must see,
By that dear language which I spake like thee,
Forget all feuds, and shed one English tear
O'er English dust. A broken heart lies here.

# WILLIAM BARNES

### 1801–1886

582      *A Winter Night*

It was a chilly winter's night;
   And frost was glittering on the ground,
And evening stars were twinkling bright;
   And from the gloomy plain around
     Came no sound,
But where, within the wood-girt tower,
The churchbell slowly struck the hour;

As if that all of human birth
  Had risen to the final day,
And soaring from the worn-out earth
  Were called in hurry and dismay,
      Far away;
And I alone of all mankind
Were left in loneliness behind.

583          *The Mother's Dream*

I'D a dream to-night
As I fell asleep,
Oh! the touching sight
Makes me still to weep:
Of my little lad,
Gone to leave me sad,
Aye, the child I had,
But was not to keep.

As in heaven high,
I my child did seek,
There, in train, came by
Children fair and meek,
Each in lily white,
With a lamp alight;
Each was clear to sight,
But they did not speak.

Then, a little sad,
Came my child in turn,
But the lamp he had,
Oh! it did not burn;
He, to clear my doubt,
Said, half turned about,
'Your tears put it out;
Mother, never mourn.'

584 *The Storm-Wind*

WHEN the swift-rolling brook, swollen deep,
   Rushes on by the alders, full speed,
And the wild-blowing winds lowly sweep
   O'er the quivering leaf and the weed,
And the willow tree writhes in each limb
Over sedge-beds that reel by the brim—

The man that is staggering by
   Holds his hat to his head by the brim;
And the girl as her hair-locks outfly,
   Puts a foot out, to keep herself trim,
And the quivering wavelings o'erspread
The small pool where the bird dips his head.

But out at my house, in the lee
   Of the nook, where the winds die away,
The light swimming airs, round the tree
   And the low-swinging ivy stem, play
So soft that a mother that's nigh
Her still cradle, may hear her babe sigh.

585 *Musings*

BEFORE the falling summer sun
   The boughs are shining all as gold,
And down below them waters run,
   As there in former years they rolled;
The poolside wall is glowing hot,
   The pool is in a dazzling glare,
And makes it seem as, ah! 'tis not,
   A summer when my life was fair.

The evening, gliding slowly by,
   Seems one of those that long have fled;
The night comes on to star the sky
   As then it darkened round my head.
A girl is standing by yon door,
   As one in happy times was there,
And this day seems, but is no more,
   A day when all my life was fair.

We hear from yonder feast the hum
  Of voices, as in summers past;
And hear the beatings of the drum
  Again come throbbing on the blast.
There neighs a horse in yonder plot,
  As once there neighed our petted mare,
And summer seems, but ah! is not
  The summer when our life was fair.


# WINTHROP MACKWORTH PRAED

### 1802–1839

586        *Good-Night to the Season*

GOOD-NIGHT to the Season! 'tis over!
  Gay dwellings no longer are gay;
The courtier, the gambler, the lover,
  Are scattered like swallows away:
There's nobody left to invite one,
  Except my good uncle and spouse;
My mistress is bathing at Brighton,
  My patron is sailing at Cowes:
For want of a better employment,
  Till Ponto and Don can get out,
I'll cultivate rural enjoyment,
  And angle immensely for trout.

Good-night to the Season!—the lobbies,
  Their changes, and rumours of change,
Which startled the rustic Sir Bobbies,
  And made all the Bishops look strange:
The breaches, and battles, and blunders,
  Performed by the Commons and Peers;
The Marquis's eloquent thunders,
  The Baronet's eloquent ears:
Denouncings of Papists and treasons,
  Of foreign dominion and oats;
Misrepresentations of reasons,
  And misunderstandings of notes.

Good-night to the Season!—the buildings
   Enough to make Inigo sick;
The paintings, and plasterings, and gildings
   Of stucco, and marble, and brick;
The orders deliciously blended,
   From love of effect, into one;
The club-houses only intended,
   The palaces only begun;
The hell where the fiend, in his glory,
   Sits staring at putty and stones,
And scrambles from story to story,
   To rattle at midnight his bones.

Good-night to the Season! the dances,
   The fillings of hot little rooms,
The glancings of rapturous glances,
   The fancyings of fancy costumes;
The pleasures which Fashion makes duties,
   The praisings of fiddles and flutes,
The luxury of looking at beauties,
   The tedium of talking to mutes;
The female diplomatists, planners
   Of matches for Laura and Jane,
The ice of her Ladyship's manners,
   The ice of his Lordship's champagne.

Good-night to the Season! the rages
   Led off by the chiefs of the throng,
The Lady Matilda's new pages,
   The Lady Eliza's new song;
Miss Fennel's macaw, which at Boodle's
   Is held to have something to say;
Mrs. Splenetic's musical poodles,
   Which bark 'Batti Batti' all day;
The pony Sir Araby sported,
   As hot and as black as a coal,
And the Lion his mother imported,
   In bearskins and grease, from the Pole.

Good-night to the Season! the Toso,
   So very majestic and tall;
Miss Ayton, whose singing was so-so,
   And Pasta, divinest of all;

The labour in vain of the Ballet,
   So sadly deficient in stars;
The foreigners thronging the Alley,
   Exhaling the breath of cigars;
The 'loge' where some heiress, how killing,
   Environed with Exquisites sits,
The lovely one out of her drilling,
   The silly ones out of their wits.

Good-night to the Season! the splendour
   That beamed in the Spanish Bazaar;
Where I purchased—my heart was so tender—
   A card-case,—a pasteboard guitar,—
A bottle of perfume,—a girdle,—
   A lithographed Riego full-grown,
Whom Bigotry drew on a hurdle
   That artists might draw him on stone,—
A small panorama of Seville,—
   A trap for demolishing flies,—
A caricature of the Devil,—
   And a look from Miss Sheridan's eyes.

Good-night to the Season! the flowers
   Of the grand horticultural fête,
When boudoirs were quitted for bowers,
   And the fashion was not to be late;
When all who had money and leisure
   Grew rural o'er ices and wines,
All pleasantly toiling for pleasure,
   All hungrily pining for pines,
And making of beautiful speeches,
   And marring of beautiful shows,
And feeding on delicate peaches,
   And treading on delicate toes.

Good-night to the Season! another
   Will come with its trifles and toys,
And hurry away like its brother,
   In sunshine, and odour, and noise.
Will it come with a rose or a briar?
   Will it come with a blessing or curse?
Will its bonnets be lower or higher?
   Will its morals be better or worse?

Will it find me grown thinner or fatter,
  Or fonder of wrong or of right,
Or married,—or buried?—no matter,
  Good-night to the Season, Good-night!


# THOMAS LOVELL BEDDOES

## 1803–1849

587                 *Song from the Waters*

THE swallow leaves her nest,
The soul my weary breast;
But therefore let the rain
    On my grave
Fall pure; for why complain?
Since both will come again
    O'er the wave.

The wind dead leaves and snow
Doth hurry to and fro;
And, once, a day shall break
    O'er the wave,
When a storm of ghosts shall shake
The dead, until they wake
    In the grave.


588                 *Wolfram's Dirge*

IF thou wilt ease thine heart
Of love and all its smart,
    Then sleep, dear, sleep;
And not a sorrow
    Hang any tear on your eyelashes;
    Lie still and deep,
    Sad soul, until the sea-wave washes
The rim o' th' sun to-morrow,
    In eastern sky.

But wilt thou cure thy heart
Of love and all its smart,
   Then die, dear, die;
'Tis deeper, sweeter,
   Than on a rose bank to lie dreaming
   With folded eye;
   And then alone, amid the beaming
Of love's stars, thou'lt meet her
   In eastern sky.

589          *Sibylla's Dirge*

WE do lie beneath the grass
   In the moonlight, in the shade
Of the yew-tree. They that pass
   Hear us not. We are afraid
   They would envy our delight,
   In our graves by glow-worm night.
Come follow us, and smile as we;
   We sail to the rock in the ancient waves,
Where the snow falls by thousands into the sea,
   And the drowned and the shipwrecked have
      happy graves.

590          *Dream-Pedlary*

IF there were dreams to sell,
   What would you buy?
Some cost a passing bell;
   Some a light sigh,
That shakes from Life's fresh crown
Only a roseleaf down.
If there were dreams to sell,
Merry and sad to tell,
And the crier rung the bell,
   What would you buy?

A cottage lone and still,
  With bowers nigh,
Shadowy, my woes to still,
  Until I die.
Such pearl from Life's fresh crown
Fain would I shake me down.
Were dreams to have at will,
This would best heal my ill,
  This would I buy.

But there were dreams to sell,
  Ill didst thou buy;
Life is a dream, they tell,
  Waking, to die.
Dreaming a dream to prize,
Is wishing ghosts to rise;
  And, if I had the spell
  To call the buried, well,
    Which one would I?

If there are ghosts to raise,
  What shall I call,
Out of hell's murky haze,
  Heaven's blue hall?
Raise my loved long-lost boy
To lead me to his joy.
  There are no ghosts to raise;
  Out of death lead no ways;
    Vain is the call.

Know'st thou not ghosts to sue?
  No love thou hast.
Else lie, as I will do,
  And breathe thy last.
So out of Life's fresh crown
Fall like a rose-leaf down.
  Thus are the ghosts to woo;
  Thus are all dreams made true,
    Ever to last!

# ELIZABETH BARRETT BROWNING
## 1806–1861

### *Sonnets from the Portuguese*

**591**                         (i)

I THOUGHT once how Theocritus had sung
  Of the sweet years, the dear and wished-for years,
  Who each one in a gracious hand appears
To bear a gift for mortals, old or young:
And, as I mused it in his antique tongue,
  I saw, in gradual vision through my tears,
  The sweet, sad years, the melancholy years,
Those of my own life, who by turns had flung
A shadow across me. Straightway I was 'ware,
  So weeping, how a mystic Shape did move
Behind me, and drew me backward by the hair;
  And a voice said in mastery, while I strove,—
'Guess now who holds thee?'—'Death,' I said. But, there,
  The silver answer rang,—'Not Death, but Love.'


**592**                         (ii)

IF thou must love me, let it be for naught
  Except for love's sake only. Do not say,
    'I love her for her smile—her look—her way
Of speaking gently,—for a trick of thought
That falls in well with mine, and certes brought
  A sense of pleasant ease on such a day'—
  For these things in themselves, Beloved, may
Be changed, or change for thee—and love, so wrought,
May be unwrought so. Neither love me for
  Thine own dear pity's wiping my cheeks dry:
A creature might forget to weep, who bore
  Thy comfort long, and lose thy love thereby!
But love me for love's sake, that evermore
  Thou mayst love on, through love's eternity.

593                 (iii)

WHEN our two souls stand up erect and strong,
   Face to face, silent, drawing nigh and nigher,
   Until the lengthening wings break into fire
At either curvèd point,—what bitter wrong
Can the earth do to us, that we should not long
   Be here contented? Think! In mounting higher,
   The angels would press on us, and aspire
To drop some golden orb of perfect song
Into our deep, dear silence. Let us stay
   Rather on earth, Beloved—where the unfit
Contrarious moods of men recoil away
   And isolate pure spirits, and permit
A place to stand and love in for a day,
   With darkness and the death-hour rounding it.


# EDWARD FITZGERALD

### 1809–1883

594     *from* The Rubaiyat of Omar Khayyam

A BOOK of Verses underneath the Bough,
A Jug of Wine, a Loaf of Bread—and Thou
   Beside me singing in the Wilderness—
O, Wilderness were Paradise enow!

Some for the Glories of This World; and some
Sigh for the Prophet's Paradise to come;
   Ah, take the Cash, and let the Credit go,
Nor heed the rumble of a distant Drum!

Look to the blowing Rose about us—'Lo,
Laughing,' she says, 'into the world I blow.
   At once the silken tassel of my Purse
Tear, and its Treasure on the Garden throw.'

And those who husbanded the Golden grain
And those who flung it to the winds like Rain,
   Alike to no such aureate Earth are turned
As, buried once, Men want dug up again.

The Worldly Hope men set their Hearts upon
Turns Ashes—or it prospers; and anon,
   Like Snow upon the Desert's dusty Face,
Lighting a little hour or two—is gone.

Think, in this battered Caravanserai
Whose Portals are alternate Night and Day,
   How Sultan after Sultan with his Pomp
Abode his destined Hour, and went his way.

They say the Lion and the Lizard keep
The Courts where Jamshyd gloried and drank deep:
   And Bahram, that great Hunter—the wild Ass
Stamps o'er his Head, but cannot break his Sleep.

I sometimes think that never blows so red
The Rose as where some buried Caesar bled;
   That every Hyacinth the Garden wears
Dropt in her Lap from some once lovely Head.

And this reviving Herb whose tender Green
Fledges the River-Lip on which we lean—
   Ah, lean upon it lightly! for who knows
From what once lovely Lip it springs unseen!

Ah, my Beloved, fill the Cup that clears
To-DAY of past Regrets and future Fears:
   *To-morrow!*—Why, To-morrow I may be
Myself with Yesterday's Seven thousand Years.

For some we loved, the loveliest and the best
That from his Vintage rolling Time hath prest,
   Have drunk their Cup a Round or two before,
And one by one crept silently to rest.

And we, that now make merry in the Room
They left, and Summer dresses in new bloom,
   Ourselves must we beneath the Couch of Earth
Descend—ourselves to make a Couch—for whom?

Ah, make the most of what we yet may spend,
Before we too into the Dust descend;
   Dust into Dust, and under Dust to lie,
Sans Wine, sans Song, sans Singer, and—sans End!

# ALFRED, LORD TENNYSON
1809–1892

595 *Mariana*

WITH blackest moss the flower-plots
    Were thickly crusted, one and all:
The rusted nails fell from the knots
    That held the pear to the gable-wall.
The broken sheds looked sad and strange:
    Unlifted was the clinking latch;
    Weeded and worn the ancient thatch
Upon the lonely moated grange.
        She only said, 'My life is dreary,
            He cometh not,' she said;
        She said, 'I am aweary, aweary,
            I would that I were dead!'

Her tears fell with the dews at even;
    Her tears fell ere the dews were dried;
She could not look on the sweet heaven,
    Either at morn or eventide.
After the flitting of the bats,
    When thickest dark did trance the sky,
    She drew her casement-curtain by,
And glanced athwart the glooming flats.
        She only said, 'The night is dreary,
            He cometh not,' she said;
        She said, 'I am aweary, aweary,
            I would that I were dead!'

Upon the middle of the night,
    Waking she heard the night-fowl crow:
The cock sung out an hour ere light:
    From the dark fen the oxen's low
Came to her: without hope of change,
    In sleep she seemed to walk forlorn,
    Till cold winds woke the gray-eyed morn
About the lonely moated grange.

She only said, 'The day is dreary,
   He cometh not,' she said;
She said, 'I am aweary, aweary,
   I would that I were dead!'

About a stone-cast from the wall
   A sluice with blackened waters slept,
And o'er it many, round and small,
   The clustered marish-mosses crept.
Hard by a poplar shook alway,
   All silver-green with gnarlèd bark:
For leagues no other tree did mark
The level waste, the rounding gray.
      She only said, 'My life is dreary,
         He cometh not,' she said;
      She said, 'I am aweary, aweary,
         I would that I were dead!'

And ever when the moon was low,
   And the shrill winds were up and away,
In the white curtain, to and fro,
   She saw the gusty shadow sway.
But when the moon was very low,
   And wild winds bound within their cell,
The shadow of the poplar fell
Upon her bed, across her brow.
      She only said, 'The night is dreary,
         He cometh not,' she said;
      She said, 'I am aweary, aweary,
         I would that I were dead!'

All day within the dreamy house,
   The doors upon their hinges creaked;
The blue fly sung in the pane; the mouse
   Behind the mouldering wainscot shrieked,
Or from the crevice peered about.
   Old faces glimmered through the doors,
   Old footsteps trod the upper floors,
Old voices called her from without.
      She only said, 'My life is dreary,
         He cometh not,' she said;
      She said, 'I am aweary, aweary,
         I would that I were dead!'

The sparrow's chirrup on the roof,
　The slow clock ticking, and the sound
Which to the wooing wind aloof
　The poplar made, did all confound
Her sense; but most she loathed the hour
　When the thick-moted sunbeam lay
　Athwart the chambers, and the day
Was sloping toward his western bower.
　　Then, said she, 'I am very dreary,
　　　He will not come,' she said;
　　She wept, 'I am aweary, aweary,
　　　Oh God, that I were dead!'


596　　　　　*The Lady of Shalott*

PART I

On either side the river lie
Long fields of barley and of rye,
That clothe the wold and meet the sky;
And through the field the road runs by
　　To many-towered Camelot;
And up and down the people go,
Gazing where the lilies blow
Round an island there below,
　　The island of Shalott.

Willows whiten, aspens quiver,
Little breezes dusk and shiver
Through the wave that runs for ever
By the island in the river
　　Flowing down to Camelot.
Four gray walls, and four gray towers,
Overlook a space of flowers,
And the silent isle imbowers
　　The Lady of Shalott.

By the margin, willow-veiled,
Slide the heavy barges trailed
By slow horses; and unhailed
The shallop flitteth silken-sailed
    Skimming down to Camelot:
But who hath seen her wave her hand?
Or at the casement seen her stand?
Or is she known in all the land,
    The Lady of Shalott?

Only reapers, reaping early
In among the bearded barley,
Hear a song that echoes cheerly
From the river winding clearly,
    Down to towered Camelot:
And by the moon the reaper weary,
Piling sheaves in uplands airy,
Listening, whispers ' 'Tis the fairy
    Lady of Shalott.'

### PART II

There she weaves by night and day
A magic web with colours gay.
She has heard a whisper say,
A curse is on her if she stay
    To look down to Camelot.
She knows not what the curse may be,
And so she weaveth steadily,
And little other care hath she,
    The Lady of Shalott.

And moving through a mirror clear
That hangs before her all the year,
Shadows of the world appear.
There she sees the highway near
    Winding down to Camelot:
There the river eddy whirls,
And there the surly village-churls,
And the red cloaks of market girls,
    Pass onward from Shalott.

Sometimes a troop of damsels glad,
An abbot on an ambling pad,
Sometimes a curly shepherd-lad,
Or long-haired page in crimson clad,
    Goes by to towered Camelot;
And sometimes through the mirror blue
The knights come riding two and two:
She hath no loyal knight and true,
    The Lady of Shalott.

But in her web she still delights
To weave the mirror's magic sights,
For often through the silent nights
A funeral, with plumes and lights
    And music, went to Camelot:
Or when the moon was overhead,
Came two young lovers lately wed;
'I am half sick of shadows,' said
    The Lady of Shalott.

### PART III

A bow-shot from her bower-eaves,
He rode between the barley-sheaves,
The sun came dazzling through the leaves,
And flamed upon the brazen greaves
    Of bold Sir Lancelot.
A red-cross knight for ever kneeled
To a lady in his shield,
That sparkled on the yellow field,
    Beside remote Shalott.

The gemmy bridle glittered free,
Like to some branch of stars we see
Hung in the golden Galaxy.
The bridle bells rang merrily
    As he rode down to Camelot:
And from his blazoned baldric slung
A mighty silver bugle hung,
And as he rode his armour rung,
    Beside remote Shalott.

All in the blue unclouded weather
Thick-jewelled shone the saddle-leather,
The helmet and the helmet-feather
Burned like one burning flame together,
    As he rode down to Camelot.
As often through the purple night,
Below the starry clusters bright,
Some bearded meteor, trailing light,
    Moves over still Shalott.

His broad clear brow in sunlight glowed;
On burnished hooves his war-horse trode;
From underneath his helmet flowed
His coal-black curls as on he rode,
    As he rode down to Camelot.
From the bank and from the river
He flashed into the crystal mirror,
'Tirra lirra,' by the river
    Sang Sir Lancelot.

She left the web, she left the loom,
She made three paces through the room,
She saw the water-lily bloom,
She saw the helmet and the plume,
    She looked down to Camelot.
Out flew the web and floated wide;
The mirror cracked from side to side;
'The curse is come upon me,' cried
    The Lady of Shalott.

### PART IV

In the stormy east-wind straining,
The pale yellow woods were waning,
The broad stream in his banks complaining,
Heavily the low sky raining
    Over towered Camelot;
Down she came and found a boat
Beneath a willow left afloat,
And round about the prow she wrote
    *The Lady of Shalott.*

And down the river's dim expanse
Like some bold seër in a trance,
Seeing all his own mischance—
With a glassy countenance
    Did she look to Camelot.
And at the closing of the day
She loosed the chain, and down she lay;
The broad stream bore her far away,
    The Lady of Shalott.

Lying, robed in snowy white
That loosely flew to left and right—
The leaves upon her falling light—
Through the noises of the night
    She floated down to Camelot:
And as the boat-head wound along
The willowy hills and fields among,
They heard her singing her last song,
    The Lady of Shalott.

Heard a carol, mournful, holy,
Chanted loudly, chanted lowly,
Till her blood was frozen slowly,
And her eyes were darkened wholly,
    Turned to towered Camelot.
For ere she reached upon the tide
The first house by the water-side,
Singing in her song she died,
    The Lady of Shalott.

Under tower and balcony,
By garden-wall and gallery,
A gleaming shape she floated by,
Dead-pale between the houses high,
    Silent into Camelot.
Out upon the wharfs they came,
Knight and burgher, lord and dame,
And round the prow they read her name,
    *The Lady of Shalott.*

Who is this? and what is here?
And in the lighted palace near
Died the sound of royal cheer;
And they crossed themselves for fear,

All the knights at Camelot:
But Lancelot mused a little space;
He said, 'She has a lovely face;
God in his mercy lend her grace,
   The Lady of Shalott.'

597 *Song of the Lotos-Eaters*

THERE is sweet music here that softer falls
Than petals from blown roses on the grass,
Or night-dews on still waters between walls
Of shadowy granite, in a gleaming pass;
Music that gentlier on the spirit lies,
Than tired eyelids upon tired eyes;
Music that brings sweet sleep down from the blissful skies.
Here are cool mosses deep,
And through the moss the ivies creep,
And in the stream the long-leaved flowers weep,
And from the craggy ledge the poppy hangs in sleep.

Why are we weighed upon with heaviness,
And utterly consumed with sharp distress,
While all things else have rest from weariness?
All things have rest: why should we toil alone,
We only toil, who are the first of things,
And make perpetual moan,
Still from one sorrow to another thrown:
Nor ever fold our wings,
And cease from wanderings,
Nor steep our brows in slumber's holy balm;
Nor harken what the inner spirit sings,
'There is no joy but calm!'
Why should we only toil, the roof and crown of things?

Lo! in the middle of the wood,
The folded leaf is wooed from out the bud
With winds upon the branch, and there
Grows green and broad, and takes no care,
Sun-steeped at noon, and in the moon
Nightly dew-fed; and turning yellow
Falls, and floats adown the air.

Lo! sweetened with the summer light,
The full-juiced apple, waxing over-mellow,
Drops in a silent autumn night.
All its allotted length of days,
The flower ripens in its place,
Ripens and fades, and falls, and hath no toil,
Fast-rooted in the fruitful soil.

Hateful is the dark-blue sky,
Vaulted o'er the dark-blue sea.
Death is the end of life; ah, why
Should life all labour be?
Let us alone. Time driveth onward fast,
And in a little while our lips are dumb.
Let us alone. What is it that will last?
All things are taken from us, and become
Portions and parcels of the dreadful Past.
Let us alone. What pleasure can we have
To war with evil? Is there any peace
In ever climbing up the climbing wave?
All things have rest, and ripen toward the grave
In silence; ripen, fall and cease:
Give us long rest or death, dark death, or dreamful ease.

How sweet it were, hearing the downward stream,
With half-shut eyes ever to seem
Falling asleep in a half-dream!
To dream and dream, like yonder amber light,
Which will not leave the myrrh-bush on the height;
To hear each other's whispered speech;
Eating the Lotos day by day,
To watch the crisping ripples on the beach,
And tender curving lines of creamy spray;
To lend our hearts and spirits wholly
To the influence of mild-minded melancholy;
To muse and brood and live again in memory,
With those old faces of our infancy
Heaped over with a mound of grass,
Two handfuls of white dust, shut in an urn of brass!

Dear is the memory of our wedded lives,
And dear the last embraces of our wives
And their warm tears: but all hath suffered change:
For surely now our household hearths are cold:
Our sons inherit us: our looks are strange:
And we should come like ghosts to trouble joy.
Or else the island princes over-bold
Have eat our substance, and the minstrel sings
Before them of the ten years' war in Troy,
And our great deeds, as half-forgotten things.
Is there confusion in the little isle?
Let what is broken so remain.
The Gods are hard to reconcile:
'Tis hard to settle order once again.
There *is* confusion worse than death,
Trouble on trouble, pain on pain,
Long labour unto agèd breath,
Sore task to hearts worn out by many wars
And eyes grown dim with gazing on the pilot-stars.

But, propt on beds of amaranth and moly,
How sweet (while warm airs lull us, blowing lowly)
With half-dropt eyelid still,
Beneath a heaven dark and holy,
To watch the long bright river drawing slowly
His waters from the purple hill—
To hear the dewy echoes calling
From cave to cave through the thick-twinèd vine—
To watch the emerald-coloured water falling
Through many a woven acanthus-wreath divine!
Only to hear and see the far-off sparkling brine,
Only to hear were sweet, stretched out beneath the pine.

The Lotos blooms below the barren peak:
The Lotos blows by every winding creek:
All day the wind breathes low with mellower tone:
Through every hollow cave and alley lone
Round and round the spicy downs the yellow Lotos-dust is blown.
We have had enough of action, and of motion we,
Rolled to starboard, rolled to larboard, when the surge was
    seething free,
Where the wallowing monster spouted his foam-fountains in the
    sea.

Let us swear an oath, and keep it with an equal mind,
In the hollow Lotos-land to live and lie reclined
On the hills like Gods together, careless of mankind.
For they lie beside their nectar, and the bolts are hurled
Far below them in the valleys, and the clouds are lightly curled
Round their golden houses, girdled with the gleaming world:
Where they smile in secret, looking over wasted lands,
Blight and famine, plague and earthquake, roaring deeps and fiery
    sands,
Clanging fights, and flaming towns, and sinking ships, and praying
    hands.
But they smile, they find a music centred in a doleful song
Steaming up, a lamentation and an ancient tale of wrong,
Like a tale of little meaning though the words are strong;
Chanted from an ill-used race of men that cleave the soil,
Sow the seed, and reap the harvest with enduring toil,
Storing yearly little dues of wheat, and wine and oil;
Till they perish and they suffer—some, 'tis whispered—down in
    hell
Suffer endless anguish, others in Elysian valleys dwell,
Resting weary limbs at last on beds of asphodel.
Surely, surely, slumber is more sweet than toil, the shore
Than labour in the deep mid-ocean, wind and wave and oar;
Oh rest ye, brother mariners, we will not wander more.


598          *Ulysses*

IT little profits that an idle king,
By this still hearth, among these barren crags,
Matched with an agèd wife, I mete and dole
Unequal laws unto a savage race,
That hoard, and sleep, and feed, and know not me.

I cannot rest from travel: I will drink
Life to the lees: all times I have enjoyed
Greatly, have suffered greatly, both with those
That loved me, and alone; on shore, and when
Through scudding drifts the rainy Hyades
Vext the dim sea: I am become a name;
For always roaming with a hungry heart
Much have I seen and known; cities of men

And manners, climates, councils, governments,
Myself not least, but honoured of them all;
And drunk delight of battle with my peers,
Far on the ringing plains of windy Troy.

    I am a part of all that I have met;
Yet all experience is an arch wherethrough
Gleams that untravelled world, whose margin fades
For ever and for ever when I move.
How dull it is to pause, to make an end,
To rust unburnished, not to shine in use!
As though to breathe were life. Life piled on life
Were all too little, and of one to me
Little remains: but every hour is saved
From that eternal silence, something more,
A bringer of new things; and vile it were
For some three suns to store and hoard myself,
And this gray spirit yearning in desire
To follow knowledge like a sinking star,
Beyond the utmost bound of human thought.

    This is my son, mine own Telemachus,
To whom I leave the sceptre and the isle—
Well-loved of me, discerning to fulfil
This labour, by slow prudence to make mild
A rugged people, and through soft degrees
Subdue them to the useful and the good.
Most blameless is he, centred in the sphere
Of common duties, decent not to fail
In offices of tenderness, and pay
Meet adoration to my household gods,
When I am gone. He works his work, I mine.

    There lies the port; the vessel puffs her sail:
There gloom the dark broad seas. My mariners,
Souls that have toiled, and wrought, and thought with me—
That ever with a frolic welcome took
The thunder and the sunshine, and opposed
Free hearts, free foreheads—you and I are old;
Old age hath yet his honour and his toil;
Death closes all: but something ere the end,
Some work of noble note, may yet be done,
Not unbecoming men that strove with Gods.

The lights begin to twinkle from the rocks:
The long day wanes: the slow moon climbs: the deep
Moans round with many voices. Come, my friends,
'Tis not too late to seek a newer world.
Push off, and sitting well in order smite
The sounding furrows; for my purpose holds
To sail beyond the sunset, and the baths
Of all the western stars, until I die.
It may be that the gulfs will wash us down:
It may be we shall touch the Happy Isles,
And see the great Achilles, whom we knew.
Though much is taken, much abides; and though
We are not now that strength which in old days
Moved earth and heaven; that which we are, we are;
One equal temper of heroic hearts,
Made weak by time and fate, but strong in will
To strive, to seek, to find, and not to yield.

## 599

O THAT 'twere possible,
    After long grief and pain,
To find the arms of my true-love
    Round me once again! . . .

A shadow flits before me—
    Not thou, but like to thee.
Ah God! that it were possible
    For one short hour to see
The souls we loved, that they might tell us
    What and where they be. . . .

## 600

BREAK, break, break,
    On thy cold gray stones, O Sea!
And I would that my tongue could utter
    The thoughts that arise in me.

O well for the fisherman's boy,
   That he shouts with his sister at play!
O well for the sailor lad,
   That he sings in his boat on the bay!

And the stately ships go on
   To their haven under the hill;
But O for the touch of a vanished hand,
   And the sound of a voice that is still!

Break, break, break,
   At the foot of thy crags, O Sea!
But the tender grace of a day that is dead
   Will never come back to me.

601             *Tears, Idle Tears*

TEARS, idle tears, I know not what they mean,
Tears from the depth of some divine despair
Rise in the heart, and gather to the eyes,
In looking on the happy Autumn-fields,
And thinking of the days that are no more.

Fresh as the first beam glittering on a sail,
That brings our friends up from the underworld,
Sad as the last which reddens over one
That sinks with all we love below the verge;
So sad, so fresh, the days that are no more.

Ah, sad and strange as in dark summer dawns
The earliest pipe of half-awakened birds
To dying ears, when unto dying eyes
The casement slowly grows a glimmering square;
So sad, so strange, the days that are no more.

Dear as remembered kisses after death,
And sweet as those by hopeless fancy feigned
On lips that are for others; deep as love,
Deep as first love, and wild with all regret;
O Death in Life, the days that are no more.

602 *Now Sleeps the Crimson Petal*

NOW sleeps the crimson petal, now the white;
Nor waves the cypress in the palace walk;
Nor winks the gold fin in the porphyry font:
The fire-fly wakens: waken thou with me.

Now droops the milkwhite peacock like a ghost,
And like a ghost she glimmers on to me.

Now lies the Earth all Danaë to the stars,
And all thy heart lies open unto me.

Now slides the silent meteor on, and leaves
A shining furrow, as thy thoughts in me.

Now folds the lily all her sweetness up,
And slips into the bosom of the lake:
So fold thyself, my dearest, thou, and slip
Into my bosom and be lost in me.

603 *Blow, Bugle, Blow*

THE splendour falls on castle walls
And snowy summits old in story:
The long light shakes across the lakes,
And the wild cataract leaps in glory.
Blow, bugle, blow, set the wild echoes flying,
Blow, bugle; answer, echoes, dying, dying, dying.

O hark, O hear! how thin and clear,
And thinner, clearer, farther going!
O sweet and far from cliff and scar
The horns of Elfland faintly blowing!
Blow, let us hear the purple glens replying:
Blow, bugle; answer, echoes, dying, dying, dying.

O love, they die in yon rich sky,
They faint on hill or field or river:
Our echoes roll from soul to soul,
And grow for ever and for ever.
Blow, bugle, blow, set the wild echoes flying,
And answer, echoes, answer, dying, dying, dying.

## *from* In Memoriam

### 604
### (i)

OLD Yew, which graspest at the stones
 That name the under-lying dead,
 Thy fibres net the dreamless head,
Thy roots are wrapt about the bones.

The seasons bring the flower again,
 And bring the firstling to the flock;
 And in the dusk of thee, the clock
Beats out the little lives of men.

O not for thee the glow, the bloom,
 Who changest not in any gale,
 Nor branding summer suns avail
To touch thy thousand years of gloom:

And gazing on thee, sullen tree,
 Sick for thy stubborn hardihood,
 I seem to fail from out my blood
And grow incorporate into thee.

### 605
### (ii)

Dark house, by which once more I stand
 Here in the long unlovely street,
 Doors, where my heart was used to beat
So quickly, waiting for a hand,

A hand that can be clasped no more—
 Behold me, for I cannot sleep,
 And like a guilty thing I creep
At earliest morning to the door.

He is not here; but far away
 The noise of life begins again,
 And ghastly through the drizzling rain
On the bald street breaks the blank day.

606                                         (iii)

CALM is the morn without a sound,
    Calm as to suit a calmer grief,
    And only through the faded leaf
The chestnut pattering to the ground:

Calm and deep peace on this high wold,
    And on these dews that drench the furze,
    And all the silvery gossamers
That twinkle into green and gold:

Calm and still light on yon great plain
    That sweeps with all its autumn bowers,
    And crowded farms and lessening towers,
To mingle with the bounding main:

Calm and deep peace in this wide air,
    These leaves that redden to the fall;
    And in my heart, if calm at all,
If any calm, a calm despair:

Calm on the seas, and silver sleep,
    And waves that sway themselves in rest,
    And dead calm in that noble breast
Which heaves but with the heaving deep.


607                                         (iv)

TONIGHT the winds begin to rise
    And roar from yonder dropping day:
    The last red leaf is whirled away,
The rooks are blown about the skies;

The forest cracked, the waters curled,
    The cattle huddled on the lea;
    And wildly dashed on tower and tree
The sunbeam strikes along the world:

And but for fancies, which aver
   That all thy motions gently pass
   Athwart a plane of molten glass,
I scarce could brook the strain and stir

That makes the barren branches loud;
   And but for fear it is not so,
   The wild unrest that lives in woe
Would dote and pore on yonder cloud

That rises upward always higher,
   And onward drags a labouring breast,
   And topples round the dreary west,
A looming bastion fringed with fire.

608                  (v)

I DREAMED there would be Spring no more,
   That Nature's ancient power was lost:
   The streets were black with smoke and frost,
They chattered trifles at the door:

I wandered from the noisy town,
   I found a wood with thorny boughs:
   I took the thorns to bind my brows,
I wore them like a civic crown:

I met with scoffs, I met with scorns
   From youth and babe and hoary hairs:
   They called me in the public squares
The fool that wears a crown of thorns:

They called me fool, they called me child:
   I found an angel of the night;
   The voice was low, the look was bright;
He looked upon my crown and smiled:

He reached the glory of a hand,
   That seemed to touch it into leaf:
   The voice was not the voice of grief,
The words were hard to understand.

609                                         (vi)

NOW fades the last long streak of snow,
    Now burgeons every maze of quick
    About the flowering squares, and thick
By ashen roots the violets blow.

Now rings the woodland loud and long,
    The distance takes a lovelier hue,
    And drowned in yonder living blue
The lark becomes a sightless song.

Now dance the lights on lawn and lea,
    The flocks are whiter down the vale,
    And milkier every milky sail
On winding stream or distant sea;

Where now the seamew pipes, or dives
    In yonder greening gleam, and fly
    The happy birds, that change their sky
To build and brood; that live their lives

From land to land; and in my breast
    Spring wakens too; and my regret
    Becomes an April violet,
And buds and blossoms like the rest.


610                                         (vii)

THERE rolls the deep where grew the tree.
    O earth, what changes hast thou seen!
    There where the long street roars, hath been
The stillness of the central sea.

The hills are shadows, and they flow
    From form to form, and nothing stands;
    They melt like mist, the solid lands,
Like clouds they shape themselves and go.

But in my spirit will I dwell,
    And dream my dream, and hold it true;
    For though my lips may breathe adieu,
I cannot think the thing farewell.

611    (viii)

Love is and was my Lord and King,
    And in his presence I attend
    To hear the tidings of my friend,
Which every hour his couriers bring.

Love is and was my King and Lord,
    And will be, though as yet I keep
    Within his court on earth, and sleep
Encompassed by his faithful guard,

And hear at times a sentinel
    Who moves about from place to place,
    And whispers to the worlds of space,
In the deep night, that all is well.


612

Come into the garden, Maud,
    For the black bat, night, has flown,
Come into the garden, Maud,
    I am here at the gate alone;
And the woodbine spices are wafted abroad,
    And the musk of the rose is blown.

For a breeze of morning moves,
    And the planet of Love is on high,
Beginning to faint in the light that she loves
    On a bed of daffodil sky,
To faint in the light of the sun she loves,
    To faint in his light, and to die.

All night have the roses heard
    The flute, violin, bassoon;
All night has the casement jessamine stirred
    To the dancers dancing in tune;
Till a silence fell with the waking bird,
    And a hush with the setting moon.

I said to the lily, 'There is but one
   With whom she has heart to be gay.
When will the dancers leave her alone?
   She is weary of dance and play.'
Now half to the setting moon are gone,
   And half to the rising day;
Low on the sand and loud on the stone
   The last wheel echoes away.

I said to the rose, 'The brief night goes
   In babble and revel and wine.
O young lord-lover, what sighs are those,
   For one that will never be thine?
But mine, but mine,' so I sware to the rose,
   'For ever and ever, mine.'

And the soul of the rose went into my blood,
   As the music clashed in the hall;
And long by the garden lake I stood,
   For I heard your rivulet fall
From the lake to the meadow and on to the wood,
   Our wood, that is dearer than all;

From the meadow your walks have left so sweet
   That whenever a March-wind sighs
He sets the jewel-print of your feet
   In violets blue as your eyes,
To the woody hollows in which we meet
   And the valleys of Paradise.

The slender acacia would not shake
   One long milk-bloom on the tree;
The white lake-blossom fell into the lake
   As the pimpernel dozed on the lea;
But the rose was awake all night for your sake,
   Knowing your promise to me;
The lilies and roses were all awake,
   They sighed for the dawn and thee.

Queen rose of the rosebud garden of girls,
    Come hither, the dances are done,
In gloss of satin and glimmer of pearls,
    Queen lily and rose in one;
Shine out, little head, sunning over with curls,
    To the flowers, and be their sun.

There has fallen a splendid tear
    From the passion-flower at the gate.
She is coming, my dove, my dear;
    She is coming, my life, my fate;
The red rose cries, 'She is near, she is near;'
    And the white rose weeps, 'She is late;'
The larkspur listens, 'I hear, I hear;'
    And the lily whispers, 'I wait.'

She is coming, my own, my sweet,
    Were it ever so airy a tread,
My heart would hear her and beat,
    Were it earth in an earthy bed;
My dust would hear her and beat,
    Had I lain for a century dead;
Would start and tremble under her feet,
    And blossom in purple and red.

## 613 *Tithonus*

THE woods decay, the woods decay and fall,
The vapours weep their burthen to the ground,
Man comes and tills the field and lies beneath,
And after many a summer dies the swan.
Me only cruel immortality
Consumes: I wither slowly in thine arms,
Here at the quiet limit of the world,
A white-haired shadow roaming like a dream
The ever-silent spaces of the East,
Far-folded mists, and gleaming halls of morn.

Alas! for this gray shadow, once a man—
So glorious in his beauty and thy choice,
Who madest him thy chosen, that he seemed
To his great heart none other than a God!

I asked thee, 'Give me immortality.'
Then didst thou grant mine asking with a smile,
Like wealthy men who care not how they give.
But thy strong Hours indignant worked their wills,
And beat me down and marred and wasted me,
And though they could not end me, left me maimed
To dwell in presence of immortal youth,
Immortal age beside immortal youth,
And all I was, in ashes. Can thy love,
Thy beauty, make amends, though even now,
Close over us, the silver star, thy guide,
Shines in those tremulous eyes that fill with tears
To hear me? Let me go: take back thy gift:
Why should a man desire in any way
To vary from the kindly race of men,
Or pass beyond the goal of ordinance
Where all should pause, as is most meet for all?

A soft air fans the cloud apart; there comes
A glimpse of that dark world where I was born.
Once more the old mysterious glimmer steals
From thy pure brows, and from thy shoulders pure,
And bosom beating with a heart renewed.
Thy cheek begins to redden through the gloom,
Thy sweet eyes brighten slowly close to mine,
Ere yet they blind the stars, and the wild team
Which love thee, yearning for thy yoke, arise,
And shake the darkness from their loosened manes,
And beat the twilight into flakes of fire.

Lo! ever thus thou growest beautiful
In silence, then before thine answer given
Departest, and thy tears are on my cheek.

Why wilt thou ever scare me with thy tears,
And make me tremble lest a saying learnt,
In days far-off, on that dark earth, be true?
'The Gods themselves cannot recall their gifts.'

Ay me! ay me! with what another heart
In days far-off, and with what other eyes
I used to watch—if I be he that watched—
The lucid outline forming round thee; saw
The dim curls kindle into sunny rings;
Changed with thy mystic change, and felt my blood
Glow with the glow that slowly crimsoned all
Thy presence and thy portals, while I lay,
Mouth, forehead, eyelids, growing dewy-warm
With kisses balmier than half-opening buds
Of April, and could hear the lips that kissed
Whispering I knew not what of wild and sweet,
Like that strange song I heard Apollo sing,
While Ilion like a mist rose into towers.

Yet hold me not for ever in thine East:
How can my nature longer mix with thine?
Coldly thy rosy shadows bathe me, cold
Are all thy lights, and cold my wrinkled feet
Upon thy glimmering thresholds, when the steam
Floats up from those dim fields about the homes
Of happy men that have the power to die,
And grassy barrows of the happier dead.
Release me, and restore me to the ground;
Thou seëst all things, thou wilt see my grave:
Thou wilt renew thy beauty morn by morn;
I earth in earth forget these empty courts,
And thee returning on thy silver wheels.

614                *In the Valley of Cauteretz*

ALL along the valley, stream that flashest white,
Deepening thy voice with the deepening of the night,
All along the valley, where thy waters flow,
I walked with one I loved two and thirty years ago.
All along the valley, while I walked today,
The two and thirty years were a mist that rolls away;
For all along the valley, down thy rocky bed,
Thy living voice to me was as the voice of the dead,
And all along the valley, by rock and cave and tree,
The voice of the dead was a living voice to me.

615                    *Crossing the Bar*

SUNSET and evening star,
  And one clear call for me!
And may there be no moaning of the bar,
  When I put out to sea,

But such a tide as moving seems asleep,
  Too full for sound and foam,
When that which drew from out the boundless deep
  Turns again home.

Twilight and evening bell,
  And after that the dark!
And may there be no sadness of farewell,
  When I embark;

For though from out our bourne of Time and Place
  The flood may bear me far,
I hope to see my Pilot face to face
  When I have crost the bar.


# ROBERT BROWNING

## 1812–1889

616                    *My Last Duchess*

THAT'S my last Duchess painted on the wall,
Looking as if she were alive. I call
That piece a wonder, now: Frà Pandolf's hands
Worked busily a day, and there she stands.
Will 't please you sit and look at her? I said
'Frà Pandolf' by design, for never read
Strangers like you that pictured countenance,
The depth and passion of its earnest glance,
But to myself they turned (since none puts by
The curtain I have drawn for you, but I)
And seemed as they would ask me, if they durst,
How such a glance came there; so, not the first
Are you to turn and ask thus. Sir, 't was not
Her husband's presence only, called that spot

Of joy into the Duchess' cheek: perhaps
Frà Pandolf chanced to say 'Her mantle laps
Over my lady's wrist too much,' or 'Paint
Must never hope to reproduce the faint
Half-flush that dies along her throat:' such stuff
Was courtesy, she thought, and cause enough
For calling up that spot of joy. She had
A heart—how shall I say?—too soon made glad,
Too easily impressed; she liked whate'er
She looked on, and her looks went everywhere.
Sir, 't was all one! My favour at her breast,
The dropping of the daylight in the West,
The bough of cherries some officious fool
Broke in the orchard for her, the white mule
She rode with round the terrace—all and each
Would draw from her alike the approving speech,
Or blush, at least. She thanked men,—good! but thanked
Somehow—I know not how—as if she ranked
My gift of a nine-hundred-years-old name
With anybody's gift. Who'd stoop to blame
This sort of trifling? Even had you skill
In speech—(which I have not)—to make your will
Quite clear to such an one, and say, 'Just this
Or that in you disgusts me; here you miss,
Or there exceed the mark'—and if she let
Herself be lessoned so, nor plainly set
Her wits to yours, forsooth, and made excuse,
—E'en then would be some stooping; and I choose
Never to stoop. Oh sir, she smiled, no doubt,
Whene'er I passed her; but who passed without
Much the same smile? This grew; I gave commands;
Then all smiles stopped together. There she stands
As if alive. Will 't please you rise? We'll meet
The company below, then. I repeat,
The Count your master's known munificence
Is ample warrant that no just pretence
Of mine for dowry will be disallowed;
Though his fair daughter's self, as I avowed
At starting, is my object. Nay, we'll go
Together down, sir. Notice Neptune, though,
Taming a sea-horse, thought a rarity,
Which Claus of Innsbruck cast in bronze for me!

617 *The Lost Mistress*

ALL'S over, then: does truth sound bitter
 As one at first believes?
Hark, 'tis the sparrows' good-night twitter
 About your cottage eaves!

And the leaf-buds on the vine are woolly,
 I noticed that, to-day;
One day more bursts them open fully
 —You know the red turns gray.

To-morrow we meet the same then, dearest?
 May I take your hand in mine?
Mere friends are we,—well, friends the merest
 Keep much that I resign:

For each glance of the eye so bright and black,
 Though I keep with heart's endeavour,—
Your voice, when you wish the snowdrops back,
 Though it stay in my soul for ever!—

Yet I will but say what mere friends say,
 Or only a thought stronger;
I will hold your hand but as long as all may,
 Or so very little longer!

618 *Home Thoughts from Abroad*

OH, to be in England
Now that April's there,
And whoever wakes in England
Sees, some morning, unaware,
That the lowest boughs and the brushwood sheaf
Round the elm-tree bole are in tiny leaf,
While the chaffinch sings on the orchard bough
In England—now!

And after April, when May follows,
And the whitethroat builds, and all the swallows!
Hark, where my blossomed pear-tree in the hedge
Leans to the field and scatters on the clover
Blossoms and dewdrops—at the bent spray's edge—
That's the wise thrush; he sings each song twice over,
Lest you should think he never could recapture
The first fine careless rapture!
And though the fields look rough with hoary dew
All will be gay when noontide wakes anew
The buttercups, the little children's dower
—Far brighter than this gaudy melon-flower!

619          *Home Thoughts from the Sea*

NOBLY, nobly Cape Saint Vincent to the North-west died away;
Sunset ran, one glorious blood-red, reeking into Cadiz Bay;
Bluish 'mid the burning water, full in face Trafalgar lay;
In the dimmest North-east distance dawned Gibraltar grand and
          gray;
'Here and here did England help me: how can I help England?'—
          say,
Whoso turns as I, this evening, turn to God to praise and pray,
While Jove's planet rises yonder, silent over Africa.

620          *Meeting at Night*

THE gray sea and the long black land;
And the yellow half-moon large and low;
And the startled little waves that leap
In fiery ringlets from their sleep,
As I gain the cove with pushing prow,
And quench its speed i' the slushy sand.

Then a mile of warm sea-scented beach;
Three fields to cross till a farm appears;
A tap at the pane, the quick sharp scratch
And blue spurt of a lighted match,
And a voice less loud, through its joys and fears,
Than the two hearts beating each to each!

621 *Parting at Morning*

ROUND the cape of a sudden came the sea,
And the sun looked over the mountain's rim:
And straight was a path of gold for him,
And the need of a world of men for me.

622 *Love among the Ruins*

WHERE the quiet-coloured end of evening smiles,
    Miles and miles
On the solitary pastures where our sheep
    Half-asleep
Tinkle homeward through the twilight, stray or stop
    As they crop—
Was the site once of a city great and gay,
    (So they say)
Of our country's very capital, its prince
    Ages since
Held his court in, gathered councils, wielding far
    Peace or war.

Now,—the country does not even boast a tree,
    As you see,
To distinguish slopes of verdure, certain rills
    From the hills
Intersect and give a name to, (else they run
    Into one)
Where the domed and daring palace shot its spires
    Up like fires
O'er the hundred-gated circuit of a wall
    Bounding all,
Made of marble, men might march on nor be pressed,
    Twelve abreast.

And such plenty and perfection, see, of grass
    Never was!
Such a carpet as, this summer time, o'erspreads
    And embeds
Every vestige of the city, guessed alone,
    Stock or stone—

Where a multitude of men breathed joy and woe
      Long ago;
Lust of glory pricked their hearts up, dread of shame
      Struck them tame;
And that glory and that shame alike, the gold
      Bought and sold.

Now,—the single little turret that remains
      On the plains,
By the caper overrooted, by the gourd
      Overscored,
While the patching houseleek's head of blossom winks
      Through the chinks—
Marks the basement whence a tower in ancient time
      Sprang sublime,
And a burning ring, all round, the chariots traced
      As they raced,
And the monarch and his minions and his dames
      Viewed the games.

And I know, while thus the quiet-coloured eve
      Smiles to leave
To their folding, all our many-tinkling fleece
      In such peace,
And the slopes and rills in undistinguished grey
      Melt away—
That a girl with eager eyes and yellow hair
      Waits me there
In the turret whence the charioteers caught soul
      For the goal,
When the king looked, where she looks now, breathless, dumb
      Till I come.

But he looked upon the city, every side,
      Far and wide,
All the mountains topped with temples, all the glades'
      Colonnades,
All the causeys, bridges, aqueducts,—and then,
      All the men!
When I do come, she will speak not, she will stand,
      Either hand

663

On my shoulder, give her eyes the first embrace
    Of my face,
Ere we rush, ere we extinguish sight and speech
    Each on each.

In one year they sent a million fighters forth
    South and North,
And they built their gods a brazen pillar high
    As the sky,
Yet reserved a thousand chariots in full force—
    Gold, of course.
Oh heart! oh blood that freezes, blood that burns!
    Earth's returns
For whole centuries of folly, noise and sin!
    Shut them in,
With their triumphs and their glories and the rest!
    Love is best!


623       *Up at a Villa—Down in the City*
      *As distinguished by an Italian person of Quality*

HAD I but plenty of money, money enough and to spare,
The house for me, no doubt, were a house in the city-square;
Ah, such a life, such a life, as one leads at the window there!

Something to see, by Bacchus, something to hear, at least!
There, the whole day long, one's life is a perfect feast;
While up at a villa one lives, I maintain it, no more than a beast.

Well now, look at our villa! stuck like the horn of a bull
Just on a mountain-edge as bare as the creature's skull,
Save a mere shag of a bush with hardly a leaf to pull!
—I scratch my own, sometimes, to see if the hair's turned wool.

But the city, oh the city—the square with the houses! Why?
They are stone-faced, white as a curd, there's something to take the
    eye!
Houses in four straight lines, not a single front awry;
You watch who crosses and gossips, who saunters, who hurries by;
Green blinds, as a matter of course, to draw when the sun gets high;
And the shops with fanciful signs which are painted properly.

What of a villa? Though winter be over in March by rights,
'Tis May perhaps ere the snow shall have withered well off the
    heights:
You've the brown ploughed land before, where the oxen steam and
    wheeze,
And the hills over-smoked behind by the faint grey olive-trees.

Is it better in May, I ask you? You've summer all at once;
In a day he leaps complete with a few strong April suns.
'Mid the sharp short emerald wheat, scarce risen three fingers well,
The wild tulip, at end of its tube, blows out its great red bell
Like a thin clear bubble of blood, for the children to pick and sell.

Is it ever hot in the square? There's a fountain to spout and splash!
In the shade it sings and springs; in the shine such foam-bows flash
On the horses with curling fish-tails, that prance and paddle and pash
Round the lady atop in her conch—fifty gazers do not abash,
Though all that she wears is some weeds round her waist in a sort of
    sash.

All the year long at the villa, nothing to see though you linger,
Except yon cypress that points like death's lean lifted forefinger.
Some think fireflies pretty, when they mix i' the corn and mingle,
Or thrid the stinking hemp till the stalks of it seem a-tingle.
Late August or early September, the stunning cicala is shrill,
And the bees keep their tiresome whine round the resinous firs on the
    hill.
Enough of the seasons,—I spare you the months of the fever and chill.

Ere you open your eyes in the city, the blessed church-bells begin:
No sooner the bells leave off than the diligence rattles in:
You get the pick of the news, and it costs you never a pin.
By-and-by there's the travelling doctor gives pills, lets blood, draws
    teeth;
Or the Pulcinello-trumpet breaks up the market beneath.
At the post-office such a scene-picture—the new play, piping hot!
And a notice how, only this morning, three liberal thieves were shot.
Above it, behold the Archbishop's most fatherly of rebukes,
And beneath, with his crown and his lion, some little new law of the
    Duke's!
Or a sonnet with flowery marge, to the Reverend Don So-and-so
Who is Dante, Boccaccio, Petrarca, Saint Jerome and Cicero,

'And moreover,' (the sonnet goes rhyming,) 'the skirts of Saint Paul
    has reached,
'Having preached us those six Lent-lectures more unctuous than ever
    he preached.'
Noon strikes,—here sweeps the procession! our Lady borne smiling
    and smart
With a pink gauze gown all spangles, and seven swords stuck in her
    heart!
*Bang-whang-whang* goes the drum, *tootle-te-tootle* the fife;
No keeping one's haunches still: it's the greatest pleasure in life.

But bless you, it's dear—it's dear! fowls, wine, at double the rate.
They have clapped a new tax upon salt, and what oil pays passing the
    gate
It's a horror to think of. And so, the villa for me, not the city!
Beggars can scarcely be choosers: but still—ah, the pity, the pity!
Look, two and two go the priests, then the monks with cowls and
    sandals,
And the penitents dressed in white shirts, a-holding the yellow candles;
One, he carries a flag up straight, and another a cross with handles,
And the Duke's guard brings up the rear, for the better prevention of
    scandals:
*Bang-whang-whang* goes the drum, *tootle-te-tootle* the fife.
Oh, a day in the city-square, there is no such pleasure in life!


624          *A Toccata of Galuppi's*

OH Galuppi, Baldassaro, this is very sad to find!
I can hardly misconceive you; it would prove me deaf and blind;
But although I take your meaning, 'tis with such a heavy mind!

Here you come with your old music, and here's all the good it brings.
What, they lived once thus at Venice where the merchants were the
    kings,
Where Saint Mark's is, where the Doges used to wed the sea with
    rings?

Ay, because the sea's the street there; and 'tis arched by . . . what
    you call
. . . Shylock's bridge with houses on it, where they kept the carnival:
I was never out of England—it's as if I saw it all.

Did young people take their pleasure when the sea was warm in May?
Balls and masks begun at midnight, burning ever to mid-day,
When they made up fresh adventures for the morrow, do you say?

Was a lady such a lady, cheeks so round and lips so red,—
On her neck the small face buoyant, like a bell-flower on its bed,
O'er the breast's superb abundance where a man might base his head?

Well, and it was graceful of them—they'd break talk off and afford
—She, to bite her mask's black velvet—he, to finger on his sword,
While you sat and played Toccatas, stately at the clavichord?

What? Those lesser thirds so plaintive, sixths diminished, sigh on
    sigh,
Told them something? Those suspensions, those solutions—'Must we
    die?'
Those commiserating sevenths—'Life might last! we can but try!'

'Were you happy?'—'Yes.'—'And are you still as happy?'—'Yes.
    And you?'
—'Then, more kisses!'—'Did *I* stop them, when a million seemed
    so few?'
Hark, the dominant's persistence till it must be answered to!

So, an octave struck the answer. Oh, they praised you, I dare say!
'Brave Galuppi! that was music! good alike at grave and gay!
'I can always leave off talking when I hear a master play!'

Then they left you for their pleasure: till in due time, one by one,
Some with lives that came to nothing, some with deeds as well undone,
Death stepped tacitly and took them where they never see the sun.

But when I sit down to reason, think to take my stand nor swerve,
While I triumph o'er a secret wrung from nature's close reserve,
In you come with your cold music till I creep thro' every nerve.

Yes, you, like a ghostly cricket, creaking where a house was burned:
'Dust and ashes, dead and done with, Venice spent what Venice earned.
'The soul, doubtless, is immortal—where a soul can be discerned.

'Yours for instance: you know physics, something of geology,
'Mathematics are your pastime; souls shall rise in their degree;
'Butterflies may dread extinction,—you'll not die, it cannot be!

667

'As for Venice and her people, merely born to bloom and drop,
'Here on earth they bore their fruitage, mirth and folly were the crop:
'What of soul was left, I wonder, when the kissing had to stop?

'Dust and ashes!' So you creak it, and I want the heart to scold.
Dear dead women, with such hair, too—what's become of all the gold
Used to hang and brush their bosoms? I feel chilly and grown old.

625                    *Love in a Life*

    Room after room,
    I hunt the house through
    We inhabit together.
    Heart, fear nothing, for, heart, thou shalt find her—
    Next time, herself!—not the trouble behind her
    Left in the curtain, the couch's perfume!
    As she brushed it, the cornice-wreath blossomed anew:
    Yon looking-glass gleamed at the wave of her feather.

    Yet the day wears,
    And door succeeds door;
    I try the fresh fortune—
    Range the wide house from the wing to the centre.
    Still the same chance! she goes out as I enter.
    Spend my whole day in the quest,—who cares?
    But 'tis twilight, you see,—with such suites to explore,
    Such closets to search, such alcoves to importune!

626                    *Two in the Campagna*

    I wonder do you feel to-day
      As I have felt since, hand in hand,
    We sat down on the grass, to stray
      In spirit better through the land,
    This morn of Rome and May?

    For me, I touched a thought, I know,
      Has tantalized me many times,
    (Like turns of thread the spiders throw
      Mocking across our path) for rhymes
    To catch at and let go.

Help me to hold it! First it left
  The yellowing fennel, run to seed
There, branching from the brickwork's cleft,
  Some old tomb's ruin: yonder weed
Took up the floating weft,

Where one small orange cup amassed
  Five beetles,—blind and green they grope
Among the honey-meal: and last,
  Everywhere on the grassy slope
I traced it. Hold it fast!

The champaign with its endless fleece
  Of feathery grasses everywhere!
Silence and passion, joy and peace,
  An everlasting wash of air—
Rome's ghost since her decease.

Such life here, through such lengths of hours,
  Such miracles performed in play,
Such primal naked forms of flowers,
  Such letting nature have her way
While heaven looks from its towers!

How say you? Let us, O my dove,
  Let us be unashamed of soul,
As earth lies bare to heaven above!
  How is it under our control
To love or not to love?

I would that you were all to me,
  You that are just so much, no more.
Nor yours nor mine, nor slave nor free!
  Where does the fault lie? What the core
O' the wound, since wound must be?

I would I could adopt your will,
  See with your eyes, and set my heart
Beating by yours, and drink my fill
  At your soul's springs,—your part my part
In life, for good and ill.

No. I yearn upward, touch you close,
  Then stand away. I kiss your cheek,
Catch your soul's warmth,—I pluck the rose
  And love it more than tongue can speak—
Then the good minute goes.

Already how am I so far
  Out of that minute? Must I go
Still like the thistle-ball, no bar,
  Onward, whenever light winds blow,
Fixed by no friendly star?

Just when I seemed about to learn!
  Where is the thread now? Off again!
The old trick! Only I discern—
  Infinite passion, and the pain
Of finite hearts that yearn.

627                    *Confessions*

WHAT is he buzzing in my ears?
  'Now that I come to die,
Do I view the world as a vale of tears?'
  Ah, reverend sir, not I!

What I viewed there once, what I view again
  Where the physic bottles stand
On the table's edge,—is a suburb lane,
  With a wall to my bedside hand.

That land sloped, much as the bottles do,
  From a house you could descry
O'er the garden-wall: is the curtain blue
  Or green to a healthy eye?

To mine, it serves for the old June weather
  Blue above lane and wall;
And that farthest bottle labelled 'Ether'
  Is the house o'ertopping all.

At a terrace, somewhere near the stopper,
  There watched for me, one June,
A girl: I know, sir, it's improper,
  My poor mind's out of tune.

Only, there was a way . . . you crept
  Close by the side, to dodge
Eyes in the house, two eyes except:
  They styled their house 'The Lodge.'

What right had a lounger up their lane?
  But, by creeping very close,
With the good wall's help,—their eyes might strain
  And stretch themselves to Oes,

Yet never catch her and me together,
  As she left the attic, there,
By the rim of the bottle labelled 'Ether',
  And stole from stair to stair,

And stood by the rose-wreathed gate. Alas,
  We loved, sir—used to meet:
How sad and bad and mad it was—
  But then, how it was sweet!

628              *May and Death*

I WISH that when you died last May,
  Charles, there had died along with you
Three parts of spring's delightful things;
  Ay, and, for me, the fourth part too.

A foolish thought, and worse, perhaps!
  There must be many a pair of friends
Who, arm in arm, deserve the warm
  Moon-births and the long evening-ends.

So, for their sake, be May still May!
  Let their new time, as mine of old,
Do all it did for me: I bid
  Sweet sights and sounds throng manifold.

Only, one little sight, one plant,
  Woods have in May, that starts up green
Save a sole streak which, so to speak,
  Is spring's blood, spilt its leaves between,—

That, they might spare; a certain wood
  Might miss the plant; their loss were small:
But I,—whene'er the leaf grows there,
  Its drop comes from my heart, that's all.


629                    *Apparent Failure*

'We shall soon lose a celebrated building.'
                              *Paris Newspaper*

No, for I'll save it! Seven years since,
  I passed through Paris, stopped a day
To see the baptism of your Prince;
  Saw, made my bow, and went my way:
Walking the heat and headache off,
  I took the Seine-side, you surmise,
Thought of the Congress, Gortschakoff,
  Cavour's appeal and Buol's replies,
So sauntered till—what met my eyes?

Only the Doric little Morgue!
  The dead-house where you show your drowned:
Petrarch's Vaucluse makes proud the Sorgue,
  Your Morgue has made the Seine renowned.
One pays one's debt in such a case;
  I plucked up heart and entered,—stalked,
Keeping a tolerable face
  Compared with some whose cheeks were chalked:
Let them! No Briton's to be baulked!

First came the silent gazers; next,
  A screen of glass, we're thankful for;
Last, the sight's self, the sermon's text,
  The three men who did most abhor
Their life in Paris yesterday,
  So killed themselves: and now, enthroned
Each on his copper couch, they lay
  Fronting me, waiting to be owned.
I thought, and think, their sin's atoned.

Poor men, God made, and all for that!
   The reverence struck me; o'er each head
Religiously was hung its hat,
   Each coat dripped by the owner's bed,
Sacred from touch: each had his berth,
   His bounds, his proper place of rest,
Who last night tenanted on earth
   Some arch, where twelve such slept abreast,—
Unless the plain asphalte seemed best.

How did it happen, my poor boy?
   You wanted to be Buonaparte
And have the Tuileries for toy,
   And could not, so it broke your heart?
You, old one by his side, I judge,
   Were, red as blood, a socialist,
A leveller! Does the Empire grudge
   You've gained what no Republic missed?
Be quiet, and unclench your fist!

And this—why, he was red in vain,
   Or black,—poor fellow that is blue!
What fancy was it turned your brain?
   Oh, women were the prize for you!
Money gets women, cards and dice
   Get money, and ill-luck gets just
The copper couch and one clear nice
   Cool squirt of water o'er your bust,
The right thing to extinguish lust!

It's wiser being good than bad;
   It's safer being meek than fierce:
It's fitter being sane than mad.
   My own hope is, a sun will pierce
The thickest cloud earth ever stretched;
   That, after Last, returns the First,
Though a wide compass round be fetched;
   That what began best, can't end worst,
Nor what God blessed once, prove accurst.

630 *Epilogue to Asolando*

AT the midnight in the silence of the sleep-time,
    When you set your fancies free,
Will they pass to where—by death, fools think, imprisoned—
Low he lies who once so loved you, whom you loved so,
    —Pity me?

Oh to love so, be so loved, yet so mistaken!
    What had I on earth to do
With the slothful, with the mawkish, the unmanly?
Like the aimless, helpless, hopeless, did I drivel!
    —Being—who?

One who never turned his back but marched breast forward,
    Never doubted clouds would break,
Never dreamed, though right were worsted, wrong would triumph,
Held we fall to rise, are baffled to fight better,
    Sleep to wake.

No, at noonday in the bustle of man's work-time
    Greet the unseen with a cheer!
Bid him forward, breast and back as either should be,
'Strive and thrive!' cry, 'Speed,—fight on, fare ever
    There as here!'

# EDWARD LEAR

## 1812–1888

631 *How pleasant to know Mr. Lear*

'HOW pleasant to know Mr. Lear!'
    Who has written such volumes of stuff!
Some think him ill-tempered and queer,
    But a few think him pleasant enough.

His mind is concrete and fastidious,
    His nose is remarkably big;
His visage is more or less hideous,
    His beard it resembles a wig.

He has ears, and two eyes, and ten fingers,
   Leastways if you reckon two thumbs;
Long ago he was one of the singers,
   But now he is one of the dumbs.

He sits in a beautiful parlour,
   With hundreds of books on the wall
He drinks a great deal of Marsala,
   But never gets tipsy at all.

He has many friends, laymen and clerical,
   Old Foss is the name of his cat:
His body is perfectly spherical,
   He weareth a runcible hat.

When he walks in a waterproof white,
   The children run after him so!
Calling out, 'He's come out in his night-
   gown, that crazy old Englishman, oh!'

He weeps by the side of the ocean,
   He weeps on the top of the hill;
He purchases pancakes and lotion,
   And chocolate shrimps from the mill.

He reads but he cannot speak Spanish,
   He cannot abide ginger-beer:
Ere the days of his pilgrimage vanish,
   How pleasant to know Mr. Lear!

632        *The Owl and the Pussy-Cat*

THE Owl and the Pussy-Cat went to sea
   In a beautiful pea-green boat,
They took some honey, and plenty of money,
   Wrapped up in a five-pound note.
The Owl looked up to the stars above,
   And sang to a small guitar,
'O lovely Pussy! O Pussy, my love,
   What a beautiful Pussy you are,
        You are,
        You are!
What a beautiful Pussy you are!'

Pussy said to the Owl, 'You elegant fowl!
　　How charmingly sweet you sing!
O let us be married! too long we have tarried:
　　But what shall we do for a ring?'
They sailed away for a year and a day,
　　To the land where the Bong-tree grows,
And there in a wood a Piggy-wig stood,
　　With a ring at the end of his nose,
　　　　His nose,
　　　　His nose,
With a ring at the end of his nose.

'Dear Pig, are you willing to sell for one shilling
　　Your ring?' Said the Piggy, 'I will.'
So they took it away, and were married next day
　　By the Turkey who lives on the hill.
They dined on mince, and slices of quince,
　　Which they ate with a runcible spoon;
And hand in hand, on the edge of the sand,
　　They danced by the light of the moon,
　　　　The moon,
　　　　The moon,
They danced by the light of the moon.


# EMILY BRONTË

### 1818–1848

633　　　　*Spellbound*

THE night is darkening round me,
The wild winds coldly blow;
But a tyrant spell has bound me
And I cannot, cannot go.

The giant trees are bending
Their bare boughs weighed with snow.
And the storm is fast descending,
And yet I cannot go.

Clouds beyond clouds above me,
Wastes beyond wastes below;
But nothing drear can move me;
I will not, cannot go.

634        *The Old Stoic*

RICHES I hold in light esteem,
And Love I laugh to scorn;
And lust of Fame was but a dream
That vanished with the morn—

And if I pray, the only prayer
That moves my lips for me
Is—'Leave the heart that now I bear,
And give me liberty.'

Yes, as my swift days near their goal,
'Tis all that I implore—
Through life and death, a chainless soul,
With courage to endure!

635        *Remembrance*

COLD in the earth—and the deep snow piled above thee,
Far, far removed, cold in the dreary grave!
Have I forgot, my only Love, to love thee,
Severed at last by Time's all-severing wave?

Now, when alone, do my thoughts no longer hover
Over the mountains, on that northern shore,
Resting their wings where heath and fern-leaves cover
Thy noble heart for ever, ever more?

Cold in the earth—and fifteen wild Decembers
From those brown hills have melted into spring—
Faithful indeed is the spirit that remembers
After such years of change and suffering!

Sweet Love of youth, forgive if I forget thee
While the world's tide is bearing me along:
Other desires and other hopes beset me,
Hopes which obscure, but cannot do thee wrong!

No later light has lightened up my heaven;
No second morn has ever shone for me:
All my life's bliss from thy dear life was given—
All my life's bliss is in the grave with thee.

But, when the days of golden dreams had perished,
And even Despair was powerless to destroy,
Then did I learn how existence could be cherished,
Strengthened, and fed without the aid of joy;

Then did I check the tears of useless passion,
Weaned my young soul from yearning after thine;
Sternly denied its burning wish to hasten
Down to that tomb already more than mine!

And, even yet, I dare not let it languish,
Dare not indulge in Memory's rapturous pain;
Once drinking deep of that divinest anguish,
How could I seek the empty world again?

636                           *The Visionary*

SILENT is the house: all are laid asleep:
One alone looks out o'er the snow-wreaths deep,
Watching every cloud, dreading every breeze
That whirls the wildering drift, and bends the groaning trees.

Cheerful is the hearth, soft the matted floor;
Not one shivering gust creeps through pane or door;
The little lamp burns straight, its rays shoot strong and far:
I trim it well, to be the wanderer's guiding-star.

Frown, my haughty sire! chide, my angry dame;
Set your slaves to spy; threaten me with shame:
But neither sire nor dame, nor prying serf shall know,
What angel nightly tracks that waste of frozen snow.

What I love shall come like visitant of air,
Safe in secret power from lurking human snare;
Who loves me, no word of mine shall e'er betray,
Though for faith unstained my life must forfeit pay.

Burn, then, little lamp; glimmer straight and clear—
Hush! a rustling wing stirs, methinks, the air:
He for whom I wait, thus ever comes to me;
Strange Power! I trust thy might; trust thou my constancy.

637 *The Prisoner*

'STILL let my tyrants know, I am not doomed to wear
Year after year in gloom, and desolate despair;
A messenger of Hope comes every night to me,
And offers for short life, eternal liberty.

'He comes with western winds, with evening's wandering airs,
With that clear dusk of heaven that brings the thickest stars,
Winds take a pensive tone, and stars a tender fire,
And visions rise, and change, that kill me with desire.

'Desire for nothing known in my maturer years,
When Joy grew mad with awe, at counting future tears.
When, if my spirit's sky was full of flashes warm,
I knew not whence they came, from sun or thunder-storm.

'But, first, a hush of peace—a soundless calm descends;
The struggle of distress, and fierce impatience ends;
Mute music soothes my breast—unuttered harmony,
That I could never dream, till Earth was lost to me.

'Then dawns the Invisible; the Unseen its truth reveals;
My outward sense is gone, my inward essence feels:
Its wings are almost free—its home, its harbour found,
Measuring the gulf, it stoops and dares the final bound.

'O! dreadful is the check—intense the agony—
When the ear begins to hear, and the eye begins to see;
When the pulse begins to throb, the brain to think again;
The soul to feel the flesh, and the flesh to feel the chain.

'Yet I would lose no sting, would wish no torture less;
The more that anguish racks, the earlier it will bless;
And robed in fires of hell, or bright with heavenly shine,
If it but herald death, the vision is divine!'

638 *Last Lines*

'The following are the last lines my sister Emily ever wrote.'
(Charlotte Brontë)

No coward soul is mine,
No trembler in the world's storm-troubled sphere:
I see Heaven's glories shine,
And faith shines equal, arming me from fear.

O God within my breast,
Almighty, ever-present Deity!
Life—that in me has rest,
As I—undying Life—have power in thee!

Vain are the thousand creeds
That move men's hearts: unutterably vain;
Worthless as withered weeds,
Or idlest froth amid the boundless main,

To waken doubt in one
Holding so fast by thine infinity;
So surely anchored on
The steadfast rock of immortality.

With wide-embracing love
Thy spirit animates eternal years,
Pervades and broods above,
Changes, sustains, dissolves, creates, and rears.

Though earth and man were gone,
And suns and universes ceased to be,
And thou were left alone,
Every existence would exist in thee.

There is not room for Death,
Nor atom that his might could render void:
Thou—thou art Being and Breath,
And what thou art may never be destroyed.

# ARTHUR HUGH CLOUGH

1819–1861

639    *Say Not the Struggle Nought Availeth*

SAY not the struggle nought availeth,
   The labour and the wounds are vain,
The enemy faints not, nor faileth,
   And as things have been, things remain.

If hopes were dupes, fears may be liars;
   It may be, in yon smoke concealed,
Your comrades chase e'en now the fliers,
   And, but for you, possess the field.

For while the tired waves, vainly breaking,
   Seem here no painful inch to gain,
Far back through creeks and inlets making
   Came, silent, flooding in, the main,

And not by eastern windows only,
   When daylight comes, comes in the light,
In front the sun climbs slow, how slowly,
   But westward, look, the land is bright.

640    *Where Lies the Land?*

WHERE lies the land to which the ship would go?
Far, far ahead, is all her seamen know.
And where the land she travels from? Away,
Far, far behind, is all that they can say.

On sunny noons upon the deck's smooth face,
Linked arm in arm, how pleasant here to pace;
Or, o'er the stern reclining, watch below
The foaming wake far widening as we go.

On stormy nights when wild north-westers rave,
How proud a thing to fight with wind and wave!
The dripping sailor on the reeling mast
Exults to bear, and scorns to wish it past.

Where lies the land to which the ship would go?
Far, far ahead, is all her seamen know.
And where the land she travels from? Away,
Far, far behind, is all that they can say.

641 *The Latest Decalogue*

THOU shalt have one God only; who
Would be at the expense of two?
No graven images may be
Worshipped, except the currency:
Swear not at all; for, for thy curse
Thine enemy is none the worse:
At church on Sunday to attend
Will serve to keep the world thy friend:
Honour thy parents; that is, all
From whom advancement may befall:
Thou shalt not kill; but need'st not strive
Officiously to keep alive:
Do not adultery commit;
Advantage rarely comes of it:
Thou shalt not steal; an empty feat,
When it's so lucrative to cheat:
Bear not false witness; let the lie
Have time on its own wings to fly:
Thou shalt not covet; but tradition
Approves all forms of competition.

The sum of all is, thou shalt love,
If anybody, God above:
At any rate shall never labour
*More* than thyself to love thy neighbour.

642 *How Pleasant it is to have Money*

As I sat at the café, I said to myself,
They may talk as they please about what they call pelf,
They may sneer as they like about eating and drinking,
But help it I cannot, I cannot help thinking,
  How pleasant it is to have money, heigh ho!
  How pleasant it is to have money.

## ARTHUR HUGH CLOUGH

I sit at my table *en grand seigneur*,
And when I have done, throw a crust to the poor;
Not only the pleasure, one's self, of good living,
But also the pleasure of now and then giving.
　So pleasant it is to have money, heigh ho!
　So pleasant it is to have money.

It was but last winter I came up to Town,
But already I'm getting a little renown;
I make new acquaintance where'er I appear;
I am not too shy, and have nothing to fear.
　So pleasant it is to have money, heigh ho!
　So pleasant it is to have money.

I drive through the streets, and I care not a damn;
The people they stare, and they ask who I am;
And if I should chance to run over a cad,
I can pay for the damage if ever so bad.
　So pleasant it is to have money, heigh ho!
　So pleasant it is to have money.

We stroll to our box and look down on the pit,
And if it weren't low should be tempted to spit;
We loll and we talk until people look up,
And when it's half over we go out and sup.
　So pleasant it is to have money, heigh ho!
　So pleasant it is to have money.

The best of the tables and best of the fare—
And as for the others, the devil may care;
It isn't our fault if they dare not afford
To sup like a prince and be drunk as a lord.
　So pleasant it is to have money, heigh ho!
　So pleasant it is to have money.

We sit at our tables and tipple champagne;
Ere one bottle goes, comes another again;
The waiters they skip and they scuttle about,
And the landlord attends us so civilly out.
　So pleasant it is to have money, heigh ho!
　So pleasant it is to have money.

It was but last winter I came up to town,
But already I'm getting a little renown;
I get to good houses without much ado,
Am beginning to see the nobility too.
   So pleasant it is to have money, heigh ho!
   So pleasant it is to have money.

O dear! what a pity they ever should lose it!
For they are the gentry that know how to use it;
So grand and so graceful, such manners, such dinners,
But yet, after all, it is we are the winners.
   So pleasant it is to have money, heigh ho!
   So pleasant it is to have money.

Thus I sat at my table *en grand seigneur,*
And when I had done threw a crust to the poor;
Not only the pleasure, one's self, of good eating,
But also the pleasure of now and then treating.
   So pleasant it is to have money, heigh ho!
   So pleasant it is to have money.

They may talk as they please about what they call pelf,
And how one ought never to think of one's self,
And how pleasures of thought surpass eating and drinking—
My pleasure of thought is the pleasure of thinking
   How pleasant it is to have money, heigh ho!
   How pleasant it is to have money.

A gondola here, and a gondola there,
'Tis the pleasantest fashion of taking the air.
To right and to left; stop, turn, and go yonder,
And let us repeat, o'er the tide as we wander,
   How pleasant it is to have money, heigh ho!
   How pleasant it is to have money.

643           *There is No God*

     'THERE is no God,' the wicked saith,
      'And truly it's a blessing,
    For what he might have done with us
      It's better only guessing.'

## ARTHUR HUGH CLOUGH

'There is no God,' a youngster thinks,
    'Or really, if there may be,
He surely didn't mean a man
    Always to be a baby.'

'There is no God, or if there is,'
    The tradesman thinks, ' 'twere funny
If he should take it ill in me
    To make a little money.'

'Whether there be,' the rich man says,
    'It matters very little,
For I and mine, thank somebody,
    Are not in want of victual.'

Some others, also, to themselves
    Who scarce so much as doubt it,
Think there is none, when they are well,
    And do not think about it.

But country folks who live beneath
    The shadow of the steeple;
The parson and the parson's wife,
    And mostly married people;

Youths green and happy in first love,
    So thankful for illusion;
And men caught out in what the world
    Calls guilt, in first confusion;

And almost everyone when age,
    Disease, or sorrows strike him,
Inclines to think there is a God,
    Or something very like him.

# MATTHEW ARNOLD

1822–1888

644 *The Song of Callicles*

THROUGH the black, rushing smoke-bursts,
Thick breaks the red flame;
All Etna heaves fiercely
Her forest-clothed frame.

Not here, O Apollo!
Are haunts meet for thee.
But, where Helicon breaks down
In cliff to the sea,

Where the moon-silvered inlets
Send far their light voice
Up the still vale of Thisbe,
O speed, and rejoice!

On the sward at the cliff-top
Lie strewn the white flocks,
On the cliff-side the pigeons
Roost deep in the rocks.

In the moonlight the shepherds,
Soft lulled by the rills,
Lie wrapt in their blankets
Asleep on the hills.

—What forms are these coming
So white through the gloom?
What garments out-glistening
The gold-flowered broom?

What sweet-breathing presence
Out-perfumes the thyme?
What voices enrapture
The night's balmy prime?—

'Tis Apollo comes leading
His choir, the Nine.
—The leader is fairest,
But all are divine.

They are lost in the hollows!
They stream up again!
What seeks on this mountain
The glorified train?—

They bathe on this mountain,
In the spring by their road;
Then on to Olympus,
Their endless abode.

—Whose praise do they mention?
Of what is it told?—
What will be for ever;
What was from of old.

First hymn they the Father
Of all things; and then,
The rest of immortals,
The action of men.

The day in his hotness,
The strife with the palm;
The night in her silence,
The stars in their calm.

645                *To Marguerite*

YES! in the sea of life enisled,
With echoing straits between us thrown,
Dotting the shoreless watery wild,
We mortal millions live *alone*.
The islands feel the enclasping flow,
And then their endless bounds they know.

MATTHEW ARNOLD

But when the moon their hollows lights,
And they are swept by balms of spring,
And in their glens, on starry nights,
The nightingales divinely sing;
And lovely notes, from shore to shore,
Across the sounds and channels pour—

Oh! then a longing like despair
Is to their farthest caverns sent;
For surely once, they feel, we were
Parts of a single continent!
Now round us spreads the watery plain—
Oh might our marges meet again!

Who ordered, that their longing's fire
Should be, as soon as kindled, cooled?
Who renders vain their deep desire?—
A God, a God their severance ruled!
And bade betwixt their shores to be
The unplumbed, salt, estranging sea.

646                    *Sohrab Dead*

So, on the bloody sand, Sohrab lay dead;
And the great Rustum drew his horseman's cloak
Down o'er his face, and sate by his dead son.
As those black granite pillars, once high-reared
By Jemshid in Persepolis, to bear
His house, now 'mid their broken flights of steps
Lie prone, enormous, down the mountain side—
So in the sand lay Rustum by his son.
    And night came down over the solemn waste,
And the two gazing hosts, and that sole pair,
And darkened all; and a cold fog, with night,
Crept from the Oxus. Soon a hum arose,
As of a great assembly loosed, and fires
Began to twinkle through the fog; for now
Both armies moved to camp, and took their meal;
The Persians took it on the open sands
Southward, the Tartars by the river marge;
And Rustum and his son were left alone.
    But the majestic river floated on,

Out of the mist and hum of that low land,
Into the frosty starlight, and there moved,
Rejoicing, through the hushed Chorasmian waste,
Under the solitary moon; he flowed
Right for the polar star, past Orgunjè,
Brimming, and bright, and large; then sands begin
To hem his watery march, and dam his streams,
And split his currents; that for many a league
The shorn and parcelled Oxus strains along
Through beds of sand and matted rushy isles—
Oxus, forgetting the bright speed he had
In his high mountain-cradle in Pamere,
A foiled circuitous wanderer—till at last
The longed-for dash of waves is heard, and wide
His luminous home of waters opens, bright
And tranquil, from whose floor the new-bathed stars
Emerge, and shine upon the Aral Sea.

647 *Requiescat*

STREW on her roses, roses,
   And never a spray of yew!
In quiet she reposes;
   Ah, would that I did too!

Her mirth the world required;
   She bathed it in smiles of glee.
But her heart was tired, tired,
   And now they let her be.

Her life was turning, turning,
   In mazes of heat and sound.
But for peace her soul was yearning,
   And now peace laps her round.

Her cabined, ample spirit,
   It fluttered and failed for breath.
To-night it doth inherit
   The vasty hall of death.

648 *The Scholar Gipsy*

Go, for they call you, shepherd, from the hill;
  Go, shepherd, and untie the wattled cotes!
    No longer leave thy wistful flock unfed,
  Nor let thy bawling fellows rack their throats,
    Nor the cropped herbage shoot another head.
      But when the fields are still,
  And the tired men and dogs all gone to rest,
    And only the white sheep are sometimes seen
    Cross and recross the strips of moon-blanched green,
  Come, shepherd, and again begin the quest!

Here, where the reaper was at work of late—
  In this high field's dark corner, where he leaves
    His coat, his basket, and his earthen cruse,
  And in the sun all morning binds the sheaves,
    Then here, at noon, comes back his stores to use—
      Here will I sit and wait,
  While to my ear from uplands far away
    The bleating of the folded flocks is borne,
    With distant cries of reapers in the corn—
  All the live murmur of a summer's day.

Screened is this nook o'er the high, half-reaped field,
  And here till sun-down, shepherd! will I be.
    Through the thick corn the scarlet poppies peep,
  And round green roots and yellowing stalks I see
    Pale pink convolvulus in tendrils creep;
      And air-swept lindens yield
  Their scent, and rustle down their perfumed showers
    Of bloom on the bent grass where I am laid,
    And bower me from the August sun with shade;
  And the eye travels down to Oxford's towers.

And near me on the grass lies Glanvil's book—
    Come, let me read the oft-read tale again!
      The story of the Oxford scholar poor,
    Of pregnant parts and quick inventive brain,
      Who, tired of knocking at preferment's door,
        One summer-morn forsook
    His friends, and went to learn the gipsy-lore,
      And roamed the world with that wild brotherhood,
      And came, as most men deemed, to little good,
    But came to Oxford and his friends no more.

But once, years after, in the country-lanes,
    Two scholars, whom at college erst he knew,
      Met him, and of his way of life enquired;
    Whereat he answered; that the gipsy-crew,
      His mates, had arts to rule as they desired
        The workings of men's brains,
    And they can bind them to what thoughts they will.
      'And I,' he said, 'the secret of their art,
      When fully learned, will to the world impart;
    But it needs heaven-sent moments for this skill.'

This said, he left them, and returned no more.—
    But rumours hung about the country-side,
      That the lost Scholar long was seen to stray,
    Seen by rare glimpses, pensive and tongue-tied,
      In hat of antique shape, and cloak of grey,
        The same the gipsies wore.
    Shepherds had met him on the Hurst in spring;
      At some lone alehouse in the Berkshire moors,
      On the warm ingle-bench, the smock-frocked boors
    Had found him seated at their entering,

But, 'mid their drink and clatter, he would fly.
    And I myself seem half to know thy looks,
      And put the shepherds, wanderer! on thy trace;
    And boys who in lone wheatfields scare the rooks
      I ask if thou hast passed their quiet place;
        Or in my boat I lie
    Moored to the cool bank in the summer-heats,
      'Mid wide grass meadows which the sunshine fills,
      And watch the warm, green-muffled Cumner hills,
    And wonder if thou haunt'st their shy retreats.

For most, I know, thou lov'st retired ground!
　Thee at the ferry Oxford riders blithe,
　　Returning home on summer-nights, have met
　Crossing the stripling Thames at Bab-lock-hithe,
　　Trailing in the cool stream thy fingers wet,
　　　As the punt's rope chops round;
　And leaning backward in a pensive dream,
　　And fostering in thy lap a heap of flowers
　　Plucked in shy fields and distant Wychwood bowers,
And thine eyes resting on the moonlit stream.

And then they land, and thou art seen no more!—
　Maidens, who from the distant hamlets come
　　To dance around the Fyfield elm in May,
　Oft through the darkening fields have seen thee roam,
　　Or cross a stile into the public way.
　　　Oft thou hast given them store
　Of flowers—the frail-leafed, white anemony,
　　Dark bluebells drenched with dews of summer eves,
　　And purple orchises with spotted leaves—
But none hath words she can report of thee.

And, above Godstow Bridge, when hay-time's here
　In June, and many a scythe in sunshine flames,
　　Men who through those wide fields of breezy grass
　Where black-winged swallows haunt the glittering Thames,
　　To bathe in the abandoned lasher pass,
　　　Have often passed thee near
　Sitting upon the river bank o'ergrown;
　　Marked thine outlandish garb, thy figure spare,
　　Thy dark vague eyes, and soft abstracted air—
But, when they came from bathing, thou wast gone!

At some lone homestead in the Cumner hills,
　Where at her open door the housewife darns,
　　Thou hast been seen, or hanging on a gate
　To watch the threshers in the mossy barns.
　　　Children, who early range these slopes and late
　　　For cresses from the rills,
　Have known thee eying, all an April-day,
　　The springing pastures and the feeding kine;
　　And marked thee, when the stars come out and shine,
Through the long dewy grass move slow away.

In autumn, on the skirts of Bagley Wood—
  Where most the gipsies by the turf-edged way
    Pitch their smoked tents, and every bush you see
With scarlet patches tagged and shreds of grey,
    Above the forest-ground called Thessaly—
      The blackbird, picking food,
Sees thee, nor stops his meal, nor fears at all;
    So often has he known thee past him stray,
    Rapt, twirling in thy hand a withered spray,
And waiting for the spark from heaven to fall.

And once, in winter, on the causeway chill
  Where home through flooded fields foot-travellers go,
    Have I not passed thee on the wooden bridge,
Wrapt in thy cloak and battling with the snow,
    Thy face toward Hinksey and its wintry ridge?
      And thou hast climbed the hill,
And gained the white brow of the Cumner range;
    Turned once to watch, while thick the snowflakes fall,
    The line of festal light in Christ-Church hall—
Then sought thy straw in some sequestered grange.

But what—I dream! Two hundred years are flown
  Since first thy story ran through Oxford halls,
    And the grave Glanvil did the tale inscribe
That thou wert wandered from the studious walls
    To learn strange arts, and join a gipsy-tribe;
      And thou from earth art gone
Long since, and in some quiet churchyard laid—
    Some country-nook, where o'er thy unknown grave
    Tall grasses and white flowering nettles wave,
Under a dark, red-fruited yew-tree's shade.

—No, no, thou hast not felt the lapse of hours!
  For what wears out the life of mortal men?
    'Tis that from change to change their being rolls;
  'Tis that repeated shocks, again, again,
    Exhaust the energy of strongest souls
      And numb the elastic powers.
Till having used our nerves with bliss and teen,
    And tired upon a thousand schemes our wit,
    To the just-pausing Genius we remit
Our worn-out life, and are—what we have been.

Thou hast not lived, why shouldst thou perish, so?
  Thou hadst *one* aim, *one* business, *one* desire;
    Else wert thou long since numbered with the dead!
  Else hadst thou spent, like other men, thy fire!
    The generations of thy peers are fled,
      And we ourselves shall go;
  But thou possessest an immortal lot,
    And we imagine thee exempt from age
    And living as thou liv'st on Glanvil's page,
  Because thou hadst—what we, alas! have not.

For early didst thou leave the world, with powers
  Fresh, undiverted to the world without,
    Firm to their mark, not spent on other things;
  Free from the sick fatigue, the languid doubt,
    Which much to have tried, in much been baffled, brings.
      O life unlike to ours!
  Who fluctuate idly without term or scope,
    Of whom each strives, nor knows for what he strives,
    And each half lives a hundred different lives;
  Who wait like thee, but not, like thee, in hope.

Thou waitest for the spark from heaven! and we,
  Light half-believers of our casual creeds,
    Who never deeply felt, nor clearly willed,
  Whose insight never has borne fruit in deeds,
    Whose vague resolves never have been fulfilled;
      For whom each year we see
  Breeds new beginnings, disappointments new;
    Who hesitate and falter life away,
    And lose to-morrow the ground won to-day—
  Ah! do not we, wanderer, await it too?

Yes, we await it!—but it still delays,
  And then we suffer! and amongst us one,
    Who most has suffered, takes dejectedly
  His seat upon the intellectual throne;
    And all his store of sad experience he
      Lays bare of wretched days;
  Tells us his misery's birth and growth and signs,
    And how the dying spark of hope was fed,
    And how the breast was soothed, and how the head,
  And all his hourly varied anodynes.

This for our wisest! and we others pine,
 And wish the long unhappy dream would end,
  And waive all claim to bliss, and try to bear;
With close-lipped patience for our only friend,
  Sad patience, too near neighbour to despair—
   But none has hope like thine!
Thou through the fields and through the woods dost stray,
  Roaming the country-side, a truant boy,
  Nursing thy project in unclouded joy,
And every doubt long blown by time away.

O born in days when wits were fresh and clear,
 And life ran gaily as the sparkling Thames;
  Before this strange disease of modern life,
With its sick hurry, its divided aims,
  Its heads o'ertaxed, its palsied hearts, was rife—
   Fly hence, our contact fear!
Still fly, plunge deeper in the bowering wood!
  Averse, as Dido did with gesture stern
  From her false friend's approach in Hades turn,
Wave us away, and keep thy solitude!

Still nursing the unconquerable hope,
 Still clutching the inviolable shade,
  With a free, onward impulse brushing through,
By night, the silvered branches of the glade—
  Far on the forest-skirts, where none pursue.
   On some mild pastoral slope
Emerge, and resting on the moonlit pales
  Freshen thy flowers as in former years
  With dew, or listen with enchanted ears,
From the dark dingles, to the nightingales!

But fly our paths, our feverish contact fly!
 For strong the infection of our mental strife,
  Which though it gives no bliss, yet spoils for rest;
And we should win thee from thy own fair life,
  Like us distracted, and like us unblest.
   Soon, soon thy cheer would die,
Thy hopes grow timorous, and unfixed thy powers,
  And thy clear aims be cross and shifting made;
  And then thy glad perennial youth would fade,
Fade, and grow old at last, and die like ours.

Then fly our greetings, fly our speech and smiles!
　—As some grave Tyrian trader, from the sea,
　　Descried at sunrise an emerging prow
　Lifting the cool-haired creepers stealthily,
　　The fringes of a southward-facing brow
　　　Among the Ægæan isles;
　And saw the merry Grecian coaster come,
　　Freighted with amber grapes, and Chian wine,
　　Green, bursting figs, and tunnies steeped in brine—
　And knew the intruders on his ancient home,

The young light-hearted masters of the waves—
　And snatched his rudder, and shook out more sail;
　　And day and night held on indignantly
　O'er the blue Midland waters with the gale,
　　Betwixt the Syrtes and soft Sicily,
　　　To where the Atlantic raves
　Outside the western straits; and unbent sails
　　There, where down cloudy cliffs, through sheets of foam,
　　Shy traffickers, the dark Iberians come;
　And on the beach undid his corded bales.

649　　　　　　　　*Thyrsis*

A Monody, to commemorate the author's friend,
Arthur Hugh Clough, who died at Florence, 1861

How changed is here each spot man makes or fills!
　In the two Hinkseys nothing keeps the same;
　　The village street its haunted mansion lacks,
　And from the sign is gone Sibylla's name,
　　And from the roofs the twisted chimney-stacks—
　　　Are ye too changed, ye hills?
　See, 'tis no foot of unfamiliar men
　　To-night from Oxford up your pathway strays!
　　Here came I often, often, in old days—
　Thyrsis and I; we still had Thyrsis then.

Runs it not here, the track by Childsworth Farm,
  Past the high wood, to where the elm-tree crowns
    The hill behind whose ridge the sunset flames?
The signal-elm, that looks on Ilsley Downs,
    The Vale, the three lone weirs, the youthful Thames?—
      This winter-eve is warm,
  Humid the air! leafless, yet soft as spring,
    The tender purple spray on copse and briers!
    And that sweet city with her dreaming spires,
  She needs not June for beauty's heightening,

Lovely all times she lies, lovely to-night!—
  Only, methinks, some loss of habit's power
    Befalls me wandering through this upland dim.
Once passed I blindfold here, at any hour;
    Now seldom come I, since I came with him.
      That single elm-tree bright
Against the west—I miss it! is it gone?
  We prized it dearly; while it stood, we said,
  Our friend, the Gipsy-Scholar, was not dead;
While the tree lived, he in these fields lived on.

Too rare, too rare, grow now my visits here,
  But once I knew each field, each flower, each stick;
    And with the country-folk acquaintance made
By barn in threshing-time, by new-built rick.
    Here, too, our shepherd-pipes we first assayed.
      Ah me! this many a year
My pipe is lost, my shepherd's holiday!
  Needs must I lose them, needs with heavy heart
  Into the world and wave of men depart;
But Thyrsis of his own will went away.

It irked him to be here, he could not rest.
  He loved each simple joy the country yields,
    He loved his mates; but yet he could not keep,
For that a shadow loured on the fields,
    Here with the shepherds and the silly sheep.
      Some life of men unblest
He knew, which made him droop, and filled his head.
  He went; his piping took a troubled sound
  Of storms that rage outside our happy ground;
He could not wait their passing, he is dead.

So, some tempestuous morn in early June,
 When the year's primal burst of bloom is o'er,
  Before the roses and the longest day—
When garden-walks and all the grassy floor
  With blossoms red and white of fallen May
   And chestnut-flowers are strewn—
So have I heard the cuckoo's parting cry,
  From the wet field, through the vext garden-trees,
  Come with the volleying rain and tossing breeze:
*The bloom is gone, and with the bloom go I!*

Too quick despairer, wherefore wilt thou go?
 Soon will the high Midsummer pomps come on,
  Soon will the musk carnations break and swell,
Soon shall we have gold-dusted snapdragon,
  Sweet-William with his homely cottage-smell,
   And stocks in fragrant blow;
Roses that down the alleys shine afar,
  And open, jasmine-muffled lattices,
  And groups under the dreaming garden-trees,
And the full moon, and the white evening-star.

He hearkens not! light comer, he is flown!
 What matters it? next year he will return,
  And we shall have him in the sweet spring-days,
With whitening hedges, and uncrumpling fern,
  And blue-bells trembling by the forest-ways,
   And scent of hay new-mown.
But Thyrsis never more we swains shall see;
  See him come back, and cut a smoother reed,
  And blow a strain the world at last shall heed—
For Time, not Corydon, hath conquered thee!

Alack, for Corydon no rival now!—
 But when Sicilian shepherds lost a mate,
  Some good survivor with his flute would go,
Piping a ditty sad for Bion's fate;
  And cross the unpermitted ferry's flow,
   And relax Pluto's brow,
And make leap up with joy the beauteous head
 Of Proserpine, among whose crowned hair
 Are flowers first opened on Sicilian air,
And flute his friend, like Orpheus, from the dead.

O easy access to the hearer's grace
  When Dorian shepherds sang to Proserpine!
    For she herself had trod Sicilian fields,
  She knew the Dorian water's gush divine,
    She knew each lily white which Enna yields,
      Each rose with blushing face;
  She loved the Dorian pipe, the Dorian strain.
    But ah, of our poor Thames she never heard!
    Her foot the Cumner cowslips never stirred;
  And we should tease her with our plaint in vain!

Well! wind-dispersed and vain the words will be,
  Yet, Thyrsis, let me give my grief its hour
    In the old haunt, and find our tree-topped hill!
  Who, if not I, for questing here hath power?
    I know the wood which hides the daffodil,
      I know the Fyfield tree,
  I know what white, what purple fritillaries
    The grassy harvest of the river-fields,
    Above by Ensham, down by Sandford, yields,
  And what sedged brooks are Thames's tributaries;

I know these slopes; who knows them if not I?—
  But many a dingle on the loved hill-side,
    With thorns once studded, old, white-blossomed trees,
  Where thick the cowslips grew, and far descried
    High towered the spikes of purple orchises,
      Hath since our day put by
  The coronals of that forgotten time;
    Down each green bank hath gone the ploughboy's team,
    And only in the hidden brookside gleam
  Primroses, orphans of the flowery prime.

Where is the girl, who by the boatman's door,
  Above the locks, above the boating throng,
    Unmoored our skiff when through the Wytham flats,
  Red loosestrife and blond meadow-sweet among
    And darting swallows and light water-gnats,
      We tracked the shy Thames shore?
  Where are the mowers, who, as the tiny swell
    Of our boat passing heaved the river-grass,
    Stood with suspended scythe to see us pass?—
  They all are gone, and thou art gone as well!

Yes, thou art gone! and round me too the night
  In ever-nearing circle weaves her shade.
    I see her veil draw soft across the day,
  I feel her slowly chilling breath invade
    The cheek grown thin, the brown hair sprent with grey;
      I feel her finger light
  Laid pausefully upon life's headlong train;—
    The foot less prompt to meet the morning dew,
    The heart less bounding at emotion new,
  And hope, once crushed, less quick to spring again.

And long the way appears, which seemed so short
  To the less practised eye of sanguine youth;
    And high the mountain-tops, in cloudy air,
  The mountain-tops where is the throne of Truth,
    Tops in life's morning-sun so bright and bare!
      Unbreachable the fort
  Of the long-battered world uplifts its wall;
    And strange and vain the earthly turmoil grows,
    And near and real the charm of thy repose,
  And night as welcome as a friend would fall.

But hush! the upland hath a sudden loss
  Of quiet!—look, adown the dusk hill-side,
    A troop of Oxford hunters going home,
  As in old days, jovial and talking, ride!
    From hunting with the Berkshire hounds they come.
      Quick! let me fly, and cross
  Into yon farther field!—'Tis done; and see,
    Backed by the sunset, which doth glorify
    The orange and pale violet evening-sky,
  Bare on its lonely ridge, the Tree! the Tree!

I take the omen! Eve lets down her veil,
  The white fog creeps from bush to bush about,
    The west unflushes, the high stars grow bright,
  And in the scattered farms the lights come out.
    I cannot reach the signal-tree to-night,
      Yet, happy omen, hail!
  Hear it from thy broad lucent Arno-vale,
    (For there thine earth-forgetting eyelids keep
    The morningless and unawakening sleep
  Under the flowery oleanders pale),

Hear it, O Thyrsis, still our tree is there!—
   Ah, vain! These English fields, this upland dim,
     These brambles pale with mist engarlanded,
   That lone, sky-pointing tree, are not for him;
     To a boon southern country he is fled,
       And now in happier air,
   Wandering with the great Mother's train divine
     (And purer or more subtle soul than thee,
     I trow, the mighty Mother doth not see)
   Within a folding of the Apennine,

Thou hearest the immortal chants of old!—
   Putting his sickle to the perilous grain
     In the hot cornfield of the Phrygian king,
   For thee the Lityerses-song again
     Young Daphnis with his silver voice doth sing;
       Sings his Sicilian fold,
   His sheep, his hapless love, his blinded eyes—
     And how a call celestial round him rang,
     And heavenward from the fountain-brink he sprang,
   And all the marvel of the golden skies.

There thou art gone, and me thou leavest here
   Sole in these fields! yet will I not despair.
     Despair I will not, while I yet descry
   'Neath the mild canopy of English air
     That lonely tree against the western sky.
       Still, still these slopes, 'tis clear,
   Our Gipsy-Scholar haunts, outliving thee!
     Fields where soft sheep from cages pull the hay,
     Woods with anemonies in flower till May,
   Know him a wanderer still; then why not me?

A fugitive and gracious light he seeks,
   Shy to illumine; and I seek it too.
     This does not come with houses or with gold,
   With place, with honour, and a flattering crew;
     'Tis not in the world's market bought and sold—
       But the smooth-slipping weeks
   Drop by, and leave its seeker still untired;
     Out of the heed of mortals he is gone,
     He wends unfollowed, he must house alone;
   Yet on he fares, by his own heart inspired.

Thou too, O Thyrsis, on like quest wast bound;
  Thou wanderedst with me for a little hour!
    Men gave thee nothing; but this happy quest,
  If men esteemed thee feeble, gave thee power,
    If men procured thee trouble, gave thee rest.
      And this rude Cumner ground,
  Its fir-topped Hurst, its farms, its quiet fields,
    Here cam'st thou in thy jocund youthful time,
    Here was thine height of strength, thy golden prime!
  And still the haunt beloved a virtue yields.

What though the music of thy rustic flute
  Kept not for long its happy, country tone;
    Lost it too soon, and learnt a stormy note
  Of men contention-tost, of men who groan,
    Which tasked thy pipe too sore, and tired thy throat—
      It failed, and thou wast mute!
  Yet hadst thou alway visions of our light,
    And long with men of care thou couldst not stay,
    And soon thy foot resumed its wandering way,
  Left human haunt, and on alone till night.

Too rare, too rare, grow now my visits here!
  'Mid city-noise, not, as with thee of yore,
    Thyrsis! in reach of sheep-bells is my home.
  —Then through the great town's harsh, heart-wearying roar,
    Let in thy voice a whisper often come,
      To chase fatigue and fear:
  *Why faintest thou? I wandered till I died.*
    *Roam on! The light we sought is shining still.*
    *Dost thou ask proof? Our tree yet crowns the hill,*
  *Our Scholar travels yet the loved hill-side.*

650 *Dover Beach*

THE sea is calm to-night.
The tide is full, the moon lies fair
Upon the straits;—on the French coast the light
Gleams and is gone; the cliffs of England stand,
Glimmering and vast, out in the tranquil bay.
Come to the window, sweet is the night-air!
Only, from the long line of spray
Where the sea meets the moon-blanched land,
Listen! you hear the grating roar
Of pebbles which the waves draw back, and fling,
At their return, up the high strand,
Begin, and cease, and then again begin,
With tremulous cadence slow, and bring
The eternal note of sadness in.

Sophocles long ago
Heard it on the Ægæan, and it brought
Into his mind the turbid ebb and flow
Of human misery; we
Find also in the sound a thought,
Hearing it by this distant northern sea.

The Sea of Faith
Was once, too, at the full, and round earth's shore
Lay like the folds of a bright girdle furled.
But now I only hear
Its melancholy, long, withdrawing roar,
Retreating, to the breath
Of the night-wind, down the vast edges drear
And naked shingles of the world.

Ah, love, let us be true
To one another! for the world, which seems
To lie before us like a land of dreams,
So various, so beautiful, so new,
Hath really neither joy, nor love, nor light,
Nor certitude, nor peace, nor help for pain;
And we are here as on a darkling plain
Swept with confused alarms of struggle and flight,
Where ignorant armies clash by night.

651 *The Last Word*

CREEP into thy narrow bed,
Creep, and let no more be said!
Vain thy onset! all stands fast.
Thou thyself must break at last.

Let the long contention cease!
Geese are swans, and swans are geese.
Let them have it how they will!
Thou art tired; best be still.

They out-talked thee, hissed thee, tore thee?
Better men fared thus before thee;
Fired their ringing shot and passed,
Hotly charged—and sank at last.

Charge once more, then, and be dumb!
Let the victors, when they come,
When the forts of folly fall,
Find thy body by the wall!

# WILLIAM CORY

## 1823–1892

652 *Mimnermus in Church*

YOU promise heavens free from strife,
  Pure truth, and perfect change of will;
But sweet, sweet is this human life,
  So sweet, I fain would breathe it still;
Your chilly stars I can forgo,
This warm kind world is all I know.

You say there is no substance here,
  One great reality above:
Back from that void I shrink in fear,
  And child-like hide myself in love:
Show me what angels feel. Till then
I cling, a mere weak man, to men.

You bid me lift my mean desires
　　From faltering lips and fitful veins
To sexless souls, ideal quires,
　　Unwearied voices, wordless strains:
My mind with fonder welcome owns
One dear dead friend's remembered tones.

Forsooth the present we must give
　　To that which cannot pass away;
All beauteous things for which we live
　　By laws of time and space decay.
But Oh, the very reason why
I clasp them, is because they die.

### 653 *Heraclitus*

THEY told me, Heraclitus, they told me you were dead,
They brought me bitter news to hear and bitter tears to shed.
I wept as I remembered how often you and I
Had tired the sun with talking and sent him down the sky.

And now that thou art lying, my dear old Carian guest,
A handful of grey ashes, long, long ago at rest,
Still are thy pleasant voices, thy nightingales, awake;
For Death, he taketh all away, but them he cannot take.

# COVENTRY PATMORE
## 1823–1896

### 654 *Departure*

IT was not like your great and gracious ways!
Do you, that have nought other to lament,
Never, my Love, repent
Of how, that July afternoon,
You went,
With sudden, unintelligible phrase,
And frightened eye,
Upon your journey of so many days,
Without a single kiss, or a good-bye?

I knew, indeed, that you were parting soon;
And so we sate, within the low sun's rays,
You whispering to me, for your voice was weak,
Your harrowing praise.
Well, it was well,
To hear you such things speak,
And I could tell
What made your eyes a growing gloom of love,
As a warm South-wind sombres a March grove.
And it was like your great and gracious ways
To turn your talk on daily things, my Dear,
Lifting the luminous, pathetic lash
To let the laughter flash,
Whilst I drew near,
Because you spoke so low that I could scarcely hear.
But all at once to leave me at the last,
More at the wonder than the loss aghast,
With huddled, unintelligible phrase,
And frightened eye,
And go your journey of all days
With not one kiss, or a good-bye,
And the only loveless look the look with which you passed:
'Twas all unlike your great and gracious ways.

655 *A Farewell*

WITH all my will, but much against my heart,
We two now part.
My Very Dear,
Our solace is, the sad road lies so clear.
It needs no art,
With faint, averted feet
And many a tear,
In our opposèd paths to persevere.
Go thou to East, I West.
We will not say
There's any hope, it is so far away.
But, O, my Best,
When the one darling of our widowhead,
The nursling, Grief,
Is dead,

And no dews blur our eyes
To see the peach-bloom come in evening skies,
Perchance we may,
Where now this night is day,
And even through faith of still averted feet,
Making full circle of our banishment,
Amazèd meet;
The bitter journey to the bourne so sweet
Seasoning the termless feast of our content
With tears of recognition never dry.

656                          *Winter*

I, SINGULARLY moved
To love the lovely that are not beloved,
Of all the Seasons, most
Love Winter, and to trace
The sense of the Trophonian pallor on her face.
It is not death, but plenitude of peace;
And the dim cloud that does the world enfold
Hath less the characters of dark and cold
Than warmth and light asleep,
And correspondent breathing seems to keep
With the infant harvest, breathing soft below
Its eider coverlet of snow.
Nor is in field or garden anything
But, duly looked into, contains serene
The substance of things hoped for, in the Spring,
And evidence of Summer not yet seen.
On every chance-mild day
That visits the moist shaw,
The honeysuckle, 'sdaining to be crost
In urgence of sweet life by sleet or frost,
'Voids the time's law
With still increase
Of leaflet new, and little, wandering spray;
Often, in sheltering brakes,
As one from rest disturbed in the first hour,
Primrose or violet bewildered wakes,
And deems 'tis time to flower;

Though not a whisper of her voice he hear,
The buried bulb does know
The signals of the year,
And hails far Summer with his lifted spear.
The gorse-field dark, by sudden, gold caprice,
Turns, here and there, into a Jason's fleece;
Lilies, that soon in Autumn slipped their gowns of green,
And vanished into earth,
And came again, ere Autumn died, to birth,
Stand full-arrayed, amidst the wavering shower,
And perfect for the Summer, less the flower;
In nook of pale or crevice of crude bark,
Thou canst not miss,
If close thou spy, to mark
The ghostly chrysalis,
That, if thou touch it, stirs in its dream dark;
And the flushed Robin, in the evenings hoar,
Does of Love's Day, as if he saw it, sing;
But sweeter yet than dream or song of Summer or Spring
Are Winter's sometime smiles, that seem to well
From infancy ineffable;
Her wandering, languorous gaze,
So unfamiliar, so without amaze,
On the elemental, chill adversity,
The uncomprehended rudeness; and her sigh
And solemn, gathering tear,
And look of exile from some great repose, the sphere
Of ether, moved by ether only, or
By something still more tranquil.

657                    *Magna est Veritas*

HERE, in this little Bay,
Full of tumultuous life and great repose,
Where, twice a day,
The purposeless, glad ocean comes and goes,
Under high cliffs, and far from the huge town,
I sit me down.
For want of me the world's course will not fail;
When all its work is done, the lie shall rot;
The truth is great, and shall prevail,
When none cares whether it prevail or not.

# WILLIAM ALLINGHAM
## 1824–1889

658                           *The Fairies*

UP the airy mountain,
　　Down the rushy glen,
We daren't go a-hunting
　　For fear of little men;
Wee folk, good folk,
　　Trooping all together;
Green jacket, red cap,
　　And white owl's feather!

Down along the rocky shore
　　Some make their home,
They live on crispy pancakes
　　Of yellow tide-foam;
Some in the reeds
　　Of the black mountain lake,
With frogs for their watch-dogs,
　　All night awake.

High on the hill-top
　　The old King sits;
He is now so old and gray
　　He's nigh lost his wits.
With a bridge of white mist
　　Columbkill he crosses,
On his stately journeys
　　From Slieveleague to Rosses;
Or going up with music
　　On cold starry nights
To sup with the Queen
　　Of the gay Northern Lights.

They stole little Bridget
　　For seven years long;
When she came down again
　　Her friends were all gone.

They took her lightly back,
  Between the night and morrow,
They thought that she was fast asleep,
  But she was dead with sorrow.
They have kept her ever since
  Deep within the lake,
On a bed of flag-leaves,
  Watching till she wake.

By the craggy hill-side,
  Through the mosses bare,
They have planted thorn-trees
  For pleasure here and there.
Is any man so daring
  As dig them up in spite,
He shall find their sharpest thorns
  In his bed at night.

Up the airy mountain,
  Down the rushy glen,
We daren't go a-hunting
  For fear of little men;
Wee folk, good folk,
  Trooping all together;
Green jacket, red cap,
  And white owl's feather!

# DANTE GABRIEL ROSSETTI
## 1828–1882

659 *The Blessed Damozel*

THE blessed damozel leaned out
  From the gold bar of Heaven;
Her eyes were deeper than the depth
  Of waters stilled at even;
She had three lilies in her hand,
  And the stars in her hair were seven.

Her robe, ungirt from clasp to hem,
   No wrought flowers did adorn,
But a white rose of Mary's gift,
   For service meetly worn;
Her hair that lay along her back
   Was yellow like ripe corn.

Herseemed she scarce had been a day
   One of God's choristers;
The wonder was not yet quite gone
   From that still look of hers;
Albeit, to them she left, her day
   Had counted as ten years.

(To one, it is ten years of years.
   . . . Yet now, and in this place,
Surely she leaned o'er me—her hair
   Fell all about my face. . .
Nothing: the autumn fall of leaves.
   The whole year sets apace.)

It was the rampart of God's house
   That she was standing on;
By God built over the sheer depth
   The which is Space begun;
So high, that looking downward thence
   She scarce could see the sun.

It lies in Heaven, across the flood
   Of ether, as a bridge.
Beneath, the tides of day and night
   With flame and darkness ridge
The void, as low as where this earth
   Spins like a fretful midge.

Around her, lovers, newly met
   'Mid deathless love's acclaims,
Spoke evermore among themselves
   Their heart remembered names;
And the souls mounting up to God
   Went by her like thin flames.

And still she bowed herself and stooped
  Out of the circling charm;
Until her bosom must have made
  The bar she leaned on warm,
And the lilies lay as if asleep
  Along her bended arm.

From the fixed place of Heaven she saw
  Time like a pulse shake fierce
Through all the worlds. Her gaze still strove
  Within the gulf to pierce
Its path; and now she spoke as when
  The stars sang in their spheres.

The sun was gone now; the curled moon
  Was like a little feather
Fluttering far down the gulf; and now
  She spoke through the still weather.
Her voice was like the voice the stars
  Had when they sang together.

(Ah sweet! Even now, in that bird's song,
  Strove not her accents there,
Fain to be hearkened? When those bells
  Possessed the mid-day air,
Strove not her steps to reach my side
  Down all the echoing stair?)

'I wish that he were come to me,
  For he will come,' she said.
'Have I not prayed in Heaven?—on earth,
  Lord, Lord, has he not prayed?
Are not two prayers a perfect strength?
  And shall I feel afraid?

'When round his head the aureole clings,
  And he is clothed in white,
I'll take his hand and go with him
  To the deep wells of light;
As unto a stream we will step down
  And bathe there in God's sight.

'We two will stand beside that shrine,
　　Occult, withheld, untrod,
Whose lamps are stirred continually
　　With prayer sent up to God;
And see our old prayers, granted, melt
　　Each like a little cloud.

'We two will lie i' the shadow of
　　That living mystic tree
Within whose secret growth the Dove
　　Is sometimes felt to be,
While every leaf that His plumes touch
　　Saith His Name audibly.

'And I myself will teach to him,
　　I myself, lying so,
The songs I sing here; which his voice
　　Shall pause in, hushed and slow,
And find some knowledge at each pause,
　　Or some new thing to know.'

(Alas! We two, we two, thou sayst!
　　Yea, one wast thou with me
That once of old. But shall God lift
　　To endless unity
The soul whose likeness with thy soul
　　Was but its love for thee?)

'We two,' she said, 'will seek the groves
　　Where the lady Mary is,
With her five handmaidens, whose names
　　Are five sweet symphonies,
Cecily, Gertrude, Magdalen,
　　Margaret and Rosalys.

'Circlewise sit they, with bound locks
　　And foreheads garlanded;
Into the fine cloth white like flame
　　Weaving the golden thread,
To fashion the birth-robes for them
　　Who are just born, being dead.

'He shall fear, haply, and be dumb:
   Then will I lay my cheek
To his, and tell about our love,
   Not once abashed or weak:
And the dear Mother will approve
   My pride, and let me speak.

'Herself shall bring us, hand in hand,
   To Him round whom all souls
Kneel, the clear-ranged unnumbered heads
   Bowed with their aureoles:
And angels meeting us shall sing
   To their citherns and citoles.

'There will I ask of Christ the Lord
   Thus much for him and me:—
Only to live as once on earth
   With Love,—only to be,
As then awhile, for ever now
   Together, I and he.'

She gazed and listened and then said,
   Less sad of speech than mild,—
'All this is when he comes.' She ceased.
   The light thrilled towards her, filled
With angels in strong level flight.
   Her eyes prayed, and she smiled.

(I saw her smile.) But soon their path
   Was vague in distant spheres:
And then she cast her arms along
   The golden barriers,
And laid her face between her hands,
   And wept. (I heard her tears.)

660                     *The Woodspurge*

THE wind flapped loose, the wind was still,
Shaken out dead from tree and hill:
I had walked on at the wind's will,—
I sat now, for the wind was still.

# DANTE GABRIEL ROSSETTI

Between my knees my forehead was,—
My lips, drawn in, said not Alas!
My hair was over in the grass,
My naked ears heard the day pass.

My eyes, wide open, had the run
Of some ten weeds to fix upon;
Among those few, out of the sun,
The woodspurge flowered, three cups in one.

From perfect grief there need not be
Wisdom or even memory:
One thing then learnt remains to me,—
The woodspurge has a cup of three.

661                    *Even So*

So it is, my dear.
All such things touch secret strings
For heavy hearts to hear.
So it is, my dear.

Very like indeed:
Sea and sky, afar, on high,
Sand and strewn seaweed,—
Very like indeed.

But the sea stands spread
As one wall with the flat skies,
Where the lean black craft like flies
Seem well-nigh stagnated,
Soon to drop off dead.

Seemed it so to us
When I was thine and thou wast mine,
And all these things were thus,
But all our world in us?

Could we be so now?
Not if all beneath heaven's pall
Lay dead but I and thou,
Could we be so now!

715

662 *Sudden Light*

I HAVE been here before,
 But when or how I cannot tell:
I know the grass beyond the door,
 The sweet keen smell,
The sighing sound, the lights around the shore.

You have been mine before,—
 How long ago I may not know:
But just when at that swallow's soar
 Your neck turned so,
Some veil did fall,—I knew it all of yore.

Has this been thus before?
 And shall not thus time's eddying flight
Still with our lives our love restore
 In death's despite,
And day and night yield one delight once more?

663 *A Superscription*

LOOK in my face; my name is Might-have-been;
 I am also called No-more, Too-late, Farewell;
 Unto thine ear I hold the dead-sea shell
Cast up thy Life's foam-fretted feet between;
Unto thine eyes the glass where that is seen
 Which had Life's form and Love's, but by my spell
 Is now a shaken shadow intolerable,
Of ultimate things unuttered the frail screen.
Mark me, how still I am! But should there dart
 One moment through thy soul the soft surprise
 Of that winged Peace which lulls the breath of sighs,—
Then shalt thou see me smile, and turn apart
Thy visage to mine ambush at thy heart
 Sleepless with cold commemorative eyes.

# GEORGE MEREDITH

1828–1909

664                    *Love in the Valley*

UNDER yonder beech-tree single on the green-sward,
    Couched with her arms behind her golden head,
Knees and tresses folded to slip and ripple idly,
    Lies my young love sleeping in the shade.
Had I the heart to slide an arm beneath her,
    Press her parting lips as her waist I gather slow,
Waking in amazement she could not but embrace me:
    Then would she hold me and never let me go?

Shy as the squirrel and wayward as the swallow,
    Swift as the swallow along the river's light
Circleting the surface to meet his mirrored winglets,
    Fleeter she seems in her stay than in her flight.
Shy as the squirrel that leaps among the pine-tops,
    Wayward as the swallow overhead at set of sun,
She whom I love is hard to catch and conquer,
    Hard, but O the glory of the winning were she won!

When her mother tends her before the laughing mirror,
    Tying up her laces, looping up her hair,
Often she thinks, were this wild thing wedded,
    More love should I have, and much less care.
When her mother tends her before the lighted mirror,
    Loosening her laces, combing down her curls,
Often she thinks, were this wild thing wedded,
    I should miss but one for many boys and girls.

Heartless she is as the shadow in the meadows
    Flying to the hills on a blue and breezy noon.
No, she is athirst and drinking up her wonder:
    Earth to her is young as the slip of the new moon.
Deals she an unkindness, 'tis but her rapid measure,
    Even as in a dance; and her smile can heal no less:
Like the swinging May-cloud that pelts the flowers with hailstones
    Off a sunny border, she was made to bruise and bless.

GEORGE MEREDITH

Lovely are the curves of the white owl sweeping
   Wavy in the dusk lit by one large star.
Lone on the fir-branch, his rattle-note unvaried,
   Brooding o'er the gloom, spins the brown eve-jar.
Darker grows the valley, more and more forgetting:
   So were it with me if forgetting could be willed.
Tell the grassy hollow that holds the bubbling well-spring,
   Tell it to forget the source that keeps it filled.

Stepping down the hill with her fair companions,
   Arm in arm, all against the raying West,
Boldly she sings, to the merry tune she marches,
   Brave in her shape, and sweeter unpossessed.
Sweeter, for she is what my heart first awaking
   Whispered the world was; morning light is she.
Love that so desires would fain keep her changeless;
   Fain would fling the net, and fain have her free.

Happy happy time, when the white star hovers
   Low over dim fields fresh with bloomy dew,
Near the face of dawn, that draws athwart the darkness,
   Threading it with colour, as yewberries the yew.
Thicker crowd the shades as the grave East deepens
   Glowing, and with crimson a long cloud swells.
Maiden still the morn is; and strange she is, and secret;
   Strange her eyes; her cheeks are cold as cold sea-shells.

\*

Mother of the dews, dark eye-lashed twilight,
   Low-lidded twilight, o'er the valley's brim,
Rounding on thy breast sings the dew-delighted skylark,
   Clear as though the dewdrops had their voice in him.
Hidden where the rose-flush drinks the rayless planet,
   Fountain-full he pours the spraying fountain-showers.
Let me hear her laughter, I would have her ever
   Cool as dew in twilight, the lark above the flowers.

All the girls are out with their baskets for the primrose;
   Up lanes, woods through, they troop in joyful bands.
My sweet leads: she knows not why, but now she loiters,
   Eyes the bent anemones, and hangs her hands.

Such a look will tell that the violets are peeping,
   Coming the rose: and unaware a cry
Springs in her bosom for odours and for colour,
   Covert and the nightingale; she knows not why.

            \*

Hither she comes; she comes to me; she lingers,
   Deepens her brown eyebrows, while in new surprise
High rise the lashes in wonder of a stranger;
   Yet am I the light and living of her eyes.
Something friends have told her fills her heart to brimming,
   Nets her in her blushes, and wounds her, and tames.—
Sure of her haven, O like a dove alighting,
   Arms up, she dropped: our souls were in our names.

            \*

Could I find a place to be alone with heaven,
   I would speak my heart out: heaven is my need.
Every woodland tree is flushing like the dogwood,
   Flashing like the whitebeam, swaying like the reed.
Flushing like the dogwood crimson in October;
   Streaming like the flag-reed South-West blown;
Flashing as in gusts the sudden-lighted whitebeam:
   All seem to know what is for heaven alone.

665              *Phoebus with Admetus*

WHEN by Zeus relenting the mandate was revoked,
   Sentencing to exile the bright Sun-God,
Mindful were the ploughmen of who the steer had yoked,
   Who: and what a track showed the upturned sod!
Mindful were the shepherds as now the noon severe
   Bent a burning eyebrow to brown evetide,
How the rustic flute drew the silver to the sphere,
   Sister of his own, till her rays fell wide.
         God! of whom music
         And song and blood are pure,
         The day is never darkened
         That had thee here obscure.

Chirping none, the scarlet cicalas crouched in ranks:
   Slack the thistle-head piled its down-silk grey:
Scarce the stony lizard sucked hollows in his flanks:
   Thick on spots of umbrage our drowsed flocks lay.
Sudden bowed the chestnuts beneath a wind unheard,
   Lengthened ran the grasses, the sky grew slate:
Then amid a swift flight of winged seed white as curd,
   Clear of limb a Youth smote the master's gate.
          God! of whom music
           And song and blood are pure,
           The day is never darkened
           That had thee here obscure.

Water, first of singers, o'er rocky mount and mead,
   First of earthly singers, the sun-loved rill,
Sang of him, and flooded the ripples on the reed,
   Seeking whom to waken and what ear fill.
Water, sweetest soother to kiss a wound and cool,
   Sweetest and divinest, the sky-born brook,
Chuckled, with a whimper, and made a mirror-pool
   Round the guest we welcomed, the strange hand shook.
          God! of whom music
           And song and blood are pure,
           The day is never darkened
           That had thee here obscure.

Many swarms of wild bees descended on our fields:
   Stately stood the wheatstalk with head bent high:
Big of heart we laboured at storing mighty yields,
   Wool and corn, and clusters to make men cry!
Hand-like rushed the vintage; we strung the bellied skins
   Plump, and at the sealing the Youth's voice rose:
Maidens clung in circle, on little fists their chins;
   Gentle beasties through pushed a cold long nose.
          God! of whom music
           And song and blood are pure,
           The day is never darkened
           That had thee here obscure.

Foot to fire in snowtime we trimmed the slender shaft:
   Often down the pit spied the lean wolf's teeth
Grin against his will, trapped by masterstrokes of craft;
   Helpless in his froth-wrath as green logs seethe!

Safe the tender lambs tugged the teats, and winter sped
   Whirled before the crocus, the year's new gold.
Hung the hooky beak up aloft the arrowhead
   Reddened through his feathers for our dear fold.
        God! of whom music
        And song and blood are pure,
        The day is never darkened
        That had thee here obscure.

Tales we drank of giants at war with Gods above:
   Rocks were they to look on, and earth climbed air!
Tales of search for simples, and those who sought of love
   Ease because the creature was all too fair.
Pleasant ran our thinking that while our work was good,
   Sure as fruits for sweat would the praise come fast.
He that wrestled stoutest and tamed the billow-brood
   Danced in rings with girls, like a sail-flapped mast.
        God! of whom music
        And song and blood are pure,
        The day is never darkened
        That had thee here obscure.

Lo, the herb of healing, when once the herb is known,
   Shines in shady woods bright as new-sprung flame.
Ere the string was tightened we heard the mellow tone,
   After he had taught how the sweet sounds came.
Stretched about his feet, labour done, 'twas as you see
   Red pomegranates tumble and burst hard rind.
So began contention to give delight and be
   Excellent in things aimed to make life kind.
        God! of whom music
        And song and blood are pure,
        The day is never darkened
        That had thee here obscure.

You with shelly horns, rams! and promontory goats,
   You whose browsing beards dip in coldest dew!
Bulls, that walk the pastures in kingly-flashing coats!
   Laurel, ivy, vine, wreathed for feasts not few!
You that build the shade-roof, and you that court the rays,
   You that leap besprinkling the rock stream-rent:
He has been our fellow, the morning of our days;
   Us he chose for housemates, and this way went.

God! of whom music
And song and blood are pure,
The day is never darkened
That had thee here obscure.

666 *Lucifer in Starlight*

ON a starred night Prince Lucifer uprose.
Tired of his dark dominion swung the fiend
Above the rolling ball in cloud part screened,
Where sinners hugged their spectre of repose.
Poor prey to his hot fit of pride were those.
And now upon his western wing he leaned,
Now his huge bulk o'er Afric's sands careened,
Now the black planet shadowed Arctic snows.
Soaring through wider zones that pricked his scars
With memory of the old revolt from Awe,
He reached a middle height, and at the stars,
Which are the brain of heaven, he looked, and sank.
Around the ancient track marched, rank on rank,
The army of unalterable law.

*from* Modern Love

667 (i)

MARK where the pressing wind shoots javelin-like
Its skeleton shadow on the broad-backed wave!
Here is a fitting spot to dig Love's grave;
Here where the ponderous breakers plunge and strike,
And dart their hissing tongues high up the sand:
In hearing of the ocean, and in sight
Of those ribbed wind-streaks running into white.
If I the death of Love had deeply planned,
I never could have made it half so sure,
As by the unblest kisses which upbraid
The full-waked sense; or failing that, degrade!
'Tis morning: but no morning can restore
What we have forfeited. I see no sin:
The wrong is mixed. In tragic life, God wot,
No villain need be! Passions spin the plot:
We are betrayed by what is false within.

668                                    (ii)

WE saw the swallows gathering in the sky,
And in the osier-isle we heard them noise.
We had not to look back on summer joys,
Or forward to a summer of bright dye:
But in the largeness of the evening earth
Our spirits grew as we went side by side.
The hour became her husband and my bride.
Love, that had robbed us so, thus blessed our dearth!
The pilgrims of the year waxed very loud
In multitudinous chatterings, as the flood
Full brown came from the West, and like pale blood
Expanded to the upper crimson cloud.
Love, that had robbed us of immortal things,
This little moment mercifully gave,
Where I have seen across the twilight wave
The swan sail with her young beneath her wings.

669                                    (iii)

THUS piteously Love closed what he begat:
The union of this ever-diverse pair!
These two were rapid falcons in a snare,
Condemned to do the flitting of the bat.
Lovers beneath the singing sky of May,
They wandered once; clear as the dew on flowers:
But they fed not on the advancing hours:
Their hearts held cravings for the buried day.
Then each applied to each that fatal knife,
Deep questioning, which probes to endless dole.
Ah, what a dusty answer gets the soul
When hot for certainties in this our life!—
In tragic hints here see what evermore
Moves dark as yonder midnight ocean's force,
Thundering like ramping hosts of warrior horse,
To throw that faint thin line upon the shore!

# CHRISTINA GEORGINA ROSSETTI
## 1830–1894

670 *A Birthday*

MY heart is like a singing bird
   Whose nest is in a watered shoot;
My heart is like an apple-tree
   Whose boughs are bent with thickset fruit;
My heart is like a rainbow shell
   That paddles in a halcyon sea;
My heart is gladder than all these
   Because my love is come to me.

Raise me a dais of silk and down;
   Hang it with vair and purple dyes;
Carve it in doves and pomegranates,
   And peacocks with a hundred eyes;
Work it in gold and silver grapes,
   In leaves and silver fleurs-de-lys;
Because the birthday of my life
   Is come, my love is come to me.

671 *Song*

WHEN I am dead, my dearest,
   Sing no sad songs for me;
Plant thou no roses at my head,
   Nor shady cypress tree:
Be the green grass above me
   With showers and dewdrops wet;
And if thou wilt, remember,
   And if thou wilt, forget.

I shall not see the shadows,
   I shall not feel the rain;
I shall not hear the nightingale
   Sing on, as if in pain;
And dreaming through the twilight
   That doth not rise nor set,
Haply I may remember,
   And haply may forget.

672 *Uphill*

DOES the road wind uphill all the way?
   Yes, to the very end.
Will the day's journey take the whole long day?
   From morn to night, my friend.

But is there for the night a resting-place?
   A roof for when the slow, dark hours begin.
May not the darkness hide it from my face?
   You cannot miss that inn.

Shall I meet other wayfarers at night?
   Those who have gone before.
Then must I knock, or call when just in sight?
   They will not keep you standing at that door.

Shall I find comfort, travel-sore and weak?
   Of labour you shall find the sum.
Will there be beds for me and all who seek?
   Yea, beds for all who come.

673 *Remember*

REMEMBER me when I am gone away,
   Gone far away into the silent land;
   When you can no more hold me by the hand,
Nor I half turn to go yet turning stay.
Remember me when no more day by day
   You tell me of our future that you planned:
   Only remember me; you understand
It will be late to counsel then or pray.
Yet if you should forget me for a while
   And afterwards remember, do not grieve:
   For if the darkness and corruption leave
   A vestige of the thoughts that once I had,
Better by far you should forget and smile
   Than that you should remember and be sad.

674

THE irresponsive silence of the land,
The irresponsive sounding of the sea,
   Speak both one message of one sense to me:—
'Aloof, aloof, we stand aloof, so stand
Thou too aloof, bound with the flawless band
   Of inner solitude; we bind not thee;
   But who from thy self-chain shall set thee free?
What heart shall touch thy heart? What hand thy hand?'—
And I am sometimes proud and sometimes meek,
   And sometimes I remember days of old
When fellowship seemed not so far to seek ,
   And all the world and I seemed much less cold,
   And at the rainbow's foot lay surely gold,
And hope felt strong, and life itself not weak.

675                   *Rest*

O EARTH, lie heavily upon her eyes;
Seal her sweet eyes weary of watching, Earth;
   Lie close around her; leave no room for mirth
With its harsh laughter, nor for sound of sighs.
She hath no questions, she hath no replies,
   Hushed in and curtained with a blessed dearth
   Of all that irked her from the hour of birth;
With stillness that is almost Paradise.
Darkness more clear than noonday holdeth her,
   Silence more musical than any song;
Even her very heart has ceased to stir:
Until the morning of Eternity
Her rest shall not begin nor end, but be;
   And when she wakes she will not think it long.

676                                    *Echo*

COME to me in the silence of the night;
   Come in the speaking silence of a dream;
Come with soft rounded cheeks and eyes as bright
      As sunlight on a stream;
         Come back in tears,
O memory, hope, love of finished years.

O dream how sweet, too sweet, too bitter sweet,
   Whose wakening should have been in Paradise,
Where souls brimfull of love abide and meet;
      Where thirsting longing eyes
         Watch the slow door
That opening, letting in, lets out no more.

Yet come to me in dreams that I may live
   My very life again though cold in death:
Come back to me in dreams, that I may give
      Pulse for pulse, breath for breath:
         Speak low, lean low,
As long ago, my love, how long ago.


677                          *A Pause of Thought*

I LOOKED for that which is not, nor can be,
   And hope deferred made my heart sick in truth:
   But years must pass before a hope of youth
      Is resigned utterly.

I watched and waited with a steadfast will:
   And though the object seemed to flee away
   That I so longed for, ever day by day
      I watched and waited still.

Sometimes I said: 'This thing shall be no more;
   My expectation wearies and shall cease;
   I will resign it now and be at peace':
      Yet never gave it o'er.

Sometimes I said: 'It is an empty name
    I long for; to a name why should I give
    The peace of all the days I have to live?'—
        Yet gave it all the same.

Alas, thou foolish one! alike unfit
    For healthy joy and salutary pain:
    Thou knowest the chase useless, and again
        Turnest to follow it.

678                            *Twice*

        I TOOK my heart in my hand
            (O my love, O my love),
        I said: Let me fall or stand,
            Let me live or die,
        But this once hear me speak—
            (O my love, O my love)—
        Yet a woman's words are weak;
            You should speak, not I.

        You took my heart in your hand
            With a friendly smile,
        With a critical eye you scanned,
            Then set it down,
        And said: It is still unripe,
            Better wait awhile;
        Wait while the skylarks pipe,
            Till the corn grows brown.

        As you set it down it broke—
            Broke, but I did not wince;
        I smiled at the speech you spoke,
            At your judgement that I heard:
        But I have not often smiled
            Since then, nor questioned since,
        Nor cared for corn-flowers wild,
            Nor sung with the singing bird.

I take my heart in my hand,
  O my God, O my God,
My broken heart in my hand,
  Thou hast seen, judge thou.
My hope was written on sand,
  O my God, O my God:
Now let thy judgement stand—
  Yea, judge me now.

This contemned of a man,
  This marred one heedless day,
This heart take thou to scan
  Both within and without:
Refine with fire its gold,
  Purge thou its dross away—
Yea, hold it in thy hold,
  Whence none can pluck it out.

I take my heart in my hand—
  I shall not die, but live—
Before thy face I stand;
  I, for thou callest such:
All that I have I bring,
  All that I am I give,
Smile thou and I shall sing,
  But shall not question much.


679                 *Somewhere or Other*

SOMEWHERE or other there must surely be
  The face not seen, the voice not heard,
The heart that not yet—never yet—ah me!
  Made answer to my word.

Somewhere or other, may be near or far;
  Past land and sea, clean out of sight;
Beyond the wandering moon, beyond the star
  That tracks her night by night.

Somewhere or other, may be far or near;
  With just a wall, a hedge, between;
With just the last leaves of the dying year
  Fallen on a turf grown green.

729

680 *Marvel of Marvels*

MARVEL of marvels, if I myself shall behold
With mine own eyes my King in his city of gold;
Where the least of lambs is spotless white in the fold,
Where the least and last of saints in spotless white is stoled,
Where the dimmest head beyond a moon is aureoled.
O saints, my beloved, now mouldering to mould in the mould,
Shall I see you lift your heads, see your cerements unrolled,
See with these very eyes? who now in darkness and cold
Tremble for the midnight cry, the rapture, the tale untold,
'The Bridegroom cometh, cometh, his Bride to enfold.'

Cold it is, my beloved, since your funeral bell was tolled:
Cold it is, O my King, how cold alone on the wold.


# CHARLES LUTWIDGE DODGSON
# (LEWIS CARROLL)

## 1832–1898

681 *Jabberwocky*

'TWAS brillig, and the slithy toves
  Did gyre and gimble in the wabe:
All mimsy were the borogoves,
  And the mome raths outgrabe.

'Beware the Jabberwock, my son!
  The jaws that bite, the claws that catch!
Beware the Jubjub bird, and shun
  The frumious Bandersnatch!'

He took his vorpal sword in hand:
  Long time the manxome foe he sought—
So rested he by the Tumtum tree,
  And stood awhile in thought.

And, as in uffish thought he stood,
  The Jabberwock, with eyes of flame,
Came whiffling through the tulgey wood,
  And burbled as it came!

One, two! One, two! And through and through
    The vorpal blade went snicker-snack!
He left it dead, and with its head
    He went galumphing back.

'And hast thou slain the Jabberwock?
    Come to my arms, my beamish boy!
O frabjous day! Callooh! Callay!'
    He chortled in his joy.

'Twas brillig, and the slithy toves
    Did gyre and gimble in the wabe:
All mimsy were the borogoves,
    And the mome raths outgrabe.

682        *The White Knight's Song*

I'LL tell thee everything I can:
    There's little to relate,
I saw an aged aged man,
    A-sitting on a gate.
'Who are you, aged man?' I said.
    'And how is it you live?'
And his answer trickled through my head,
    Like water through a sieve.

He said 'I look for butterflies
    That sleep among the wheat:
I make them into mutton-pies,
    And sell them in the street.
I sell them unto men', he said,
    'Who sail on stormy seas;
And that's the way I get my bread—
    A trifle, if you please.'

But I was thinking of a plan
    To dye one's whiskers green,
And always use so large a fan
    That they could not be seen.
So, having no reply to give
    To what the old man said,
I cried 'Come, tell me how you live!'
    And thumped him on the head.

His accents mild took up the tale:
    He said 'I go my ways,
And when I find a mountain-rill,
    I set it in a blaze;
And thence they make a stuff they call
    Rowland's Macassar-Oil—
Yet two-pence-halfpenny is all
    They give me for my toil.'

But I was thinking of a way
    To feed oneself on batter
And so go on from day to day
    Getting a little fatter.
I shook him well from side to side,
    Until his face was blue:
'Come, tell me how you live,' I cried,
    'And what it is you do!'

He said 'I hunt for haddocks' eyes
    Among the heather bright,
And work them into waistcoat-buttons
    In the silent night.
And these I do not sell for gold
    Or coin of silvery shine,
But for a copper halfpenny,
    And that will purchase nine.

I sometimes dig for buttered rolls,
    Or set limed twigs for crabs:
I sometimes search the grassy knolls
    For wheels of Hansom-cabs.
And that's the way' (he gave a wink)
    'By which I get my wealth—
And very gladly will I drink
    Your Honour's noble health.'

I heard him then, for I had just
    Completed my design
To keep the Menai bridge from rust
    By boiling it in wine.
I thanked him much for telling me
    The way he got his wealth,
But chiefly for his wish that he
    Might drink my noble health.

## CHARLES LUTWIDGE DODGSON (LEWIS CARROLL)

And now, if e'er by chance I put
  My fingers into glue,
Or madly squeeze a right-hand foot
  Into a left-hand shoe,
Or if I drop upon my toe
  A very heavy weight,
I weep, for it reminds me so
Of that old man I used to know—
Whose look was mild, whose speech was slow
Whose hair was whiter than the snow,
Whose face was very like a crow,
With eyes, like cinders, all aglow,
Who seemed distracted with his woe,
Who rocked his body to and fro,
And muttered mumblingly and low,
As if his mouth were full of dough,
Who snorted like a buffalo—
That summer evening long ago,
  A-sitting on a gate.


# RICHARD WATSON DIXON

## 1833–1900

683               *Song*

THE feathers of the willow
Are half of them grown yellow
  Above the swelling stream;
And ragged are the bushes,
And rusty now the rushes,
  And wild the clouded gleam.

The thistle now is older,
His stalk begins to moulder,
  His head is white as snow;
The branches all are barer,
The linnet's song is rarer,
  The robin pipeth now.

# WILLIAM MORRIS

## 1834–1896

684 *Summer Dawn*

PRAY but one prayer for me 'twixt thy closed lips;
  Think but one thought of me up in the stars.
The summer night waneth, the morning light slips,
  Faint and grey 'twixt the leaves of the aspen,
    betwixt the cloud-bars,
That are patiently waiting there for the dawn:
  Patient and colourless, though Heaven's gold
Waits to float through them along with the sun.
Far out in the meadows, above the young corn,
  The heavy elms wait, and restless and cold
The uneasy wind rises; the roses are dun;
Through the long twilight they pray for the dawn,
Round the lone house in the midst of the corn.
  Speak but one word to me over the corn,
  Over the tender, bowed locks of the corn.

685 *Riding Together*

FOR many, many days together
  The wind blew steady from the East;
For many days hot grew the weather,
  About the time of our Lady's Feast.

For many days we rode together,
  Yet met we neither friend nor foe;
Hotter and clearer grew the weather,
  Steadily did the East wind blow.

We saw the trees in the hot, bright weather,
  Clear-cut, with shadows very black,
As freely we rode on together
  With helms unlaced and bridles slack.

And often as we rode together,
  We, looking down the green-banked stream,
Saw flowers in the sunny weather,
  And saw the bubble-making bream.

And in the night lay down together,
  And hung above our heads the rood,
Or watched night-long in the dewy weather,
  The while the moon did watch the wood.

Our spears stood bright and thick together,
  Straight out the banners streamed behind,
As we galloped on in the sunny weather,
  With faces turned towards the wind.

Down sank our threescore spears together,
  As thick we saw the pagans ride;
His eager face in the clear fresh weather,
  Shone out that last time by my side.

Up the sweep of the bridge we dashed together,
  It rocked to the crash of the meeting spears,
Down rained the buds of the dear spring weather,
  The elm-tree flowers fell like tears.

There as we rolled and writhed together,
  I threw my arms above my head,
For close by my side, in the lovely weather,
  I saw him reel and fall back dead,

I and the slayer met together,
  He waited the death-stroke there in his place,
With thoughts of death, in the lovely weather,
  Gapingly mazed at my maddened face.

Madly I fought as we fought together;
  In vain: the little Christian band
The pagans drowned, as in stormy weather,
  The river drowns low-lying land.

They bound my blood-stained hands together,
  They bound his corpse to nod by my side:
Then on we rode, in the bright March weather,
  With clash of cymbals did we ride.

We ride no more, no more together;
  My prison-bars are thick and strong,
I take no heed of any weather,
  The sweet Saints grant I live not long.

686                 *A Garden by the Sea*

I KNOW a little garden-close,
Set thick with lily and red rose,
Where I would wander if I might
From dewy morn to dewy night,
And have one with me wandering.

And though within it no birds sing,
And though no pillared house is there,
And though the apple-boughs are bare
Of fruit and blossom, would to God
Her feet upon the green grass trod,
And I beheld them as before.

There comes a murmur from the shore,
And in the close two fair streams are,
Drawn from the purple hills afar,
Drawn down unto the restless sea:
Dark hills whose heath-bloom feeds no bee,
Dark shore no ship has ever seen,
Tormented by the billows green
Whose murmur comes unceasingly
Unto the place for which I cry.
For which I cry both day and night,
For which I let slip all delight,
Whereby I grow both deaf and blind,
Careless to win, unskilled to find,
And quick to lose what all men seek.

Yet tottering as I am and weak,
Still have I left a little breath
To seek within the jaws of death
An entrance to that happy place,
To seek the unforgotten face,
Once seen, once kissed, once reft from me
Anigh the murmuring of the sea.

# JAMES THOMSON ('B.V.')

1834–1882

*from* The City of Dreadful Night

(i)

687                    *The City*

Lo, thus, as prostrate, 'In the dust I write
  My heart's deep languor and my soul's sad tears.'
Yet why evoke the spectres of black night
  To blot the sunshine of exultant years?
Why disinter dead faith from mouldering hidden?
Why break the seals of mute despair unbidden,
  And wail life's discords into careless ears?

Because a cold rage seizes one at whiles
  To show the bitter old and wrinkled truth
Stripped naked of all vesture that beguiles,
  False dreams, false hopes, false masks and modes of youth;
Because it gives some sense of power and passion
In helpless impotence to try to fashion
  Our woe in living words howe'er uncouth.

Surely I write not for the hopeful young,
  Or those who deem their happiness of worth,
Or such as pasture and grow fat among
  The shows of life and feel nor doubt nor dearth,
Or pious spirits with a God above them
To sanctify and glorify and love them,
  Or sages who foresee a heaven on earth.

For none of these I write, and none of these
  Could read the writing if they deigned to try:
So may they flourish, in their due degrees,
  On our sweet earth and in their unplaced sky.
If any cares for the weak words here written,
It must be some one desolate, Fate-smitten,
  Whose faith and hope are dead, and who would die.

737

## JAMES THOMSON ('B.V.')

Yes, here and there some weary wanderer
   In that same city of tremendous night,
Will understand the speech, and feel a stir
   Of fellowship in all-disastrous fight;
'I suffer mute and lonely, yet another
Uplifts his voice to let me know a brother
   Travels the same wild paths though out of sight.'

O sad Fraternity, do I unfold
   Your dolorous mysteries shrouded from of yore?
Nay, be assured; no secret can be told
   To any who divined it not before:
None uninitiate by many a presage
Will comprehend the language of the message,
   Although proclaimed aloud for evermore.

               *

The street-lamps burn amidst the baleful glooms,
   Amidst the soundless solitudes immense
Of rangèd mansions dark and still as tombs.
   The silence which benumbs or strains the sense
Fulfils with awe the soul's despair unweeping:
Myriads of habitants are ever sleeping,
   Or dead, or fled from nameless pestilence!

Yet as in some necropolis you find
   Perchance one mourner to a thousand dead,
So there; worn faces that look deaf and blind
   Like tragic masks of stone. With weary tread,
Each wrapt in his own doom, they wander, wander,
Or sit foredone and desolately ponder
   Through sleepless hours with heavy drooping head.

Mature men chiefly, few in age or youth,
   A woman rarely, now and then a child:
A child! If here the heart turns sick with ruth
   To see a little one from birth defiled,
Or lame or blind, as preordained to languish
Through youthless life, think how it bleeds with anguish
   To meet one erring in that homeless wild.

738

They often murmur to themselves, they speak
　　To one another seldom, for their woe
Broods maddening inwardly and scorns to wreak
　　Itself abroad; and if at whiles it grow
To frenzy which must rave, none heeds the clamour,
Unless there waits some victim of like glamour,
　　To rave in turn, who lends attentive show.

The City is of Night, but not of Sleep;
　　There sweet sleep is not for the weary brain;
The pitiless hours like years and ages creep,
　　A night seems termless hell. This dreadful strain
Of thought and consciousness which never ceases,
Or which some moments' stupor but increases,
　　This, worse than woe, makes wretches there insane.

They leave all hope behind who enter there:
　　One certitude while sane they cannot leave,
One anodyne for torture and despair;
　　The certitude of Death, which no reprieve
Can put off long; and which, divinely tender,
But waits the outstretched hand to promptly render
　　That draught whose slumber nothing can bereave.


(ii)

688　　　　　　*The City's Queen*

ANEAR the centre of that northern crest
　　Stands out a level upland bleak and bare,
From which the city east and south and west
　　Sinks gently in long waves; and thronèd there
An Image sits, stupendous, superhuman,
The bronze colossus of a wingèd Woman,
　　Upon a graded granite base foursquare.

Low-seated she leans forward massively,
　　With cheek on clenched left hand, the forearm's might
Erect, its elbow on her rounded knee;
　　Across a clasped book in her lap the right
Upholds a pair of compasses; she gazes
With full set eyes, but wandering in thick mazes
　　Of sombre thought beholds no outward sight.

739

# JAMES THOMSON ('B.V.')

Words cannot picture her; but all men know
   That solemn sketch the pure sad artist wrought
Three centuries and threescore years ago,
   With phantasies of his peculiar thought:
The instruments of carpentry and science
Scattered about her feet, in strange alliance
   With the keen wolf-hound sleeping undistraught;

Scales, hour-glass, bell, and magic-square above;
   The grave and solid infant perched beside,
With open winglets that might bear a dove,
   Intent upon its tablets, heavy-eyed;
Her folded wings as of a mighty eagle,
But all too impotent to lift the regal
   Robustness of her earth-born strength and pride;

And with those wings, and that light wreath which seems
   To mock her grand head and the knotted frown
Of forehead charged with baleful thoughts and dreams,
   The household bunch of keys, the housewife's gown
Voluminous, indented, and yet rigid
As if a shell of burnished metal frigid,
   The feet thick-shod to tread all weakness down;

The comet hanging o'er the waste dark seas,
   The massy rainbow curved in front of it
Beyond the village with the masts and trees;
   The snaky imp, dog-headed, from the Pit,
Bearing upon its batlike leathern pinions
Her name unfolded in the sun's dominions,
   The 'MELENCOLIA' that transcends all wit.

Thus has the artist copied her, and thus
   Surrounded to expound her form sublime,
Her fate heroic and calamitous;
   Fronting the dreadful mysteries of Time,
Unvanquished in defeat and desolation,
Undaunted in the hopeless conflagration
   Of the day setting on her baffled prime.

**the pure sad artist]** Albrecht Dürer

## JAMES THOMSON ('B.V.')

Baffled and beaten back she works on still,
  Weary and sick of soul she works the more,
Sustained by her indomitable will:
  The hands shall fashion and the brain shall pore,
And all her sorrow shall be turned to labour,
Till Death the friend-foe piercing with his sabre
  That mighty heart of hearts ends bitter war.

But as if blacker night could dawn on night,
  With tenfold gloom on moonless night unstarred,
A sense more tragic than defeat and blight,
  More desperate than strife with hope debarred,
More fatal than the adamantine Never
Encompassing her passionate endeavour,
  Dawns glooming in her tenebrous regard:

The sense that every struggle brings defeat
  Because Fate holds no prize to crown success;
That all the oracles are dumb or cheat
  Because they have no secret to express;
That none can pierce the vast black veil uncertain
Because there is no light beyond the curtain;
  That all is vanity and nothingness.

Titanic from her high throne in the north,
  That City's sombre Patroness and Queen,
In bronze sublimity she gazes forth
  Over her Capital of teen and threne,
Over the river with its isles and bridges,
The marsh and moorland, to the stern rock-ridges,
  Confronting them with a coëval mien.

The moving moon and stars from east to west
  Circle before her in the sea of air;
Shadows and gleams glide round her solemn rest.
  Her subjects often gaze up to her there:
The strong to drink new strength of iron endurance,
The weak new terrors; all, renewed assurance
  And confirmation of the old despair.

# ALGERNON CHARLES SWINBURNE
### 1837–1909

689       Chorus from *Atalanta in Calydon*

WHEN the hounds of spring are on winter's traces,
   The mother of months in meadow or plain
Fills the shadows and windy places
   With lisp of leaves and ripple of rain;
And the brown bright nightingale amorous
Is half assuaged for Itylus,
For the Thracian ships and the foreign faces,
   The tongueless vigil, and all the pain.

Come with bows bent and with emptying of quivers,
   Maiden most perfect, lady of light,
With a noise of winds and many rivers,
   With a clamour of waters, and with might;
Bind on thy sandals, O thou most fleet,
Over the splendour and speed of thy feet;
For the faint east quickens, the wan west shivers,
   Round the feet of the day and the feet of the night.

Where shall we find her, how shall we sing to her,
   Fold our hands round her knees, and cling?
O that man's heart were as fire and could spring to her,
   Fire, or the strength of the streams that spring!
For the stars and the winds are unto her
As raiment, as songs of the harp-player;
For the risen stars and the fallen cling to her,
   And the southwest-wind and the west-wind sing.

For winter's rains and ruins are over,
   And all the season of snows and sins;
The days dividing lover and lover,
   The light that loses, the night that wins;
And time remembered is grief forgotten,
And frosts are slain and flowers begotten,
And in green underwood and cover
   Blossom by blossom the spring begins.

The full streams feed on flower of rushes,
    Ripe grasses trammel a travelling foot,
The faint fresh flame of the young year flushes
    From leaf to flower and flower to fruit;
And fruit and leaf are as gold and fire,
And the oat is heard above the lyre,
And the hoofèd heel of a satyr crushes
    The chestnut-husk at the chestnut-root.

And Pan by noon and Bacchus by night,
    Fleeter of foot than the fleet-foot kid,
Follows with dancing and fills with delight
    The Mænad and the Bassarid;
And soft as lips that laugh and hide
The laughing leaves of the trees divide,
And screen from seeing and leave in sight
    The god pursuing, the maiden hid.

The ivy falls with the Bacchanal's hair
    Over her eyebrows hiding her eyes;
The wild vine slipping down leaves bare
    Her bright breast shortening into sighs;
The wild vine slips with the weight of its leaves,
But the berried ivy catches and cleaves
To the limbs that glitter, the feet that scare
    The wolf that follows, the fawn that flies.

690           *A Leave-Taking*

LET us go hence, my songs; she will not hear.
Let us go hence together without fear;
Keep silence now, for singing-time is over,
And over all old things and all things dear.
She loves not you nor me as we all love her.
Yea, though we sang as angels in her ear,
    She would not hear.

Let us rise up and part; she will not know.
Let us go seaward as the great winds go,
Full of blown sand and foam; what help is here?
There is no help, for all these things are so,
And all the world is bitter as a tear.
And how these things are, though ye strove to show,
     She would not know.

Let us go home and hence; she will not weep.
We gave love many dreams and days to keep,
Flowers without scent, and fruits that would not grow,
Saying, 'If thou wilt, thrust in thy sickle and reap.'
All is reaped now; no grass is left to mow;
And we that sowed, though all we fell on sleep,
     She would not weep.

Let us go hence and rest; she will not love.
She shall not hear us if we sing hereof,
Nor see love's ways, how sore they are and steep.
Come hence, let be, lie still; it is enough.
Love is a barren sea, bitter and deep;
And though she saw all heaven in flower above,
     She would not love.

Let us give up, go down; she will not care.
Though all the stars made gold of all the air,
And the sea moving saw before it move
One moon-flower making all the foam-flowers fair;
Though all those waves went over us, and drove
Deep down the stifling lips and drowning hair,
     She would not care.

Let us go hence, go hence; she will not see.
Sing all once more together; surely she,
She too, remembering days and words that were,
Will turn a little toward us, sighing; but we,
We are hence, we are gone, as though we had not been there.
Nay, and though all men seeing had pity on me,
     She would not see.

691         *The Garden of Proserpine*

HERE, where the world is quiet;
  Here, where all trouble seems
Dead winds' and spent waves' riot
  In doubtful dreams of dreams;
I watch the green field growing
For reaping folk and sowing,
For harvest-time and mowing,
  A sleepy world of streams.

I am tired of tears and laughter,
  And men that laugh and weep;
Of what may come hereafter
  For men that sow to reap:
I am weary of days and hours,
Blown buds of barren flowers,
Desires and dreams and powers
  And everything but sleep.

Here life has death for neighbour,
  And far from eye or ear
Wan waves and wet winds labour,
  Weak ships and spirits steer;
They drive adrift, and whither
They wot not who make thither;
But no such winds blow hither,
  And no such things grow here.

No growth of moor or coppice,
  No heather-flower or vine,
But bloomless buds of poppies,
  Green grapes of Proserpine,
Pale beds of blowing rushes
Where no leaf blooms or blushes
Save this whereout she crushes
  For dead men deadly wine.

Pale, without name or number,
  In fruitless fields of corn,
They bow themselves and slumber
  All night till light is born;
And like a soul belated,
In hell and heaven unmated,
By cloud and mist abated
  Comes out of darkness morn.

Though one were strong as seven,
  He too with death shall dwell,
Nor wake with wings in heaven,
  Nor weep for pains in hell;
Though one were fair as roses,
His beauty clouds and closes;
And well though love reposes,
  In the end it is not well.

Pale, beyond porch and portal,
  Crowned with calm leaves, she stands
Who gathers all things mortal
  With cold immortal hands;
Her languid lips are sweeter
Than love's who fears to greet her
To men that mix and meet her
  From many times and lands.

She waits for each and other,
  She waits for all men born;
Forgets the earth her mother,
  The life of fruits and corn;
And spring and seed and swallow
Take wing for her and follow
Where summer song rings hollow
  And flowers are put to scorn.

There go the loves that wither,
  The old loves with wearier wings;
And all dead years draw thither,
  And all disastrous things;
Dead dreams of days forsaken,
Blind buds that snows have shaken,
Wild leaves that winds have taken,
  Red strays of ruined springs.

## ALGERNON CHARLES SWINBURNE

We are not sure of sorrow,
   And joy was never sure;
To-day will die to-morrow;
   Time stoops to no man's lure;
And love, grown faint and fretful,
With lips but half regretful
Sighs, and with eyes forgetful
   Weeps that no loves endure.

From too much love of living,
   From hope and fear set free,
We thank with brief thanksgiving
   Whatever gods may be
That no life lives for ever;
That dead men rise up never;
That even the weariest river
   Winds somewhere safe to sea.

Then star nor sun shall waken,
   Nor any change of light:
Nor sound of waters shaken,
   Nor any sound or sight:
Nor wintry leaves nor vernal,
Nor days nor things diurnal;
Only the sleep eternal
   In an eternal night.

692      *Ave atque Vale*

### IN MEMORY OF CHARLES BAUDELAIRE

*Nous devrions pourtant lui porter quelques fleurs;*
*Les morts, les pauvres morts, ont de grandes douleurs,*
*Et quand Octobre souffle, émondeur des vieux arbres,*
*Son vent mélancolique à l'entour de leurs marbres,*
*Certe, ils doivent trouver les vivants bien ingrats.*
        —'Les Fleurs du Mal.'

SHALL I strew on thee rose or rue or laurel,
   Brother, on this that was the veil of thee?
   Or quiet sea-flower moulded by the sea,
Or simplest growth of meadow-sweet or sorrel,
   Such as the summer-sleepy Dryads weave,
   Waked up by snow-soft sudden rains at eve?

Or wilt thou rather, as on earth before,
    Half-faded fiery blossoms, pale with heat
    And full of bitter summer, but more sweet
To thee than gleanings of a northern shore
    Trod by no tropic feet?

For always thee the fervid languid glories
    Allured of heavier suns in mightier skies;
    Thine ears knew all the wandering watery sighs
Where the sea sobs round Lesbian promontories,
    The barren kiss of piteous wave to wave
    That knows not where is that Leucadian grave
Which hides too deep the supreme head of song.
    Ah, salt and sterile as her kisses were,
    The wild sea winds her and the green gulfs bear
Hither and thither, and vex and work her wrong,
    Blind gods that cannot spare.

Thou sawest, in thine old singing season, brother,
    Secrets and sorrows unbeheld of us:
    Fierce loves, and lovely leaf-buds poisonous,
Bare to thy subtler eye, but for none other
    Blowing by night in some unbreathed-in clime;
    The hidden harvest of luxurious time,
Sin without shape, and pleasure without speech;
    And where strange dreams in a tumultuous sleep
    Make the shut eyes of stricken spirits weep;
And with each face thou saw'st the shadow on each,
    Seeing as men sow men reap.

O sleepless heart and sombre soul unsleeping,
    That were athirst for sleep and no more life
    And no more love, for peace and no more strife!
Now the dim gods of death have in their keeping
    Spirit and body and all the springs of song,
    Is it well now where love can do no wrong,
Where stingless pleasure has no foam or fang
    Behind the unopening closure of her lips?
    Is it not well where soul from body slips
And flesh from bone divides without a pang
    As dew from flower-bell drips?

It is enough; the end and the beginning
  Are one thing to thee, who art past the end.
  O hand unclasped of unbeholden friend,
For thee no fruits to pluck, no palms for winning,
  No triumph and no labour and no lust,
  Only dead yew-leaves and a little dust.
O quiet eyes wherein the light saith nought,
  Whereto the day is dumb, nor any night
  With obscure finger silences your sight,
Nor in your speech the sudden soul speaks thought,
  Sleep, and have sleep for light.

Now all strange hours and all strange loves are over,
  Dreams and desires and sombre songs and sweet,
  Hast thou found place at the great knees and feet
Of some pale Titan-woman like a lover,
  Such as thy vision here solicited,
  Under the shadow of her fair vast head,
The deep division of prodigious breasts,
  The solemn slope of mighty limbs asleep,
  The weight of awful tresses that still keep
The savour and shade of old-world pine-forests
  Where the wet hill-winds weep?

Hast thou found any likeness for thy vision?
  O gardener of strange flowers, what bud, what bloom,
  Hast thou found sown, what gathered in the gloom?
What of despair, of rapture, of derision,
  What of life is there, what of ill or good?
  Are the fruits grey like dust or bright like blood?
Does the dim ground grow any seed of ours,
  The faint fields quicken any terrene root,
  In low lands where the sun and moon are mute
And all the stars keep silence? Are there flowers
  At all, or any fruit?

Alas, but though my flying song flies after,
  O sweet strange elder singer, thy more fleet
  Singing, and footprints of thy fleeter feet,
Some dim derision of mysterious laughter
  From the blind tongueless warders of the dead,
  Some gainless glimpse of Proserpine's veiled head,

Some little sound of unregarded tears
   Wept by effaced unprofitable eyes,
    And from pale mouths some cadence of dead sighs—
These only, these the hearkening spirit hears,
   Sees only such things rise.

Thou art far too far for wings of words to follow,
   Far too far off for thought or any prayer.
   What ails us with thee, who art wind and air?
What ails us gazing where all seen is hollow?
   Yet with some fancy, yet with some desire,
   Dreams pursue death as winds a flying fire,
Our dreams pursue our dead and do not find.
   Still, and more swift than they, the thin flame flies,
   The low light fails us in elusive skies,
Still the foiled earnest ear is deaf, and blind
   Are still the eluded eyes.

Not thee, O never thee, in all time's changes,
   Not thee, but this the sound of thy sad soul,
   The shadow of thy swift spirit, this shut scroll
I lay my hand on, and not death estranges
   My spirit from communion of thy song—
   These memories and these melodies that throng
Veiled porches of a Muse funereal—
   These I salute, these touch, these clasp and fold
   As though a hand were in my hand to hold,
Or through mine ears a mourning musical
   Of many mourners rolled.

I among these, I also, in such station
   As when the pyre was charred, and piled the sods,
   And offering to the dead made, and their gods,
The old mourners had, standing to make libation,
   I stand, and to the gods and to the dead
   Do reverence without prayer or praise, and shed
Offering to these unknown, the gods of gloom,
   And what of honey and spice my seedlands bear,
   And what I may of fruits in this chilled air,
And lay, Orestes-like, across the tomb
   A curl of severed hair.

But by no hand nor any treason stricken,
　　Not like the low-lying head of Him, the King,
　　The flame that made of Troy a ruinous thing,
Thou liest, and on this dust no tears could quicken
　　There fall no tears like theirs that all men hear
　　Fall tear by sweet imperishable tear
Down the opening leaves of holy poets' pages.
　　Thee not Orestes, not Electra mourns;
　　But bending us-ward with memorial urns
The most high Muses that fulfil all ages
　　Weep, and our God's heart yearns.


For, sparing of his sacred strength, not often
　　Among us darkling here the lord of light
　　Makes manifest his music and his might
In hearts that open and in lips that soften
　　With the soft flame and heat of songs that shine.
　　Thy lips indeed he touched with bitter wine,
And nourished them indeed with bitter bread;
　　Yet surely from his hand thy soul's food came,
　　The fire that scarred thy spirit at his flame
Was lighted, and thine hungering heart he fed
　　Who feeds our hearts with fame.


Therefore he too now at thy soul's sunsetting,
　　God of all suns and songs, he too bends down
　　To mix his laurel with thy cypress crown,
And save thy dust from blame and from forgetting.
　　Therefore he too, seeing all thou wert and art,
　　Compassionate, with sad and sacred heart,
Mourns thee of many his children the last dead,
　　And hallows with strange tears and alien sighs
　　Thine unmelodious mouth and sunless eyes,
And over thine irrevocable head
　　Sheds light from the under skies.


And one weeps with him in the ways Lethean,
　　And stains with tears her changing bosom chill:
　　That obscure Venus of the hollow hill,
That thing transformed which was the Cytherean,
　　With lips that lost their Grecian laugh divine
　　Long since, and face no more called Erycine;

A ghost, a bitter and luxurious god.
   Thee also with fair flesh and singing spell
   Did she, a sad and second prey, compel
Into the footless places once more trod,
   And shadows hot from hell.

And now no sacred staff shall break in blossom,
   No choral salutation lure to light
   A spirit sick with perfume and sweet night
And love's tired eyes and hands and barren bosom.
   There is no help for these things; none to mend
   And none to mar; not all our songs, O friend,
Will make death clear or make life durable.
   Howbeit with rose and ivy and wild vine
   And with wild notes about this dust of thine
At least I fill the place where white dreams dwell
   And wreathe an unseen shrine.

Sleep; and if life was bitter to thee, pardon,
   If sweet, give thanks; thou hast no more to live;
   And to give thanks is good, and to forgive.
Out of the mystic and the mournful garden
   Where all day through thine hands in barren braid
   Wove the sick flowers of secrecy and shade,
Green buds of sorrow and sin, and remnants grey,
   Sweet-smelling, pale with poison, sanguine-hearted,
   Passions that sprang from sleep and thoughts that started,
Shall death not bring us all as thee one day
   Among the days departed?

For thee, O now a silent soul, my brother,
   Take at my hands this garland, and farewell.
   Thin is the leaf, and chill the wintry smell,
And chill the solemn earth, a fatal mother,
   With sadder than the Niobean womb,
   And in the hollow of her breasts a tomb.
Content thee, howsoe'er, whose days are done;
   There lies not any troublous thing before,
   Nor sight nor sound to war against thee more,
For whom all winds are quiet as the sun,
   All waters as the shore.

693 *A Forsaken Garden*

In a coign of the cliff between lowland and highland,
  At the sea-down's edge between windward and lee,
Walled round with rocks as an inland island,
  The ghost of a garden fronts the sea.
A girdle of brushwood and thorn encloses
  The steep square slope of the blossomless bed
Where the weeds that grew green from the graves of its roses
    Now lie dead.

The fields fall southward, abrupt and broken,
  To the low last edge of the long lone land.
If a step should sound or a word be spoken,
  Would a ghost not rise at the strange guest's hand?
So long have the grey bare walks lain guestless,
  Through branches and briars if a man make way,
He shall find no life but the sea-wind's, restless
    Night and day.

The dense hard passage is blind and stifled
  That crawls by a track none turn to climb
To the strait waste place that the years have rifled
  Of all but the thorns that are touched not of time.
The thorns he spares when the rose is taken;
  The rocks are left when he wastes the plain.
The wind that wanders, the weeds wind-shaken,
    These remain.

Not a flower to be pressed of the foot that falls not;
  As the heart of a dead man the seed-plots are dry;
From the thicket of thorns whence the nightingale calls not,
  Could she call, there were never a rose to reply.
Over the meadows that blossom and wither
  Rings but the note of a sea-bird's song;
Only the sun and the rain come hither
    All year long.

The sun burns sere and the rain dishevels
  One gaunt bleak blossom of scentless breath.
Only the wind here hovers and revels
  In a round where life seems barren as death.

Here there was laughing of old, there was weeping,
  Haply, of lovers none ever will know,
Whose eyes went seaward a hundred sleeping
    Years ago.

Heart handfast in heart as they stood, 'Look thither,'
  Did he whisper? 'look forth from the flowers to the sea;
For the foam-flowers endure when the rose-blossoms wither,
  And men that love lightly may die—but we?'
And the same wind sang and the same waves whitened,
  And or ever the garden's last petals were shed,
In the lips that had whispered, the eyes that had lightened,
    Love was dead.

Or they loved their life through, and then went whither?
  And were one to the end—but what end who knows?
Love deep as the sea as a rose must wither,
  As the rose-red seaweed that mocks the rose.
Shall the dead take thought for the dead to love them?
  What love was ever as deep as a grave?
They are loveless now as the grass above them
    Or the wave.

All are at one now, roses and lovers,
  Not known of the cliffs and the fields and the sea.
Not a breath of the time that has been hovers
  In the air now soft with a summer to be.
Not a breath shall there sweeten the seasons hereafter
  Of the flowers or the lovers that laugh now or weep,
When as they that are free now of weeping and laughter
    We shall sleep.

Here death may deal not again for ever;
  Here change may come not till all change end.
From the graves they have made they shall rise up never,
  Who have left nought living to ravage and rend.
Earth, stones, and thorns of the wild ground growing,
  While the sun and the rain live, these shall be;
Till a last wind's breath upon all these blowing
    Roll the sea.

Till the slow sea rise and the sheer cliff crumble,
　　Till terrace and meadow the deep gulfs drink,
Till the strength of the waves of the high tides humble
　　The fields that lessen, the rocks that shrink,
Here now in his triumph where all things falter,
　　Stretched out on the spoils that his own hand spread,
As a god self-slain on his own strange altar,
　　　　Death lies dead.


# THOMAS HARDY

## 1840–1928

694

I LOOK into my glass,
And view my wasting skin,
And say, 'Would God it came to pass
My heart had shrunk as thin!'

For then, I, undistrest
By hearts grown cold to me,
Could lonely wait my endless rest
With equanimity.

But Time, to make me grieve,
Part steals, lets part abide;
And shakes this fragile frame at eve
With throbbings of noontide.

695

I NEED not go
Through sleet and snow
To where I know
She waits for me;
She will tarry me there
Till I find it fair,
And have time to spare
From company.

When I've overgot
The world somewhat,
When things cost not
Such stress and strain,
Is soon enough
By cypress sough
To tell my Love
I am come again.

And if some day,
When none cries nay,
I still delay
To seek her side,
(Though ample measure
Of fitting leisure
Await my pleasure)
She will not chide.

What—not upbraid me
That I delayed me,
Nor ask what stayed me
So long? Ah, no!—
New cares may claim me,
New loves inflame me,
She will not blame me,
But suffer it so.

696                          *Wives in the Sere*

NEVER a careworn wife but shows,
    If a joy suffuse her,
Something beautiful to those
    Patient to peruse her,
Some one charm the world unknows
    Precious to a muser,
Haply what, ere years were foes,
    Moved her mate to choose her.

But, be it a hint of rose
    That an instant hues her,
Or some early light or pose
    Wherewith thought renews her—
Seen by him at full, ere woes
    Practised to abuse her—
Sparely comes it, swiftly goes,
    Time again subdues her.

697          *The Darkling Thrush*

I LEANT upon a coppice gate
    When Frost was spectre-gray,
And Winter's dregs made desolate
    The weakening eye of day.
The tangled bine-stems scored the sky
    Like strings of broken lyres,
And all mankind that haunted nigh
    Had sought their household fires.

The land's sharp features seemed to be
    The Century's corpse outleant,
His crypt the cloudy canopy,
    The wind his death-lament.
The ancient pulse of germ and birth
    Was shrunken hard and dry,
And every spirit upon earth
    Seemed fervourless as I.

At once a voice arose among
    The bleak twigs overhead
In a full-hearted evensong
    Of joy illimited;
An agèd thrush, frail, gaunt, and small,
    In blast-beruffled plume,
Had chosen thus to fling his soul
    Upon the growing gloom.

So little cause for carolings
    Of such ecstatic sound
Was written on terrestrial things
    Afar or nigh around,

That I could think there trembled through
  His happy good-night air
Some blessed Hope, whereof he knew
  And I was unaware.

698          *The Self-Unseeing*

HERE is the ancient floor,
Footworn and hollowed and thin,
Here was the former door
Where the dead feet walked in.

She sat here in her chair,
Smiling into the fire;
He who played stood there,
Bowing it higher and higher.

Childlike, I danced in a dream;
Blessings emblazoned that day;
Everything glowed with a gleam;
Yet we were looking away!

699          *In Tenebris*

WINTERTIME nighs;
But my bereavement-pain
It cannot bring again:
  Twice no one dies.

  Flower-petals flee;
But, since it once hath been,
No more that severing scene
  Can harrow me.

  Birds faint in dread:
I shall not lose old strength
In the lone frost's black length:
  Strength long since fled!

Leaves freeze to dun;
But friends can not turn cold
This season as of old
    For him with none.

Tempests may scath;
But love can not make smart
Again this year his heart
    Who no heart hath.

Black is night's cope;
But death will not appal
One who, past doubtings all,
    Waits in unhope.

700         *Shut Out that Moon*

CLOSE up the casement, draw the blind,
    Shut out that stealing moon,
She wears too much the guise she wore
    Before our lutes were strewn
With years-deep dust, and names we read
    On a white stone were hewn.

Step not forth on the dew-dashed lawn
    To view the Lady's Chair,
Immense Orion's glittering form,
    The Less and Greater Bear:
Stay in; to such sights we were drawn
    When faded ones were fair.

Brush not the bough for midnight scents
    That come forth lingeringly,
And wake the same sweet sentiments
    They breathed to you and me
When living seemed a laugh, and love
    All it was said to be.

Within the common lamp-lit room
    Prison my eyes and thought;
Let dingy details crudely loom,
    Mechanic speech be wrought:
Too fragrant was Life's early bloom,
    Too tart the fruit it brought!

701 *On the Departure Platform*

WE kissed at the barrier; and passing through
She left me, and moment by moment got
Smaller and smaller, until to my view
　　She was but a spot;

A wee white spot of muslin fluff
That down the diminishing platform bore
Through hustling crowds of gentle and rough
　　To the carriage door.

Under the lamplight's fitful glowers,
Behind dark groups from far and near,
Whose interests were apart from ours,
　　She would disappear,

Then show again, till I ceased to see
That flexible form, that nebulous white;
And she who was more than my life to me
　　Had vanished quite.

We have penned new plans since that fair fond day,
And in season she will appear again—
Perhaps in the same soft white array—
　　But never as then!

—'And why, young man, must eternally fly
A joy you'll repeat, if you love her well?'
—O friend, nought happens twice thus; why,
　　I cannot tell!

702 *A Church Romance*

(*Mellstock: circa 1835*)

SHE turned in the high pew, until her sight
Swept the west gallery, and caught its row
Of music-men with viol, book, and bow
Against the sinking sad tower-window light.

She turned again; and in her pride's despite
One strenuous viol's inspirer seemed to throw
A message from his string to her below,
Which said: 'I claim thee as my own forthright!'

Thus their hearts' bond began, in due time signed.
And long years thence, when Age had scared Romance,
At some old attitude of his or glance
That gallery-scene would break upon her mind,
With him as minstrel, ardent, young, and trim,
Bowing 'New Sabbath' or 'Mount Ephraim'.

703                    *The Roman Road*

THE Roman Road runs straight and bare
As the pale parting-line in hair
Across the heath. And thoughtful men
Contrast its days of Now and Then,
And delve, and measure, and compare;

Visioning on the vacant air
Helmed legionaries, who proudly rear
The Eagle, as they pace again
                    The Roman Road.

But no tall brass-helmed legionnaire
Haunts it for me. Uprises there
A mother's form upon my ken,
Guiding my infant steps, as when
We walked that ancient thoroughfare,
                    The Roman Road.

704                    *After the Visit*

COME again to the place
Where your presence was as a leaf that skims
Down a drouthy way whose ascent bedims
        The bloom on the farer's face.

Come again, with the feet
That were light on the green as a thistledown ball,
And those mute ministrations to one and to all
        Beyond a man's saying sweet.

Until then the faint scent
Of the bordering flowers swam unheeded away,
And I marked not the charm in the changes of day
 As the cloud-colours came and went.

Through the dark corridors
Your walk was so soundless I did not know
Your form from a phantom's of long ago
 Said to pass on the ancient floors,

 Till you drew from the shade,
And I saw the large luminous living eyes
Regard me in fixed inquiring-wise
 As those of a soul that weighed,

 Scarce consciously,
The eternal question of what Life was,
And why we were there, and by whose strange laws
 That which mattered most could not be.

705      *Beyond the Last Lamp*
      (*Near Tooting Common*)

WHILE rain, with eve in partnership,
Descended darkly, drip, drip, drip,
Beyond the last lone lamp I passed
 Walking slowly, whispering sadly,
 Two linked loiterers, wan, downcast;
Some heavy thought constrained each face,
And blinded them to time and place.

The pair seemed lovers, yet absorbed
In mental scenes no longer orbed
By love's young rays. Each countenance
 As it slowly, as it sadly
 Caught the lamplight's yellow glance,
Held in suspense a misery
At things which had been or might be.

When I retrod that watery way
Some hours beyond the droop of day,
Still I found pacing there the twain
    Just as slowly, just as sadly,
      Heedless of the night and rain.
One could but wonder who they were
And what wild woe detained them there.

Though thirty years of blur and blot
Have slid since I beheld that spot,
And saw in curious converse there
    Moving slowly, moving sadly
      That mysterious tragic pair,
Its olden look may linger on—
All but the couple; they have gone.

Whither? Who knows, indeed. . . . And yet
To me, when nights are weird and wet,
Without those comrades there at tryst
    Creeping slowly, creeping sadly,
      That lone lane does not exist.
There they seem brooding on their pain,
And will, while such a lane remain.

706        *The Going*

WHY did you give no hint that night
That quickly after the morrow's dawn,
And calmly, as if indifferent quite,
You would close your term here, up and be gone
    Where I could not follow
    With wing of swallow
To gain one glimpse of you ever anon!

    Never to bid good-bye,
    Or lip me the softest call,
Or utter a wish for a word, while I
Saw morning harden upon the wall,
    Unmoved, unknowing
    That your great going
Had place that moment, and altered all.

Why do you make me leave the house
And think for a breath it is you I see
At the end of the alley of bending boughs
Where so often at dusk you used to be;
       Till in darkening dankness
       The yawning blankness
Of the perspective sickens me!

       You were she who abode
       By those red-veined rocks far West,
You were the swan-necked one who rode
Along the beetling Beeny Crest,
       And, reining nigh me,
       Would muse and eye me,
While Life unrolled us its very best.

Why, then, latterly did we not speak,
Did we not think of those days long dead,
And ere your vanishing strive to seek
That time's renewal? We might have said,
       'In this bright spring weather
       We'll visit together
Those places that once we visited.'

       Well, well! All's past amend,
       Unchangeable. It must go.
I seem but a dead man held on end
To sink down soon. . . . O you could not know
       That such swift fleeing
       No soul foreseeing—
Not even I—would undo me so!

707

       I FOUND her out there
       On a slope few see,
       That falls westwardly
       To the salt-edged air,
       Where the ocean breaks
       On the purple strand,
       And the hurricane shakes
       The solid land.

I brought her here,
And have laid her to rest
In a noiseless nest
No sea beats near.
She will never be stirred
In her loamy cell
By the waves long heard
And loved so well.

So she does not sleep
By those haunted heights
The Atlantic smites
And the blind gales sweep,
Whence she often would gaze
At Dundagel's famed head,
While the dipping blaze
Dyed her face fire-red;

And would sigh at the tale
Of sunk Lyonnesse,
As a wind-tugged tress
Flapped her cheek like a flail;
Or listen at whiles
With a thought-bound brow
To the murmuring miles
She is far from now.

Yet her shade, maybe,
Will creep underground
Till it catch the sound
Of that western sea
As it swells and sobs
Where she once domiciled,
And joy in its throbs
With the heart of a child.

708          *The Haunter*

HE does not think that I haunt here nightly:
　　How shall I let him know
That whither his fancy sets him wandering
　　I, too, alertly go?—

Hover and hover a few feet from him
    Just as I used to do,
But cannot answer the words he lifts me—
    Only listen thereto!

When I could answer he did not say them:
    When I could let him know
How I would like to join in his journeys
    Seldom he wished to go.
Now that he goes and wants me with him
    More than he used to do,
Never he sees my faithful phantom
    Though he speaks thereto.

Yes, I companion him to places
    Only dreamers know,
Where the shy hares print long paces,
    Where the night rooks go;
Into old aisles where the past is all to him,
    Close as his shade can do,
Always lacking the power to call to him,
    Near as I reach thereto!

What a good haunter I am, O tell him!
    Quickly make him know
If he but sigh since my loss befell him
    Straight to his side I go.
Tell him a faithful one is doing
    All that love can do
Still that his path may be worth pursuing,
    And to bring peace thereto.

709                 *At Castle Boterel*

As I drive to the junction of lane and highway,
    And the drizzle bedrenches the waggonette,
I look behind at the fading byway,
    And see on its slope, now glistening wet,
        Distinctly yet

# THOMAS HARDY

Myself and a girlish form benighted
  In dry March weather. We climb the road
Beside a chaise. We had just alighted
  To ease the sturdy pony's load
    When he sighed and slowed.

What we did as we climbed, and what we talked of
  Matters not much, nor to what it led,—
Something that life will not be balked of
  Without rude reason till hope is dead,
    And feeling fled.

It filled but a minute. But was there ever
  A time of such quality, since or before,
In that hill's story? To one mind never,
  Though it has been climbed, foot-swift, foot-sore,
    By thousands more.

Primaeval rocks form the road's steep border,
  And much have they faced there, first and last,
Of the transitory in Earth's long order;
  But what they record in colour and cast
    Is—that we two passed.

And to me, though Time's unflinching rigour,
  In mindless rote, has ruled from sight
The substance now, one phantom figure
  Remains on the slope, as when that night
    Saw us alight.

I look and see it there, shrinking, shrinking,
  I look back at it amid the rain
For the very last time; for my sand is sinking,
  And I shall traverse old love's domain
    Never again.

710        *The Phantom Horsewoman*

QUEER are the ways of a man I know:
    He comes and stands
    In a careworn craze,
    And looks at the sands
    And the seaward haze
    With moveless hands
    And face and gaze,
    Then turns to go . . .
And what does he see when he gazes so?

They say he sees as an instant thing
    More clear than to-day,
    A sweet soft scene
    That was once in play
    By that briny green;
    Yes, notes alway
    Warm, real, and keen,
    What his back years bring—
A phantom of his own figuring.

Of this vision of his they might say more:
    Not only there
    Does he see this sight,
    But everywhere
    In his brain—day, night,
    As if on the air
    It were drawn rose-bright—
    Yea, far from that shore
Does he carry this vision of heretofore:

A ghost-girl-rider. And though, toil-tried
    He withers daily,
    Time touches her not,
    But she still rides gaily
    In his rapt thought
    On that shagged and shaly
    Atlantic spot,
    And as when first eyed
Draws rein and sings to the swing of the tide.

711 *The Oxen*

CHRISTMAS EVE, and twelve of tne clock.
  'Now they are all on their knees,'
An elder said as we sat in a flock
  By the embers in hearthside ease.

We pictured the meek mild creatures where
  They dwelt in their strawy pen,
Nor did it occur to one of us there
  To doubt they were kneeling then.

So fair a fancy few would weave
  In these years! Yet, I feel,
If someone said on Christmas Eve,
  'Come; see the oxen kneel,

'In the lonely barton by yonder coomb
  Our childhood used to know,'
I should go with him in the gloom,
  Hoping it might be so.

712 *Great Things*

SWEET cyder is a great thing,
  A great thing to me,
Spinning down to Weymouth town
  By Ridgway thirstily,
And maid and mistress summoning
  Who tend the hostelry:
O cyder is a great thing,
  A great thing to me!

The dance it is a great thing,
  A great thing to me,
With candles lit and partners fit
  For night-long revelry;
And going home when day-dawning
  Peeps pale upon the lea:
O dancing is a great thing,
  A great thing to me!

Love is, yea, a great thing,
  A great thing to me,
When, having drawn across the lawn
  In darkness silently,
A figure flits like one a-wing
  Out from the nearest tree:
O love is, yes, a great thing,
  A great thing to me!

Will these be always great things,
  Great things to me? . . .
Let it befall that One will call,
  'Soul, I have need of thee':
What then? Joy-jaunts, impassioned flings
  Love, and its ecstasy,
Will always have been great things,
  Great things to me!

713           *Midnight on the Great Western*

In the third-class seat sat the journeying boy,
    And the roof-lamp's oily flame
Played down on his listless form and face,
Bewrapt past knowing to what he was going,
    Or whence he came.

In the band of his hat the journeying boy
    Had a ticket stuck; and a string
Around his neck bore the key of his box,
That twinkled gleams of the lamp's sad beams
    Like a living thing.

What past can be yours, O journeying boy
    Towards a world unknown,
Who calmly, as if incurious quite
On all at stake, can undertake
    This plunge alone?

Knows your soul a sphere, O journeying boy
    Our rude realms far above,
Whence with spacious vision you mark and mete
This region of sin that you find you in
    But are not of?

714     *In Time of 'The Breaking of Nations'*

ONLY a man harrowing clods
        In a slow silent walk
With an old horse that stumbles and nods
        Half asleep as they stalk.

Only thin smoke without flame
        From the heaps of couch-grass;
Yet this will go onward the same
        Though Dynasties pass.

Yonder a maid and her wight
        Come whispering by:
War's annals will cloud into night
        Ere their story die.


715                     *Afterwards*

WHEN the Present has latched its postern behind my tremulous stay,
        And the May month flaps its glad green leaves like wings,
Delicate-filmed as new-spun silk, will the neighbours say,
        'He was a man who used to notice such things'?

If it be in the dusk when, like an eyelid's soundless blink,
        The dewfall-hawk comes crossing the shades to alight
Upon the wind-warped upland thorn, a gazer may think,
        'To him this must have been a familiar sight.'

If I pass during some nocturnal blackness, mothy and warm,
        When the hedgehog travels furtively over the lawn,
One may say, 'He strove that such innocent creatures should come to
        no harm,
        But he could do little for them; and now he is gone.'

If, when hearing that I have been stilled at last, they stand at the door,
        Watching the full-starred heavens that winter sees,
Will this thought rise on those who will meet my face no more,
        'He was one who had an eye for such mysteries'?

And will any say when my bell of quittance is heard in the gloom,
  And a crossing breeze cuts a pause in its outrollings,
Till they rise again, as they were a new bell's boom,
  'He hears it not now, but used to notice such things'?


# ROBERT BRIDGES

## 1844–1930

716                    *London Snow*

WHEN men were all asleep the snow came flying,
In large white flakes falling on the city brown,
Stealthily and perpetually settling and loosely lying,
    Hushing the latest traffic of the drowsy town;
Deadening, muffling, stifling its murmurs failing;
Lazily and incessantly floating down and down:
    Silently sifting and veiling road, roof and railing;
Hiding difference, making unevenness even,
Into angles and crevices softly drifting and sailing.
    All night it fell, and when full inches seven
It lay in the depth of its uncompacted lightness,
The clouds blew off from a high and frosty heaven;
    And all woke earlier for the unaccustomed brightness
Of the winter dawning, the strange unheavenly glare:
The eye marvelled—marvelled at the dazzling whiteness;
    The ear hearkened to the stillness of the solemn air;
No sound of wheel rumbling nor of foot falling,
And the busy morning cries came thin and spare.
    Then boys I heard, as they went to school, calling,
They gathered up the crystal manna to freeze
Their tongues with tasting, their hands with snowballing;
    Or rioted in a drift, plunging up to the knees;
Or peering up from under the white-mossed wonder,
'O look at the trees!' they cried, 'O look at the trees!'
    With lessened load a few carts creak and blunder,
Following along the white deserted way,
A country company long dispersed asunder:
    When now already the sun, in pale display
Standing by Paul's high dome, spread forth below
His sparkling beams, and awoke the stir of the day.

For now doors open, and war is waged with the snow;
And trains of sombre men, past tale of number,
Tread long brown paths, as toward their toil they go:
But even for them awhile no cares encumber
Their minds diverted; the daily word is unspoken,
The daily thoughts of labour and sorrow slumber
At the sight of the beauty that greets them, for the charm
    they have broken.


717             *On a Dead Child*

PERFECT little body, without fault or stain on thee,
  With promise of strength and manhood full and fair!
      Though cold and stark and bare,
The bloom and the charm of life doth awhile remain on thee.

Thy mother's treasure wert thou;—alas! no longer
  To visit her heart with wondrous joy; to be
      Thy father's pride;—ah, he
Must gather his faith together, and his strength make stronger.

To me, as I move thee now in the last duty,
  Dost thou with a turn or gesture anon respond;
      Startling my fancy fond
With a chance attitude of the head, a freak of beauty.

Thy hand clasps, as 'twas wont, my finger, and holds it:
  But the grasp is the clasp of Death, heartbreaking and stiff;
      Yet feels to my hand as if
'Twas still thy will, thy pleasure and trust that enfolds it.

So I lay thee there, thy sunken eyelids closing,—
  Go lie thou there in thy coffin, thy last little bed!—
      Propping thy wise, sad head,
Thy firm, pale hands across thy chest disposing.

So quiet! doth the change content thee?—Death, whither hath he
    taken thee?
  To a world, do I think, that rights the disaster of this?
      The vision of which I miss,
Who weep for the body, and wish but to warm thee and awaken thee?

Ah! little at best can all our hopes avail us
　To lift this sorrow, or cheer us, when in the dark,
　　Unwilling, alone we embark,
And the things we have seen and have known and have heard of, fail us.


718

　　　AWAKE, my heart, to be loved, awake, awake!
　　　The darkness silvers away, the morn doth break,
　　　It leaps in the sky: unrisen lustres slake
　　　The o'ertaken moon. Awake, O heart, awake!

　　　She too that loveth awaketh and hopes for thee;
　　　Her eyes already have sped the shades that flee,
　　　Already they watch the path thy feet shall take:
　　　Awake, O heart, to be loved, awake, awake!

　　　And if thou tarry from her,—if this could be,—
　　　She cometh herself, O heart, to be loved, to thee;
　　　For thee would unashamèd herself forsake:
　　　Awake to be loved, my heart, awake, awake!

　　　Awake, the land is scattered with light, and see,
　　　Uncanopied sleep is flying from field and tree:
　　　And blossoming boughs of April in laughter shake;
　　　Awake, O heart, to be loved, awake, awake!

　　　Lo all things wake and tarry and look for thee:
　　　She looketh and saith, 'O sun, now bring him to me.
　　　Come more adored, O adored, for his coming's sake,
　　　And awake my heart to be loved: awake, awake!'


719　　　　　　　　　*Nightingales*

　　　BEAUTIFUL must be the mountains whence ye come,
　　　And bright in the fruitful valleys the streams, wherefrom
　　　　　　Ye learn your song:
　　Where are those starry woods? O might I wander there,
　　　Among the flowers, which in that heavenly air
　　　　　　Bloom the year long!

Nay, barren are those mountains and spent the streams:
Our song is the voice of desire, that haunts our dreams,
A throe of the heart,
Whose pining visions dim, forbidden hopes profound,
No dying cadence nor long sigh can sound,
For all our art.

Alone, aloud in the raptured ear of men
We pour our dark nocturnal secret; and then,
As night is withdrawn
From these sweet-springing meads and bursting boughs of May,
Dream, while the innumerable choir of day
Welcome the dawn.

720

My delight and thy delight
Walking, like two angels white,
In the gardens of the night:

My desire and thy desire
Twining to a tongue of fire,
Leaping live, and laughing higher;
Thro' the everlasting strife
In the mystery of life.

Love, from whom the world begun,
Hath the secret of the sun.

Love can tell, and love alone,
Whence the million stars were strewn,
Why each atom knows its own,
How, in spite of woe and death,
Gay is life, and sweet is breath:

This he taught us, this we knew,
Happy in his science true,
Hand in hand as we stood
Neath the shadows of the wood.
Heart to heart as we lay
In the dawning of the day.

721 *Eros*

WHY hast thou nothing in thy face?
Thou idol of the human race,
Thou tyrant of the human heart,
The flower of lovely youth that art;
Yea, and that standest in thy youth
An image of eternal Truth,
With thy exuberant flesh so fair,
That only Pheidias might compare,
Ere from his chaste marmoreal form
Time had decayed the colours warm;
Like to his gods in thy proud dress,
Thy starry sheen of nakedness.

Surely thy body is thy mind,
For in thy face is nought to find,
Only thy soft unchristened smile,
That shadows neither love nor guile,
But shameless will and power immense,
In secret sensuous innocence.

O king of joy, what is thy thought?
I dream thou knowest it is nought,
And wouldst in darkness come, but thou
Makest the light where'er thou go.
Ah yet no victim of thy grace,
None who e'er longed for thy embrace,
Hath cared to look upon thy face.

# GERARD MANLEY HOPKINS
## 1844–1889

722 *Heaven-Haven*

*A nun takes the veil*

I HAVE desired to go
    Where springs not fail,
To fields where flies no sharp and sided hail
    And a few lilies blow.

And I have asked to be
Where no storms come,
Where the green swell is in the havens dumb,
And out of the swing of the sea.

723 *The Wreck of the Deutschland*

*To the
happy memory of five Franciscan nuns
exiles by the Falck Laws
drowned between midnight and morning of
Dec. 7th, 1875*

PART THE FIRST

1

THOU mastering me
God! giver of breath and bread;
World's strand, sway of the sea;
Lord of living and dead;
Thou hast bound bones and veins in me, fastened me flesh,
And after it almost unmade, what with dread,
Thy doing: and dost thou touch me afresh?
Over again I feel thy finger and find thee.

2

I did say yes
O at lightning and lashed rod;
Thou heardst me truer than tongue confess
Thy terror, O Christ, O God;
Thou knowest the walls, altar and hour and night:
The swoon of a heart that the sweep and the hurl of thee trod
Hard down with a horror of height:
And the midriff astrain with leaning of, laced with fire of stress.

3

The frown of his face
Before me, the hurtle of hell
Behind, where, where was a, where was a place?
I whirled out wings that spell
And fled with a fling of the heart to the heart of the Host.
My heart, but you were dovewinged, I can tell,
Carrier-witted, I am bold to boast,
To flash from the flame to the flame then, tower from the grace to the
grace.

4

I am soft sift
In an hourglass—at the wall
Fast, but mined with a motion, a drift,
    And it crowds and it combs to the fall;
I steady as a water in a well, to a poise, to a pane,
But roped with, always, all the way down from the tall
    Fells or flanks of the voel, a vein
Of the gospel proffer, a pressure, a principle, Christ's gift.

5

I kiss my hand
To the stars, lovely-asunder
Starlight, wafting him out of it; and
    Glow, glory in thunder;
Kiss my hand to the dappled-with-damson west:
Since, tho' he is under the world's splendour and wonder,
    His mystery must be instressed, stressed;
For I greet him the days I meet him, and bless when I understand.

6

Not out of his bliss
Springs the stress felt
Nor first from heaven (and few know this)
    Swings the stroke dealt—
Stroke and a stress that stars and storms deliver,
That guilt is hushed by, hearts are flushed by and melt—
    But it rides time like riding a river
(And here the faithful waver, the faithless fable and miss).

7

It dates from day
Of his going in Galilee;
Warm-laid grave of a womb-life grey;
    Manger, maiden's knee;
The dense and the driven Passion, and frightful sweat:
Thence the discharge of it, there its swelling to be,
    Though felt before, though in high flood yet—
What none would have known of it, only the heart, being hard at bay,

8

Is out with it! Oh,
We lash with the best or worst
Word last! How a lush-kept plush-capped sloe
Will, mouthed to flesh-burst,
Gush!—flush the man, the being with it, sour or sweet,
Brim, in a flash, full!—Hither then, last or first,
To hero of Calvary, Christ,'s feet—
Never ask if meaning it, wanting it, warned of it—men go.

9

Be adored among men,
God, three-numberèd form;
Wring thy rebel, dogged in den,
Man's malice, with wrecking and storm.
Beyond saying sweet, past telling of tongue,
Thou art lightning and love, I found it, a winter and warm;
Father and fondler of heart thou hast wrung:
Hast thy dark descending and most art merciful then.

10

With an anvil-ding
And with fire in him forge thy will
Or rather, rather then, stealing as Spring
Through him, melt him but master him still:
Whether at once, as once at a crash Paul,
Or as Austin, a lingering-out swéet skíll,
Make mercy in all of us, out of us all
Mastery, but be adored, but be adored King.

PART THE SECOND

11

'Some find me a sword; some
The flange and the rail; flame,
Fang, or flood' goes Death on drum,
And storms bugle his fame.
But wé dream we are rooted in earth—Dust!
Flesh falls within sight of us, we, though our flower the same,
Wave with the meadow, forget that there must
The sour scythe cringe, and the blear share come.

779

12

On Saturday sailed from Bremen,
American-outward-bound,
Take settler and seamen, tell men with women,
Two hundred souls in the round—
O Father, not under thy feathers nor ever as guessing
The goal was a shoal, of a fourth the doom to be drowned;
Yet did the dark side of the bay of thy blessing
Not vault them, the million of rounds of thy mercy not reeve even
them in?

13

Into the snows she sweeps,
Hurling the haven behind,
The Deutschland, on Sunday; and so the sky keeps,
For the infinite air is unkind,
And the sea flint-flake, black-backed in the regular blow,
Sitting Eastnortheast, in cursed quarter, the wind;
Wiry and white-fiery and whirlwind-swivellèd snow
Spins to the widow-making unchilding unfathering deeps.

14

She drove in the dark to leeward,
She struck—not a reef or a rock
But the combs of a smother of sand: night drew her
Dead to the Kentish Knock;
And she beat the bank down with her bows and the ride of her
keel:
The breakers rolled on her beam with ruinous shock;
And canvas and compass, the whorl and the wheel
Idle for ever to waft her or wind her with, these she endured.

15

Hope had grown grey hairs,
Hope had mourning on,
Trenched with tears, carved with cares,
Hope was twelve hours gone;
And frightful a nightfall folded rueful a day
Nor rescue, only rocket and lightship, shone,
And lives at last were washing away:
To the shrouds they took,—they shook in the hurling and horrible airs.

16

One stirred from the rigging to save
        The wild woman-kind below,
    With a rope's end round the man, handy and brave—
        He was pitched to his death at a blow,
For all his dreadnought breast and braids of thew:
    They could tell him for hours, dandled the to and fro
        Through the cobbled foam-fleece. What could he do
With the burl of the fountains of air, buck and the flood of the wave?

17

They fought with God's cold—
        And they could not and fell to the deck
    (Crushed them) or water (and drowned them) or rolled
        With the sea-romp over the wreck.
Night roared, with the heart-break hearing a heart-broke rabble,
    The woman's wailing, the crying of child without check—
        Till a lioness arose breasting the babble,
A prophetess towered in the tumult, a virginal tongue told.

18

Ah, touched in your bower of bone,
        Are you! turned for an exquisite smart,
    Have you! make words break from me here all alone,
        Do you!—mother of being in me, heart.
O unteachably after evil, but uttering truth,
    Why, tears! is it? tears; such a melting, a madrigal start!
        Never-eldering revel and river of youth,
What can it be, this glee? the good you have there of your own?

19

Sister, a sister calling
        A master, her master and mine!—
    And the inboard seas run swirling and hawling;
        The rash smart sloggering brine
Blinds her; but she that weather sees one thing, one;
    Has one fetch in her: she rears herself to divine
        Ears, and the call of the tall nun
To the men in the tops and the tackle rode over the storm's brawling.

20

She was first of a five and came
Of a coifèd sisterhood.
(O Deutschland, double a desperate name!
O world wide of its good!
But Gertrude, lily, and Luther, are two of a town,
Christ's lily and beast of the waste wood:
From life's dawn it is drawn down,
Abel is Cain's brother and breasts they have sucked the same.)

21

Loathed for a love men knew in them,
Banned by the land of their birth,
Rhine refused them, Thames would ruin them;
Surf, snow, river and earth
Gnashed: but thou art above, thou Orion of light;
Thy unchancelling poising palms were weighing the worth,
Thou martyr-master: in thy sight
Storm flakes were scroll-leaved flowers, lily showers—sweet heaven
was astrew in them.

22

Five! the finding and sake
And cipher of suffering Christ.
Mark, the mark is of man's make
And the word of it Sacrificed.
But he scores it in scarlet himself on his own bespoken,
Before-time-taken, dearest prizèd and priced—
Stigma, signal, cinquefoil token
For lettering of the lamb's fleece, ruddying of the rose-flake.

23

Joy fall to thee, father Francis,
Drawn to the Life that died;
With the gnarls of the nails in thee, niche of the lance, his
Lovescape crucified
And seal of his seraph-arrival! and these thy daughters
And five-livèd and leavèd favour and pride,
Are sisterly sealed in wild waters,
To bathe in his fall-gold mercies, to breathe in his all-fire glances.

24

Away in the loveable west,
On a pastoral forehead of Wales,
I was under a roof here, I was at rest,
And they the prey of the gales;
She to the black-about air, to the breaker, the thickly
Falling flakes, to the throng that catches and quails
Was calling 'O Christ, Christ, come quickly':
The cross to her she calls Christ to her, christens her wild-worst Best.

25

The majesty! what did she mean?
Breathe, arch and original Breath.
Is it love in her of the being as her lover had been?
Breathe, body of lovely Death.
They were else-minded then, altogether, the men
Woke thee with a *We are perishing* in the weather of Gennesareth.
Or is it that she cried for the crown then,
The keener to come at the comfort for feeling the combating keen?

26

For how to the heart's cheering
The down-dugged ground-hugged grey
Hovers off, the jay-blue heavens appearing
Of pied and peeled May!
Blue-beating and hoary-glow height; or night, still higher,
With belled fire and the moth-soft Milky Way,
What by your measure is the heaven of desire,
The treasure never eyesight got, nor was ever guessed what for the
hearing?

27

No, but it was not these.
The jading and jar of the cart,
Time's tasking, it is fathers that asking for ease
Of the sodden-with-its-sorrowing heart,
Not danger, electrical horror; then further it finds
The appealing of the Passion is tenderer in prayer apart:
Other, I gather, in measure her mind's
Burden, in wind's burly and beat of endragonèd seas.

28

But how shall I . . . make me room there:
Reach me a . . . Fancy, come faster—
Strike you the sight of it? look at it loom there,
Thing that she . . . There then! the Master,
*Ipse*, the only one, Christ, King, Head:
He was to cure the extremity where he had cast her;
Do, deal, lord it with living and dead;
Let him ride, her pride, in his triumph, despatch and have done with
his doom there.

29

Ah! there was a heart right!
There was single eye!
Read the unshapeable shock night
And knew the who and the why;
Wording it how but by him that present and past,
Heaven and earth are word of, worded by?—
The Simon Peter of a soul! to the blast
Tarpeïan-fast, but a blown beacon of light.

30

Jesu, heart's light,
Jesu, maid's son,
What was the feast followed the night
Thou hadst glory of this nun?—
Feast of the one woman without stain.
For so conceivèd, so to conceive thee is done;
But here was heart-throe, birth of a brain,
Word, that heard and kept thee and uttered thee outright.

31

Well, she has thee for the pain, for the
Patience; but pity of the rest of them!
Heart, go and bleed at a bitterer vein for the
Comfortless unconfessed of them—
No not uncomforted: lovely-felicitous Providence
Finger of a tender of, O of a feathery delicacy, the breast of the
Maiden could obey so, be a bell to, ring of it, and
Startle the poor sheep back! is the shipwrack then a harvest, does
tempest carry the grain for thee?

32

I admire thee, master of the tides,
　　Of the Yore-flood, of the year's fall;
The recurb and the recovery of the gulf's sides,
　　The girth of it and the wharf of it and the wall;
Stanching, quenching ocean of a motionable mind;
Ground of being, and granite of it: past all
　　Grasp God, throned behind
Death with a sovereignty that heeds but hides, bodes but abides;

33

With a mercy that outrides
　　The all of water, an ark
For the listener; for the lingerer with a love glides
　　Lower than death and the dark;
A vein for the visiting of the past-prayer, pent in prison,
The-last-breath penitent spirits—the uttermost mark
　　Our passion-plungèd giant risen,
The Christ of the Father compassionate, fetched in the storm of his
　　strides.

34

Now burn, new born to the world,
　　Double-naturèd name,
The heaven-flung, heart-fleshed, maiden-furled
　　Miracle-in-Mary-of-flame,
Mid-numberèd he in three of the thunder-throne!
Not a dooms-day dazzle in his coming nor dark as he came;
　　Kind, but royally reclaiming his own;
A released shower, let flash to the shire, not a lightning of fire hard-
　　hurled.

35

Dame, at our door
　　Drowned, and among our shoals,
Remember us in the roads, the heaven-haven of the reward:
　　Our King back, Oh, upon English souls!
Let him easter in us, be a dayspring to the dimness of us, be a
　　crimson-cresseted east,
More brightening her, rare-dear Britain, as his reign rolls,
　　Pride, rose, prince, hero of us, high-priest,
Our hearts' charity's hearth's fire, our thoughts' chivalry's throng's
　　Lord.

724 *God's Grandeur*

THE world is charged with the grandeur of God.
  It will flame out, like shining from shook foil;
  It gathers to a greatness, like the ooze of oil
Crushed. Why do men then now not reck his rod?
Generations have trod, have trod, have trod;
  And all is seared with trade; bleared, smeared with toil;
  And wears man's smudge and shares man's smell: the soil
Is bare now, nor can foot feel, being shod.

And for all this, nature is never spent;
  There lives the dearest freshness deep down things;
And though the last lights off the black West went
  Oh, morning, at the brown brink eastward, springs—
Because the Holy Ghost over the bent
  World broods with warm breast and with ah! bright wings.

725 *Spring*

NOTHING is so beautiful as Spring—
  When weeds, in wheels, shoot long and lovely and lush;
  Thrush's eggs look little low heavens, and thrush
Through the echoing timber does so rinse and wring
The ear, it strikes like lightnings to hear him sing;
  The glassy peartree leaves and blooms, they brush
  The descending blue; that blue is all in a rush
With richness; the racing lambs too have fair their fling.

What is all this juice and all this joy?
  A strain of the earth's sweet being in the beginning
In Eden garden.—Have, get, before it cloy,

  Before it cloud, Christ, lord, and sour with sinning,
Innocent mind and Mayday in girl and boy,
  Most, O maid's child, thy choice and worthy the winning.

726                         *The Windhover*

                          *To Christ our Lord*

I CAUGHT this morning morning's minion, king-
      dom of daylight's dauphin, dapple-dawn-drawn Falcon, in his
         riding
Of the rolling level underneath him steady air, and striding
High there, how he rung upon the rein of a wimpling wing
In his ecstasy! then off, off forth on swing,
      As a skate's heel sweeps smooth on a bow-bend: the hurl and
         gliding
Rebuffed the big wind. My heart in hiding
Stirred for a bird,—the achieve of, the mastery of the thing!

Brute beauty and valour and act, oh, air, pride, plume, here
      Buckle! AND the fire that breaks from thee then, a billion
Times told lovelier, more dangerous, O my chevalier!

No wonder of it: shéer plód makes plough down sillion
Shine, and blue-bleak embers, ah my dear,
      Fall, gall themselves, and gash gold-vermilion.


727                          *Pied Beauty*

      GLORY be to God for dappled things—
         For skies of couple-colour as a brinded cow;
            For rose-moles all in stipple upon trout that swim;
      Fresh-firecoal chestnut-falls; finches' wings;
         Landscape plotted and pieced—fold, fallow, and plough;
            And áll trádes, their gear and tackle and trim.

      All things counter, original, spare, strange;
         Whatever is fickle, freckled (who knows how?)
            With swift, slow; sweet, sour; adazzle, dim;
      He fathers-forth whose beauty is past change:
                                                   Praise him

728 *Felix Randal*

FELIX Randal the farrier, O is he dead then? my duty all ended,
Who have watched his mould of man, big-boned and hardy-handsome
Pining, pining, till time when reason rambled in it and some
Fatal four disorders, fleshed there, all contended?

Sickness broke him. Impatient, he cursed at first, but mended
Being anointed and all; though a heavenlier heart began some
Months earlier, since I had our sweet reprieve and ransom
Tendered to him. Ah well, God rest him all road ever he offended!

This seeing the sick endears them to us, us too it endears.
My tongue had taught thee comfort, touch had quenched thy tears,
Thy tears that touched my heart, child, Felix, poor Felix Randal;

How far from then forethought of, all thy more boisterous years,
When thou at the random grim forge, powerful amidst peers,
Didst fettle for the great grey drayhorse his bright and battering sandal!

729 *Spring and Fall*

*to a young child*

MÁRGARÉT, áre you gríeving
Over Goldengrove unleaving?
Léaves, líke the things of man, you
With your fresh thoughts care for, can you?
Áh! ás the heart grows older
It will come to such sights colder
By and by, nor spare a sigh
Though worlds of wanwood leafmeal lie,
And yet you *will* weep and know why.
Now no matter, child, the name:
Sórrow's spríngs áre the same.
Nor mouth had, no nor mind, expressed
What heart heard of, ghost guessed:
It ís the blight man was born for,
It is Margaret you mourn for.

730      ## 'No Worst, there is None'

No worst, there is none. Pitched past pitch of grief,
More pangs will, schooled at forepangs, wilder wring.
Comforter, where, where is your comforting?
Mary, mother of us, where is your relief?
My cries heave, herds-long; huddle in a main, a chief-
woe, world-sorrow; on an age-old anvil wince and sing—
Then lull, then leave off. Fury had shrieked 'No ling-
ering! Let me be fell: force I must be brief'.
O the mind, mind has mountains; cliffs of fall
Frightful, sheer, no-man-fathomed. Hold them cheap
May who ne'er hung there. Nor does long our small
Durance deal with that steep or deep. Here! creep,
Wretch, under a comfort serves in a whirlwind: all
Life death does end and each day dies with sleep.

731      ## 'I Wake and feel the Fell of Dark'

I WAKE and feel the fell of dark, not day.
What hours, O what black hoürs we have spent
This night! what sights you, heart, saw; ways you went!
And more must, in yet longer light's delay.

With witness I speak this. But where I say
Hours I mean years, mean life. And my lament
Is cries countless, cries like dead letters sent
To dearest him that lives alas! away.

I am gall, I am heartburn. God's most deep decree
Bitter would have me taste: my taste was me;
Bones built in me, flesh filled, blood brimmed the curse.

Selfyeast of spirit a dull dough sours. I see
The lost are like this, and their scourge to be
As I am mine, their sweating selves; but worse.

732          *'Thou art indeed Just, Lord'*

THOU art indeed just, Lord, if I contend
With thee; but, sir, so what I plead is just.
Why do sinners' ways prosper? and why must
Disappointment all I endeavour end?

Wert thou my enemy, O thou my friend,
How wouldst thou worse, I wonder, than thou dost
Defeat, thwart me? Oh, the sots and thralls of lust
Do in spare hours more thrive than I that spend,

Sir, life upon thy cause. See, banks and brakes
Now, leavèd how thick! lacèd they are again
With fretty chervil, look, and fresh wind shakes

Them; birds build—but not I build; no, but strain,
Time's eunuch, and not breed one work that wakes.
Mine, O thou lord of life, send my roots rain.

# ALICE MEYNELL

## 1847–1922

733          *Renouncement*

I MUST not think of thee; and, tired yet strong,
   I shun the thought that lurks in all delight—
   The thought of thee—and in the blue Heaven's height,
And in the sweetest passage of a song.
O just beyond the fairest thoughts that throng
   This breast, the thought of thee waits hidden yet bright;
   But it must never, never come in sight;
I must stop short of thee the whole day long.
But when sleep comes to close each difficult day,
   When night gives pause to the long watch I keep
   And all my bonds I needs must loose apart,
Must doff my will as raiment laid away,—
   With the first dream that comes with the first sleep
   I run, I run, I am gathered to thy heart.

734 *Christ in the Universe*

WITH this ambiguous earth
His dealings have been told us. These abide:
The signal to a maid, the human birth,
The lesson, and the young Man crucified.

    But not a star of all
The innumerable host of stars has heard
How he administered this terrestrial ball.
Our race have kept their Lord's entrusted Word.

    Of his earth-visiting feet
None knows the secret, cherished, perilous
The terrible, shamefast, frightened, whispered, sweet,
Heart-shattering secret of his way with us.

    No planet knows that this
Our wayside planet, carrying land and wave,
Love and life multiplied, and pain and bliss,
Bears, as chief treasure, one forsaken grave.

    Nor, in our little day,
May his devices with the heavens be guessed,
His pilgrimage to thread the Milky Way,
Or his bestowals there be manifest.

    But, in the eternities,
Doubtless we shall compare together, hear
A million alien Gospels, in what guise
He trod the Pleiades, the Lyre, the Bear.

    O be prepared, my soul!
To read the inconceivable, to scan
The million forms of God those stars unroll
When, in our turn, we show to them a Man.

# WILLIAM ERNEST HENLEY
## 1849–1903

735

Out of the night that covers me,
  Black as the Pit from pole to pole,
I thank whatever gods may be
  For my unconquerable soul.

In the fell clutch of circumstance
  I have not winced nor cried aloud.
Under the bludgeonings of chance
  My head is bloody, but unbowed.

Beyond this place of wrath and tears
  Looms but the Horror of the shade,
And yet the menace of the years
  Finds, and shall find, me unafraid.

It matters not how strait the gate,
  How charged with punishments the scroll,
I am the master of my fate:
  I am the captain of my soul

736          *Margaritae Sorori, I.M.*

A late lark twitters from the quiet skies;
And from the west,
Where the sun, his day's work ended,
Lingers as in content
There falls on the old, gray city
An influence luminous and serene,
A shining peace.

The smoke ascends
In a rosy-and-golden haze. The spires
Shine, and are changed. In the valley
Shadows rise. The lark sings on. The sun,
Closing his benediction,

Sinks, and the darkening air
Thrills with a sense of the triumphing night—
Night with her train of stars
And her great gift of sleep.

So be my passing!
My task accomplished and the long day done,
My wages taken, and in my heart
Some late lark singing,
Let me be gathered to the quiet west,
The sundown splendid and serene,
Death.

# ROBERT LOUIS STEVENSON

## 1850–1894

### *The House Beautiful*

737

*A naked house, a naked moor,*
*A shivering pool before the door,*
*A garden bare of flowers and fruit*
*And poplars at the garden foot:*
*Such is the place that I live in,*
*Bleak without and bare within.*

Yet shall your ragged moor receive
The incomparable pomp of eve,
And the cold glories of the dawn
Behind your shivering trees be drawn;
And when the wind from place to place
Doth the unmoored cloud-galleons chase,
Your garden gloom and gleam again,
With leaping sun, with glancing rain.
Here shall the wizard moon ascend
The heavens, in the crimson end
Of day's declining splendour; here
The army of the stars appear.
The neighbour hollows dry or wet,
Spring shall with tender flowers beset;
And oft the morning muser see
Larks rising from the broomy lea,

And every fairy wheel and thread
Of cobweb dew-bediamonded.
When daisies go, shall winter time
Silver the simple grass with rime;
Autumnal frosts enchant the pool
And make the cart-ruts beautiful;
And when snow-bright the moor expands,
How shall your children clap their hands!
To make this earth, our hermitage,
A cheerful and a changeful page,
God's bright and intricate device
Of days and seasons doth suffice.

738                          *Requiem*

UNDER the wide and starry sky,
Dig the grave and let me lie.
Glad did I live and gladly die,
    And I laid me down with a will.

This be the verse you grave for me:
*Here he lies where he longed to be;*
*Home is the sailor, home from sea,*
    *And the hunter home from the hill.*

739

SING me a song of a lad that is gone,
    Say, could that lad be I?
Merry of soul he sailed on a day
    Over the sea to Skye.

Mull was astern, Rum on the port,
    Eigg on the starboard bow;
Glory of youth glowed in his soul:
    Where is that glory now?

Sing me a song of a lad that is gone,
    Say, could that lad be I?
Merry of soul he sailed on a day
    Over the sea to Skye.

Give me again all that was there,
  Give me the sun that shone!
Give me the eyes, give me the soul,
  Give me the lad that's gone!

Sing me a song of a lad that is gone,
  Say, could that lad be I?
Merry of soul he sailed on a day
  Over the sea to Skye.

Billow and breeze, islands and seas,
  Mountains of rain and sun,
All that was good, all that was fair,
  All that was me is gone.

740      *To S. R. Crockett*

BLOWS the wind today, and the sun and the rain are flying,
  Blows the wind on the moors today and now,
Where about the graves of the martyrs the whaups are crying,
  My heart remembers how!

Grey recumbent tombs of the dead in desert places,
  Standing-stones on the vacant wine-red moor,
Hills of sheep, and the howes of the silent vanished races,
  And winds, austere and pure.

Be it granted me to behold you again in dying,
  Hills of home! and to hear again the call;
Hear about the graves of the martyrs the peewees crying,
  And hear no more at all.

# OSCAR WILDE
## 1856–1900

OSCAR WILDE

741     *from* The Ballad of Reading Gaol

HE did not wear his scarlet coat,
  For blood and wine are red,
And blood and wine were on his hands
  When they found him with the dead,
The poor dead woman whom he loved,
  And murdered in her bed.

He walked amongst the Trial Men
  In a suit of shabby grey;
A cricket cap was on his head,
  And his step seemed light and gay;
But I never saw a man who looked
  So wistfully at the day.

I never saw a man who looked
  With such a wistful eye
Upon that little tent of blue
  Which prisoners call the sky,
And at every drifting cloud that went
  With sails of silver by.

I walked, with other souls in pain,
  Within another ring,
And was wondering if the man had done
  A great or little thing,
When a voice behind me whispered low,
  *'That fellow's got to swing.'*

Dear Christ! the very prison walls
  Suddenly seemed to reel,
And the sky above my head became
  Like a casque of scorching steel;
And, though I was a soul in pain,
  My pain I could not feel.

I only knew what hunted thought
   Quickened his step, and why
He looked upon the garish day
   With such a wistful eye;
The man had killed the thing he loved,
   And so he had to die.

\*

Yet each man kills the thing he loves,
   By each let this be heard,
Some do it with a bitter look,
   Some with a flattering word,
The coward does it with a kiss,
   The brave man with a sword!

Some kill their love when they are young,
   And some when they are old;
Some strangle with the hands of Lust,
   Some with the hands of Gold:
The kindest use a knife, because
   The dead so soon grow cold.

Some love too little, some too long,
   Some sell, and others buy;
Some do the deed with many tears,
   And some without a sigh:
For each man kills the thing he loves,
   Yet each man does not die.

He does not die a death of shame
   On a day of dark disgrace,
Nor have a noose about his neck,
   Nor a cloth upon his face,
Nor drop feet foremost through the floor
   Into an empty space.

742

### *Theocritus*

#### *A Villanelle*

O SINGER of Persephone!
   In the dim meadows desolate
Dost thou remember Sicily?

Still through the ivy flits the bee
    Where Amaryllis lies in state;
O Singer of Persephone!

Simaetha calls on Hecate
    And hears the wild dogs at the gate;
Dost thou remember Sicily?

Still by the light and laughing sea
    Poor Polypheme bemoans his fate;
O Singer of Persephone!

And still in boyish rivalry
    Young Daphnis challenges his mate;
Dost thou remember Sicily?

Slim Lacon keeps a goat for thee,
    For thee the jocund shepherds wait;
O Singer of Persephone!
Dost thou remember Sicily?

# JOHN DAVIDSON

## 1857–1909

743                     *London*

ATHWART the sky a lowly sigh
From west to east the sweet wind carried;
The sun stood still on Primrose Hill;
    His light in all the city tarried:
The clouds on viewless columns bloomed
Like smouldering lilies unconsumed.

'Oh sweetheart, see! how shadowy,
    Of some occult magician's rearing,
Or swung in space of heaven's grace
    Dissolving, dimly reappearing,
Afloat upon ethereal tides
St Paul's above the city rides!'

A rumour broke through the thin smoke
  Enwreathing abbey, tower, and palace,
The parks, the squares, the thoroughfares,
  The million-peopled lanes and alleys,
An ever-muttering prisoned storm,
The heart of London beating warm.

744            *Thirty Bob a Week*

I COULDN'T touch a stop and turn a screw,
  And set the blooming world a-work for me,
Like such as cut their teeth—I hope, like you—
  On the handle of a skeleton gold key;
I cut mine on a leek, which I eat it every week:
  I'm a clerk at thirty bob as you can see.

But I don't allow it's luck and all a toss;
  There's no such thing as being starred and crossed;
It's just the power of some to be a boss,
  And the bally power of others to be bossed:
I face the music, sir; you bet I ain't a cur;
  Strike me lucky if I don't believe I'm lost!

For like a mole I journey in the dark,
  A-travelling along the underground
From my Pillar'd Halls and broad Suburbean Park,
  To come the daily dull official round;
And home again at night with my pipe all alight,
  A-scheming how to count ten bob a pound.

And it's often very cold and very wet,
  And my missis stitches towels for a hunks;
And the Pillar'd Halls is half of it to let—
  Three rooms about the size of travelling trunks.
And we cough, my wife and I, to dislocate a sigh,
  When the noisy little kids are in their bunks.

But you never hear her do a growl or whine,
  For she's made of flint and roses, very odd;
And I've got to cut my meaning rather fine,
  Or I'd blubber, for I'm made of greens and sod:
So p'r'aps we are in Hell for all that I can tell,
  And lost and damn'd and served up hot to God.

# JOHN DAVIDSON

I ain't blaspheming, Mr Silver-tongue;
  I'm saying things a bit beyond your art:
Of all the rummy starts you ever sprung,
  Thirty bob a week's the rummiest start!
With your science and your books and your the'ries about spooks,
  Did you ever hear of looking in your heart?

I didn't mean your pocket, Mr, no:
  I mean that having children and a wife,
With thirty bob on which to come and go,
  Isn't dancing to the tabor and the fife:
When it doesn't make you drink, by Heaven! it makes you think,
  And notice curious items about life.

I step into my heart and there I meet
  A god-almighty devil singing small,
Who would like to shout and whistle in the street,
  And squelch the passers flat against the wall;
If the whole world was a cake he had the power to take,
  He would take it, ask for more, and eat it all.

And I meet a sort of simpleton beside,
  The kind that life is always giving beans;
With thirty bob a week to keep a bride
  He fell in love and married in his teens:
At thirty bob he stuck; but he knows it isn't luck:
  He knows the seas are deeper than tureens.

And the god-almighty devil and the fool
  That meet me in the High Street on the strike,
When I walk about my heart a-gathering wool,
  Are my good and evil angels if you like.
And both of them together in every kind of weather
  Ride me like a double-seated bike.

That's rough a bit and needs its meaning curled.
  But I have a high old hot un in my mind—
A most engrugious notion of the world,
  That leaves your lightning 'rithmetic behind—
I give it at a glance when I say 'There ain't no chance,
  Nor nothing of the lucky-lottery kind.'

And it's this way that I make it out to be:
  No fathers, mothers, countries, climates—none;
Not Adam was responsible for me,
  Nor society, nor systems, nary one:
A little sleeping seed, I woke—I did, indeed—
  A million years before the blooming sun.

I woke because I thought the time had come;
  Beyond my will there was no other cause;
And everywhere I found myself at home,
  Because I chose to be the thing I was;
And in whatever shape of mollusc or of ape
  I always went according to the laws.

I was the love that chose my mother out;
  I joined two lives and from the union burst;
My weakness and my strength without a doubt
  Are mine alone for ever from the first:
It's just the very same with a difference in the name
  As 'Thy will be done.' You say it if you durst!

They say it daily up and down the land
  As easy as you take a drink, it's true;
But the difficultest go to understand,
  And the difficultest job a man can do,
Is to come it brave and meek with thirty bob a week,
  And feel that that's the proper thing for you.

It's a naked child against a hungry wolf;
  It's playing bowls upon a splitting wreck;
It's walking on a string across a gulf
  With millstones fore-and-aft about your neck;
But the thing is daily done by many and many a one;
  And we fall, face forward, fighting, on the deck.

# FRANCIS THOMPSON

## 1859–1907

745                    *In No Strange Land*

O WORLD invisible, we view thee,
O world intangible, we touch thee,
O world unknowable, we know thee,
Inapprehensible, we clutch thee!

Does the fish soar to find the ocean,
The eagle plunge to find the air—
That we ask of the stars in motion
If they have rumour of thee there?

Not where the wheeling systems darken,
And our benumbed conceiving soars!—
The drift of pinions, would we hearken,
Beats at our own clay-shuttered doors.

The angels keep their ancient places;—
Turn but a stone, and start a wing!
'Tis ye, 'tis your estrangèd faces,
That miss the many-splendoured thing.

But (when so sad thou canst not sadder)
Cry;—and upon thy so sore loss
Shall shine the traffic of Jacob's ladder
Pitched betwixt Heaven and Charing Cross.

Yea, in the night, my Soul, my daughter,
Cry,—clinging Heaven by the hems;
And lo, Christ walking on the water,
Not of Gennesareth, but Thames!

## ALFRED EDWARD HOUSMAN
1859–1936

**746**

ON Wenlock Edge the wood's in trouble;
 His forest fleece the Wrekin heaves;
The gale, it plies the saplings double,
 And thick on Severn snow the leaves.

'Twould blow like this through holt and hanger
 When Uricon the city stood:
'Tis the old wind in the old anger,
 But then it threshed another wood.

Then, 'twas before my time, the Roman
 At yonder heaving hill would stare:
The blood that warms an English yeoman,
 The thoughts that hurt him, they were there.

There, like the wind through woods in riot,
 Through him the gale of life blew high;
The tree of man was never quiet:
 Then 'twas the Roman, now 'tis I.

The gale, it plies the saplings double,
 It blows so hard, 'twill soon be gone:
To-day the Roman and his trouble
 Are ashes under Uricon.

**747**

ON the idle hill of summer,
 Sleepy with the flow of streams,
Far I hear the steady drummer
 Drumming like a noise in dreams.

Far and near and low and louder
 On the roads of earth go by,
Dear to friends and food for powder,
 Soldiers marching, all to die.

East and west on fields forgotten
  Bleach the bones of comrades slain,
Lovely lads and dead and rotten;
  None that go return again.

Far the calling bugles hollo,
  High the screaming fife replies,
Gay the files of scarlet follow:
  Woman bore me, I will rise.


748

INTO my heart an air that kills
  From yon far country blows:
What are those blue remembered hills,
  What spires, what farms are those?

That is the land of lost content,
  I see it shining plain,
The happy highways where I went
  And cannot come again.


749

HER strong enchantments failing,
  Her towers of fear in wreck,
Her limbecks dried of poisons
  And the knife at her neck,

The Queen of air and darkness
  Begins to shrill and cry,
'O young man, O my slayer,
  To-morrow you shall die.'

O Queen of air and darkness,
  I think 'tis truth you say,
And I shall die to-morrow;
  But you will die to-day.

750     *Epitaph on an Army of Mercenaries*

THESE, in the day when heaven was falling,
    The hour when earth's foundations fled,
Followed their mercenary calling
    And took their wages and are dead.

Their shoulders held the sky suspended;
    They stood, and earth's foundations stay;
What God abandoned, these defended,
    And saved the sum of things for pay.

751

TELL me not here, it needs not saying,
    What tune the enchantress plays
In aftermaths of soft September
    Or under blanching mays,
For she and I were long acquainted
    And I knew all her ways.

On russet floors, by waters idle,
    The pine lets fall its cone;
The cuckoo shouts all day at nothing
    In leafy dells alone;
And traveller's joy beguiles in autumn
    Hearts that have lost their own.

On acres of the seeded grasses
    The changing burnish heaves;
Or marshalled under moons of harvest
    Stand still all night the sheaves;
Or beeches strip in storms for winter
    And stain the wind with leaves.

Possess, as I possessed a season,
    The countries I resign,
Where over elmy plains the highway
    Would mount the hills and shine,
And full of shade the pillared forest
    Would murmur and be mine.

For nature, heartless, witless nature,
  Will neither care nor know
What stranger's feet may find the meadow
  And trespass there and go,
Nor ask amid the dews of morning
  If they are mine or no.


752

Crossing alone the nighted ferry
  With the one coin for fee,
Whom, on the wharf of Lethe waiting,
  Count you to find? Not me.

The brisk fond lackey to fetch and carry,
  The true, sick-hearted slave,
Expect him not in the just city
  And free land of the grave.


753                    *Parta Quies*

Good-night; ensured release,
Imperishable peace,
    Have these for yours,
While sea abides, and land,
And earth's foundations stand,
    And heaven endures.

When earth's foundations flee,
Nor sky nor land nor sea
    At all is found,
Content you, let them burn:
It is not your concern;
    Sleep on, sleep sound.

# ERNEST DOWSON

## 1867–1900

754    *Non sum qualis eram bonae sub regno Cynarae*

LAST night, ah, yesternight, betwixt her lips and mine
There fell thy shadow, Cynara! thy breath was shed
Upon my soul between the kisses and the wine;
And I was desolate and sick of an old passion,
    Yea, I was desolate and bowed my head:
I have been faithful to thee, Cynara! in my fashion.

All night upon mine heart I felt her warm heart beat,
Night-long within mine arms in love and sleep she lay;
Surely the kisses of her bought red mouth were sweet;
But I was desolate and sick of an old passion,
    When I awoke and found the dawn was gray:
I have been faithful to thee, Cynara! in my fashion.

I have forgot much, Cynara! gone with the wind,
Flung roses, roses riotously with the throng,
Dancing, to put thy pale, lost lilies out of mind;
But I was desolate and sick of an old passion,
    Yea, all the time, because the dance was long:
I have been faithful to thee, Cynara! in my fashion.

I cried for madder music and for stronger wine,
But when the feast is finished and the lamps expire,
Then falls thy shadow, Cynara! the night is thine;
And I am desolate and sick of an old passion,
    Yea, hungry for the lips of my desire:
I have been faithful to thee, Cynara! in my fashion.


755    *Vitae summa brevis spem nos vetat incohare longam*

THEY are not long, the weeping and the laughter,
    Love and desire and hate:
I think they have no portion in us after
    We pass the gate.

ERNEST DOWSON

They are not long, the days of wine and roses:
    Out of a misty dream
Our path emerges for a while, then closes
    Within a dream.


# LIONEL JOHNSON
## 1867–1902

756             *The Dark Angel*

DARK Angel, with thine aching lust
To rid the world of penitence:
Malicious Angel, who still dost
My soul such subtile violence!

Because of thee, no thought, no thing,
Abides for me undesecrate:
Dark Angel, ever on the wing,
Who never reachest me too late!

When music sounds, then changest thou
Its silvery to a sultry fire:
Nor will thine envious heart allow
Delight untortured by desire.

Through thee, the gracious Muses turn
To Furies, O mine Enemy!
And all the things of beauty burn
With flames of evil ecstasy.

Because of thee, the land of dreams
Becomes a gathering place of fears:
Until tormented slumber seems
One vehemence of useless tears.

When sunlight glows upon the flowers,
Or ripples down the dancing sea:
Thou, with thy troop of passionate powers,
Beleaguerest, bewilderest, me.

# LIONEL JOHNSON

Within the breath of autumn woods,
Within the winter silences:
Thy venomous spirit stirs and broods,
O Master of impieties!

The ardour of red flame is thine,
And thine the steely soul of ice:
Thou poisonest the fair design
Of nature, with unfair device.

Apples of ashes, golden bright;
Waters of bitterness, how sweet!
O banquet of a foul delight,
Prepared by thee, dark Paraclete!

Thou art the whisper in the gloom,
The hinting tone, the haunting laugh:
Thou art the adorner of my tomb,
The minstrel of mine epitaph.

I fight thee, in the Holy Name!
Yet, what thou dost, is what God saith:
Tempter! should I escape thy flame,
Thou wilt have helped my soul from Death:

The second Death, that never dies,
That cannot die, when time is dead:
Live Death, wherein the lost soul cries,
Eternally uncomforted.

Dark Angel, with thine aching lust!
Of two defeats, of two despairs:
Less dread, a change to drifting dust,
Than thine eternity of cares.

Do what thou wilt, thou shalt not so,
Dark Angel! triumph over me:
*Lonely, unto the Lone I go;*
*Divine, to the Divinity.*

757   *By the Statue of King Charles*
*At Charing Cross*

Sombre and rich, the skies;
Great glooms, and starry plains.
Gently the night wind sighs;
Else a vast silence reigns.

The splendid silence clings
Around me: and around
The saddest of all kings
Crowned, and again discrowned.

Comely and calm, he rides
Hard by his own Whitehall:
Only the night wind glides:
No crowds, nor rebels, brawl.

Gone, too, his Court: and yet,
The stars his courtiers are:
Stars in their stations set;
And every wandering star.

Alone he rides, alone,
The fair and fatal king:
Dark night is all his own,
That strange and solemn thing.

Which are more full of fate:
The stars; or those sad eyes?
Which are more still and great:
Those brows; or the dark skies?

Although his whole heart yearn
In passionate tragedy:
Never was face so stern
With sweet austerity.

Vanquished in life, his death
By beauty made amends:
The passing of his breath
Won his defeated ends.

## LIONEL JOHNSON

Brief life, and hapless? Nay:
Through death, life grew sublime.
*Speak after sentence?* Yea:
And to the end of time.

Armoured he rides, his head
Bare to the stars of doom:
He triumphs now, the dead,
Beholding London's gloom.

Our wearier spirit faints,
Vexed in the world's employ:
His soul was of the saints;
And art to him was joy.

King, tried in fires of woe!
Men hunger for thy grace:
And through the night I go,
Loving thy mournful face.

Yet, when the city sleeps;
When all the cries are still:
The stars and heavenly deeps
Work out a perfect will.


# RUDYARD KIPLING

## 1865–1936

758                          *Mandalay*

BY the old Moulmein Pagoda, lookin' lazy at the sea,
There's a Burma girl a-settin', and I know she thinks o' me;
For the wind is in the palm-trees, and the temple-bells they say:
'Come you back, you British soldier; come you back to Mandalay!'
        Come you back to Mandalay,
        Where the old Flotilla lay:
        Can't you 'ear their paddles chunkin' from Rangoon to
            Mandalay?
        On the road to Mandalay,
        Where the flyin'-fishes play,
        An' the dawn comes up like thunder outer China 'crost the
            Bay!

'Er petticoat was yaller an' 'er little cap was green,
An' 'er name was Supi-yaw-lat—jes' the same as Theebaw's Queen,
An' I seed her first a-smokin' of a whackin' white cheroot,
An' a-wastin' Christian kisses on an 'eathen idol's foot:
   Bloomin' idol made o' mud—
   Wot they called the Great Gawd Budd—
   Plucky lot she cared for idols when I kissed 'er where she
    stud!
   On the road to Mandalay . . .

When the mist was on the rice-fields an' the sun was droppin' slow,
She'd git 'er little banjo an' she'd sing '*Kulla-lo-lo!*'
With 'er arm upon my shoulder an' 'er cheek agin my cheek
We useter watch the steamers an' the *hathis* pilin' teak.
   Elephints a-pilin' teak
   In the sludgy, squdgy creek,
   Where the silence 'ung that 'eavy you was 'arf afraid to speak!
   On the road to Mandalay . . .

But that's all shove be'ind me—long ago an' fur away,
An' there ain't no 'buses runnin' from the Bank to Mandalay;
An' I'm learnin' 'ere in London what the ten-year soldier tells:
'If you've 'eard the East a-callin', you won't never 'eed naught else.'
   No! you won't 'eed nothin' else
   But them spicy garlic smells,
   An' the sunshine an' the palm-trees an' the tinkly temple-
    bells;
   On the road to Mandalay . . .

I am sick o' wastin' leather on these gritty pavin'-stones,
An' the blasted English drizzle wakes the fever in my bones;
Tho' I walks with fifty 'ousemaids outer Chelsea to the Strand,
An' they talks a lot o' lovin', but wot do they understand?
   Beefy face an' grubby 'and—
   Law! wot do they understand?
   I've a neater, sweeter maiden in a cleaner, greener land!
   On the road to Mandalay . . .

Ship me somewheres east of Suez, where the best is like the worst,
Where there aren't no Ten Commandments an' a man can raise a
    thirst;
For the temple-bells are callin', an' it's there that I would be—
By the old Moulmein Pagoda, looking lazy at the sea;

On the road to Mandalay,
Where the old Flotilla lay,
With our sick beneath the awnings when we went to
   Mandalay!
O the road to Mandalay,
Where the flyin'-fishes play,
An' the dawn comes up like thunder outer China 'crost the
   Bay!

759               *Danny Deever*

'WHAT are the bugles blowin' for?' said Files-on-Parade.
'To turn you out, to turn you out,' the Colour-Sergeant said.
'What makes you look so white, so white?' said Files-on-Parade.
'I'm dreadin' what I've got to watch,' the Colour-Sergeant said.
  For they're hangin' Danny Deever, you can hear the Dead March
    play,
    The Regiment's in 'ollow square—they're hangin' him to-day;
    They've taken of his buttons off an' cut his stripes away,
    An' they're hangin' Danny Deever in the mornin'.

'What makes the rear-rank breathe so 'ard?' said Files-on-Parade.
'It's bitter cold, it's bitter cold,' the Colour-Sergeant said.
'What makes that front-rank man fall down?' said Files-on-Parade.
'A touch o' sun, a touch o' sun,' the Colour-Sergeant said.
    They are hangin' Danny Deever, they are marchin' of 'im round,
    They 'ave 'alted Danny Deever by 'is coffin on the ground;
    An' 'e'll swing in 'arf a minute for a sneakin' shootin' hound—
    O they're hangin' Danny Deever in the mornin'!

' 'Is cot was right-'and cot to mine,' said Files-on-Parade.
' 'E's sleepin' out an' far to-night,' the Colour-Sergeant said.
'I've drunk 'is beer a score o' times,' said Files-on-Parade.
' 'E's drinkin' bitter beer alone,' the Colour-Sergeant said.
    They are hangin' Danny Deever, you must mark 'im to 'is place,
    For 'e shot a comrade sleepin'—you must look 'im in the face;
    Nine 'undred of 'is county an' the Regiment's disgrace,
    While they're hangin' Danny Deever in the mornin'.

'What's that so black agin the sun?' said Files-on-Parade.
'It's Danny fightin' 'ard for life,' the Colour-Sergeant said.
'What's that that whimpers over'ead?' said Files-on-Parade.
'It's Danny's soul that's passin' now,' the Colour-Sergeant said.
  For they're done with Danny Deever, you can 'ear the quickstep
    play,
  The Regiment's in column, an' they're marchin' us away;
  Ho! the young recruits are shakin', an' they'll want their beer to-day,
  After hangin' Danny Deever in the mornin'!

760         *'Cities and Thrones and Powers'*

    CITIES and Thrones and Powers
      Stand in Time's eye,
    Almost as long as flowers,
      Which daily die:
    But, as new buds put forth
      To glad new men,
    Out of the spent and unconsidered Earth
      The Cities rise again.

    This season's Daffodil
      She never hears
    What change, what chance, what chill,
      Cut down last year's;
    But with bold countenance,
      And knowledge small,
    Esteems her seven days' continuance
      To be perpetual.

    So Time that is o'erkind
      To all that be,
    Ordains us e'en as blind,
      As bold as she:
    That in our very death,
      And burial sure,
    Shadow to shadow, well persuaded, saith,
      'See how our works endure!'

761 *The Way through the Woods*

THEY shut the road through the woods
Seventy years ago.
Weather and rain have undone it again,
And now you would never know
There was once a road through the woods
Before they planted the trees.
It is underneath the coppice and heath
And the thin anemones.
Only the keeper sees
That, where the ring-dove broods,
And the badgers roll at ease,
There was once a road through the woods.

Yet, if you enter the woods
Of a summer evening late,
When the night-air cools on the trout-ringed pools
Where the otter whistles his mate,
(They fear not men in the woods,
Because they see so few.)
You will hear the beat of a horse's feet,
And the swish of a skirt in the dew,
Steadily cantering through
The misty solitudes,
As though they perfectly knew
The old lost road through the woods. . . .
But there is no road through the woods.

762 *Recessional*

June 22, 1897

GOD of our fathers, known of old,
    Lord of our far-flung battle-line,
Beneath whose awful Hand we hold
    Dominion over palm and pine—
Lord God of Hosts, be with us yet,
Lest we forget—lest we forget!

The tumult and the shouting dies;
  The Captains and the Kings depart:
Still stands thine ancient sacrifice,
  An humble and a contrite heart.
Lord God of Hosts, be with us yet,
Lest we forget—lest we forget!

Far-called, our navies melt away;
  On dune and headland sinks the fire:
Lo, all our pomp of yesterday
  Is one with Nineveh and Tyre!
Judge of the Nations, spare us yet,
Lest we forget—lest we forget!

If, drunk with sight of power, we loose
  Wild tongues that have not thee in awe,
Such boastings as the Gentiles use,
  Or lesser breeds without the Law—
Lord God of Hosts, be with us yet,
Lest we forget—lest we forget!

For heathen heart that puts her trust
  In reeking tube and iron shard,
All valiant dust that builds on dust,
  And guarding, calls not thee to guard,
For frantic boast and foolish word—
Thy mercy on thy People, Lord!

# WILLIAM BUTLER YEATS

## 1865–1939

763          *The Lake Isle of Innisfree*

I WILL arise and go now, and go to Innisfree,
And a small cabin build there, of clay and wattles made:
Nine bean-rows will I have there, a hive for the honey-bee,
And live alone in the bee-loud glade.

And I shall have some peace there, for peace comes dropping slow,
Dropping from the veils of the morning to where the cricket sings;
There midnight's all a glimmer, and noon a purple glow,
And evening full of the linnet's wings.

I will arise and go now, for always night and day
I hear lake water lapping with low sounds by the shore;
While I stand on the roadway, or on the pavements grey,
I hear it in the deep heart's core.

764          *Who goes with Fergus?*

WHO will go drive with Fergus now,
And pierce the deep wood's woven shade,
And dance upon the level shore?
Young man, lift up your russet brow,
And lift your tender eyelids, maid,
And brood on hopes and fear no more.

And no more turn aside and brood
Upon love's bitter mystery;
For Fergus rules the brazen cars,
And rules the shadows of the wood,
And the white breast of the dim sea
And all dishevelled wandering stars.

765          *No Second Troy*

WHY should I blame her that she filled my days
With misery, or that she would of late
Have taught to ignorant men most violent ways,
Or hurled the little streets upon the great,
Had they but courage equal to desire?
What could have made her peaceful with a mind
That nobleness made simple as a fire,
With beauty like a tightened bow, a kind
That is not natural in an age like this,
Being high and solitary and most stern?
Why, what could she have done, being what she is?
Was there another Troy for her to burn?

766 *An Irish Airman foresees his Death*

I KNOW that I shall meet my fate
Somewhere among the clouds above;
Those that I fight I do not hate,
Those that I guard I do not love;
My country is Kiltartan Cross,
My countrymen Kiltartan's poor,
No likely end could bring them loss
Or leave them happier than before.
Nor law, nor duty bade me fight,
Nor public men, nor cheering crowds,
A lonely impulse of delight
Drove to this tumult in the clouds;
I balanced all, brought all to mind,
The years to come seemed waste of breath,
A waste of breath the years behind
In balance with this life, this death.

767 *Easter 1916*

I HAVE met them at close of day
Coming with vivid faces
From counter or desk among grey
Eighteenth-century houses.
I have passed with a nod of the head
Or polite meaningless words,
Or have lingered awhile and said
Polite meaningless words,
And thought before I had done
Of a mocking tale or a gibe
To please a companion
Around the fire at the club,
Being certain that they and I
But lived where motley is worn:
All changed, changed utterly:
A terrible beauty is born.

That woman's days were spent
In ignorant good-will,
Her nights in argument
Until her voice grew shrill.
What voice more sweet than hers
When, young and beautiful,
She rode to harriers?
This man had kept a school
And rode our wingèd horse;
This other his helper and friend
Was coming into his force;
He might have won fame in the end,
So sensitive his nature seemed,
So daring and sweet his thought.
This other man I had dreamed
A drunken, vainglorious lout.
He had done most bitter wrong
To some who are near my heart,
Yet I number him in the song;
He, too, has resigned his part
In the casual comedy;
He, too, has been changed in his turn,
Transformed utterly:
A terrible beauty is born.

Hearts with one purpose alone
Through summer and winter seem
Enchanted to a stone
To trouble the living stream.
The horse that comes from the road,
The rider, the birds that range
From cloud to tumbling cloud,
Minute by minute they change;
A shadow of cloud on the stream
Changes minute by minute;
A horse-hoof slides on the brim,
And a horse plashes within it;
The long-legged moor-hens dive,
And hens to moor-cocks call;
Minute by minute they live:
The stone's in the midst of all.

Too long a sacrifice
Can make a stone of the heart.
O when may it suffice?
That is Heaven's part, our part
To murmur name upon name,
As a mother names her child
When sleep at last has come
On limbs that had run wild.
What is it but nightfall?
No, no, not night but death;
Was it needless death after all?
For England may keep faith
For all that is done and said.
We know their dream; enough
To know they dreamed and are dead;
And what if excess of love
Bewildered them till they died?
I write it out in a verse—
MacDonagh and MacBride
And Connolly and Pearse
Now and in time to be,
Wherever green is worn,
Are changed, changed utterly:
A terrible beauty is born.

768                    *The Second Coming*

TURNING and turning in the widening gyre
The falcon cannot hear the falconer;
Things fall apart; the centre cannot hold;
Mere anarchy is loosed upon the world,
The blood-dimmed tide is loosed, and everywhere
The ceremony of innocence is drowned;
The best lack all conviction, while the worst
Are full of passionate intensity.

Surely some revelation is at hand;
Surely the Second Coming is at hand.
The Second Coming! Hardly are those words out
When a vast image out of *Spiritus Mundi*
Troubles my sight: somewhere in sands of the desert
A shape with lion body and the head of a man,

A gaze blank and pitiless as the sun,
Is moving its slow thighs, while all about it
Reel shadows of the indignant desert birds.
The darkness drops again; but now I know
That twenty centuries of stony sleep
Were vexed to nightmare by a rocking cradle,
And what rough beast, its hour come round at last,
Slouches towards Bethlehem to be born?

769            *Sailing to Byzantium*

THAT is no country for old men. The young
In one another's arms, birds in the trees
—Those dying generations—at their song,
The salmon-falls, the mackerel-crowded seas,
Fish, flesh, or fowl, commend all summer long
Whatever is begotten, born, and dies.
Caught in that sensual music all neglect
Monuments of unageing intellect.

An agèd man is but a paltry thing,
A tattered coat upon a stick, unless
Soul clap its hands and sing, and louder sing
For every tatter in its mortal dress,
Nor is there singing school but studying
Monuments of its own magnificence;
And therefore I have sailed the seas and come
To the holy city of Byzantium.

O sages standing in God's holy fire
As in the gold mosaic of a wall,
Come from the holy fire, perne in a gyre,
And be the singing-masters of my soul.
Consume my heart away; sick with desire
And fastened to a dying animal
It knows not what it is; and gather me
Into the artifice of eternity.

Once out of nature I shall never take
My bodily form from any natural thing,
But such a form as Grecian goldsmiths make
Of hammered gold and gold enamelling

To keep a drowsy Emperor awake;
Or set upon a golden bough to sing
To lords and ladies of Byzantium
Of what is past, or passing, or to come.

## *from* Meditations in Time of Civil War

### (i)

770         *The Road at My Door*

AN affable Irregular,
A heavily-built Falstaffian man,
Comes cracking jokes of civil war
As though to die by gunshot were
The finest play under the sun.

A brown Lieutenant and his men,
Half dressed in national uniform,
Stand at my door, and I complain
Of the foul weather, hail and rain,
A pear-tree broken by the storm.

I count those feathered balls of soot
The moor-hen guides upon the stream,
To silence the envy in my thought;
And turn towards my chamber, caught
In the cold snows of a dream.

### (ii)

771         *The Stare's Nest by My Window*

THE bees build in the crevices
Of loosening masonry, and there
The mother birds bring grubs and flies.
My wall is loosening; honey-bees,
Come build in the empty house of the stare.

We are closed in, and the key is turned
On our uncertainty; somewhere
A man is killed, or a house burned,
Yet no clear fact to be discerned:
Come build in the empty house of the stare.

A barricade of stone or of wood;
Some fourteen days of civil war;
Last night they trundled down the road
That dead young soldier in his blood:
Come build in the empty house of the stare.

We had fed the heart on fantasies,
The heart's grown brutal from the fare;
More substance in our enmities
Than in our love; O honey-bees,
Come build in the empty house of the stare.

772                   *Two Songs from a Play*

(i)

I saw a staring virgin stand
Where holy Dionysus died,
And tear the heart out of his side,
And lay the heart upon her hand
And bear that beating heart away;
And then did all the Muses sing
Of Magnus Annus at the spring,
As though God's death were but a play.

Another Troy must rise and set,
Another lineage feed the crow,
Another Argo's painted prow
Drive to a flashier bauble yet.
The Roman Empire stood appalled:
It dropped the reins of peace and war
When that fierce virgin and her Star
Out of the fabulous darkness called.

(ii)

In pity for man's darkening thought
He walked that room and issued thence
In Galilean turbulence;
The Babylonian starlight brought
A fabulous, formless darkness in;
Odour of blood when Christ was slain
Made all Platonic tolerance vain
And vain all Doric discipline.

Everything that man esteems
Endures a moment or a day.
Love's pleasure drives his love away,
The painter's brush consumes his dreams;
The herald's cry, the soldier's tread
Exhaust his glory and his might:
Whatever flames upon the night
Man's own resinous heart has fed.

773                    *Leda and the Swan*

A SUDDEN blow: the great wings beating still
Above the staggering girl, her thighs caressed
By the dark webs, her nape caught in his bill,
He holds her helpless breast upon his breast.

How can those terrified vague fingers push
The feathered glory from her loosening thighs?
And how can body, laid in that white rush,
But feel the strange heart beating where it lies?

A shudder in the loins engenders there
The broken wall, the burning roof and tower
And Agamemnon dead.
                              Being so caught up,
So mastered by the brute blood of the air,
Did she put on his knowledge with his power
Before the indifferent beak could let her drop?

774                    *Among Schoolchildren*

I WALK through the long schoolroom questioning;
A kind old nun in a white hood replies;
The children learn to cipher and to sing,
To study reading-books and histories,
To cut and sew, be neat in everything
In the best modern way—the children's eyes
In momentary wonder stare upon
A sixty-year-old smiling public man.

I dream of a Ledaean body, bent
Above a sinking fire, a tale that she
Told of a harsh reproof, or trivial event
That changed some childish day to tragedy—
Told, and it seemed that our two natures blent
Into a sphere from youthful sympathy,
Or else, to alter Plato's parable,
Into the yolk and white of the one shell.

And thinking of that fit of grief or rage
I look upon one child or t'other there
And wonder if she stood so at that age—
For even daughters of the swan can share
Something of every paddler's heritage—
And had that colour upon cheek or hair,
And thereupon my heart is driven wild:
She stands before me as a living child.

Her present image floats into the mind—
Did Quattrocento finger fashion it
Hollow of cheek as though it drank the wind
And took a mess of shadows for its meat?
And I though never of Ledaean kind
Had pretty plumage once—enough of that,
Better to smile on all that smile, and show
There is a comfortable kind of old scarecrow.

What youthful mother, a shape upon her lap
Honey of generation had betrayed,
And that must sleep, shriek, struggle to escape
As recollection or the drug decide,
Would think her son, did she but see that shape
With sixty or more winters on its head,
A compensation for the pang of his birth,
Or the uncertainty of his setting forth?

Plato thought nature but a spume that plays
Upon a ghostly paradigm of things;
Solider Aristotle played the taws
Upon the bottom of a king of kings;
World-famous golden-thighed Pythagoras
Fingered upon a fiddle-stick or strings
What a star sang and careless Muses heard:
Old clothes upon old sticks to scare a bird.

Both nuns and mothers worship images,
But those the candles light are not as those
That animate a mother's reveries,
But keep a marble or a bronze repose.
And yet they too break hearts—O Presences
That passion, piety or affection knows,
And that all heavenly glory symbolise—
O self-born mockers of man's enterprise;

Labour is blossoming or dancing where
The body is not bruised to pleasure soul,
Nor beauty born out of its own despair,
Nor blear-eyed wisdom out of midnight oil.
O chestnut-tree, great-rooted blossomer,
Are you the leaf, the blossom or the bole?
O body swayed to music, O brightening glance,
How can we know the dancer from the dance?

775                          *Byzantium*

THE unpurged images of day recede;
The Emperor's drunken soldiery are abed;
Night resonance recedes, night-walkers' song
After great cathedral gong;
A starlit or a moonlit dome disdains
All that man is,
All mere complexities,
The fury and the mire of human veins.

Before me floats an image, man or shade,
Shade more than man, more image than a shade;
For Hades' bobbin bound in mummy-cloth
May unwind the winding path;
A mouth that has no moisture and no breath
Breathless mouths may summon;
I hail the superhuman;
I call it death-in-life and life-in-death.

Miracle, bird or golden handiwork,
More miracle than bird or handiwork,
Planted on the star-lit golden bough,
Can like the cocks of Hades crow,

Or, by the moon embittered, scorn aloud
In glory of changeless metal
Common bird or petal
And all complexities of mire or blood.

At midnight on the Emperor's pavement flit
Flames that no faggot feeds, nor steel has lit,
Nor storm disturbs, flames begotten of flame,
Where blood-begotten spirits come
And all complexities of fury leave,
Dying into a dance,
An agony of trance,
An agony of flame that cannot singe a sleeve.

Astraddle on the dolphin's mire and blood,
Spirit after spirit! The smithies break the flood,
The golden smithies of the Emperor!
Marbles of the dancing floor
Break bitter furies of complexity,
Those images that yet
Fresh images beget,
That dolphin-torn, that gong-tormented sea.

776

## Lapis Lazuli

I HAVE heard that hysterical women say
They are sick of the palette and fiddle-bow,
Of poets that are always gay,
For everybody knows or else should know
That if nothing drastic is done
Aeroplane and Zeppelin will come out,
Pitch like King Billy bomb-balls in
Until the town lie beaten flat.

All perform their tragic play,
There struts Hamlet, there is Lear,
That's Ophelia, that Cordelia;
Yet they, should the last scene be there,
The great stage curtain about to drop,
If worthy their prominent part in the play,
Do not break up their lines to weep.
They know that Hamlet and Lear are gay;

Gaiety transfiguring all that dread.
All men have aimed at, found and lost;
Black out; Heaven blazing into the head:
Tragedy wrought to its uttermost.
Though Hamlet rambles and Lear rages,
And all the drop-scenes drop at once
Upon a hundred thousand stages,
It cannot grow by an inch or an ounce.

On their own feet they came, or on shipboard,
Camel-back, horse-back, ass-back, mule-back,
Old civilisations put to the sword.
Then they and their wisdom went to rack:
No handiwork of Callimachus,
Who handled marble as if it were bronze,
Made draperies that seemed to rise
When sea-wind swept the corner, stands:
His long lamp-chimney shaped like the stem
Of a slender palm, stood but a day;
All things fall and are built again,
And those that build them again are gay.

Two Chinamen, behind them a third,
Are carved in lapis lazuli,
Over them flies a long-legged bird,
A symbol of longevity;
The third, doubtless a serving-man,
Carries a musical instrument.

Every discoloration of the stone,
Every accidental crack or dent,
Seems a water-course or an avalanche,
Or lofty slope where it still snows
Though doubtless plum or cherry-branch
Sweetens the little half-way house
Those Chinamen climb towards, and I
Delight to imagine them seated there;
There, on the mountain and the sky,
On all the tragic scene they stare.
One asks for mournful melodies;
Accomplished fingers begin to play.
Their eyes mid many wrinkles, their eyes,
Their ancient, glittering eyes, are gay.

777 *Long-Legged Fly*

THAT civilisation may not sink,
Its great battle lost,
Quiet the dog, tether the pony
To a distant post;
Our master Caesar is in the tent
Where the maps are spread,
His eyes fixed upon nothing,
A hand under his head.
*Like a long-legged fly upon the stream*
*His mind moves upon silence.*

That the topless towers be burnt
And men recall that face,
Move most gently if move you must
In this lonely place.
She thinks, part woman, three parts a child,
That nobody looks; her feet
Practise a tinker shuffle
Picked up on a street.
*Like a long-legged fly upon the stream*
*Her mind moves upon silence.*

That girls at puberty may find
The first Adam in their thought,
Shut the door of the Pope's chapel,
Keep those children out.
There on that scaffolding reclines
Michael Angelo.
With no more sound than the mice make
His hand moves to and fro.
*Like a long-legged fly upon the stream*
*His mind moves upon silence.*

778 *The Circus Animals' Desertion*

I SOUGHT a theme and sought for it in vain,
I sought it daily for six weeks or so.
Maybe at last, being but a broken man,
I must be satisfied with my heart, although
Winter and summer till old age began
My circus animals were all on show,
Those stilted boys, that burnished chariot,
Lion and woman and the Lord knows what.

What can I but enumerate old themes?
First that sea-rider Oisin led by the nose
Through three enchanted islands, allegorical dreams,
Vain gaiety, vain battle, vain repose,
Themes of the embittered heart, or so it seems,
That might adorn old songs or courtly shows;
But what cared I that set him on to ride,
I, starved for the bosom of his faery bride?

And then a counter-truth filled out its play,
*The Countess Cathleen* was the name I gave it;
She, pity-crazed, had given her soul away,
But masterful Heaven had intervened to save it.
I thought my dear must her own soul destroy,
So did fanaticism and hate enslave it,
And this brought forth a dream and soon enough
This dream itself had all my thought and love.

And when the Fool and Blind Man stole the bread
Cuchulain fought the ungovernable sea;
Heart-mysteries there, and yet when all is said
It was the dream itself enchanted me:
Character isolated by a deed
To engross the present and dominate memory.
Players and painted stage took all my love,
And not those things that they were emblems of.

Those masterful images because complete
Grew in pure mind, but out of what began?
A mound of refuse or the sweepings of a street,
Old kettles, old bottles, and a broken can,
Old iron, old bones, old rags, that raving slut
Who keeps the till. Now that my ladder's gone,
I must lie down where all the ladders start,
In the foul rag-and-bone shop of the heart.

# LAURENCE BINYON

1869–1943

779

## *For the Fallen*
### (*1914*)

WITH proud thanksgiving, a mother for her children,
England mourns for her dead across the sea.
Flesh of her flesh they were, spirit of her spirit,
Fallen in the cause of the free.

Solemn the drums thrill: Death august and royal
Sings sorrow up into immortal spheres.
There is music in the midst of desolation
And a glory that shines upon our tears.

They went with songs to the battle, they were young,
Straight of limb, true of eye, steady and aglow.
They were staunch to the end against odds uncounted,
They fell with their faces to the foe.

They shall grow not old, as we that are left grow old:
Age shall not weary them, nor the years condemn.
At the going down of the sun and in the morning
We will remember them.

They mingle not with their laughing comrades again;
They sit no more at familiar tables of home;
They have no lot in our labour of the day-time;
They sleep beyond England's foam.

But where our desires are and our hopes profound,
Felt as a well-spring that is hidden from sight,
To the innermost heart of their own land they are known
As the stars are known to the Night;

As the stars that shall be bright when we are dust,
Moving in marches upon the heavenly plain,
As the stars that are starry in the time of our darkness,
To the end, to the end, they remain.

780        *The Burning of the Leaves*

*(1942)*

Now is the time for the burning of the leaves.
They go to the fire; the nostril pricks with smoke
Wandering slowly into a weeping mist.
Brittle and blotched, ragged and rotten sheaves!
A flame seizes the smouldering ruin and bites
On stubborn stalks that crackle as they resist.

The last hollyhock's fallen tower is dust;
All the spices of June are a bitter reek,
All the extravagant riches spent and mean.
All burns! The reddest rose is a ghost;
Sparks whirl up, to expire in the mist: the wild
Fingers of fire are making corruption clean.

Now is the time for stripping the spirit bare,
Time for the burning of days ended and done,
Idle solace of things that have gone before:
Rootless hope and fruitless desire are there;
Let them go to the fire, with never a look behind.
The world that was ours is a world that is ours no more.

They will come again, the leaf and the flower, to arise
From squalor of rottenness into the old splendour,
And magical scents to a wondering memory bring;
The same glory, to shine upon different eyes.
Earth cares for her own ruins, naught for ours.
Nothing is certain, only the certain spring.

# HILAIRE BELLOC
## 1870–1953

781        *On a General Election*

THE accursèd power which stands on Privilege
(And goes with Women, and Champagne and Bridge)
Broke—and Democracy resumed her reign:
(Which goes with Bridge, and Women and Champagne).


782        *The Statesman*

I KNEW a man who used to say,
Not once but twenty times a day,
That in the turmoil and the strife
(His very words) of Public Life
The thing of ultimate effect
Was Character—not Intellect.
He therefore was at strenuous pains
To atrophy his puny brains
And registered success in this
Beyond the dreams of avarice,
Till, when he had at last become
Blind, paralytic, deaf and dumb,
Insensible and cretinous,
He was admitted ONE OF US.
They therefore, (meaning Them by 'They')
His colleagues of the N.C.A.,
The T.U.C., the I.L.P.,
Appointed him triumphantly
To bleed the taxes of a clear
200,000 Francs a year
(Swiss), as the necessary man
For Conferences at Lausanne,
Geneva, Basle, Locarno, Berne:
A salary which he will earn,
Yes—*earn* I say—until he Pops,
Croaks, passes in his checks and Stops:—
When he will be remembered for
A week, a month, or even more.

783

## *Matilda*
### *Who Told Lies, and was Burned to Death*

MATILDA told such Dreadful Lies,
It made one Gasp and Stretch one's Eyes;
Her Aunt, who, from her Earliest Youth,
Had kept a Strict Regard for Truth,
Attempted to Believe Matilda:
The effort very nearly killed her,
And would have done so, had not She
Discovered this Infirmity.
For once, towards the Close of Day,
Matilda, growing tired of play,
And finding she was left alone,
Went tiptoe to the Telephone
And summoned the Immediate Aid
Of London's Noble Fire-Brigade.
Within an hour the Gallant Band
Were pouring in on every hand,
From Putney, Hackney Downs, and Bow
With Courage high and Hearts a-glow
They galloped, roaring through the Town
'Matilda's House is Burning Down!'
Inspired by British Cheers and Loud
Proceeding from the Frenzied Crowd,
They ran their ladders through a score
Of windows on the Ball Room Floor;
And took Peculiar Pains to Souse
The Pictures up and down the House,
Until Matilda's Aunt succeeded
In showing them they were not needed;
And even then she had to pay
To get the Men to go away!

It happened that a few Weeks later
Her Aunt was off to the Theatre
To see that Interesting Play
*The Second Mrs Tanqueray*.
She had refused to take her Niece
To hear this Entertaining Piece:
A Deprivation Just and Wise
To Punish her for Telling Lies.

That Night a Fire *did* break out—
You should have heard Matilda Shout!
You should have heard her Scream and Bawl,
And throw the window up and call
To People passing in the Street—
(The rapidly increasing Heat
Encouraging her to obtain
Their confidence)—but all in vain!
For every time She shouted 'Fire!'
They only answered 'Little Liar'!
And therefore when her Aunt returned,
Matilda, and the House, were Burned.

# WILLIAM HENRY DAVIES

## 1871–1940

784

### *The Kingfisher*

IT was the Rainbow gave thee birth,
    And left thee all her lovely hues;
And, as her mother's name was Tears,
    So runs it in thy blood to choose
For haunts the lonely pools, and keep
In company with trees that weep.

Go you and, with such glorious hues,
    Live with proud Peacocks in green parks;
On lawns as smooth as shining glass,
    Let every feather show its marks;
Get thee on boughs and clap thy wings
Before the windows of proud kings.

Nay, lovely Bird, thou art not vain;
    Thou hast no proud, ambitious mind;
I also love a quiet place
    That's green, away from all mankind;
A lonely pool, and let a tree
Sigh with her bosom over me.

785                                     *Leisure*

WHAT is this life if, full of care,
We have no time to stand and stare.

No time to stand beneath the boughs
And stare as long as sheep or cows.

No time to see, when woods we pass,
Where squirrels hide their nuts in grass.

No time to see, in broad daylight,
Streams full of stars like skies at night.

No time to turn at Beauty's glance,
And watch her feet, how they can dance.

No time to wait till her mouth can
Enrich that smile her eyes began.

A poor life this if, full of care,
We have no time to stand and stare.


786                                   *The Inquest*

I TOOK my oath I would inquire,
    Without affection, hate, or wrath,
Into the death of Ada Wright—
    So help me God! I took that oath.

When I went out to see the corpse,
    The four months' babe that died so young,
I judged it was seven pounds in weight,
    And little more than one foot long.

One eye, that had a yellow lid,
    Was shut—so was the mouth, that smiled;
The left eye open, shining bright—
    It seemed a knowing little child.

For as I looked at that one eye,
   It seemed to laugh, and say with glee:
'What caused my death you'll never know—
   Perhaps my mother murdered me.'

When I went into court again,
   To hear the mother's evidence—
It was a love-child, she explained.
   And smiled, for our intelligence.

'Now, Gentlemen of the Jury,' said
   The coroner—'this woman's child
By misadventure met its death.'
   'Aye, aye,' said we. The mother smiled.

And I could see that child's one eye
   Which seemed to laugh, and say with glee:
'What caused my death you'll never know—
   Perhaps my mother murdered me.'

787                  *The Cat*

WITHIN that porch, across the way,
   I see two naked eyes this night;
Two eyes that neither shut nor blink,
   Searching my face with a green light.

But cats to me are strange, so strange—
   I cannot sleep if one is near;
And though I'm sure I see those eyes
   I'm not so sure a body's there!

## RALPH HODGSON
### 1871–1962

788 *The Bells of Heaven*

'TWOULD ring the bells of Heaven
The wildest peal for years,
If Parson lost his senses
And people came to theirs,
And he and they together
Knelt down with angry prayers
For tamed and shabby tigers
And dancing dogs and bears,
And wretched, blind pit ponies,
And little hunted hares.

789 *The Hammers*

NOISE of hammers once I heard,
Many hammers, busy hammers,
Beating, shaping, night and day,
Shaping, beating dust and clay
To a palace; saw it reared;
Saw the hammers laid away.

And I listened, and I heard
Hammers beating, night and day,
In the palace newly reared,
Beating it to dust and clay:
Other hammers, muffled hammers,
Silent hammers of decay.

# WALTER DE LA MARE
## 1873–1956

### *Fare Well*

790

WHEN I lie where shades of darkness
Shall no more assail mine eyes,
Nor the rain make lamentation
    When the wind sighs;
How will fare the world whose wonder
Was the very proof of me?
Memory fades, must the remembered
    Perishing be?

Oh, when this my dust surrenders
Hand, foot, lip, to dust again,
May these loved and loving faces
    Please other men!
May the rusting harvest hedgerow
Still the Traveller's Joy entwine,
And as happy children gather
    Posies once mine.

Look thy last on all things lovely,
Every hour. Let no night
Seal thy sense in deathly slumber
    Till to delight
Thou have paid thy utmost blessing;
Since that all things thou wouldst praise
Beauty took from those who loved them
    In other days.

### *All That's Past*

791

VERY old are the woods;
    And the buds that break
Out of the brier's boughs,
    When March winds wake,
So old with their beauty are—
    Oh, no man knows
Through what wild centuries
    Roves back the rose.

Very old are the brooks;
   And the rills that rise
Where snow sleeps cold beneath
   The azure skies
Sing such a history
   Of come and gone,
Their every drop is as wise
   As Solomon.

Very old are we men
   Our dreams are tales
Told in dim Eden
   By Eve's nightingales;
We wake and whisper awhile,
   But, the day gone by,
Silence and sleep like fields
   Of amaranth lie.

792         *The Listeners*

'Is there anybody there?' said the Traveller,
   Knocking on the moonlit door;
And his horse in the silence champed the grasses
   Of the forest's ferny floor:
And a bird flew up out of the turret,
   Above the Traveller's head:
And he smote upon the door again a second time;
   'Is there anybody there?' he said.
But no one descended to the Traveller;
   No head from the leaf-fringed sill
Leaned over and looked into his grey eyes,
   Where he stood perplexed and still.
But only a host of phantom listeners
   That dwelt in the lone house then
Stood listening in the quiet of the moonlight
   To that voice from the world of men:
Stood thronging the faint moonbeams on the dark stair,
   That goes down to the empty hall,
Hearkening in an air stirred and shaken
   By the lonely Traveller's call.

And he felt in his heart their strangeness,
  Their stillness answering his cry,
While his horse moved, cropping the dark turf,
  'Neath the starred and leafy sky;
For he suddenly smote on the door, even
  Louder, and lifted his head:—
'Tell them I came, and no one answered,
  That I kept my word,' he said.
Never the least stir made the listeners,
  Though every word he spake
Fell echoing through the shadowiness of the still house
  From the one man left awake:
Ay, they heard his foot upon the stirrup,
  And the sound of iron on stone,
And how the silence surged softly backward,
  When the plunging hoofs were gone.

793                     *Napoleon*

        'WHAT is the world, O soldiers?
              It is I:
        I, this incessant snow,
              This northern sky;
        Soldiers, this solitude
              Through which we go
              Is I.'

794                     *The Ghost*

    'WHO knocks?' 'I, who was beautiful,
      Beyond all dreams to restore,
    I, from the roots of the dark thorn am hither.
      And knock on the door.'

    'Who speaks?' 'I—once was my speech
      Sweet as the bird's on the air,
    When echo lurks by the waters to heed;
      'Tis I speak thee fair.'

'Dark is the hour!' 'Ay, and cold.'
  'Lone is my house.' 'Ah, but mine?'
'Sight, touch, lips, eyes yearned in vain.'
  'Long dead these to thine . . .'

Silence. Still faint on the porch
  Brake the flames of the stars.
In gloom groped a hope-wearied hand
  Over keys, bolts, and bars.

A face peered. All the grey night
  In chaos of vacancy shone;
Nought but vast sorrow was there—
  The sweet cheat gone.


795          *The Song of the Mad Prince*

WHO said, 'Peacock Pie'?
  The old King to the sparrow:
Who said, 'Crops are ripe'?
  Rust to the harrow:
Who said, 'Where sleeps she now?
  Where rests she now her head,
Bathed in eve's loveliness'?
  That's what I said.

Who said, 'Ay, mum's the word';
  Sexton to willow:
Who said, 'Green dusk for dreams,
  Moss for a pillow'?
Who said, 'All Time's delight
  Hath she for narrow bed;
Life's troubled bubble broken'?
  That's what I said.

# GILBERT KEITH CHESTERTON
## 1874–1936

796  *The Rolling English Road*

BEFORE the Roman came to Rye or out to Severn strode,
The rolling English drunkard made the rolling English road.
A reeling road, a rolling road, that rambles round the shire,
And after him the parson ran, the sexton and the squire;
A merry road, a mazy road, and such as we did tread
The night we went to Birmingham by way of Beachy Head.

I knew no harm of Bonaparte and plenty of the Squire,
And for to fight the Frenchman I did not much desire;
But I did bash their baggonets because they came arrayed
To straighten out the crooked road an English drunkard made,
Where you and I went down the lane with ale-mugs in our hands,
The night we went to Glastonbury by way of Goodwin Sands.

His sins they were forgiven him; or why do flowers run
Behind him; and the hedges all strengthening in the sun?
The wild thing went from left to right and knew not which was which,
But the wild rose was above him when they found him in the ditch.
God pardon us, nor harden us; we did not see so clear
The night we went to Bannockburn by way of Brighton Pier.

My friends, we will not go again or ape an ancient rage,
Or stretch the folly of our youth to be the shame of age,
But walk with clearer eyes and ears this path that wandereth,
And see undrugged in evening light the decent inn of death;
For there is good news yet to hear and fine things to be seen,
Before we go to Paradise by way of Kensal Green.

797 *Antichrist, or the Reunion of Christendom: an Ode*

'A Bill which has shocked the conscience of every
Christian community in Europe.'—Mr. F. E. Smith,
on the Welsh Disestablishment Bill.

ARE they clinging to their crosses,
   F. E. Smith,
Where the Breton boat-fleet tosses,
   Are they, Smith?
Do they, fasting, trembling, bleeding,
  Wait the news from this our city?
Groaning 'That's the Second Reading!'
  Hissing 'There is still Committee!'
If the voice of Cecil falters,
  If McKenna's point has pith,
Do they tremble for their altars?
   Do they, Smith?

Russian peasants round their pope
   Huddled, Smith,
Hear about it all, I hope,
   Don't they, Smith?
In the mountain hamlets clothing
  Peaks beyond Caucasian pales,
Where Establishment means nothing
  And they never heard of Wales,
Do they read it all in Hansard—
  With a crib to read it with—
'Welsh Tithes: Dr. Clifford Answered.'
   Really, Smith?

In the lands where Christians were,
   F. E. Smith,
In the little lands laid bare,
   Smith, O Smith!
Where the Turkish bands are busy,
  And the Tory name is blessed
Since they hailed the Cross of Dizzy
  On the banners from the West!
Men don't think it half so hard if
  Islam burns their kin and kith,
Since a curate lives in Cardiff
   Saved by Smith.

It would greatly, I must own,
                Soothe me, Smith!
If you left this theme alone,
                Holy Smith!
For your legal cause or civil
      You fight well and get your fee;
For your God or dream or devil
      You will answer, not to me.
Talk about the pews and steeples
      And the Cash that goes therewith!
But the souls of Christian peoples . . .
                Chuck it, Smith!

# JOHN MASEFIELD

## 1878–1967

798 *Cargoes*

QUINQUIREME of Nineveh from distant Ophir
Rowing home to haven in sunny Palestine,
With a cargo of ivory,
And apes and peacocks,
Sandalwood, cedarwood, and sweet white wine.

Stately Spanish galleon coming from the Isthmus,
Dipping through the Tropics by the palm-green shores,
With a cargo of diamonds,
Emeralds, amethysts,
Topazes, and cinnamon, and gold moidores.

Dirty British coaster with a salt-caked smoke stack
Butting through the Channel in the mad March days,
With a cargo of Tyne coal,
Road-rail, pig-lead,
Firewood, iron-ware, and cheap tin trays.

799                          *Up on the Downs*

Up on the downs the red-eyed kestrels hover,
Eyeing the grass.
The field-mouse flits like a shadow into cover
As their shadows pass.

Men are burning the gorse on the down's shoulder;
A drift of smoke
Glitters with fire and hangs, and the skies smoulder,
And the lungs choke.

Once the tribe did thus on the downs, on these downs burning
Men in the frame.
Crying to the gods of the downs till their brains were turning
And the gods came.

And to-day on the downs, in the wind, the hawks, the grasses,
In blood and air,
Something passes me and cries as it passes.
On the chalk downland bare.


# EDWARD THOMAS
## 1878–1917

800                          *The Owl*

DOWNHILL I came, hungry, and yet not starved;
Cold, yet had heat within me that was proof
Against the North wind; tired, yet so that rest
Had seemed the sweetest thing under a roof.

Then at the inn I had food, fire, and rest,
Knowing how hungry, cold, and tired was I.
All of the night was quite barred out except
An owl's cry, a most melancholy cry

Shaken out long and clear upon the hill,
No merry note, nor cause of merriment,
But one telling me plain what I escaped
And others could not, that night, as in I went.

And salted was my food, and my repose,
Salted and sobered, too, by the bird's voice
Speaking for all who lay under the stars,
Soldiers and poor, unable to rejoice.

801          *In Memoriam (Easter, 1915)*

THE flowers left thick at nightfall in the wood
This Eastertide call into mind the men,
Now far from home, who, with their sweethearts, should
Have gathered them and will do never again.

802          *Adlestrop*

YES. I remember Adlestrop—
The name, because one afternoon
Of heat the express-train drew up there
Unwontedly. It was late June.

The steam hissed. Someone cleared his throat.
No one left and no one came
On the bare platform. What I saw
Was Adlestrop—only the name

And willows, willow-herb, and grass,
And meadowsweet, and haycocks dry,
No whit less still and lonely fair
Than the high cloudlets in the sky.

And for that minute a blackbird sang
Close by, and round him, mistier,
Farther and farther, all the birds
Of Oxfordshire and Gloucestershire.

803 *Lights Out*

I HAVE come to the borders of sleep,
The unfathomable deep
Forest where all must lose
Their way, however straight,
Or winding, soon or late;
They cannot choose.

Many a road and track
That, since the dawn's first crack,
Up to the forest brink,
Deceived the travellers,
Suddenly now blurs,
And in they sink.

Here love ends,
Despair, ambition ends;
All pleasure and all trouble,
Although most sweet or bitter,
Here ends in sleep that is sweeter
Than tasks most noble.

There is not any book
Or face of dearest look
That I would not turn from now
To go into the unknown
I must enter, and leave, alone,
I know not how.

The tall forest towers;
Its cloudy foliage lowers
Ahead, shelf above shelf;
Its silence I hear and obey
That I may lose my way
And myself.

804 *The New House*

Now first, as I shut the door,
  I was alone
In the new house; and the wind
  Began to moan.

Old at once was the house,
  And I was old;
My ears were teased with the dread
  Of what was foretold,

Nights of storm, days of mist, without end;
  Sad days when the sun
Shone in vain: old griefs and griefs
  Not yet begun.

All was foretold me; naught
  Could I foresee;
But I learned how the wind would sound
  After these things should be.

805 *Out in the Dark*

Out in the dark over the snow
The fallow fawns invisible go
With the fallow doe;
And the winds blow
Fast as the stars are slow.

Stealthily the dark haunts round
And, when the lamp goes, without sound
At a swifter bound
Than the swiftest hound,
Arrives, and all else is drowned;

And star and I and wind and deer,
Are in the dark together,—near,
Yet far,—and fear
Drums on my ear
In that sage company drear.

How weak and little is the light,
All the universe of sight,
Love and delight,
Before the might,
If you love it not, of night.

# JAMES JOYCE

## 1882–1941

806                    *'I hear an army'*

I HEAR an army charging upon the land,
    And the thunder of horses plunging, foam about their knees:
Arrogant, in black armour, behind them stand,
    Disdaining the reins, with fluttering whips, the charioteers.

They cry unto the night their battle-name:
    I moan in sleep when I hear afar their whirling laughter.
They cleave the gloom of dreams, a blinding flame,
    Clanging, clanging upon the heart as upon an anvil.

They come shaking in triumph their long, green hair:
    They come out of the sea and run shouting by the shore.
My heart, have you no wisdom thus to despair?
    My love, my love, my love, why have you left me alone?

# JAMES ELROY FLECKER

## 1884–1915

807          *The Golden Journey to Samarkand*
       *At the Gate of the Sun, Bagdad, in olden time*

*The Merchants*
*(together)*

Away, for we are ready to a man!
    Our camels sniff the evening and are glad.
Lead on, O Master of the Caravan:
    Lead on the Merchant-Princes of Bagdad.

## JAMES ELROY FLECKER

### The Chief Draper

Have we not Indian carpets dark as wine,
  Turbans and sashes, gowns and bows and veils,
And broideries of intricate design,
  And printed hangings in enormous bales?

### The Chief Grocer

We have rose-candy, we have spikenard,
  Mastic and terebinth and oil and spice,
And such sweet jams meticulously jarred
  As God's own Prophet eats in Paradise.

### The Principal Jews

And we have manuscripts in peacock styles
  By Ali of Damascus; we have swords
Engraved with storks and apes and crocodiles,
  And heavy beaten necklaces, for Lords.

### The Master of the Caravan

But you are nothing but a lot of Jews.

### The Principal Jews

Sir, even dogs have daylight, and we pay.

### The Master of the Caravan

But who are ye in rags and rotten shoes,
  You dirty-bearded, blocking up the way?

### The Pilgrims

We are the Pilgrims, master; we shall go
  Always a little further: it may be
Beyond that last blue mountain barred with snow,
  Across that angry or that glimmering sea,

White on a throne or guarded in a cave
  There lives a prophet who can understand
Why men were born: but surely we are brave,
  Who make the Golden Journey to Samarkand.

### The Chief Merchant

We gnaw the nail of hurry. Master, away!

### One of the Women

O turn your eyes to where your children stand.
Is not Bagdad the beautiful? O stay!

### The Merchants
#### (*in chorus*)

We take the Golden Road to Samarkand.

### An Old Man

Have you not girls and garlands in your homes,
   Eunuchs and Syrian boys at your command?
Seek not excess: God hateth him who roams!

### The Merchants
#### (*in chorus*)

We make the Golden Journey to Samarkand.

### A Pilgrim with a Beautiful Voice

Sweet to ride forth at evening from the wells
   When shadows pass gigantic on the sand,
And softly through the silence beat the bells
   Along the Golden Road to Samarkand.

### A Merchant

We travel not for trafficking alone:
   By hotter winds our fiery hearts are fanned:
For lust of knowing what should not be known
   We make the Golden Journey to Samarkand.

### The Master of the Caravan

Open the gate, O watchman of the night!

### The Watchman

Ho, travellers, I open. For what land
Leave you the dim-moon city of delight?

### The Merchants
#### (*with a shout*)

We make the Golden Journey to Samarkand.

*(The Caravan passes through the gate)*

*The Watchman*
(*consoling the women*)

What would ye, ladies? It was ever thus.
  Men are unwise and curiously planned.

*A Woman*

They have their dreams, and do not think of us.

*Voices of the Caravan*
(*in the distance, singing*)

We make the Golden Journey to Samarkand.


# DAVID HERBERT LAWRENCE

1885–1930

808             *Piano*

SOFTLY, in the dusk, a woman is singing to me;
Taking me back down the vista of years, till I see
A child sitting under the piano, in the boom of the tingling strings
And pressing the small, poised feet of a mother who smiles as she sings.

In spite of myself, the insidious mastery of song
Betrays me back, till the heart of me weeps to belong
To the old Sunday evenings at home, with winter outside
And hymns in the cosy parlour, the tinkling piano our guide.

So now it is vain for the singer to burst into clamour
With the great black piano appassionato. The glamour
Of childish days is upon me, my manhood is cast
Down in the flood of remembrance, I weep like a child for the past.


809          *Giorno Dei Morti*

ALONG the avenue of cypresses,
All in their scarlet cloaks and surplices
Of linen, go the chanting choristers,
The priests in gold and black, the villagers. . . .

853

And all along the path to the cemetery
The round dark heads of men crowd silently,
And black-scarved faces of womenfolk, wistfully
Watch at the banner of death, and the mystery.

And at the foot of a grave a father stands
With sunken head; and forgotten, folded hands;
And at the foot of a grave a mother kneels
With pale shut face, nor either hears nor feels

The coming of the chanting choristers
Between the avenue of cypresses
The silence of the many villagers,
The candle-flames beside the surplices.

810                          *Snake*

A SNAKE came to my water-trough
On a hot, hot day, and I in pyjamas for the heat,
To drink there.

In the deep, strange-scented shade of the great dark carob-tree
I came down the steps with my pitcher
And must wait, must stand and wait, for there he was at the trough
    before me.

He reached down from a fissure in the earth-wall in the gloom
And trailed his yellow-brown slackness soft-bellied down, over the
    edge of the stone trough
And rested his throat upon the stone bottom,
And where the water had dripped from the tap, in a small clearness,
He sipped with his straight mouth,
Softly drank through his straight gums, into his slack long body,
Silently.

Someone was before me at my water-trough,
And I, like a second comer, waiting.

He lifted his head from his drinking, as cattle do,
And looked at me vaguely, as drinking cattle do,
And flickered his two-forked tongue from his lips, and mused a
    moment,

And stooped and drank a little more,
Being earth-brown, earth-golden from the burning bowels of the earth
On the day of Sicilian July, with Etna smoking.

The voice of my education said to me
He must be killed,
For in Sicily the black, black snakes are innocent, the gold are
    venomous.

And voices in me said, If you were a man
You would take a stick and break him now, and finish him off.

But must I confess how I liked him,
How glad I was he had come like a guest in quiet, to drink at my
    water-trough
And depart peaceful, pacified, and thankless,
Into the burning bowels of this earth?

Was it cowardice, that I dared not kill him?
Was it perversity, that I longed to talk to him?
Was it humility, to feel so honoured?
I felt so honoured.

And yet those voices:
*If you were not afraid, you would kill him!*

And truly I was afraid, I was most afraid,
But even so, honoured still more
That he should seek my hospitality
From out the dark door of the secret earth.

He drank enough
And lifted his head, dreamily, as one who has drunken,
And flickered his tongue like a forked night on the air, so black;
Seeming to lick his lips,
And looked around like a god, unseeing, into the air,
And slowly turned his head,
And slowly, very slowly, as if thrice adream,
Proceeded to draw his slow length curving round
And climb again the broken bank of my wall-face.

And as he put his head into that dreadful hole,
And as he slowly drew up, snake-easing his shoulders, and entered
    farther,
A sort of horror, a sort of protest against his withdrawing into that
    horrid black hole,
Deliberately going into the blackness, and slowly drawing himself
    after,
Overcame me now his back was turned.

I looked round, I put down my pitcher,
I picked up a clumsy log
And threw it at the water-trough with a clatter.

I think it did not hit him,
But suddenly that part of him that was left behind convulsed in
    undignified haste,
Writhed like lightning, and was gone
Into the black hole, the earth-lipped fissure in the wall front,
At which, in the intense still noon, I stared with fascination.

And immediately I regretted it.
I thought how paltry, how vulgar, what a mean act!
I despised myself and the voices of my accursed human education.

And I thought of the albatross,
And I wished he would come back, my snake.

For he seemed to me again like a king,
Like a king in exile, uncrowned in the underworld,
Now due to be crowned again.

And so, I missed my chance with one of the lords
Of life.
And I have something to expiate;
A pettiness.

811                   *Bavarian Gentians*

NOT every man has gentians in his house
in Soft September, at slow, Sad Michaelmas.

Bavarian gentians, big and dark, only dark
darkening the day-time torch-like with the smoking blueness of
    Pluto's gloom,
ribbed and torch-like, with their blaze of darkness spread blue
down flattening into points, flattened under the sweep of white day
torch-flower of the blue-smoking darkness, Pluto's dark-blue daze,
black lamps from the halls of Dis, burning dark blue,
giving off darkness, blue darkness, as Demeter's pale lamps give off
    light,
lead me then, lead me the way.

Reach me a gentian, give me a torch
let me guide myself with the blue, forked torch of this flower
down the darker and darker stairs, where blue is darkened on blueness,
even where Persephone goes, just now, from the frosted September
to the sightless realm where darkness is awake upon the dark
and Persephone herself is but a voice
or a darkness invisible enfolded in the deeper dark
of the arms Plutonic, and pierced with the passion of dense gloom,
among the splendour of torches of darkness, shedding darkness on the
    lost bride and her groom.


# EZRA POUND

## 1885–1972

812            *The River-Merchant's Wife:*
            *A Letter* after *Rihaku*

WHILE my hair was still cut straight across my forehead
I played about the front gate, pulling flowers.
You came by on bamboo stilts, playing horse,
You walked about my seat, playing with blue plums.
And we went on living in the village of Chokan:
Two small people, without dislike or suspicion.

At fourteen I married My Lord you.
I never laughed, being bashful.
Lowering my head, I looked at the wall.
Called to, a thousand times, I never looked back.

At fifteen I stopped scowling,
I desired my dust to be mingled with yours
For ever and for ever and for ever.
Why should I climb the look out?

At sixteen you departed,
You went into far Ku-to-yen, by the river of swirling eddies,
And you have been gone five months.
The monkeys make sorrowful noise overhead.

You dragged your feet when you went out.
By the gate now, the moss is grown, the different mosses,
Too deep to clear them away!
The leaves fall early this autumn, in wind.
The paired butterflies are already yellow with August
Over the grass in the West garden;
They hurt me. I grow older.
If you are coming down through the narrows of the river Kiang,
Please let me know beforehand,
And I will come out to meet you
             As far as Cho-fu-Sa.

813         *from* Hugh Selwyn Mauberley

(i)

THE tea-rose tea-gown, etc.
Supplants the mousseline of Cos,
The pianola 'replaces'
Sappho's barbitos.

Christ follows Dionysus,
Phallic and ambrosial
Made way for macerations;
Caliban casts out Ariel.

All things are a flowing,
Sage Heracleitus says;
But a tawdry cheapness
Shall outlast our days.

Even the Christian beauty
Defects—after Samothrace;
We see τὸ καλὸν
Decreed in the market place.

Faun's flesh is not to us,
Nor the saint's vision.
We have the Press for wafer;
Franchise for circumcision.

All men, in law, are equals.
Free of Pisistratus,
We choose a knave or an eunuch
To rule over us.

O bright Apollo,
τίν' ἄνδρα, τίν' ἥρωα, τίνα θεὸν,
What god, man, or hero
Shall I place a tin wreath upon!

(ii)

These fought in any case,
and some believing,
pro domo, in any case . . .

Some quick to arm,
some for adventure,
some from fear of weakness,
some from fear of censure,
some for love of slaughter, in imagination,
learning later . . .
some in fear, learning love of slaughter;

Died some, pro patria,
non 'dulce' non 'et decor' . . .
walked eye-deep in hell
believing in old men's lies, then unbelieving
came home, home to a lie,
home to many deceits,
home to old lies and new infamy;
usury age-old and age-thick
and liars in public places.

τὸ καλὸν] (tŏ kalon) beauty      τίν' ἄνδρα, τίν' ἥρωα, τίνα θεὸν,] tin' andra, tin'
hērōa, tina theon,) what man, what hero, what god,

Daring as never before, wastage as never before.
Young blood and high blood,
fair cheeks, and fine bodies;

fortitude as never before

frankness as never before,
disillusions as never told in the old days,
hysterias, trench confessions,
laughter out of dead bellies.

(iii)

There died a myriad,
And of the best, among them,
For an old bitch gone in the teeth,
For a botched civilization,

Charm, smiling at the good mouth,
Quick eyes gone under earth's lid,

For two gross of broken statues,
For a few thousand battered books.

814                    *from* The Pisan Cantos

WHAT thou lovest well remains,
                              the rest is dross
What thou lov'st well shall not be reft from thee
What thou lov'st well is thy true heritage
Whose world, or mine or theirs
                              or is it of none?
First came the seen, then thus the palpable
      Elysium, though it were in the halls of hell,
What thou lovest well is thy true heritage
What thou lov'st well shall not be reft from thee

# EZRA POUND

The ant's a centaur in his dragon world.
Pull down thy vanity, it is not man
Made courage, or made order, or made grace,
    Pull down thy vanity, I say pull down.
Learn of the green world what can be thy place
In scaled invention or true artistry,
Pull down thy vanity,
                        Paquin pull down!
The green casque has outdone your elegance.

'Master thyself, then others shall thee beare'
    Pull down thy vanity
Thou art a beaten dog beneath the hail,
A swollen magpie in a fitful sun,
Half black half white
Nor knowst'ou wing from tail
Pull down thy vanity
                How mean thy hates
Fostered in falsity,
                Pull down thy vanity,
Rathe to destroy, niggard in charity,
Pull down thy vanity,
                I say pull down.

But to have done instead of not doing
                this is not vanity
To have, with decency, knocked
That a Blunt should open
            To have gathered from the air a live tradition
or from a fine old eye the unconquered flame
This is not vanity.
        Here error is all in the not done,
all in the diffidence that faltered.

Blunt] Wilfred Scawen Blunt (1840–1922), explorer, politician, and poet,
opponent of British Imperialism

# SIEGFRIED SASSOON
### 1886–1967

815 *Everyone Sang*

EVERYONE suddenly burst out singing;
And I was filled with such delight
As prisoned birds must find in freedom,
Winging wildly across the white
Orchards and dark-green fields; on—on—and
    out of sight.

Everyone's voice was suddenly lifted;
And beauty came like the setting sun:
My heart was shaken with tears; and horror
Drifted away . . . O, but Everyone
Was a bird; and the song was wordless; the singing
    will never be done.

816 *Attack*

AT dawn the ridge emerges massed and dun
In the wild purple of the glow'ring sun,
Smouldering through spouts of drifting smoke that shroud
The menacing scarred slope; and, one by one,
Tanks creep and topple forward to the wire.
The barrage roars and lifts. Then, clumsily bowed
With bombs and guns and shovels and battle-gear,
Men jostle and climb to meet the bristling fire.
Lines of grey, muttering faces, masked with fear,
They leave their trenches, going over the top,
While time ticks blank and busy on their wrists,
And hope, with furtive eyes and grappling fists,
Flounders in mud. O Jesus, make it stop!

# RUPERT BROOKE
## 1887–1915

817                              *The Soldier*

IF I should die, think only this of me:
    That there's some corner of a foreign field
That is for ever England. There shall be
    In that rich earth a richer dust concealed;
A dust whom England bore, shaped, made aware,
    Gave, once, her flowers to love, her ways to roam,
A body of England's, breathing English air,
    Washed by the rivers, blest by suns of home.

And think, this heart, all evil shed away,
    A pulse in the eternal mind, no less
        Gives somewhere back the thoughts by England given;
Her sights and sounds; dreams happy as her day;
    And laughter, learnt of friends; and gentleness,
        In hearts at peace, under an English heaven.


818                              *Heaven*

FISH (fly-replete, in depth of June,
Dawdling away their wat'ry noon)
Ponder deep wisdom, dark or clear,
Each secret fishy hope or fear.
Fish say, they have their Stream and Pond;
But is there anything Beyond?
This life cannot be All, they swear,
For how unpleasant, if it were!
One may not doubt that, somehow, Good
Shall come of Water and of Mud;
And, sure, the reverent eye must see
A Purpose in Liquidity.
We darkly know, by Faith we cry,
The future is not Wholly Dry.
Mud unto mud!—Death eddies near—
Not here the appointed End, not here!
But somewhere, beyond Space and Time,
Is wetter water, slimier slime!

And there (they trust) there swimmeth One
Who swam ere rivers were begun,
Immense, of fishy form and mind,
Squamous, omnipotent, and kind;
And under that Almighty Fin,
The littlest fish may enter in.
Oh! never fly conceals a hook,
Fish say, in the Eternal Brook,
But more than mundane weeds are there,
And mud, celestially fair;
Fat caterpillars drift around,
And Paradisal grubs are found;
Unfading moths, immortal flies,
And the worm that never dies.
And in that Heaven of all their wish,
There shall be no more land, say fish.

# EDWIN MUIR

## 1887–1959

819                  *Ballad of Hector in Hades*

YES, this is where I stood that day,
    Beside this sunny mound.
The walls of Troy are far away,
    And outward comes no sound.

I wait. On all the empty plain
    A burnished stillness lies,
Save for the chariot's tinkling hum,
    And a few distant cries.

His helmet glitters near. The world
    Slowly turns around,
With some new sleight compels my feet
    From the fighting ground.

I run. If I turned back again
    The earth must turn with me,
The mountains planted on the plain,
    The sky clamped to the sea.

The grasses puff a little dust
  Where my footsteps fall.
I cast a shadow as I pass
  The little wayside wall.

The strip of grass on either hand
  Sparkles in the light;
I only see that little space
  To the left and to the right,

And in that space our shadows run,
  His shadow there and mine,
The little flowers, the tiny mounds,
  The grasses frail and fine.

But narrower still and narrower!
  My course is shrunk and small,
Yet vast as in a deadly dream,
  And faint the Trojan wall.
The sun up in the towering sky
  Turns like a spinning ball.

The sky with all its clustered eyes
  Grows still with watching me,
The flowers, the mounds, the flaunting weeds
  Wheel slowly round to see.

Two shadows racing on the grass,
  Silent and so near,
Until his shadow falls on mine.
  And I am rid of fear.

The race is ended. Far away
  I hang and do not care,
While round bright Troy Achilles whirls
  A corpse with streaming hair.

820 *The Combat*

IT was not meant for human eyes,
That combat on the shabby patch
Of clods and trampled turf that lies
Somewhere beneath the sodden skies
For eye of toad or adder to catch.

And having seen it I accuse
The crested animal in his pride,
Arrayed in all the royal hues
Which hide the claws he well can use
To tear the heart out of the side.

Body of leopard, eagle's head
And whetted beak, and lion's mane,
And frost-grey hedge of feathers spread
Behind—he seemed of all things bred.
I shall not see his like again.

As for his enemy, there came in
A soft round beast as brown as clay;
All rent and patched his wretched skin;
A battered bag he might have been,
Some old used thing to throw away.

Yet he awaited face to face
The furious beast and the swift attack.
Soon over and done. That was no place
Or time for chivalry or for grace.
The fury had him on his back.

And two small paws like hands flew out
To right and left as the trees stood by.
One would have said beyond a doubt
This was the very end of the bout,
But that the creature would not die.

For ere the death-stroke he was gone,
Writhed, whirled, huddled into his den,
Safe somehow there. The fight was done,
And he had lost who had all but won.
But oh his deadly fury then.

A while the place lay blank, forlorn,
Drowsing as in relief from pain.
The cricket chirped, the grating thorn
Stirred, and a little sound was born.
The champions took their posts again.

And all began. The stealthy paw
Slashed out and in. Could nothing save
These rags and tatters from the claw?
Nothing. And yet I never saw
A beast so helpless and so brave.

And now, while the trees stand watching, still
The unequal battle rages there.
The killing beast that cannot kill
Swells and swells in his fury till
You'd almost think it was despair.

821             *One Foot in Eden*

ONE foot in Eden still, I stand
And look across the other land.
The world's great day is growing late,
Yet strange these fields that we have planted
So long with crops of love and hate.
Time's handiworks by time are haunted,
And nothing now can separate
The corn and tares compactly grown.
The armorial weed in stillness bound
About the stalk; these are our own.
Evil and good stand thick around
In the fields of charity and sin
Where we shall lead our harvest in.

Yet still from Eden springs the root
As clean as on the starting day.
Time takes the foliage and the fruit
And burns the archetypal leaf
To shapes of terror and of grief
Scattered along the winter way.

But famished field and blackened tree
Bear flowers in Eden never known.
Blossoms of grief and charity
Bloom in these darkened fields alone.
What had Eden ever to say
Of hope and faith and pity and love
Until was buried all its day
And memory found its treasure trove?
Strange blessings never in Paradise
Fall from these beclouded skies.

822                                   *The Horses*

BARELY a twelvemonth after
The seven days war that put the world to sleep,
Late in the evening the strange horses came.
By then we had made our covenant with silence,
But in the first few days it was so still
We listened to our breathing and were afraid.
On the second day
The radios failed; we turned the knobs; no answer.
On the third day a warship passed us, heading north,
Dead bodies piled on the deck. On the sixth day
A plane plunged over us into the sea. Thereafter
Nothing. The radios dumb;
And still they stand in corners of our kitchens,
And stand, perhaps, turned on, in a million rooms
All over the world. But now if they should speak,
If on a sudden they should speak again,
If on the stroke of noon a voice should speak,
We would not listen, we would not let it bring
That old bad world that swallowed its children quick
At one great gulp. We would not have it again.
Sometimes we think of the nations lying asleep,
Curled blindly in impenetrable sorrow,
And then the thought confounds us with its strangeness.
The tractors lie about our fields; at evening
They look like dank sea-monsters couched and waiting.
We leave them where they are and let them rust:
'They'll moulder away and be like other loam'.
We make our oxen drag our rusty ploughs,
Long laid aside. We have gone back
Far past our fathers' land.

> And then, that evening
> Late in the summer the strange horses came.
> We heard a distant tapping on the road,
> A deepening drumming; it stopped, went on again
> And at the corner changed to hollow thunder.
> We saw the heads
> Like a wild wave charging and were afraid.
> We had sold our horses in our fathers' time
> To buy new tractors. Now they were strange to us
> As fabulous steeds set on an ancient shield
> Or illustrations in a book of knights.
> We did not dare go near them. Yet they waited,
> Stubborn and shy, as if they had been sent
> By an old command to find our whereabouts
> And that long-lost archaic companionship.
> In the first moment we had never a thought
> That they were creatures to be owned and used.
> Among them were some half-a-dozen colts
> Dropped in some wilderness of the broken world,
> Yet new as if they had come from their own Eden.
> Since then they have pulled our ploughs and borne our loads,
> But that free servitude still can pierce our hearts.
> Our life is changed; their coming our beginning.

# EDITH SITWELL

## 1887–1964

### *The Innocent Spring*

823

> IN the great gardens, after bright spring rain,
> We find sweet innocence come once again,
> White periwinkles, little pensionnaires
> With muslin gowns and shy and candid airs,
>
> That under saint-blue skies, with gold stars sown,
> Hide their sweet innocence by spring winds blown,
> From zephyr libertines that like Richelieu
> And d'Orsay their gold-spangled kisses blew;

And lilies of the valley whose buds blonde and tight
Seem curls of little school-children that light
The priests' procession, when on some saint's day
Along the country paths they make their way;

Forget-me-nots, whose eyes of childish blue,
Gold-starred like heaven, speak of love still true;
And all the flowers that we call 'dear heart',
Who say their prayers like children, then depart

Into the dark. Amid the dew's bright beams
The summer airs, like Weber waltzes, fall
Round the first rose who, flushed with her youth, seems
Like a young Princess dressed for her first ball.

Who knows what beauty ripens from dark mould
After the sad wind and the winter's cold?—
But a small wind sighed, colder than the rose
Blooming in desolation, 'No one knows.'

824                        *Neptune—Polka*

' "TRA la la la—
            See me dance the polka," '
Said Mr. Wagg like a bear,
'With my top hat
And my whiskers that—
(Tra la la la) trap the Fair.

Where the waves seem chiming haycocks
I dance the polka; there
Stand Venus' children in their gay frocks,—
Maroon and marine,—and stare

To see me fire my pistol
Through the distance blue as my coat;
Like Wellington, Byron, the Marquis of Bristol,
Buzbied great trees float.

While the wheezing hurdy-gurdy
Of the marine wind blows me
To the tune of 'Annie Rooney', sturdy,
Over the sheafs of the sea;

And bright as a seedsman's packet
With zinnias, candytufts chill,
Is Mrs. Marigold's jacket
As she gapes at the inn door still,

Where at dawn in the box of the sailor,
Blue as the decks of the sea,
Nelson awoke, crowed like the cocks,
Then back to the dust sank he.

And Robinson Crusoe
Rues so
The bright and foxy beer,—
But he finds fresh isles in a negress' smiles,—
The poxy doxy dear,

As they watch me dance the polka,'
Said Mr. Wagg like a bear,
'In my top hat and my whiskers that,—
Tra la la la, trap the Fair.

Tra la la la la—
Tra la la la la—
Tra la la la la la la la la
                          La
                          La
                          La!'


825      *Still Falls the Rain*

*(The Raids, 1940. Night and Dawn)*

STILL falls the Rain—
Dark as the world of man, black as our loss—
Blind as the nineteen hundred and forty nails
Upon the Cross.

Still falls the Rain
With a sound like the pulse of the heart that is changed to the hammer-
    beat
In the Potters' Field, and the sound of the impious feet

On the Tomb:

            Still falls the Rain
In the Field of Blood where the small hopes breed and the human
    brain
Nurtures its greed, that worm with the brow of Cain.

Still falls the Rain
At the feet of the Starved Man hung upon the Cross.
Christ that each day, each night, nails there, have mercy on us—
On Dives and on Lazarus:
Under the Rain the sore and the gold are as one.

Still falls the Rain—
Still falls the Blood from the Starved Man's wounded Side
He bears in his Heart all wounds,—those of the light that died,
The last faint spark
In the self-murdered heart, the wounds of the sad uncomprehending
    dark,
The wounds of the baited bear,—
The blind and weeping bear whom the keepers beat
On his helpless flesh . . . the tears of the hunted hare.

Still falls the Rain—
Then—O Ile leape up to my God: who pulles me doune—
See, see where Christ's blood streames in the firmament:
It flows from the Brow we nailed upon the tree
Deep to the dying, to the thirsting heart
That holds the fires of the world,—dark-smirched with pain
As Caesar's laurel crown.

Then sounds the voice of One who like the heart of man
Was once a child who among beasts has lain—
'Still do I love, still shed my innocent light, my Blood, for thee.'

# THOMAS STEARNS ELIOT
### 1888–1965

826     *The Love Song of J. Alfred Prufrock*

LET us go then, you and I,
When the evening is spread out against the sky
Like a patient etherised upon a table;
Let us go, through certain half-deserted streets,
The muttering retreats
Of restless nights in one-night cheap hotels
And sawdust restaurants with oyster-shells:
Streets that follow like a tedious argument
Of insidious intent
To lead you to an overwhelming question . . .
Oh, do not ask, 'What is it?'
Let us go and make our visit.

In the room the women come and go
Talking of Michelangelo.

The yellow fog that rubs its back upon the window-panes,
The yellow smoke that rubs its muzzle on the window-panes
Licked its tongue into the corners of the evening,
Lingered upon the pools that stand in drains,
Let fall upon its back the soot that falls from chimneys,
Slipped by the terrace, made a sudden leap,
And seeing that it was a soft October night,
Curled once about the house, and fell asleep.

And indeed there will be time
For the yellow smoke that slides along the street
Rubbing its back upon the window-panes;
There will be time, there will be time
To prepare a face to meet the faces that you meet;
There will be time to murder and create,
And time for all the works and days of hands
That lift and drop a question on your plate;
Time for you and time for me,
And time yet for a hundred indecisions,
And for a hundred visions and revisions,
Before the taking of a toast and tea.

In the room the women come and go
Talking of Michelangelo.

And indeed there will be time
To wonder, 'Do I dare?' and, 'Do I dare?'
Time to turn back and descend the stair,
With a bald spot in the middle of my hair—
(They will say: 'How his hair is growing thin!')
My morning coat, my collar mounting firmly to the chin,
My necktie rich and modest, but asserted by a simple pin—
(They will say: 'But how his arms and legs are thin!')
Do I dare
Disturb the universe?
In a minute there is time
For decisions and revisions which a minute will reverse.

For I have known them all already, known them all—
Have known the evenings, mornings, afternoons,
I have measured out my life with coffee spoons;
I know the voices dying with a dying fall
Beneath the music from a farther room.
  So how should I presume?

And I have known the eyes already, known them all—
The eyes that fix you in a formulated phrase,
And when I am formulated, sprawling on a pin,
When I am pinned and wriggling on the wall,
Then how should I begin
To spit out all the butt-ends of my days and ways?
  And how should I presume?

And I have known the arms already, known them all—
Arms that are braceleted and white and bare
(But in the lamplight, downed with light brown hair!)
Is it perfume from a dress
That makes me so digress?
Arms that lie along a table, or wrap about a shawl.
  And should I then presume?
  And how should I begin?

    .   .   .   .

Shall I say, I have gone at dusk through narrow streets
And watched the smoke that rises from the pipes
Of lonely men in shirt-sleeves, leaning out of windows? . . .

I should have been a pair of ragged claws
Scuttling across the floors of silent seas.

      .     .     .     .     .

And the afternoon, the evening, sleeps so peacefully!
Smoothed by long fingers,
Asleep . . . tired . . . or it malingers,
Stretched on the floor, here beside you and me.
Should I, after tea and cakes and ices,
Have the strength to force the moment to its crisis?
But though I have wept and fasted, wept and prayed,
Though I have seen my head (grown slightly bald) brought in upon a
    platter,
I am no prophet—and here's no great matter;
I have seen the moment of my greatness flicker,
And I have seen the eternal Footman hold my coat, and snicker,
And in short, I was afraid.

And would it have been worth it, after all,
After the cups, the marmalade, the tea,
Among the porcelain, among some talk of you and me,
Would it have been worth while,
To have bitten off the matter with a smile,
To have squeezed the universe into a ball
To roll it towards some overwhelming question,
To say: 'I am Lazarus, come from the dead,
Come back to tell you all, I shall tell you all'—
If one, settling a pillow by her head,
    Should say: 'That is not what I meant at all.
    That is not it, at all.'

And would it have been worth it, after all,
Would it have been worth while,
After the sunsets and the dooryards and the sprinkled streets,
After the novels, after the teacups, after the skirts that trail along the
    floor—
And this, and so much more?—
It is impossible to say just what I mean!
But as if a magic lantern threw the nerves in patterns on a screen:

Would it have been worth while
If one, settling a pillow or throwing off a shawl,
And turning toward the window, should say:
   'That is not it at all,
   That is not what I meant, at all.'

     .    .    .    .    .

No! I am not Prince Hamlet, nor was meant to be;
Am an attendant lord, one that will do
To swell a progress, start a scene or two,
Advise the prince; no doubt, an easy tool,
Deferential, glad to be of use,
Politic, cautious, and meticulous;
Full of high sentence, but a bit obtuse;
At times, indeed, almost ridiculous—
Almost, at times, the Fool.

I grow old . . . I grow old . . .
I shall wear the bottoms of my trousers rolled.

Shall I part my hair behind? Do I dare to eat a peach?
I shall wear white flannel trousers, and walk upon the beach.
I have heard the mermaids singing, each to each.

I do not think that they will sing to me.

I have seen them riding seaward on the waves
Combing the white hair of the waves blown back
When the wind blows the water white and black.

We have lingered in the chambers of the sea
By sea-girls wreathed with seaweed red and brown
Till human voices wake us, and we drown.

827       *Sweeney Among the Nightingales*

    APENECK Sweeney spreads his knees
    Letting his arms hang down to laugh,
    The zebra stripes along his jaw
    Swelling to maculate giraffe.

The circles of the stormy moon
Slide westward toward the River Plate,
Death and the Raven drift above
And Sweeney guards the hornèd gate.

Gloomy Orion and the Dog
Are veiled; and hushed the shrunken seas;
The person in the Spanish cape
Tries to sit on Sweeney's knees

Slips and pulls the table cloth
Overturns a coffee-cup,
Reorganised upon the floor
She yawns and draws a stocking up;

The silent man in mocha brown
Sprawls at the window-sill and gapes;
The waiter brings in oranges
Bananas figs and hothouse grapes;

The silent vertebrate in brown
Contracts and concentrates, withdraws;
Rachel *née* Rabinovitch
Tears at the grapes with murderous paws;

She and the lady in the cape
Are suspect, thought to be in league;
Therefore the man with heavy eyes
Declines the gambit, shows fatigue,

Leaves the room and reappears
Outside the window, leaning in,
Branches of wistaria
Circumscribe a golden grin;

The host with someone indistinct
Converses at the door apart,
The nightingales are singing near
The Convent of the Sacred Heart,

And sang within the bloody wood
When Agamemnon cried aloud,
And let their liquid siftings fall
To stain the stiff dishonoured shroud.

828

## *The Waste Land*

### *I. The Burial of the Dead*

APRIL is the cruellest month, breeding
Lilacs out of the dead land, mixing
Memory and desire, stirring
Dull roots with spring rain.
Winter kept us warm, covering
Earth in forgetful snow, feeding
A little life with dried tubers.
Summer surprised us, coming over the Starnbergersee
With a shower of rain; we stopped in the colonnade,
And went on in sunlight, into the Hofgarten,
And drank coffee, and talked for an hour.
Bin gar keine Russin, stamm' aus Litauen, echt deutsch.
And when we were children, staying at the arch-duke's,
My cousin's, he took me out on a sled,
And I was frightened. He said, Marie,
Marie, hold on tight. And down we went.
In the mountains, there you feel free.
I read, much of the night, and go south in the winter.

  What are the roots that clutch, what branches grow
Out of this stony rubbish? Son of man,
You cannot say, or guess, for you know only
A heap of broken images, where the sun beats,
And the dead tree gives no shelter, the cricket no relief,
And the dry stone no sound of water. Only
There is shadow under this red rock,
(Come in under the shadow of this red rock),
And I will show you something different from either
Your shadow at morning striding behind you
Or your shadow at evening rising to meet you;
I will show you fear in a handful of dust.
                    *Frisch weht der Wind*
                    *Der Heimat zu*
                    *Mein Irisch Kind,*
                    *Wo weilest du?*
'You gave me hyacinths first a year ago;
'They called me the hyacinth girl.'
—Yet when we came back, late, from the hyacinth garden,

Your arms full, and your hair wet, I could not
Speak, and my eyes failed, I was neither
Living nor dead, and I knew nothing,
Looking into the heart of light, the silence.
*Oed' und leer das Meer.*

    Madame Sosostris, famous clairvoyante,
Had a bad cold, nevertheless
Is known to be the wisest woman in Europe,
With a wicked pack of cards. Here, said she,
Is your card, the drowned Phoenician Sailor,
(Those are pearls that were his eyes. Look!)
Here is Belladonna, the Lady of the Rocks,
The lady of situations.
Here is the man with three staves, and here the Wheel,
And here is the one-eyed merchant, and this card,
Which is blank, is something he carries on his back,
Which I am forbidden to see. I do not find
The Hanged Man. Fear death by water.
I see crowds of people, walking round in a ring.
Thank you. If you see dear Mrs. Equitone,
Tell her I bring the horoscope myself:
One must be so careful these days.

    Unreal City,
Under the brown fog of a winter dawn,
A crowd flowed over London Bridge, so many,
I had not thought death had undone so many.
Sighs, short and infrequent, were exhaled,
And each man fixed his eyes before his feet.
Flowed up the hill and down King William Street,
To where Saint Mary Woolnoth kept the hours
With a dead sound on the final stroke of nine.
There I saw one I knew, and stopped him, crying: 'Stetson!
'You who were with me in the ships at Mylae!
'That corpse you planted last year in your garden,
'Has it begun to sprout! Will it bloom this year?
'Or has the sudden frost disturbed its bed?
'Oh keep the Dog far hence, that's friend to men,
'Or with his nails he'll dig it up again!
'You! hypocrite lecteur!—mon semblable,—mon frère!'

## II. A Game of Chess

The Chair she sat in, like a burnished throne,
Glowed on the marble, where the glass
Held up by standards wrought with fruited vines
From which a golden Cupidon peeped out
(Another hid his eyes behind his wing)
Doubled the flames of sevenbranched candelabra
Reflecting light upon the table as
The glitter of her jewels rose to meet it,
From satin cases poured in rich profusion;
In vials of ivory and coloured glass
Unstoppered, lurked her strange synthetic perfumes,
Unguent, powdered, or liquid—troubled, confused
And drowned the sense in odours; stirred by the air
That freshened from the window, these ascended
In fattening the prolonged candle-flames,
Flung their smoke into the laquearia,
Stirring the pattern on the coffered ceiling.
Huge sea-wood fed with copper
Burned green and orange, framed by the coloured stone,
In which sad light a carvèd dolphin swam.
Above the antique mantel was displayed
As though a window gave upon the sylvan scene
The change of Philomel, by the barbarous king
So rudely forced; yet there the nightingale
Filled all the desert with inviolable voice
And still she cried, and still the world pursues,
'Jug Jug' to dirty ears.
And other withered stumps of time
Were told upon the walls; staring forms
Leaned out, leaning, hushing the room enclosed.
Footsteps shuffled on the stair.
Under the firelight, under the brush, her hair
Spread out in fiery points
Glowed into words, then would be savagely still.

'My nerves are bad to-night. Yes, bad. Stay with me.
'Speak to me. Why do you never speak. Speak.
   'What are you thinking of? What thinking? What?
'I never know what you are thinking. Think.'

I think we are in rats' alley
Where the dead men lost their bones.

'What is that noise?'
                    The wind under the door.
'What is that noise now? What is the wind doing?'
                    Nothing again nothing.
                                        'Do
'You know nothing? Do you see nothing? Do you remember
'Nothing?'

        I remember
Those are pearls that were his eyes.
'Are you alive, or not? Is there nothing in your head?'
                                        But

O O O O that Shakespeherian Rag—
It's so elegant
So intelligent
'What shall I do now? What shall I do?'
'I shall rush out as I am, and walk the street
'With my hair down, so. What shall we do tomorrow?
'What shall we ever do?'
                    The hot water at ten.
And if it rains, a closed car at four.
And we shall play a game of chess,
Pressing lidless eyes and waiting for a knock upon the door.

    When Lil's husband got demobbed, I said—
I didn't mince my words, I said to her myself,
HURRY UP PLEASE ITS TIME
Now Albert's coming back, make yourself a bit smart.
He'll want to know what you done with that money he gave you
To get yourself some teeth. He did, I was there.
You have them all out, Lil, and get a nice set,
He said, I swear, I can't bear to look at you.
And no more can't I, I said, and think of poor Albert,
He's been in the army four years, he wants a good time,
And if you don't give it him, there's others will, I said.
Oh is there, she said. Something o' that, I said.
Then I'll know who to thank, she said, and give me a straight look.
HURRY UP PLEASE ITS TIME
If you don't like it you can get on with it, I said.
Others can pick and choose if you can't.

But if Albert makes off, it won't be for lack of telling.
You ought to be ashamed, I said, to look so antique.
(And her only thirty-one.)
I can't help it, she said, pulling a long face,
It's them pills I took, to bring it off, she said.
(She's had five already, and nearly died of young George.)
The chemist said it would be all right, but I've never been the same.
You *are* a proper fool, I said.
Well, if Albert won't leave you alone, there it is, I said,
What you get married for if you don't want children?
HURRY UP PLEASE ITS TIME
Well, that Sunday Albert was home, they had a hot gammon,
And they asked me in to dinner, to get the beauty of it hot—
HURRY UP PLEASE ITS TIME
HURRY UP PLEASE ITS TIME
Goonight Bill. Goonight Lou. Goonight May. Goonight.
Ta ta. Goonight. Goonight.
Good night, ladies, good night, sweet ladies, good night, good night.


## III. The Fire Sermon

The river's tent is broken: the last fingers of leaf
Clutch and sink into the wet bank. The wind
Crosses the brown land, unheard. The nymphs are departed.
Sweet Thames, run softly, till I end my song.
The river bears no empty bottles, sandwich papers,
Silk handkerchiefs, cardboard boxes, cigarette ends
Or other testimony of summer nights. The nymphs are departed.
And their friends, the loitering heirs of City directors;
Departed, have left no addresses.
By the waters of Leman I sat down and wept . . .
Sweet Thames, run softly till I end my song,
Sweet Thames, run softly, for I speak not loud or long.
But at my back in a cold blast I hear
The rattle of the bones, and chuckle spread from ear to ear.

A rat crept softly through the vegetation
Dragging its slimy belly on the bank
While I was fishing in the dull canal
On a winter evening round behind the gashouse
Musing upon the king my brother's wreck
And on the king my father's death before him.
White bodies naked on the low damp ground

And bones cast in a little low dry garret,
Rattled by the rat's foot only, year to year.
But at my back from time to time I hear
The sound of horns and motors, which shall bring
Sweeney to Mrs. Porter in the spring.
O the moon shone bright on Mrs. Porter
And on her daughter
They wash their feet in soda water
*Et O ces voix d'enfants, chantant dans la coupole!*

Twit twit twit
Jug jug jug jug jug jug
So rudely forc'd.
Tereu

   Unreal City
Under the brown fog of a winter noon
Mr. Eugenides, the Smyrna merchant
Unshaven, with a pocket full of currants
C.i.f. London: documents at sight,
Asked me in demotic French
To luncheon at the Cannon Street Hotel
Followed by a weekend at the Metropole.

   At the violet hour, when the eyes and back
Turn upward from the desk, when the human engine waits
Like a taxi throbbing waiting,
I Tiresias, though blind, throbbing between two lives,
Old man with wrinkled female breasts, can see
At the violet hour, the evening hour that strives
Homeward, and brings the sailor home from sea,
The typist home at teatime, clears her breakfast, lights
Her stove, and lays out food in tins.
Out of the window perilously spread
Her drying combinations touched by the sun's last rays,
On the divan are piled (at night her bed)
Stockings, slippers, camisoles, and stays.
I Tiresias, old man with wrinkled dugs
Perceived the scene, and foretold the rest—
I too awaited the expected guest.
He, the young man carbuncular, arrives,
A small house agent's clerk, with one bold stare,
One of the low on whom assurance sits

As a silk hat on a Bradford millionaire.
The time is now propitious, as he guesses,
The meal is ended, she is bored and tired,
Endeavours to engage her in caresses
Which still are unreproved, if undesired.
Flushed and decided, he assaults at once;
Exploring hands encounter no defence;
His vanity requires no response,
And makes a welcome of indifference.
(And I Tiresias have foresuffered all
Enacted on this same divan or bed;
I who have sat by Thebes below the wall
And walked among the lowest of the dead.)
Bestows one final patronising kiss,
And gropes his way, finding the stairs unlit . . .

She turns and looks a moment in the glass,
Hardly aware of her departed lover;
Her brain allows one half-formed thought to pass:
'Well now that's done: and I'm glad it's over.'
When lovely woman stoops to folly and
Paces about her room again, alone,
She smoothes her hair with automatic hand,
And puts a record on the gramophone.

'This music crept by me upon the waters'
And along the Strand, up Queen Victoria Street.
O City city, I can sometimes hear
Beside a public bar in Lower Thames Street,
The pleasant whining of a mandoline
And a clatter and a chatter from within
Where fishmen lounge at noon: where the walls
Of Magnus Martyr hold
Inexplicable splendour of Ionian white and gold.

   The river sweats
   Oil and tar
   The barges drift
   With the turning tide
   Red sails
   Wide
   To leeward, swing on the heavy spar.

THOMAS STEARNS ELIOT

The barges wash
Drifting logs
Down Greenwich reach
Past the Isle of Dogs.
         Weialala leia
         Wallala leialala

Elizabeth and Leicester
Beating oars
The stern was formed
A gilded shell
Red and gold
The brisk swell
Rippled both shores
Southwest wind
Carried down stream
The peal of bells
White towers
         Weialala leia
         Wallala leialala

'Trams and dusty trees.
Highbury bore me. Richmond and Kew
Undid me. By Richmond I raised my knees
Supine on the floor of a narrow canoe.'

'My feet are at Moorgate, and my heart
Under my feet. After the event
He wept. He promised "a new start."
I made no comment. What should I resent?'

'On Margate Sands.
I can connect
Nothing with nothing.
The broken fingernails of dirty hands.
My people humble people who expect
Nothing.'
         la la

To Carthage then I came

Burning burning burning burning
O Lord Thou pluckest me out
O Lord Thou pluckest

burning


## IV. Death By Water

Phlebas the Phoenician, a fortnight dead,
Forgot the cry of gulls, and the deep sea swell
And the profit and loss.
              A current under sea
Picked his bones in whispers. As he rose and fell
He passed the stages of his age and youth
Entering the whirlpool.
              Gentile or Jew
O you who turn the wheel and look to windward,
Consider Phlebas, who was once handsome and tall as you.


## V. What the Thunder said

After the torchlight red on sweaty faces
After the frosty silence in the gardens
After the agony in stony places
The shouting and the crying
Prison and palace and reverberation
Of thunder of spring over distant mountains
He who was living is now dead
We who were living are now dying
With a little patience

Here is no water but only rock
Rock and no water and the sandy road
The road winding above among the mountains
Which are mountains of rock without water
If there were water we should stop and drink
Amongst the rock one cannot stop or think
Sweat is dry and feet are in the sand
If there were only water amongst the rock
Dead mountain mouth of carious teeth that cannot spit
Here one can neither stand nor lie nor sit

There is not even silence in the mountains
But dry sterile thunder without rain
There is not even solitude in the mountains
But red sullen faces sneer and snarl
From doors of mudcracked houses
                              If there were water

    And no rock
    If there were rock
    And also water
    And water
    A spring
    A pool among the rock
    If there were the sound of water only
    Not the cicada
    And dry grass singing
    But sound of water over a rock
    Where the hermit-thrush sings in the pine trees
    Drip drop drip drop drop drop drop
    But there is no water

    Who is the third who walks always beside you?
When I count, there are only you and I together
But when I look ahead up the white road
There is always another one walking beside you
Gliding wrapt in a brown mantle, hooded
I do not know whether a man or a woman
—But who is that on the other side of you?

    What is that sound high in the air
Murmur of maternal lamentation
Who are those hooded hordes swarming
Over endless plains, stumbling in cracked earth
Ringed by the flat horizon only
What is the city over the mountains
Cracks and reforms and bursts in the violet air
Falling towers
Jerusalem Athens Alexandria
Vienna London
Unreal

    A woman drew her long black hair out tight
And fiddled whisper music on those strings
And bats with baby faces in the violet light

Whistled, and beat their wings
And crawled head downward down a blackened wall
And upside down in air were towers
Tolling reminiscent bells, that kept the hours
And voices singing out of empty cisterns and exhausted wells.

In this decayed hole among the mountains
In the faint moonlight, the grass is singing
Over the tumbled graves, about the chapel
There is the empty chapel, only the wind's home.
It has no windows, and the door swings,
Dry bones can harm no one.
Only a cock stood on the rooftree
Co co rico co co rico
In a flash of lightning. Then a damp gust
Bringing rain

Ganga was sunken, and the limp leaves
Waited for rain, while the black clouds
Gathered far distant, over Himavant.
The jungle crouched, humped in silence.
Then spoke the thunder
DA
*Datta :* what have we given?
My friend, blood shaking my heart
The awful daring of a moment's surrender
Which an age of prudence can never retract
By this, and this only, we have existed
Which is not to be found in our obituaries
Or in memories draped by the beneficent spider
Or under seals broken by the lean solicitor
In our empty rooms
DA
*Dayadhvam :* I have heard the key
Turn in the door once and turn once only
We think of the key, each in his prison
Thinking of the key, each confirms a prison
Only at nightfall, aethereal rumours
Revive for a moment a broken Coriolanus

DA
*Damyata :* The boat responded
Gaily, to the hand expert with sail and oar
The sea was calm, your heart would have responded
Gaily, when invited, beating obedient
To controlling hands

                          I sat upon the shore
Fishing, with the arid plain behind me
Shall I at least set my lands in order?
London Bridge is falling down falling down falling down
*Poi s'ascose nel foco che gli affina*
*Quando fiam uti chelidon*—O swallow swallow
*Le Prince d'Aquitaine à la tour abolie*
These fragments I have shored against my ruins
Why then Ile fit you. Hieronymo's mad againe.
Datta. Dayadhvam. Damyata.
                   Shantih shantih shantih

829          *Eyes that last I saw in tears*

EYES that last I saw in tears
Through division
Here in death's dream kingdom
The golden vision reappears
I see the eyes but not the tears
This is my affliction.

This is my affliction
Eyes I shall not see again
Eyes of decision
Eyes I shall not see unless
At the door of death's other kingdom
Where, as in this,
The eyes outlast a little while
A little while outlast the tears
And hold us in derision.

830 *Marina*

WHAT seas what shores what grey rocks and what islands
What water lapping the bow
And scent of pine and the woodthrush singing through the fog
What images return
O my daughter.

Those who sharpen the tooth of the dog, meaning
Death
Those who glitter with the glory of the hummingbird, meaning
Death
Those who sit in the sty of contentment, meaning
Death
Those who suffer the ecstasy of the animals, meaning
Death

Are become unsubstantial, reduced by a wind,
A breath of pine, and the woodsong fog
By this grace dissolved in place

What is this face, less clear and clearer
The pulse in the arm, less strong and stronger—
Given or lent? more distant than stars and nearer than the eye

Whispers and small laughter between leaves and hurrying feet
Under sleep, where all the waters meet.

Bowsprit cracked with ice and paint cracked with heat.
I made this, I have forgotten
And remember.
The rigging weak and the canvas rotten
Between one June and another September.
Made this unknowing, half conscious, unknown, my own.
The garboard strake leaks, the seams need caulking.
This form, this face, this life
Living to live in a world of time beyond me; let me
Resign my life for this life, my speech for that unspoken,
The awakened, lips parted, the hope, the new ships.

What seas what shores what granite islands towards my timbers
And woodthrush calling through the fog
My daughter.

831 *Little Gidding*

I

MIDWINTER spring is its own season
Sempiternal though sodden towards sundown,
Suspended in time, between pole and tropic.
When the short day is brightest, with frost and fire,
The brief sun flames the ice, on pond and ditches,
In windless cold that is the heart's heat,
Reflecting in a watery mirror
A glare that is blindness in the early afternoon.
And glow more intense than blaze of branch, or brazier,
Stirs the dumb spirit: no wind, but pentecostal fire
In the dark time of the year. Between melting and freezing
The soul's sap quivers. There is no earth smell
Or smell of living thing. This is the spring time
But not in time's covenant. Now the hedgerow
Is blanched for an hour with transitory blossom
Of snow, a bloom more sudden
Than that of summer, neither budding nor fading,
Not in the scheme of generation.
Where is the summer, the unimaginable
Zero summer?

If you came this way,
Taking the route you would be likely to take
From the place you would be likely to come from,
If you came this way in may time, you would find the hedges
White again, in May, with voluptuary sweetness.
It would be the same at the end of the journey,
If you came at night like a broken king,
If you came by day not knowing what you came for,
It would be the same, when you leave the rough road
And turn behind the pig-sty to the dull façade
And the tombstone. And what you thought you came for
Is only a shell, a husk of meaning
From which the purpose breaks only when it is fulfilled
If at all. Either you had no purpose
Or the purpose is beyond the end you figured
And is altered in fulfilment. There are other places

Which also are the world's end, some at the sea jaws,
Or over a dark lake, in a desert or a city—
But this is the nearest, in place and time,
Now and in England.

                         If you came this way,
Taking any route, starting from anywhere,
At any time or at any season,
It would always be the same: you would have to put off
Sense and notion. You are not here to verify,
Instruct yourself, or inform curiosity
Or carry report. You are here to kneel
Where prayer has been valid. And prayer is more
Than an order of words, the conscious occupation
Of the praying mind, or the sound of the voice praying.
And what the dead had no speech for, when living,
They can tell you, being dead: the communication
Of the dead is tongued with fire beyond the language of the living.
Here, the intersection of the timeless moment
Is England and nowhere. Never and always.

## II

Ash on an old man's sleeve
Is all the ash the burnt roses leave.
Dust in the air suspended
Marks the place where a story ended.
Dust inbreathed was a house—
The wall, the wainscot and the mouse.
The death of hope and despair,
     This is the death of air.

There are flood and drouth
Over the eyes and in the mouth,
Dead water and dead sand
Contending for the upper hand.
The parched eviscerate soil
Gapes at the vanity of toil,
Laughs without mirth.
     This is the death of earth.

Water and fire succeed
The town, the pasture and the weed.
Water and fire deride
The sacrifice that we denied.
Water and fire shall rot
The marred foundations we forgot,
Of sanctuary and choir.
    This is the death of water and fire.


In the uncertain hour before the morning
  Near the ending of interminable night
  At the recurrent end of the unending
After the dark dove with the flickering tongue
  Had passed below the horizon of his homing
  While the dead leaves still rattled on like tin
Over the asphalt where no other sound was
  Between three districts whence the smoke arose
  I met one walking, loitering and hurried
As if blown towards me like the metal leaves
  Before the urban dawn wind unresisting.
  And as I fixed upon the down-turned face
That pointed scrutiny with which we challenge
  The first-met stranger in the waning dusk
  I caught the sudden look of some dead master
Whom I had known, forgotten, half recalled
  Both one and many; in the brown baked features
  The eyes of a familiar compound ghost
Both intimate and unidentifiable.
  So I assumed a double part, and cried
  And heard another's voice cry: 'What! are *you* here?'
Although we were not. I was still the same,
  Knowing myself yet being someone other—
  And he a face still forming; yet the words sufficed
To compel the recognition they preceded.
  And so, compliant to the common wind,
  Too strange to each other for misunderstanding,
In concord at this intersection time
  Of meeting nowhere, no before and after,
  We trod the pavement in a dead patrol.
I said: 'The wonder that I feel is easy,
  Yet ease is cause of wonder. Therefore speak:
  I may not comprehend, may not remember.'

And he: 'I am not eager to rehearse
  My thought and theory which you have forgotten.
  These things have served their purpose: let them be.
So with your own, and pray they be forgiven
  By others, as I pray you to forgive
  Both bad and good. Last season's fruit is eaten
And the fullfed beast shall kick the empty pail.
  For last year's words belong to last year's language
  And next year's words await another voice.
But, as the passage now presents no hindrance
  To the spirit unappeased and peregrine
  Between two worlds become much like each other,
So I find words I never thought to speak
  In streets I never thought I should revisit
  When I left my body on a distant shore.
Since our concern was speech, and speech impelled us
  To purify the dialect of the tribe
  And urge the mind to aftersight and foresight,
Let me disclose the gifts reserved for age
  To set a crown upon your lifetime's effort.
  First, the cold friction of expiring sense
Without enchantment, offering no promise
  But bitter tastelessness of shadow fruit
  As body and soul begin to fall asunder.
Second, the conscious impotence of rage
  At human folly, and the laceration
  Of laughter at what ceases to amuse.
And last, the rending pain of re-enactment
  Of all that you have done, and been; the shame
  Of motives late revealed, and the awareness
Of things ill done and done to others' harm
  Which once you took for exercise of virtue.
  Then fools' approval stings, and honour stains.
From wrong to wrong the exasperated spirit
  Proceeds, unless restored by that refining fire
  Where you must move in measure, like a dancer.'
The day was breaking. In the disfigured street
  He left me, with a kind of valediction,
  And faded on the blowing of the horn.

## III

There are three conditions which often look alike
Yet differ completely, flourish in the same hedgerow:
Attachment to self and to things and to persons, detachment
From self and from things and from persons; and, growing
     between them, indifference
Which resembles the others as death resembles life,
Being between two lives—unflowering, between
The live and the dead nettle. This is the use of memory:
For liberation—not less of love but expanding
Of love beyond desire, and so liberation
From the future as well as the past. Thus, love of a country
Begins as attachment to our own field of action
And comes to find that action of little importance
Though never indifferent. History may be servitude,
History may be freedom. See, now they vanish,
The faces and places, with the self which, as it could, loved them,
To become renewed, transfigured, in another pattern.
Sin is Behovely, but
All shall be well, and
All manner of thing shall be well.
If I think, again, of this place,
And of people, not wholly commendable,
Of no immediate kin or kindness,
But some of peculiar genius,
All touched by a common genius,
United in the strife which divided them;
If I think of a king at nightfall,
Of three men, and more, on the scaffold
And a few who died forgotten
In other places, here and abroad,
And of one who died blind and quiet,
Why should we celebrate
These dead men more than the dying?
It is not to ring the bell backward
Nor is it an incantation
To summon the spectre of a Rose.
We cannot revive old factions
We cannot restore old policies
Or follow an antique drum.

These men, and those who opposed them
And those whom they opposed
Accept the constitution of silence
And are folded in a single party.
Whatever we inherit from the fortunate
We have taken from the defeated
What they had to leave us—a symbol:
A symbol perfected in death.
And all shall be well and
All manner of thing shall be well
By the purification of the motive
In the ground of our beseeching.

IV

The dove descending breaks the air
With flame of incandescent terror
Of which the tongues declare
The one discharge from sin and error.
The only hope, or else despair
   Lies in the choice of pyre or pyre—
   To be redeemed from fire by fire.

Who then devised the torment? Love.
Love is the unfamiliar Name
Behind the hands that wove
The intolerable shirt of flame
Which human power cannot remove.
   We only live, only suspire
   Consumed by either fire or fire.

V

What we call the beginning is often the end
And to make an end is to make a beginning.
The end is where we start from. And every phrase
And sentence that is right (where every word is at home,
Taking its place to support the others,
The word neither diffident nor ostentatious,
An easy commerce of the old and the new,
The common word exact without vulgarity,
The formal word precise but not pedantic,
The complete consort dancing together)
Every phrase and every sentence is an end and a beginning,

Every poem an epitaph. And any action
Is a step to the block, to the fire, down the sea's throat
Or to an illegible stone: and that is where we start.
We die with the dying:
See, they depart, and we go with them.
We are born with the dead:
See, they return, and bring us with them.
The moment of the rose and the moment of the yew-tree
Are of equal duration. A people without history
Is not redeemed from time, for history is a pattern
Of timeless moments. So, while the light fails
On a winter's afternoon, in a secluded chapel
History is now and England.

With the drawing of this Love and the voice of this Calling

We shall not cease from exploration
And the end of all our exploring
Will be to arrive where we started
And know the place for the first time.
Through the unknown, remembered gate
When the last of earth left to discover
Is that which was the beginning;
At the source of the longest river
The voice of the hidden waterfall
And the children in the apple-tree
Not known, because not looked for
But heard, half-heard, in the stillness
Between two waves of the sea.
Quick now, here, now, always—
A condition of complete simplicity
(Costing not less than everything)
And all shall be well and
All manner of thing shall be well
When the tongues of flame are in-folded
Into the crowned knot of fire
And the fire and the rose are one.

# WALTER JAMES TURNER
## 1889–1946

832  *Romance*

WHEN I was but thirteen or so
   I went into a golden land,
Chimborazo, Cotopaxi
   Took me by the hand.

My father died, my brother too,
   They passed like fleeting dreams.
I stood where Popocatapetl
   In the sunlight gleams.

I dimly heard the Master's voice
   And boys far-off at play,
Chimborazo, Cotopaxi
   Had stolen me away.

I walked in a great golden dream
   To and fro from school—
Shining Popocatapetl
   The dusty streets did rule.

I walked home with a gold dark boy
   And never a word I'd say,
Chimborazo, Cotopaxi
   Had taken my speech away:

I gazed entranced upon his face
   Fairer than any flower—
O shining Popocatapetl
   It was thy magic hour:

The houses, people, traffic seemed
   Thin fading dreams by day,
Chimborazo, Cotopaxi
   They had stolen my soul away!

## ISAAC ROSENBERG
### 1890–1918

833              *August 1914*

WHAT in our lives is burnt
In the fire of this?
The heart's dear granary?
The much we shall miss?

Three lives hath one life—
Iron, honey, gold.
The gold, the honey gone—
Left is the hard and cold.

Iron are our lives
Molten right through our youth.
A burnt space through ripe fields
A fair mouth's broken tooth.

834         *Break of Day in the Trenches*

THE darkness crumbles away—
It is the same old druid Time as ever.
Only a live thing leaps my hand—
A queer sardonic rat—
As I pull the parapet's poppy
To stick behind my ear.
Droll rat, they would shoot you if they knew
Your cosmopolitan sympathies.
Now you have touched this English hand
You will do the same to a German—
Soon, no doubt, if it be your pleasure
To cross the sleeping green between.
It seems you inwardly grin as you pass
Strong eyes, fine limbs, haughty athletes
Less chanced than you for life,
Bonds to the whims of murder,
Sprawled in the bowels of the earth,
The torn fields of France.

What do you see in our eyes
At the shrieking iron and flame
Hurled through still heavens?
What quaver—what heart aghast?
Poppies whose roots are in man's veins
Drop, and are ever dropping;
But mine in my ear is safe,
Just a little white with the dust.


# WILFRED OWEN

## 1893–1918

835                    *Anthem for Doomed Youth*

WHAT passing-bells for these who die as cattle?
   Only the monstrous anger of the guns.
Only the stuttering rifles' rapid rattle
   Can patter out their hasty orisons.
No mockeries now for them; no prayers nor bells,
   Nor any voice of mourning save the choirs,—
The shrill, demented choirs of wailing shells;
   And bugles calling for them from sad shires.

What candles may be held to speed them all?
   Not in the hands of boys, but in their eyes
Shall shine the holy glimmers of good-byes.
The pallor of girls' brows shall be their pall;
   Their flowers the tenderness of patient minds,
   And each slow dusk a drawing-down of blinds.


836                    *Strange Meeting*

IT seemed that out of battle I escaped
Down some profound dull tunnel, long since scooped
Through granites which titanic wars had groined.
Yet also there encumbered sleepers groaned,
Too fast in thought or death to be bestirred.
Then, as I probed them, one sprang up, and stared

With piteous recognition in fixed eyes,
Lifting distressful hands as if to bless.
And by his smile I knew that sullen hall,
By his dead smile I knew we stood in Hell.
With a thousand pains that vision's face was grained;
Yet no blood reached there from the upper ground,
And no guns thumped, or down the flues made moan.
'Strange friend,' I said, 'here is no cause to mourn.'
'None,' said the other, 'save the undone years,
The hopelessness. Whatever hope is yours,
Was my life also; I went hunting wild
After the wildest beauty in the world,
Which lies not calm in eyes, or braided hair,
But mocks the steady running of the hour,
And if it grieves, grieves richlier than here.
For by my glee might many men have laughed,
And of my weeping something had been left,
Which must die now. I mean the truth untold,
The pity of war, the pity war distilled.
Now men will go content with what we spoiled,
Or, discontent, boil bloody, and be spilled.
They will be swift with swiftness of the tigress,
None will break ranks, though nations trek from progress.
Courage was mine, and I had mystery,
Wisdom was mine, and I had mastery;
To miss the march of this retreating world
Into vain citadels that are not walled.
Then, when much blood had clogged their chariot-wheels
I would go up and wash them from sweet wells,
Even with truths that lie too deep for taint.
I would have poured my spirit without stint
But not through wounds; not on the cess of war.
Foreheads of men have bled where no wounds were.
I am the enemy you killed, my friend.
I knew you in this dark; for so you frowned
Yesterday through me as you jabbed and killed.
I parried; but my hands were loath and cold.
Let us sleep now . . .'

837                                   *Miners*

THERE was a whispering in my hearth,
        A sigh of the coal,
Grown wistful of a former earth
        It might recall.

I listened for a tale of leaves
        And smothered ferns;
Frond-forests; and the low, sly lives
        Before the fawns.

My fire might show steam-phantoms simmer
        From Time's old cauldron,
Before the birds made nests in summer,
        Or men had children.

But the coals were murmuring of their mine,
        And moans down there
Of boys that slept wry sleep, and men
        Writhing for air.

And I saw white bones in the cinder-shard.
        Bones without number;
For many hearts with coal are charred
        And few remember.

I thought of some who worked dark pits
        Of war, and died
Digging the rock where Death reputes
        Peace lies indeed.

Comforted years will sit soft-chaired
        In rooms of amber;
The years will stretch their hands, well-cheered
        By our lives' ember.

The centuries will burn rich loads
        With which we groaned,
Whose warmth shall lull their dreaming lids
        While songs are crooned.
But they will not dream of us poor lads
        Lost in the ground.

# ROBERT GRAVES

1895–

ROBERT GRAVES

838

## *Full Moon*

As I walked out that sultry night,
  I heard the stroke of One.
The moon, attained to her full height,
  Stood beaming like the sun:
She exorcized the ghostly wheat
To mute assent in love's defeat,
  Whose tryst had now begun.

The fields lay sick beneath my tread,
  A tedious owlet cried,
A nightingale above my head
  With this or that replied—
Like man and wife who nightly keep
Inconsequent debate in sleep
  As they dream side by side.

Your phantom wore the moon's cold mask,
  My phantom wore the same;
Forgetful of the feverish task
  In hope of which they came,
Each image held the other's eyes
And watched a grey distraction rise
  To cloud the eager flame—

To cloud the eager flame of love,
  To fog the shining gate;
They held the tyrannous queen above
  Sole mover of their fate,
They glared as marble statues glare
Across the tessellated stair
  Or down the halls of state.

And now warm earth was Arctic sea,
   Each breath came dagger-keen;
Two bergs of glinting ice were we,
   The broad moon sailed between;
There swam the mermaids, tailed and finned,
And love went by upon the wind
    As though it had not been.

839                  *Sick Love*

O LOVE, be fed with apples while you may,
And feel the sun and go in royal array,
A smiling innocent on the heavenly causeway,

Though in what listening horror for the cry
That soars in outer blackness dismally,
The dumb blind beast, the paranoiac fury:

Be warm, enjoy the season, lift your head,
Exquisite in the pulse of tainted blood,
That shivering glory not to be despised.

Take your delight in momentariness,
Walk between dark and dark—a shining space
With the grave's narrowness, though not its peace.

840                  *Welsh Incident*

'BUT that was nothing to what things came out
From the sea-caves of Criccieth yonder.'
'What were they? Mermaids? dragons? ghosts?'
'Nothing at all of any things like that.'
'What were they, then?'
                'All sorts of queer things,
Things never seen or heard or written about,
Very strange, un-Welsh, utterly peculiar
Things. Oh, solid enough they seemed to touch,
Had anyone dared it. Marvellous creation,
All various shapes and sizes, and no sizes,
All new, each perfectly unlike his neighbour,
Though all came moving slowly out together.'

'Describe just one of them.'
                      'I am unable.'
'What were their colours?'
                  'Mostly nameless colours,
Colours you'd like to see; but one was puce
Or perhaps more like crimson, but not purplish.
Some had no colour.'
               'Tell me, had they legs?'
'Not a leg nor foot among them that I saw.'
'But did these things come out in any order?
What o'clock was it? What was the day of the week?
Who else was present? How was the weather?'
'I was coming to that. It was half-past three
On Easter Tuesday last. The sun was shining.
The Harlech Silver Band played *Marchog Jesu*
On thirty-seven shimmering instruments
Collecting for Caernarvon's (Fever) Hospital Fund.
The populations of Pwllheli, Criccieth,
Portmadoc, Borth, Tremadoc, Penrhyndeudraeth,
Were all assembled. Criccieth's mayor addressed them
First in good Welsh and then in fluent English,
Twisting his fingers in his chain of office,
Welcoming the things. They came out on the sand,
Not keeping time to the band, moving seaward
Silently at a snail's pace. But at last
The most odd, indescribable thing of all,
Which hardly one man there could see for wonder,
Did something recognizably a something.'
'Well, what?'
            'It made a noise.'
                        'A frightening noise?'

'No, no.'
        'A musical noise? A noise of scuffling?'
'No, but a very loud, respectable noise—
Like groaning to oneself on Sunday morning
In Chapel, close before the second psalm.'
'What did the mayor do?'
                  'I was coming to that'.

841        *She tells her love while half asleep*

> SHE tells her love while half asleep
>        In the dark hours,
>              With half-words whispered low:
> As Earth stirs in her winter sleep
>        And puts out grass and flowers
>              Despite the snow,
>              Despite the falling snow.

842              *A Slice of Wedding Cake*

WHY have such scores of lovely, gifted girls
       Married impossible men?
Simple self-sacrifice may be ruled out,
       And missionary endeavour, nine times out of ten.

Repeat 'impossible men': not merely rustic,
       Foul-tempered or depraved
(Dramatic foils chosen to show the world
       How well women behave, and always have behaved).

Impossible men: idle, illiterate,
       Self-pitying, dirty, sly,
For whose appearance even in City parks
       Excuses must be made to casual passers-by.

Has God's supply of tolerable husbands
       Fallen, in fact, so low?
Or do I always over-value woman
       At the expense of man?
                     Do I?
                              It might be so.

# EDMUND BLUNDEN
## 1896–

843        *Forefathers*

HERE they went with smock and crook,
  Toiled in the sun, lolled in the shade,
Here they mudded out the brook
  And here their hatchet cleared the glade:
Harvest supper woke their wit,
Huntsman's moon their wooings lit.

From this church they led their brides,
  From this church themselves were led
Shoulder-high; on these waysides
  Sat to take their beer and bread.
Names are gone—what men they were
These their cottages declare.

Names are vanished, save the few
  In the old brown Bible scrawled;
These were men of pith and thew,
  Whom the city never called;
Scarce could read or hold a quill,
Built the barn, the forge, the mill.

On the green they watched their sons
  Playing till too dark to see,
As their fathers watched them once,
  As my father once watched me;
While the bat and beetle flew
On the warm air webbed with dew.

Unrecorded, unrenowned,
  Men from whom my ways begin,
Here I know you by your ground
  But I know you not within—
There is silence, there survives
Not a moment of your lives.

Like the bee that now is blown
  Honey-heavy on my hand,
From his toppling tansy-throne
  In the green tempestuous land
I'm in clover now, nor know
Who made honey long ago.


844                  *Report on Experience*

I HAVE been young, and now am not too old;
And I have seen the righteous forsaken,
His health, his honour and his quality taken.
  This is not what we were formerly told.

I have seen a green country, useful to the race,
Knocked silly with guns and mines, its villages vanished,
Even the last rat and last kestrel banished—
  God bless us all, this was peculiar grace.

I knew Seraphina; Nature gave her hue,
Glance, sympathy, note, like one from Eden.
I saw her smile warp, heard her lyric deaden;
  She turned to harlotry;—this I took to be new.

Say what you will, our God sees how they run.
These disillusions are his curious proving
That he loves humanity and will go on loving;
  Over there are faith, life, virtue in the sun.


845                 *The Midnight Skaters*

THE hop-poles stand in cones,
  The icy pond lurks under,
The pole-tops steeple to the thrones
  Of stars, sound gulfs of wonder;
But not the tallest there, 'tis said,
Could fathom to this pond's black bed.

EDMUND BLUNDEN

Then is not death at watch
    Within those secret waters?
What wants he but to catch
    Earth's heedless sons and daughters?
With but a crystal parapet
Between, he has his engines set.

Then on, blood shouts, on, on,
    Twirl, wheel and whip above him,
Dance on this ball-floor thin and wan,
    Use him as though you love him;
Court him, elude him, reel and pass,
And let him hate you through the glass.


# STEVIE SMITH

1902–1971

846        *Not Waving But Drowning*

NOBODY heard him, the dead man,
But still he lay moaning:
I was much further out than you thought
And not waving but drowning.

Poor chap, he always loved larking
And now he's dead
It must have been too cold for him his heart gave way,
They said.

Oh, no no no, it was too cold always
(Still the dead one lay moaning)
I was much too far out all my life
And not waving but drowning.

## CECIL DAY-LEWIS

### 1904–1972

*A Failure*

THE soil was deep and the field well-sited,
  The seed was sound.
Average luck with the weather, one thought,
  And the crop would abound.

If harrowing were all that is needed for
  Harvest, his field
Had been harrowed enough, God knows, to warrant
  A record yield.

He gazed from a hill in the breezy springtime:
  That field was aflow
With wave upon wave like a sea's green shallows
  Breathing below.

He looked from a gate one summer morning
  When the mists uprolled:
Headland to headland those fortunate acres
  Seemed solid gold.

He stood by the field as the day of harvest
  Dawned. But, oh,
The fruit of a year's work, a lifetime's lore,
  Had ceased to grow.

No wickedest weather could thus have turned,
  As it were overnight,
His field to so wan and weedy a showing:
  Some galloping blight

From earth's metabolism must have sprung
  To ruin all;
Or perhaps his own high hopes had made
  The wizened look tall.

But it's useless to argue the why and wherefore.
  When a crop is so thin,
There's nothing to do but to set the teeth
  And plough it in.

# SIR JOHN BETJEMAN
## 1906–

848              *Death of King George V*

'New King arrives in his capital by air . . .'
*Daily Newspaper.*

SPIRITS of well-shot woodcock, partridge, snipe
    Flutter and bear him up the Norfolk sky:
In that red house in a red mahogany book-case
    The stamp collection waits with mounts long dry.

The big blue eyes are shut which saw wrong clothing
    And favourite fields and coverts from a horse;
Old men in country houses hear clocks ticking
    Over thick carpets with a deadened force;

Old men who never cheated, never doubted,
    Communicated monthly, sit and stare
At the new suburb stretched beyond the run-way
    Where a young man lands hatless from the air.


849              *Parliament Hill Fields*

RUMBLING under blackened girders, Midland, bound for Crickle-
    wood,
Puffed its sulphur to the sunset where that Land of Laundries stood.
Rumble under, thunder over, train and tram alternate go,
Shake the floor and smudge the ledger, Charrington, Sells, Dale and
    Co.,
Nuts and nuggets in the window, trucks along the lines below.

When the Bon Marché was shuttered, when the feet were hot and
    tired,
Outside Charrington's we waited, by the 'STOP HERE IF REQUIRED',
Launched aboard the shopping basket, sat precipitately down,
Rocked past Zwanziger the baker's, and the terrace blackish brown,
And the curious Anglo-Norman parish church of Kentish Town.

Till the tram went over thirty, sighting terminus again,
Past municipal lawn tennis and the bobble-hanging plane;
Soft the light suburban evening caught our ashlar-speckled spire,
Eighteen-sixty Early English, as the mighty elms retire
Either side of Brookfield Mansions flashing fine French-window fire.

Oh the after-tram-ride quiet, when we heard a mile beyond,
Silver music from the bandstand, barking dogs by Highgate Pond;
Up the hill where stucco houses in Virginia creeper drown—
And my childish wave of pity, seeing children carrying down
Sheaves of drooping dandelions to the courts of Kentish Town.

850                    *The Cottage Hospital*

AT the end of a long-walled garden
    in a red provincial town,
A brick path led to a mulberry—
    scanty grass at its feet.
I lay under blackening branches
    where the mulberry leaves hung down
Sheltering ruby fruit globes
    from a Sunday-tea-time heat.
Apple and plum espaliers
    basked upon bricks of brown;
The air was swimming with insects,
    and children played in the street.

Out of this bright intentness
    into the mulberry shade
*Musca domestica* (housefly)
    swung from the August light
Slap into slithery rigging
    by the waiting spider made
Which spun the lithe elastic
    till the fly was shrouded tight.
Down came the hairy talons
    and horrible poison blade
And none of the garden noticed
    that fizzing, hopeless fight.

Say in what Cottage Hospital
  whose pale green walls resound
With the tap upon polished parquet
  of inflexible nurses' feet
Shall I myself be lying
  when they range the screens around?
And say shall I groan in dying,
  as I twist the sweaty sheet?
Or gasp for breath uncrying,
  as I feel my senses drown'd
While the air is swimming with insects
  and children play in the street?


# WILLIAM EMPSON

## 1906–

851                *To an Old Lady*

RIPENESS is all; her in her cooling planet
Revere; do not presume to think her wasted.
Project her no projectile, plan nor man it;
Gods cool in turn, by the sun long outlasted.

Our earth alone given no name of god
Gives, too, no hold for such a leap to aid her;
Landing, you break some palace and seem odd;
Bees sting their need, the keeper's queen invader.

No, to your telescope; spy out the land;
Watch while her ritual is still to see,
Still stand her temples emptying in the sand
Whose waves o'erthrew their crumbled tracery;

Still stand uncalled-on her soul's appanage;
Much social detail whose successor fades,
Wit used to run a house and to play Bridge,
And tragic fervour, to dismiss her maids.

Years her precession do not throw from gear.
She reads a compass certain of her pole;
Confident, finds no confines on her sphere,
Whose failing crops are in her sole control.

Stars how much further from me fill my night.
Strange that she too should be inaccessible,
Who shares my sun. He curtains her from sight,
And but in darkness is she visible.

852                    *Missing Dates*

SLOWLY the poison the whole blood stream fills.
It is not the effort nor the failure tires.
The waste remains, the waste remains and kills.

It is not your system or clear sight that mills
Down small to the consequence a life requires;
Slowly the poison the whole blood stream fills.

They bled an old dog dry yet the exchange rills
Of young dog blood gave but a month's desires.
The waste remains, the waste remains and kills.

It is the Chinese tombs and the slag hills
Usurp the soil, and not the soil retires.
Slowly the poison the whole blood stream fills.

Not to have fire is to be a skin that shrills.
The complete fire is death. From partial fires
The waste remains, the waste remains and kills.

It is the poems you have lost, the ills
From missing dates, at which the heart expires.
Slowly the poison the whole blood stream fills.
The waste remains, the waste remains and kills.

# WYSTAN HUGH AUDEN

1907–

853                    *O Where are you Going?*

'O WHERE are you going?' said reader to rider,
'That valley is fatal when furnaces burn,
Yonder's the midden whose odours will madden,
That gap is the grave where the tall return.'

'O do you imagine,' said fearer to farer,
'That dusk will delay on your path to the pass,
Your diligent looking discover the lacking
Your footsteps feel from granite to grass?'

'O what was that bird,' said horror to hearer,
'Did you see that shape in the twisted trees?
Behind you swiftly the figure comes softly,
The spot on your skin is a shocking disease.'

'Out of this house'—said rider to reader,
'Yours never will'—said farer to fearer,
'They're looking for you'—said hearer to horror,
As he left them there, as he left them there.


854                    *A I walked out one Evening*

As I walked out one evening,
    Walking down Bristol Street,
The crowds upon the pavement
    Were fields of harvest wheat.

And down by the brimming river
    I heard a lover sing
Under an arch of the railway:
    'Love has no ending.

'I'll love you, dear, I'll love you
    Till China and Africa meet,
And the river jumps over the mountain
    And the salmon sing in the street,

'I'll love you till the ocean
  Is folded and hung up to dry
And the seven stars go squawking
  Like geese about the sky.

The years shall run like rabbits,
  For in my arms I hold
The Flower of the Ages,
  And the first love of the world.'

But all the clocks in the city
  Began to whirr and chime:
'O let not Time deceive you,
  You cannot conquer Time.

'In the burrows of the Nightmare
  Where Justice naked is,
Time watches from the shadow
  And coughs when you would kiss.

'In headaches and in worry
  Vaguely life leaks away,
And Time will have his fancy
  To-morrow or to-day.

'Into many a green valley
  Drifts the appalling snow;
Time breaks the threaded dances
  And the diver's brilliant bow.

'O plunge your hands in water,
  Plunge them in up to the wrist;
Stare, stare in the basin
  And wonder what you've missed.

'The glacier knocks in the cupboard,
  The desert sighs in the bed,
And the crack in the tea-cup opens
  A lane to the land of the dead.

'Where the beggars raffle the banknotes
  And the Giant is enchanting to Jack,
And the Lily-white Boy is a Roarer,
  And Jill goes down on her back.

'O look, look in the mirror,
  O look in your distress;
Life remains a blessing
  Although you cannot bless.

'O stand, stand at the window
  As the tears scald and start;
You shall love your crooked neighbour
  With your crooked heart.'

It was late, late in the evening,
  The lovers they were gone;
The clocks had ceased their chiming,
  And the deep river ran on.

855                    *Lullaby*

LAY your sleeping head, my love,
Human on my faithless arm;
Time and fevers burn away
Individual beauty from
Thoughtful children, and the grave
Proves the child ephemeral:
But in my arms till break of day
Let the living creature lie,
Mortal, guilty, but to me
The entirely beautiful.

Soul and body have no bounds:
To lovers as they lie upon
Her tolerant enchanted slope
In their ordinary swoon,
Grave the vision Venus sends
Of supernatural sympathy,
Universal love and hope;
While an abstract insight wakes
Among the glaciers and the rocks
The hermit's carnal ecstasy.

Certainty, fidelity
On the stroke of midnight pass
Like vibrations of a bell
And fashionable madmen raise
Their pedantic boring cry:
Every farthing of the cost,
All the dreaded cards foretell,
Shall be paid, but from this night
Not a whisper, not a thought,
Not a kiss nor look be lost.

Beauty, midnight, vision dies:
Let the winds of dawn that blow
Softly round your dreaming head
Such a day of welcome show
Eye and knocking heart may bless,
Find our mortal world enough;
Noons of dryness find you fed
By the involuntary powers,
Nights of insult let you pass
Watched by every human love.

856                    *Musée des Beaux Arts*

ABOUT suffering they were never wrong,
The Old Masters: how well they understood
Its human position; how it takes place
While someone else is eating or opening a window or just walking
    dully along;
How, when the aged are reverently, passionately waiting
For the miraculous birth, there always must be
Children who did not specially want it to happen, skating
On a pond at the edge of the wood:
They never forgot
That even the dreadful martyrdom must run its course
Anyhow in a corner, some untidy spot
Where the dogs go on with their doggy life and the torturer's horse
Scratches its innocent behind on a tree.

In Brueghel's *Icarus*, for instance: how everything turns away
Quite leisurely from the disaster; the ploughman may
Have heard the splash, the forsaken cry,
But for him it was not an important failure; the sun shone
As it had to on the white legs disappearing into the green
Water; and the expensive delicate ship that must have seen
Something amazing, a boy falling out of the sky,
Had somewhere to get to and sailed calmly on.

857            *In Memory of W. B. Yeats*

*(d. Jan. 1939)*

I

HE disappeared in the dead of winter:
The brooks were frozen, the airports almost deserted,
And snow disfigured the public statues;
The mercury sank in the mouth of the dying day.
What instruments we have agree
The day of his death was a dark cold day.

Far from his illness
The wolves ran on through the evergreen forests,
The peasant river was untempted by the fashionable quays;
By mourning tongues
The death of the poet was kept from his poems.

But for him it was his last afternoon as himself,
An afternoon of nurses and rumours;
The provinces of his body revolted,
The squares of his mind were empty,
Silence invaded the suburbs,
The current of his feeling failed; he became his admirers.

Now he is scattered among a hundred cities
And wholly given over to unfamiliar affections,
To find his happiness in another kind of wood
And be punished under a foreign code of conscience.
The words of a dead man
Are modified in the guts of the living.

But in the importance and noise of to-morrow
When the brokers are roaring like beasts on the floor of the Bourse,
And the poor have the sufferings to which they are fairly accustomed,
And each in the cell of himself is almost convinced of his freedom,
A few thousand will think of this day
As one thinks of a day when one did something slightly unusual.
What instruments we have agree
The day of his death was a dark cold day.

## II

You were silly like us; your gift survived it all:
The parish of rich women, physical decay,
Yourself. Mad Ireland hurt you into poetry.
Now Ireland has her madness and her weather still,
For poetry makes nothing happen: it survives
In the valley of its making where executives
Would never want to tamper, flows on south
From ranches of isolation and the busy griefs,
Raw towns that we believe and die in; it survives,
A way of happening, a mouth.

## III

Earth, receive an honoured guest:
William Yeats is laid to rest.
Let the Irish vessel lie
Emptied of its poetry.

In the nightmare of the dark
All the dogs of Europe bark,
And the living nations wait,
Each sequestered in its hate;

Intellectual disgrace
Stares from every human face,
And the seas of pity lie
Locked and frozen in each eye.

Follow, poet, follow right
To the bottom of the night,
With your unconstraining voice
Still persuade us to rejoice;

With the farming of a verse
Make a vineyard of the curse,
Sing of human unsuccess
In a rapture of distress;

In the deserts of the heart
Let the healing fountain start,
In the prison of his days
Teach the free man how to praise.

858                    *The Shield of Achilles*

    SHE looked over his shoulder
      For vines and olive trees,
    Marble well-governed cities
      And ships upon untamed seas,
    But there on the shining metal
      His hands had put instead
    An artificial wilderness
      And a sky like lead.

A plain without a feature, bare and brown,
    No blade of grass, no sign of neighbourhood,
Nothing to eat and nowhere to sit down,
    Yet, congregated on its blankness, stood
    An unintelligible multitude,
A million eyes, a million boots in line,
Without expression, waiting for a sign.

Out of the air a voice without a face
    Proved by statistics that some cause was just
In tones as dry and level as the place:
    No one was cheered and nothing was discussed;
    Column by column in a cloud of dust
They marched away enduring a belief
Whose logic brought them, somewhere else, to grief.

She looked over his shoulder
   For ritual pieties,
White flower-garlanded heifers,
   Libation and sacrifice,
But there on the shining metal
   Where the altar should have been,
She saw by his flickering forge-light
   Quite another scene.

Barbed wire enclosed an arbitrary spot
   Where bored officials lounged (one cracked a joke)
And sentries sweated for the day was hot:
   A crowd of ordinary decent folk
   Watched from without and neither moved nor spoke
As three pale figures were led forth and bound
To three posts driven upright in the ground.

The mass and majesty of this world, all
   That carries weight and always weighs the same
Lay in the hands of others; they were small
   And could not hope for help and no help came:
   What their foes liked to do was done, their shame
Was all the worst could wish; they lost their pride
And died as men before their bodies died.

She looked over his shoulder
   For athletes at their games,
Men and women in a dance
   Moving their sweet limbs
Quick, quick, to music,
   But there on the shining shield
His hands had set no dancing-floor
   But a weed-choked field.

A ragged urchin, aimless and alone,
   Loitered about that vacancy, a bird
Flew up to safety from his well-aimed stone:
   That girls are raped, that two boys knife a third,
   Were axioms to him, who'd never heard
Of any world where promises were kept,
Or one could weep because another wept.

The thin-lipped armourer,
  Hephaestos hobbled away,
Thetis of the shining breasts
  Cried out in dismay
At what the god had wrought
  To please her son, the strong
Iron-hearted man-slaying Achilles
  Who would not live long.

# LOUIS MACNEICE

1907–1963

859                    *Snow*

THE room was suddenly rich and the great bay-window was
Spawning snow and pink roses against it
Soundlessly collateral and incompatible:
World is suddener than we fancy it.

World is crazier and more of it than we think,
Incorrigibly plural. I peel and portion
A tangerine and spit the pips and feel
The drunkenness of things being various.

And the fire flames with a bubbling sound for world
Is more spiteful and gay than one supposes—
On the tongue on the eyes on the ears in the palms of one's hands—
There is more than glass between the snow and the huge roses.

860              *The Sunlight on the Garden*

THE sunlight on the garden
Hardens and grows cold,
We cannot cage the minute
Within its nets of gold,
When all is told
We cannot beg for pardon.

Our freedom as free lances
Advances towards its end;
The earth compels, upon it
Sonnets and birds descend;
And soon, my friend,
We shall have no time for dances.

The sky was good for flying
Defying the church bells
And every evil iron
Siren and what it tells:
The earth compels,
We are dying, Egypt, dying

And not expecting pardon,
Hardened in heart anew,
But glad to have sat under
Thunder and rain with you,
And grateful too
For sunlight on the garden.

861                        *Bagpipe Music*

It's no go the merrygoround, it's no go the rickshaw,
All we want is a limousine and a ticket for the peepshow.
Their knickers are made of crêpe-de-chine, their shoes are made of
     python,
Their halls are lined with tiger rugs and their walls with heads of bison.

John MacDonald found a corpse, put it under the sofa,
Waited till it came to life and hit it with a poker,
Sold its eyes for souvenirs, sold its blood for whisky,
Kept its bones for dumb-bells to use when he was fifty.

It's no go the Yogi-Man, it's no go Blavatsky,
All we want is a bank balance and a bit of skirt in a taxi.

Annie MacDougall went to milk, caught her foot in the heather,
Woke to hear a dance record playing of Old Vienna.
It's no go your maidenheads, it's no go your culture,
All we want is a Dunlop tyre and the devil mend the puncture.

The Laird o'Phelps spent Hogmanay declaring he was sober,
Counted his feet to prove the fact and found he had one foot over.
Mrs. Carmichael had her fifth, looked at the job with repulsion,
Said to the midwife 'Take it away; I'm through with over-production'.

It's no go the gossip column, it's no go the ceilidh,
All we want is a mother's help and a sugar-stick for the baby.

Willie Murray cut his thumb, couldn't count the damage,
Took the hide of an Ayrshire cow and used it for a bandage.
His brother caught three hundred cran when the seas were lavish,
Threw the bleeders back in the sea and went upon the parish.

It's no go the Herring Board, it's no go the Bible,
All we want is a packet of fags when our hands are idle.

It's no go the picture palace, it's no go the stadium,
It's no go the country cot with a pot of pink geraniums,
It's no go the Government grants, it's no go the elections,
Sit on your arse for fifty years and hang your hat on a pension.

It's no go my honey love, it's no go my poppet;
Work your hands from day to day, the winds will blow the profit.
The glass is falling hour by hour, the glass will fall for ever,
But if you break the bloody glass you won't hold up the weather.

862                          *Prognosis*

                         *Spring 1939*

                 GOODBYE, Winter,
                 The days are getting longer,
                 The tea-leaf in the teacup
                 Is herald of a stranger.

                 Will he bring me business
                 Or will he bring me gladness
                 Or will he come for cure
                 Of his own sickness?

                 With a pedlar's burden
                 Walking up the garden
                 Will he come to beg
                 Or will he come to bargain?

Will he come to pester,
To cringe or to bluster,
A promise in his palm
Or a gun in his holster?

Will his name be John
Or will his name be Jonah
Crying to repent
On the Island of Iona?

Will his name be Jason
Looking for a seaman
Or a mad crusader
Without rhyme or reason?

What will be his message—
War or work or marriage?
News as new as dawn
Or an old adage?

Will he give a champion
Answer to my question
Or will his words be dark
And his ways evasion?

Will his name be Love
And all his talk be crazy?
Or will his name be Death
And his message easy?

863        *The British Museum Reading Room*

UNDER the hive-like dome the stooping haunted readers
Go up and down the alleys, tap the cells of knowledge—
    Honey and wax, the accumulation of years—
Some on commission, some for the love of learning,
Some because they have nothing better to do
Or because they hope these walls of books will deaden
    The drumming of the demon in their ears.

Cranks, hacks, poverty-stricken scholars,
In pince-nez, period hats or romantic beards
    And cherishing their hobby or their doom
Some are too much alive and some are asleep
Hanging like bats in a world of inverted values,
Folded up in themselves in a world which is safe and silent:
    This is the British Museum Reading Room.

Out on the steps in the sun the pigeons are courting,
Puffing their ruffs and sweeping their tails or taking
    A sun-bath at their ease
And under the totem poles—the ancient terror—
Between the enormous fluted Ionic columns
There seeps from heavily jowled or hawk-like foreign faces
    The guttural sorrow of the refugees.

864                    *Brother Fire*

*1943*

WHEN our brother Fire was having his dog's day
Jumping the London streets with millions of tin cans
Clanking at his tail, we heard some shadow say
'Give the dog a bone'—and so we gave him ours;
Night after night we watched him slaver and crunch away
The beams of human life, the tops of topless towers.

Which gluttony of his for us was Lenten fare
Who mother-naked, suckled with sparks, were chill
Though cotted in a grille of sizzling air
Striped like a convict—black, yellow and red;
Thus were we weaned to knowledge of the Will
That wills the natural world but wills us dead.

O delicate walker, babbler, dialectician Fire,
O enemy and image of ourselves,
Did we not on those mornings after the All Clear,
When you were looting shops in elemental joy
And singing as you swarmed up city block and spire,
Echo your thought in ours? 'Destroy! Destroy!'

865 *The Truisms*

His father gave him a box of truisms
Shaped like a coffin, then his father died;
The truisms remained on the mantelpiece
As wooden as the playbox they had been packed in
Or that other his father skulked inside.

Then he left home, left the truisms behind him
Still on the mantelpiece, met love, met war,
Sordor, disappointment, defeat, betrayal,
Till through disbeliefs he arrived at a house
He could not remember seeing before,

And he walked straight in; it was where he had come from
And something told him the way to behave.
He raised his hand and blessed his home;
The truisms flew and perched on his shoulders
And a tall tree sprouted from his father's grave.

866 *Thalassa*

Run out the boat, my broken comrades;
Let the old seaweed crack, the surge
Burgeon oblivious of the last
Embarkation of feckless men,
Let every adverse force converge—
Here we must needs embark again.

Run up the sail, my heartsick comrades;
Let each horizon tilt and lurch—
You know the worst: your wills are fickle,
Your values blurred, your hearts impure
And your past life a ruined church—
But let your poison be your cure.

Put out to sea, ignoble comrades,
Whose record shall be noble yet;
Butting through scarps of moving marble
The narwhal dares us to be free;
By a high star our course is set,
Our end is Life. Put out to sea.

# KATHLEEN RAINE
1908–

867

*Envoi*

TAKE of me what is not my own,
my love, my beauty, and my poem—
the pain is mine, and mine alone.

See how against the weight in the bone
the hawk hangs perfect in mid-air—
the blood pays dear to raise it there,
the moment, not the bird, divine.

And see the peaceful trees extend
their myriad leaves in leisured dance—
they bear the weight of sky and cloud
upon the fountain of their veins.

In rose with petals soft as air
I bind for you the tides and fire—
the death that lives within the flower,
oh gladly, love, for you I bear!


# STEPHEN SPENDER
1909–

868

WHAT I expected was
Thunder, fighting,
Long struggles with men
And climbing.
After continual straining
I should grow strong;
Then the rocks would shake
And I should rest long.

929

What I had not foreseen
Was the gradual day
Weakening the will
Leaking the brightness away,
The lack of good to touch
The fading of body and soul
Like smoke before wind
Corrupt, unsubstantial.

The wearing of Time,
And the watching of cripples pass
With limbs shaped like questions
In their odd twist,
The pulverous grief
Melting the bones with pity,
The sick falling from earth—
These, I could not foresee.

For I had expected always
Some brightness to hold in trust,
Some final innocence
To save from dust;
That, hanging solid,
Would dangle through all
Like the created poem
Or the dazzling crystal.

## 869

I THINK continually of those who were truly great.
Who, from the womb, remembered the soul's history
Through corridors of light where the hours are suns
Endless and singing. Whose lovely ambition
Was that their lips, still touched with fire,
Should tell of the Spirit clothed from head to foot in song.
And who hoarded from the Spring branches
The desires falling across their bodies like blossoms.

What is precious is never to forget
The essential delight of the blood drawn from ageless springs
Breaking through rocks in worlds before our earth.
Never to deny its pleasure in the morning simple light
Nor its grave evening demand for love.
Never to allow gradually the traffic to smother
With noise and fog the flowering of the spirit.

Near the snow, near the sun, in the highest fields
See how these names are fêted by the waving grass
And by the streamers of white cloud
And whispers of wind in the listening sky.
The names of those who in their lives fought for life,
Who wore at their hearts the fire's centre.
Born of the sun they travelled a short while towards the sun,
And left the vivid air signed with their honour.

870

   MOVING through the silent crowd
   Who stand behind dull cigarettes
   These men who idle in the road,
   I have the sense of falling light.

   They lounge at corners of the street
   And greet friends with a shrug of shoulder
   And turn their empty pockets out,
   The cynical gestures of the poor.

   Now they've no work, like better men
   Who sit at desks and take much pay
   They sleep long nights and rise at ten
   To watch the hours that drain away.

   I'm jealous of the weeping hours
   They stare through with such hungry eyes.
   I'm haunted by these images,
   I'm haunted by their emptiness.

STEPHEN SPENDER

871        *The Room above the Square*

THE light in the window seemed perpetual
Where you stayed in the high room for me;
It flowered above the trees through leaves
Like my certainty.

The light is fallen and you are hidden
In sunbright peninsulas of the sword:
Torn like leaves through Europe is the peace
Which through me flowed.

Now I climb alone to the dark room
Which hangs above the square
Where among stones and roots the other
Peaceful lovers are.


# ROY FULLER

1912–

872        *The Statue*

THE noises of the harbour die, the smoke is petrified
Against the thick but vacant, fading light, and shadows slide
From under stone and iron, darkest now. The last birds glide.

Upon this black-boned, white-splashed, far receding vista of grey
Is an equestrian statue, by the ocean, trampling the day,
Its green bronze flaked like petals, catching night before the bay.

Distilled from some sad, endless, sordid period of time,
As from the language of disease might come a consummate rhyme,
It tries to impose its values on the port and on the lime—

The droppings that by chance and from an uncontrollable
And savage life have formed a patina upon the skull;
Abandoned, have blurred a bodied vision once thought spare but full—

932

On me, as authority recites to boys the names of queens.
Shall I be dazzled by the dynasties, the gules and greens,
The unbelievable art, and not recall their piteous means?

Last night I sailed upon that sea whose starting place is here,
Evaded the contraptions of the enemy, the mere
Dangers of water, saw the statue and the plinth appear.

Last night between the crowded, stifling decks I watched a man,
Smoking a big curved pipe, who contemplated his great wan
And dirty feet while minute after tedious minute ran—

This in the city now, whose floor is permanent and still,
Among the news of history and sense of an obscure will,
Is all the image I can summon up, my thought's rank kill;

As though there dominated this sea's threshold and this night
Not the raised hooves, the thick snake neck, the profile, and the might,
The wrought, eternal bronze, the dead protagonist, the fight,

But that unmoving, pale but living shape that drops no tears,
Ridiculous and haunting, which each epoch reappears,
And is what history is not. O love, O human fears!

873        *Translation*

Now that the barbarians have got as far as Picra,
And all the new music is written in the twelve-tone scale,
And I am anyway approaching my fortieth birthday,
        I will dissemble no longer.

I will stop expressing my belief in the rosy
Future of man, and accept the evidence
Of a couple of wretched wars and innumerable
        Abortive revolutions.

I will cease to blame the stupidity of the slaves
Upon their masters and nurture, and will say,
Plainly, that they are enemies to culture,
        Advancement and cleanliness.

From progressive organisations, from quarterlies
Devoted to daring verse, from membership of
Committees, from letters of various protest
   I shall withdraw forthwith.

When they call me reactionary I shall smile,
Secure in another dimension. When they say
'Cinna has ceased to matter' I shall know
   How well I reflect the times.

The ruling class will think I am on their side
And make friendly overtures, but I shall retire
To the side farther from Picra and write some poems
   About the doom of the whole boiling.

Anyone happy in this age and place
Is daft or corrupt. Better to abdicate
From a material and spiritual terrain
   Fit only for barbarians.


# ANNE RIDLER

## 1912–

874    *Choosing a Name*

MY little son, I have cast you out
 To hang heels upward, wailing over a world
 With walls too wide.
My faith till now, and now my love:
 No walls too wide for that to fill, no depth
 Too great for all you hide.

I love, not knowing what I love,
 I give, though ignorant for whom
 The history and power of a name.
I conjure with it, like a novice
 Summoning unknown spirits: answering me
 You take the word, and tame it.

Even as the gift of life
  You take the famous name you did not choose
  And make it new.
You and the name exchange a power:
  Its history is changed, becoming yours,
  And yours by this: who calls this, calls you.

Strong vessel of peace, and plenty promised,
  Into whose unsounded depths I pour
  This alien power;
Frail vessel, launched with a shawl for sail,
  Whose guiding spirit keeps his needle-quivering
  Poise between trust and terror,

And stares amazed to find himself alive;
  This is the means by which you say *I am*,
  Not to be lost till all is lost,
When at the sight of God you say *I am nothing*,
  And find, forgetting name and speech at last,
  A home not mine, dear outcast.

# HENRY REED

### 1914–

## Lessons of the War

*Vixi duellis nuper idoneus*
*Et militavi non sine gloria*

### (i)

### *Naming of Parts*

TO-DAY we have naming of parts. Yesterday,
We had daily cleaning. And to-morrow morning,
We shall have what to do after firing. But to-day,
To-day we have naming of parts. Japonica
Glistens like coral in all of the neighbouring gardens,
    And to-day we have naming of parts.

875

This is the lower sling swivel. And this
Is the upper sling swivel, whose use you will see,
When you are given your slings. And this is the piling swivel,
Which in your case you have not got. The branches
Hold in the gardens their silent, eloquent gestures,
    Which in our case we have not got.

This is the safety-catch, which is always released
With an easy flick of the thumb. And please do not let me
See anyone using his finger. You can do it quite easy
If you have any strength in your thumb. The blossoms
Are fragile and motionless, never letting anyone see
    Any of them using their finger.

And this you can see is the bolt. The purpose of this
Is to open the breech, as you see. We can slide it
Rapidly backwards and forwards: we call this
Easing the spring. And rapidly backwards and forwards
The early bees are assaulting and fumbling the flowers:
    They call it easing the Spring.

They call it easing the Spring: it is perfectly easy
If you have any strength in your thumb: like the bolt,
And the breech, and the cocking-piece, and the point of balance,
Which in our case we have not got; and the almond-blossom
Silent in all of the gardens and the bees going backwards and forwards,
    For to-day we have naming of parts.


(ii)

876                    *Judging Distances*

    NOT only how far away, but the way that you say it
    Is very important. Perhaps you may never get
    The knack of judging a distance, but at least you know
    How to report on a landscape: the central sector,
    The right of arc and that, which we had last Tuesday,
        And at least you know

That maps are of time, not place, so far as the army
Happens to be concerned—the reason being,
Is one which need not delay us. Again, you know
There are three kinds of tree, three only, the fir and the poplar,
And those which have bushy tops to; and lastly
    That things only seem to be things.

A barn is not called a barn, to put it more plainly,
Or a field in the distance, where sheep may be safely grazing.
You must never be over-sure. You must say, when reporting:
At five o'clock in the central sector is a dozen
Of what appear to be animals; whatever you do,
    Don't call the bleeders *sheep*.

I am sure that's quite clear; and suppose, for the sake of example,
The one at the end, asleep, endeavours to tell us
What he sees over there to the west, and how far away,
After first having come to attention. There to the west,
On the fields of summer the sun and the shadows bestow
    Vestments of purple and gold.

The still white dwellings are like a mirage in the heat,
And under the swaying elms a man and a woman
Lie gently together. Which is, perhaps, only to say
That there is a row of houses to the left of arc,
And that under some poplars a pair of what appear to be humans
    Appear to be loving.

Well that, for an answer, is what we might rightly call
Moderately satisfactory only, the reason being,
Is that two things have been omitted, and those are important.
The human beings, now: in what direction are they,
And how far away, would you say? And do not forget
    There may be dead ground in between.

There may be dead ground in between; and I may not have got
The knack of judging a distance; I will only venture
A guess that perhaps between me and the apparent lovers,
(Who, incidentally, appear by now to have finished,)
At seven o'clock from the houses, is roughly a distance
    Of about one year and a half.

# ALUN LEWIS

## 1915–1944

877                    *All Day it has Rained . . .*

ALL day it has rained, and we on the edge of the moors
Have sprawled in our bell-tents, moody and dull as boors,
Groundsheets and blankets spread on the muddy ground
And from the first grey wakening we have found
No refuge from the skirmishing fine rain
And the wind that made the canvas heave and flap
And the taut wet guy-ropes ravel out and snap.
All day the rain has glided, wave and mist and dream,
Drenching the gorse and heather, a gossamer stream
Too light to stir the acorns that suddenly
Snatched from their cups by the wild south-westerly
Pattered against the tent and our upturned dreaming faces.
And we stretched out, unbuttoning our braces,
Smoking a Woodbine, darning dirty socks,
Reading the Sunday papers—I saw a fox
And mentioned it in the note I scribbled home;—
And we talked of girls, and dropping bombs on Rome,
And thought of the quiet dead and the loud celebrities
Exhorting us to slaughter, and the herded refugees;
—Yet thought softly, morosely of them, and as indifferently
As of ourselves or those whom we
For years have loved, and will again
Tomorrow maybe love; but now it is the rain
Possesses us entirely, the twilight and the rain.

And I can remember nothing dearer or more to my heart
Than the children I watched in the woods on Saturday
Shaking down burning chestnuts for the schoolyard's merry play,
Or the shaggy patient dog who followed me
By Sheet and Steep and up the wooded scree
To the Shoulder o' Mutton where Edward Thomas brooded long
On death and beauty—till a bullet stopped his song.

# KEITH DOUGLAS

## 1920–1944

878

### *How to Kill*

UNDER the parabola of a ball,
a child turning into a man,
I looked into the air too long.
The ball fell in my hand, it sang
in the closed fist: *Open Open*
*Behold a gift designed to kill.*

Now in my dial of glass appears
the soldier who is going to die.
He smiles, and moves about in ways
his mother knows, habits of his.
The wires touch his face: I cry
Now. Death, like a familiar, hears

and look, has made a man of dust
of a man of flesh. This sorcery
I do. Being damned, I am amused
to see the centre of love diffused
and the waves of love travel into vacancy.
How easy it is to make a ghost.

The weightless mosquito touches
her tiny shadow on the stone,
and with how like, how infinite
a lightness, man and shadow meet.
They fuse. A shadow is a man
when the mosquito death approaches.

# DYLAN THOMAS

## 1914–1953

879 *The force that through the green fuse drives the flower*

THE force that through the green fuse drives the flower
Drives my green age; that blasts the roots of trees
Is my destroyer.
And I am dumb to tell the crooked rose
My youth is bent by the same wintry fever.

The force that drives the water through the rocks
Drives my red blood; that dries the mouthing streams
Turns mine to wax.
And I am dumb to mouth unto my veins
How at the mountain spring the same mouth sucks.

The hand that whirls the water in the pool
Stirs the quicksand; that ropes the blowing wind
Hauls my shroud sail.
And I am dumb to tell the hanging man
How of my clay is made the hangman's lime.

The lips of time leech to the fountain head;
Love drips and gathers, but the fallen blood
Shall calm her sores.
And I am dumb to tell a weather's wind
How time has ticked a heaven round the stars.

And I am dumb to tell the lover's tomb
How at my sheet goes the same crooked worm.

880 *The hand that signed the paper*

THE hand that signed the paper felled a city;
Five sovereign fingers taxed the breath,
Doubled the globe of dead and halved a country;
These five kings did a king to death.

The mighty hand leads to a sloping shoulder,
The finger joints are cramped with chalk;
A goose's quill has put an end to murder
That put an end to talk.

The hand that signed the treaty bred a fever,
And famine grew, and locusts came;
Great is the hand that holds dominion over
Man by a scribbled name.

The five kings count the dead but do not soften
The crusted wound nor stroke the brow;
A hand rules pity as a hand rules heaven;
Hands have no tears to flow.

881    *A Refusal to Mourn the Death, by Fire, of
a Child in London*

NEVER until the mankind making
Bird beast and flower
Fathering and all humbling darkness
Tells with silence the last light breaking
And the still hour
Is come of the sea tumbling in harness

And I must enter again the round
Zion of the water bead
And the synagogue of the ear of corn
Shall I let pray the shadow of a sound
Or sow my salt seed
In the least valley of sackcloth to mourn

The majesty and burning of the child's death.
I shall not murder
The mankind of her going with a grave truth
Nor blaspheme down the stations of the breath
With any further
Elegy of innocence and youth.

Deep with the first dead lies London's daughter,
Robed in the long friends,
The grains beyond age, the dark veins of her mother,
Secret by the unmourning water
Of the riding Thames.
After the first death, there is no other.


882        *Do not go gentle into that good night*

Do not go gentle into that good night,
Old age should burn and rave at close of day;
Rage, rage against the dying of the light.

Though wise men at their end know dark is right,
Because their words had forked no lightning they
Do not go gentle into that good night.

Good men, the last wave by, crying how bright
Their frail deeds might have danced in a green bay,
Rage, rage against the dying of the light.

Wild men who caught and sang the sun in flight,
And learn, too late, they grieved it on its way,
Do not go gentle into that good night.

Grave men, near death, who see with blinding sight
Blind eyes could blaze like meteors and be gay,
Rage, rage against the dying of the light.

And you, my father, there on the sad height,
Curse, bless, me now with your fierce tears, I pray.
Do not go gentle into that good night.
Rage, rage against the dying of the light.

## 883 *Fern Hill*

NOW as I was young and easy under the apple boughs
About the lilting house and happy as the grass was green,
    The night above the dingle starry,
      Time let me hail and climb
    Golden in the heydays of his eyes,
And honoured among wagons I was prince of the apple towns
And once below a time I lordly had the trees and leaves
      Trail with daisies and barley
    Down the rivers of the windfall light.

And as I was green and carefree, famous among the barns
About the happy yard and singing as the farm was home,
    In the sun that is young once only,
      Time let me play and be
    Golden in the mercy of his means,
And green and golden I was huntsman and herdsman, the calves
Sang to my horn, the foxes on the hills barked clear and cold,
      And the sabbath rang slowly
    In the pebbles of the holy streams.

All the sun long it was running, it was lovely, the hay
Fields high as the house, the tunes from the chimneys, it was air
    And playing, lovely and watery
      And fire green as grass.
    And nightly under the simple stars
As I rode to sleep the owls were bearing the farm away,
All the moon long I heard, blessed among stables, the nightjars
      Flying with the ricks, and the horses
      Flashing into the dark.

And then to awake, and the farm, like a wanderer white
With the dew, come back, the cock on his shoulder: it was all
    Shining, it was Adam and maiden,
      The sky gathered again
    And the sun grew round that very day.
So it must have been after the birth of the simple light
In the first, spinning place, the spellbound horses walking warm
      Out of the whinnying green stable
      On to the fields of praise.

And honoured among foxes and pheasants by the gay house
Under the new made clouds and happy as the heart was long,
    In the sun born over and over,
        I ran my heedless ways,
    My wishes raced through the house high hay
And nothing I cared, at my sky blue trades, that time allows
In all his tuneful turning so few and such morning songs
    Before the children green and golden
        Follow him out of grace,

Nothing I cared, in the lamb white days, that time would take me
Up to the swallow thronged loft by the shadow of my hand,
    In the moon that is always rising,
        Nor that riding to sleep
    I should hear him fly with the high fields
And wake to the farm forever fled from the childless land.
Oh as I was young and easy in the mercy of his means,
    Time held me green and dying
    Though I sang in my chains like the sea.

# EPILOGUE

## LOUIS MACNEICE

884       *A Fanfare for the Makers*

A CLOUD of witnesses. To whom? To what?
To the small fire that never leaves the sky.
To the great fire that boils the daily pot.

To all the things we are not remembered by,
Which we remember and bless. To all the things
That will not even notice when we die,

Yet lend the passing moment words and wings.

       \*

So Fanfare for the Makers: who compose
A book of words or deeds who runs may write
As many do who run, as a family grows

At times like sunflowers turning towards the light,
As sometimes in the blackout and the raids
One joke composed an island in the night,

As sometimes one man's kindliness pervades
A room or house or village, as sometimes
Merely to tighten screws or sharpen blades

Can catch a meaning, as to hear the chimes
At midnight means to share them, as one man
In old age plants an avenue of limes

And before they bloom can smell them, before they span
The road can walk beneath the perfected arch,
The merest greenprint when the lives began

Of those who walk there with him, as in default
Of coffee men grind acorns, as in despite
Of all assaults conscripts counterassault,

As mothers sit up late night after night
Moulding a life, as miners day by day
Descend blind shafts, as a boy may flaunt his kite

In an empty nonchalant sky, as anglers play
Their fish, as workers work and can take pride
In spending sweat before they draw their pay,

As horsemen fashion horses while they ride,
As climbers climb a peak because it is there,
As life can be confirmed even in suicide:

To make is such. Let us make. And set the weather fair.

# NOTES AND REFERENCES

TEXTS are based on the author's final version, with a few exceptions noted below. Spelling and punctuation have been modernized, except for poems in the Scottish dialect, and for the poems of Spenser and Chatterton whose spelling is part of their deliberate archaism. In medieval poems, and occasionally after, a dot over the vowel indicates that it has syllabic value. Throughout -èd is used to indicate the uncontracted form of the weak past tense and past participle, and an acute accent indicates that the syllable takes stress.

Titles have throughout been supplied for extracts from poems, for songs from plays and novels, and for the many poems up to the beginning of the seventeenth century which their authors left untitled. Beyond this point, when the practice of giving titles to lyrics had become established, titles have not been supplied to poems their authors thought fit to leave without them. In a few cases titles have been slightly expanded by the provision of dates or explanatory information.

The sources of passages excerpted from poems, and of songs from plays or novels, are given below, as well as line or stanza references where omissions from a poem are substantial. No references are given for poems by authors whose collected poems are easily available, since these can be found by consulting first-line indexes. But references are supplied for authors whose poems have not been collected, or, if they have been, are difficult to obtain.

1-5. ANON. Texts from *The Oxford Book of Medieval English Verse*.

6. WILLIAM LANGLAND, *Piers Plowman*, C Text, II.149-56.

7-10. GEOFFREY CHAUCER: 7. *Troilus and Criseyde*, V.547-81, 638-44, 1688-1701; 8. Ibid., 1835-48; 9. Prologue to *The Legend of Good Women*, F Text, 249-69; 10. *Cant. Tales*, General Prologue, 118-62.

11-18. ANON. Texts from *The Oxford Book of Medieval English Verse*. 11. There are two poems with the refrain '*Quia Amore Langueo*', which is taken from the Song of Songs. In the other, beginning 'In a tabernacle of a tower', the Virgin is the speaker.

19. ANON., British Museum MS. Harley 7578.

20. WILLIAM CORNISH, British Museum MS. Additional 31922.

21. ANON., British Museum MS. Royal Appendix 58.

22. WILLIAM DUNBAR. Ten stanzas, in which Dunbar interrupts his *danse macabre* to commemorate dead Scottish poets (mostly unknown to fame), are omitted. The poem gained its traditional title from these stanzas. The refrain, used here as title, is from the Office of the Dead.

24. JOHN SKELTON, *The Book of Philip Sparrow* (c. 1545: written c. 1505-7), 1-63, 108-46, 386-575. The poem (1,382 lines in all) continues

with the speaker, Jane Scrope, apologizing for her lack of poetic skill and with the 'commendations' of Jane.

39. ROBERT WEVER, *Lusty Juventus* (*c.* 1560).

40. THOMAS SACKVILLE, EARL OF DORSET, Induction to *The Mirror for Magistrates* (1563), stanzas 56–68.

41. GEORGE GASCOIGNE, from 'The Adventures of Master F.I.' in *A Hundred Sundry Flowers* (1573).

54. CHIDIOCK TICHBORNE, *Verses of Praise and Joy* (1586). Tichborne wrote these verses in the Tower three days before his execution for complicity in the Babington conspiracy.

55–63. EDMUND SPENSER: 55. *The Shepherds' Calendar* (1579), 'April , 37–153; 58–63. *The Faerie Queene* (1590, 1596, and 1609), I.ix.33–44; II.xii.70–5; III.vi.30–42; III.xii.7–18; VI.x.10–16; VII.vii.57–9, VII.viii.1–2.

64. ANTHONY MUNDAY, in *England's Helicon* (1600).

65 and 67. JOHN LYLY, *Campaspe* (1584); texts of the songs were first printed in 1632.

68–70. NICHOLAS BRETON: 68. *Entertainment at Elvetham* (1591); 69. *The Arbour of Amorous Devices* (1594); 70. In *England's Helicon* (1600).

71. THOMAS LODGE, *Rosalynde* (1590).

72–7. GEORGE PEELE: 72. *The Arraignment of Paris* (1584); 73. *The Hunting of Cupid* (1591), Drummond MS., Library of the Society of Antiquaries, Edinburgh; 74. *Polyhymnia* (1590); 75. *David and Bethsabe* (1599); 76 and 77. *The Old Wife's Tale* (1595).

78 and 79. ROBERT GREENE, *Menaphon* (1589).

83. ROBERT SOUTHWELL, 'Upon the Image of Death'. Although printed as Southwell's, the mood and style of this poem suggests it was written at an earlier date, probably in the first half of the sixteenth century.

84 and 85. THOMAS NASHE, *Summer's Last Will and Testament* (1600).

86 and 87. CHRISTOPHER MARLOWE, *Hero and Leander* (1598), I.131–76 and II.153–206.

89 and 90. SIR WALTER RALEGH. Both these poems are only doubtfully Ralegh's, though accepted by his latest editor, Agnes Latham. 'The Nymph's Reply', printed as by 'Ignoto' in *England's Helicon* (1600), was attributed to Ralegh by Izaak Walton in *The Compleat Angler* (1653). 'Walsingham', a poem based on an earlier popular ballad, is attributed to Ralegh only in Bodleian MS. Rawlinson 85.

96. FULKE GREVILLE, LORD BROOKE, last chorus from *Mustapha, Certain Learned and Elegant Works* (1633).

97. GEORGE CHAPMAN, *Hero and Leander* (1598), V.432–47.

98. MARK ALEXANDER BOYD. This sonnet was first printed by Q in *The Oxford Book of English Verse* (1900), from a single leaf then in the possession of Miss Boyd of Penkill Castle, a descendant of the poet; the leaf is now in the National Library of Scotland. 'I suppose this is the

most beautiful sonnet in the language, at any rate it has one nomination' (Ezra Pound, *ABC of Reading* (1934)).

99–107. SAMUEL DANIEL: 104. *Musophilus* (1599), 939–80; 106. *Tethys' Festival* (1610); 107. *Hymen's Triumph* (1615).

113. MICHAEL DRAYTON, 'Epistle to Reynolds', 1–40.

115 and 116. WILLIAM SHAKESPEARE, *Venus and Adonis* (1593), 259–324; *The Rape of Lucrece* (1594), 876–910.

132 and 133. WILLIAM SHAKESPEARE, 'Sweet Music's Power', *Henry VIII*, and 'A Bridal Song', *The Two Noble Kinsmen*. These may be by John Fletcher.

166. ANON., 'Hierusalem my Happy Home'. The text is from British Museum MS. Additional 15255, a commonplace-book compiled by a Catholic, where the poem has twenty-six stanzas. A shorter version (nineteen stanzas) with some inferior readings, was printed in *The Song of Mary the Mother of Christ* (1601). There exists also a longer version (fifty-five stanzas) which is plainly derivative.

167–75. POEMS FROM SONG-BOOKS. Texts can be found in Fellowes, *English Madrigal Verse* (3rd ed., rev. Sternfeld and Greer, 1967).

176. ANON., 'A Madrigal', in Davison's *Poetical Rhapsody* (1602).

177. ANON., 'Aubade'. This is a better version of the first stanza of a poem in two stanzas set by Dowland in 1612. It appears in the 1669 edition of Donne's *Poems* wrongly prefixed to Donne's poem 'Break of Day', which is in a different metre and is spoken by a woman.

178. HENRY CHETTLE, in *England's Helicon* (1600).

179–81. SIR HENRY WOTTON, *Reliquiae Wottonianae* (1651).

182–4. SIR JOHN DAVIES, *Orchestra* (1596), stanzas 17–19, 39–52; *Nosce Teipsum* (1599), stanzas 38–45 and 225–31. Complete texts of both poems can be found in E. Arber, *English Garner*, v (1882), or A. H. Bullen, *Some Longer Elizabethan Poems* (1903).

185–203. JOHN DONNE: 185. 'Satire III', 72–110; 187. 'The Storm', 37–74. Texts from *Satires and Verse-Letters*, ed. Wesley Milgate (1967). Texts of the other poems are from *Elegies and Songs and Sonnets* and *Divine Poems*, ed. Helen Gardner (1965 and 1952). (A conjectural reading in 'The Ecstasy' has been withdrawn.) 203. 'Hymn'. In the first (posthumous) edition of Donne's poems in 1633 the title was 'Hymn to God the Father'; but in all manuscript copies the title is either 'To Christ' or 'Christo Salvatori'. As the text here follows the manuscripts, whose readings make the established title unsuitable, I have used the non-committal 'Hymn'.

204–19. BEN JONSON: 204. *Cynthia's Revels* (acted 1600); 205. *The Silent Woman* (acted 1609); 212. *The Masque of Queens* (acted 1609); *The Golden Age Restored* (acted 1615). Texts from *Works* (1616). 218. *The Sad Shepherd*, *Works* (1640); 219. 'To the Memory of Shakespeare', 17–65, the First Folio (1623).

220. RICHARD BARNFIELD, *Poems in Diverse Humours* (1598).

**221-5.** JOHN FLETCHER: **221.** *The Faithful Shepherdess* (*c.* 1609); **222.** *The Maid's Tragedy* (*ante* 1611) (possibly by Beaumont); **223.** *The Captain* (*ante* 1612); **224** and **225.** *Valentinian* (*ante* 1614). Beaumont and Fletcher, *Works* (1647 and 1679).

**226-8.** JOHN WEBSTER: **226.** *The White Devil* (1612); **227.** *The Duchess of Malfi* (1623: acted *c.* 1613); **228.** *The Devil's Law Case* (1623: acted ?1610).

**234.** SIR JOHN BEAUMONT, *Bosworth Field* (1629).

**235.** AURELIAN TOWNSHEND, in Henry Lawes, *Airs and Dialogues* (1655).

**236.** ?FRANCIS BEAUMONT, 'On the Tombs in Westminster Abbey'. First printed as 'A Memento for Mortality' in *A Help to Discourse*, by W. B. and E.P. (1619). Ault suggested that William Basse was the author; but there is no reason to identify W.B. with Basse, and, even if there were, no reason to suppose poems he printed were his own. It appeared, also anonymously, in J. Weever, *Ancient Funeral Monuments* (1631). A shortened version (1-4, 19-30 and a concluding couplet based on 33-4), headed 'On the Tombs in Westminster', was included in Francis Beaumont's *Poems* (1653). The original poem may well be his. It is not unusual to find shortened versions of poems in the seventeenth-century manuscripts which were the source of posthumous collections of an author's works.

**241.** GILES FLETCHER, *Christ's Victory and Triumph* (1610), IV, stanzas 39-42.

**242.** JOHN FORD, *The Broken Heart* (1633).

**243.** SIR FRANCIS KYNASTON, *Leoline and Sydanis* (1642), included in Saintsbury (ed.), *Minor Caroline Poets*, ii.

**246.** WILLIAM BROWNE, *Inner Temple Masque*, Emmanuel College MS., first printed in *Works* (1772).

**278.** ANON., 'Preparations', Christ Church, Oxford MS.

**279.** THOMAS CAREW, lines 25-70 of Carew's Elegy on Donne, printed in *Poems by J.D.* (1633).

**284** and **285.** JAMES SHIRLEY, *Poems* (1646) and *Ajax and Ulysses* (1659).

**286.** WILLIAM STRODE. This stanza was highly popular and much imitated in manuscript. It was first printed in W. Porter, *Madrigals and Airs* (1632).

**291-4.** SIR WILLIAM DAVENANT, *Works* (1673).

**296.** SIR EDMUND WALLER, 'Old Age', last two stanzas of 'Of the Last Verses in the Book', *Poems* (1686).

**297.** SIR RICHARD FANSHAWE, *Il Pastor Fido* (1648).

**298-313.** JOHN MILTON: **298.** The four stanzas that introduce the Hymn are omitted; **308-11.** *Paradise Lost* (1667), I.76-124; III.1-55; IV.598-656; XII.624-49; **312** and **313.** *Samson Agonistes* (1671), 1268-96, 1745-58.

317. SIDNEY GODOLPHIN, Bodleian MS. Malone 13.

318 and 319. JAMES GRAHAM, MARQUIS OF MONTROSE, in Watson, *Choice Collection* (1711).

320. THOMAS JORDAN, *The Triumphs of London* (1675), last four stanzas omitted. Q's version appears to be a *rifacimento*.

321-5. RICHARD CRASHAW: 322. 'An Hymn of the Nativity *etc.*' The introductory chorus (sixteen lines) is omitted. The text is from *Steps to the Temple* (1648), a revised and expanded version of the poem in the first edition of 1646. The last two lines of each solo verse are repeated by the chorus. 323. 'A Hymn to . . . Saint Teresa': text from the revised and expanded version of 1648; 324. 'The Flaming Heart', 93–108 (conclusion).

326 and 327. SAMUEL BUTLER, *Hudibras*, Part I (1662), 1–14, 187–234 and 451–6, 473–518.

331. ABRAHAM COWLEY, 'On the Death of Mr. William Harvey', first six stanzas of a poem in nineteen stanzas.

343. ANDREW MARVELL, 'Appleton House', stanzas 37–43.

353. JOHN BUNYAN, *The Pilgrim's Progress*, Part 2 (1684).

355-60. BALLADS. Texts are from *The Oxford Book of Ballads*, ed. James Kinsley (1969).

361. ANON., 'A Lyke Wake Dirge', Scott, *Minstrelsy of the Scottish Border* (1802).

362. ANON., 'Loving Mad Tom', British Museum MS. Additional 24665.

363-72. JOHN DRYDEN: 363. *Annus Mirabilis* (1667), stanzas 293–300; 364. *Mac Flecknoe* (1682: written 1678), 1–28; 365 and 366. *Absalom and Achitophel* (1681), 140–99 and 529–68; 367. *The Medal* (1682), 82–112; 369. *The Hind and the Panther* (1687), 1.62–92; 370. *The Spanish Friar* (1681).

373. CHARLES SACKVILLE, EARL OF DORSET, *Works* (1749).

374-6. SIR CHARLES SEDLEY, *Miscellaneous Works* (1702).

377. APHRA BEHN, *Poems* (1684).

381. JOHN WILMOT, EARL OF ROCHESTER, 'A Satire against Reason and Mankind', *Poems* (1680), 1–30.

390. JONATHAN SWIFT, 'Verses on the Death of Dr. Swift', Faulkner's Dublin edition (1739), 73–116, 299–374, 459–88 (conclusion).

392 and 393. ISAAC WATTS, *Horae Lyricae* (1709 and 1706).

394-6. JOHN GAY: 394-5. *The Beggars' Opera* (1728); 396. *Acis and Galatea* (1732).

397-412. ALEXANDER POPE: 397. *Pastorals, Poet. Misc.* (1709) 'Summer', 59–76; 398. *An Essay on Criticism* (1711), 215–32; 399 and 400. *The Rape of the Lock* (1714), 1.121–48 and 11.1–18, 47–68; 404. *An Essay on Man* (1733), 11.1–18; 405. *Epistle to Bathurst* (1733), 299–314; 406 and 407. *Epistle to Dr. Arbuthnot* (1735), 193–214 and 305–33; 408. *Epistle to a Lady*

(1735), 157–80; **409**. *Epistle to Dr. Arbuthnot* 334–59; **410** and **411**. *Epilogue to the Satires* (1738), I.137–72 and II.197–227; **412**. *The Dunciad* (1743), IV.627–56.

**413**. HENRY CAREY, *Poems* (1729).

**414**. ANON. In *The British Musical Miscellany*, i (1734).

**415**. JOHN BYROM, *Miscellaneous Poems* (1773).

**416–18**. JAMES THOMSON, *The Seasons* (1746), 'Winter', 722–46; 'Spring', 524–52; 'Autumn', 1080–1100.

**420–2**. SAMUEL JOHNSON, *The Vanity of Human Wishes* (1749), 135–64, 191–222 and 343–68 (conclusion).

**435**. WILLIAM COLLINS, 'Ode on the Popular Superstitions of the Highlands', stanzas 9 and 10: written *c.* 1749, first printed in *Trans. Royal Society of Edinburgh* (1788).

**436**. CHRISTOPHER SMART, *A Song to David* (1763), stanzas 1–3 and 49–86.

**438** and **439**. OLIVER GOLDSMITH: **438**. *The Vicar of Wakefield* (1766); **439**. *The Deserted Village* (1760), 1–56.

**440**. THOMAS OSBERT MORDAUNT. This stanza, from 'Verses Written during the War 1756–1763', *The Bee*, Edinburgh (1791), was used by Scott as a heading for chapter 33 of *Old Mortality*, ascribed to 'Anon.'. It was for long supposed that Scott was its author.

**441**. JOHN SCOTT OF AMWELL. *Poetical Works* (1782).

**448–52**. GEORGE CRABBE: **448**. *The Village* (1783), I.39–84; **449**. *The Parish Register* (1807), III.233–311; **450**. *The Borough* (1810), Letter XXII, 171–204; **451**. 'Sir Eustace Grey', *Poems* (1807), stanzas 22, 35–40; **452**. Crabbe's son, in his Life of his father, in *Works* (1834), quotes these lines as 'found written on a paper in which my dear mother's wedding-ring nearly worn through before she died, was wrapped'.

**453–68**. WILLIAM BLAKE: **464**. *The Book of Thel* (1789), IV; **467** and **468**. *Milton* (1804–8), Preface and II.34.

**469–77**. ROBERT BURNS. Texts are from the first printings, and not from critical texts based on manuscripts.

**478**. SAMUEL ROGERS, *An Ode to Superstition* etc. (1786).

**496** and **497**. WILLIAM WORDSWORTH, *The Prelude*, (1805 text, first printed in 1925) I.305–50 and 428–89.

**502–7**. SIR WALTER SCOTT: **502**. *The Lay of the Last Minstrel* (1805), VI.i and ii; **503**. *Marmion* (1808), V.xii; **504**. *The Lady of the Lake* (1810), I.xxxi; **505**. *Rokeby* (1813), III.xxviii; **506**. *The Heart of Midlothian* (1818), chapter 40; **507**. *The Bride of Lammermuir* (1819), chapter 2.

**531**. THOMAS LOVE PEACOCK, *The Misfortunes of Elphin* (1829), chapter 11.

**534–44**. GEORGE GORDON NOEL, LORD BYRON: **536** and **537**. *Childe Harold*, III (1816), xxi–xxviii and IV (1818), cxl–xli; **538**. *The Prisoner of Chillon* (1816), xi–xiv (conclusion); **540**. *Beppo* (1818), xli–xlix; **542** and

543. *Don Juan*, I (1819), ccxiii–ccxx and III (1821), after stanza lxxxvi.

545. CHARLES WOLFE, in *Newry Telegraph*, 19 April 1817.

546–58. PERCY BYSSHE SHELLEY: 548. *Prometheus Unbound* (1820), II.v.48–110; 551. 'A Letter to Maria Gisborne', 132–74, 192–291, *Posthumous Poems* (1824); 552. *Adonais* (1821), stanzas 39–44, 52–5 (conclusion); 553. *Hellas* (1822), the last chorus.

559. JOHN CLARE, *The Shepherds' Calendar* (1827).

563. JOHN KEATS, *Endymion* (1818), IV.182–272.

575 and 576. GEORGE DARLEY, *Nepenthe* (1835), I.152–221 and II.432–55.

587–9. THOMAS LOVELL BEDDOES, *Death's Jest Book* (1850).

594. EDWARD FITZGERALD, *The Rubaiyat of Omar Khayyam* (4th ed., 1879) stanzas 12–24.

595–615. ALFRED, LORD TENNYSON: 597. 'The Lotos-Eaters', introductory stanzas (1–46) omitted. 599. These are the first and third stanzas of a poem published as 'Stanzas' in 1837, which finally, with revision, found a place in *Maud* (1855), Part II, 141–4, 151–6; 604–11. *In Memoriam* (1850), ii, vii, xi, xv, lxix, cxv, cxxiii, cxxvi; 612. *Maud*, I.xxii.

636 and 637. EMILY JANE BRONTË. In Emily Brontë's transcription of the 'Gondal Poems' in the British Museum these two poems form part of a long poem headed 'Julian M. and A.G. Rochelle'. Charlotte Brontë published the first three stanzas, with two additional stanzas, which may be her own, under the title of 'The Visionary' in poems added to the 1850 edition of *Wuthering Heights*. Emily had already lifted fifteen stanzas from the manuscript poem and published them as 'The Prisoner: A Fragment', with an additional concluding stanza, in *Poems* by Currer, Ellis, and Acton Bell (1846).

639–43. ARTHUR HUGH CLOUGH. *Poems* ed. A. L. P. Norrington (1968); 642 and 643. *Dipsychus*, iv. 130–203 and v, 134–85.

644 and 645. MATTHEW ARNOLD: 644. 'Empedocles on Etna', II.417–68, *Empedocles* etc. (1852); 645. 'Sohrab and Rustum', 857–92 (conclusion), *Poems* (1853).

652 and 653. WILLIAM CORY, *Ionica* (1858).

658. WILLIAM ALLINGHAM, *Poems* (1850).

664. GEORGE MEREDITH, 'Love in the Valley', the revised and extended version (1883) of a poem first published in 1851, stanzas 1–7, 10–11, 23, and 26 (conclusion).

681 and 682. CHARLES LUTWIDGE DODGSON (LEWIS CARROLL), *Through the Looking Glass* (1872), chapters 1 and 8.

683. RICHARD WATSON DIXON, *Historic Odes* (1864).

687 and 688. JAMES THOMSON, *The City of Dreadful Night* (1880), Proem and Part I. 43–84; Part XXI.

741. OSCAR WILDE, *The Ballad of Reading Gaol* (1898), first ten stanzas.

813 and 814. EZRA POUND, *Hugh Selwyn Mauberley* (1920), iii, iv, v, and *Pisan Cantos* (1949), Canto lxxxi (conclusion).

823. EDITH SITWELL, *The Sleeping Beauty* (1924), viii.

EPILOGUE: Louis MacNeice, *Autumn Sequel* (1935), vii, omitting lines 8–105.

# INDEX OF AUTHORS

The references are to the numbers of the poems

954

# INDEX OF AUTHORS

# INDEX OF AUTHORS

# INDEX OF FIRST LINES

# INDEX OF FIRST LINES

# INDEX OF FIRST LINES

# INDEX OF FIRST LINES

# INDEX OF FIRST LINES

# INDEX OF FIRST LINES

# INDEX OF FIRST LINES

# INDEX OF FIRST LINES

# INDEX OF FIRST LINES